CITY DIRECTORIES
FOR
CHARLESTON, SOUTH CAROLINA

FOR THE YEARS

1803, 1806, 1807, 1809 AND 1813

James W. Hagy

CLEARFIELD

Printed for
Clearfield Company, Inc. by
Genealogical Publishing Co., Inc.
Baltimore, Maryland
1995

Reprinted for
Clearfield Company, Inc. by
Genealogical Publishing Co., Inc.
Baltimore, Maryland
2000

International Standard Book Number: 0-8063-4536-5

CONTENTS

INTRODUCTION

This volume contains the city directories for Charleston, South Carolina for the years 1803, 1806, 1807, 1809, and 1813. No more are known to exist during this time. Each of the directories cost $1 at the time of publication. This work represents a continuing effort to republish the directories of the city prior to the Civil War. A previous volume contained the city directories for the years 1782, 1785, 1790, 1794, 1796, 1801, and 1802 as well as the census reports for 1790 and 1800 which appeared under the title of *People and Professions of Charleston, South Carolina, 1782-1802* (Baltimore: Clearfield, 1992)

Due to the growth of the city the directories become larger. As a result, the census information has not been included, and the number of directories per volume has decreased.

In an effort to make the researcher's work the least confusing as possible, a number of changes have been made from the original entries. For example, most of the abbreviations used in the directories have been spelled out. Some of them, such as "v. m." for "vendue master" can be figured out with a little effort; however, others such as "o. d. c." for "outdoor clerk" take a considerable time to decipher. A few abbreviations could not be deciphered such as "q.m." In those cases they have been retained. The abbreviation "c. h." proved to be confusing; it could mean "custom house," as it clearly does in some cases, or "counting house." An attempt was made to distinguish between the two, but errors may have occurred. There are some words for professions which could not be found in dictionaries. They, too, have been kept. Also, spellings have been modernized where appropriate such as "tailor" for "taylor." On the other hand, the names have been kept as they are spelled in the directories even when they are recognized to be incorrect At times the directories are very faded, torn, or are difficult to read for other reasons such as part of the name being hidden by the binding. Often these people could be found in other directories and the entries made complete. In a few cases, however, part of a name is missing In addition, some street numbers could not be read. If the number could be found in another directory, it was included; otherwise the house number was omitted. This, though, did not happen very often.

The following abbreviations have been used for common words: Al = Alley; Cont'd. = Continued; cor. = corner; E. = East; Ln. = Lane; N. = North; S. = South; S. C. = South Carolina; St. = Street; W. = West; Whf. = Wharf.

The 1806 directory contains the following information on streets and some of the important places in the city:

Amen St. ran east to west from 66 Church St. to East Bay.

Anson Street ran south to north from Quince St. to Scarborough St.

Archdale St. ran south to north from Queen St. to Beaufain St.

Bank of South Carolina was at the corner of Broad and Church streets.

Beaufain St. ran east to west from King Street to the River.

Berresford Alley ran west to east from 187 Meeting to Church St.

Berresford St. ran east to west from King St. to 22 Archdale St.

Black Bird Alley ran east to west from 157 King St. to Meeting St.

Blake's Wharf was on South Bay southwest of Legare St

Boundary St. ran east to west from Gadsden's Wharf to Cannon's Mill.

Centurion Street ran east to west from 26 East Bay Cont'd to the corner of Anson & Society streets.

Chalmers Alley ran east to west from 10 Union St. to Church St

Charles St. ran north to south from Pinckney St. to Ellery St.

Charleston Theatre was at the southwest end of Broad St between New & Savage Sts.

Church St. Cont'd. ran north to south to South Bay.

Church St. ran south to north from Water St. to Ellery St.

City Theatre was at 26 Church St.

Clifford St. ran west to east from 80 King St. to Archdale St.

Clifford's Alley ran west to east from 68 King St. to Archdale St.

Cock Lane ran south to north from Pinckney St. to Motte's Lane.

Coming St. ran south to north from corner of 15 Beaufain St

Crafts' Wharves, South and North, ran from 134 to 139 East Bay.

Cumberland Street ran east to west from 52 Church to Moore St.

Custom House & Stores were at Geyer's Fourth Range at 151 East Bay.

East Bay Cont'd. ran south to north from Governor's Bridge to Front St.

East Bay St. ran south to north from New East Bay St. to Governor's Bridg.

Ellery St ran east to west from Governor's Bridge at 1 East Bay Cont'd. to Meeting St.

Elliott St. Cont'd ran eastwardly to Beale's Wharf.

Elliott St. ran west to east from Church St. to 36 East Bay.

Federal St. ran from 179 King St. north to Society St.

Fish Market was at the east end of Prioleau's Beef Market Wharf

Gadsden's Wharf was east of Front St. and southeast of Boundary St.

George St. ran east to west from Scarborough Coming St.

Geyer's Wharf lay east from 146 Bay St. to the Custom House

Gibbes St. ran east to west from Legare St. to the river.

Gibbes Wharf was at the west end of South Bay.

Goodby Alley ran from Pinckney St. south to Guignard St.

Governor's Bridge ran south to north from 90 East Bay

Guard House (1) was at the northwest corner of Meeting St. Cont'd. and Tobacco Street

Guard House (2) was at the southwest corner of Broad and Meeting streets.

Ham's Wharf (1) was southeast of Governor's Bridge

Ham's Wharf (2) was east of Mazyckborough.

Harleston's Green was west of Coming St.

Hay Market (1) was on Prioleau's Wharf on East Bay

Hay Market (2) was on southwest end of South Bay

Ingles Lane ran from 29 Bay St. to Bedon's Alley.

King St. Cont'd. ran south to north from Boundary St. to the Tobacco Inspection.

King St. ran south to north from South Bay to Boundary St.

King St. Road ran south from the Tobacco Inspection north to Augusta.

Legare St. ran south to north from South Bay to 63 Tradd St.

Liberty St. ran from east to west from 124 King St. to St. Philip's St.

Library Society of Charleston was on the third story of the State House.

Lightwood's Alley ran east to west from 220 Meeting St. to Church St. Cont'd.

Linguard St. ran east to west from 63 Church St. to Union St. Cont'd.

Longitude Lane ran west to east from 101 Church St. to 14 East Bay.

Lynch St. ran south to north from the Ashley River to Cannonborough

Lynch's Court ran from Lynch's Lane south to north.

Lynch's Lane ran east to west from New East Bay St to Lightwood's Alley
Magazine St. ran east to west from 4 Archibald St. to the Ashley River
Maiden lane ran south to north from 15 Ellery St. to Hasell St.
Marine Hospital was on Magazine St. behind the jail
Mazyck St ran south from corner of 88 Broad St. to north Beaufain St.
Meeting St. Cont'd. ran south from Boundary north to the Tobacco Inspection
Meeting St. ran south from corner of Port St. & South Bay to Boundary St. north.
Mey's Wharf was east from Pinckney St.
Minority St. ran west to east from Wall St. to Front St.
Montague St. ran east to west from Coming St. to the Ashley River
National Bank Square ran south from 110 Broad St. northwest to 196 Meeting St
National Branch Bank was at the corner Broad and Meeting streets.
Orange St. ran north from 53 Broad St. to Tradd St
Orphan Church was north of the Orphan House fronting Vanderhorst St
Orphan House was at the southeast corner of St. Philip's St. fronting Boundary St.
Parsonage Lane ran east to west from 97 King St to Archdale St.
Pinckney St. ran from Maiden Lane to Mey's Wharf
Pitt St. ran south to north from west end of Beaufain St.
Poor House was at the southwest corner of Mazyck and Magazgine streets.
Port Street ran from the south end of New East Bay St. to South Bay
Post Office was at 99 Tradd St
Powder Magazine was south of the jail in the enclosure of the Marine Hospital
Price's Alley ran east to west from 21 Meeting St. to King St.
Prioleau's Wharf was east from 109 to 117 East Bay.
Prison was southwest of Magazine St. & north of the Marine Hospital.
Pritchard's Wharf had been changed to Fitzsimon's Wharf and was east of 90 East Bay.
Race Ground was to the left of King St Road West of the two mile stone
Raper's Lane ran south to north from the corner of Ellery St. to Guignard St
Rope Lane cul-de-sac was between 203 and 204 Meeting St.
Roper's Wharf had become D'Oyley's Wharf.
Saint Michael's Alley ran east to west from 32 Church to Meeting St.
Savage St. ran from the west end of Broad St to the Ashley River
Scarborough St. ran from Anson St. north to Boundary St.
Short Street ran east from 1 Mazyck St. to the Ashley River.
Smith Street ran south to north from the Ashley River to the corner of Beaufain St.
Smith's Lane ran east from 7 Meeting St. West into Lamboll St
Smith's Wharf was at South Bay.
Society St. ran east to west from the corner of 130 Meeting St. to Anson St.
South Bay St. ran east to west from Port St.
St. Philip's St. ran south to north from 35 Beaufain St.
State Bank was at 128 Broad St.
State House Square was at 33 Meeting St. & 109 Broad St.
Stoll's Alley ran east to west from 4 East Bay to Church St.
Tobacco Inspection ran east to west from Meeting St. & King St. Roads.
Tobacco St. was south from the Inspection & north from Lowndes St
Tradd St. ran from east to west from 32 East Bay to the Ashley River
Trott St. ran east to west from 24 East Bay Cont'd to King St.
Union St. Cont'd. ran south to north from 123 Queen St. to Market .
Union St. ran south to north from 140 Broad St. to 8 Queen St.
Unity Alley ran east to west from 59 East Bay to Union St.
Vanderhorst St. ran east to west from King St. Road to Cannon's Mills.

Vanderhorst's Wharf was east from 140 to 144 East Bay.
Vanxhall Garden was at 93 Broad St.
Wall St ran south to north from Minority St. to Boundary St.
Water St. ran east to west from New Bay St. West to Meeting St.
Wentworth St. Cont'd ran to Lynch St., Wyatt's Mills
Wentworth St. ran east to west from 117 King St. to Coming St.
West St. ran east to west from 8 Archdale St. to Mazyck St.
Whim Court ran west to east into a cul-de-sac at 280 King St.
Williams' Wharf was northeast of Governor's Bridge at 44 East Bay Cont'd.
Work House was south of Magazine St. contiguous to the Jail.
Wyatt's Lot was north of Linguard St & northwest of Union St. Cont'd.

The assistance of Antoinette Dickson and Doug Mellard in the preparation of this volume is especially appreciated.

Chapter 1

THE 1803 DIRECTORY

This directory was compiled by Eleazer Elizer and published under the title of *A Directory for 1803, Containing the Names of all the House-Keepers and Traders in the City of Charleston, Alphabetically Arranged. Their Particular Professions, and Their Residence* (Charleston: Printed and Sold by W P Young, 41 Broad St, 1803, 64 pages)

In addition to the 2,191 entries included here, it contains the names of streets, public places, and wharves

Elizer was a Jewish resident of the city who was employed in the city assessor's office. He collected his information by making the rounds of the city and using the assessor's records. Originally he intended to include a list of the directors of banks, city and state office holders, and other information but decided this would add too much to the cost of the volume

----

Abbot, William, Merchant, 143 Bay St
Abendanone, David, Broker, 244 King St
Abendanone, Joseph, Broker, 244 King St
Abendanone, Zipporah, Shop Keeper, 244 King St
Abrahams, Israel, Shop Keeper, 125½ King St
Abrahams, Jacob, Shop Keeper, 4 Queen St
Abrahams, Judith, 11 Berresford St
Ackis, John, Shoe Maker, 6 East Bay Cont'd.
Adams, David, Factor, Vanderhorst's Whf
Adams, Ezekiel, House Carpenter, 6 Maiden Ln
Adams, John S, Distillery, 5 Quince St
Aertsen, Guilliam, Teller, State Bank, 128 Broad St
Aiken, William, Merchant, 31 Broad St
Ainger, Edward, Planter, 15 Ellery St
Air, James, Physician, Savage's Back St
Akeen, Helena, Shop Keeper, 32 Pinckney St
Akin, Ann, Boarding School, 117 King St, cor. Wentworth
Akin, Thomas, Physician, 117 King St, cor Wentworth
Alexander, Abraham, Jr, Shop Keeper, 183 King St
Alexander, Abraham, Sr, Scrivener, 129 King St.
Alexander, David, Merchant, 10 Broad St
Alexander, Judah, Shop Keeper, 109 King St
Alexander, Moses, Vendue Cryer, 109 King St
Alexander, Rachel, 56 Trott St
Alexander, William, Accountant, 13 Amen St
Allan, Mason & Ewing, Merchants, 113 Tradd St
Allan, William, Merchants, 5 Federal St
Allison, James, Cooper, 6 Champneys St
Allport, John, Blacksmith & Farrier, 113 King St
Allston, Joseph, 93 Church St
Allston, William, Planter, 13 King St

Ancrum, James H, Planter, 30 Hasel St
Ancrum, William, Planter, 22 Ellery St
Anderson, Ann, 4 Minority St
Anderson, Robert, Store Keeper, 18 Tradd St
Anderson, William, Stay Maker, 204 Meeting St
Andrew, Moses, Sea Captain, 4 Stoll's Al
Annely & Lewis, Merchants, 96 Church St
Anome, John & Co, Carvers & Gilders, 6 Broad St
Anthony, John, Saddler, 192 Meeting St
Antonio, Manuel, Merchant, Bull St
Appleton, Joseph, Sea Captain, 42 Elliot St
Arms, Sylvester, Sea Captain, 44 Trott St
Armstrong, Rachel, 8 Charles St
Armstrong, William, Saddler, 103 King St
Arthur, George, Shop Keeper, 242 Trott St
Artman, John, Cabinet Maker, 28 Meeting St.
Ash, Elizabeth, 5 Lamboll St
Ash, Hannah, 19 King St
Ash, John, Planter, 17 South Bay
Ash, Samuel E, Coach Maker, 169 Meeting St
Atkinson, William, Savage's Back St
Atmar, Ralph, State Bank, Out Door Clerk, 1 Lynch's Ln
Auld, Isaac, Physician, 46 Meeting St
Austen, James, Hatter, 7 Queen St
Austin, Catherine, Shop Keeper, 47 Bay St
Austin, William, Broker, 90 Meeting St
Avery, Park, Grocer, House, Champneys St
Axsom, ——, Mrs, 22 King St
Axsom, Jacob, S C Bank, Book Keeper, 91 King St
Axsom, Samuel E, House Carpenter, 22 King St
Ayrault, Peter, Merchant, Store, 120 Bay, Res, 40 Church St
Baas, Thomas, Block Maker, 1 Gillon St
Bacot, Henry, Attorney, 25 & 26 Tradd St
Bacot, Thomas W, Post Master & Cashier, S C Bank, 99 Tradd St
Badger, James, House, Painter & Glazier, 6 Berresford's Al, House, 7 Archdale St
Bailey & Waller, Merchant, 122 Broad St
Bailey, Antony, Shoe Maker, 2 Unity Al
Bailey, David, Merchant, 122 Broad St
Bailey, George C, Commission Store, 26 Church St
Bailey, Henry, Attorney, 42 Church St
Bain, Archibald, Merchant, 83 Church St
Baker, Amelia, W End of Wentworth St
Baker, Francis, Brick Layer, 37 King St
Baker, John, Boarding House, 20 Bay St
Baker, Joseph, Carpenter, 7 Society St
Baker, Samuel, Shop Keeper, 31 Beaufain St
Baker, Thomas, Brick Layer, 38 King St
Baker, Thomas, Insurance Broker, 23 Bay St
Ball, Archibald, Planter, 2 Liberty St
Ball, Elizabeth, 5 Church St
Ball, John, Planter, 31 Hasell St

Ball, Thomas, Factor, 9 Church St Cont'd,
Counting House, Roper's Whf
Ballon, Andrew, Shop Keeper, 133 Queen St
Bampfield, Henry, Scrivener, 77 Queen St
Bampfield, James, Scrivener, 77 Queen St
Bampfield, Thomas, Scrivener, 77 Queen St
Banks & Lockwood, Merchants, 116 Tradd St
Barker, Joseph S , Merchant, 93 Bay St
Barnard, —, Sea Captain, 42 Trott St
Barnet, Samuel, 46 Church St
Barrett, —, Mrs , 67 Meeting St
Barrett, James, Gardener, Bull St
Barrett, Judah, Shop Keeper, 230 King St
Barron, Alexander, Physician, W End of
Wentworth St
Barron, James, Merchant, Crafts' S Whf
Barron, John, Wine Merchant, 11 Bay St
Basileau, Lewis, Mariner, 29 Beaufain St
Bay, Elihu II , Associate Judge, 197 Meeting St
Beale, John, 32 Bay St
Beale, Joseph, Accountant, 95 Bay St
Beard, Elizabeth, 140 Broad St
Beard, Frederick, Teller, S C Bank, Montague cor
Coming
Beckman, Adolphus, Painter & Glazier, 161
Meeting St
Bee, Elizabeth, 12 Amen St
Bee, John S , Carpenter, 16 Amen St
Bee, Peter Smith, Planter, 22 Church St
Bee, Thomas, At the College
Bee, Thomas, Federal District Judge, 4 Short St
Bee, William, Accountant, 24 Church St Cont'd
Beekman, Eliza, 17 Bay St Cont'd
Beekman, Samuel, Pump Maker, Shop, 128 Bay St ,
House, 102 Queen St
Beiler, Joseph, Butcher, 23 Archdale St
Beissiere, Anthony, Taylor, 27 Church St
Belamy, —, Pilot, Lynch's Al
Bell, David, Accountant, 6 Middle St
Bellamy, Samuel, Merchant, 12 Broad St
Bellinger, George, Physician, 24 Mazyck St
Bellisle, Peter, Baker, Guignard St
Bennet, Asher, House Carpenter, 3 Lodge Al
Bennett, Henry, Counting House, 9 Liberty St
Bennett, Thomas, Jr , Sawmills, Bull St
Bennett, Thomas, Sr , Sawmills, Bull St
Benoist, Baptist, Baker, 138 Meeting St
Benoit, Teresa, Confectioner Shop, 25 Church St
Bentham, James, Q U & Notary Public, 39 Bay St
Benthel, Ebent, Mariner, Wyatt's Square
Bering, John, Silver Smith & Jeweller, Shop, 141
Broad St , House 192 King St
Bernard, Rene, Hair Dresser, 4 Tradd St
Berney, John, Broker, 28 King St
Bernstine, Henry, Shop Keeper, 2 Berresford Al.
Berresford, Richard, Planter, 2 St Michael's Al
Best, William, Rev , Greek Latin, & English
Academy, 193 King St
Bethune, Angus & Co , Merchants, 11 Broad St.

Bevin, Francis, Shop Keeper, 16 Union St Cont'd
Bezel, John, Shop Keeper, 30 Queen St
Bigelow, Elizabeth, 55 Trott St
Bishop, —, Sea Captain, 45 George St
Bixby, Joseph, Merchant, Crafts' N Whf
Bize, Daniel, House Carpenter, 33 Hasell St
Black, Ann, Boarding House, 13 Chalmer's Al
Black, James, Ship Carpenter, 92 East Bay St
Black, John, Ironmongery Store, 13 Broad St
Black, Nathaniel, 28 Meeting St
Blacklock & Bower, Merchants, 134 East Bay St
Blacklock, William, Merchant, Res , Bull St
Blackwood, Thomas, Merchant, Montague St
Blair, William, Ship Carpenter, 39 Church St
Cont'd
Blair, William, Vendue Master, 1 Stoll's Al
Blake & Magwood, Factor, Blake's Whf
Blake, John, President of State Bank, 5 South Bay
Blake, Peter, Work House, Upper End of Broad St
Blakely, Samuel & Co , Merchants, 29 Broad St &
Boundary St , cor King
Blakie, Elizabeth, 4 Church St
Blamyer, William, Weigher, Custom House, 21
Wall St
Bleakely, Seth, Tailor, 7 Clifford's Al
Blomberg, Peter, Accountant, 23 Guignard St.
Blood, Charles, Coach & Chair Maker, 14 Church
St
Blooms, Jean, Baker, 21 Berresford's Al
Blum, Andrew, 191 King St
Boatcher, Theobold, Accountant, 16 Scarborough
St
Bocquett, Elizabeth, Sr , 12 St Philip's St
Boisgerard, Constant & Fidelle, Merchants, 7 Anson
St
Boissou, Peter, Shop Keeper, 106 King St
Bold, Rodes & Otis, Factors, 14 East Bay St
Bollough, E , Shoe Maker, 88 Queen St
Bonneau, Eleanor, 59 Church St
Bonsall, Elizabeth, 5 Wentworth St
Bonthron, John, Grocer, 90 Queen St.
Boon, Thomas, Carpenter, 16 Ellery St
Booner, Christian, Shop Keeper, 95 Queen St
Booth, Benjamin, Merchant, 18 Front South Bay
Boothroy'd, Jabez, Grocer, 18 Archdale St
Bordroit, Joseph, Accountant, 68 Meeting St
Borley, Joshua, Grocer, 163 King St
Bounetheau, Edward, House Carpenter, 141
Meeting St
Bounetheau, Elizabeth, 67 Church St.
Bounetheau, Gabriel, M C C , 3 Quince St.
Bourgeois, Alexander, Shop Keeper, 106 King St
Bow, Ann, 76 Meeting St
Bowen, T. B., Printer, 3 Broad St.
Bowens, C , Grocer, 20 Quince St
Bowering, Henry, Merchant, 12 Tradd St
Bowers, Alexander, Merchant, 15 Friend St
Bowey, James, Ship Carpenter, 1 Federal Green or
Boundary St

Bowman, John, Planter, 31 Wentworth St
Boyd, Benjamin, Merchant, 134 King St
Boyden, Daniel, Shop Keeper, 230 King St
Boyer, Mary, 223 King St
Boyle, Jane, Ladies Boarding House, 23 Union St
Bradford, Lydia Ann, Boarding House, Church St
Bradford, Thomas, Music Store, 76 Church St
Bradley, Eleanor, Boarding House, 9 Stoll's Al.
Brailsford, Edward, Physician, 84 Meeting St
Brailsford, Morton, Accountant, 22 Tradd St
Brailsford, William, Planter, 32 Church St Cont'd
Brandford, Mary, 17 Legare St
Brandon, David, Confectioner, 68 King St
Brebner & Hueston, Merchant Tailors, 11 Tradd St
Bremar, Francis, 6 Wentworth St
Brenan, Martin, Grocer, 51 Queen St
Brennan, Mathew & R, Merchants, 146 Broad St.
Bride, Elizabeth, Umbrella Maker, 184 Meeting St
Bridey, Eleanor, School Mistress, 25 Meeting St
Brisky, Sarah, Boarding House, Champney St
Broaduss, Bartholemew, Boarding House, 34 Union
   St
Brockway, Martha, 173 King St
Brockway, Samuel, House Carpenter, 27 Trott St
Brodie, —, Painter, 2 Guignard St
Brodie, Robert, Carpenter, 56 Tradd St.
Brooks & Potter, Merchants, 7 Crafts' N Whf
Bross, John, Blacksmith, 30 Union St Cont'd
Broughton, Ann, 72 Queen St
Brower, Jeremiah, 6 Society St
Brown & Borrow, Merchants, 16 Broad St
Brown, Ann, Boarding House, 11 Berresford's Al
Brown, Daniel, Carpenter, 31 Church St. Cont'd
Brown, Daniel, Grocer, 100 Church St
Brown, John, Pilot, Kinloch Court
Brown, Jonathan, Shop Keeper, 165 Meeting St
Brown, Joshua, Broker, 2 Short St
Brown, Mary, 12 East Bay Cont'd
Brown, William, Boarding House, 23 Berresford's
   Al
Brown, William, Sea Captain, 14 Ellery St
Brown, William, Sea Captain of Savannah Packet, 2
   Maiden Ln
Browne, James, City Marshall, 164 Meeting St
Brownlee, John, Merchant, 14 St Philip's St
Bruckner, Daniel, Porter, S C Bank, 35 Church St
Brunston, John, Boundary St
Bryan, Jonathan, Store Keeper, 130 Broad St
Buchanan, Archibald, Brass Founder, Swinton's Ln
Buckle, George, Ship Carpenter, 31 Boundary St.
Budd, Abigail, Boarding House, 13 Church St
Buford, —, Miss, Milliner, 30 Church St
Buist, George, Minister Presbyterian Church, 3
   Church St Cont'd
Buley, Jacob, Shop Keeper, 164 King St
Bulgin, James, Merchant, 54 Church St.
Bulkley, P C, Grocer, 124 Queen St
Bulkley, Stephen, Merchant, 24 East Bay St
Bulow, John & Charles, Merchants, 166 King St

Burch, H T & Co, Merchants, 7 East Bay St,
   House, 71 East Bay St
Burden, Kinsy, Factor, Store, 10 Crafts' S Whf,
   House, 224 King St
Burgein, Susannah, Boarding House, 4 Union St
Burger, David, 97 Queen St
Burges, James, Merchant, 41 Church St, 123 Tradd
   St
Burk, Patrick, Cabinet Maker, 87 Queen St
Burke, —, Sea Captain, 12 Pinckney St
Burkemeyer, John, Butcher, W End of Wentworth
   St
Burkett, John, Boarding House, 32 Union St
Burn, John, Grocer, 131 Meeting St
Burnham, Thomas, Carpenter, 3 Maiden Ln
Burr, Nehemiah, Mariner, 35 Pinckney St
Burrows, Frederick, Pilot, 5 Trott St.
Butler, C P, Goldsmith & Jeweller, 236 King St
Butler, Joseph, Painter, 113 King St
Butler, Robert, Merchant, 54 Queen St
Byers, Joseph, Merchant, Store, 3 Blake's Whf,
   House, 76 Queen St
Bynam, Thomas, School Master, 2 Wentworth St
Byrnes, Patrick, Sail Maker, 37 Hasell St
Bythwood, Daniel, Sea Captain, 17 Coming St
Bythwood, Thomas, Sea Captain, 14 Amen St
Cabos, John, 101 Tradd St
Calder, Alexander, Cabinet Maker, 113 Queen St
Caldwell, Henry, Shop Keeper, 99 Church St
Caldwell, John, Carpenter, 1 Clifford St
Caldwell, John, Merchant, 5 Elliot St
Caldwell, Sarah, Lynch's Ln
Calhoun, John, Factor, 223 Meeting St
Calhoun, William, Merchant, Store, 6 Crafts' N
   Whf, House 8 Lamboll St
Calvert, Elizabeth, Boarding House, 152 Broad St
Calvert, J J, Brick Layer, 4 Maiden Ln
Cambridge, Eliza, 45 King St
Cambridge, Tobias, Vendue Master, Store,
   Exchange St, House, 6 Orange St
Cameron, Alexander, Dray Keeper, 81 King St.
Cameron, Lewis, Merchant, 23 Church St
Cameron, Samuel, Mariner, Wyatt's Square
Cameron, Samuel, Ship Carpenter, 4 Trott St
Cammer, Peter, 18 Wall St
Campbell, Colin, Broker, House, 3 Bedon's Al
Campbell, Laurence, Vendue Master, 10 St Philip's
   St
Campbell, M'Laughlan & Co, Merchants, 6 Tradd
   St
Campbell, M'Millan, Vendue Master, House, 31
   Church St
Canter, Emanuel & J, Shipping Merchants, 10
   Champneys St, House, 4 Savage St
Canter, Isaac, 28 Church St
Canter, Jacob, Sr.,
Canter, Joshua, Portrait & Minature Painter, 60
   Broad St
Canty, Ann, 2 Tanner's Ln.

Cape, Bryan, Notary Public, Factor, 77 East Bay St
Cape, Jonathan, 47 Trott St
Card, John, Baker, 31 Meeting St
Cardoza, David, Lumber Measurer, 17 Meeting St
Carmand, Peter, Tailor, 228 King St
Carnes, Lawrence, Shop Keeper, Upper End of King St
Carnes, Susannah, 25 Hasell St
Carnes, Thomas W, Grocer, 124 East Bay St
Carrach, ——, Shop Keeper, 28 Meeting St
Carriere, Charles, Teacher of French Language, 13 Hasell St
Carrison, ——, Sea Captain, 16 Friend St
Carson, James, Merchant, Store, 10 Broad St
Cart, John, Factor, Bull St
Carter, George, Physician, 110 Meeting St
Cary, Edward, Block Maker, 3 Ellery St
Cary, Thomas, Ship Carpenter, Pritchard's New Whf
Casey, Benjamin, Coach Maker, Shop, 121 Broad St, House, 121 Broad St
Castro, Jacob, Cigar Maker, 8 Berresford St
Cating, ——, Accountant, 2 Longitude Ln
Caught, Mary, Shop Keeper, 30 East Bay St Cont'd
Caulker, Thomas, Shipwright, 30 Pinckney St.
Caveneau, Thomas, Grocer, 5 East Bay St Cont'd.
Chalmers, Gilbert, Carpenter, 16 Beaufain St
Chambers, William S, Grocer, 21 Union St
Champney, ——, Madame, Shop Keeper, 130 Meeting St
Champneys, John, Planter, 95 King St.
Chancognie, S J, Commercial Agent, French Republic, 5 Charles St
Chandler, ——, Mrs., 52 Broad St
Chanet, Anthony, Shop Keeper, 8 Queen St
Charles, Andrew, Merchant, 14 Liberty St
Chattelin, ——, Madame, 4 Trott St
Cheves, Langdon, Attorney at Law, House, 32 George St
Cheves, Susannah, Shop Keeper, 97 King St
Chichester, John, Physician, 205 Meeting St
Chinners, John, 16 Pinckney St
Chion, J F, Merchant, Store, 17 East Bay St, House, 16 Broad St
Chisolm, Alexander, Planter, 287 King St
Chisolm, George, Factor, 30 Church St Cont'd
Chitty, William, Accountant, 46 Trott St
Chollet, Alexander, Distillery, 2 Coming St.
Chouler, Joseph, Physician & Apothecary, 147 Broad St
Christian, William, Shop Keeper, 18 Federal St
Christie, Alexander, Baker, 96 Queen St
Chupein, Lewis, Hair Dresser, 7 Elliot St.
Clarke, David, Shop, 141 Broad St, Watchmaker, House, 3 Price's Al
Clarke, James, Tailor, 11 Elliot St cr Bedon's Al, Chair Maker, 156 Meeting St
Clarke, Margaret, Boarding House, 35 Union St

Clarke, Marian, 50 Church St
Clarkson, William, Jr, Factor, House, 44 Meeting St, Store, 9 Champneys Whf
Clastiere, John, 286 King St
Claybrook, Richard, Boarding House, 22 Union St
Cleapor, Charles, Sail Maker, House, 17 Ellery St, Sail Loft, Nicholls' Whf
Cleary, John R, School Master, 20 Hasell St
Clement, Sarah, 44 Queen St
Clement, William, Planter, 76 Tradd St
Clime, Martin, House Carpenter, 130 King St
Clisse, Raymond, Coach & Harness Maker, 78 Church St
Clitheral, ——, Mrs, 33 East Bay St Cont'd
Club, Alexander, Grocer, Shop, 7 Tradd St
Club, Alexander, House, 21 Meeting St
Coats, William A, Grocer, 5 Prioleau's Whf
Cobia, ——, 12 Berresford St
Cochran, Charles, Federal Marshal, 20 Amen St
Cochran, Margaret, Shop Keeper, 243 King St
Cochran, Thomas, Sr, Factor, 122 East Bay St
Coffin, Ebenezer, Merchant, Bull St
Cogdell, John S, Attorney at Law, House, 1 St Michael's Al
Cogdell, Mary Ann, Boarding School, 1 St Michael's Al
Cohen & Moses, Vendue Masters, Store, Exchange Cellar
Cohen, Celia, 49 Church St
Cohen, Jacob & Co., Vendue Masters, Exchange St
Cohen, Joseph, Sexton of the Synagogue, 195 King St
Cohen, Mordecai, Shop Keeper, 210 King St
Cohen, Moses, Shop Keeper, 49 East Bay St
Cohen, Philip, Vendue Master, House, 10 Orange St
Cohen, Rebecca, Shop Keeper, 240 King St
Cohen, Solomon, Shop Keeper, 164 King St
Coils, Margaret, 10 Pinckney St
Coit, Jonathan & Co, Merchants, Crafts' S. Whf
Coit, Jonathan, Merchant, 54 Broad St
Colcock, Melicent, Boarding School, 6 Lamboll St
Cole, S, Nurse, 2 Clifford Al
Collins, ——, Boarding School, 34 King St
Collins, ——, Mrs, 4 Lynch's Ln
Collins, Daniel, Tavern Keeper, 7 Chalmers' Al
Colzy, C, Tailor, 19 Church St.
Condy, Jeremiah, Notary Public & Attorney, 31 East Bay St
Connolly, John, Sea Captain, 17 Meeting St
Connor, Bryan, Shoe Store, 126 Queen St
Connover, William, Printer, 4 Broad St
Conolly, William, 12 Bottle Al
Contey, Ann, 20 Wall St
Conty, George, House Carpenter, 36 King St.
Conyers, Elizabeth, School Mistress, 264 King St, Conyers, William, Sea Captain, 27 Pinckney St
Coram, Thomas, Limner, 70 Queen St
Corbett, Samuel, Tavern Keeper, 191 Meeting St

Corbett, Thomas, Jr, Merchant, 1 Roper's St
Corbett, Thomas, Sr, Merchant, 10 Cumberland St
Corkle, Thomas, Mariner, 17 Amen St
Cormick, Thomas, Grocer, 5 Union St Cont'd
Cormick, Thomas, Grocer, 71 East Bay St
Cornwall, Abraham, Carpenter, 17 Wall St
Corps, John, Mariner, 60 Church St
Corre, C G, Merchant, 54 King St
Corrie, Alexander & John, Merchants, 2 Prioleau's
    Middle Range
Corse, ——, Madame, 123 Meeting St
Cortould, Samuel, 69 Tradd St
Cosney, John, Physician, 40 Trott St
Cotton, James W, Carver & Gilder, 63 Meeting St
Cotton, Nancy, 13 Berresford's Al
Couie, John, Grocer, 41 Tradd St
Courtey, John, Grocer, 29 Union St
Courtney, Edward, Wine Merchant, 137 Broad St
Courtney, Humphrey, Merchant, 34 Meeting St
Courtney, James, Merchant Tailor, 36 Meeting St
Courtois, ——, Madame, Shop Keeper, 215 King St
Couzins, E, Boarding House, 26 Broad St
Coveny & Martin, Grocers, 6 Prioleau's N Whf
Coveny, Thomas, House, 28 Pinckney St
Cowen, John, Rigger, 35 East Bay Cont'd
Cox & Sheppard, Printers of the Times, 124 Tradd
    St, Res, 41 Broad St.
Cox, James, Merchant, 10 Church St Cont'd
Cox, John C R, Brick Layer, 2 Federal St
Cox, John, Tailor, 24 Queen St
Cox, Joseph D, House Carpenter, 126 Meeting St
Cox, Susanna, 126 Meeting St
Cox, Thomas Campbell, Printer, 124 Tradd St,
    Res, 41 Broad St
Crafts, Ebenezer, Merchant, 21 Tradd St.
Crafts, W & E, Merchants, Crafts' S Whf
Craig & Monor, Hair Dressers, 21 Queen St
Crane, Joseph, Boot & Shoe Store, 63 King St
Crask, Philip, Painter, 25 Quince St
Crawford, Alexander, Painter & Glazier, 212
    Meeting St
Crawford, James, Grocer, 68 Queen St
Crawford, John, Grocer, 23 King St
Crawford, John, Grocer, 33 King St
Crawford, William, Grocer, 88 East Bay St
Cripps, John Splatt, Merchant, 52 Meeting St
Crocker & Hichborn, Merchants, 8 Crafts' N Whf
Croft, Edward, Attorney, 39 Tradd St
Crofts, Peter, Factor, Prioleau's S Whf
Crombie, Joseph, Merchant, 15 Broad St.
Cromwell, Oliver, Attorney, 35 Tradd St
Crosby, Josiah, Sea Captain, 22 Scarborough St
Cross, George, Sea Captain, 19 East Bay St
    Cont'd.
Cross, James, Dyer, 5 Berresford St
Cross, John, Carpenter, 3 Pitt St
Cross, William, Brick Layer, Kinloch's Court
Crouch, Abraham, Notary Public, Counting House,
    Res, Broad St

Crovat, Peter, Shop Keeper, 26 Broad St
Crow & Query, Booksellers, 129 Broad St
Crowley, Michael, Merchant, 105 Broad St
Cruckshanks, Daniel, Shoe Maker, 120 Queen St
Cruckshanks, William, Grocer, 66 Broad St
Cruckshanks, William, Shoe Maker, 40 Elliot St
Cruger, David, Factor, House, 30 Meeting St, 3
    Cochran's Whf
Cruger, Elizabeth, 7 Guignard St
Cuckow, William, Pilot, 21 East Bay St Cont'd
Cudworth, Benjamin, Montague St
Cudworth, Nathaniel, 21 Trott St
Cumming, John, 172 King St
Cunningham & O'Neil, Merchants, 148 King St
Cunningham, Charles, 152 King St
Cunningham, Eleanor, 5 Bedon's Al
Curry & Thompson, Shoe Store, 65 King St
Custer, James, Factor, House, 38 Meeting St
Custer, Robert, Sea Captain, 213 Meeting St, at
    Prioleau's S Whf
D'Azevedo, Isaac, Shop Keeper, 79 King St
D'Oyley, Daniel, State Treasurer, 1 St. Philip's St
Dabney, William, Merchant, 29 Church St
DaCosta, Joseph, 1 Wentworth St
Daker, Charles & Co, Grocers, 88 Meeting St
Daker, Frederick, Grocer, 24 Union St
Dalcho, Frederick, Physician, 29 East Bay St
Daley, Henrietta, Boarding School, 37 Tradd St
Dalton, James, Medical Store, 127 Broad St
Darby, Artemas B, Deputy Surveyor General, 29
    Wentworth St
Darby, John, Shop Keeper, 5 Beaufain St
Darby, Robert, Tailor, 26 Union St Cont'd
Darrell, Keziah, 3 Water St
Dart & Simons, Factors, 7 Crafts' S Whf
Dart, Benjamin, Factor, Prioleau's S Range
Dart, Isaac Motte, Factor, Lynch's St
Dart, John, Attorney at Law, 28 Union St
Datty, J, French School, 29 Hasell St
Davidson, Gilbert, Merchant, 17 Broad St
Davis, ——, Accountant, 20 Queen St
Davis, Israel, Shop Keeper, 128 King St
Davis, John M, Broker & Commission Merchant,
    23 East Bay St.
Davis, Thomas, Shop Keeper, 185 King St
Davison, John, Charleston Librarian, House, 5
    Society St
Dawson, ——, Mrs, 16 Elliot St
Dawson, John & William, Merchants, 7 Broad St
Dawson, John, Jr., Merchant, Dwelling, 28 Hasell
    St
Dawson, John, Sr, Planter, 2 East Bay St Cont'd
Day, George, Goldsmith, 2 Champneys St
Deas, Charles, Merchant, 13 East Bay St Cont'd
Deas, David, Intendent of City, 66 Tradd St
Deas, Henry, Planter, 1 Friend St
Deas, Robert, Physician, 57 Queen St
Deas, Seaman, Planter, 13 East Bay St Cont'd
Deas, William Allen, Planter, 1 Meeting St.

DeBesse & Co , Dwelling, 120 King St
DeBesse & Co , Merchants, 106 East Bay St
DeBow, John, Grocer, 88 Meeting St
DeBow, William, Physician, 2 Queen St
DeCottes, ——, Madame, 15 Wall St.
DeLaHogue, J B , 8 Federal St
DeLaire & Canut, Factors, Nicholls' Whf
DeLaRue, R , Merchant, Store, 5 Gaillard's Whf.
DeLeon, Jacob, Vendue Master, House, 80 Tradd
St
DeLieben, Israel, Shop Keeper, 48 East Bay,
Vendue Store, Exchange St
DeLorme, Francis, Upholsterer, 42 Broad St
Dener, George, Tanner, 25 Archdale St
Dennis, Richard, 11 Hasell St
Dennison, James, Cooper, 38 Elliot St
Denny, Thomas, Physician, 13 Church St.
Denoon, David, Factor, 38 Trott St
Denton, James, 5 St Philip's St
Depass, Ralph, Vendue Master, House, 194 King
St , Store, Champneys St
Depau, ——, Merchant, 17 Society St
Depau & Toutain, Merchants, 95 East Bay St
DeSaussure & Ford, Office, 29 Tradd St
DeSaussure, H W , Attorney at Law, 206 Meeting
St
Desbeau, John, Cooper, 3 Cumberland St
Desel, Charles, Cabinet Maker, 50 Broad St
Desjardans, ——, Shop Keeper, 20 Queen St
DeVago, Moses, Shop Keeper, 66 King St
DeVeaux, Jacob, Sr , 23 Meeting St
DeVilliers, L , Music Master, 257 King St
Dewar, Robert, Director of S C Bank, 82 Tradd St
Dewees, William, Factor, Prioleau's S Range
Dickinson, Francis, Attorney at Law, 7 Cumberland
St
Dickinson, J F , Merchant, 121 Tradd St
Dickinson, Joseph, Carpenter, 203 Meeting St
Dickinson, Joseph, Inspector of Exports, 61 Meeting
St
Dickinson, Samuel, Vendue Master, Store, 1
Champneys St
Dierson, Barnard, Grocer, 3 Union St
Dilio, ——, 171 King St
Dill, Jane, 9 Price's Al
Dill, Susanna, 274 King St
Dixon, Samuel, School Master, 143 King St
Dobel, Joseph, Boarding House, 61 Meeting St
Don, Alexander, Mariner, 21 Federal St
Donaldson, James, Carpenter, 103 Tradd St
Doughty, Thomas, Factor, House, 51 Meeting St ,
Store, 2 Gaillard's Whf
Doughty, William, Planter, 2 Smith's St
Douglas, Alexander, Tailor, 105 Tradd St
Douglas, James, Shop Keeper, 97 Church St
Douglas, James, Turner, 186 Meeting St
Douglas, John, Cabinet Maker, 186 Meeting St.
Drake, John, Block Maker, 6 Trott St

Drayton, Jacob, Prothonotary, House, 96 Tradd St ,
Office, State House
Drayton, John, Planter, 74 Queen St
Drenniss, George, Baker, 34 Beaufain St
Drouillard, James, 37 Trott St
Drummond, James, Shoe Maker, 121 Queen St
Drummond, John, Shoe Maker, 2 Broad St
Dryburgh, ——, Sea Captain, 14 Pinckney St
Dubard, Peter, Hair Dresser, 84 Tradd St
Dubarre, Stephen, 18 Pinckney St
Dubois & Ross, Tailors, 39 Meeting St
Duboise, D , Grocer, 32 Church St
Duboise, Peter, Carpenter, Meeting St , Wyatt's
Square
Duddle, James, Cabinet Maker, 209 Meeting St
Dueston, Stephen, Lt , City Guard, 4 Pitt St
Duffus, John, Merchant, 18 Elliot St
Duffy, Patrick, Grocer, 234 King St
Dulles, Joseph, Merchant, House, 7 Church St
Cont'd , Store, 33 East Bay St
Dumoutet, John, Goldsmith & Jeweller, 120 Broad
St
Duncan, Archibald, Blacksmith, 103 Queen St ,
Store, 118 Queen St
Duncan, James C , Factor, 5 Cumberland St
Duncan, John, Merchant, House, 46 Tradd St ,
Store, 6 Champneys Whf
Dunlop & Johnston, Medical Store, 5 Broad St
Dunlop, Robert, Physician, 5 Broad St.
Dunseeth, James A , Physician, Rope Ln
Dupree, Benjamin, Tailor, 75 East Bay St
Dupuis, Claudias, Merchant, 175 King St
Dutch, Stephen, Accountant, 5 Guignard St
Duvall, John, Carpenter, 107 Church St.
Dwight, O D , Merchant, 83 Church St
Dyre, Kendall, Grocer, 139 Broad St
Easton, Robert, Merchant, 46 Meeting St
Easton, William, Blockmaker, 9 Guignard St
Eberly, Barbary, 17 Guignard St
Eckhard, Jacob, Organist & Music Teach , 47 Tradd
St
Eddy, John, Carpenter, 22 St Philip's St
Edward, George, Planter, 90 Tradd St
Edwards, Alexander, Attorney & Recorder of the
Inferior Court, 3 St Michael's Al.
Edwards, Isaac, Factor, Prioleau's S. Whf , House,
10 Friend St
Edwards, James, Factor, Geyer's S Whf
Egleston, John, Grocer, 67 Bay
Ehlers & Weets, Grocers, 33 Union St
Ehney & Chinners, Tailors, 1 Elliot St
Ehney, Frederick, Accountant, 18 Magazine St
Ehney, Peter, Merchant Tailor, 32 Church St
Ehrick, John M , Broker & Commission Merchant,
107 Broad St
Elfe, Thomas, Carpenter, 17 Wentworth St
Elizer, Eleazer, Notary Public, 195 King St
Elizer, Isaac, 195 King St
Elliot, ——, Mrs Thomas O , 15 Legare St

Elliot, Barnard, Planter, 29 George St
Elliot, Mary, 17 Legare St
Elliot, Thomas, Planter, 5 Gibbes St
Elliott, Ann, 29 Wentworth St
Ellis, Thomas, Carver, 14 Scarborough St
Ellison, Henry, Grocer, 125 Bay St
Ellison, John, Shop Keeper, 216 King St
Ellison, William, Grocer, 62 King St
Ellmore, Dorcas, 92 Church St
Ellstob, Simon, Painter & Glazier, 64 Meeting St
Ellsworth, John T, Shop Keeper, King St
Ellsworth, Theophilus, Guager, W End of
    Wentworth
England, Alexander, Baker, 100 Tradd St
English, Ann, 7 King St
Enguard, Oliver, Grocer, 89 Queen St
Ernest, Jacob, Taylor, 22 Queen St
Eschauffe, Guilliam, Mattress Maker, 42 Meeting
    St
Estell, Bordman, Brick Layer, Wyatt's Ln, from
    Union St Cont'd
Evans, James, Shoe Maker, 36 Broad St
Evans, John, Printer, 11 Maiden Ln
Evans, Leacraft, 85 Queen St.
Evringham, John, Merchant, 136 King St
Ewing, John, Merchant, 214 Meeting St
Faber, John C, Minister of German Church, Moore
    St.
Fair & Haig, Grocers, 181 Meeting St
Fair, Richard, Shoe & Boot Maker, 107 King St
Fair, Robert, Shoe & Boot Maker, 94 King St
Fair, William, Shoe & Leather Warehouse, Upper
    End of King St
Fairchilds, Aaron, Blacksmith, 15 George St
Fairley, Hance, Cabinet Maker, 65 Meeting St
Fanning, Maria, Mantua Maker, 241 King St
Farley, J, Boot & Shoe Store, 27 Broad St
Farrow, Thomas, Shoe Maker, 254 King St
Fasche, Sarah, Shopkeeper, 247 King St
Faures, F, Merchant, House, 15 Society St
Fayolle, Peter, Dancing Master, 260 King St
Fayssoux, Ann, 67 Tradd St
Fearreau, M, 162 King St
Fell, Thomas, Sr, Shop Keeper, 24 Broad St.
Ferguson & Gunter, Merchants, 87 Church St
Ferguson, Ann, 3 Liberty St
Fiddy, William, Vendue Master & Grocer, 8 Gillon
    St
Fields, William B, Clerk, St. Philip's Church, 12
    Ellery St
Finlay & Turnbull, Factors, 5 Cocham's Whf
Finlay, Jacob, Brick Layer, 1 Mazyck St
Finlay, John, Factor, Prioleau's N Whf
Fisher, James, 16 S Bay
Fisher, Peter, Merchant, 39 Trott St
Fitzpatrick & Thompson, Tailors, 107 Tradd St
Fitzsimmons, Christopher, Distillery, 6 Quince St
Fitzsimmons, Christopher, Merchant, 73 East Bay
Flagg, George, Sr, 212 King St

Flagg, Samuel H, Dentist, 26 Queen St
Fleming, Robert, Merchant, cor of King & George
    St
Fletcher, Thomas, Merchant, 6 Crafts' S Whf
Flin, Margaret, Shop Keeper, 9 King St
Flint, Joseph, Grocer, 31 Union St Cont'd
Florence, Zachariah, Shop Keeper, 126 King St
Florin, Lucas, 32 Guignard St
Fogartie, James, Factor, Prioleau's S Whf
Foissine, ——, Mrs, Boarding House, 89 Tradd St
Folker, John Casper, 38 Beaufain St
Folmer, J, Taylor & Habit Maker, 106 Tradd St
Foltz, J F, Merchant, Dwelling, 2 Longitude Ln
Footman, John W, Broker & Scrivener, Office, 105
    Broad St, House, Lynch's St
Forbes, John, Tin Plate Worker, 134 Queen St
Ford, Jacob, Attorney at Law, 19 Tradd St
Ford, John, Mariner, 140 Meeting St
Ford, Timothy, Attorney at Law, 29 Tradd St
Forneau, John, Pilot, 26 Pinckney St
Forrest, C, 2 Hasell St
Forrest, Thomas Hunter, Cooper, 262 King St
Foster, Nathan, Grocer, 13 Elliott St
Foster, Robert H., Merchant, 35 Elliott St.
Foster, Robert, Shop Keeper, 3 Tradd St
Foster, Thomas, National Bank, Outdoor Clerk,
    House, 285 King St
Foucard, ——, Musician, 256 King St
Fouchett, Charles, Shop Keeper, 119 King St
Fowler, Mary, Boarding House, 36 East Bay
    Cont'd
Francis, Amelia, Boarding House, 7 Champneys
    Row
Fraser, John M, House Carpenter, 26 Trott St
Fraser, Mary, 27 King St
Fraser, Thomas, Planter, 86 Meeting St
Frederick, John, National Bank Guard, 1 Price's Al
Freeman, William, Teller, National Bank, 91 Tradd
    St
Freneau & Williams, Printers, City Gazette, 44 East
    Bay
Freneau, Peter, Printer, 34 George St
Friend, Ulrick, Baker, 22 East Bay Cont'd
Frish, Charles, Shop Keeper, 181 King St.
Fronti, Michael, Physician, 11 Moore St.
Frost, Thomas, Rev, St Philip's Church,
    Wentworth St
Fuller, Oliver, Sea Captain, 16 Society St.
Furman, Richard, Rev, Baptist Church, 10 Church
    St
Furman, Wood, School Master, 10 Stoll's Al
Futerrell, James, Teller, S C Bank
Fyle, James, Cooper, House, 4 Champneys St,
    Shop, 18 Bay
Gabeau, Anthony, Tailor, 190 Meeting St
Gadsden, Christopher, Factor, 16 Front St, Bay
Gadsden, James, Factor, 73 Queen St
Gadsden, Martha, 19 Front St, Bay
Gadsden, Philip, Factor, 8 Front St. Bay

Gaillard & Mazyck, Factors, 1 Gaillard's Whf
Gaillard, Bartholomew, Merchant, Dwelling, 1
  Anson St , Store, 94 East Bay
Gaillard, Theodore, Attorney at Law, 45 Meeting
  St
Gaillard, Theodore, Jr , Montague St
Gaillard, Theodore, Sr , 78 East Bay
Gairdner, Edwin, Merchant, 72 East Bay
Galbraith, Robert, Carpenter, 14 George St
Gallachattt, Mary, Shop Keeper, 77 Meeting St
Gallagher, S. F , Rev , Minister of Roman Catholic
  Church, 28 Wentworth St
Galloway, Alfred, Pilot, 8 Church St
Gamboll, ——, Mrs , Shop Keeper, Upper End of
  King St
Gandowin, Isidore, Shop Keeper, 58 East Bay
Gappin, William, Chair Maker, 7 Liberty St
Garden, Alexander, Physician, 121 East Bay
Garden, John, Block Maker, Ellery St
Gardner, John, Blacksmith, 5 Maiden Ln
Gardner, Samuel, Tailor, 35 Broad St
Gardon, Anthony, Shop Keeper, 14 Union St
  Cont'd
Garnett, William, Boarding House, 196 Meeting St
Gates, Jacob, Grocer & Wagon Yard, Upper End of
  King St
Gaultier, Joseph, Vendue Master, 81 Tradd St
Geddes, Henry, Shop Keeper, 176 King St
Geddes, John, Attorney, Dwelling, 15 Beaufain St ,
  Office, 120 Broad St
Geddes, Robert, Shop Keeper, 156 King St.
Gennerick, John F , Shop Keeper, 150 King St
Gensel, John, Keeper of the Jail, Green
George, James, Shipwright, 31 East Bay Cont'd
George, Mark, Grocer, 289 King St
George, Mary, Shop Keeper, 204 King St
Gerhard, John, Cigar Maker, 11 Mazyck St
Gerke, Frederick, Confectioner, 37 Queen St
Gerrard, Philip, Grocer, 30 Pinckney St
Gervais, ——, Mrs , 85 Broad St
Gervais, St Clair D , Attorney at Law, 85 Broad St
Geyer, Greenman, Carpenter, 9 Berresford St
Geyer, John, Merchant, 35 King St. (Dwelling)
Geyer, John W , Factor, 3 Geyer's S Whf
Gibbes, George, Baker, 29 Elliott St
Gibbes, John, Planter, 48 Church St Cont'd
Gibbes, Lewis, Planter, 8 South Bay
Gibbes, Robert R , Planter, 8 Meeting St
Gibbes, Sarah, 14 Meeting St
Gibbes, William H , Master in Equity, State House
  Square
Gibson & Broadfoot, Merchants, 143 East Bay
Gibson, James, Coach Maker, 58 Broad St & 55
  Meeting St
Gibson, Patrick, Merchant, 31 Church St
Gidiere, Margaret, Grocer, Upper End of King St.
Gidney, Isaac, House Carpenter, 5 Minority St
Gilbert, Elizabeth, 25 Church St Cont'd

Gilbert, J J , Saddler & Harness Maker, 21 Hasell
  St
Gilbertz, Peter, Brewer, 1 Magazine St
Gilchrist, Adam, President, National Bank, 12
  Church St
Gill, John, Livery Stable, Market Square
Gillespie & Mackay, Merchants, 30 East Bay
Gillon, Ann P , 2 Wall St
Gillon, Archibald, Counting House, 23 King St
Gist, Nathaniel & F , Merchants, 146 King St
Given, Mary, 161 King St
Gladden, Joseph, Carpenter, 20 Pinckney St
Glenn, John, Planter, 54 Tradd St
Glover, Charles, Jr , Physician, 168 King St
Glover, Charles, Sr , Register of Mesne
  Conveyance, 168 King St , Office, State House
Glover, Wilson, Planter, 2 Meeting St
Godard, Rene, Broker, 2 Moore St
Godfrey, Elizabeth, 280 King St
Godfrey, Thomas, Carpenter, 25 King St
Godfrey, William, Champneys St
Gojahn, Theodore, Cigar Maker, Upper End of
  Meeting St.
Goldfinch, Charles, Boarding House, 39 Union St
Goldsmith, Abraham, 127 King St
Goldsmith, Morris, Shop Keeper, 127 King St
Gomez, Jacob, Shop Keeper, 75 King St
Gomez, Lewis, Turnkey of the Jail
Gondrand, Antony, Ship Carpenter, 2 Trott St
Goods, Sarah, School Mistress, 42 King St
Goodton, Peter, Mariner, 136 Meeting St
Goodwin, Mary, Amen St.
Gordon & M'Call, Grocers, 27 Wentworth St
Gordon & Miller, Merchants, 26 East Bay
Gordon, Andrew, Brick Layer, 101 Queen St
Gordon, Martha, 4 Parsonage Ln
Gordon, Thomas, Cashier, Counting House, 8
  Orange St
Gordon, Thomas, Grocer, 68 Bay, cor Queen St
Gordon, William & R , Grocers, 87 King St
Gowdy, ——, Mrs , 58 King St
Grado, ——, Mariner, 4 Ellery St
Graeser, Jacob C , Merchant, 100 Queen St.
Graeser, Lewis A & Co , Merchants, 9 Tradd St.
Grant, ——, Mrs , School Mistress, 43 Trott St
Grant, Adrian, 34 Pinckney St
Grant, Alexander, Merchant, 92 Church St.
Grant, Joseph, Rigger, 63 Church St
Grascoll, Anthony, Musical Instrument Maker, 7
  Chalmer's Al
Gravenstine, Frederick, Shop Keeper, 2 Berresford
  St
Graves & Swinton, Factors, Geyer's S. Range
Graves, Charles, Factor, 55 Tradd St
Graves, Massey, 8 Smith's Ln
Gray, Benjamin, Planter, Montague St
Gray, Caleb, Shop Keeper, 140 King St
Gray, E , Shop Keeper, 20 Tradd St
Gray, William Russell, Brick Layer, Whim Court

8

Green, J C , Shop Keeper, 14 Trott St.
Green, John, Fruit Shop, 6 Queen St
Greenhill, Hume, Carpenter, 63 Tradd St
Greenland, George, Factor, 31 Meeting St , Store, Prioleau's S Whf
Greenwood, William, Jr , Merchant, 1 Ellery St
Greenwood, William, Sr , Planter, 17 Beaufain St
Gregorie, James, Jr & Cosby, Merchants, 133 Broad St
Gregorie, James, Merchant, 133 Broad St
Grierson, James, Tavern Keeper, 65 East Bay
Griffin, Lewis, Harness Maker, 183 Meeting St
Griffiths & Mancie, Grocers, 118 East Bay
Griggs, Isaac, Attorney at Law, 80 East Bay
Grimball, John, Planter, 21 Church St Cont'd
Grimke, J. F , Associate Judge, 6 Front S. Bay
Gripon, Baptist, Shop Keeper, Trott St
Groning, Lewis & R , Merchants, 144 East Bay
Grosman, Mary, Shop Keeper, 2 Mazyck St
Gruber, Catharine, W End of Wentworth St
Gruber, Christian, School Master, 15 Berresford St
Gruber, Samuel, 6 Chalmer's Al
Guilbert, Eugene, Professor of Music, 1 Wall St
Guilou, Samuel, Tailor, 109 Queen St
Gunn, William, Gunsmith, 5 Queen St
Gunter, William, 11 Trott St
Guy, Christopher, House Carpenter, Wyatt's Square
Guy, James, Tailor, Boundary St
Hackell & Oswald, Tailors, 20 Elliott St
Hackerty, ——, Mrs , Boarding House, 8 Friend St
Hadden, Gardnir, Tailor, 95 Church St
Hagar, James, 10 Water St.
Hagarthy, Jane, Boarding House, 18 Champneys Al
Haig, David, Cooper, 132 Meeting St
Haig, Robert, Carpenter, 42 Trott St
Hall, ——, Misses, 216 Meeting St
Hall, Daniel, Factor, Dwelling, 2 State House Square
Hall, Dominick A , 25 Elliott St
Hall, James, Stone Cutter, 5 Ellery St
Hall, Mary A , 19 Magazine St
Hall, Thomas, Planter & Clerk of Federal Court, 33 Broad St
Hall, William & Co , Merchants, 17 Broad St
Hall, William, Sea Captain, 7 Front St. Bay
Halliday, Hugh, Cooper, 11 Champneys St
Ham, Samuel, Ship Carpenter, Dwelling, 11 Amen St , Ham's Whf ,
Ham, Thomas, Factor, 9 Anson St.
Hamett, Charlotte, 14 Elliott St
Hamilton, Malborough, School Master, German Society House, Archdale St
Hamilton, Paul, Comptroller, Dwelling, 12 Legare St , Office, State House
Hanby, John & Co , Grocers, 145 Meeting St
Hancock, Richard, Sea Captain, 9 Union St
Hands, John, Sea Captain, 6 Cumberland St

Harby, Solomon, Vendue Master & Commission Merchant, 198 King St , Store, Exchange St
Hare, ——, Mrs , 1 Bull St
Hare, Francis, Shop Keeper, 16 Union St
Hargreaves, J & J , Merchants, Store, 7 Gillon St
Hargreaves, Joseph, Merchant, 3 Parsonage Ln
Harleston, Ann, 83 Meeting St
Harleston, William, Planter, 90 Broad St.
Harper, James, Baker, 43 Tradd St
Harper, John, Iron Monger Shop, 122 Queen St
Harriott, ——, Shop Keeper, 257 King St
Harris, ——, Mrs , Shop Keeper, 222 King St
Harris, Andrew, Shop Keeper, 58 East Bay
Harris, Jacob, Shop Keeper, 159 King St
Harris, Tucker, Physician, 71 King St
Harrison, Thomas, Rigger, 11 Bottle Al.
Hart, Daniel, Shop Keeper, 54 East Bay
Hart, Dorcas, School Mistress, 17 Federal St
Hart, Joseph, Shop Keeper, 45 East Bay
Hart, Sarah, Shop Keeper, 4 Queen St
Hart, Simon M , Merchant, 190 King St
Hart, Stewart & Co, Vendue Masters, Store, Exchange St
Harth, John, Planter, 1 South Bay
Harvey, ——, Mrs , cor of George & King St
Harvey, Archibald, Deputy Sheriff, 10 Society St
Harvey, Benjamin, Brick Layer, Lynch St
Harvey, Elizabeth, 120 Meeting St
Harvey, Samuel, Sea Captain, 28 Guignard St
Haslett, John, Merchant, 6 Bedon's Al , Store, 2 Blake's Whf
Haslett, John, Painter, 7 Stoll's Al
Hatch, Robert, Sea Captain, 15 Union St Cont'd
Hatter, Elizabeth B , 32 Queen St
Hattier, H , Grocer, 117 East Bay
Hauck, John, Grocer, 10 Anson St
Hawie & Avery, Grocers, 120 East Bay
Hawie, Thomas, Grocer, 13 Amen St
Hawkings, ——, Mrs , 83 Tradd St
Hazard, ——, Sea Captain, 23 East Bay Cont'd
Hazlehurst, Robert, Merchant, 14 East Bay
Heavy, Dennis, Tailor, 220 King St
Hemmett, Thomas, Chair Maker, 112 Meeting St
Hemmett, William, Rev , 8 Maiden Ln
Henderson, Daniel, Lock Smith & Bell Hanger, 24 Queen St.
Henderson, Robert, Mail Coach Office, Market Square
Henry, ——, Grocer, 28 Union St
Henry, Ann, Milliner, 22 Elliott St
Henry, Jacob, Shop Keeper, 200 King St
Henry, Julian, Cabinet Maker, 183 Meeting St
Henson, Archibald, Carpenter, 1 Minority St
Henwood, Robert, Boat Builder, 6 Wall St
Henwood, S B , Merchant, 6 Wall St
Heron, John, Merchant, 145 King St
Hertz, Henry, Shop Keeper, 131 King St
Heyward, ——, Mrs , Planter, 10 Legare St
Heyda, David, Grocer, 154 Meeting St

Heyward, Nathaniel, Planter, 26 East Bay
Heyward, Thomas, Planter, 9 Church St
Hildreth, Benjamin, Sail Maker, 22 Wall St , Loft,
  Champneys St
Hill, Hannah, Miss, 24 Meeting St
Hill, Paul, Cane & Wire Worker, 28 Archdale St
Hill, Thomas, 10 Broad St
Hillegas, Philip, Distiller, Savage's Back St
Hillstrup, Thomas J , 57 Church St
Himely John G , Watch & Clock Maker, 135 Broad
  St
Himley, John M , Academy, Price's Al
Hinds, Thomas, Attorney at Law, 33 Broad St
Hipper, ——, Sea Captain, 8 Pinckney St
Hipper, Peter, Grocer, 146 Meeting St
Hislop, Robert B , Tailor, 58 Church St
Hislop, Robert, Factor, 80 East Bay
Hitchborn, ——, Merchant, 23 Tradd St
Hodgson, Mary, 41 King St
Hogarth, William, 9 Quince St
Hollingshead, William, Minister of Independent
  Church, 79 Meeting St
Holmes, Abel, Merchant, 188 Meeting St
Holmes, Andrew, Merchant, 4 Pinckney St
Holmes, Isaac, Planter, 13 Legare St
Holmes, John B , Attorney at Law, 6 Meeting St
Holmes, Thomas, Counting House, Wyatt's Ln
Holmes, William & Co , Vendue Masters, 129 East
  Bay
Holmes, William, Vendue Master, Dwelling,
  Manigault St
Honeywood, Elizabeth, Blacksmith, 59 Meeting St
Honor, John, Saddler, 13 Coming St
Hook, Conrod, Carpenter, 8 Ellery St
Hope, ——, City Hotel, 55 East Bay
Hopkins & Charles, Merchants, 5 Crafts' S Whf
Hopkins, Ebenezer & Co , Grocers, 16 Church St
Hopkins, John, Merchant, 98 Tradd St
Hore, Thomas, Grocer, 8 Champneys St
Horlbeck, George, Chair & Coach Maker, 149
  Meeting St
Horlbeck, Henry, Brick Layer, 3 Moore St
Horlbeck, John, Jr , Brick Layer, 9 Moore St
Horlbeck, John, Sr , Brick Layer, 8 Moore St
Hornby, Hannah, Boarding School, 203 King St
Horry, Elias Lynch, Planter, 81 Broad St
Horry, Elias, Planter
Horry, Harriott, 59 Tradd St.
Horry, Thomas, Jr , Planter, 225 Meeting St
Horry, Thomas, Sr , Planter, 27 Meeting St
Horst, Antony, Black Smith, 20 Berresford's Al
Hosier, James, Store, 5 Gillon St
Houlton, James, 4 Cumberland St
House, Samuel, Justice of the Peace & Notary
  Public
Houser, Elias, Weigher of Hay, 4 Smith's Ln
Houston, James, Carpenter, 3 Wall St.
Howard, Ann, 1 George St
Howard, John, Brick Layer, 1 George St

Howard, Richard, Cooper, 4 Gillon St
Howard, Robert, Tax Collector, 1 George St ,
  Office, Exchange
Hoyland, Ann, School Mistress, 102 Broad St
Hrabowskie, John, Planter, 45 Broad St
Hueston, Samuel, 16 Berresford St
Huff, John, Carpenter, Unity Al
Huger, ——, Misses, 85 Meeting St
Huger, Daniel E , Planter, 12 Legare St
Huger, Daniel, Secretary of State, Dwelling, 82
  Queen St , Office, Guard House
Huger, John, Planter, 88 Broad St
Hugg, Abigail, Spinster, 241 King St
Hughes, Edward, Planter, 3 Lynch's Ln
Hughes, Edward, Teacher, 36 Tradd St
Hughes, Henry, Merchant, 44 Church St
Hughes, James, 3 Amen St
Hughes, John, Accountant, 212 Meeting St
Hughes, Mary, Boarding House, 7 Trott St
Hulbert, Thomas, Saddler, 115 King St
Humbert, Godfrey, Carpenter, 5 Lynch's Ln
Hume, John, Planter, Montague St
Humphreville, T B , Merchant, 3 Champneys St.
Hunter, James, Grocer, 66 East Bay
Hunter, James, Ship Carpenter, 2 Minority St
Hunter, John, Hair Dresser, 28 Queen St
Hunter, Thomas, Sea Captain, 64 Church St
Huray, M , Madame, Mantua Maker, 167 Meeting
  St
Hussey, Benjamin, Pilot, 12 Water St
Hutchinson, ——, Mrs , South Bay
Hutchinson, Jeremiah, Chair Maker, Pitt St
Hutchinson, John, Chair Maker, 5 Archdale St
Hutley & Wood, Chair & Harness Makers, 115
  King St
Hutton, James, Factor, Dwelling, Bull St , Office,
  12 South Bay
Huxhams, ——, Misses, Milliners, 13 Tradd St
Hyams, David, Shop Keeper, 182 King St
Hyams, Samuel, Vendue Master, Dwelling, 62 East
  Bay, Store, Exchange Cellar
Hyams, Solomon & Co., Vendue Masters,
  Exchange St
Hyslop, Christiana, Shop Keeper, 3 Union St.
  Cont'd.
Icardon, L. & C , Grocers, 13 Trott St
Inglesby & Monk, Merchant Tailors, 126 Broad St
Inglesby, William, Merchant Tailor, 24 Tradd St
Ingraham, Nathaniel, Merchant, 292 King St , Store,
  149 East Bay
Ireland, Benjamin & Co , Grocers, 93 Queen St.
Irving, Mathew, Physician, 7 Meeting St
Izard, Henry, Planter, Bull St
Izard, Ralph, Jr , Planter, 99 Broad St
Izard, Ralph, Sr , Planter, 1 Meeting St
Jacks, ——, Mrs , 125 Broad St
Jackson & Donnan, Shoestore & Factors, 130
  Queen St
Jackson, George, Boarding House, 12 Chalmers' Al

Jackson, John, Watchmaker, Dwelling, 19 Quince
  St
Jacob, Eliza, Spinster, 7 Wentworth St
Jacobs, Barnett, Shop Keeper, 13 Queen St
Jacobson, C H, Shop Keeper, 98 King St
Jacques, Victor, Fisherman, 123 East Bay
Jahan, Joseph, Architect, Upper End of Meeting St
James, ——, Mrs, Milliner, 21 Archdale St
James, Elizabeth, 3 Liberty St
James, John, House Carpenter, 21 Archdale St
Jeannerett, C, Clerk of the State Bank, 20 East Bay
Jeffe, Sarah, 49 Broad St
Jeffers, ——, Mrs, 5 Price's Al
Jeffers, Mary, Mantua Maker, 5 Price's Al
Jeffers, Samuel, Tailor, 21 Pinckney St
Jenkins, Edward, Minister, St Michael's Church, 10
  Lamboll St
Jenkins, Elias, Brick Layer, 13 Liberty St
Jenkins, Micah, Planter, 75 Tradd St
Jennings, Elizabeth, 9 East Bay
Jenny, John, Baker, 3 Berresford's Al
Jessop, J, Hotel, 127 East Bay
Jewell, Benjamin, Shop Keeper, 59 East Bay
Johnson & Dunlop, Physicians, 5 Broad St
Johnson, Elizabeth, Shop Keeper, 83 King St
Johnson, Jabez W, Watch Maker, 138 Broad St
Johnson, John, Jr, Blacksmith, Shop & Counting
  House, 3 Gillon St, Dwelling, 7 East Bay Cont'd
Johnson, John, Sr, Justice of the Peace, 158 King
  St
Johnson, Joseph, Physician, 48 Broad St
Johnson, William, Jr, Judge, 66 Church St
Johnson, William P, Shop Keeper, 158 King St
Johnson, William, Sr, Blacksmith, 10 Charles St
Johnston, David, Deputy Collector, 82 Queen St
Johnston, John W, Attorney at Law, 82 Queen St
Johnston, Robert, Planter, 10 South Bay
Johnston, Sarah, 8 Liberty St
Jones, Alexander, Merchant, 78 Tradd St.
Jones, Daniel, Tailor, 2 Union St Cont'd
Jones, Edward, Physician, 4 Orange St
Jones, Henry, Merchant, 18 Church St
Jones, Henry, Ship Carpenter, 6 Maiden Ln
Jones, Joseph, Shop Keeper, 14 Tradd St
Jones, Margaret, 29 King St
Jones, Nathaniel, 8 Tradd St
Jones, Samuel B, S C Bank, 1 Charles St
Jones, Samuel, Shop Keeper, 248 King St
Jones, Sarah, Boarding School, 2 Anson St
Jones, Thomas, President, S.C. Bank, 1 Guignard
  St
Jones, Thomas, Tailor, 25 Berresford's Al
Jones, Thomas, Tailor, 43 Church St
Josephs, Israel, Merchant, 44 Broad St
Josephs, Lazarus, Shop Keeper, 132 King St
Joy, Susannah, 2 Quince St
Kahlne, J H, Counting House, Boundary St
Kampth, ——, Mrs, 13 Bottle Al
Karnes, Mary, Boarding House, 14 Union St

Kavel, William, Merchant, 91 Church St Cont'd
Kay, James, Grocer, 20 Meeting St
Keating, William, Merchant, 90 Church St
Keen, Thomas, Sea Captain, 25 Union St Cont'd
Keil, Peter, Carpenter, Upper End of King St
Keirnan, James, Wharfinger, Geyer's Whf
Keith, Isaac, Minister, Independent Church, 50
  Tradd St
Keith, S & Co, Merchants, 100 East Bay
Kelly, Mary, Shop Keeper, 114 King St
Kemnitz, F N, Grocer, Williman's Whf
Kempton, Ann, Shop Keeper, 30 King St
Kempton, George, Accountant, 14 King St
Kenan, George, Grocer, 24 Church St Cont'd
Kenan, George, Grocer, McKenzie's Whf, South
  Bay
Kenan, Thomas, Grocer, 1 Church St
Kennedy, James, Planter, 8 Mazyck St
Kennedy, Peter, Grocer, 82 Meeting St
Kenny, John, Grocer, 112 King St
Keon, William, Boarding House, 5 Unity Al
Ker, Samuel, Attorney at Law, 41 Meeting St
Kern, John F, Merchant, Dwelling, 184 King St,
  Store, 4 Gaillard's Whf
Kerr, Andrew, Boarding House, 118 Broad St
Kerr, John, Hatter, 46 East Bay
Kerr, Margaret, Boarding House, 118 Broad St
Kershaw, Charles, Merchant, 97 Tradd St
Kessick, Margaret, Boarding House, 2 Union St
King, D S, Tailor, 86 Queen St
King, Eleanor, Shop Keeper, 13 Union St Cont'd
Kingman, David, Blacksmith, S East Bay
Kingman, Eliab, Shoe Shop, 17 Tradd St
Kirk & Lukens, Merchants, 56 East Bay
Kirk, R, Dyer, 85 Tradd St
Kirkland, Joseph, Physician & Dispensary, 194
  Meeting St
Kirkpatrick, James, Merchant, 84 Church St.
Kirkpatrick, John, Merchant, 89 Church St
Kirkwood, Jeffy, Shop Keeper, 19 Wall St
Knipping & Steinmitz, Merchants, 136 East Bay
Knox & Upham, Grocers, 18 Amen St
Knox, Mathew, Counting House, 288 King St
Knox, Walter, House Carpenter, 5 Wall St
Kogly (or Kugly), George, Tailor, 14 Mazyck St.
Kogly (or Kugly), John, Carpenter, 15 Mazyck St
Kohne, Frederick, Merchant, 28 East Bay
Koskey, Ann C, Shop Keeper, 88 King St
Kreitner, Barbary, Shop Keeper, 33 Queen St
Krips, Ann, Shop Keeper, Upper End of King St
LaBat, David, Shop Keeper, 119 Queen St
LaBlon, Henry, Shoe Maker, 7 Liberty St
LaBorde, Francis, Shop Keeper & Public Chairs,
  133 King St
Lacey, Thomas, Carpenter, 126 Queen St
LaComb, John, Sea Captain, 18 Ellery St
Ladevise, Joseph, Shop Keeper, 85 King St
Ladson, Elizabeth, Boarding House, 44 Church St
Ladson, James, Planter, 13 Meeting St

Lafar, Catherine, 21 Guignard St
Lafilly, Francis, Accountant, 4 Wentworth St
Lamb, David, Merchant, 34 East Bay
Lamb, Thomas, Grocer, 3 Prioleau's Middle Range
Lambert & Bordman, Shoe Store, 14 Queen St
Lambert, Joseph, State Constable, 1 Berresford's Al
Lance, Ann, 11 Friend St
Lance, Lambert, Attorney at Law, 81 Queen St
Landry, Baptist, Grocer, 118 King St
Lane, Robert, Merchant, 108 East Bay
Lane, Samuel, Carpenter, 6 Society St
Lane, William, Blacksmith, 9 Magazine St, Dwelling, 11 Ellery St
Lang, Charles, Shoe Maker, 26 Union St
Langdon, John, Accountant, 23 Union St Cont'd
Lange, J H & Co, Merchants, Roper's Whf
Lange, Jacob H, Merchant, 1 Church St Cont'd
Langstaff & Frink, Factors & Commission Merchants, Beale's Whf
Langstaff, Benjamin, Shop Keeper, 127 Meeting St
Lanneau, Basil, Tanner, 1 Pitt St
Larouffelier, Peter, Goldsmith & Jeweller, 108 King St
Larry, Robert, Carpenter, 57 Church St
Larue, Francis, Shop Keeper, 81 Meeting St
Latham, Daniel, Distiller, 1 Hasell St
Latham, Joseph, Distiller, 6 Hasell St
Laurens, Henry, Planter, 28 East Bay
Laval, ----, Planter, 19 Federal St
Lawrans, Peter, Grocer, 167 King St
Lawrence & Brailsford, Factors, Crafts' S Whf
Lawrence, Elizabeth, 17 Pinckney St
Lawrence, R D, Factor, 44 George St
Lawton, Winborn, Planter, 1 Lightwood's Al
Lazarus, Mark, 33 King St
Lazarus, R, Shop Keeper, 103 King St
Leacraft, William, Carpenter, 26 Pinckney St
Leadbetter, Agnes, 10 Liberty St
Leaumont, R, Professor of Music, 4 Berresford's Al
Leavitt, Joshua, Grocer, 80 East Bay
Leavitt, S & H, Grocers, 1 Tradd St
Lebby, Nathaniel, Blockmaker, 55 Church St
Lebby, Robert, 55 Church St
Lecat, F, Teacher of Music, 39 Meeting St
Lecat, R, Confectioner, 39 Meeting St
Lecider, Francis, Confectioner, 27 Queen St.
Lee, James, Merchant, Dwelling, 6 Anson St, Store, 1 Crafts' S Whf
Lee, John & Co, Merchants, 206 King St
Lee, Stephen, Attorney at Law, 55 King St
Lee, Stephen, Planter, 40 Tradd St
Lee, Timothy, Factor, Crafts' S Whf
Lee, William, Jr, Attorney, 55 King St, Office, Exchange
Lee, William, Merchant, 1 Archdale St
Lee, William, Sr, Watchmaker, 55 King St, Shop, 110 Broad St

Lefevre, Stephen, Merchant, 171 Meeting St, Store, Nicholls' Whf.
Lefoi, Mary, 8 Wentworth St
Legare, Elizabeth, 4 Federal St
Legare, Elizabeth, Mazyck St
Legare, Joseph, Factor, Prioleau's S Whf
Legare, Mary, 283 King St
Legare, Solomon, Planter, 10 Friend St
Legare, Thomas, Planter, 1 Gibbs' St
Lege, J M, Dancing Master, 104 Queen St
Legge, Edward, Jr, Attorney at Law, 57 Trott St
Legge, Edward, Sr, Accountant, 57 Trott St
Legge, James, Brick Layer, 4 Lamboll St
Legge, Joseph, Shop Keeper, 184 King St
Legoux, ----, Watchmaker, 10 Queen St
Lehre, ----, Mrs, 1 Lownde's St
Lehre, Ann, 37 St Phillips' St
Lehre, Mary, 12 Liberty St
Lehre, Thomas, Sheriff, Charleston District, 272 King St, Office, State House
Leindharst, Henry, Grocer, 27 Church St Cont'd
Lennox, William, Merchant, 36 King St
Lennox, William, Merchant, 6 Cumberland St
Lenorment, Andrew, Goldsmith, 102 King St
Lesesne, Elizabeth, Upper End of Meeting St
Lesesne, Hannah, Boarding House, 43 East Bay Cont'd
Levrier, Peter, Teacher of the French Lanuage, 24 Meeting St
Levy, Bella, Shop Keeper, 126 ½ King St
Levy, Eleazer, Shop Keeper, 53 East Bay
Levy, Emaneul & Co, Shop Keeper, 50 East Bay
Levy, Lyon, 189 King St
Levy, Moses C, Shop Keeper, 217 King St
Levy, Nathan, Shop Keeper, 115 King St
Levy, Reuben, 37 Broad St
Levy, Samuel & Co, Merchants, 17 Friend St, Store, 101 Broad St
Levy, Simon, Shop Keeper, 232 King St
Lewis & You, Merchants, 111 Tradd St
Lewis, Charles & Co, Merchants, 10 Tradd St
Lewis, Charles I, Dwelling, Champney St
Lewis, Charles, Mariner, 23 Quince St
Lewis, Henry, Deputy Sheriff, 9 Berresford's alley
Lewis, Isaac & A, Merchants, 20 Broad St
Lewis, John, Grocer, 290 King St
Lewis, John, Merchant, Dwelling, 7 Charles St
Ley, Francis, Shop Keeper, Upper End of King St
Liber, John, Shop Keeper, 157 King St
Lightburn, Francis, Sea Captain, 16 Federal St
Lightwood, Edward, Attorney, 220 Meeting St
Lightwood, Elizabeth, 220 Meeting St
Limehouse, Robert, 64 Tradd St
Lining, Charles, Ordinary, 8 Legare St
Little, Robert, Carpenter, 22 Union St
Livingston, William, Sea Captain, 29 East Bay Cont'd
Lloyd, ----, Cabinet Maker, 8 Guignard St
Lloyd, J P, Venetian Blind Maker, 75 Meeting St

Lloyd, John, Factor, 2 Geyer's S Whf
Lloyd, John, Jr, Merchant, 166 Meeting St
Lloyd, John, Sr, Planter, 119 Broad St.
Lockey & Naylor, Merchants, 105 East Bay
Lockwood, Joshua, Jr, Planter, 170 Meeting St
Lockwood, Joshua, Sr, 1 Smith's Ln
Logan, ——, Mrs, 18 Queen St
Logan, ——, Mrs, Nurse, 12 Coming St
Logan, C M. & Co, Merchants, 110 Queen St.
Logan, William, Jr, Attorney at Law, 14 Moore St
Loger, John, Baker, 1 Trott St
Long, John, Accountant, 31 George St
Lopez, Aaron, 33 Beaufain St
Lopez, David, Vendue Master, Dwelling, 237 King St, Store, Exchange St
Lord, Richard, Factor, 17 Berresford's St
Lothrop, Seth, Merchant, 109 East Bay
Loughbridge, Daniel, Grocer, 9 Maiden Ln
Love, Duncan, Grocer, 6 Church St
Love, Elizabeth, 24 St Phillip's St
Love, Mary, 3 Lowndes' St
Loveday, John, Powder Inspector, 10 Moore St
Lovitt, William, Carpenter, 3 Lamboll St
Lowndes, William, Attorney at Law, 89 Broad St
Loyd & Snyder, Shop Keepers, 227 King St
Loyd, Joseph, Shop Keeper, 227 King St
Lucian, ——, Confectioner, Upper End of Meeting St
Lukens, John, Merchant, 98 Tradd St
Lunt, Mary, Shop Keeper, 26 Union St Cont'd
Luscomb, George, Sea Captain, 7 Federal St
Lynah, James, Physician, 47 Meeting St
Lynn & Weyman, Merchants, 107 East Bay
Lynn, John, Merchant, 2 Front St, Bay
Lyon, Mordecai, Shop Keeper, 225 King St
M'Bride, James, Merchant, 57 East Bay
M'Calkin, Arthur, 4 Lowndes' St
M'Call, Ann, 105 Church St
M'Call, Elizabeth, 14 Meeting St
M'Calla, Thomas H, Physician, 10 Elliott St
M'Cann, Edward, Clerk of the Fish Market, 6 Price's Al
M'Cartney & Crawford, Grocers, 135 Queen St
M'Cartney, James, Wharfinger, 44 Church St
M'Carty, John, State Constable, 16 Hasell St
M'Cauley, George & Son, Merchants, 111 Tradd St
M'Cauley, George, Merchant, 18 Broad St.
M'Clardy, Neil, Boat Builder, 23 East Bay Cont'd
M'Cleary, Jane, Boarding House, 12 Berresford's Al
M'Cleish, Alexander, Brass Founder, Shop, 56 Meeting St, Dwelling, 8 St Philip's St
M'Cloud, ——, Mrs., 46 East Bay Cont'd
M'Clure, A & J, Merchants, 23 Broad St
M'Cormick, William, Grocer, 21 East Bay
M'Coy, Malcolm, Grocer, 44 King St
M'Cready & Cogdell, Attornies at Law, 34 Broad St

M'Cready, David & Co, Merchants, 8 Broad St
M'Cready, John, Attorney, 34 Broad St
M'Credie, John, Merchant, 169 King St
M'Donald, Christopher, Shop Keeper, 269 King St
M'Donald, Richard, Shop Keeper, 132 Queen St
M'Donald, Susan E, Store Keeper, 22 East Bay
M'Dowell & Blair, Merchants, 143 Broad St
M'Dowell, Alexander, Saddler, 221 King St
M'Dowell, James, Merchant, 65 King St
M'Dowell, John, Merchant, 144 King St
M'Farlane, ——, Baker, 2 South Bay
M'Gann, Patrick, Watch Maker, 132 East Bay
M'Gillivray, A H & Co, Factors & Brokers, 104 Broad St
M'Ginnis, Patrick, Grocer, 70 King St
M'Grath, ——, Carpenter, 61 Meeting St
M'Illhenny, J, Sea Captain, 7 Lynch's Ln
M'Intosh, Simon, Planter, 18 Friend St
M'Kenzie & M'Neil, Grocers, 123 Broad St
M'Kenzie, Elizabeth, Boarding House, 8 Unity Al
M'Kie, ——, Mrs, Shop Keeper, 277 King St
M'Kie, John, Brick Layer, 277 King St
M'Lean, Evan, Grocer, 188 Meeting St
M'Lean, Lauchlan, Grocer, 53 Tradd St
M'Leod, William, Planter, 286 King St
M'Millan, Richard, Public House & Wagon Yard, Upper End of King St
M'Neil, C, Shop Keeper, 36 Hasell St
M'Neil, Neil, Sea Captain, 21 King St
M'Pherson, Daniel, Wheelwright, 29 East Bay Cont'd
M'Pherson, Duncan, Shop Keeper, 72 King St
M'Pherson, John, Planter, 97 Broad St
M'Taggart, David & Co, Merchants, 139 East Bay
M'Whann, William & Nephew, Merchants, 9 Broad St
Macadam, James & Co, Merchants, 145 East Bay
Macbeth, Henry & Co., Merchants, 119 Tradd St
Mackay, Crafts, Watchmaker, 37 Union St
Magwood, Simon, Factor, 99 Queen St
Main, John, Merchant, 271 King St
Maine, Susannah, Shop Keeper, 3 Meeting St
Mair & Means, Merchants, 136 Broad St
Mair, Patrick & Co, Merchants, 25 East Bay
Mair, Thomas & Co, Merchants, 34 East Bay
Makkay, Ann, 3 Berresford's St
Makkay, John, Carpenter, 33 Tradd St
Makkay, Sarah, 95 Meeting St
Malcolm, Thomas, Lumber Merchant, 56 Church St
Man & Foltz, Merchants, Geyer's N Whf
Manigault, Gabriel, Planter, 121 Meeting St
Manigault, Joseph, Planter, 7 Maiden Ln
Mann, Margaret, School Mistress, 148 Meeting St
Manson, George, Boat Builder, 6 Wall St
Manuel & Fairborn, Merchants, 11 East Bay Cont'd
Marchal, Francis, Professor of Music, 46 Meeting St

13

Markley, Abraham, Merchant, 122 King St
Marks, Humphrey, Shop Keeper, 137 King St
Marks, Joseph, Fruit Shop, 131 Queen St
Marks, S M , Shop Keeper, 91 King St
Marlin, Edward, 6 Guignard St
Marlin, Francis, Tailor, 31 Elliott St
Marlin, William, Cabinet Maker, Cock Ln
Marr, Ann, 43 Church St Cont'd
Marsh, James, Shipwright, 24 Guignard St
Marshall, Dorothea, 106 King St
Marshall, Eleanor, 24 Wall St
Marshall, Elizabeth, 86 Tradd St.
Marshall, John, Broker, 106 King St
Marshall, John, Cabinet Maker, Upper End of
  Meeting St
Marshall, Mary, 250 King St
Marshall, William, Sea Captain, 33 Guignard St
Marshall, William, Vendue Master, 3 Middle St ,
  Store, Exchange St
Martin, Brunett, Fruit Shop, 38 Union St
Martin, Charles, Brick Layer, 18 Scarborough St
Martin, Elizabeth, 26 St Philip's St
Martin, Henry, Upper End of Meeting St
Martin, Jacob, Book Keeper, S C Bank, 174
  Meeting St
Martin, James, 2 Lowndes St
Martin, John C , Planter, 15 Guignard St.
Martin, John C , Planter, 214 King St
Martin, Mary, Seamstress, 249 King St
Martin, Thomas, Merchant, 72 Tradd St
Mason, Mary, Boarding House, 22 Berresford's Al
Mason, William, Academy, 19 Ellery St
Mathews, ——, Mrs , Rutledge St , Harleston
Mathews, George, Vendue Master, cor Wentworth
  & Bull St
Mathews, James, Attorney at Law, Meeting St
Mathews, Mary, 7 Friend St
Mattuce, John, Rutledge St , Harleston
Mauger, John, Vendue Master & Commission
  Broker, 24 East Bay
Mauran, J H , Grocer & Boarding House, 123
  Queen St
Maverick, Samuel, Merchant, 165 King St
Maxwell, John, Shoe Maker, 8 Archdale St
Maxwell, Nathaniel G , Accountant, 13 Church St
Mazyck & Cyples, Merchants, 132 Broad St
Mazyck, Daniel, Smith St , Harleston
Mazyck, Elizabeth, 57 Meeting St
Mazyck, Nathaniel, Planter, 57 Meeting St
Mazyck, William, Factor, 3 Archdale St
McComb, Joseph, Shop Keeper, 139 King St
Meeks, Joseph, Grocer, 4 St Philip's St
Meley, William, Accountant, 6 King St
Melhado, Benjamin, 1 Berresford St
Mellise, Anthony, Joiner, 137 Meeting St
Merchant, Peter T , 15 Broad St
Merrell, Benjamin, Livery Stables, 37 Church St
Merry, Patrick H , Sea Captain, 22 Guignard St
Mey, Florian Charles, Merchant, 43 Pinckney St

Michaw, John, Grocer, 4 East Bay Cont'd
Middleton, Ann, 95 Broad St
Middleton, S , Tailor & Habit Maker, 128 King St
Miller & Robertson, Merchants, Dwelling, 12
  Scarborough St , Store, 7 Geyer's N Whf
Miller, Catherine, Boarding House, 179 King St
Miller, Elizabeth, 4 Friend St
Miller, Frederick, Butcher, 2 Burns' Ln.
Miller, James, Merchant, 114 Tradd St
Miller, James, Wine Merchant, 61 East Bay
Miller, John D , Silversmith, 51 Trott St , Shop, 111
  Broad St
Miller, John, Drayman, 88 Meeting St
Miller, John J , House Carpenter, W End of
  Wentworth St
Miller, John Theodore, Carpenter, 24 Beaufain St
Miller, Morrison & Co , Merchants, 82 Church St
Miller, Nicholas, Baker, 16 George St
Miller, Stephen, Boarding House, 40 Church St
Miller, William, Tailor, 1 Union St Cont'd , Shop,
  2 Queen St
Millet, Thomas, Teacher of French, 7 Moore St
Milligan, Joseph, Shop Keeper, 73 King St
Milligan, William, Merchant, 1 Crafts' N Whf
Milligan, William, Merchant, 11 Meeting St
Mills, ——, Mrs , 45 East Bay Cont'd
Mills, Henry, Merchant, 109 Tradd St
Mills, Thomas, Merchant, 108 Tradd St
Milner, George, Black Smith, 72 Church St
Miner, M , Ship Master, 21 East Bay Cont'd
Minot, Thomas & John, Carpenters, 11 Stoll's Al
Minsey, Robert, Shoe Maker, 29 Queen St
Miott, Frances, Boarding House, 46 Meeting St
Mitchals, Elis, Cook Shop, 10 Berresford's Al
Mitchell, ——, Mrs , 14 Coming St
Mitchell, Ann, 218 Meeting St
Mitchell, James, Cooper, 18 Meeting St
Mitchell, John H , Notary Public & Justice of the
  Peace, Office, 133 Coates's Row
Mitchell, John, Q U & Notary Public, 29 East Bay
Mitchell, Thomas, Planter, 42 Pinckney St
Moles, James, Blacksmith, Shop, Champneys'Whf ,
  House, 19 Amen St
Moncrieff, John, Carpenter, 9 East Bay Cont'd
Moncrieff, John, Factor, 2 Church St
Monk, James, Silversmith & Jeweller, 21 Broad St
Monpoey, Honore, Grocer, 40 Union St
Montain, Anthony, Shop Keeper, 31 Broad St
Mood, Peter, Silversmith, 223 King St
Moodie, Benjamin, British Consul, 12 Hasell St
Mooney, Patrick, Grocer, 125 Queen St.
Moore, ——, Mrs , 1 Market Square
Moore, J P , Physician, 47 King St.
Moore, John, Planter, 33 Trott St
Moore, Joseph, Drayman, 8 East Bay Cont'd
Moore, Philip, Cabinet Maker, 28 Meeting St
Morales, Jacob, Shop Keeper, 77 King St
Morgan, Charles, Ship Carpenter, 2 Pinckney St
Morgan, Edward, Cooper, 52 Queen St

Morgan, Henry, Boarding House, 11 Union St
Cont'd
Morgan, Isaac, Carpenter, 67 Church St
Morgan, William, Physician, 52 Broad St
Morphy, Diego, Spanish Consul, 261 King St
Morris, George, Carpenter, 16 Archdale St
Morris, Lewis, Planter, 215 Meeting St
Morris, Thomas, Merchant, 58 Trott St
Morrison & Murdock, Shop Keepers, Upper End of
    King St
Morrison, John, Merchant, 98 Church St
Morrison, John, Sea Captain, 37 George St
Mortimer & Heron, Merchants, 14 Broad St
Mortimer, William, Upper End of Meeting St.
Morton, Alexander, Grocer, 231 King St
Moser, Philip, Physician & Apothecary, 124 Broad
    St
Moses, Henry, Shop Keeper, 51 East Bay
Moses, Isaac & Co, Vendue Masters, 78 King St
Moses, Isaac C & Co, Shop Keepers, 237 King
    St, Dwelling, 7 Orange St
Moses, Isaiah, Shop Keeper, 197 King St
Moses, Joseph, Shop Keeper, 233 King St
Moses, Lyon, Swinton's Ln
Moses, Philip, 268 King St
Moses, Solomon, Shop Keeper, 188 King St
Motta, Emanuel D L, Vendue Master, 48 Tradd
    St, Store, Exchange St
Motte, Abraham, Planter, 38 East Bay Cont'd
Motte, Francis, Factor, House, Meeting St,
    Counting House, Vanderhorst's Whf
Motte, Jacob, Merchant, 2 Cock Ln
Motte, Mary, 217 Meeting St
Moubray, Martha, Baker, 90 King St
Moulin, Peter, Grocer, 10 King St
Moultrie, Alexander, Attorney at Law, 2
    Cumberland St
Moultrie, James, Physician, 87 Meeting St
Mouzon, Henry, Shoe Maker, 2 Parsonage Ln
Muck, Philip, Musician, 252 King St
Muckilmoy, William, Accountant, 9 King St
Muckinfee, John, Carpenter, 7 St Philip's St.
Muckinfuss, Henry, Brick Layer, W End of
    Wentworth St
Muckinfuss, Michael, Cabinet Maker, 53 King St
Muir, William, Merchant, Bull St, Store, 1 Geyer's
    N Whf
Mulligan, Barnard, Factor, Champneys St
Mulligan, Francis, Collector of Excise, 133 Coates's
    Row
Mulligan, John, Grocer, 131 Coates's Row, Bay
Munds, Israel, Minister of Trinity Church, 6 Union
    St Cont'd
Munro, Catherine, Midwife, 19 Tradd St
Munro, John, Watchmaker, 8 Elliott St
Murdock & M'Quintin, Shop Keepers, 141 King St
Murray, Catherine, Boarding House, 4 Berresford's
    Al
Myers, ——, Mrs, 6 Berresford St

Myers, Francis, Cigar Maker, 115 King St
Myers, Michael, Vendue Cryer, 9 Parsonage Ln
Myers, Samuel, Tailor, 28 King St
Myers, Sarah, 4 Quince St
Mylne, James, Baker, 17 Union St
Napier, Thomas, Merchant, Store, 9 Crafts' N Whf
Nathans, Solomon, Shop Keeper, 229 King St
Naylor, Robert, Merchant, 23 Elliott St
Naylor, Thomas, Wine Merchant, House, 1 Moore
    St
Nazer, Philip, Baker, 84 King St
Nebuhr, J D, Shop Keeper, 186 King St
Negrin, John J, Translator & Printing Office, 43
    East Bay
Neilson, James, Attorney at Law, 49 Broad St
Nelson, Ambrose, Sea Captain, 53 Trott St
Nelson, Francis, Ship Carpenter, 24 East Bay
Cont'd
Nelson, Jane, 73 Church St
Neufville, Isaac, Book Keeper, National Bank, W
    End of Wentworth St
Neufville, John, Commissioner of Loans, 75 Queen
    St
Neville, Joshua, Cabinet Maker, 43 Queen St
Nevison, John, Carpenter, Fort Ln
Newman, ——, Miss, 6 Front St, Bay
Neyle, Charles, Deputy City Sheriff, 253 King St
Nicholls, George & Co, Commission Merchants &
    Grain Store, 6 Gaillard's Whf
Nicholson, James, Attorney at Law, 51 Broad St.
Nicholson, Joseph, Carpenter, 61 Meeting St
Nicolls, Thomas, Merchant, 79 Bay, Counting
    House, Nicolls Whf
Niel, Peter, Planter, 35 Trott St
Nipper, David H, Bookbinder, 100 King St
Nobbs, Samuel, Inspector of Customs, 77 Meeting
    St
Noble, Ezekiel, Merchant, 153 King St
Noble, John, Physician, 189 King St
Nonoy, Francis, Tobacconist, Upper End of Meeting
    St.
Norr, Moses, Shop Keeper, 43 King St.
Norris, ——, Mrs, St Philip's St
Norris, James, Turner, 80 Meeting St
North, John, 15 Church St
North, Richard, 15 Church St
North, Susannah, 28 Tradd St
Norwell, George H, Mariner, 30 Pinckney St
Nott, E, Boarding House, 36 Bay, cor Elliott St
Nowell, Thomas, Clerk, S C Bank, 16 Broad St
Nugent, Margaret, 12 Lamboll St
O'Connor, Thomas, Grocer, 1 King St
O'Dener, Peter, 19 Wall St
O'Hara, Charles, Merchant, 6 Smith's Ln
O'Hara, Daniel & Son, Merchants, 144 Board St
O'Hear, James, Factor, 28 Church St, Store,
    Geyer's S Range
O'Kelly, John, Tutor, 193 King St
Oeland, John, Grocer, 8 Union St Cont

Ogden, George, Clothing Shop, 28 Elliott St
Ogier & M'Kinny, Merchants, 146 East Bay, Store,
  Geyer's N Whf
Ogier & Marwell, Factors, 9 Crafts' S Whf
Ogier, Lewis, Factor, 75 Tradd St
Ogilvie, J. A., Planter, 41 George St
Oliphant & Hayson, Ornamental Furniture Dealers,
  118 Broad St
Oliphant, David, Painter, 9 Ellery St
Oliver, James, Brick Layer, 10 Wall St
Olman, Henneguin, Confectioner, 127 Queen St
Ominsetter, John, Tanner, 27 Archdale St
Ormond, ——, Mrs, 10 East Bay Cont'd
Osborn, Henry, 65 Queen St
Osborn, Thomas, Planter & Sheriff of Colleton, 6
  South Bay
Otis, Joseph, Jr, Factor, 46 Queen St
Otto, John, Drayman, 109 Meeting St
Owens, John, Factor, 27 Tradd St
Pacque, Francis G, 2 Boundary St or Federal
  Green
Paine, Thomas, Sea Captain, 265 King St
Palmer, Job, Carpenter, 32 Trott St
Palmer John, Corporal, City Gaurd, 4 Price's Al
Parker, ——, Mrs, Pitt St
Parker, Catherine, Milliner, 180 Meeting St
Parker, Florida, 26 Guignard St
Parker, George, Planter, 83 East Bay
Parker, Isaac, Planter, 9 Legare St
Parker, John, Planter, 36 Trott St
Parker, John, Planter, 83 East Bay
Parker, Phineas, Dyer, 27 Hasell St
Parker, Thomas & Co, Ironmongery Shop, 113
  East Bay
Parker, Thomas, Attorney at Law, 33 Meeting St
Parker, Thomas C, School Master, 89 Meeting St
Parker, William, Physician, 39 Hasell St
Parks & Elliott, Shop Keepers, 6 Union St
Parks, John, Shoe Store, 92 King St
Parks, John, Shoe Maker, 6 St Philip's St
Parks, Samuel, Shoe Store, 41 Meeting St
Patch, ——, Mrs, 2 Bottle Al
Paton, John, Clerk in Counting House, 61 Meeting
  St
Patterson, David, Sea Captain, 7 Bedon's Al
Patterson, Hugh, Insurance Broker & Commission
  Merchant, 3 Broad St
Paxton, Henry, Clerk in Counting House, 8 Stoll's
  Al
Payne & Collier, Merchants, 131 Broad St.
Payne, William, Merchant, 131 Broad St
Payne, William R, Grocer, 77 King St
Peace & Cheves, Attornies at Law, Office, 1 State
  House Square
Peace, Joseph, Attorney at Law, 1 State House
  Square
Pearce & Tillinghast, Shoe Store, 27 Elliott St
Pearson, Benjamin, Sea Captain, 21 Scarborouth St.
Pebarte, John, Planter, 18 George St.

Peigne, Lewis, Hair Dresser, 195 Meeting St
Pendleton, ——, Mrs, Lynch's Ln
Pennall, James, Grocer, 180 King St
Pennington, Edward, Lt, Revenue Cutter, 65 East
  Bay
Pepoon, Benjamin, Grocer & Corn Store, 10 Queen
  St
Peppin, Joseph, Merchant, 103 Chruch St
Perault, Paul, 4 Wall St
Perronneau, William, Planter, 9 George St
Perry, Isabella, Midwife, 54 Meeting St
Peters, P, Merchant, cor Broad & Bay
Petre, Alexander, Factor, 1 Orange St
Petrie, George, School Master, 9 Federal St
Phelon, Edmund M, Grocer, cor Meeting & Queen
  St
Phillips, Benjamin, Shop Keeper, Upper End of
  King St
Phillips, David, Broker, 29 Meeting St
Phillips, Dorothy, Shop Keeper, 69 Queen St
Phillips, E B, Shoe Maker, 23 Elliott St
Phillips, John C & Co, Grocers, 3 Prioleau's
  Middle Range
Phillips, John, Painter & Glazier, 46 Broad St
Philps, Anson G, Saddler & Harness Maker, 191
  King St
Philson, Alexander, Broker, 196 King St
Pike, Nathaniel, Grocer, 2 King St
Pillans, ——, Mrs, Boarding House, 110 Tradd St
Pillsbury, Samuel, Clerk in Counting House, 4
  Charles St
Pilote, Onesime, Grocer, 6 Elliott St
Pinckney, Charles Coatesworth, Planter, 1 East Bay
  Cont'd
Pinckney, Frances, 14 Legare St
Pinckney, Thomas H, Planter, 2 Price's Al
Pinckney, Thomas, Planter, 42 George St
Placide, Alexander, Manager of Charleston Theatre,
  93 Broad St
Platt, Eleazer, Baker, 39 King St
Plessonau & Borch, Sail Makers, 2 Cochran's Whf
Plessonau, John, Sail Maker, Dwelling, 49 Broad
  St
Plume, A, Shop Keeper, 255 King St
Pohl, Elias, Shop Keeper, 224 King St
Poinsett, Elisha, Physician, 294 King St
Poissenou, Nicholas I, Shop Keeper, 19
  Berresford's Al
Poissignon, Antony, Tin Plate Worker, 12 Queen St
Polock, Solomon, Horse Dealer, Bull St
Polony, Jean L, Physician, 17 Church St Cont'd.
Pool, Isaac, Shop Keeper, 142 ½ King St
Pooser, N H., Tailor, 107 Queen St
Porter, Benjamin R, Cabinet Maker, 175 Meeting
  St
Porter, Peter, Blacksmith, 245 King St
Porter, William, Boarding House, 13 Union St
Porter, William, Vendue Master, Dwelling, 39
  Elliott St, Store, Exchange St.

Postell, Edward, Chair Maker, 12 George St
Potter, John, Merchant, 19 Broad St
Poulton, Edward, Sea Captain, 20 Church St
  Cont'd
Poyas, John E, Planter, 29 Meeting St
Poyas, John L, Carpenter, 1 Cumberland St.
Pratt, ——, Sea Captain, 41 East Bay
Pratt, Samuel H, Grocer, 35 East Bay
Prendergast, P E, School Master, 4 Cumberland St
Prentice, John, Chair Maker, Dwelling & Shop, 30
  Archdale St
Pressley, ——, Misses, Mantua Makers, 20
  Berresford St
Pressley, William, Grocer, 85 King St
Price, Ann, 79 East Bay
Price, Charles, Tailor, W End of Wentworth St
Price, John, Merchant, Dwelling, 8 Church St
  Cont'd.
Price, Thomas, Planter, 24 Hasell St
Price, William, Planter, 2 Orange St
Primrose, Catherine, 21 St Philip's St
Primrose, James, 21 Bereford St
Prince, Charles, Tin Plate Worker, 246 King St
Pringle, John Julius, Attorney General, 93 Tradd St
Pringle, M, 1 Cock Ln
Pringle, Robert, Dr, Planter, 101 Tradd St
Prioleau, Ann, Boarding House, 82 Queen St
Prioleau, J & Co, Factors, Prioleau's S Whf
Prioleau, John, Accountant, 10 Maiden Ln
Prioleau, John Cordes, 76 East Bay
Prioleau, Philip G, Physician, 49 Meeting St
Prioleau, Samuel, Factor, 49 Meeting St
Pritchard, Joseph, Accountant, 57 King St
Pritchard, Paul, Sr, Shipwright, 89 East Bay
Pritchard, Paul, Jr, Shipwright, 6 Charles St
Pritchard, William, Jr, Shipwright, 2 Charles St
Pritchard, William, Sr, Shipwright, 1 Pinckney St
Proys, John P., Accountant, Champneys St
Purcell, A, Widow of Rev Henry, 1 Legare St.
Purcell, Joseph, Land Surveyor, 123 King St
Purdy, Joseph, Mariner, 41 Pinckney St
Purse, William, Silver Smith & Jeweller, 117 Broad
  St
Purvis, William, Merchant, Upper End of Meeting
  St.
Pyeatt, ——, Mrs, 25 St. Philip's St
Pyne, ——, Mrs, Nurse, 6 Liberty St
Quackinbush, Laurence, Cabinet Maker, 3
  Wentworth St
Quash, Robert, Planter, 91 Broad St
Quigging, ——, Mrs, Boarding House, Lodge Al
Quinby, Joseph, Carpenter, 7 Pinckney St
Quinn, James, Boarding House, 6 Unity Al
Quinning, Dennis, Tobacconist, 14 Hasell St
Radcliffe, Thomas, Planter, 39 George St
Raine, Thomas, Scrivener, 222 King St.
Ramage, Frances, Boarding House, 187 Meeting St
Rame, Michael, Planter, 42 Broad St
Ramousin & Sons, 30 Beaufain St

Ramsay, ——, Mrs, 41 Trott St.
Ramsay, David, Physician, 106 Broad St.
Ramsay, George, Shop Keeper, 5 Chalmers's Al
Ramsay, John, Liquor Merchant, 111 Queen St
Ramsay, John, Planter, 37 Meeting St
Ramsay, Joseph H., Physician, 30 Tradd St
Rane, Sarah, 83 Tradd St
Rankin, James, Grocer, 233 King St
Ravel, ——, Mrs, Shop Keeper, 23 Scarborough St
Ravenel, Daniel, Planter, 115 Broad St
Ravenel, Elizabeth, 67 Meeting St
Ravenel, Stephen, 2 W End of Boundary St
Raynol, Lewis, Accountant, 18 Hasell St
Read, John, Wheelwright, 173 Meeting St
Read, William, Physician, 19 Church St Cont'd
Rebb, Adam, Baker, 5 Meeting St
Rechon, David, Tailor, 110 King St
Redman, James, Rigger, 25 Beaufain St
Reeves, Enos, Silversmith, Dwelling, 3 W St,
  Shop, 112 Broad St
Reiar, H, Grocer, Williman's Whf, South Bay
Reid, George, Notary Public, 12 East Bay
Reid, George, Tailor & Habit Maker, 196 Meeting
  St
Reid, James, Clerk of the National Bank, 196
  Meeting St
Reid, John, Tin Plate Worker, 36 Church St
Reigne, John, Baker, 9 Elliott St
Reilly, Thomas, Physician, 45 Trott St
Reily, James, Harness Maker, 15 Church St
Remondo, Peter, Grocer, 30 Elliott St
Renauld, John, Shop Keeper, 34 Tradd St
Repon, Mary, Boarding House, 1 Chalmers's Al
Reside, William, Cabinet Maker, 189 Meeting St
Reynolds & Cannere, Grocers, 33 Pinckney St
Ricard, Francis, Grocer, Prioleau's N Whf.
Ricard, Peter, Grocer, 40 Pinckney St
Ricardo, Benjamin, Merchant, 91 Church St
Ricardo, Benjamin, Shop Keeper, 89 King St
Richards, ——, Sea Captain, 14 East Bay Cont'd
Richardson, J. B, Governor of the State, 56 King
  St
Richardson, James, Grocer, 7 Berresford's Al
Richardson, John, Counting House, 27 Elliott St
Ridgway, John, State Constable, Trott St
Righton, Joseph, Cooper, 1 Water St
Righton, M'Cully, Cooper, 2 Water St
Rigou, Peter, Shop Keeper, 4 Middle St
Risher, Mary, 3 Meeting St
Rivers, Abraham R, 4 Clifford's Al
Rivers, Francis, 142 Meeting St
Rivers, Mary Ann, 3 Short St
Rivers, Samuel, Boat Builder, 6 Water St
Rivers, Thomas, Jr., Butcher, 48 Trott St
Rivers, Thomas, Sr, Planter, 1 Stoll's Al
Roach, William, City Treasurer, Dwelling, 15
  Quince St, Office, Exchange
Roberts, ——, Mrs, 1 Bottle Al
Roberts, Ann, 7 Church St

Roberts, Susannah, Boarding House, 88 East Bay
Roberts, William, Chair Maker, 78 Queen St
Robertson, Alexander & Sons, Merchants, 147 King St
Robertson, John & Co, Merchants, 118 Tradd St
Robertson, William, Attorney at Law, 56 King St
Robine, ——, 250 King St
Robinson, Frances, Whim Court
Robinson, John, Merchant, 142 King St
Robinson, Peter, Painter, 8 Parsonage Ln.
Robinson, William, Hotel, 105 Queen St
Robiou, ——, Mrs, 250 King St
Robiou, Charles, 6 Federal St
Roche, John, Grocer, 10 Union St
Rodgers, Samuel, Organist, W End of Wentworth St
Rodick, Thomas & Co, Merchants, 3 Geyer's N Whf
Rodman, Thomas, Boarding House, 25 Union St
Rogers, Christopher, 25 Tradd St
Rogers, Sampson, Boatman, 115 Meeting St
Rogers, Sarah, 26 Church St Cont'd
Roper, Thomas, Planter, 71 East Bay
Rose, John, Factor, 19 Hasell St
Rosignoll, ——, Madame, 15 Wall St
Ross, Elizabeth, Shop Keeper, 69 King St
Ross, Thomas, Sea Captain, 21 Ellery St
Ross, William, Shop Keeper, 138 King St
Roulain, R, Brick Layer, 43 George St
Roupell, Elizabeth, Planter, 73 Tradd St
Rouse, William, Tanner & Leather Dresser, 70 Meeting St
Rout, ——, Mrs, 17 Archdale St
Roux, Lewis, 153 Meeting St
Rowand, Charles E, Planter, 2 Friend St
Rowe, Daniel, 17 George St
Ruberry, John, Carpenter, 7 Smith's Ln & 6 Stoll's Al
Russell, ——, Mrs, 16 Trott St
Russell, Daniel, Carpenter, 2 Ellery St
Russell, John, Blacksmith, Shop, Governor's Bridge
Russell, Nathaniel, Merchant, 16 East Bay
Russell, Samuel, Tobacco Manufactory, 162 Meeting St
Russell, William & Co, Merchants, 34 Elliott St
Russell, William, 29 Guignard St
Rutledge, Charles, Planter, 27 East Bay Cont'd
Rutledge, Edward, Planter, 94 Tradd St
Rutledge, Frederick, Planter, 59 Tradd St.
Rutledge, Henry Middleton, Planter, Wentworth St.
Rutledge, Hugh, Chancellor in Equity, 15 St Philip's St
Ryan, Elizabeth, Shop Keeper, 52 East Bay
Ryan, James, Register of the Court of Equity, 16 Broad St
Ryley, Terrance, Dyer, 23 Mazyck St
Ryne, Elizabeth, W End of Wentworth St
Sabb, John, Book Keeper, State Bank, 36 Elliott St.
Saint, Mary, Boarding House, 173 King St

Saltus & Yates, Ship Chandlers, 41 East Bay, Factors, 4 Crafts's S Whf
Samory, C, Grocer, 19 Queen St
Sanders, ——, Mrs, 170 King St
Sandi, Angelo, Confectioner, 60 King St
Sarrazin, Catherine & Mary, Spinsters, 12 Wentworth St
Sarrazin, Jonathan, 12 Wentworth St
Sarrois, P, Merchant, 2 Society St
Sasportas, Abraham, Merchant, 15 Queen St
Sass, Jacob, Cabinet Maker, 35 Queen St.
Savage, Martha, 72 Broad St
Sawyer, ——, 16 Legare St
Schepeler & Sudermann, Merchants, 112 East Bay
Schmidt, John F, 116 East Bay
Schurman, J E, Cooper, 95 Queen St
Schutt, Caspar C, Merchant, 8 East Bay
Scot, Campbell & Co, Vendue Masters, Exchange St
Scot, James, Vendue Master, 5 Champneys St
Scott, John, Watch & Clock Maker, 111 Broad St
Scott, William E & Co, Shop Keepers, 232 King St
Scrimzeour, J & C, Merchants, 2 Middle St, Store, 110 Tradd St
Scriven, Thomas, Planter, 110 Church St
Seabrook, Benjamin, Planter, 86 Broad St
Sebbin, Sebbe, Grocer, 14 Church St
Secreess, Martin, Sea Captain, 24 Union St Cont'd
Seile, Daniel, Butcher, 12 Coming St
Serjeant, Mary, Shop Keeper, 97 Church St
Severs, John, 4 Unity Al
Seyle, Samuel, Saddler, 101 King St
Seymour, Bartholomew, Shop Keeper, 1 Unity Al
Seymour, Isaac, Sea Captain, 20 King St
Seymour, Stephen, Harbor Master, 5 Orange St
Shackelford, Nathaniel, Factor, Dwelling, Kinloch's Court
Shackelford, Nathaniel, Store, 4 Gaillard's Whf
Shand, Robert, Inspector Customs, 178 Meeting St
Sharp, John, Blockmaker, 9 Charles St
Shaw, James, Factor, 1 Blake's Whf
Shaw, Richard, Tailor, 4 Smith's Ln
Shaw, William, Attorney at Law, 106 Queen St
Shephard, James, Saddler, 7 Coming St
Sheppard, Thomas, Printer, 16 Elliott St
Sherman & M'Neil, Shop Keepers, 155 King St
Shirer, John, Carpenter, 19 Coming St
Shirtliffe, William, Factor, 4 Prioleau's N Whf
Shively, George, Grocer, 117 Meeting St
Shoolbred, James, Planter, 7 Lamboll St
Shrewsburg, Stephen, Book Keeper, S C Bank, 8 Cumberland St.
Shrewsbury, Mary, 12 Guignard St
Shriner, Nicholas, Grocer, 6 Coming St
Shutz, John, Grocer, 2 Smith's Ln.
Simons, ——, Tailor, 2 Bull St.
Simons, Benjamin, Physician, 226 Meeting St.
Simons, James, Collector, 21 Church St

Simons, Keating & Son, Factors, 3 Orange St,
  Store, 150 East Bay
Simons, Keating Lewis, Attorney at Law, 3 Orange
  St
Simons, Sampson, Shop Keeper, 105 King St.
Simons, Samuel, Broker, 19 Berresford St
Simons, Sarah R, Planter, 58 Tradd St
Simons, Thomas, Factor, 44 East Bay Cont'd
Simons, Thomas, Merchant, 2 Gaillard's Whf
Simons, William, Carpenter, Upper End of King St
Simpson, John, Ship Chandler, 104 East Bay
Sims, William, Millwright, Upper End of King St.
Sinclair, Alexander & Co, Merchants, 17 Elliott St
Singletary, Joseph, Grocer, Upper End of King St
Singleton, Mary, 3 Trott St
Singleton, S, Boundary St
Sisk, Susannah, Boarding House, 74 East Bay
Skirving, Charlotte, 16 Church St Cont'd
Skirving, William, Jr, Planter, 9 Archdale St
Skirving, William, Sr, Planter, 13 Meeting St
Skrine, Mary, Mantua Maker, 8 Bedon's Al
Slack, Mary, Boarding House, 16 Broad St
Sloman, Henry, Tailor, 114 Meeting St
Slout, John, Boarding House, 33 Union St Cont'd
Smallwood, Robert, Accountant, 22 Pinckney St
Smart, John T, Shoe Maker, 113 Broad St
Smerdon, Elias, Broker, 38 East Bay
Smiser, Hannah, 48 Church St
Smith, ----, Mrs, 71 Church Ln
Smith, ----, Mrs, Milliner, 10 Mazyck St
Smith & Duncan, Attornies at Law, 28 Maiden Ln
Smith, Agnes, Boarding House, 7 Broad St
Smith, Amos, Boarding House, 7 Union St.
Smith, Ann, 30 Trott St
Smith, Archibald, 20 Quince St
Smith, Christopher F, Kolf-baan, 132 King St.
Smith, Daniel, City Assessor, 5 Society St
Smith, Elizabeth, Shop Keeper, 26 Broad St
Smith, Esther, Grocer, 8 Middle St
Smith, George, Factor, National Bank Branch
Smith, George, Musician, 117 Tradd St
Smith, Henry, Ship Carpenter, 6 Maiden Ln
Smith, Jane, 21 Friend St
Smith, John Rutledge, Planter, 11 Liberty St
Smith, John, School Master, 82 Broad St
Smith, John, Ship Carpenter, 5 Middle St
Smith, John, Upholsterer, 84 Queen St
Smith, Josiah, National Branch Bank
Smith, Margaret, Shop Keeper, 187 King St
Smith, Mary, 57 King St
Smith, Nomia, 4 Coming St
Smith, Obrian, Planter, 11 Church St
Smith, Peter, Lumber Merchant & Factor, Dwelling,
  South Bay, 24 Mazyck St
Smith, Peter, Planter, 2 South Bay
Smith, Rebecca, 73 Queen St
Smith, Roger, Planter, 3 Coming St
Smith, Sally, 8 Berresford's Al
Smith, Samuel, Factor, 39 Broad St

Smith, Samuel, Wine Merchant, 142 Broad St
Smith, Sarah, 22 Church St
Smith, Thomas B, Physician, 1 Middle St
Smith, Thomas, Planter, 1 Burns's Ln or Blackbird
  Al
Smith, Thomas Rhett, Planter, 56 Tradd St
Smith, Thomas, Sea Captain, 111 Queen St
Smith, Whitford, Grocer, 56 Church St
Smith, William, Carpenter, 23 Wall St
Smith, William, Ironmongery Store, 21 Elliott St
Smith, William, Merchant, 43 East Bay Cont'd
Smith, William, Ship Carpenter, 11 Pinckney St
Smith, William, Sr, Commission Merchant &
  Factor, Beale's Whf
Smith, William Stevens, Attorney at Law, 38 Broad
  St
Smith, William, Tailor, King St, Upper End
Smither, Mary, Shop Keeper, 5 Berresford's Al
Smithers, A, 32 Church St Cont'd
Smylie, Susannah, 7 South Bay
Smyth, John & Co, Store Keepers, 178 King St
Smyth, John, Merchant, 20 Ellery St
Snipes, Benjamin, Factor, 6 East Bay, Dwelling, 13
  Water St
Snowden, Charles, Merchant, 60 East Bay
Sollee, John, City Theatre Long Rooms, 26 Church
  St
Solomons, Alexander, Shop Keeper, 187 King St
Solomons, Chapman, Shop Keeper, 184 King St
Solomons, Joseph, Shop Keeper, 185 King St
Solomons, Nathan, Shop Keeper, 3 Union St
  Cont'd
Somarsall, Thomas, Merchant, 10 East Bay
Somarsall, William, Merchant, 3 East Bay
Sparks, Rachel, 39 Queen St
Spears, James, Carpenter, 3 Society St
Speiren, Patrick, Shop Keeper, 177 King St
Speiren, Thomas P, 40 Tradd St
Speissegar, John, Musical Instrument Maker, 4
  Hasell St
Spencer, George, Brick Layer, 168 Meeting St
Spencer, James, Sea Captain, 16 Queen St
Spencer, Sebastian, 168 Meeting St
Spencer, William, Brick Layer, 168 Meeting St
Spidle, Elizabeth, 3 Clifford St
Spidle, John G, Carpenter, 24 Archdale St
Spinler, J, Hair Dresser, 108 Queen St
Spright, Nicholas, Ship Carpenter, Fort Ln
Stall, Thomas D, Coach Maker, 29 Trott St
Stanke, Christopher, 26 Tradd St
Stankie, Christopher, Grocer, 5 Union St.
Starkey, ----, Mrs, Shop Keeper, 164 King St
Stecher, Christopher, Butcher, 164 King St
Steedman, Charles, Carpenter, 133 Meeting St
Steedman, Charles, Cooper, 39 Trott St
Steedman, Elizabeth, 39 Trott St
Steinmire, George, Baker, Boundary St
Steinmitz & Lorent, Merchants, Dwelling, 52 Tradd
  St.

Stent, John, Brick Layer, 21 Quince St
Stevens & Ramsay, Physicians, 44 East Bay
Stevens, Daniel, Planter, 30 George St
Stevens, Jervis Henry, City Sheriff, Dwelling, 68
  Tradd St , Office, Exchange
Stevens, William, Factor, 15 Pinckney St , Store,
  Nicholls' Whf
Stevens, William S , Physician, 15 King St
Stevenson, Mary, 40 King St
Stewart, ——, Misses, Boarding School, 58 Meeting
  St
Stewart, Alexander, House Carpenter, 275 King St
Stewart, Henry, Carpenter, 28 St Philip's St
Stewart, Robert, Ship Chandler, 29 East Bay
Stewart, Thomas, Cordage Store, 2 Gillon St
Stock, Margaret, 6 Legare St
Stoddard, Elijah, Grocer, 63 Church St
Stoll, Catherine, 17 Magazine St
Stoll, Justinus, Brick Layer, 119 Meeting St
Stone, E , 18 Coming St
Stone, Michael, 7 Gaillard's Whf
Stoney, John, Merchant, 8 Hasell St
Stoops, Benjamin T , Shoe Maker, 111 King St
Stowe, Richard R , Sea Captain, 52 King St
Strobel, Daniel, Tanner, 118 Meeting St
Strobel, Jacob, Butcher, 10 Magazine St
Strobel, John, Butcher, 1 Smith St
Strobel, Lewis, Brick Layer, 53 Meeting St
Strohecker, John, Blacksmith, 154 Meeting St
Stromer, J H , Merchant, 19 Elliott St
Stroub, Jacob, Carpenter, 5 Burns' Ln
Sturgis, Josiah, Merchant, 4 Crafts' S Whf.
Suares, Jacob, Sr , Shop Keeper, 79 King St
Suder, John & Joseph, Tailors, 2 Elliott St
Suder, Peter, Shoe Maker, 10 Federal St
Sullivan, ——, Champneys St
Sutcliffe, Eli, House Carpenter, 26 Archdale St
Sutherland & Carmichael, Merchants, 86 Church St
Sutherland & Jackson, Shoe Store, 61 King St
Sutherland & Reader, Shoe Store, 3 Queen St
Swain, Joseph, Sea Captain, 24 East Bay Cont'd
Swain, L , Mrs , 3 Stoll's Al
Sweeny & Atkinson, Grocers, 40 East Bay Cont'd
Sweeny, James, Vendue Master, Store, Exchange
  Cellar
Swinton, Hugh, Factor, 74 Meeting St
Swinton, James, Factor, 74 Meeting St
Switzer, John R , Saddler, 218 King St
Taite, James, Sea Captain, 114 Queen St
Taite, Wilson & Co , Wholesale & Retail Grocers,
  110 East Bay
Tarver, John, 107 Tradd St
Tavel, Frederick, 13 Pinckney St
Tavina, Peter, 69 Meeting St
Taylor, Joseph G , Grocer, 7 Prioleau's N Whf
Taylor, Joseph, Sea Captain, 3 Charles St
Taylor, Margaret, 140 Meeting St
Taylor, Maria, 13 Friend St
Taylor, Sarah, 10 Quince St

Teasdale, Isaac, Merchant, 112 Queen St
Teasdale, John, Merchant, 2 Bay, Counting House,
  36 Bay
Terill, Mary, 20 Union St Cont'd
Teronna, Anthony, Print Shop, 30 Broad St.
Teus, Simeon, Cashier, State Bank, 238 King St
Tew, Charles, Notary Public & Q U , 43 Elliott St
Thayer, Ebenezer, Broker, 79 Tradd St
Theadcraft, Bethel, Watch Maker, 235 King St
Theus, Rosanna, 94 Queen St
Thibaud, ——, French Teacher, 12 Middle St
Thom, Jacob, Cabinet Maker, 68 Meeting St
Thomas, Ebenezer S , Bookseller, 121 Broad St
Thomas, Francis, Discount Clerk, National Bank, 29
  Archdale St
Thomas, John, Grocer, 31 Union St
Thomas, John, Hair Dresser, 11 Bedon's Al
Thomas, Mary Lamboll, 12 King St
Thomas, Sarah, Shop Keeper, 41 East Bay Cont'd
Thomas, Stephen, Shop Keeper, 33 Elliott St
Thompson, John, 10 Chalmers' Al
Thompson, Margaret, 19 Beaufain St
Thompson, Margaret, Boarding House, 63 East Bay
Thompson, Thomas, Boarding House, 4 Lodge Al
Thompson, William, Windsor Chair Maker, 40
  Queen St
Thomson, James, Boarding Officer & Keeper of the
  Carolina Coffee House, 115 Tradd St
Thorn, John G , Sail Maker, 3 Guignard St., Sail
  Loft, Pritchard's Whf
Thornhill, John, Merchant, 17 Church St
Thron, John, Grocer, 60 Meeting St
Thynnes, William, Grocer, 70 East Bay
Tidyman, ——, Mrs , 9 Meeting St
Tidyman, Philip, Physician, 7 Legare St
Timmons, William, Merchant, 34 Trott St
Timothy, Benjamin F , Printer, 33 George St
Tobias, Isaac, 202 King St
Tofel, John, Confectioner, 20 Church St
Tordham, Richard, Shipwright, 59 Church St
Torel, Thomas, Grocer, 135 Meeting St
Tores, Abraham, Shop Keeper, 84 King St
Torrance, James, Grocer, 157 Meeting St
Torrance, W H , Attorney at Law, 20 Trott St
Torry, Charles & Co , Opticians, Etc , 32 Broad St
Toussiger, Elizabeth, 4 Water St
Tovey, ——, Block Maker, 9 Pinckney St
Tovey & Sharp, Blockmakers, 100 East Bay
Trencelet, ——, Madame, 167 Meeting St
Trenholm, William, Grocer, 2 Prioleau's N Whf
Trescot, Edward, Planter, 72 Meeting St
Trezevant, Lewis, Associate Judge, 98 Queen St
Trezevant, Peter, Discount Clerk, State Bank, 100
  Broad St
Troup, ——, Mrs , 104 Tradd St
Truchelet, Joseph, Baker, 128 Queen St
Truel, Jacques, Tailor, 38 Union St Cont'd
Truxham, Elizabeth, Lynch's Ln
Tucker, Mary, 5 Price's Al

Tucker, Sarah, School Mistress, 108 Church St
Tunno & Cox, Merchants, 27 East Bay
Tunno & Price, Merchants, 4 Geyer's N Whf
Tunno, Adam, Merchant, 27 East Bay
Tunno, William, Planter, 81 East Bay
Turnbull, James, Lumber Merchant, 42 Church St. Cont'd
Turnbull, John, 211 Meeting St
Turnbull, Robert J, Attorney at Law, 198 Meeting St
Turner, Daniel Watson, Deputy City Sheriff, Whim Court
Turner, Thomas, Dancing Master, 7 Parsonage Ln
Turner, William, 105 Church St
Turner, William, Shop Keeper, Upper End of King St
Turpin, ----, Mrs, Boarding House, 28 Elliott St
Turpin, William, Merchant, 149 King St
Tweed, Alexander, Planter, 3 Pinckney St
Twing, Edward, Grocer, 15 Union St
Ulmo, A, Physician & Family Medicine Store, 179 Meeting St
Vanbrune, L, Cigar Maker, 37 Union St Cont'd
Vanderbolt, Timothy W, Shoestore, 28 Elliott St
Vanderherchen, A, Tailor, 209 King St
Vanderhorst, Arnoldus, Planter, 15 East Bay
Vanderhorst, Chisolm & Taylor, Factors & Commission Merchants, Vanderhorst's Whf
Vandraff, Cornelius, Shoe Maker, 19 Middle St
VanRyne, A E, Store Keeper, 134 Broad St
Vardell, Elizabeth, 24 King St
Varley, ----, Misses, 26 Beaufain St
Veitch, William, Brick Layer, 1 South Bay
Vernon, Nathaniel & Co, Jewellers & Silversmiths, 140 Broad St
Verree & Blair, Vendue Masters, Exchange St.
Verree, George, 3 Church St
Verree, Joseph, Vendue Master, 3 Church St
Verree, Mary, 3 Church St
Verree, Robert, Merchant, 15 Tradd St
Verree, Samuel, 3 Church St
Verree, William, 3 Church St
Versmester, ----, Accountant, 16 Broad St
Vesey, Charles, Accountant, 5 Parsonage Ln
Vesiene, Antoine, Cigar Maker, 14 Berresford St.
Vieyra, Joseph, 253 King St
Villeneuve, J B, Merchant, 9 Society St, Store, 111 East Bay
Villeponteau, ----, Mrs, 6 East Bay
Vincent, Thomas, Grocer, 5 Tradd St
Virgent, Elizabeth, 34 King St
Voss, Andrew, Merchant, 32 Beaufain St
Wadsworth, ----, Mrs, Upper End of King St
Wadsworth, Joel, Saddler, 125 King St
Wagner, Christopher, Drayman, 6 Trott St
Wagner, George, Planter, 101 Broad St
Wainwright, ----, Mrs, 92 Tradd St
Waite, William, Coach Maker, 66 Meeting St
Wales, Horatio, Shop Keeper, 17 Amen St.

Walker & Evans, Stone Cutters, 24 Trott St
Walker, David, Grocer, 253 King St
Walker, Robert, House Carpenter, 10 Middle St
Walker, William, Cabinet Maker, 23 Hasell St
Wall, Richard, Boarding House, 27 Union St
Wallace, Alexander, Shop Keeper, 288 King St
Wallace, James, Deputy Sheriff
Wallace, Thomas, Cabinet Maker, 25 Queen St
Waller, Bayfield, Merchant, 13 Magazine St
Walsh, George, Tailor, Boundary St
Walton, ----, Mrs, 6 Moore St
Walton & Pagan, Merchants, 151 King St
Ward, ----, Mr, School Master, 13 Berresford St
Ward & Gilbert, Academy, 104 Church St
Ward, Daniel, Master of the Work House, 62 Tradd St or 6 Adams' St
Ward, James M, Attorney at Law, 176 Meeting St
Ward, John, Attorney at Law, 47 Church St
Waring & Smith, Factors, Roper's Whf
Waring, Daniel, Planter, 13 Scarborough St
Waring, Mary, 32 Wentworth St
Waring, Morton, Factor, Dwelling, 273 King St
Waring, Thomas, Sr, Naval Officer, 32 Meeting St
Warley, Elizabeth, 6 Beaufain St
Warley, Felix, Planter, 8 Trott St
Warner, Penelope, Shop Keeper, 202 Meeting St
Warnock, Joseph, Jr, Carpenter, 23 St Philip's St
Warren, Peter, Sea Captain, 13 Wall St
Washburn, Eli, Sea Captain, 16 King St
Washington, William, Planter, 6 Church St Cont'd
Watson & M'Lean, Grocers, 69 East Bay
Watson, Alexander, Factor, Dwelling, East Bay Cont'd
Watson, John, Cabinet Maker, 26 King St
Watson, William, Shop Keeper, 73 Meeting St
Watts, Charles, Cabinet Maker, 39 Church St
Watts, James, Grocer, 29 Church St Cont'd.
Watts, Robert, 14 Friend St
Webb, Benjamin, Planter, 16 Beaufain St
Webb, John, 14 Moore St
Webb, William, Teller of the State Bank, 14 Moore St
Weissinger, John, Baker, 174 King St
Wells, Frances C, 18 Church St Cont'd
Wells, Samuel, Mariner, 52 Trott St
Welsh, John, Cabinet Maker, 80 Meeting St
Welsh, Samuel, Sail Maker, 77 Tradd St
Welsh, Thomas, Carver & Gilder, 16 Hasell St
Wershing, Catherine, 3 Burns' Ln
West, J D, Physician, 49 Tradd St
West, Simon, Sea Captain, 9 Wall St
West, Thomas, Sea Captain, 9 Charles St
Westerburgh, John, Ship Carpenter, Cock Ln
Westermyer, Andrew, Goldsmith, 19 Union St
Westner, Henry, Baker, 5 Mazyck St
Weston, Isaac M, Merchant, Broad St
Weston, Plowden, Planter, 31 Queen St.
Whaley, Thomas, Planter, 293 King St
Whalley & Broadfoot, Merchants, 122 Tradd St

Wheeler & Parmele, Grocers, 101 Church St
Wheeler & Warren, Merchants, 6 Bedons' Al
White, George K., Merchant, 44 Church St
White, Henry, Sea Captain, 3 Wall St.
White, James, Grocer, 129 Queen St
White, John, Factor, Dwelling, 124 Meeting St,
Store, 8 Geyer's N Whf
White, William, Factor, 1 Bedons' Al
White, William, Rigger, 3 Bottle Al
Whitfield, George, Merchant, 2 Bedons' Al
Whitney, James, Upper End of King St.
Whitney, Thomas H, Carver & Gilder, 195
Meeting St
Wigfall, Constantia, 46 George St
Wightman, William, Jeweller, 185 Meeting St.
Wilcox, ——, Painter & Glazier, 26 Queen St
Wilcox & Flagg, Painter & Glazier, 104 East Bay
Wildman, Seymore, Hatter, 143 King St
Wilhelmi, J P, Boarding House, 1 Tradd St cor.
East Bay
Wilkie, William, 116 Meeting St
Wilkinson, Mary, Boarding House, 11 Chalmers'
Al
Will, Charlotte, 9 Middle St
Will, Philip, Deputy Federal Marshal, 9 Middle St
Williams, Charles, Custon House, Waytt's Ln
Williams, Isham, Planter, Williams' Whf
Williams, James, Custon House, 35 Union St
Cont'd
Williams, John, Tin Plate Worker, 29 Pinckney St
Williams, R D, Printer, Dwelling, 109 Church St
Williams, William, Portrait Painter, 78 Meeting St
Williamson & Stoney, Merchants, 3 Gaillard's Whf
Williamson, Amelia, 104 King St
Williamson, John, Union St Cont'd
Williman, Christopher, Planter, 211 King St
Williman, Jacob, Physician, 226 King St
Williman, Jacob, Tanner, Montague St
Willis & Miller, Bakers, 102 East Bay
Willis, Mary, 1 Boundary St
Wilson, Elizabeth, 22 Mazyck St
Wilson, Frederick, Rev, 186 Meeting St
Wilson, John, Cabinet Maker, 125 Meeting St.
Wilson, Margaret, 267 King St
Wilson, Robert, Physician, 35 Meeting St
Wilson, Robert, Sr, Physician, Dwelling, 87 Broad
St, Shop, 88 Church St
Wilson, Samuel, Physician, 43 Broad St
Wilson, Susannah, 15 Scarborough St
Wilson, Thomas, Planter, 1 Federal St
Winkins, J H, Grocer, 36 Union St
Winn, Joseph, Grocer, Dwelling, 10 Beaufain St,
Shop, 20 Union St
Winstanly, Thomas, Attorney at Law, 86 East Bay
Winthrop, Joseph, Merchant, 57 Tradd St
Wish & Bryan, Merchants, 130 Broad St
Wish, Ann, 59 Queen St
Wish, Catherine, 58 Queen St
Wish, William, Merchant, 10 Meeting St

Wissmann & Lorent, Merchants, 135 East Bay
Withers, Thomas, Ship Carpenter, Cock Ln
Witte, M J., Merchant, 120 Tradd St
Wittich, Charles, Silver Smith & Jeweller, 25 Broad
St
Woddrop, John, Merchant, 9 East Bay, Dwelling,
106 Church St
Wolf, George, Grocer, 5 Hasell St
Wolf, Mathias, Butcher, 18 Mazyck St
Wolf, Rachel, 259 King St
Wolfe, John, Grocer, 182 King St
Wood, James, Montague St
Wood, William, Counting House, 15 Archdale St
Wood, William, Rigger, 10 Bottle Al
Woodhill, John A, Cabinet Maker, 199 King St
Woodrouffe, E L, Merchant, 22 Broad St
Woodward & Green, Factors, 145 Broad St
Worthington, Joseph, Upholsterer, 177 Meeting St
Wragg, Samuel, Planter, 5 Front St, Bay
Wragg, William, Planter, 82 East Bay
Wrainch, John, School Master, 61 Meeting St
Wrainch, Richard, City Scavenger, 62 Meeting St
Wright, ——, Plasterer, Bull St
Wright, Elizabeth, 9 Orange St
Wurdemann, J G, Grocer, 9 Queen St
Wyatt, ——, Mrs, 65 Church St
Wyatt, Elizabeth, 55 Church St
Wyatt, Peter, Lynch St
Yates, Deborah, Fort St
Yates, Joseph, Cooper, 11 Church St Cont'd
Yates, Seth, Carpenter, Lynch's Ln
Yeadon, Richard, Teller, National Bank, 18 King
St
Yeadon, William, Attorney at Law, 18 King St
Yoer, Jacob, Shoe Maker, 92 Queen St
Yon, Elizabeth, 31 Archdale St
Young, ——, Mr, Tallow Chandler, 3 Union St
Young, Frances, 16 Meeting St
Young, John & Co, Merchants, 15 Elliott St
Young, Margaret, 8 Chalmers' Al
Young, Margaret, Boarding House, 12 Union St
Young, William Price, Bookstore & Printing Office,
41 Broad St
Zalic, Abraham, Shop Keeper, 219 King St
Zealy, Joseph, Shop Keeper, 263 King St
Zylstra, Peter, Shop Keeper, 64 East Bay

Chapter 2

THE 1806 DIRECTORY

The 1806 directory was compiled by J. J. Negrin under the title of *Negrin's Directory, and Almanac, for the Year 1806 Containing Every Article of General Utility* (Charleston: J J Negrin's Press), 126 pages) Among other things, Negrin, a refugee from St Domingo, present Haiti, lists himself as an interpreter, tutor of French and English, printer, and compiler of the directory. In his introduction, he states that he was again presenting to the public a new directory, indicating that this was not his first; however, his previous directory has not been found Interspersed among the 3,003 entries presented here are lists of streets, public officers, clubs, lodges, societies, military units, lawyers, banks, school masters, company officers, justices of the peace, and other such information This information has not been included here as most of the people can be found in the listings; however, anyone wishing to find information on a particular individual would be advised to check these lists Especially important is information found in the "Appendix of Index and Supplement to the Charleston Directory " Here one can find bank officers and employees, militia leaders, custom house officials, insurance company officials, and justices of the peace for all the districts in South Carolina.

———

Abbott, William, Merchant, Geyer's Whf , Res., 1 N Centurion St
Abelard, Anthony, Shop Keeper, 5 W Middle St
Abelard, Joseph, Dr , 38 King St
Abendanone, Joseph, Shop Keeper, 244 King St
Abercrombie, Sarah, Mrs , 9 Berresford St
Abrahams, ——, Mrs Judah, 10 Berresford St
Abrahams, Jacob, Shop Keeper, 4 Queen St.
Abrahams, Moise, Vendue Master, 24 Hasell St
Ackis, John E , Shoe Maker, 17 Union St
Adams & Lawrence, Factors, 4 Geyer's Whf.
Adams, David, Merchant, 37 Hasell St
Adams, John S , Merchant, 98 East Bay
Adger, Eliza, Mrs , Widow, 46 King St
Adger, James, Merchant, 3 W King St. Cont'd.
Adickes, E J , Grocer, 6 N E cor Prioleau Market Whf
Aiken, William, Merchant, 3 E King St Road
Air, George, Carpenter, 10 Archdale St
Air, James A , Dr , N E End Boundary St

Air, Mary, Boarding House, 7 Union St
Akeen, Helena, Shop Keeper, 30 Pinckney St
Akin, Ann, Mrs , Misses Boarding School, 117 King St
Akin, Thomas, Dr , cor King & Wentworth St
Aldrich, Robert, Book Store 121 Broad St
Alexander, Abraham, Jr , Shop Keeper, 129 King St
Alexander, Abraham, Sr , Store Keeper, 129 King St
Alexander, David, Merchant, 10 Broad St.
Alexander, Joseph, Grocer, 16 Church St
Alexander, Samuel, 8 Archdale St.
Alexander, William, Planter, 5 Charles St
Allan, John, Carpenter, 160 King St
Allan, Lucien, Grocer, 34 King St
Allan, Mason & Ewing, Merchants, 113 Tradd St
Allan, William, Merchant, 5 Federal St
Allen, John, Planter, 3 Pinckney St
Allman, Robert, Merchant, 24 E King St Road
Allon, James, Cooper, 2 Champneys Whf
Allon, William, Boat Builder, 3 Hard Al
Allport, John, Smith & Farrier, 113 King St
Alson, William, Planter, 13 King St
Alston, J W , Planter, 3 Front St
Alston, Joseph, Planter, 93 Church St
Ancrum, James, Planter, 30 Hasell St
Ancrum, William, Planter, 22 Ellery St
Anderson, Ann, Mrs , cor Middle & Minority St
Anderson, George, Capt , Mariner, 30 East Bay Cont'd
Anderson, Hannah & Son, Merchants, 18 Tradd St
Anderson, John, Carpenter, N E Middle St
Anderson, Rebecca, Mrs , 30 East Bay Cont'd
Anderson, William, Stay Maker, 204 Meeting St
Andrew & Co , Merchants, 116 Bay, Res , 4 Pinckney St
Andrews, Loring, Proprietor of the Courier, 115 Queen St
Annely, George W , Merchant, 1 S W Middle St
Anone & Co , Print Sellers, 16 Broad St
Anthony, John, Harness Maker, 192 Meeting St
Antonio, Manoel, Merchant, Columbia, 13 N Bull St
Appleton, Mary, Boarding House, 38 Union St
Arms, Elizabeth, Mantua Maker, 44 Trott St
Armstrong, Rebecca, Widow, 14 Pinckney St
Arnold, Amos, Planter's Overseer, 132 Queen St
Arthur, George, Planter, 16 Pinckney St
Artman & Jordan, Coach Makers, 29 Trott St
Ash, Elizabeth, Mrs , Widow, 5 Lamboll St
Ash, Hannah, Mrs , 19 King St
Ash, John, Planter, 17 South Bay
Ash, Samuel E & Co , Coach & Harness Makers, 149 Meeting St
Askew, Ann, Widow, 24 Archdale St
Assalit, Joseph, French Tutor, 163 Meeting St
Atkins, William, Victualler, Pinckney St , Over Cannon's Bridge

Atmar, Ralph, Out Door Clerk, State Bank, 8 Lynch's Ln
Austen, Catherine, Shop Keeper, 47 East Bay
Austin, William, Broker, 91 Meeting St
Avery, Mary, Mrs, Baker, 94 Church St
Axson, Jacob, Bill Book Keeper, S C Bank, Res, 62 Tradd St
Axson, Samuel, Carpenter, 63 Tradd St
Aydelot, Joshua, Mercantile, 77 Church St
Ayrault, Peter, Merchant, 118 East Bay
Baas & Fordham, Mast, Block & Pump Makers, cor Bay & Gillon Streets
Baas, Thomas, Block Maker, Gillon St, Res, 84 Bay
Babcock, Amon & John, Proprietor, Southern Mail Stage, National Bank Square
Bachelier, Thomas, Jr, Merchant Tailor, 117 Queen St
Bachelier, Thomas, Sr, Tailor, 117 Queen St
Backman, Gerhard, Grocer, 11 Mazyck St
Bacot Henry, Attorney at Law, 26 Tradd St
Bacot, Thomas W, Post Master & Cashier, S C Bank, 99 Tradd St
Badger, James, Painter & Glazier, 6 Berresford's Al, Res, 30 Trott St
Bailey & Waller, Merchants, 121 Broad St
Bailey, George G, Commission Store, 187 Meeting St
Bailey, H B, Lodging House, 187 Meeting St
Bailey, Henry, Attorney at Law, 42 Church St
Bailly, Anthony, Shoe Maker, 5 Unity Al
Baker, ——, Mrs, 4 N Wenthworth St Cont'd
Baker, Francis, Mason, 37 King St
Baker, J J, Grocer, 20 East Bay
Baker, Joseph, Lumber Merchant, 1 South Bay & Gibbes St
Baker, Samuel, Planter, 5 St Philip's St
Baker, Thomas, Commission Merchant & Vendue Master, 36½ Bay, Res, 15 Federal St
Baker, Thomas, Mason, 38 King St
Baldwin, Robert, Carpenter, 23 Beaufain St
Ball, ——, Mrs Thomas, 9 Church St Cont'd
Ball, Archibald, Planter, 5 S E Cannon St
Ball, Elizabeth, Widow, 5 Church St
Ball, John, Jr, Planter, 12 Hasell St
Ball, John, Planter, 31 Hasell St.
Ballon, Andrew, Grocer, 132 Queen St
Bampfield, George, Mariner, 11 Society St
Bampfield, Sarah, Mrs, 8 George St
Bampfield, Thomas, James & Henry, Planters, 15 Pinckney St
Banks, Charles, Merchant, Crafts' S Whf, Res, 1 W Logan St
Barelli, John, Print Seller & Mathematical Instrument Maker, 32 Broad St
Barker, Joseph S, Merchant, 94 Bay, Res, 1 Anson St
Barksdale, Thomas, Jr., Planter, 90 Tradd St
Barnard, Alexander, Store, 53 King St

Barnett, Samuel, 12 W Wall St.
Barnett, Samuel, Planter, 19 Scarborough St
Baron & Wilson, Physicians, 218 Meeting St
Baron, Alexander, Dr, 53 Broad St
Barrett, Esther, Shop Keeper, 62 King St
Barreyre, Peter, Baker, 9 Berresford St
Barron, John, Wine Merchant, 11 East Bay
Barton, Eliza, Mantua Maker, 17 Hasell St
Basile, Margaret, Refugee, St Domingo, 19 Union St Cont'd
Bay, Elihu, Judge, Court of Sessions & Common Pleas, 197 Meeting St
Beach, Mary, Mrs, Widow, 12 King St
Beale, John E, Esq, Whf Owner, 32 Bay
Beale, Joseph, Accountant, N W End, Lynch's Court
Beard, Frederick, Teller, S C Bank
Beard, —— Mrs, Widow, 104 Broad St
Beard, William, Porter, S C Bank, Res, 35 Church St
Beath, David, Wharfinger, Chisolm's Whf, Res, Guignard & Charles St
Beattie, Edward, Merchant, 46 East Bay
Beatty, Robert, Merchant, 28 Broad St
Beauboeuf, Michel, Dr, Refugee, St Domingo, 12 Society St
Beckman, Adolph, Painter & Glazier, 77 Meeting St
Beckstrom, Jonas, Mariner, 21 East Bay Cont'd
Bee, David, Planter, 10 Stoll's Al
Bee, Eliza, Mrs, Widow, 63 Tradd St
Bee, John, Factor, 22 Church St
Bee, John, House Carpenter, 16 Mazyck St
Bee, Smith, Planter, 22 Church St
Bee, Thomas, Jr, Principal of the College
Bee, Thomas, Judge, Admiralty Court, S C, 4 Short St
Bee, William, Book Keeper, 10 Meeting St
Bee, William, Planter, 14 Church St Cont'd
Beekman, Samuel, Pump Maker, 129 East Bay, Res, 28 Hasell St.
Beggs & Coan, Grocers, S W cor King St Road & Vanderhorst St
Beile, John C, Store Keeper, 119 King St
Bell, Boor, Jr, Capt, Mariner of Bermuda
Bell, Daniel, Gardener, 24 St Philip's St
Bell, David, Book Keeper, 7 Society St
Bellamy, Esther, Mrs, Widow, 41 Tradd St
Bellinger, George, Dr, Planter, 24 Mazyck St
Bellisle, Peter, Baker & Grocer, 5 Maiden Ln.
Belser, Christian, Victualler, 15 East King St
Belsher, Robert, Merchant, 7 E King St Road
Benbenon, Lolotte, Fruit Shop, 253 King St
Bennett, A, House Carpenter, 1 Trott St
Bennett, George, Merchant, 16 Berresford St
Bennett, Henry, Counting House Store Keeper, 22 King St
Bennett, Mary, Boarding House, 8 Chalmer's Al

Bennett, Thomas, Jr, Lumber Merchant, at his Mills, Bull St

Benoist, Charles, Chair Maker, 3 Meeting St Cont'd

Benoist, John B, Baker, 138 Meeting St

Benoit, John, Capt, Mariner, 4 Maiden Ln

Benoit, Therese, See Hanotau

Benson, Laurence, Grocer, 233 King St

Bentham, James, Notary Public & Q U, 39 East Bay

Bering, Ann, Mrs, Dry Goods Store, 192 King St

Bering, John, Jeweller, 192 King St

Bernard, R, Dr, 39 King St

Bernard, Rene, Perfumer, 4 Tradd St

Berney, John, Merchant, 2 Geyer's N Whf, Res, 28 Meeting St

Bernstine, Henry, Grocer, Boundary St, N W cor. Coming

Berry, Andrew, Grocer, N E cor Boundary & Meeting St Cont'd

Berry, Hesley, Tailor, 19 Trott St

Besden, Laurence, Shipwright, 14 Pinckney St

Besseleu, Charles, Carpenter, 24 Beaufain St

Besseleu, Elizabeth, Mrs, Nurse, 29 Beaufain St

Besseleu, Lewis, Cabinet Maker, 29 Beaufain St

Besseleu, Mark Anthony, Carpenter, 24 Beaufain St

Bessiere, J, Tailor, at Mr Guilou

Beswicke, John, Wharfinger, Prioleau's Whf

Beswicke, S, Mrs, School, 3 Society St

Bethune, Angus, Merchant, 11 Broad St

Bevin, Francis, House Carpenter, 16 Union St Cont'd.

Bicaisse, Clodius, Cabinet Maker, 135 Meeting St

Bieller, Joseph, Butcher, 23 Archdale St

Billing, J, Livery Stables, 214 King St

Bingley, Nathaniel, Capt, Mariner, 80 Bay

Bird, Sarah, Nurse, 7 Mazyck St

Bishop, Charles, Capt, Mariner, 77 Queen St

Bishop, Eliza, 12 N Bull St

Bishop, Henry, Grocer, South Bay, M'Kenzie's Whf

Bivette, Catharine, 1 Union St Cont'd

Bixby, Nathaniel, Merchant, 8 Crafts' Whf, Res, 35 King St

Bize, Daniel, Carpenter, Meeting St. Road, 2d street above the Inspection

Bizeuil, Julien, Grocer, 80 Church St

Blacan, Peter, Turner, 89 Queen St.

Black & Birnie, Ironmongers, 116 Tradd St.

Black & Birnie, Merchants, 11 Broad St

Black & Yates, Coopers, Beale's & Crafts' N Whf

Black, James, Shipwright, 92 East Bay

Black, Johanna, Widow, 9 Guignard St

Black, William, 116 Tradd St

Blacklock, William, Merchant, 134 Bay, Res, cor Bull St & Coming

Blackwood, Thomas, Merchant, 19 Bay, Res., 37 Tradd St

Bladen, Thomas D, Rev, Guignard St

Blair, James, Vendue Merchant & Commission Merchant, 2 Stoll's Al

Blair, John, Merchant, 107 Broad St

Blair, William, Shipwright, 39 Church St Cont'd

Blake & Magwood, Factors, Blake's Whf

Blake, John, Capt, Whf Owner, President, State Bank, Res, 5 South Bay

Blake, Peter, Assistant, Work House

Blakeley, Elizabeth, Widow, 4 Church St

Blakeley, Robert, Merchant, 4 King St Cont'd

Blamyer, William, Weight Master, Custom House, 4 N. E. Wall St

Blancken, George, Grocer, 16 Wentworth St cor Coming

Bland, Richard, Boarding House, 5 Union St

Bleakley, Seth, Tailor, 27 Church St, Res, 19 Amen St

Blewer, Peter, Grocer, 10 E King St Road

Blomberg, Peter, Accountant, at Mr Villeneuve's

Blome & Bonay, Bakers, 21 Berresford's Al

Blome, John, Surgeon, 21 Berresford's Al

Blume, Andrew, Butcher, 101 King St

Blumestock, Michael, Grocer, cor St Philip's & Liberty St

Bocquet, Elizabeth, Mrs, Widow, 12 St Philip's St

Bolchoz, Alexander, Capt, 17 Guignard St

Bolick, Lucretia, Laundress, N E Scarborough St

Bollough, E, Shoe Maker, 88 Queen St

Bomkamper, Frederick, Grocer, 8 W Wall St

Bonay, Peter J, Baker, 21 Berresford St

Bones, John, Shop, 160 King St.

Bonneau, John, 58 Broad St

Bonsall, Elizabeth, Mrs, 5 Wentworth St

Bonthron, John, Grocer, 90 Queen St

Boone, James, Planter, cor Blake & Drake St, Hampstead

Booner, Christian, Hotel, 97 Queen St

Borch, Peter, Fruit Shop, 87 Queen St

Bosgerard, C & F, Merchants, 1 Crafts' N Whf, Res, 196 King St

Bouchanneau, Isaac, Carpenter, 4 W Meeting St

Bouchanneau, Sarah, Mrs, Widow, Drake St, Hampstead

Bouisselin, Peter, Capt, 127 East Bay Boundary & Mill St, Cannonborough

Bounetheau, Elizabeth, Mrs, 69 Church St

Bounetheau, G M, Justice of the Peace, Clerk of Council, Printer, 3 Broad St

Bourg, Peter, Refugee, Santo Domingo, 7 Middle St

Boutan, Peter Bernard, Merchant, Citizen U S, 104 East Bay

Boutet, Francis, Tobacconist, 5 Ellery St

Bowen, Nathaniel, Rev, 2 Front St

Bowering, Henry, Merchant, 78 King St

Bowers, Alexander, Merchant, 81 Tradd St

Bowhay, Joseph, Butcher Stall 23, Res, 18 E King St Road

Bowles, Tobias, Maj , Planter, cor Drake & Nassau St , Hampstead
Bowman, John, Esq , N W End Montagu St
Boyd, Benjamin, Merchant, 134 King St
Boyd, James, Grocer, 10 Union St
Boyd, William, Merchant, 103 Church St
Bradford, Christiana, Mrs , Music Store, 6 Broad St
Bradford, Lydia, Mrs , Hotel, 21 Church St
Bradley, Charles, Printer, 36 George St
Bradley, Mathew, Grocer, 81 King St cor Clifford St.
Brailsford, John, Jr , Planter, 5 East Bay
Brailsford, Robert, Planter, 4 West St
Brailsford, Samuel, Mrs , 32 Church St.
Brailsford, William, Planter, 18 Beaufain St
Brainerd, Elijah, Shoestore, 209 King St
Branan, Martin, Grocer, South Bay
Brandford, Mary, Mrs , 17 Legare St
Brandon, David, Confectioner, cor Meeting St Cont'd & Boundary
Brebner, Archibald, Merchant Tailor, 11 Tradd St
Bremar, Francis, Esq , 2 miles W King St Road
Brenan, Mathew & Richard, Merchants, 146 Broad St
Bride, E , Mrs , Umbrella Maker, 186 Meeting St
Bridie, Eleonora, Mrs , Boarding School, 25 Meeting St
Brisbane, William, Planter, 3 Smith's Ln
Brissat, F A , Baker, 2 Trott St
Broadfoot, James & Co , Merchants, 151 Bay, Res , 7 Cumberland St
Broadfoot, M , Merchant, 86 Broad St
Brochard, Charlotte, Refugee, St Domingo, 1 Maiden Ln
Brockway, Martha, Widow, 173 King St
Brockway, Samuel, House Carpenter, 27 Trott St
Brodie, Alexander, Student in Divinity, 2 Clifford St
Brodie, Robert, House Carpenter, 56 Tradd St
Brooks & Potter, Merchants, 9 Crafts' N Whf
Broskie, Sarah, Mrs , Boarding House, East Bay
Bross, John, Boarding House, 63 Meeting St
Broughton, ——, Mrs , Planter, 51 Meeting St.
Broughton, Ann, Miss, 72 Queen St
Broun, ——, Mrs , 12 East Bay Cont'd
Brower, Christina, Mrs , Widow, 6 Society St
Brown & Hyams, Auctioneers & Commission Merchants, N E of the Exchange
Brown & Pottle, Cotton Ginned & Moated on Toll, 1½ Mile, King St Road
Brown, Daniel, Capt , 31 Church St Cont'd.
Brown, Daniel, Grocer, 1 Church St
Brown, Jonathan, Capt , Mariner, 14 Maidenlane
Brown, Jonathan, Capt Second, Two Friends, 23 Bay Cont'd
Brown, Joseph, Custom House Inspector, S E End Prioleau's Whf S

Brown, Joshua, Vendue Master & Commission Merchant, Res , W Short St
Brown, Moses, Drum Major, 50 King St , Barber Shop, 7 Union St
Brown, Rebecca, Widow, 22 St Philip's St
Brown, Samuel S , 87 East Bay
Brown, Sarah, Shop Keeper, 21 Quince St.
Brown, Thomas, Capt , 15 Hasell St
Brown, William, Broker, 7 Wentworth St
Brown, William, Capt , Savannah Packet, 5 Guignard St
Browne, James, City Marshal, 56 Queen St
Browne, S , Commission Broker, 163 King St
Browne, Samuel, Shop, 162 King St
Brownlee, John, Merchant, 14 St Philip's St
Bruce, David, Mariner, 7 Lodge Al
Bruckner, Daniel, Commission Merchant, 7 N Montague St
Brunet, Joseph, Refugee St Domingo, 38 Meeting St
Bryan, Lydia, Mrs , Widow, 85 East Bay
Bryant, John, Clerk of the Market, 9 W King St Road
Bryce, Nicol, Auctioneer & Commission Merchant, 5 N Champneys St
Buchanan, A , Brass Founder, 21 Queen St , Res , 14 W King St Road
Budd, Abigail, Mrs , Boarding House, 40 Church St
Buford, Abigail, Mrs , Boarding House, 115 Queen St
Buist, G , Rev Dr , Principal of the College of Charleston
Buist, G , Rev Dr , Rector of the Scotch Presbyterian Church, 3 Church St Cont'd
Bulit, Catharine, Shop Keeper, 164 King St
Bulkley, Stephen, Ship Chandler, 74 East Bay,
Bull, Thomas, Shoe Maker, 2 Chalmer's Al
Bulow, John & Charles, Merchants, 166 King St
Bunce, Jacob, Boat Builder, Hard Al
Bunel, Jeanne D , 53 Trott St.
Burch, Henry J , Merchant, 71 Queen St
Burd, Rebecca, 5 Smith's Ln
Burden, James, Merchant, 41 Church St
Burden, Kinsey & Thomas, Factors, 10 Crafts' Whf
Burden, Kinsey, Factor, Crafts' S Whf, Res , 51 Tradd St
Burgoyne, William, Dr , Apothecary & Druggist, 147 Broad St
Burk, Thomas, Capt., Mariner, 123 East Bay
Burkmeyer, John, Victualler Stall 8, Res , 2 N Wentworth St. Cont'd
Burn, John, Grocer, 131 Meeting St
Burnet, Andrew, Planter, 198 Meeting St
Burr, Mary, Mrs , Mantua Maker, cor Pinckney & Charles St
Burr, Nehemiah, Capt , cor Pinckney & Charles St
Burrows, Frederick, Pilot, 5 Trott St.

Burrows, Sarah, Seamstress, 2 N Lingard St
Busquel, Anthony, Capt, 5 E Wall St
Butler, ——, Misses, Quilters, 14 N W Wall St
Butler, Charles P, Jeweller, 238 King St
Butler, Daniel, Rigger, 9 Chalmer's Al
Butler, Joseph, City Deputy Sheriff, 49 Church St
Butler, Robert, Capt, Mariner, 54 Trott St
Butner, William, Boarding House, 7 Chalmer's Al
Bynum, T, Misses Academy, cor King and
  Wentworth St
Byrne, Patrick, Sail Maker, Champneys Whf, Res,
  13 Pinckney St
Byrnes & Bennett, Merchants, 114 East Bay
Byrnes, Joseph, Merchant, Res, 34 Pinckney St
Bythewood, Thomas, Capt, 3 E Kinloch's Court
Cabos, John, 127 East Bay
Calder, Alexander, Cabinet Maker & Upholsterer,
  29 Broad St
Caldwell, John, Carpenter, N W cor College &
  Green St
Calhoun, William, Merchant
Callaghan, John, Merchant, 5 Elliott St
Calvert, Eliza, Mrs, Boarding House, 132 Broad St
Calvert, John, Mason, 17 Federal St
Calwell, Henry, Merchant, 14 Bedon's Al
Calwell, Sarah, Mrs, 212 Meeting St
Cambridge, Eliza, Mrs, Widow, 1 S E No Name
  Al
Cambridge, James H, Vendue Master, cor S E
  End Vendue Row & Beale's Whf
Cambridge, Tobias, Vendue Master, cor S E End
  Vendue Row & Beale's Whf, Res, 6 Orange St
Cameron, Alexander, Dray Keeper, 168 King St
Cameron, David, Victualler, 4 N Cannon St
Cameron, Lewis, Merchant, 23 Church St
Cameron, Samuel, Shipwright, 13 Chalmer's Al
Cammer, Peter, Grocer, 22 N W Wall St
Camolt, John, Mariner, 19 N W Wall St
Campbell, Alexander, Capt, Mariner, 14 Amen St
Campbell, Colin, Merchant, 3 Bedon's Al
Campbell, Elizabeth, Mrs, Widow, 11 St Philip's
  St
Campbell, McMillan, Vendue Master and
  Commission Merchant, 5 S Champney St, Res,
  31 Church St
Camps, Ann Carth, 4 Clifford Al
Cannon, Martha, Miss, Plantress, 1 Hudson or Mill
  St, Cannonborough
Canter, Isaac, Auctioneer, 28 Hasell St
Canter, Joshua, Mariner, 13 Legare St
Cantor, J, Merchant, Diedcrick & Co
Cantor, Jacob, 116 Tradd St
Canut, Francis, Firm Delaire & Canut, Res, 8
  Ellery St
Cape, Brian, Factor, Geyer's Whf, Res, 20 East
  Bay Cont'd
Cape, Mary, Mrs, Widow, 20 East Bay Cont'd
Cape, Thomas, Planter, Res., 20 East Bay Cont'd
Capers, Sarah, Mrs, Plantress, 5 N Montague St

Card, Mary, Mrs, Seamstress, 105 Tradd St
Cardozo, David, Lumber Measurer, 17 King St
Carew, Edward, Block & Pump Maker, Etc, Res,
  4 S Ellery St
Carew, Thomas, Shipwright, 64 Church St
Carmand, Peter & Son, Tailors, 230 King St
Carmichael, Eliza, Mrs, Lynch's Ln
Carne, Susannah, Mrs, Plantress, 17 Archdale St
Carne, Thomas W, Messenger of Council &
  Keeper of Exchange
Carnes, Samuel, Rope Maker, 27 Beaufain St
Carns, Thomas William, Book Keeper, 26 St
  Philip's St
Carpenter, Joseph, Victualler Stall 15, Res, 10
  S. Cannon St
Carpenter, S C, Editor of the Courier, 39 Hasell
  St
Carr, Ann, Mrs, Widow, 14 Quince St
Carrere, Charles, French Teacher, 78 Meeting St
Carrere, Francis, Tailor, 25 Union St
Carroll, Bartholomew, Planter, 8 N W Boundary
  St
Carroll, James P Planter, 4 N W Boundary St
Carroll John, Merchant, 106 East Bay, Lothrop's
  Row
Carson, James, Merchant, 7 Broad St, Res, 78
  Tradd St
Cart & Faber, Lumber Merchant, Cochran's Whf
Cart, John, Factor, Cochran's Whf, Res, 9 N W
  Bull St
Cart, Sarah, Mrs, Widow, 7 E Kinloch's Court
Carter, Elizabeth, Widow, 7 St Philip's St
Carter, George, Physician, 64 S W End Tradd St
Carter, Solomon, Shoe Maker, 37 Union St
Carty, William, Supercargo, 4 Cumberland St
Carver, William & Co, Farrier & Livery Stables, 1
  Kinloch's Court
Carvin, Elizabeth, Madame, 28 Church St
Casceaux, Dominic, Shop Keeper, 207 King St
Casey, Benjamin, Coach Maker, 116 Broad St
Cashman, John & Co, Grocer, 28 Union St
Catlet, M, Boarding House, 23 Berresford's Al
Catonnet, Peter, Merchant, 118 Broad St
Catonnet, Peter, Merchant, 42 Broad St
Cattle, Catherine, Mantua Maker, Whim Court
Cattle, William, Planter, 75 Tradd St
Cauffe, Aimee, Madame, 35 Trott St
Caught, Thomas, Ship Builder, 31 Bay Cont'd
Cave, Thomas, Distiller, Mazyckborough
Caveneau, Mary, Mrs, Plantress, 5 N. Cannon St
Caw, Rachel, Mrs., Plantress, 1 Legare St
Chafe, Archiles, Custom House Inspector, 1 N Pitt
  St, Federal Green
Chaihou, Laurette, Seamstress, 6 Kinloch's Court
Chalmers, Gilbert, Mrs, Widow, 16 Beaufain St
Chalmers, Margaretta, Mrs, 1 Trott St
Chamberlin, William, Tailor, 4 Clifford's Al
Chambers, Ann, Seamstress, 21 Berresford St
Chambers, William, Boarding House, 6 Union St

Chambers, William Seth, Capt , Sullivan Packet, 21 Union St

Champlin, Joseph, Grocer, 14 Elliot St.

Champman, Joseph, Carpenter, S W Vanderhorst's Whf

Champney, John, Whf. Owner, Planter, 95 King St

Champy, A Edme, Madame, 130 Meeting St

Chanceaulme, Mary, Madame, 8 Berresford St

Chancognie, Simon J , Merchant, 7 N Pitt St . Gadsden's Green

Chanet, Anthony, Grocer, 8 Queen St

Chanler, Catharine, Mrs , Widow, 52 Broad St or 64 Meeting St

Charles, Andrew, Merchant, Firm Ilopkins & Co , 14 Liberty St

Chatelain, Marie L , 4 Trott St

Chaudeux, Nicholas, Boarding House, 41 East Bay Cont'd

Cheramy, Luce, 41 Trott St

Cheves, Langdon, Attorney at Law, Firm Peace & Co , N W End State House Square

Chew, Sarah, Seamstress, 10 Trott St

Chichester, John, Dr

Chigarin, Elizabeth, Couturiere, 53 Meeting St

Child, Eliza, Mrs , Milliner & Mantua Maker, 101 King St

Chinners, John, Tailor, 8 Pinckney St

Chion, J F , Merchant, 17 East Bay

Chisolm, Alexander, Planter, 287 King St

Chisolm, George, Factor, Whf Owner, Faber's N Range, Chisolm's Whf , Res , 93 Bay

Chisolm, George, Res , 30 Church St Cont'd , Counting House, Chisolm's Whf

Chittey, William John, Porter, State Bank, 30 Wentworth St

Choinard, Charles P , Grocer, 16 St Phillip's St cor George St

Chollit, Alexander, Distiller, 2 S E Coming St

Chouler, Mary, Mrs , Widow, 11 Liberty St

Chrietzburg, Conrad, Victualler, South Bay, Res , 4 S Cannon St

Christie, Alexander, Merchant, 93 Church St

Chupein, Lewis, Merchant, Perfumer, 137 Broad St

Church, Henry, Capt , Mariner, 10 East Bay Cont'd

Church, Slocum, Carpenter, N cor Boundary & Meeting St Cont'd

Claims, Martin, Carpenter, 130 King St

Clapperson, Harriot, Grocer, 157 Meeting St

Clark, David, Watch Maker, 9 Anson St

Clark, David, Watch Maker's Shop, 74 East Bay

Clark, E , Dr , 131 Queen St or at Dr Mackey's

Clark, Isabella, Seamstress, 7 Union St. Cont'd

Clark, James, Coach Maker, 75 Meeting St

Clark, James, Tailor, 12 Elliott St

Clarkson, William, Merchant, 3 Champneys St , Res., 83 Meeting St.

Clastrier, John, Capt , 256 King St

Clastrier, Maximin, Starch & Powder Manufacturer, S W End Vanderhorst's St

Cleapor, Charles, Sail Maker's Loft, 5 Keith's Whf , 17 Ellery St

Cleary, John R , School Master, 20 Hasell St

Cleary, Robert W , Grocer, 120 Bay, Res , 11 Amen St

Clement, John P , Mercantile, 44 Queen St

Clement, Sarah, Mrs , Widow, 44 Queen St

Clissey, Raymond, Coach & Harness Maker, 78 Church St

Cliterall, George C , Planter, Removed, 33 Bay Cont'd

Club, Alexander, Merchant, 7 Tradd St , Res , 21 Meeting St

Coates, Thomas, Capt , Coates' Row Proprietor, Res , King St Road

Coates, William A , Grocer, 4 Prioleau's N Range

Cobia, Daniel, Butcher Stall 34, Res , 12 Berresford St

Coburn, Seth S , Broker, cor Coming & Wentworth St

Cochran, Charles B , Intendant, 67 Meeting St

Cochran, John, Mercantile, 122 East Bay

Cochran, Margaret, Mrs , Store, 242 King St

Cochran, Robert E , Federal Marshal, 6 Wentworth St

Cochran, Susannah, Mrs , Widow, 122 East Bay

Cochran, Thomas, Merchant, 120 East Bay

Codd, Francis, Planter, 80 Queen St

Coffskey, Ann Catharine, Widow, Shop Keeper, 88 King St

Cogdell, John S , Attorney at Law, 2 St Michael's Al

Cogdell, Mary Ann E , Mrs , Boarding School, 1 St Michael's Al

Cohen & Moses, Auctioneers & Commercial Merchants, S of the Exchange

Cohen, Barnard, Grocer, 7 N Cannon St

Cohen, Jacob & Co , Auctioneers & Commission Merchants, S Exchange, Vendue Row

Cohen, Joseph, Sexton, Synagogue, 140 Meeting St

Cohen, Mordecai, Merchant, 124 King St

Cohen, Philip, Vendue Master, 10 Orange St

Cohen, Rebecca, Mrs , Shop Keeper, 240 King St

Cohen, Solomon, Shop Keeper, 164 King St

Cohin, Nathaniel, Wharfinger, Geyer's Whf

Coils, Margaret, Seamstress, 19 Pinckney St

Coit, Jonathan, Merchant, 3 Crafts' Whf

Colas, John, Esq , 105 Queen St

Colcock, Mellisscent, Mrs , Misses Boarding House, 6 Lamboll St , Summer Res , N W. End cor

Cole, Ruth

Cole, Sarah, Nurse, 30 King St

Coleman, Benjamin, Grocer, 33 Union St

Coleman, S , Shop Keeper, 182 King St

Colhoun, John, Factor, 223 Meeting St

Colin, Ann, Mrs , Boarding House, 42 Queen St.

Colley, Thomas, Grocer, 20 Union St

Collier, William, Merchant, 53 Trott St

Collignon, Josephine, Couturier, 53 Meeting St

Collins, Catharine, Mantua Maker, 21 Berresford St

Collins, Mary, Mrs, Widow, 18 Hasell St

Colzy, Charlemagne, Tailor, 20 Church St

Combe, John, Carpenter, 3 Hudson St or Mill St, Cannonborough

Connolly, John, Capt, Mariner, 17 Meeting St

Connor, Brian, Merchant, 126 Queen St

Conolly, Thomas, Capt, Mariner, 24 Queen St

Conover, William, Printer, 138 Broad St

Conte, John, Merchant, 10 W Wall St

Conton, John, Dr, at Mrs Reigne, Elliott St

Conyers, Elizabeth, Mrs., Boarding School, 264 King St

Conyers, William, Capt, Mariner, 27 Pinckney St

Cook, Joseph, Mason, 18 Federal St

Cooper, William, Shoe Maker, 255 King St

Coram, Francis, Factor, Prioleau's Whf, Res, 20 George St

Coram, Thomas, Painter & Engraver, 70 Queen St

Corbet, Thomas, Jr, Planter, 1 Raper's Ln

Corbett, Samuel, Tavern Keeper, 191 Meeting St

Corbett, Thomas, Sr, Planter, 1 Cumberland St

Cordes, Rebecca, Mrs., Widow, 13 Society St

Cordier, Peter, Grocer, 12 E King St Road cor Reed St

Corkel, Thomas, Mariner, 9 S Cock Ln

Corker, Thomas, Shipwright, S E cor Maiden Ln & Guignard St

Cormick, Thomas, Grocer & Contractor, 71 East Bay

Cormier, Francis, Shipwright, 21 N W Wall St.

Corneille, Francis, Tinsmith, 8 Meeting St Road Cont'd

Corneille, John B, Tinsmith, 10 W King St Road

Cornely, James, Carpenter, 20 E King St Road

Corps, Elizabeth, Boarding House, 14 Union St Cont'd

Corr, Charles, Tailor, 50 King St

Corre, Charles G, Merchant 54 King St

Corrie & Kehr, Auctioneers & Commission Merchants, 2 N Vendue Row

Corrie, Alexander, Cambridge's Store, 5 Orange St.

Corrie, Samuel, Wheelwright, 10 W King St Road

Costan, John, Laborer, 23 Trott St

Cosuay, John, Dr, Surveyor & Wood Measurer, 14 Queen St

Cotten, Ann, Boarding & Lodging, 14 Berresford's Al

Cottingam, Ann, Mantua Maker, 4 Berresford's Al

Cotton, James W, Carver & Gilder, 63 Meeting St

Courtnay, Edward, Wine Merchant, Apply to Mr Samuel Smith

Courtney, Humphrey, Merchant, 34 Meeting St

Courtney, James, Merchant, 37 Meeting St

Courty, John, Grocer, 30 Union St

Courty, Mary, Mrs, Boarding House, 13 Union St

Coveney, Thomas, Grocer, 5 East Bay Cont'd

Coventry, Alexander, Dyer, 85 Tradd St

Cowen, John, Rigger, 36 East Bay Cont'd

Cox & Sheppard, Printers, Editors of the Times, 124 Tradd St

Cox, James, Merchant, Firm Tunno & Co, 10 Church St Cont'd

Cox, John, Mason, 2 Federal St

Cox, Joseph D, Carpenter, 127 Meeting St

Cox, Thomas, Coach Maker, 1 Clifford St

Cox, Thomas, Proprietor, Times Office, 19 Meeting St

Cozzens, Elizabeth, Mrs, Boarding House, S Lingard St

Crafts, William & Ebenezer, Merchants, Whf Owners, Crafts' Wharves, Counting House, E End Scale House

Craib, Thomas, Carpenter, 26 Beaufainn St

Cralk, Philip, Painter & Glazier, 12 Pinckney St cor King St

Crane, Joseph & Co, Shoe Store, 101 Broad St cor of King St

Crask, Philip, Painter & Glazier, 12 Pinckney St

Crawford, Alexander, Painter & Glazier, 213 Meeting St

Crawford, James, Grocer, 68 Queen St

Crawford, John, Wharfinger, Vanderhorst's Whf, 71 Tradd St

Crawford, William, at M O'Connor, King St

Crawley, ——, Miss, School Mistress, 12 Stoll's Al

Creighton, Edward, Hair Dresser, 5 & 21 Union St Cont'd

Creighton, James, Hair Dresser, 4 Elliott St

Creighton, Joseph, Hair Dresser, 12 Union St

Creighton, Perth, Hair Dresser, 16 Guignard St

Creighton, Samuel, Hair Dresser, 19 Union St Cont'd

Creighton, William, Hair Dresser, 39 Pickney St

Creyer, Valentin, 2 N Minority St

Cripps, John S, Merchant, 52 Meeting St

Cristian, Jacob, Carpenter, 4 Smith's Ln

Crocker & Hichborn, Merchant, 10 Crafts' N Whf, Res, 24 Tradd St

Croft, Arnoldus, Book Keeper, Res, Hampstead

Croft, Edward, Attorney at Law, 44 Meeting St

Croft, Peter, Accountant, Jones Court cor 108 King St

Croft, Peter, Factor, 4 Prioleau's Whf, Res, Hampstead

Crolbey, Josiah, Capt, Grain Merchant, 23 Scarborough St.

Crombie, Joseph, Merchant

Cromwell, Oliver, Attorney, Sheriff's Office, Res, 9 Stoll's Al

Croper, Elizabeth, Mantua Maker, 33 King St

Crosby, Josiah, Grain & Commission Merchant, Chisolm's N Whf

Cross, G Warren, Jr, Attorney at Law, 1 Federal St, Office, 102 Queen St

Cross, George, Capt, Merchant, 1 Federal St

Cross, James, Black & Fancy Dyer, 36 Broad St

Cross, Matthew, William, Mason, 4 Kinloch's Court
Cross, Samuel, John, Carpenter, 8 Society St
Crouch, Abraham, Notary Public, Counting House
Crovat, Peter, Grocer, Descoudres & Co
Crow, John, Bookbinder, 74 East Bay
Crowell, Jeremiah, Grocer, 93 Queen St
Crowley, Ann, Mrs, 105 Broad St
Cruckshanks, Daniel, Boot & Shoe Maker, 126 Queen St
Cruckshanks, William, Boot & Shoe Maker, 40 Elliot St
Cruger, Elizabeth, Mrs, Widow, 7 Guignard St
Cruger, Elizabeth, Mrs, Widow, 30 Meeting St
Cudworth, Benjamin, Stewart, Orphan House
Cudworth, Nathaniel, Principal Tutor, S C Society School
Cuigno, Lewis, Tobacconist, 27 Union St
Culliat, Elizabeth, Shop Keeper, 4 Trott St
Cummings, John, Carpenter 42 Church St Cont'd
Cummins, John, Carpenter, 42 Church St
Cunningham, Charles, Merchant, 2 E King St Road
Cunningham, John, Merchant & Commissioner, Cotton House Co, 148 King St
Cunnington, ——, Mrs, Col, Widow, Hampstead
Curlet, Lewis, Boarding House, 49 Church St
Curry & Thompson, Merchants, Boot & Shoe Store, 65 King St
Curtis, Francis, Master of the Poor House
Custer, James, Factor, Prioleau's Whf, Res, 38 Meeting St
Cutter, Robert, Capt, Mariner, 7 Smith's Ln
D'Arasse, Adelaide, Planter, Guadaloupe, 31 Beaufain St
Dabney, William, Merchant, Grocer, 101 Church St cor Longitude Ln
Dacosta, Joseph, Broker, 2 Wentworth St
Dacqueny, John, Printer, 151 Meeting St
Daker, Charles, Grocer, 134 Meeting St
Daker, Frederick, Grocer, 147 Meeting St
Dalcho, Frederick, Dr, 87 Tradd St, formerly 54 Meeting St
Dalton, James, Dr, Apothecary & Chemist, 17 Church St cor Tradd St
Damgee, Francis, Store Keeper, 6 Queen St
Damsey, Mary, Grocer, 23 Scarborough St
Daniel, Margaret, Mrs, Pastry Cook, 22 Archdale St.
Danton, James, Carter, cor St Philip's & Wentworth St
Darby, Artemas B, Deputy Surveyor General
Darby, John, Grocer, 3 Beaufain St. cor. Archdale St
Darby, Margaret, Mrs, Mantua Maker, 11 Maiden Ln
Darby, Robert A., Tailor, 75 East Bay
Darraugh, John, Tailor, 9 W King St Cont'd
Darrel, Kesia, Mrs, Widow, 3 Water St

Darrell, Nicholas, Capt, Mariner, 2 St Michael's Al
Darrett, John, Boarding House, 14 Chalmer's Al
Dart & Simmons, Factors, 7 Crafts' S Whf
Dart, Benjamin S, Factor, Res, 28 Tradd St
Dart, Isaac M, Attorney & Factor, Crafts' Whf, Res, 8 N W Montague St
Dart, John M, Attorney at Law, Res, 28 Tradd St
Dastas, ——, Messrs, Merchant, 26 King St
Datty, Julie, Mademoiselle, Misses Boarding Academy, 24 Wentworth St
Datty, Marc, French Academy, 24 Wentworth St
Daubee, ——, Navigation School, Etc, 116 Queen St
Davezac de Castra, Peter, V D J, Refugee, St Domingo, 11 W Wall St
Davidson & Blocker, Merchants, 1 East King St Road
Davidson, Gilbert, Merchant, 17 Broad St
Davidson, John, Charleston Librarian, State House, Res, 5 Society St
Davidson, Sibella, Mantua Maker, 4 S W Wall St
Davis, Israel, Store Keeper, 128 King St
Davis, John M, Marine Insurance Broker, 37 East Bay, Res, Pinckney St, Cannonborough
Davis, John, Merchant, 29 Wentworth St.
Davis, Polly, Seamstress, 26 Trott St
Dawes, Hugh P, Factor & Commission Merchant, Gadsden's Whf
Dawnie, Robert, Tin Smith & Plumber, 15 Tradd St
Dawson, Ann, Mrs, 39 Beaufain cor King St
Dawson, John & William, Merchants, 115 East Bay
Dawson, John, Esq, Planter, 2 East Bay Cont'd
Dawson, John, Jr, Merchant, Res, 6 N Bull St
Dawson, John, Merchant, 122 Queen St
Dawson, William, Merchant, Firm J & W, 9 Church St
Day, George, Goldsmith & Jeweller, at Mr Lowe
Dayton, Shipwright, over Cannon's Bridge
Dazevedo, Rachel, Mrs, Store, 223 King St
Deas, Charles & Thomas, Factors & Commission Merchants, Faber's Range, Chisolm's Whf
Deas, Charles D, Factor, 2 Faber's S Range
Deas, David, Attorney at Law, 66 Tradd St.
Deas, Henry, Esq., Planter, 1 Friend St
Deas, Robert, Dr, Planter, 57 Queen St
Deas, William Allen, Esq, Planter, 1 Meeting St
Deblieux, Alexander, 23 Trott St
Debogarin, D, Madame, Seamstress, 17 Hasell St
Debow, John, Grocer, 90 Meeting St
Debow, William, Dr, Apothecary & Druggist, 43 East Bay
Debroussses, Jeanne, 53 Trott St.
Debruhl, M S., Watchmaker, 35 Union St Cont'd
Decamps, James, 61 Meeting St
Deglanne, John, Grocer, 28 Pinckney St
Deirson, Bernard, Grocer, 3 Union St

Delaire & Canut, Merchants, 10 Faber's N Range, Chisolm's Whf
Delaire, James, Res , 7 Charles St.
Delajonchere, A Francis, Merchant, 215 King St
Delane, John A , Capt , Mariner, 9 Charles St
Delany, Michael, Pilot, Lynch's Court
Delcon, Jacob, Vendue Master, 3 N E Vendue Row, Exchange St , Res , 2 S New St
Delieben & Co , Vendue Masters & Commission Merchants, 3 S Vendue Row Cont'd
Delieben, Israel, 41 East Bay
Deliesselines, Francis G , Merchant, 1 Faber's S Range, Res , 27 Bay Cont'd cor Centurion St
Delorme, John F , Planter, 42 Broad St
Delozear, Ezra, 157 King St
Dener, George, Tanner & Currier, 9 Mazyck St
Dennis, Eliza, Mrs , 41 Church St
Dennison, James, Capt , 39 Elliott St
Dennon, David, Mrs , Widow, 38 Trott ST
Denny, Thomas, Physician, 48 Broad St
Depass, Ralph, Vendue Master, 8 S Champneys St
Depau & Toutain, Merchants, 7 & 8 Faber's N Range, Chisolm's Whf , Res , 17 Society St
Dereck, Peter, Shop Keeper, 1 Lamboll St
Desaussure & Ford, Attornies at Law, Office, 29 Tradd St
Desaussure, H W , Esq , Attorney at Law, 206 Meeting St
Desclaw, Joseph, Mariner, 2 N E Wall St
Descoudres, L P & Co , Merchants, Grocers, 110 Church St cor Queen St
Desel, Charles, Cabinet Maker, 50 Broad St
Desguer, P A , 161 King St
Desir, Joseph, Hair Dresser, 6 Bay Cont'd
Desjardins, J A , Merchant, 60 King St
Desportes, P , Grocer, 88 East Bay
Desrivaux, Melanie, Cake Shop, 107 Queen St
Detargny, Martin, Rev , Minister, French Protestant Calvinic Church, 75 Church St , at the Parsonage House
Deveaux, Jacob, Esq , Planter, 23 Meeting St ,
Devega, Moses, Shop Keeper, 199 King St
Devillers, L , Professor of Music, 258 King St
Dewar, Robert, Director, S C Bank, 82 Tradd St
Dewees, Sarah, Widow, 92 Meeting St
Dewees, William, Factor, 2 Prioleau's Range, Res , cor Charlotte & Alexander St , Mazyckborough
Diamond, John, Land Surveyor, 119 Meeting St
Dickinson, Francis, Attorney at Law, 35 Meeting St
Dickinson, J F , Merchant, 121 Tradd St
Dickinson, Joseph, Capt of the Guard, Res , 23 Church St
Dickinson, Joseph, Carpenter, 209 Meeting St
Dickinson, Samuel, Vendue Master & Commission Merchant, 5 Champneys St
Dickson, Samuel, Stables & Wagon Yard Keeper, 143 King St
Dieckert & Co , Grocers, 71 East Bay

Diedericks, Franz & Co , Merchants, 123 Tradd St
Dike, Jonathan, Musical Instrument Maker, City Hotel or 8 Trott St
Dikes, William Henry, Comedian, Savage St
Dile, P , Baker, 12 W King St Cont'd
Dill, Jane, E , Mrs , Widow, 9 Price's Al
Dill, Susannah, Mrs , Widow, 274 King St
Dillon, Thomas P , Grocer, 11 Union St Cont'd
Disher, Mary, Seamstress, 10 Trott St
Dixon, John, Tallow Chandler, 12 W King St Road
Dixon, Robert, Butler, 19 East King St. Road
Doane, Joseph, Capt , Mariner, 9 W Wall St
Dobbins, Rosa, 1 Parsonage Ln
Dogan, John, Mason, 17 W King St Road
Dogarthy, George, Gunsmith, 249 King St
Domec, Marc, Merchant, 39 Elliot St.
Donaldson, James, Carpenter, 103 Tradd St
Donaldson, Mary, Mrs , 22 Tradd St
Donnal, Catherine, Boarding House, 20 King St
Donneadieu, Michael, Director French Theatre, 94 Meeting St
Donnill, Mary, Mrs , Milliner & Dress Making, 97 Church St
Dorrell & Braund, Factor, Cochran's Whf
Dorrell, Robert, Factor, 3 N W Boundary St
Dougherty, John, Stucco Plasterer, N E. cor Charlotte & Washington St , Mazyckborough
Doughty, Thomas, Factor, 2 Faber's S Range, Res , 83 Bay & 4 Anson St
Doughty, William, Esq , Planter, 2 E Smith St , Harleston Green
Douglass, Alexander, Tailor, 14 Elliot St
Douglass, George, Mason, 5 St Michael's Al
Douglass, James K , Merchant, 89 Church St
Douglass, James, Turner, 186 Meeting St
Douglass, John, Cabinet Maker, 62 Meeting St
Dove, Sarah, Mrs , Store Keeper, 6 Charles St
Doyle, Michael, Mason, 70 Church St
Doyle, Daniel & Co , Whf Owners, Factors, Doyley's Whf , late Roper's
Drayton, Jacob, Prothonotary, State House, S cor , Res , Smith & Wentworth St Cont'd
Drayton, John, Esq , Late Governor, Planter, 40 Church St Cont'd
Drayton, Thomas, Planter, 31 Wentworth St
Drayton, William, Attorney at Law, 96 Tradd St
Drennis, George, Baker, 34 Beaufain St cor St Philip's St
Dresler & Drewes, Grocers, 60 Meeting St
Drummond, James, Boot & Shoe Maker, 121 Queen St
Dryburg, James, Capt , Mariner, 27 Church St Cont'd
Dubarry, Stephen, Grocer, 93 King St
Dubert, Frederick, Grocer, 17 East King St Road
Dubois, Berranger & Co , John, Grocers, 88 East Bay

Dubois, Lewis, Grocer & Paper Hanger, 32 Church St
Dubois, Peter, Carpenter, 14 S Cannon St
Dubuard, Peter, F, Hair Dresser, 47 Broad St
Ducarau, Marie I, Seamstress, 18 Trott St
Duchene, Francis, 2 W King St Road
Dudan, Mary F, 111 King St
Duddell, James, Cabinet Maker
Dueston, Stephen, Carpenter
Duff, Mary, Lowndes St
Duffus, John, Merchant, 6 Mazyck St
Duhadway, C B, Saddler & Harness Maker, 31 Broad St,
Dulles, Joseph, Merchant 33 East Bay, Res, 7 Church St Cont'd
Dumaine, John, Dr, Chemist, 17 Church St Cont'd
Dumont, W, Dr, School, 16 King St
Dumouche, Elizabeth, 25 Church St
Dumoutet, John B, Goldsmith & Jeweller, 120 Broad St
Dumpsey, Mary, Shop, cor Anson & Scarborough St
Duncan & North, Attornies at Law, Office, 28 Church St
Duncan, James, Attorney at Law, 46 Tradd St
Duncan, John, Merchant, 46 Tradd St
Duncan, Patrick, Tallow Chandler, Pinckney St, Cannonborough
Dunn, Joel, Capt, Mariner at M Segerstrom
Dunn, John, Grocer, 66 East Bay
Duplat, Rose, Goldsmith, 1 Queen St
Dupont, Delorme, cor. Wall & Pitt St
Dupont, John, Planter, 34 Church St
Dupont, Joseph, Grocer, 181 Meeting St
Dupont, Nancy, Seamstress, Rope Ln
Duprat, Raymond, Commission Broker, 15 Queen St 3d Story
Dupre, Benjamin, Livery Stable, 37 & 38 Church St
Dupuy, Elizabeth, 3 N E Wall St
Dupuy, John, Merchant, 7 W Wall St
Durant, Levy, Mason, Hampstead
Durbec, Joseph, Grocer, 133 Queen St
Durrett, George, Hotel, 196 Meeting St
Duvall, John, Carpenter, 107 Church St
Duvergie, Catherine, 55 Trott St
Dykes, William Henry, Comedian, 12 Magazine St
Dyre, Kendall, Mason, cor Beaufain & Archdale St.

Eagar, Sarah, Seamstress, William's Whf
Eason, James, Liquor Store, 35 Elliot St, Res, 262 King St
Eason, Robert, Merchant, 4 S Champney St
Easton, Susannah, Seamstress, Montague St
Eaton, Robert, Shipwright, 46 Trott St
Eberly, Barbara, Widow, 18 Guignard St.
Eckert, Robert D, Grocer, 6 Church St
Eckhard, Jacob, Professor of Music, Organist, German Church, 47 Tradd St.

Eden, William, Turner, 6 Amen St
Edmondston, Charles, 30 East Bay
Edward, Chair Maker, 12 George St
Edwards, Alexander, Esq, Judge, Recorder of the Inferior City Court, 3 St Michael's Al
Edwards, Catherine, Mrs, Widow, 3 S W Lynch's St
Edwards, Edward, Planter, Pinckney St, Cannonborough
Edwards, George, Planter
Edwards, Isaac, Factor 1 S End Prioleau's Whf, Res., 10 Friend St
Edwards, James, Factor, Geyer's Whf
Egleston & Hopkins, Grain Merchant, 4 Faber's N Range, Chislom's Whf
Egleston, John, Merchant, Grocer, 67 E Bay cor Queen St, Res, 15 Union St
Ehney, George, Carpenter, 4 Smith St
Ehney, Jacob, Mason, 29 Guignard St
Ehney, Peter E, Tailor, 263 King St
Ehney, William F, Accountant, D'Oyley's Whf, Res, 26 Beaufain St
Ehney, William, Tailor, Whim Court & 1 Elliott St
Ehrich, John M, Merchant, 7 Crafts' N Whf, Res, 74 Queen St
Elf, Benjamin, Cart Man, 5 Charlotte St, Mazyckborough
Elfe, Benjamin, Carter, Hampstead
Elfe, Thomas, Carpenter, 8 George St
Elford, James, Capt, Navigation School, 35 Union St Cont'd
Elfworth, John, Gauger, City Council, 130 Queen St
Elfworth, Theophilus, Gauger, Custom House, Res, S E cor Pitt & Wentworth St Cont'd
Eliezer, Elisha, City Deputy Sheriff, 5 Berresford St
Eliezer, Isaac, 5 Berresford St
Elliott, Barnard, Planter, 29 George St cor St Philip's St
Elliott, C R, Painter & Glazier, 13 Queen St
Elliott, Charles, Planter, 290 King St
Elliott, T O, Mrs, Plantress, 15 Legare St
Elliott, Thomas, Planter, 3 Gibbes St
Ellis, Matthew, Cabinet Maker
Ellis, Thomas, Carpenter, 5 Amen St
Ellis, Thomas, Sr, Wood Measurer, 14 Scarborough St
Ellison, John, Store Keeper, 52 King St
Ellison, William, Merchant, Columbia, 62 King St
Elmore, Dorcas, Mrs., Widow, 92 Church St
Emanuel, Flora, Mrs, Shop, 45 East Bay
England, Alexander, Baker, 1 Tradd St.
England, James, Jeweller, 75 King St
Ernest, Jacob, Tailor, 22 Queen St
Eschaussse, William, Mattress Maker, 42 Meeting St
Establier, Joseph, Sausage Maker, 14 Union St
Etenaud, Stephen, Baker, 127 East Bay

Evans, James, Shoe Maker, 10 N Bull St
Evans, John, Boot & Shoe Maker, 80 Church St,
Res, 126 Meeting St
Evans, John J, Printer, 11 Maiden Ln
Everingham & Bineham, Factors & Commission
Merchants, Champneys Whf
Everingham, John, Merchant, Champneys Whf cor
Gillon St
Ewing & Ross, A, Merchants, 29 East Bay
Ewing, John, Merchant, 214 Meeting St
E[?]renstrom, ——, Capt, Mariner, City Hotel
Fabeaux, Lewis, Merchant, 4 Coming St
Faber, Charles, Rev, Minister, German Lutheran
Church, 2 S W Lynch's St, Harleston Green
Faber, Christian H, Factor, 1 Faber's S Range
Faber, John C, Rev, Whf Owner, 12 Moore St
Faber, William, Merchant, Cochran's Whf, Res, 23
George St
Faesch, Sarah, Store 247 King St
Fair, John, Boot & Shoe Store, 141 King St
Fair, Richard, Boot & Shoe Maker, 190 King St
Fair, Robert, Boot & Shoe Store, 94 King St.
Fair, William, Tanner & Currier, cor Bull & Pitt
St
Fairchild, Aaron, Blacksmith, Ham's Whf, Res, 15
George St
Fairley, Hance, Cabinet Maker, 66 Meeting St
Faissoux, Ann, Mrs, Plantress, 67 Meeting St
Faissoux, James H, Dr, Planter, 67 Meeting St
Fanning, Maria, Mrs., Mantua Maker, 116 ½ King
St
Farley, James, Boot & Shoe Maker, 27 Broad St
Faroux, Nicholas, Grocer, 106 King St
Farr, Elizabeth, Mrs, Widow, 11 Hasell St
Farrow, Thomas, Shoe & Boot Maker, 255 King St
Fasbender, J H, Watchmaker, 46 East Bay
Faures, Francis, Merchant, 15 Society St
Faures, Sophie, Madame, Widow, 4 S Minority St
Fayolle, Peter, Dancing Master, 260 King St
Febve, Benjamin, Refugee, St Domingo, 6 W
Middle St
Fell, Eliza, Mrs, Millinery Store, 24 Broad St
Fell, Thomas, Merchant, 24 Broad St
Ferguson, Ann, Mrs, Widow, 3 Liberty St
Ferguson, Edmond, Carpenter, 1 Berresford St
Ferguson, Sarah, Laundress, 68 Church St
Fernald, Denni, Guard, 2 Berresford's Al
Ferret, Marie L, Seamstress, 22 Hasell St
Ferret, Polotte, Couturiere, 152 Meeting St
Fiddy, William, Merchant, 1 S Gillon St
Field, William, Mrs, Widow, at Mr Cleapor's
Fife, Mary, Mrs, Widow, 8 Coming St
Fillette, Francis, Store Keeper, 124 Queen St.
Finch, Joseph, Nail Manufacturer, 4 Gillon St
Findley, Jacob, Mason, Whim Court
Finengan, Michael, Slater, 29 Church St Cont'd.
Finore, Alexander, Grocer, 117 Tradd St
Firth, ——, Mrs, Millinery Store, 49 Broad St

Fishbourn, William, Col, Planter, 26 Wentworth
St
Fisher, ——, Capt, 2 N End Kinloch's Court
Fisher & Hitchcock, Saddlers, 191 King St cor
Hasell St
Fisher, James A, Saddler & Harness Maker, 116
King St
Fisher, James, Esq, 16 South Bay
Fitzpatrick, Peter, Tailor, 117 Tradd St
Fitzsimons, Christopher, Merchant, Whf Owner,
Res, 73 East Bay
Flagg, George, Painter & Glazier, Firm Wilcox &
Flagg, Res, 11 East Bay
Flagg, George, Sr, Esq, 212 King St
Flagg, Samuel, Dr, Dentist, 26 Queen St
Fleming, James, Grocer, 41 Tradd St
Fleming, William, Merchant, 23 E. King St Road
Flemming, R, Merchant, 135 King St cor George
St
Fletcher, Thomas, Merchant, 7 Crafts' Whf
Flint, Joseph, Grocer, 31 Union St Cont'd
Florance, Zacharia, Dentist, 120 King St
Florin, Lucas, 32 Guignard St
Fogartie, James, Factor, 3 Prioleau's Whf, Res, 15
Scarsborough St
Fogartie, Mary, Mrs, Widow, 14 Ellery St
Foissin, Esther, Mrs, Widow, 89 Tradd St
Foissin, Peter, Dr, Planter, 67 Tradd St
Foley, Daniel, Tailor, 83 Tradd St
Foley, Joshua, Rigger, 4 Unity Al
Folker, John Caspar, Planter, 28 Beaufain St
Follin, Michael, Tobacconist, 89 King St
Footman, John W., Broker, 11 Beaufain St
Forbes, Alexander, Merchant, 41 Church St
Forbes, J G, Merchant, 23 Bay St, Res, 39
Church St
Forbes, John, Tin Plate Worker, 187 King St
Ford, Jacob, Attorney at Law, 29 Tradd St
Ford, Timothy, Barrister, 208 Meeting St
Fordham, Richard, Shipwright, 59 Church St
Forrest, Aberdeen, Cooper, N Boundary St
between Meeting St & King St Cont'd
Forrest, Charity, Mrs, Widow, 2 Hasell St
Forrest, Thomas H, Cooper, D'Oyley's Whf, Res,
1 Bedon's Al
Forrester, Susannah, Mrs, Plantress, Hampstead
Forseith, John & Walker, Merchants, 138 King St
Foster, ——, Mrs, Misses Academy
Foster, Robert, Grocer, 13 & 30 Elliott St
Foster, Robert, Merchant, 106 Church St
Foster, Thomas, Out Door Clerk, National Bank,
Res, 285 King St
Foucard, Peter J, Music Master, 256 King St
Fouchy, Josephine, Madame, 119 King St
Fouchy, Olimpie & Sisters, 12 Ellery St.
Fourneau, John, Pilot, 63 Church St
Fowke, Mary, Mrs., Plantress, 7 Church St
Fowler, John, Carpenter, 1 & 4 Longitude Ln
Fowler, William, Boarding House, 34 Union St

Frances, Amelia, Mrs , Boarding House, 30 Church St
Fraser, John, Maj., Planter, 80 Tradd St
Fraser, Mary James, Mrs , Widow, 1 East Bay
Fraser, Mary, Mrs , Widow, Plantress, 27 King St
Fraser, Phillip, Coach Maker, 28 Beaufain St
Frazer, John M , Carpenter, 26 Trott St
Freeman, E William, Mrs., Widow, 71 Tradd St
Freeman, William, Grocer, 2 Queen St
Freer, Charles, Planter, 7 N Wentworth St Cont'd
Freneau, Peter, Proprietor & Editor City Gazette, 44 E Bay, Res , 34 George St
Friday, William, Victualler, 6 N Cannon St
Friend, Ulric, Baker, 22 East Bay Cont'd
Frink, Thomas, Wharfinger, Beale's Whf , Res , 38 Pinckney St
Frish, Charles, Merchant, 181 King St
Fronty, Michael, Dr , Physician, 11 Moore St
Frost, Elizabeth, Mrs , Widow, 5 West St
Fuller, Christopher, Dr , 2 Savage St.
Fuller, Oliver, Capt , Mariner, 56 Trott St
Fullilove, Thomas, Mill Wright, 11 Ellery St
Fulmer, John, Coach Maker, 3 Blackbird Al
Fuquet, ——, Mr , Res , Mr Bowman, W End Montague St
Furches, John, Tailor, 4 Amen St
Furman, Richard, Rev Dr , Minister, Baptist Incorporated Church, 10 Church St
Furman, Wood, A B Academy, 1 Stoll's Al
Futerell, James, Teller, S C Bank
Fyholl, John, Supercargo, 10 Queen St
F[?]rnum, J F , Merchant, Shoe Store, 102 East Bay
Gabeau, Anthony, Tailor, 190 Meeting St
Gabeau, James, Cooper, 6 Crafts' N Range
Gadsden, ——, Mrs , Widow of General, 16 Front St , Gadsden's Green
Gadsden, M , Mrs , Widow, 19 Front St
Gadsden, Philip, Res , 3 S Pitt St , Gadsden's Green
Gadsden, Philip, Whf Owner, Merchant, 8 Front St , Counting House, Gadsden's Whf
Gaillard & Mazyck, Factors, 5 Geyer's N Range
Gaillard, Bartholomew, Merchant
Gaillard, Peter, Planter
Gaillard, Theodore, Attorney at Law, 45 Meeting St
Gaillard, Theodore, Jr , Factor, N W Montague St
Gaillard, Theodore, Sr , Planter, 78 East Bay
Galais, Louisa L , 42 King St
Galbraith, Robert, Carpenter, Cannon's Mill
Gallagher, S S T D , Rev , Roman Catholic Church, 28 Wentworth St
Gallaway, Alford, Pilot, 4 Lynch Ln
Gamble, Jane, Shop Keeper, 11 W King St Cont'd.
Gandouin, John, Merchant Hatter, Etc , 58 East Bay

Gantt, Esther, Mrs , Misses Boarding School, 45 Trott St
Gappin, William, Chairmaker, 14 Trott St
Garden, Alexander, Dr , Physician, 121 East Bay
Garden, Alexander, Planter, N E cor. Coming & Bull St
Gardener, Sophy, Seamstress, Archdale St
Gardiner, Ruth, Widow, 19 Quince St
Gardner, John, Blacksmith, Governor's Bridge, Res , 4 Maiden Ln
Garnons, William, Carver, William's Whf
Gaskin, Henry, Grain Measurer
Gaspar, Zannite, 12 Ellery St
Gasper, Francis, Shipwright, 21 Trott St
Gates, Jacob, Grocer, 16 W King St Road
Gaujan, Peter B , & Sisters, Refugees, St Domingo, Mary St , Wraggsboro
Gaultier, Joseph, Vendue Master, 271 King St
Gauth, Francis, Grocer, Williman's Whf , Res , 8 W King St
Geddes, Henry, Merchant, 176 King St
Geddes, John, Attorney at Law, 104 Broad St , Res , 15 Beaufain St
Geddes, Robert, Merchant, 156 King St
Gell, John, Livery Stables, National Bank Square
Gennerick, John F , Merchant, 150 King St
Gennert, Lewis, Boot Maker, 3 Cumberland St
Gensel, John, 1 Coming St
George, James, Shipwright, 33 East Bay Cont'd
George, Mary, Mrs , Shop Keeper, 204 King St
Gerard, Philip, Grocer, 7 King St Cont'd
Gere, Greenman, Ship Master
Gerley, John, Late Master, Poor House, Invalid, 2 Union St
Gervais, Mary, Mrs , Plantress, 85 Broad St
Gervais, R L , 85 Broad St
Geyer, John, Capt., Merchant, Counting House, Whf , Res , 1 St Philip's St
Geyer, John, Shipwright, 3 Amen St.
Geyer, John William, Factor, Geyer's Whf
Gibbes, John, Planter, 121 Meeting St
Gibbes, Lewis, Planter, 8 South Bay
Gibbes, Robert R , Planter, 8 South Bay
Gibbes, William Hasell, Master in Equity, 103 Broad St
Gibbs, George, Baker, 29 Elliott St
Gibert, J J., Saddler & Harness Maker
Gibson & Broadfoot, Merchant, 143 East Bay
Gibson, James, Coach Maker, 55 Meeting St
Gibson, Robert, Blacksmith, 4 Archdale St
Gibson, Robert, Store Keeper, 232 King St
Gidiere, Marguerite, Madame, Grocer, 2 E King St
Gidney, Isaac, Carpenter, 8 S Minority St.
Gilbeet, Elizabeth, Mrs , Widow, 25 Church St Cont'd.
Gilbert, Seth H , Book Keeper, 25 Church St Cont'd
Gilchrist, Adam, Merchant 16 East Bay, Res , 12 Church St

34

Gilles, Othneil J., Factor, Keith's Whf, Res, 6 Beaufain St
Gillespie & Mackay, Merchant, 30 East Bay
Gillon, Ann, O, Mrs, Widow, 2 W Wall St
Gissendenner, L, Nurse, S. 5 Bull St
Gissendenner, Susannah, Widow, 24 Beaufain St.
Gist, N & F, Merchants, 146 King St
Given, Mary, Shop Keeper, 29 Queen St
Glading, Joseph, Carpenter, 23 Trott St
Gleise, Lewis, Commission Merchant, 16 Elliott St
Gleise, Stephen, Dr, 252 King St
Glement, Lewis, Shop Keeper, W King St Road
Glen, John, Planter, 54 Tradd St
Glover, Charles, Mesne Conveyance, 3d Story, State House, Res, S cor Bull & Smith St, Harleston Glover, Glover, Wilson, Planter, 2 Meeting St
Godard, Rene, French Tutor, 2 Moore St
Godber, William, Book Keeper, 2 Stolls Al
Goddet, ——, Madame, Refugee, St Domingo, 12 Society St
Goddet, John, Shoe Maker, 23 Trott St
Godfrey, Catherine, Widow, 25 King St
Goldsmith, Abraham, Store Keeper, 112 King St
Goldsmith, Morris, Store Keeper, 112 King St
Goldsmith, Samuel, Store Keeper, 10 Queen St
Gomez, Jacob, Store Keeper, 245 King St
Good, Sarah, School Mistress, 42 King St
Goodtown, Peter, Mariner, 136 Meeting St
Gordon, A, Mason, 101 Queen St
Gordon, James, Merchant, 26 East Bay
Gordon, John, Factor & Grocer, 15 South Bay
Gordon, Mul, Mason, 6 W Coming St
Gordon, Thomas, Cashier, Counting House, 18 Church St. Cont'd
Gordon, Thomas, Grocer, 44 Tradd St
Gordon, William, Grocer, 87 King St
Gosian, ——, Monsieur, Refugee, St Domingo, 10 W Meeting St Cont'd
Goubron, James, Upholsterer, Band Box Maker, Etc, 7 Ellery St see Marc
Gough, John, 18 Quince St
Gourgnes, Dominic, Merchant, 49 Church St
Gowen, Sarah, Laundress, 25 Trott St
Gradick, Christian, Butcher, Mary St, Wraggsborough
Grado, Mariano, Boarding House, 60 Church St
Graeser, C J, Merchant, 1 Queen St
Graham, George, Painter & Engraver, 24 Quince St
Grant, Alexander, Merchant, 92 Church St, Res, 25 Friend St
Grant, Joseph, Rigger, 63 Church St
Graves & Swinton, Factors, Geyer's Whf
Graves, Charles, Factor, Res, 55 Tradd St
Graves, James, Planter at Chyhaw, Res., 2 N Pinckney St, Cannonborough
Gray, Benjamin, Lumber Merchant, 4 N Montague St
Gray, Caleb, Tailor, 140 King St.

Gray, Francis, Mrs, School, 169 King St
Gray, Henry, Justice of the Peace, cor Liberty & King St
Gray, William, Mason, Whim Court
Green & Lawson, Factors & Commission Merchants, 145 Broad St
Green, Edmund, Factor, 145 Broad St
Green Glover, Joseph, Dr, Physician, Dispensary, 14 Archdale St
Green, John Gray, Umbrella Maker, 33 Queen St
Green, John, Shop Keeper, 14 Trott St
Green, Robert, Mariner, N E Middle St
Green, William, Grocer, 2 N Prioleau's Market Whf
Green, William J, Grocer, 6 Union St
Greenhill, Hume, Carpenter, 63 Tradd St
Greenland, George, Factor, 32 Meeting St
Greenwood, William, Sr, Planter, 17 Beaufain St
Griffin, Peter, Merchant, 142 Broad St
Gregorie, James, Jr, Merchant, 133 Broad St
Gregorie, James, Sr, Merchant, 133 Broad St
Gregorie, Junior & Smith, Merchants, 133 Broad St
Greiner, Meinrad, Merchant, 9 East King St Cont'd
Griersan, James, Tavern Keeper, 65 East Bay
Griggs, Isaac, Attorney at Law, 37 East Bay
Grimball, Eliza, Mrs, Plantress, 21 South Bay
Grimke, John F, Associate Judge, 6 Front St
Grippon, John, Grocer, 42 Elliott St.
Groasman, Henry, Whf Filler, 6 W Coming St
Groasman, Mary, Old Widow, 2 Mazyck St
Grochan, John, Merchant, 32 Beaufain St
Groning, Lewis & R, Merchants, 144 East Bay
Gros & Lee, Cabinet Makers, 76 Meeting St
Groscoll, Anthony, Instrument Maker & Turner, cor Church & 1 Chalmers Al
Gruan, Francis Paul, Mariner, 35 Hasell St
Gruber, Catherine, Widow, Wentworth St Cont'd
Gruber, Christian, School Master, 15 Berresford St
Gruber, Martin, Cooper, 5 Mazyck St
Guieu, Philip C & Brothers, 14 Queen St
Guilbert, Eugene, Professor of Music, cor Wall & Pitt Sts
Guillame, Dom & Joseph, Shoe Makers, 23 Trott St
Guillaume, Magdalen, Widow, 23 Trott St
Guillotin, Francis X, 96 ½ Queen St N E cor Meeting St
Guilon, Samuel, Tailor, 109 Queen St
Guimarins, Sophy, Madame, Store, Grocer, 19 Church St
Gunn, William, Gun & Blacksmith, 5 Queen St
Gunter, Isaac, Capt, 15 Hasell St.
Gunter, Philis, Seamstress, 14 Berresford St
Guy, James, Tailor, N Boundary St 2 doors off Lowndes St
Gyles, Thomas, Factor & Lumber Measurer, 3 Price's Al

Hackell & Oswald, Tailors, 20 Elliott St
Hacket, Jane, Mistress, Misses Boarding House, 61 King St
Hadden, Gardner, Tailor, 3 Meeting St
Hadden, Sittlington, Mercantile, 81 King St
Hagen, Richard, Grocer, 92 King St
Hagens, Enrietta, Seamstress, 2 Clifford's Al
Haig, David, Cooper Crafts' Whf, Res, 132 Meeting St
Haig, Robert, Carpenter, 42 Trott St
Halbert, Rene, Merchant, 141 Meeting St
Hall, —, Misses, 294 King St
Hall, Daniel, Factor, 2 State House Square
Hall, George, Dr, Marine Hospital Physician, Res, 294 King St
Hall, James, Stone Cutter, 5 Ellery St
Hall, Mary Ann, Mrs, Widow, 19 Magazine St.
Hall, Thomas, Clerk, Admiralty & Registerer Copyright, 33 Broad St
Hall, Thomas, Mason, S W End Vanderhorst St
Hall, William & Co, Merchants, 17 Broad St
Hall, William, Capt, Mariner, 7 Front St
Hall, William, Merchant, 21 Broad St cor Church St
Halliday, Hugh, Cooper, 6 N Champneys St
Halsall, William, Victualler Stall 30, King St Road above mile stone
Ham, Samuel, Shipwright, Whf Owner, Ham's Whf., Res, 10 Amen St
Ham, Thomas, Commission Merchant, Fitzsimons' Whf
Ham, Thomas, Factor, Res, Hampstead
Hamett, Charlotte, Widow, 14 Elliott St
Hamett, Thomas, Chair Maker, 112 Meeting St cor Boundary St
Hamett, Thomas, Grocer, cor Pinckney & Quince St
Hamilton, James, Merchant, 132 Broad St
Hamilton, James, Planter, Pinckney St, Islington, Cannonborough
Hamilton, Marlborough S, Academy, 36 Queen St
Hamilton, Paul, Esq, Governor & Commander in Chief of S C, Res, 18 Front St
Hamilton, Rachel, Miss, 98 King St cor. Parsonage Ln
Hampton, William, Cabinet Maker, 6 W Boundary St
Hanahan, John, Planter, Res, 5 Stoll's Al
Hanahan, Maria, Laundress, 6 Clifford St
Hanby, John, Grocer, 48 King St
Hands, Jane, Mrs, School Mistress, 58 Church St
Hanmer, John, Yeoman, at Mr Roche, Church St
Hanothau, Therese & Sister, Fruit Shop, 25 Church St
Happold, John Philip, Victualler, 10 N. W. Boundary St.
Happold, John, Victualler, Coming St opposite the Burial Ground
Harby, Rebecca, Mrs, Widow, 249 King St

Harden, Richard, Tailor & Habit Maker, 196 Meeting St
Hare, Francis, Mrs, Widow, 16 Union St
Hargraves, J, Merchant
Harleston, Ann, Mrs, Plantress, 83 Meeting St
Harleston, Edward, Painter, 19 St Philip's St
Harleston, Elizabeth, Mrs, Plantress, 94 Tradd St
Harleston, Nicholas, Planter, 3 W Bull St
Harleston, William Planter, 90 Broad St
Harper, James, Baker, 43 Tradd St
Harper, John, Merchant, Columbia
Harris, Andrew, Store, 178 King St
Harris, Elizabeth, Shop Keeper, 116 King St
Harris, Jacob, Store, 13 Queen St
Harris, John, Drayman, 125 Meeting St
Harris, Thomas, Grocer, 10 N Bull St
Harris, Tucker, Dr, 71 King St
Harrison, George, Nail & Iron Store 4 Broad St, Res, 48 Trott St
Harrison, Thomas, Rigger, 8 Clifford's Al
Harrison, Thomas, Rigger, cor Vanderhorst & St Philip's St Cont'd
Hart, Daniel, Vendue Master, 54 East Bay
Hart, Joseph, Store, 48 Bay
Hart, Nathan, Store, 183 King St
Hart, Samuel Moses, Store, 227 King St
Harth, John, Planter, 1 N W End South Bay
Hartt, Moses, Carpenter, 1 Society St
Harvey, Archibald, Merchant, 10 Society St
Harvey, Benjamin, Capt, Planter, N of Islington, Cannonborough
Harvey, Elizabeth, Widow, 120 Meeting St
Harvey, Elizabeth, Widow, 27 Hasell St
Harvey, James, Carpenter, Fort Mechanic
Harvey, John, Grocer, 19 Berresford Al
Harvey, John S, Printer, 120 Meeting St
Harvey, Samuel, Capt, Mariner, 13 Guignard St
Hasell, James, Factor, 8 Hasell St
Hasell, William S, Attorney at Law, 43 Elliott St Res, 39 Bay Cont'd
Haslett, John, Merchant, 25 East Bay
Hatch, R, Capt, 14 Union St. Cont'd
Hatter, E B, Mrs, Widow, 32 Queen St
Hattier, Henry, Grocer, 117 East Bay
Hauck, John, Grocer, 10 Anson St cor Pitt St
Hauser, Elizabeth, Widow, 21 Archdale St
Havens, Samuel, Boarding House, Chalmer's Al
Haydon, William, Custom House Inspector, E St Philip's St Cont'd
Hayne, William, Capt, Planter, 17 Legare St
Hazlehurst, Robert & Co, Merchants, 14 East Bay
Hazlehurst, Robert, Res, 8 Front St
Healey, Patrick, School Master, 23 Hasell St
Heath & Bryne, Sail Makers Loft, Champneys Whf
Heath, James, Sail Maker, 3 S. W. Wall St
Hedderly, William, Bell Hanger, 86 Queen St, 2 doors N W King St
Hedderly, William, Bell Hanger & Founder, 36 Queen St

Heffernan, John, Cabinet Maker, 76 King St
Heir, Henry, Drayman, 5 N W Boundary St
Helfred, John, Constable, 3 Lodge Al
Henderson, D, Locksmith & Bell Hanger, 24 Queen St
Henderson, Elizabeth, Boarding House, 15 Trott St
Henderson, Robert, Stage Office Owner
Hendlen, John, Mason, 8 Lynch Ln
Hennequin, John B Olman, Confectioner, 126 Queen St
Hennon, Thomas, Gun & Locksmith, 39 Queen St
Henrickson, B, Carpenter, W Meeting St Road
Henry, Alexander, Carpenter, 44 Trott St
Henry, Alexander, Merchant, 135 King St. cor of George St
Henry, Andrew & Co, Grocers, 68 East Bay
Henry, Ann, Mrs & Son, Millinery & Dry Goods Store, 118 Tradd
Henry, J, Cabinet Maker, 39 Church St
Henry, Jacob, Merchant, 5 W King St Road
Henson, Archibald, Carpenter, ½ N Minority St
Henwood, Samuel, Merchant, 3 N E Wall St
Herbemont, Nicholas, French Tutor, 37 Beaufain St
Heriot, R, Merchant, 132 Broad St
Heriot, R, Merchant, 3 Crafts' S Whf, Res, 2 Centurion St
Herron & Martindale, Merchants, 142 King St
Herron, John, Merchant, 145 King St
Heyda, David, Grocer, 153 Meeting St
Heyward, Hannah, Mrs, Plantress, 10 Legare St
Heyward, Nathaniel, Planter, 25 East Bay Cont'd
Heyward, Samuel, Capt, Mariner, 21 Mazyck St
Heyward, Thomas, Planter, 221 Meeting St
Hibbern, Susannah, 278 King St
Hignet, Henry, Mariner, 245 King St.
Hill, Asa, Victualler Stall 6, 2 N Cannon St
Hill, Francis C, Painter, 28 Archdale St
Hill, Hannah, Miss, Misses Boarding House, 19 Meeting St
Hill, Hannah, Mrs, 19 Meeting St
Hill, Helena, Mrs, Widow, Blake St, Hampstead
Hill, Henry, Coach Maker, 25 Guignard St
Hill, Paul, Distiller, Cane Wire Worker, Clerk, German Church, 28 Archdale St
Hill, Thomas, Clothes Warehouse, 26 Church St
Hillegas, Phillip, Distiller, 20 W King St Road
Himley, J J, Merchant, Watch & Clock Maker, 135 Broad St, Summer Res., 7 S E Cannon St
Hinds, Thomas, Attorney at Law, 33 Broad St
Hinson, Sarah, Nurse, 266 King St
Hinson, Susan, Seamstress, Moser's Lot, 209 Meeting St
Hippius, Phebe, Mrs, 8 Pinckney St
Hislop, Christiana, Nurse, 3 Union St Cont'd
Hislop, John, Carpenter, 61 Church St
Hislop, Robert, Lumber Merchant, 1 S Pitt St, Gadsden's Green
Hislop, Robert, Tailor, 103 Queen St
Hobrecker, John G, Gunsmith, 91 King St

Hobs, John, Carpenter, 5 Ellery St
Hodge, John, Grocer, 14 Berresford's Al
Hodgson, Martha, Nurse, 41 King St
Hoey, Ann Anglish, Grocer, 7 King St
Hogarth, William Jr, Shoe Maker, 3 East Bay Cont'd
Hogarth, William, Sr, Shoe Maker, 12 Union St, Res, 13 Mazyck St
Hollan, Andrew, Mariner, 37 Church St
Holland, Diana, Laundress, 8 Price's Al
Holland, John, Merchant, 12 Church St
Hollinshead, William, Rev Dr, Pastor, Independent Church, 7 Maiden Ln
Holloway, Richard, Carpenter, 7 Archdale St
Holme, William & Co, Vendue Masters & Commission Merchants, S W cor Coming & Boundary St,
Holmes, Charles, Academy, Islington, N W Cannon St
Holmes, John B, Advocate, Planter, 6 Meeting St
Holmes, Mary, Mrs, Widow, 8 St Philip's St
Holmes, Thomas, Carpenter, 2 N Montague St
Holyday, Mary, 4 Beaufain St
Honeywood, Arthur, Engraver, 1 N E cor of Coming & Cannon St
Honeywood, Elizabeth, Mrs, Widow, 59 Meeting St
Hook, Esther, Mrs, Widow, Blake St, Hampstead
Hook, Peter, Boarding House, 20 Union St Cont'd
Hope, Jonathan, City Hotel, 55 East Bay
Hopkins & Charles, Merchants, 125 East Bay
Hopkins, Ebenezer, Grain Merchant, 23 Union St Cont'd
Hopkins, Henry, Mariner, 6 Trott St
Hopton, Robert, Carpenter, 3 S. Bull St
Horden, John, Tobacconist, 35 Broad St & 167 Meeting St
Hore, Thomas, 3 Champneys St
Horlbeck, George, Coach Maker
Horlbeck, Henry, Mason, 3 Moore St
Horlbeck, John Jr, Mason, 8 Moore St
Horlbeck, John, Sr, Mason, 8 Moore St
Hornby, ----, Misses Boarding School, 205 King St
Horry, Elias, Planter, 225 Meeting St
Horry, Harriott, Mrs, Plantress, 59 Tradd St
Horry, Jonah, Planter, Mazyckborough cor Charlotte & Elizabeth St
Horry, Lynch, Planter, 81 Broad St
Horry, Thomas, Planter, 27 Meeting St
Horwood, Mary, Nurse, 43 Church St Cont'd
Horwood, William, Tailor, 43 Church St Cont'd
Hosmer & Haslett, Painters & Glaziers, 1 Elliott St Cont'd., Res, 7 Stoll's Al
Houlton, James, Broker, 4 Cumberland St
House, Samuel, Q U. & Notary Public, Comptroller's Office, Res, 54 Meeting St
Howard, John, Mason, 43 George St

Howard, Richard, Cooper, Gillon St , Blake's Whf , Res , 122 Meeting St
Howard, Robert, Tax Collector, Exchange, Res , 1 George St
Hoyland, Ann M , Mrs , Boarding School, 102 Broad St
Hrabowski, John S , Planter, 45 Broad St
Huff, Abigail, Mrs , Widow, 241 King St
Huff, John, Carpenter, 6 Unity Al
Huffey, Brian, Pilot, 13 Water St
Huger, Ann John, Mrs , Plantress, Widow, 88 Broad St
Huger, Carlos, Tailor, 7 Queen St Cont'd
Huger, Daniel E , Secretary of State, Res , 81 Queen St , Office, 2d Story, Guard House
Hughes & Lusher, Merchants, 7 East Bay, Res , 3 Lynch's Ln
Hughes & Lusher, Merchants, Grocery Store, 120 Bay
Hughes, Edward, Teacher, Misses Academy, 79 Tradd St
Humbert, Godfrey, Carpenter, 3 Lynch's Ln
Humphreville, J B , Commission Merchant, Champneys St , Res , 18 Magazine St
Hunt, Joseph, Capt , Mariner, 4 E Boundary St
Hunt, Mary, Mrs , Boarding House, 14 Elliott St.
Hunt, Thomas, Planter, 34 Trott St
Hunter, ——, Mrs , Dry Goods Store, 108 Queen St
Hunter, John, Hair Dresser, 108 Queen St
Hunter, John, Shoe Maker, 31 Church St Cont'd
Hunter, William Taylor, Mrs , Widow, 7 Elliott St. Cont'd
Huston, James, Merchant Tailor, 27 Church St
Hutchinson, Ann, Mrs , 8 N Bull St
Hutchinson, Charlotte, Miss, 8 N Bull St
Hutchinson, Elizabeth L , Mrs , Widow, 4 Federal St
Hutchinson, Hugh, Capt , Mariner, 4 N Champneys St
Hutchinson, Jeremiah, 1 mile W Meeting St Road
Hutson, James H , Carpenter, 3 W Wall St
Hutson, Rebecca, Seamstress, 18 Wentworth St
Hutton, Frederick, Tailor, 4 Cumberland St
Hutton, James, Factor, 12 South Bay
Huxham, ——, Miss, Millinery Store, 13 Tradd St
Hyams, David, Store, 203 King St
Hyams, Samuel, Mrs , Store, 63 East Bay
Hynes, James, Grocer, 41 Union St
Icarden, Lewis & Co , Grocers, 13 Trott St
Imar, ——, Confectioner Shop, 40 Meeting St
Ingels, Catharine, Seamstress, 30 Pinckney St
Inglesby, Henry, Mercer, Merchant Tailor, 96 Broad St.
Inglesby, William, Sr , Planter, 23 Tradd St
Ingraham, Nathaniel, Capt , Merchant, 292 King St
Ireland, Benjamin, Carpenter, 94 Queen St.
Ireland, Edward, Cart Keeper, 18 W King St Road
Irvin, Moses, 16 Trott St
Irvine, Mathew, Dr , 7 Meeting St

Isaacks, Abraham, Vendue Master, Champneys St & Bedon's Al
Isaacs, J , Mrs , Boarding House, 124 East bay
Izard, Henry, Planter, 1 Meeeting St.
Izard, Ralph, Planter, 99 Broad St
Izard, Ralph, Sr , Mrs , Widow, 1 Meeting St
Jacks, James, Merchant Jeweller, 125 Broad St
Jackson, John, Watchmaker, 131 Bay, Res , 17 Pinckney St
Jackson, Montague, Deputy Sheriff, 10 Berresford's Al
Jackson, William, Shoe & Boot Store, 77 East Bay
Jacobs, Fanny, Seamstress, 20 Trott St
Jacobs, Hannah, Shop, 162 King St
Jacobson, Christopher, Grocer, 58 Church St & 3 Tradd St
Jahan, Joseph, Architect Builder, 2 W Meeting St Cont'd
James & Bracy (Holloway & Xenophon), Geyer's Whf
James, John, Carpenter, 7 Trott St
Jaudong, Isaac, Tailor, 5 Meeting St Cont'd
Javin, Peter, Dry Goods Store, 70 ½ King St
Jeanneret, C , Collection Clerk, State Bank, Res , 5 East Boundary St
Jeffers, Mary, Mrs., Plantress, Pinckney St , Cannonborough
Jefferson, John, Turner
Jeffords, John, Tailor, 21 Pinckney St
Jenkins, ——, Mrs , Plantress, 20 South Bay
Jenkins, Edward, Rev Dr , Pastor, Episcopal Church, 10 Lamboll St
Jenkins, Elias, Mason, 3 Federal St
Jenkins, Michael, Planter, 16 Meeting St
Jennings, Elizabeth, Mrs., Widow, 3 Short St
Jenny, John, Baker, 2 Berresford's Al
Jesse, Sarah, Miss, S E cor Broad & King St
Jessop, J , Planter, Four Mile House, King St Road
Jewell, Benjamin, Merchant, 59 East Bay
John, Carter, 21 George St
John, Watchmaker & Jeweller, 111 Broad St
Johnson, Aaron, Mason, 4 Lamboll St & 5 Magazine St
Johnson, Barbara, Doctress, Widow, 9 Wentworth St
Johnson, Benjamin, Carpenter, 21 Guignard St
Johnson, Bernard, Academy, 6 Cumberland St
Johnson, Jabez W , Watchmaker, 179 Meeting St
Johnson, John, Blacksmith, Gillon St., Res , 87 Bay or at his Foundary, King St Road
Johnson, John, Esq., 158 King St
Johnson, John, Grocer, 24 Pinckney St
Johnson, John, Hair Dresser, 16 Ellery St
Johnson, Joseph, Dr , Apothecary & Druggist, 5 Broad St.
Johnson, Sarah, Mrs , Widow, 8 Liberty St
Johnson, William, Judge, Admiralty, 1 Charles St
Johnson, William P , Merchant, 158 King St.

Johnson, William, Sr , Blacksmith, Gillon St.,
Res , 10 Charles St
Johnston, Alexander, School Master, 44 Trott St
Johnston, Archibald, Merchant, 20 Elliott St
Johnston, Charles, Esq , Sail Maker, Wingfield's
Loft, Beale's Whf
Johnston, David, Deputy Collector, Custom House,
Res , 44 Queen St
Johnston, Edward, Grocer, 15 Amen St
Johnston, Jane, Miss, Plantress, 214 Meeting St
Johnston, John William, Attorney at Law 133 Bay,
Res , 83 Queen St
Johnston, Peter, Printer, 8 Pinckney St
Johnston, Robert M , Whf Owner & Planter, 11
South Bay
Jones, ----, Capt , Mariner, 10 W Cock Ln
Jones, Abner, Tailor, 16 Amen St
Jones, Alexander, Esq , 78 Tradd St
Jones, Benjamin, Jone's Court, 180 King St
Jones, Daniel, Tailor, 33 Church St
Jones, Edward, Dr , Physician, 4 Orange St.
Jones, Henry, Merchant, 18 Church St , Res , 37
George St
Jones, Henry, Shipwright, 7 Maiden Ln
Jones, Jacob, Planter, Pinckney St , Cannonborough
Jones, Jehu, Mrs , Pastry Cook, 42 Trad St
Jones, Jehu, Tailor, 110 Broad St , Res , 42 Tradd
St
Jones, Joseph, Merchant, 14 Tradd St
Jones, Marguaret, Mrs , Widow, 29 King St
Jones, Nathaniel, Merchant, 8 Tradd St
Jones, Samuel, Bank of S C, 1 Guignard St
Jones, Samuel, Store, 248 King St
Jones, Sarah, Boarding School
Jones, Sarah, Seamstress, 11 Trott St
Jones, Thomas, President, S C. Bank, 2 Guignard
St cor of Charles St.
Jones, William, Planter, 3 S. W Coming St
Joseph, Joseph, Shop Keeper, 133 King St
Joseph, Marian, Widow, 44 Broad St
Joseph, Samuel, Shop Keeper, 230 King St
Jousseaume, Mathieu, Inspector, Custom House, 20
Pinckney St
Jousset, John, Capt , Mariner, 19 Amen St
Joyner, Mary, Mantua Maker, 24 Bay Cont'd
Just, George, Guardman, 3 Clifford Al
Kahnle, John H., Cooper, 2 S E. Boundary St
opposite Lownde St
Kaiser, John J , Victualler, King St Road
Karwon, Thomas, Planter, 2 Hasell St
Katle, Frances, 6 Berresford St
Kay, James, Grocer, 20 Meeting St
Keating, William, Broker & Commission Merchant,
Beale's Whf , Res , 90 Church St
Keddie, Charles, Merchant, 83 Church St
Keenan, George, Grocer, 23 Church St Cont'd
Keenan, Thomas, Grocer, 1 Church St cor Water
St

Kehr, John D , Firm, Corrie & Kehr, Auctioneers &
Commission Merchants
Keils, Peter, Carpenter, 11 E King St Road
Keith, Isaac, Rev Dr , Pastor, Independent
Presbyterian Church, 50 Church St
Keith, Silvanus, Merchant, Whf Owner, 109 East
Bay
Kelly, Christopher, Grocer, 11 Union St
Kelly, John, Pilot, 2 Lodge Al
Kelly, Mary, Mrs , Store, 114 King St
Kelly, William, Butcher, Hampstead
Kemnitz, Francis F , Grocer, 2 Smith Ln
Kempton, George, Factor, 20 Queen St
Kennedy, Ann, Mrs , Charlotte St , Mazyckborough
Kennedy, Edward & Lawson, Merchants, 5 Crafts'
S Whf , Res , 45 Tradd St
Kennedy, Edward, Factor (late Kennedy &
Lawson), 5 Crafts' S Whf
Kennedy, James, Planter, 8 Mazyck St
Kennedy, P , Grocer, 82 Meeting St & 53 Tradd
St
Kenny, John, Grocer, 145 Meeting St
Ker, Henry & John, Merchants, 10 Tradd St
Ker, John, Grain Inspector, 16 Society St
Kern, John F , Merchant 9 Faber's S Whf , 185
King St
Kerr, Andrew, Merchant, 136 Broad St
Kershaw, Charles, Factor, 23 East Bay
Ketelsen, Nicholas, Grocer, 2 Berresford's Al
Kiddel, Charles, Merchant, 83 Church St
King, ----, Mr , Grocer, 23 King St
King, Benjamin, Carpenter, Hard Al
King, Christian, Tailor, 2 King St
King, John, Grocer, 117 Tradd St
King, John, Grocer, 5 Tradd St
King, Mary, Miss, 224 King St
King, William, Boarding House, 32 Union St
Kingman, E , Shoe Store, 17 Tradd St
Kingman, H , Shoe Warehouse, 97 Church St
Kinmont, David, Blacksmith, Fort Mechanic, New
Bay St
Kirk & Luckens, John, Merchants, 56 East Bay
Kirk, John D , Harness Maker, No Name Al
Kirkland, Joseph, Dr , Physician, Dispensary, 34
Broad St
Kirkpatrick, James, Merchant, 84 Church St
Kittle, David, Carpenter, 1 Lynch's Ln
Knarston, James, Millwright, 3 S Spring St
Knipping & Steinmetz, Merchants, 136 Bay, Res ,
52 Tradd St
Knoff, Mary, Victualler, 12 W King St Road
Knox, Matthew, Crier of the Court of Sessions, 284
King St
Knox, Sarah, Mrs , Boarding House, 4 Meeting St
Knust, Henry, Grocer, 103 Meeting St
Koffkey, Ann Catharine, Shop Keeper, 88 King St
Kohne, Frederick, Merchant, 28 East Bay
Kreps, Ann, Mrs., Widow, 12 W King St Cont'd
Kreps, John, Engraver, 12 W King St Cont'd

Kugley, John, Carpenter, 15 Mazyck St
L'homaca, J D, Physician & Apothecary
Labatt, David, Shop Keeper, 119 Queen St
Labattut, Peter, Drawing Master, 171 King St
Laborde, Francis, Livery Stables & Public Chairs,
  173 King St
Laborde, Henriette, 253 King St
Labosse, Peter, Baker, 8 Coming St
Lacassagne, Mary, Refugee, St Domingo, 9 Middle
  St
Lacombe, Geraud, Tobacconist, 224 King St
Lacombe, Stephen, Dr, 3 Maiden Ln
Lacoste, Stephen, Merchant, 109 Church St
Lacoudre, Gnertin, Dr, 31 Elliott St
Lacroix, Francis Joseph, Cabinet Maker, 53 Meeting
  St
Ladeveze, Joseph, Merchant, 85 King St
Ladson, James, Maj, Planter, 13 Meeting St
Lafar, Catharine, Widow, 31 Guignard St
Lafar, Peter & John, Goldsmith & Jewellers, 154
  Meeting St
Lafilly, Francis, Book Keeper, 4 Wentworth St
Lafrantz, Peter, Merchant, 270 King St
Lagrange, Francis, Dr, 25 Union St Cont'd
Laidler, William, Capt, Mariner, 19 Guignard St
Lajus, Paul, Confectioner, 139 Broad St
Lalande, A J P, Broker, 22 Guignard St
Lamb, David, Merchant, 2 Bedon's Al
Lamb, James, Shipmaster, 8 Bedon's Al
Lambert, Jane, Mrs, 13 Friend St.
Lambert, Lewis, Dr, 102 King St
Lamont, Helena, Boarding House, 26 Elliott St.
Lance, Ann, Mrs, Widow, 11 Friend St
Lance, Lambert, Mrs, Widow, 81 Queen St
Lane, Robert, Merchant, 108 East Bay, Lothrop
  Row
Lane, Samuel, Carpenter, 6 Society St
Lane, William, Planter, 79 Queen St
Lange, J H & Co, Merchants, 18 East Bay
Lange, Jacob, Res, 1 Church St Cont'd.
Langley, William, Equestrian, 21 Scarborough St
Langlois, DeBarville, Refugee, St Domingo, 19
  Federal St
Langlois, Maria, Madame, Boarding House, 94
  Tradd St
Langstaff & Fink, Wharfingers, Beale's Whf
Langstaff, Benjamin, Factor, Beale's Whf
Langstaff, Benjamin, Merchant, Beale's Whf, 36
  Trott St
Langton, John, Accountant, 6 Hasell St
Lanneau, Bazile, Esq, 1 S W Pitt St Road cor
  Beaufain St
Lapenne, Joseph, Grocer, 11 E King St Road cor
  Read St
Lapierre, Bernard, Billiard & Cabinet Maker, 30
  Union St
Laporte, R, Refugee, St Domingo
Lardy, Sarah, Mrs, Midwifery, 29 East Bay Cont'd
Laroche, Deliah, Widow, 1 N Lingard St

Laroche, Elizabeth, Widow, 29 Beaufain St
Larrey, Robert, Carpenter, 57 Church St
Lartigau, Dominick, Grocer, 145 Meeting St
Lasser, Eliza, Commere, 13 Friend St
Lassit, Marie A E, Madame, Widow, Mary St,
  Wraggsborough
Latham, Daniel, Distiller, 1 Hasell St
Latham, Joseph, Distiller, Cannonborough
Latthausen, J W, at Mr Mauran
Latts, J, Dr, Physician, 179 King St.
Laughfin, Mary, Shop Keeper 98 Church St
Laurans, Peter, Grocer, 167 King St
Laurence, Henry, Planter, 28 East Bay Cont'd
Laurence, Thomas, Factor, Geyer's Whf
Laval, Jacint, Sheriff, Charleston District, Office,
  State House, Res, 2 W Middle St
Lavaudan, Paul, Trader, 193 Meeting St
Lavintendiere, H, Shop Keeper, 7 W King St
  Road
Lawrence, Elizabeth, Mrs, Widow, 18 Pinckney St
Lawrence, Robert D, Factor, Crafts' E End, Res,
  1 State House Square
Lawrence, Sarah, Mrs, Widow, 44 George St
Lawson, William, Fruit Shop, 87 Queen St
Lawton, Winborn, Planter, 1 Lightwood Al
Lazarus, Marks, Store Keeper, 102 King St
Leacraft, William, Carpenter, 25 Pinckney St
Leadbetter, Agnes, Mrs, School Mistress, 9 Liberty
  St
Leaumont, R, Professor of Music, N W cor
  Middle & Minority St
Leavitt, Joshua, Grocer, 112 East Bay
Lebby, Nathaniel, Block, Mast & Pump Maker,
  Governor's Bridge, Res, 55 Church St
Leblong, Henry, Shoe Maker, 7 Liberty St
Lebreton, John B, Store Keeper
Lecat, P, Madame, Confectioner Shop, 89 King St
Lecat, P, Professor of Music, 89 King St
Lechais, A, Assistant Post Master, 13 Church St
Lee & Beekman, Auctioneers, 128 East Bay
Lee & Co, John, Merchants, 206 King St
Lee, Abigail, Seamstress, 222 Meeting St
Lee, James, Merchant, Geyer's Whf, Res, 6 Anson
  St
Lee, John & Co, Merchants, 206 King St
Lee, Mercier, Rev, Roman Catholic Church, Hasell
  St
Lee, Paul S, Adjutant, 28th Regiment, 40 Broad St
Lee, Stephen, Attorney at Law, 55 King St
Lee, Stephen, Planter, 40 Broad St
Lee, Thomas, Comptroller General Office, Office,
  3d Story, W State House, Res, Harleston's Green
Lee, Timothy, Factor, Crafts's E Whf
Lee, William, Attorney at Law, Clerk, Inferior
  Court, 55 King St
Lee, William, Merchant, 1 Archdale St
Leese, Benjamin, Merchant, Firm Campbell,
  M'Lachlan & Co., Res, 262 King St

Lefeve, John, Glass Engraver, 181 Meeting St cor Queen St
Lefevre, Stephen, Merchant, 171 Meeting St
Lefoi, Mary, Madame, 16 Scarborough St
Legare, James, Planter, 2 New St
Legare, John, Capt, Mariner, 45 George St
Legare, John, Planter, Santee, 5 Anson St
Legare, Mary, Mrs, Plantress, 19 Federal St
Legare, Mary, Mrs, Widow, 283 King St
Legare, Solomon, Planter, 19 Friend St
Legare, Thomas, Planter, 2 Gibbes St
Lege, J M, Dancing Master Academy, 104 Queen St
Leger, Elizabeth, Mrs, Widow, 4 Federal St
Legg, Catharine, Mrs., Widow, 7 St Philip's St
Legg, Joseph, Store Keeper, 184 King St
Legge, Ann, Mrs, Widow, 57 Trott St
Legoux, J Francis, Watch Maker
Lehre, Ann, Mrs, Widow, 27 St Philip's St
Lehre, Mary, Mrs, Widow, 12 Liberty St
Lehre, Thomas, Planter, 127 King St
Lelly & Sibley, Stephen, Distillers, Turpentine, Mazyckborough
Lemke, Christian, Grocer, 27 Wentworth St cor St Philip's St
Lengle, John, Merchant, 14 N W Middle St
Lenormant, Andrew, Goldsmith & Jeweller, 101 King St
Lequeux, John, Factor, Keith's Whf.
Leroy, ----, Mademoiselle, Refugee St Domingo, 13 Moore St
Leroy, Firmin, Dr, 14 Meeting St
Leseigneur, Vincent, Dr, Res, 3 E Savage St, Hospital for Negroes, S W End cor Broad & Savage St.
Lesesne, Hanah, Mrs, Widow, 43 East Bay Cont'd
Lesesne, Thomas, Merchant, 15 Broad St, Res, 4 Front St or 12 Bay Cont'd
Lester, Johanna, Seamstress, Goodby Al.
Leuder, F, Mrs, Confectioner, 27 Queen St, Candle & Soap Manufacture, 6 W Meeting St Road
Levrier, Peter, French Teacher, 42 Meeting St
Levy, Bella, Shop, 167 King St
Levy, Eliazer, Umbrella Maker, Shop Keeper, 186 King St
Levy, Lyon, Clerk, State Treasurer, 189 King St
Levy, Manuel, Store 230 King St
Levy, Moses C, Store, 217 King St
Levy, Moses, Tailor, 116 King St
Levy, Nathan, Shop Keeper, 115 King St
Levy, Rubben, Broker, 1 Magazine St
Levy, Simon, Store, 229 King St
Levy, Solomon, Merchant, 1 N W cor Broad & King St
Lewis, Isaac, Merchant, 20 Broad St
Lewis, John & Co., Grocers, 24 Union St
Lewis, John, Carpenter, 71 Meeting St

Lewis John, Merchant, 23 East Bay, Res, Mazyckborough cor Alexander & Charles St
Lewis, Joseph, Merchant, 112 Tradd St
Ley, Francis, Shop Keeper, 14 W King St Cont'd
Lightwood, Edward, Attorney at Law, Res, 220 Meeting St, Office, Thomas Parker, Esq
Lightwood, Elizabeth, Mrs, Widow, 220 Meeting St
Limehouse, Robert, Lumber Merchant, 64 Tradd St
Lind, George, Dr, Physician, 28 Guignard St cor Charles St.
Lindsay, Eliza, Laundress, 23 Pinckney St
Lindsay, Robert, Carpenter, 27 Church St Cont'd
Linguard, Mary, Mrs, Widow, 65 Church St
Lining, Charles, Attorney at Law, Ordinary, Charleston, District, 8 Legare St
Lissenhoff, F H
Little, Robert, Carpenter, 3 Pinckney St
Little, Thomas, Boarding House, 11 Chalmers Al
Livingston, J H, Printer, 16 Archdale St
Livingston, William, Capt, Mariner, 29 Bay Cont'd
Lockey, George, Merchant 106 East Bay
Lockey, Murley & Naylor, Merchants, 105 East Bay
Lockmazickes, Catherine, 2 Maiden Ln
Lockwood, Joshua, Planter, 1 Smith Ln
Logan, Ann, Widow, 257 King St.
Logan, C M, Factor, Geyer's Whf
Logan, Christian M, Factor, 14 Moore St
Logan, George, Dr, 31 Tradd St
Logan, Honoria, Mrs, Plantress, 31 Tradd St
Logan, Judith, Seamstress, 7 Price's Al
Logan, Thomas, Grocer, 132 Queen St
Logan, William, Attorney at Law, 14 Moore St
Long, Abraham W, Boarding House, 3 Chalmer's Al
Long, John, Book Keeper, 31 George St
Long, Mary, Nurse, 6 Coming St
Longbothom, B T, Dr, Dentist, 8 Orange St, formerly 55 Meeting St
Lopez, Aaron, Merchant, 33 Beaufain St
Lopez, David, Auctioneer & Commission Merchant, cor Blake's Whf, Res, 237 King St
Lopez, David, Commission Merchant, 237 King St
Lord, Jacob N, Boot Maker, 2 S W King St Cont'd
Lormore, Ann, Mrs., 10 Guignard St
Loughridge, David & Co., Grocers, 62 King St.
Love, Elizabeth, Seamstress, 56 Trott St
Loveday, Sarah, Mrs, Widow, 10 Moore St
Lovell, M, Merchant, 115 Queen St
Lovett, William, Carpenter, 3 Lamboll St
Lowe, John, Jeweller, 33 Church St
Lowndes, James, Planter, 215 Meeting St
Lowndes, Jane, Mrs, Plantress, 7 Church St
Lowndes, William, Planter, 89 Broad St.
Lowndes, William, Planter, at the Grove, 58 Tradd St
Lowrey, Charles, Tailor, 45 Church St

Loyd, John, Factor, 3 Geyer's Whf, Res, 166 Meeting St
Loyd, John P, Bedstead, Venetian Blind Maker, Etc, Meeting St
Loyd, John, Sr, Planter, 119 Broad St
Lucas, John, Lumber Merchant, Lucas Mills, Cannonborough
Lucas, Jonathan, Planter, Mill Owner, Pinckney St, Cannonborough
Luckens, John, Merchant, 56 East Bay, Res, 14 Bay Cont'd
Lundquist, Magnust, Shipwright, 35 Bay Cont'd
Lupken, Henry, Boarding House, 39 Union St
Luther, Giles & Co, Shoe & Boot Store, 186 Meeting St
Lynah, James, Dr, Physician, 47 Meeting St
Lynn, John, Merchant, 2 Front St
Lyon, Mordecay, Shop Keeper, 225 King St
M'Beth, Henry & Co, Merchants, 119 Tradd St
M'Bride, Mary, Mrs, Store Keeper, 57 East Bay
M'Call, ——, Mrs, Widow, 105 Church St
M'Call, Duncan, Grocer, 275 King St
M'Call, Elizabeth, Mrs, Widow, 14 Meeting St
M'Call, James, Planter, 3 W King St Road Opposite 1 Mile Stone
M'Call, John H, Planter, 15 Church St
M'Calla, Thomas H, Dr, Physician, 10 Elliott St
M'Can, Edward, Clerk, Fish Market, 6 Price's Al
M'Carthy, Christiana, Widow, 2 Berresford St
M'Carthy, John, Constable, 16 Hasell St
M'Carthy, John, Grocer, 234 King St
M'Carthy, Patrick, State Constable, 5 Chalmer's Al
M'Causlin, Rebecca, Mantua Maker, 17 Wentworth St
M'Cliesh, Alexander, Brass Founder, Mathematical Instrument Maker, 56 Meeting St, Res, 9 St Philip's St
M'Clure, Alexander & John, Merchants, 23 Broad St
M'Cormick, Eliza, Boarding House, Champneys Whf.
M'Cormick, William, Grocer, 21 East Bay & cor Tradd St
M'Couarta, Margaret, 5 Beaufain St
M'Credie, David & Co, Merchants, 8 Broad St
M'Credie, Jane, Mrs, Widow, 42 East Bay Cont'd
M'Credie, M, Mrs, Millinery Store, 209 King St
M'Credie, William, 209 King St
M'Dannald, William, Carpenter, 27 Beaufain St.
M'Donnald, Christopher, Grocer, 269 King St
M'Donnald, S E, Mrs, Merchant, 111 East Bay
M'Dow, William, Tutor, Academy, 3 S W Montague St
M'Dowall & Blair, Merchants, 143 Broad St
M'Dowall, Alexander, Merchant, 32 Broad St
M'Dowall, Alexander, Saddler, 80 King St
M'Dowall, James, Merchant, 64 King St.
M'Dowall, John, Merchant, 144 King St
M'Dowall, John, Merchant, 169 King St

M'Elmoyle, William, Grocer, 276 King St
M'Farlane, Catharine, Widow, 36 Hasell St
M'Fie, Dugald, Merchant, Firm Weir & Co, 26 Church St Cont'd
M'Gann, Patrick, Watchmaker, 132 East Bay
M'Gillivray, Alexander H, Vendue Master & Commission Merchant, 3 Lynch's Ln
M'Gillivray, Ann, 1 N Wentworth St Cont'd
M'Ginness, Patrick, Grocer, 70 King St & cor Queen & Mazyck St
M'Grath, Edward, Architect, 26 Archdale St
M'Gregor, A L, Mason, 15 Quince St
M'Gregor, Neil, Planter, S W End Vanderhorst St
M'Ilhenny, James, Pilot, Lynch's Ln
M'Ilraith, Eliza, Widow, by Cannon's Bridge
M'Intosh & Foulda, Cabinet Makers, 133 Meeting St
M'Intosh, Samuel, Attorney at Law, 18 Friend St
M'Kay, Ann, Mrs, Doctress
M'Kay, Barbera, Shop Keeper, 1 Quince St
M'Kay, George, Merchant, 97 King St
M'Kay, Malcolm, Grocer, 53 Tradd St
M'Kee, John, Mason, 277 King St
M'Kee, John, Mrs, Shop Keeper, 277 King St
M'Kelvey, David, Book Keeper
M'Kenzie & M'Neill, Merchants, Grocers, 123 Broad St
M'Kenzie, Ann, Butcher, Spring St
M'Kenzie, Catharine, 279 King St.
M'Kenzie, Eliza, Boarding House, 3 N Unity Al
M'Kenzie, Hannah, Mantua Maker, 53 Queen St
M'Kenzie, Hannah, Mrs, 21 King St
M'Kernan, James, Wharfinger, Keith's Whf, 8 Church St
M'Kerns, Michael, Grocer, 28 Union St
M'Key, John, Dr, Physician, Jailer, Magazine St
M'Kie, Sarah N, Mrs, Charlotte St, Mazyckborough
M'Kinley, Dugald, Merchant, 31 Church St
M'Lachlan, Campbell & Co, Merchants, 6 Tradd St
M'Lachlin, Philip, Capt, Mariner, 164 Meeting St.
M'Lane, Margaret, Widow, 20 N W Wall St
M'Lean, Evan, Grocer, 188 Meeting St
M'Millan, Ann, Mrs, Widow, 77 Tradd St
M'Millan, Richard, Merchant (Stables & Wagon Yard Keeper), 63 King St Cont'd
M'Millan, Thomas, Carpenter, 77 Tradd St
M'Neal, Catharine, Shop Keeper, 36 Hasell St
M'Neil, Neil, Capt., Mariner, 21 King St
M'Pherson, Daniel, Wheelwright, 29 East Bay Cont'd
M'Pherson, Duncan, Shop Keeper, 72 King St
M'Pherson, John, Gen, Planter, 97 Broad S
M'Quiston, Archibald, Store, 79 King St
M'Taggart, David, Merchant, 7 Cumberland St.
M'Whann & Nephew, Merchants, 9 Broad St.
Macadam, James & Co, Merchants, 153 East Bay, D'Oyley's Whf., Res, S W End Cannon St

Macaulay, George & Son, Merchants, 111 Tradd St
Macaulay, George, Merchant, 18 Broad St
Madelmond, John, School Master, 11 Society St
Madon, Peter, Baker, 4 W King St Road
Maguire F & J, Boot & Shoe Makers, 106 Tradd St
Magwood, Simon, Factor, Blake's Whf, Res, 99 Queen St
Mahan, Thomas, Coach Painter, 15 Guignard St
Maheo, Louis, Merchant, 42 Broad St
Maine, John, Commission Merchant, Keith's Whf, Res, 43 East Bay Cont'd
Mair & Fraser, Merchants, 136 Broad St.
Mair, Ann, Mrs, Widow, 43 Church St Cont'd
Mair, James, Planter, 7 N Bull St
Mair, Thomas, Merchant, 34 East Bay
Makky, John, Carpenter, 113 Meeting St
Malcomson, Catharine, Mrs, Widow, 20 St Philip's St.
Manigault, Gabriel, Planter, 122 Meeting St
Manigault, Joseph, Planter, cor Meeting St Road & John St
Mann, Henry W, Grain Inspector, 10 Beaufain St
Mann, Margaret, Boarding House, 141 Meeting St
Mann, Spencer John, Merchant, Chisolm's Whf, Res, 20 Federal St
Manson, George, Boat Builder, 84 Bay Cont'd.
Mansui, ——, Madame, 4 W Meeting St Cont'd
Manuel, Philip, Tailor, 86½ Queen St
Manuel, Sylvey, 7 Clifford's Al
Marc & Goubron, Upholsterers, Painters & Glaziers, No 7 Ellery St
Marc, George, Grocer, 288 King St
Marchal, Francis, Professor of Music, 40 Church St
Marchant, Peter T, Courier Office, 16 Bay Cont'd
Margart, John H, Black & White Smith, 65 Meeting St, Res, 2 Blackbird Al
Marinaux, Poline, Veuve, 256 King St
Markley, Abraham, Merchant, 122 King St
Marks, Humphrey, Merchant, 137 King St
Marks, Joseph, Grocer, 125 Queen St
Marks, S. M., Shop Keeper, 127 King St
Marks, Solomon & Co, Umbrella Makers, 111 King St formerly 29 Queen St.
Marlin, Edward, Sr, Custom House Inspector, 1 Cock Ln
Marsh, James, Shipwright, 24 Guignard St.
Marshall, Elizabeth, Miss, 86 Tradd St
Marshall, Helena, Shop Keeper, 6 East Wall St
Marshall, J, Cutler & Surgeon's Instrument Maker, 110 Broad St
Marshall, John, Planter, 12 W Meeting St Cont'd
Marshall, Mary, Mrs, Widow, 251 King St
Marston, Benjamin, Book Keeper, Hampstead
Martin & Ricard, Grocers, 3 N. Prioleau's Range
Martin, Charles, Mason, 17 Scarsborough St
Martin, Christian, Grocer, 5 N Prioleau's Range
Martin, Henry, Invalid, Blind Man, 10 Meeting St Cont'd

Martin, Henry, School Master, German Friendly Society
Martin, Jacob, Book Keeper, S C Bank, Res, 174 Meeting St
Martin, John & Thomas, Assistant Clerks, National Bank
Martin, Nicholas, Mason, 114 Meeting St
Martin, Thomas, Merchant, 8 Geyer's N Range, Res., 79 Bay
Mashbourn, Nicholas, Carpenter, 92 East Bay
Maspero, P A, Print Seller, Carver, Guilder, & Profile Taker, 27 Broad St
Massot, Horace, Watch Maker, 96 ½ Queen St
Mathews, Benjamin, Mrs, Widow 1 S Bull St
Mathews, D, Capt, Mariner, 21 Queen St
Mathews, Edward, 7 Parsonage Ln
Mathews, George, Vendue Master & Commission Merchant, S E cor Bull St. & Rutledge St
Mathews, James, Attorney at Law, 83 East Bay
Mathews, James, Shoe Maker, 23 King St
Mathews, Martha Ann, Planter, 1 W New St
Mathews, Mary, Seamstress, 11 Lamboll St
Mathews, Sarah, Mrs, S W cor Rutledge & Wentworth St Cont'd
Mathews, Thomas, Planter, 226 Meeting St
Mathieu, J B, Hair Worker, Etc, 20 Tradd St
Mathieu, J B, Hair Worker, 275 King St
Matthews, Philip, Rev, Trinity Church, 9 Maiden Ln
Matthiesen, C F, Grocer, 69 East Bay
Matuce, John, Butcher, 2 N W Boundary St
Maubant, P, Merchant Tailor, 42 King St
Mauger, John, Ship Broker, 24 East Bay
Mauran, John R, Merchant Grocer, 123 Queen St.
Maury, Everist, Teacher Piano Forte, 78 King St
Maverick, Samuel, Merchant, 2 W King St Road, Res, S Boundary opposite Orphan House
Maxwell, Harriot, Mrs, 48 Meeting St
Maxwell, Robert, Merchant, 97 Tradd St
May, John, Tavern, 243 King St
Mayas, Francis, Tobacconist, 114 King St
Mayberry, Thomas, Steward, Marine Hospital, 9 N. Magazine St
Mays, James, Grocer, 3 Tradd St
Mazyck, Alex, Mrs, 86 Meeting St
Mazyck, Daniel, Planter, N E cor Smith & Montague St
Mazyck, Hannah, Seamstress, 53 Queen St.
Mazyck, Mary, Mrs, 36 Meeting St
Mazyck, Nathaniel B, Firm Weston & Mazyck
Mazyck, Stephen, Planter, 5 Short St.
Mazyck, William, Firm Gaillard & Mazyck, 3 Archdale St
Mealy, William, Grocer, 13 Archdale St
Means & Fraser, Merchants, 129 Broad St
Mecomb, Joseph, Merchant, 155 King St
Meed, James, Grocer, 32 Hasell St
Meeds, William, Coffee House, 1 S E cor Cannon & Coming St Cont'd

Meeks, Joseph, High Constable, 4 St Philip's St
Meentz, D C A, Grocer, 180 King St
Melhado, Benjamin, Auctioneer, 88 Tradd St
Mellard, James H, Rev, Methodist Church, N W
cor Pitt St & W Boundary St
Mellicham, S L, Planter, 2 S Montague St
Melmies, Anthony, Turner, 137 Meeting St
Menagh, William, Wharfinger, Doyley's Whf
Mensey, Robert, Boot Maker, 2 Hard Al
Merchant, Peter, Book Keeper, Courier Office,
Res, 16 Bay Cont'd
Mercier, Matthews, Grocer, 33 Pinckney St
Meriam, John H, Boot & Shoe Store, 22 Elliott St
Mersey, John, Mariner, 53 Church St
Mesnier, Mary J, Refugee, St Domingo, 33 Union
St Cont'd
Meteyer, Peter, Merchant, 138 Broad St
Metivier, Stephen & Feis, Bakers, 3 Berresford's
Al
Meurset, Amelia, Widow, 21 Archdale St
Mey, Florian C, Merchant, Mey's Whf, Res, 43
Pinckney St
Michael, Henry, Public Chairs Keeper, 1 Parsonage
Ln.
Michel, Lazard, Capt, Mariner, 6 Parsonage Ln
Michel, Marie, Madame, Veuve, 6 W Coming St
Middleston, Ann, Mrs, Plantress, 95 Broad St
Middleton, Solomon, Tailor, 129 King St
Miles, William, Planter, 28 Church St Cont'd
Millar, Nicholas, Baker, 16 George St
Millar, William, Baker, 23 Queen St
Miller, Anson, Shipwright, 18 N W Wall St
Miller, Benjamin, Butcher, Opposite the Mile
Stone, King St Road
Miller, Catharine, Mrs, Boarding House, 179 King
St cor Federal St
Miller, Elizabeth, Widow, 4 Friend St
Miller, Ferdinand, Merchant, 13 East King St
Cont'd
Miller, Frederick, Butcher, 13 E. King St Road
Miller, Jacob H, Rope Maker, 7 Federal St
Miller, James, Merchant, 110 Tradd St
Miller, James, Sr, Merchant, Geyer's Whf, Res,
12 Scarborough
Miller, James, Wine Merchant, 61 East Bay
Miller, John D, Gold, Silver, & Gunsmith &
Jeweller, 111 Broad St, Res, 2 East Boundary
St cor Wall
Miller, John James, Carpenter, W End Wentworth
St Cont'd
Miller, John T, Carpenter, 2 N Pitt St.
Gadsden's Green
Miller, William, Tailor, 102 Queen St
Millet, Thomas, French Tutor, 3 Cumberland St
Milligan, Joseph, Store Keeper, 73 King St
Milligan, William, Merchant, 124 Bay, Res, 48
Church St Cont'd
Mills, Andrew, Carpenter, 5 Magazine St
Mills, Eliza, Miss, School, 4 Mazyck St

Mills, Henry, National Bank Porter, 116 Meeting
St
Mills, Rebecca, Mrs, Widow, 45 East Bay Cont'd
Mills, Thomas, Merchant, 108 Tradd St
Milner, George, Blacksmith & Chair Shop, 72
Church St
Minott, Benjamin, Factor, 6 East Bay
Minott, Dorcas, 5 Smith's Ln
Minott, William, Planter, 4 Gibbes St
Miott, John, Lumber Measurer, 19 W King St
Road
Mitchell, Alexander, Harness Maker, 21 Hasell St
Mitchell, Andrew, Plasterer, 10 Clifford's Al
Mitchell, Ann, Mrs, Plantress, 188 Meeting St
Mitchell, Dennison & Co, Coopers, Vanderhorst's
Whf
Mitchell, Eliza, Widow, 9 Amen St
Mitchell, James, Carpenter, 3 West St
Mitchell, James, Cooper, Vanderhorst's Whf, Res,
18 Meeting St
Mitchell, James D, Attorney at Law, 218 Meeting
St, Secretary to the Governor
Mitchell, John, Col, Notary Public & Q U, 29
East Bay
Mitchell, John H, Notary Public & Justice of the
Peace, 134 Bay, Res, 15 Guignard St
Mitchell, Thomas, Planter, Blake's Whf, Res, cor
Smith & Wentworth St Cont'd.
Modd, Peter, Goldsmith & Jeweller, 222 King St
Modern, James, Boarding House, 10 Queen St
Moer, William, Cooper & Inspector of Tobacco,
Charlotte St, Mazyckborough
Moise, Cherry, Broker & Agent for J Cohen &
Co, Res, 35 Tradd St.
Moles, ——, Mrs, Dry Goods Store, 193 King St
Moles, James, Black Smith, William's Whf, Res,
193 King St
Molly, John, Constable, 9 Chalmer's Al
Moncrieffe, John, Merchant, 2 Church St
Moncrieffe, Mary, Mrs, Widow, 82 Tradd St
Monetelot, Esaias, Merchant, 286 King St
Monk & Meuset, Gold & Silversmiths, 21 Broad St
Monk, James, Gold & Silversmith, 21 Broad St,
Res, 203 Meeting St
Monnar, Lewis, Hair Dresser, 21 & 131 Queen St
Monpoey & Heyns, Grocers, 41 Union St
Monpoey, Honore, Grocer, 118 King St
Montamar, Margaret, 22 Trott St
Montmain, Lewis C. H, Refugee, St Domingo, 42
Broad St or 85 King St
Moodie, Benjamin, His Majesty's British Consul,
Res, 65 Tradd St.
Mooney, Patrick, Merchant, Champneys Whf., 22
Bay, Res, 8 S Cannon St.
Moore, ——, Mrs, 8 King St
Moore, John E, Planter, 33 Trott St
Moore, Joseph, Drayman & Public Chair Keeper, 8
Bay Cont'd

Moore, Mary, Mrs, Widow, 1 National Bank
Square
Moore, Philip, Cabinet Maker, 28 Meeting St
Moore, Richard, Painter & Glazier, 11 Wentworth
St.
Moore, S W, Jr, Wharfinger, Blake's Whf, Res,
Lynch's Ln
Moorehouse, John, Tailor, 95 Tradd St
Morales, Jacob, 10 Wentworth St
Moran, Christopher, Board & Lodging, 4 Union St
Cont'd
Mordecai, David, Commission Merchant, 10
Berresford St
Mordecai, Jacob, Broker, 250 King St
More, P J, Dr., Surgeon, Dentist & Midwifery, 47
King St
Morgan, Charles, Mrs, Widow, 2 Pinckney St
Morin, Jeanne, Seamstress, 23 Guignard St
Morisson, A B, Mrs, Millinery Store, 9 Tradd St
Morphy, Don Diego, His Catholic Majesty's Consul
for Spain, 263 King St
Morris, George, Carpenter, 16 Archdale St
Morris, Lewis, Col, Planter, 215 Meeting St
Morris, Thomas, Col, Merchant, 58 Trott St cor
Bay Cont'd
Morrison, John, Capt, Mariner, 89 Tradd St
Morrisson, Samuel, Capt, 7 S Linguard St
Morten, Joseph, Drayman, 3 W Pitt St,
Harleston's Green
Mortimer & Heron, Merchants, 14 Broad St
Morton, Alexander, Grocer, 231 King St
Morton, E, Mrs, Nurse, 41 King St
Moser, Philip, Dr, Apothecary & Druggist, 124
Broad St., Res, 1 New St
Moses & Isaak, Vendue Masters & Commission
Merchants, 7 S Champneys St
Moses, Chapman, Store, 116 King St
Moses, Henry, Shop Keeper, 51 East Bay
Moses, Isaac C, Merchant, 237 King St
Moses, Isaiah, Store, 197 King St
Moses, Levy & Isaia, Store, 220 King St
Moses, Lyon, Broker, 18 Archdale St
Moses, Myer, Firm Cohen & Moses, Res, 10 N
Cannon St, Islington
Moses, Philip, Store, 36 King St
Moses, Planter, 14 Federal St
Moses, Solomon, Constable, 188 King St
Motta, E D L, Auctioneer & Commission
Merchant, 48 Tradd St, N Vendue Row,
Exchange Square
Motta, J A, Store Keeper, 75 King St
Motte, Abraham, Planter, 39 East Bay Cont'd
Motte, Alexander B, Planter, 217 Meeting St
Motte, Francis, Factor, Vanderhorst's Whf, Res,
209 Meeting St
Motte, Jacob, Custom House Inspector, 2 S Cock
Ln
Motte, Mary, Mrs, Widow, 217 Meeting St
Mouat, John, Mrs., Widow, 3 Trott St.

Moubray, Martha, Mrs, Baker, 90 King St
Mouchel, A F, Printer, 14 Queen St
Moulin, Peter, Shop Keeper, 10 King St
Moullin, Matthew, Grocer, 17 Trott St
Moullins, Sarah, Widow, 17 Church St
Moultrie, Alex, Councilor & Advocate at Law, 2
Cumberland St
Moultrie, Ann, Mrs, Plantress, 62 Tradd St.
Moultrie, H, Mrs., Planter, 84 Meeting St
Moultrie, James, Dr, Port Physician, 87 Meeting
St
Moultrie, William A, Planter, 84 Meeting St
Moultrie, William, Gen, 84 Meeting St
Mouzon, Charles, Boot & Shoe Maker, 45 Church
St
Muck, Philip, Music Master, 254 King St
Muckenfuss, Henry, Mason, 3 N Wentworth St
Cont'd
Muckenfuss, Michael, Cabinet Maker, 53 King St
Muir, William, Merchant, Geyer's Whf, Res, 8
Magazine St
Mulin, Rose, Mantua Maker, 31 Trott St
Mulligan, Bernard, Wharfinger, Champneys Whf
Mulligan, Francis, Esq, Justice of the Peace, 3
Washington St, Mazyckborough
Mulligan, Joseph, Shop Keeper, 69 King St
Muncreef, Susannah, Mrs, Widow, 34 Hasell St
Muncreeff, John, Jr, House Carpetner, 9 Bay
Cont'd
Muncreeff, John, Sr, House Carpenter, 9 Bay
Cont'd
Munds, Israel, Rev, Academy, 6 Union St Cont'd
Munro, Catharine, Mrs, Midwife, 43 Elliott St
cor of the Bay
Munro, John, Jewellery Store, 6 Elliott St
Murphy, Sarah, Boarding House, 6 Champneys St
Murray, Darby, Boarding House, 10 Chalmers Al
Murray, Eliza, Seamstress, 13 W Wall St
Murray, John, Accountant, William Pritchard's
Whf, Res, 1 N E Wall St
Mushett, John, Blacksmith, 10 Ellery St, Res, 68
Meeting St
Mushrooms, James, Capt, Mariner, 57 East Bay
Mussault, Ann M., Madame, Refugee, St Domingo,
Mary St, Wraggsborough
Myer, Michael, Auctioneer, 5 Parsonage Ln
Myers, John, Guard, 5 Clifford's Al
Myers, Samuel, Tailor, 208 King St
Myers, Sarah, Widow, 5 Quince St
Mylne, James, Mrs, 31 Union St Cont'd
Naar, Moise, Shop Keeper, 43 King St
Napier, Smith & Co, Merchants, Crafts' N Whf,
East End
Nasar, Philip, Baker, 84 King St
Nathan, David, Store, 123 King St
Nathan, Solomon, Shop Keeper, 228 King St
Navarro, Esther, Boarding House, 11 Berresford St
Naylor, Thomas, Merchant, Firm Lockey, Murley &
Naylor, 106 Bay

Neal, Robert, Boarding House, 18 Amen St
Nebuhr, J David, Store, 188 King St
Negrin, J J., Interpreter & Tutor of the French &
English Languages, Printer, Compiler of the
Directory, and Director of the Intelligence Office,
124 East Bay
Neilson, James S , Attorney at Law, Prothonotary
Office, 176 Meeting St
Nelson, Ambrose, Capt , Mariner, 53 Trott St
Nelson, Francis, Shipwright, 8 Pitt St , Gadsden
Green
Nelson, Isaac, Boarding House, 16 E King St
Road
Nelson, Jane, Mrs , Widow, 73 Church St
Neusville, Ann, Mrs , Widow, 169 King St
Neusville, Edward, Planter, 89 Broad St
Neusville, Elizabeth, Mrs , 75 Queen St
Neusville, Isaac, Book Keeper, National Bank, 8 N
Wentworth St Cont'd
Neusville, John, Attorney at Law, Commissioner of
Loans, & Notary Public, 75 Queen St
Neville, Joshua, Cabinet Maker, 40 Tradd St
Newton, Mary, Victualler or Butcher, 12 N Cannon
St
Newton, Sarah, Laundress, 31 King St
Neyle, Philip, Planter, 12 Legare St
Nicholls, George & Co , Capt , Grain Merchants, 6
Faber's N Range Chisolm's Whf
Nicholson, James, Attorney at Law, Prothonotary
Office, 176 Meeting St
Nicholson, James, Planter, over Cannon's Bridge
Niderburg, Simon, Dr , 55 Queen St
Nipper, David H , Book Binder, 1 King St.
Nobbs, Samuel, Inspector, Custom House, Shoe
Store, 191 King St
Noble, Ezekiel, Merchant, 153 King St
Noble, John, Dr , Apothecary & Druggist, 175 King
St
Noble, Paul, Carpenter, 11 Lamboll St
Noel, Sarah A , Madame, Mantua Maker, 20 Tradd
St
Noel, William, Professor of Music, 20 Tradd St
Noldens, Peter, Merchant Tailor, 116 Queen St
Nolen, James, Carpenter, 3 N Pitt St , Gadsden's
Green
Noney & Mulligan, Factors & Commission
Merchants, Champneys Whf
Noney, William, Merchant, 22 Bay cor Tradd St.
Norris, James, Turner, 5 Guignard St
Norris, Stephen, Shipwright, 16 Hasell St
Norroy, J C F, Tobacconist, 18 George St.
North & Webb, Factors, Geyer's S Whf
North, Richard B , Merchant, 15 Church St
North, Susannah, Widow, 38 Tradd St
Nowel, John, Commission Merchant, 17 Berresford
St
Nowell, John, Factor, 118 East Bay
Nowell Thomas S , Discount Clerk, S.C Bank, 16
Magazine St

Nuffer, Mary, N W End Wentworth St Cont'd
Nugent, Margaret & Daughters, 13 Lamboll St.
O'Brien, Isabella, Miss, Jewellery store, 120 Broad
St
O'Connor, Eliza, Laundress, 4 Beaufain St
O'Connor, Thomas, Clerk, Hay Market, South Bay,
Grocer, 1 King St
O'Hara, Charles, Merchant, 6 Smith's Ln
O'Hara, James & Son, Merchants, 144 Broad St
O'Hear, James, Accountant, 1 W Pitt St ,
Harleston's Green
O'Kelly, John, Mathematic, Navigation, Etc
Academy, 245 King St
O'Kelly, John, Tutor
O'Neale, Charles, Merchant, Firm Pagan &
O'Neale, Wentworth St
O'Neale, Elizabeth, Nurse, 3 Clifford St
Oats, Mary, Widow, 6 Meeting St Cont'd
Oeland, John, Grocery Store, 8 Union St Cont'd
Ogden, George W , Clothier & Salesman, 49 East
Bay
Ogier, Lewis & Co , Factors, 9 Crafts' S Whf ,
Res , Friend St
Ogier, Rosinette, Couturiere, 6 Columbus St
Ogier, Thomas, Merchant 146 Bay, Res , 74 Tradd
St
Ogilvie, John Alex, Mrs , Plantress, Islington,
Cannonborough
Ohlweiller, M , Baker & Grocer, 14 Church St.
Oleron, Jane, Widow, 79 ½ Church St
Oliphant, David, Painter, 9 Ellery St
Oliphant, Thomas, Upholsterer, 26 Broad St
Oliver, James, Butcher, 22 E King St Road
Oliver, James, Mason, 23 St Philip's St.
Oliver, Sarah, Boarding House, 4 Bedon's Al
Osborn, Richard, Factor, 5 Blake's Whf
Osborn, Thomas, Planter, 6 South Bay
Otis, Joseph & Co , Factors, 13 East Bay
Otto, Hannah, Widow, 7 Federal St
Otzel, John, Grocer, 21 Archdale St
Owen, Hannah, Miss, 9 Parsonage Ln.
Owen, John, Merchant, 27 Tradd St
Owen, John, Millwright, W End Bull St
Owens, Thomas, Mariner, 1 Hard Al
Pagan & O'Neale (Archibald), Merchants, 151 King
St
Paine & Son, Thomas, Merchants, 13 Hasell St
Palmer, Job, Carpenter, Clerk Independent
Congregational Church, Meeting St., Professor,
Harmonical School,
Palmer, John, Sergeant, City Guard, 44 Church St
Paque, F Gabriel, Architect Builder, 106 King St
Parke, George, Planter, 90 East Bay
Parker, ——, Merchant, 3 New St
Parker, ——, 44 George St
Parker, Ann, Widow, 7 Legare St
Parker, Catharine, Mrs , Millinery Store, 180
Meeting St
Parker, E , Mrs , Millinery Store, 193 King St

Parker, Florida, Mrs , Widow, 26 Guignard St
Parker, Henry, Coach Painter, 6 Berresford St
Parker, Isaac, Planter, 9 Legare St & Gibbes St
Parker, John, Planter, 9 Archdale St
Parker, Mary, Mrs , Widow, 6 George St
Parker, Phineas, Dyer, 89 Meeting St
Parker, Thomas & Co., Merchants, 113 East Bay
Parker, Thomas, District Attorney, Office, State
  House Square, Res , 33 Meeting St
Parks, Samuel, Shoe Ware House, 82 King St
Parmele, David, Grocer, 16 Tradd St
Parret, John, Hair Dresser, 109 King St
Parsons, Joseph, Grocer, Firm Dieckert & Co ,
  Res , 6 Boundary St between Meeting & King St
Patch, Francis, Mrs , Clifford's Al
Paterson, Hugh, Notary Public, Insurance Broker,
  83 Church St
Patin, —, Madame, 119 King St
Paton, John, Book Keeper, Custom House
Patterson, David, Capt , Mariner, 6 N Champneys
  St
Patterson, Robert, Carpenter, 25 Beaufain St
Paul, D , Merchant, 224 King St
Payne, James, Capt , Revenue Cutter, Sullivan's
  Island
Payne, W R , Stone Cutter & Marble Mason, 77
  King St
Payne, William, Commission Broker, 131 Broad St
Peace & Cheves (Joseph), Attornies at Law, 3 N
  W State House Square, Summer Res , Hampstead
  cor Nassau & Drake
Peak, Pearce & Tillinghast (Reuben), Shoe
  Warehouse, 22 Elliott St
Pearce, John, Painter & Glazier, 5 Bedon's Al
Pearson, Benjamin, Capt , Mariner, 22 Scarborough
  St
Peart, John, Shipwright, 9 Quince St
Pearton, Henry, Book Keeper, Custom House
Pebarte, John, Refugee, St Domingo, 17 George St
Peigne, C H , Madame, Mantua Maker
Peigne, Lewis, 195 Meeting St
Pellissier, John B , Store Keeper, 53 East Bay
Pemble, David, Tailor, Foreman, Mr Brener
Pennall, James, Merchant, 6 W King St Road
Pennington, Edward, Lt., Revenue Cutter, 5 Black
  Bird Al
Pennington, Thomas, Mason, 2 Berresford Al
Pepoon, Benjamin, Grain Merchant, 118 Queen St ,
  Res., 10 Union St Cont'd
Perdrian, Peter, Carpenter, 13 Ellery St
Perinchief, Francis, Mrs , Widow, 7 Archdale St
Peronne, Cesar, Capt , Mariner, 13 Liberty St
Peronneau, William, Planter, 9 George St
Perrault, P , Drawing & Mathematic Master, 7 Bay
  Cont'd
Perrie, Isabella, Mrs , Midwife, 96 Queen St.
Perry, Ann, Widow, Hampstead
Perry, Nathaniel, Shoe Store, 5 Tradd St.
Peters, William, Shipwright

Petit, Francis, Planter
Pett [bottom of page 62 of directory is garbled]
Peyton, Violetta, Mrs , Widow, cor. Linguard &
  Church St
Pezant, J L'aimable, Fisher & Net Maker,
  Gadsden's Market, E End Boundary St
Phelon, Edmond M , Grocer & Liquor Store, 182
  Meeting St.
Philip, Dorethea, Mrs , Widow, 69 Queen St
Philips & Gardner, Merchants Market, Prioleau's N
  Range
Philips, E & B , Boot & Shoe Store, 23 Elliott St
Philips, John, Painter & Glazier, 14 King St
Pickton, Charles & Thomas, Carpenters
Pieckenpack, John, Grocer, 32 Archdale St
Pikes, Nathaniel, Plasterer, 13 Berresford St
Pillans, Ann, Mrs , Widow, 110 Tradd St
Pillot, John, Grocer, East King St Road No 14
Pillot, Onesime, Grocer, 6 Elliott St
Pilsbury, Amos, School Master, 3 & 13 Amen St
Pilsbury, Samuel, Custom House Inspector, 4
  Charles St
Pincel, William, Tin Plate Worker, 184 Meeting St
Pinckeny, Charles, American Ambassador to Spain,
  Res , 217 Meeting St
Pinckeny, Thomas, Planter, 93 Meeting St
Pinckney, Charles Cotelworth, Gen , Planter, 1 East
  Bay Cont'd
Pinckney, Frances, S , Mrs (Roger), 14 Legare St
Pinckney, Thomas, Maj , Planter, 42 George St
Pinnan, Charles, Merchant, 95 Church St
Piot, Elizabeth P , Mrs , Plantress, 25 St Philip's
  St
Placide, Alexander, Charleston Theatre Manager &
  Dancing Master, 93 Broad St , Vaux Hall Garden
Platt, S , Broker & Commission Merchant, 102
  King St
Plissonneau & Bork, Sail Makers, 119 Bay
  Cochran's Whf
Plissonneau, John, Grocer, 44 King St
Plum, E , Stage Office, National Bank Square
Plumet, John, Dr , 45 King St
Pogson, Milward, Rev Dr , Rector, St James',
  Goose Creek & St John's Berkeley, 4 S Pitt St
  Gadsden's Green
Poincignon, P A , Tin Plate Worker, 12 Queen St
Poissenot, Joseph, Mrs , Shop Keeper, 18
  Berresford Al.
Pollard, James, Capt , Lynch's Ln
Pollock, Solomon, Mrs , 4 Bull St
Polony, Jean Louis, Dr , Physician, 17 Church St
  Cont'd
Porcher, Isaac, Planter, S Charlotte St ,
  Mazyckborough
Porcher, Peter, Planter, 2 Lamboll St
Porter, Benjamin R , Cabinet Maker, 175 Meeting
  St
Porter, Peter, Blacksmith, 1 West St

47

Porter, William, Auctioneer & Commission Merchant, S Vendue Row, Exchange Square, Res , 36 Elliott
Postell, Edward, Chair Marker, 12 George St
Postell, William, Capt , Planter, 41 George St
Potter, John, Merchant, 19 Broad St
Poulnot, Nicholas, French Boot & Shoe Maker, 39 Meeting St
Poulton, Edward, Capt , Mariner, 20 Church St Cont'd
Poupel, Jeanne M , Madame, Widow, 4 Cumberland St
Power, E , Grocer, 80 East Bay
Power, Maurice, Planter, 41 Tradd St
Poyas, John E , Dr , Planter, 29 Meeting St
Poyas, John Lewis, House Carpenter
Pratt, John, Capt , Mariner, 21 Elliott St
Pratt, Samuel H , Merchant, Grocery Store, 107 East Bay
Prendergast, P E , Tutor
Prentice, John, Coach & Chair Maker, 4 & 30 Archdale St
Presley, William, Merchant, Grocery Store, 86 King St
Pressley, M & C , Misses, Mantua Makers, 116 Meeting St
Price, John, Merchant, 8 Church St Cont'd
Price, Thomas William, Planter, 89 Tradd St
Price, William, Merchant, 98 Tradd St.
Price, William, Planter, 2 Orange St
Prieur, Marie E , Madame, Refugee, St Domingo, 61 Meeting St
Primrose, Catharine, Mrs , Widow, 21 St Philip's St
Prince, Charles, Tin Plate Worker, 246 King St
Prince, Harriot, Mrs , Widow, 3 New St
Pringle, John J , Attorney General, 93 Tradd St
Pringle, Robert, Dr , Physician, 7 Friend St cor Broad St
Prioleau, A E , Mrs , Widow, 82 Queen St
Prioleau, Isaac, Factor, 49 Meeting St
Prioleau, Jane B , Mrs , School Mistress, 10 Maiden Ln
Prioleau, John Cordes, Capt , Merchant, 76 East Bay
Prioleau, John, Wharfinger Crafts' Whf
Prioleau, Philip G , Dr , Physician, 49 Meeting St
Prioleau, Samuel, Factor, Whf Owner, Prioleau's Whf , 49 Meeting St
Prioleau, Thomas G , 82 Queen St
Pritchard, Benjamin F , Printer, 238 King St
Pritchard, Joseph, Factor, Wharfinger & Lumber Merchant, Gadsden's Whf , Res , 57 King St
Pritchard, Paul, Jr , Shipwright, 24 Guignard St
Pritchard, Paul, Shipwright & Whf Owner is now Planter & Resides on his Plantation
Pritchard, William, Jr , Shipwright, 2 Charles St

Pritchard, William, Sr , Shipwright, 1 Pinckney St
Proby, M , Widow, 4 East Cock Ln
Procter, John, Indian Doctor, 5 N E Lowndes St
Provand, Baird & Macmurrich, Merchants
Provaux, Elizabeth, Mrs , Plantress, 32 George St
Provaux, Joseph, 37 King St
Provaux, Marie, Madame, 2 Union St Cont'd
Puppo, Daniel C , Commission Merchant, 19 East Bay
Purcel, Sarah Blake, Mrs , (Rev Dr Widow), 1 Legare St
Purcell, Joseph, Land Surveyor, 11 George St
Purcell, Joseph R , Capt , Mariner, 34 East Bay Cont'd
Purkson, M , Rev Dr , 82 East Bay
Purse, Elizabeth, Mrs , Mantua Maker, 117 Broad St
Purse, William, Watch Maker & Jeweller, 117 Broad St
Purvis, William, Merchant, cor Boundary & Middle St
Quackinbush, Laurence, Cabinet Maker, 3 East Cock Ln
Quash, Robert, Planter, 91 Broad St
Query, John, Auction Store, Verree & Blair, 4 Mazyck St
Quigging, ——, Mrs , Boarding House, 3 N Lodge Al
Quin, Thomas F , Grocer, 22 Quince St
Quinby, Joseph, Carpenter, Grocer, 6 & 7 Pinckney St
Quinlon, Michael, Grocer, cor Mazyck & Magazine St
Quinning, Dennis, Boarding House, 17 Union St.
Quinning, Denny, Tobacconist, 14 Hasell St
Radcliffe, Thomas, Sr , Planter, 39 & 40 George St
Rade, J C , Dr , Physician & Apothecary, 216 King St
Rain, Samuel, Pilot, 7 Lynch's Ln
Raine, Thomas, Store, 221 King St
Rall, Lewis, Baker, 40 Union St
Ralston, George, Merchant, 4 Elliott St Cont'd
Ramage, F , Mrs , Boarding House
Ramley, Barbara, Mrs , Laundresss, 5 Coming St
Ramley, Michael, Carpenter, 6 N W Boundary St
Ramsay, David, Dr , Physician, 106 Broad St
Ramsay, George, Shop Keeper, 25 Church St Cont'd
Ramsay, John, Dr , Planter, 74 Tradd St
Ramsay, Joseph, Dr , 30 Tradd St
Randell, Elizabeth, Mrs , Widow, 76 Queen St.
Ravenel, Daniel J , Justice of the Peace, State Secretary Office
Ravenel, Daniel, Planter, 115 Broad St
Ravenel, Stephen
Raworth, George, Trimmer, 21 Hasell St
Raynal, Lewis, Accountant, Custom House, Res , 104 Tradd St

Raynal, P E B, Goldsmith, 105 Tradd St
Read, William, Dr, Physician, 19 Church St
Cont'd.
Reader, Philip, Shoe Store, 3 Queen St
Rechon, David, Tailor, 110 King St
Redlich, William, Notary Public & Broker
Redman, James, Rigger
Redman, Samuel, Painter, 7 S Cock Ln
Reed, Ezra & Lucas, Merchants, 7 Stoll's Al
Reed, Sarah, Seamstress, No Name Al
Reeves, Enos, Jeweller, 112 Broad St
Reiar, Henry, Grocer, William's Whf, South Bay
Reid, George, Notary Public, Agent Batavian
Republic, 12 East Bay
Reid, John, Tinplate Worker, 36 Church St
Reid, John, Wheelwright, 173 Meeting St
Reigne, Dupuy, Madame, Refugee, St Domingo, 4
E Wall St
Reigne, John, Baker, 9 Elliott St
Reilley, James, Saddler & Harness Maker, 24
Church St
Remington, Francis, Tailor, 6 Amen St
Remoussin, Daniel, Planter, 123 Meeting St
Remoussin, M P D, Planter, St Domingo, 30
Beaufain St
Remoussin, Rose, Laundress, 157 King St
Renauld, John, Fruit Shop, 34 Tradd St
Rennie, George, Marble Stone Cutter, 62 Broad St
Renty, George, Tailor, 61 Church St
Renty, Jesse, Grocer, 8 Archdale St
Repon, Bernard, Boarding House, 8 Union St
Res, 30 Tradd St
Reside, William, Cabinet Maker, 189 Meeting St
Revel, Hannah, Mrs, Widow, 23 Scarborough St
Revell, George, Book Keeper, 4 W Coming St
Revell, John, Mariner, 39 Queen St
Reynard, L Cabeuil, Tailor, 152 Meeting St
Rhind, Elizabeth, Mrs, 11 N W Wentworth St
Cont'd
Rhodes & Otis, Factors, 13 East bay
Ricard, Francis, Grocer, 35 East Bay
Ricardo, R J & Co, Store Keepers, 240 King St
Richards, Samuel, Broker, 11 Bedon's Al
Richardson, ——, Miss, 98 King St cor
Parsonage Ln
Richardson, J B, Late Governor S C, at his seat
Jamesville
Richardson, John, 26 Elliott St
Richardson, John, Attorney at Law, 26 Tradd St
Richardson, Thomas, Capt, Tavern, 4 S Bull St
Richmond, John C, Hair Dresser, 8 Amen St
Rickard, William, Tailor, 2 Elliott St
Ridgway, John, Constable, 6 Chalmer's Al
Rigaud, Peter, Manufacturer, Soap & Candles, 10
W Meeting St Road
Righton, F, Mrs, 3 Stoll's Al
Righton, Joseph, Cooper, 1 Water St
Righton, M'Cully, Esq, 2 Water St

Ring, David, Painter, Glazier & Paper Hanger, 201
King St
Rivers, Frances, Mrs, Widow, 172 King St
Rivers, Frances, Widow, 142 Meeting St
Rivers, Francis, Planter, 12 Amen St
Rivers, Gracia, Mrs, Widow, cor Short & Mazyck
St
Rivers, Samuel, Shipwright, 6 Water St
Rivers, Thomas, Jr, 47 Trott St
Rivers, Thomas, Planter, 1 Stoll's Al
Riviere, Jean l', Grocer, 81 Meeting St
Riviere, Marie Louis Ferret, Fruit Shop, 144
Meeting St
Roach, William, City Treasurer, Exchange, Res, 15
Quince St cor Liberty St
Roberts, Catharine, Widow, 2 Clifford St
Roberts, William, Coach Maker, 66 Meeting St
Robertson, Alexander, Merchant, 147 King St
Robertson, Francis, Factor, 8 Elliott St
Robertson, John, Merchant, 8 Crafts' S Whf, Res,
47 Church St Cont'd
Robertson, Samuel & George, Merchants, Opposite
the Tobacco Inspection
Robin, Andrew, Broker, 252 King St
Robinet, Frances, Madame, N W End Wentworth
St Cont'd
Robinson & Long, Merchants, 136 King St cor
George St
Robinson, Frances, Miss, Seamstress, 277 King St.
Robinson, John, Firm
Robinson, Mary, Mrs, Store, 38 Queen St
Robinson, P, Seamstress, 17 St Philip's St
Robinson, Peter, Painter & Glazier, 8 Parsonage
Ln
Robinson, Robert S, Tavern, 81 King St cor
Clifford St
Robinson, Thomas J, Boot & Shoe Maker, at Mr
Rouse's
Robinson, William, Hotel, 105 Queen St
Robinson, William, Insurance Broker, 36 East Bay
Robiou, Charles, Merchant, E cor King St Cont'd
& Boundary St
Roche, John, Grocer, 78 Church St.
Rodgers, Samuel, Organist, St Michael's Church, 4
N Wentworth St Cont'd
Rodick, Thomas & Co, Merchants, Geyer's Whf
Rodman, Mary, Boarding House, 24 Pinckney St
Rodrigues, Abraham, Merchant, 54 King St
Rodrigues, Moise, Merchant, 8 Wentworth St
Roger, Abraham, Shoe Maker, 8 Water St
Rogers, Christopher, House Carpenter, 25 Tradd St
Rogers, Eliza, Mrs, Widow, 115 Meeting St
Rogers, Sarah, Mrs., Widow, 26 Church St Cont'd
Roper, Thomas, Planter, 71 East Bay
Roper, William, Planter, 5 East Bay
Rosainville, ——, Mr, Confectioner, 102 King
St
Rose, John S, Accountant, 15 Ellery St.
Rose, William S, Merchant, 14 Broad St

Ross, Daniel, Saw Mills, 63 Tradd St
Ross, David, Tailor, 46 Broad St
Ross, Elizabeth, Nurse, 1 N Linguard St
Ross, Thomas, Capt , Mariner, 21 Ellery St
Rosse, Paul, Print Seller & Frame Maker, 31 Broad
  St
Rossignol, ——, Madame, Refugee, St Domingo,
  17 N W Wall St
Roturean, Charles, Grocer, 163 King St.
Rou, M., Cabinet Maker, 17 George St
Roulain, Robert, Mason, 3 Friend St
Roupell, E , Mrs , Plantress, 73 Tradd St
Rour, Lewis, Merchant, Liquor Store, 37 Bay, Res ,
  153 Meeting St
Rouse, William, Tanner & Leather Manufacturer,
  170 Meeting St
Rout, ——, Mrs , Widow, 16 Friend St
Rowand, Charles E , Planter, 2 Friend St
Rowand, Robert
Rowed, John, Merchant, 122 Tradd St
Ruberry, B W , Painter, 65 Tradd St
Ruberry, John, Carpenter, 6 Stoll's Al.
Ruberry, William, Carpenter, 65 Tradd St
Ruddock, Samuel A , A M Academy, 6 St
  Michael's Al
Ruhlman, George, Tailor, 4 Union St
Rulain, Catharine, Miss, 270 King St
Russel, ——, Mrs , 9 Clifford St
Russel, Benjamin, Mason, 29 Guignard St
Russel, Nathaniel, Merchant, 15 East Bay
Russell, Daniel, Carpenter, 2 Ellery St
Russell, John, Blacksmith, Governor's Bridge, Res ,
  41 Trott St
Russell, William & Co , 34 Elliott St
Rutledge, Charles, Planter, S W cor Wentworth
  St Cont'd & Rutledge St
Rutledge, Edward, Planter, 30 Hasell St
Rutledge, Frederick, Planter, 59 Tradd St
Rutledge, Henry, Maj , Planter, 25 Wentworth St
Rutledge, Hugh, Judge of the Court of Equity, 15
  St Philip's St
Rutledge, Sarah, Miss, 22 Church St
Rutledge, William, N E cor Chapel & Elizabeth
  St , Mazyckborough
Ryan, Elizabeth, Mrs , Store, 52 East Bay
Ryan, James, Register in Equity, 75 Church St
Saint Cellery, Peter, Hair Dresser, 3 Elliott St
Salmon, David D , Saddler & Harness Maker, 13
  W King St
Salomon, Lewis, Grocery Store, 14 Queen St
Salomon, Salomon, Store, 186 King St
Saltus & Yates, Ship Chandlers, 41 East Bay & 2
  Crafts' S Whf
Samory, Claude Nicholas, Grocery Store, 19 Queen
  St
Samuel, Hyman, Watchmaker, 50, Res , 123 East
  Bay
Sanders, E , Mrs , Widow, 170 King St
Sanders, E P , Planter, 170 King St

Sanders, Elkeny, Boarding House, 10 Queen St
Sanford, Moses, School Master, German Friendly
  Society School
Santi, Angelo & Co, Merchants, Confectioners, 60
  King St
Sarrazin, Catharine & Mary, Spinsters, 12
  Wentworth St
Sarrazin, Jonathan, Esq , 12 Wentworth St
Sartoris, Peter, Merchant, 128 Meeting St
Sasportas, Abraham, Buildings, 14 & 15 Queen St
Sass, Jacob, Cabinet Maker, 34 & 35 Queen St
Savage, Martha, Mrs , Widow, cor Broad & Savage
  St
Savage, Samuel, Carpenter, S Cannon St
Savala, Joseph, Fruit Shop, 99 King St
Sayre, Stephen, Ship Joiner, Pritchard's Whf , Res ,
  33 Guignard St
Schem, J F , Watchmaker, at Mr Himley
Schirer, ——, Mrs , Milliner & Mantua Maker, 177
  Meeting St
Schirer, John, Gunsmith, 177 Meeting St.
Schmidt, Elizabeth, Mrs , Widow, S E cor Pitt &
  Montague St
Schmierle, John, Carpenter, 59 Queen St
Schmiser, Henry, Grocer, 50 Trott St
Schnell & Smitzers, Grocers, Cochran's Whf
Schodde, Margaret, Mrs , Mantua Maker, 3 Hasell
  St
Schutt, Margaret D , Mrs , Merchant, Firm A
  Holmes & Co , 8 East Bay
Schwartz, John, Grocer, 27 Church St
Scirmer, John Frederick, Grocer, 70 Bay
Sconder, Susan, Mantua Maker, 97 King St
Scott, Alexander, Drayman, 20 Scarborough St
Scott, Ann, Shop Keeper, 40 Queen St
Scott, James, Auctioneer & Commission Merchant,
  cor Champney St and N Venue Row, Res , 101
  Tradd Scott, Scott, William, Boarding House, 36
  Union St Cont'd
Scress, ——, Mrs , Boarding House, Union St
  Cont'd
Screven, Thomas, Mrs , Widow, 110 Church St
Seabrook, Benjamin, Planter, 1 N W Bull St
Seaver, Abraham, House Carpenter, 36 Pinckney St
Seavey, John, Mariner, 2 Spring St
Secress, Martin, Capt , Mariner, cor Amen &
  Union St Cont'd
Segerstrom, J G Grocer, 2 Elliott St Cont'd
Seixas, ——, Mrs & Daughters, 7 Moore St
Seixas, I M , Mercantile
Selby, George, Store Keeper
Serjant, Mary, Store, 222 King St
Seyler, Sarah, Seamstress, cor Bull & Coming St
Seymour, Stephen, Harbor Master, 83 Tradd St
Shackelford, Nathan, Merchant, Wraggsborough
Shand, Robert, Custom House Inspector, 6 S
  Linguard St
Sharp, John, Mast, Pump & Block Maker,
  Governor's Bridge

Shaw, Terrance, Plasterer, 18 Berresford St
Shaw, William, Attorney at Law, 106 Queen St
Shecut, John L , Dr , Apothecary & Druggist, 109
King St cor Beaufain St
Sheively, George, Grocer, 117 Meeting St
Shephard, James, Harness Maker, 7 Coming St
Sheppard, Thomas, Proprietor of the Times, 14
Water St
Shirras, Alexander, Merchant, 129 Broad St
Shirtliff, William, Merchant, 5 N Pitt St cor
Wall St.
Shiter, John, Carpenter, 1 S W Coming St
Shoolbred, James, Planter, 8 Lamboll St
Shrewsbury, Edward, Carpenter, 6 Ellery St
Shrewsbury, Jeremiah, Carpenter, Res , 6 Ellery
St
Shrewsbury, Mary Ann, Mrs , Widow, 12 Guignard
St
Shrewsbury, Stephen, Book & Collector Clerk, S C
Bank, 8 Cumberland St
Shrimer, Nicholas, Grocer, cor George & Coming
St
Shroder, John & Cutler, Grocers, 5 Hasell St
Sibley, Joseph, Grocer, 40 East Bay
Sigwald, Thomas, Cabinet Maker, S W cor King
& Queen St
Simmons, ——, Dr , Physician, 15 East Bay
Simmons & Sweeny, Grocers, cor East Bay &
Broad St
Simmons, Francis, Planter, 18 Legare St
Simmons, John, Planter, 3 N Cannon St
Simmons, Thomas, Planter, 5 N W Bull St
Simmons, William, Tailor, 6 S Bull St
Simms, William, Tavern, 16 W. King St Road
Simonet, ——, Madame, Confectioner, 29 Queen St
Simons & Murden, Commission Merchants, 2
Prioleau's N Range
Simons, James, Collector Custom House, Res , 56
King St
Simons, Keating & Son, Factors, 9 Geyer's Whf N
Range, Res , 3 Orange St
Simons, Keating Lewis, Attorney at Law, 3 Orange
St
Simons, Robert, Planter, 6 W King St Cont'd
Simons, Samuel, Broker, 20 Berresford St
Simons, Sarah R , Mrs , Plantress, 58 Tradd St
Simons, Simpson, Shop Keeper, 105 King St
Simons, William, Carpenter, 8 East King St
Cont'd
Simpson, George, Merchant, 26 Meeting St
Simpson, John, Ship Chandler, 72 Bay
Simpson, Lydia, Seamstress, 266 King St
Simpson, William, Planter, 1 Ellery St
Sims, William, Millwright, 13 W King St Cont'd
Sinclair, Alex & Co , Merchants, 2 Blake's Whf
Singleton, Mary, Mrs , Widow, 3 Trott St
Singleton, Sarah, N Boundary between King &
Meeting St Cont'd
Singleton, Tobitha, Seamstress, 19 Trott St

Sisk, Susannah, Mrs , Boarding House, 20 Pinckney
St
Skirmer, John, Cooper, 95 Queen St
Skirving, Charlotte, Mrs , Widow, 16 Church St
Cont'd
Skirving, William, Col , Planter, Ladson &
Skirving's Court, 13 Meeting St
Slade, Laben, Shipwright, 9 Pinckney St
Slade, Margarite, Boarding House, 11 Stoll's Al
Slann, Ann Catharine, Miss, Seamstress, W Pitt St ,
Harleston Green
Slowman, Henry, Tailor, 32 East Bay Cont'd
Smallwood, Richard, Deputy Weigher, Custom
House, 22 Pinckney St
Smart, John T , Boot & Shoe Maker, 30 & 136
Broad St
Smerdon, Elias, Marine Insurance & Ship Broker,
38 Bay
Smerdon, Henry, Auctioneer, Commission
Merchant, Vendue Row, 38 Bay
Smilie, Susannah, Mrs , Widow, 7 South Bay
Smisser, Hannah, Mrs , 48 Church St
Smith & Bacot, Attornies at Law, 26 Tradd St
Smith & Faust, Grocers, 201 King St
Smith & Montague St
Smith, Agnes, Mrs , Boarding House, 7 Broad St
Smith, Agnes, Mrs , Plantress, 10 Mazyck St
Smith, Ann, Miss, 8 King St
Smith, Benjamin Burgh, Editor & Proprietor of the
Courier, 6 Legare St
Smith, Christopher F , Kolfbaan Keeper, 132 King
St
Smith, Daniel, Assessor, City Tax Collector,
Exchange, 5 Society St
Smith, E D , Dr , Physician, 57 Meeting St.
Smith, Eliza, Store Keeper, 142 King St
Smith, George, Carpenter, 6 Guignard St
Smith, George Elias, Cabinet Maker, 135 Meeting
St
Smith, George, Merchant, 8 Anson St
Smith, George, Professor of Music
Smith, George S D , Book Keeper, City Gazette,
36 Tradd St
Smith, Henry, Shipwright, 6 Maiden Ln
Smith, James B , Rigger, 2 Cock Ln
Smith, James, Carpenter, 7 Beaufain St
Smith, Jane, Mrs , Widow, 21 Friend St
Smith, John (L L D.), Academy, 38 Broad St
Smith, John M , Boarding & Lodging, 13 Union St
Cont'd
Smith, John R , Planter, 8 Meeting St
Smith, Josiah, Cashier, National Bank, Res , 8
Anson St
Smith, M'Pherson, Planter, Drake St , Hampstead
Smith, Margaret, Shop Keeper, 187 King St
Smith, Marian, School, 69 Church St
Smith, Mary, J C , Mrs , Plantress, 57 King St
Smith, Mary, Mrs (Caleb), Widow, 71 Church St
Smith, Mary, Mrs , 187 King St

Smith, Mary Roger, Mrs, Widow, 3 Coming St
Smith, Naomi, Miss, 4 Coming St
Smith, O'Brien, Planter, 11 Church St
Smith, Peter, Capt, Lumber Merchant, South Bay, Res, 23 Mazyck St
Smith, Peter, Mariner, 20 Quince St
Smith, Peter, Planter, 2 South Bay
Smith, Peter, St Andrew's Parish, 288 King St
Smith, Puck, Miss & Miss, 74 Tradd St
Smith, Rebecca, Mrs, Widow, 73 Queen St
Smith, Roger Moore, Mrs, Widow, 5 West St
Smith, Samuel, Factor, 39 Broad St
Smith, Samuel, Grocer, 2 Champneys St
Smith, Samuel, Miniature Painter, 2 Champneys St
Smith, Sarah, Boarding House, 8 Union St
Smith, Sarah, Mrs, Widow, 22 Church St
Smith, Thomas B, Hampstead
Smith, Thomas, Capt, Merchant, 132 Broad St
Smith, Thomas, Jr, Planter, 2 W King St Road Opposite One Mile Stone
Smith, Thomas, Planter, Mazyckborough
Smith, Thomas Rhett, Planter, 56 Tradd St or Col Ewing's Court, 13 Meeting St
Smith, Thomas Y & M W, 21 Friend St
Smith, Whiteford, Grocer, 56 Church St
Smith, William, Capt, Mariner, 23 Bay Cont'd
Smith, William, Carpenter, 6 N Wall St
Smith, William, Ironmonger, 21 Elliott St
Smith, William L, Attorney at Law, 92 Tradd St
Smith, William S, Attorney at Law, 38 Broad St.
Smith, William, Shipwright, 3 Charles St
Smith William, Shipwright, Ham's Whf, Res, 11 Pinckney St.
Smith, William, Sr, Merchant, Fitzsimmon's Whf, Res, 42 Pinckney St
Smylie, Andrew, Merchant, 102 Church St cor Longitude Ln
Smyth, John & Co, Merchants, 5 E King St Road
Smyth, John, Planter, 33 Hasell St
Snelling, Ann, Pastry Cook, 8 Friend St
Snelling, Michael, Carpenter, 1 Liberty St
Snitter, Bristol, Rope Maker, Rope Ln
Snowden, Ann, Mrs, Widow, 2 Quince St
Sollee, John, Proprietor City Theatre, 26 Church St
Solomon, Alexander, Store, 188 King St
Solomon, Catharine, Widow, 279 King St
Solomon, Chapman, Shop Keeper, 185 King St
Solomon, Joseph, Shop Keeper, 195 King St
Solomon, Levy, Store Keeper, 63 East Bay
Somarsall, Thomas, Merchant, 10 East Bay
Somarsall, William, Merchant, 3 East Bay
Somers, Rosa, Mantua Maker, 54 Queen St
Soult, John Francis, Commissary of the Commercial Relations for the French Empire, 85 Meeting St.
Sparks, Thomas, Mrs, 39 Queen St
Sparrow, James, Butcher, 6 S E Cannon St
Spears, James, Carpenter, 3 Society St

Speissegger, John, Music & Instrument Maker, 4 Hasell St
Spencer, Frederick, Auction Rooms, 113 Queen St
Spencer, Joseph, Capt, Mariner, 16 Queen St
Spencer, Sebastian, Former Shoe Maker, 168 Meeting St
Spencer, William & George, Masons, 168 Meeting St
Spengler, Frederick, Merchant, Keith's Whf, Res, 8 E. King St Road
Spidle, Eliza, Widow, 4 Clifford St
Spidle, John G, House Builder, 24 Archdale St
Spierin, Patrick, 5 Trott St
Spierin, Thomas P
Spreth, Nicholas, Grocer, cor Lynch & New Bay St
Spring, John, Powder Inspector, 4 Blackbird Al
Stank, Christopher, Grocer, 4 W King St Cont'd
Stanyarne, Ann, Miss, Plantress, 216 Meeting St
Stanyarne, James, Planter, 18 South Bay
Stecker, Christopher, Butcher, 7 W Coming St
Stedman, T, Teller, State Bank
Steinmyer, George William, Baker, S Boundary Opposite Lowndes St
Stent, John H., Mason, 2 West St
Stent, John, Jr, Carpenter, 19 Mazyck St
Stent, Mary C, Mrs, Widow, 34 Church St
Stephen, Thomas, Commission Merchant, at the Times
Stephen, William, Factor, 16 N W Wall St
Stephen, William, Merchant, 15 East King St Cont'd
Stephens, Emanuel, Merchant
Stevens & Ramsay, Physicians, 44 East Bay
Stevens, Daniel, Coach Maker, 169 Meeting St.
Stevens, Daniel, Col, Supervisor, 30 George St
Stevens, Jervis H, City Sheriff, Exchange, Res, 68 Tradd St
Stevens, William, Dr, Physician, 44 Bay, Res, 19 King St
Stevenson, John, Mason, 40 King St
Stewart, Ann, M, Misses Boarding School, 12 Moore St, formerly 1 Cumberland St
Stewart, Charles, Attorney at Law, 1 Wentworth St
Stewart, Daniel, Painter & Glazier, 7 Clifford St
Stewart, Daniel, Painter & Glazier, 13 King St
Stewart, R, Planter, 14 Society St
Stewart, William, Academy, 44 Wentworth St
Stock, Margaret, Mrs, Plantress, 6 Legare St
Stocker, Henry, Boat Builder, Governor's Bridge, Res, 9 Charles
Stodder, Elijah, Capt, Mariner, 40 Church St Cont'd
Stoll, Justinus, Baker, 139 Meeting St.
Stone, Charles, Mrs, 24 King St
Stone, Isabella, Mrs, Widow, 2 W Coming St
Stone, William, Professor of Music
Stoney, John, Merchant, 3 Faber's S Range, Chisholm's Whf, Res, 66 Church St.

Stoops, Benjamin T, Boot & Shoe Maker, 2 Broad St

Story, ——, Mr, Comedian, 194 Meeting St

Story, ——, Mr, of the Charleston Theatre, 11 Magazine St

Stowe, Richard R, Capt, Mariner, 29 Hasell St

Strobel, Jacob, Butcher, Meeting St Market, Res, 104 King St

Stroble, Daniel, Sr, Tanner & Currier, 118 Meeting St

Stroble, John, Boot & Shoe Store, 63 King St, Res, S End Smith St cor.

Strohecker, J, Blacksmith, 154 Meeting St

Stromer, J H, Merchant, 19 Elliott St

Strother, Mary, Widow, 3 Blackbird Al

Stroub, George, Carpenter, 2 Blackbird Al

Stroub, Jacob, Carpenter, 2 Blackbird Al

Sturis & Lovell, Josiah, Merchants, 4 Crafts' S Whf, Res, 40 Church St

Suares, David, Mercantile, 21 Berresford St

Suares, Jacob, Rev, Synagogue

Suau, Peter, Merchant, 12 N W Middle St

Sullivan, Timothy, Auctioneer & Commission Merchant, N Vendue Row

Sully, Mathew, Comedian, 17 Friend St

Sutcliffe, Ely, Mrs, at Mrs Peigne

Sutherland, ——, Mr, Merchant, 187 Meeting St

Swain, Joseph, Pilot, 35 East Bay Cont'd

Swain, Rebecca, Mrs, Widow, 3 Stoll's Al

Swan, Robert, Carpenter, 133 Meeting St

Swaney, William, Cabinet Maker, 1 Magazine St

Sweeny, Bryan, Grocer, 40 East Bay Cont'd

Sweeny, James, Merchant, 83 King St

Sweet, ——, Mrs, Widow, 114 Queen St

Sweetzer, John R, Saddler, 218 King St

Swinton, Hugh, Planter, 74 Meeting St

Symonds, Hannah, Mrs., 2 Guignard St

Sysan, John, Butcher, 21 East King St Road

Taggart, Mary, Mrs, Widow, 17 Meeting St

Tait & Wilson, Merchants, Grocers, 23 Broad St

Talvande, Rose, Madame, 102 Tradd St

Tamerus, Christian, Cabinet Maker, 9 E King St Road

Tardy, Alexander, Tinplate Worker, 131 Queen St

Tarone, Anthony & Co, Print Sellers, Etc, 30 Broad St

Tate, James, Capt, Mariner, 114 Queen St

Tate, James, Mrs, Store Keeper, 114 Queen St

Tavel, Frederick, Merchant, 1 Keith's Whf, Res, 8 E. King St Road

Taylor, James, Capt, Mariner, 9 Water St

Taylor, Joseph, Capt, Mariner, 3 Charles St

Taylor, Maria, Miss, 33 King St

Taylor, Paul, Carpenter, 15 S Cannon St

Taylor, Sarah, Widow, 10 Quince St

Taylor, William, Boarding House, 23 Union St

Taylor, William, Planter, S E End Lynch St, Harleston

Teasdale, Isaac, Merchant, 118 Queen St

Teasdale, John, Merchant, 2 East Bay

Teddeman, ——, Mrs, Widow, 3 Front St

Teddeman, Philip, Dr, 22 Wentworth St

Terraf, Philip, Mariner, 53 Church St

Tew, Charles, Notary Public & Justice of the Peace, 123 King St

Thackam, Thomas, Mercantile, S Pinckney St, Cannonborough

Thayer, Ebenezer, Broker, 43 Elliott St, Res, 49 Tradd St

Theus, James, Planter, 11 Meeting St

Theus, Simeon, Cashier, State Bank, 239 King St

Thevenin, Peter, Refugee, St Domingo, 69 Meeting St

Thomas, E S, Bookseller & Stationer, 121 Broad St

Thomas, Francis, National Bank, Discount Clerk, 29 Archdale St

Thomas, John, Capt, Mariner, 41 East Bay Cont'd

Thomas, John D, Grocer, 22 Union St

Thomas, John, Grocer, 31 Union St

Thomas, John, Hair Dresser, 178 Meeting St

Thomas, John J, Merchant, East Middle St

Thomas, John R, Refugee, St Domingo, 6 Federal St

Thomas, John, Store Keeper, 37 Broad St

Thomas, Mary Lamboll, Mrs, Widow, 12 King St

Thomas, Stephen, Merchant, 7 E King St Cont'd

Thomas, Stephen, Merchant Tailor, 28 Elliott St

Thompson, Aaron, Factor, 11 Crafts' N Whf, Res, 3 Quince St

Thompson, Alexander, Mason, 21 Trott St

Thompson, Daniel, Shop Keeper, 13 South Bay

Thompson, Eliza, Mrs, 21 Friend St

Thompson, Henry, Painter, 24 Bay Cont'd

Thompson, James D, Tailor, First Lieutenant, Guard, 20 Tradd St.

Thompson, John, Shipmaster, 41 East Bay Cont'd

Thompson, Lesley, Tailor, 85 Church St

Thompson, Margaret, Shop Keeper, 21 Beaufain St

Thompson, William, Windsor Chair Maker

Thomson, James, Boarding Officer, Custom House, Planter's Hotel, 46 Meeting St

Thorne, John Gardner, Sail Maker, Beale's Whf, Res, 6 Bedon's Al

Threadcraft, Bethel & Co, Watch & Clock Makers, Res, 58 King St

Thwing, David, Ship Joiner, Governor's Bridge, 29 Pinckney St

Thwing, Edward, House Builder, 73 Meeting St

Thynnes, William, Commission Merchant, 110 East Bay

Time, Joseph, Monsieur, Confectioner, 80 Meeting St

Timmons, William, Merchant, 119 Broad St, Res, 6 N Pitt St, Gadsden's Green

Timothy, Benjamin F, Late Editor, State Gazette, 33 George St.

Timothy, Factor, Crafts' East Whf

Tobias, Judith, Widow, 202 King St.
Tofel, Catharine, Mrs , Dry Goods Store, 20 Church St
Tofel, John, Confectioner, 20 Church St
Tomalty, Henry, Carpenter, 26 Trott St
Tomkins, Margaret, Mrs , Boarding House, 20 Queen St
Tomlins, James, Music Master, Mazyckborough
Tongue, Susannah, Mrs , Widow, 44 Church St Cont'd
Toomer, Ann, Mrs., 7 Legare St
Torrance, James, Grocer
Torrans, ——, Miss, 32 Queen St
Torres, Abraham, Shop Keeper, 84 King St
Torrey, William, Capt , Mariner, 1 S End New St
Torry & Co , Opticians
Tourette, Thomas, French Boarding House, 65 Meeting St
Toussiger, Margaret, Widow, 4 Water St
Tovey, Henry, Mast, Pump & Block Maker, 1 Bay, Res , 38 Hasell St
Trajetta, Philip, Music Master, 4 Cumberland St
Trapier, ——, Mr., Planter, S Alexander St , Mazyckborough
Trenholm, William, Grocer & Grain Merchant, 1 N Prioleau's Market Whf
Trescot, Edward, Planter, 108 Broad St
Treuil, Louisa, Madame, Refugee, St Domingo, 10 W Middle St
Trezevant, Lewis, Associate Judge, Court of Sessions and Common Pleas, 273 King St
Trezevant, Peter, Discount Clerk, State Bank, 98 Queen St
Triggay, William, Printer, 14 N W Middle St Trott St
Trouche, Adel, Madame, Refugee, St Domingo, 10 Liberty St
Troup, Eliza, Mrs , Boarding School, 91 Queen St
Truchelut, Joseph, Merchant & Baker, 128 Queen St
Truelle, James, Tailor, 38 Union St Cont'd
Tucker, Mary, Mrs & Mrs C Stone, 24 King St
Tucker, Sarah, Mrs , 108 Church St
Tunno & Cox, Merchants, 27 East Bay
Tunno & Price, Merchants, 6 Geyer's N Whf
Tunno, Adam, Firm
Tunno, William, Planter, 81 East Bay
Turnbull, Gavin, Charleston Theatre, 21 Mazyck St
Turnbull, James, Lumber Merchant, South Bay
Turnbull, Robert J , Attorney at Law, 4 St Michael's Al , Res , N Broad St
Turner, Dan W , City Deputy Sheriff, 1 Clifford's Al
Turner, Francis, Mariner, 40 Pinckney St
Turner, Thomas, Boarding House, 18 Union St
Turner, Thomas, Capt , Dancing Master, 7 Parsonage Ln
Turner, William, Broker, 8 Charles St
Turner, William, Merchant, 4 W King St Cont'd.

Turpin, William, Esq , Planter, 149 King St
Ulmo, A , Dr , Apothecary & Druggist, 176 Meeting St
Ummensetter, John, Tanner & Courier, cor Pitt & Beaufain, Res , 2 Archdale St
Underwood, John, Grocer, 16 Ellery St
Underwood, William, Boarding House, 2 Unity Al
Vaillant, Clement, 14 Queen St , Monsieur Salon
Valance, Moses & Son, Traders, 42 Tradd St
Valburne, Leonard, Tobacconist, see Cuigno, Union St
Vale, J D , Planter, 9 N W Cannon St
Valentine, Antionette, 32 King St
Valentine, Mary, Boarding House, 35 Union St
Valk, Jacob, R , Merchant, Crafts' N Whf
Vanderbusche, ——, Tobacconist, 161 King St
Vanderchen, Andrew, Tailor, Lieutenant, Guard, 210 King St
Vanderhoff, Cornelius, Shoe & Boot Maker, 130 King St
Vanderhorst & Taylor, Factors, Vanderhorst's Whf
Vanderhorst, Arnoldus, Gen., Planter, 16 East Bay
Vanderhorst, John S , Merchant, 15 East Bay
VanNorden, Abraham, Tailor, 24 St Philip's St
VanRhyn, A E , Miss, Merchant, 134 Broad St
Vardel, Robert, Carter, Drake St , Hampstead
Vaughn, Jeffe, Custom House Inspector, 12 E King St Cont'd
Vernon & Co , Jewellers & Goldsmiths, 140 Broad St
Verree & Blair, Auctioneers & Commission Merchants, N Vendue Row
Verree, Joseph, Vendue Master, 3 Church St
Verree, Mary, Mrs , Widow, 3 Church St
Verree, Rebecca, Mrs , Widow, Distillery, Mazyckborough
Vesey, Charles M , Book Keeper, Fitzsimmon's Whf., 5 Parsonage Ln
Vesey, John, Mercantile, W King St Road
Vesey, Joseph, Capt , Academy, 13 N W Middle St
Vieyra, Joseph, Grain Inspector, 55 King St
Vigie, Anthony, Tobacconist, Late Planter, St Domingo, 20 Archdale St
Vignier, Arnoldus, Merchant, 128 Meeting St
Villaneuve, John B & Co , Merchant, 99 East Bay
Villepigue, Lise, Madame, Widow, 40 Trott St
Vincent, Eliza, Mrs , Boarding House, 5 Tradd St
Vinro, Sarah, Widow, 26 Union St Cont'd
Virgent, Elizabeth, Mrs., Widow, Hampstead
Vitau, James, Refugee, St Domingo, 15 N W Wall St
VonHagen, George, Grocer, cor Boundary & Scarborough St
Waggner, Mary, Widow, 6 Trott St
Wagner, George, Planter, 101 Broad St
Wainwright & Bee, Factors, Prioleau's S Whf
Wainwright, Ann, Mrs , Widow, 265 King St
Walker & Evans, Marble Cutters, 24 Trott St

54

Walker, Caleb, Carpenter, 14 Magazine St
Walker, Margaret, Nurse, 20 Trott St
Walker, Robert, Cabinet Maker, 39 Church St
Walker, Robert, House Carpenter, 11 W Middle St
Walker, William, Cabinet Maker, 12 Archdale St
Wall, Richard, Boarding House, 27 Union St,
Wallace, Alexander, Grocery Store, 2 Queen St
Wallace, James, District Deputy Sheriff, cor
  Boundary & Lowndes St
Wallace, Thomas, Cabinet Maker, 25 Queen St
Waller, Bayfield, Firm Bailey & Waller, 13
  Magazine St
Walsh, Edmond, Grocery Stores, 2 Amen St &
  Union St, Res, 18 Friend St
Walton, William & Co, S. W cor King St Cont'd
  & Boundary St
Ward, Daniel, Master, Work House
Ward, James M, Attorney at Law, 18 Queen St
Ward, John, Attorney at Law, 47 Church St
Ward, Sarah, Mrs, Widow, 210 Meeting St
Wardenburg, Peter, Grocer, 183 Meeting St
Waring, Daniel, Attorney at Law, 13 Scarborough
  St
Waring, Mary, Mrs (John), Widow, 32 Wentworth
  St
Waring, Morton & Co, Factors, 152 East Bay,
  Res, 55 Broad St
Waring, Thomas, Planter, Mazyckborough
Waring, Thomas, Sr, Naval Officer, 38 Meeting St
Warley, ——, Mrs, Widow, 6 Beaufain St
Warley, Christina & Daughters, Mrs, 26 Beaufain
  St
Warley, Felix, State Treasurer, State House, Res,
  8 Trott St
Warner, Penelope, Widow, 202 Meeting St
Warnock, Joseph, Boarding House & Stables, 15
  Queen St
Warnock, Joseph, Jr, Carpenter, 77 Meeting St
Warren, Samuel, Col, Planter, St James Santee,
  Planter's Hotel or Isaac M Dart, factor
Washbourn, Eleazar, Capt, Merchant, 54 King St
Washington, William, Gen, Planter, Port St cor
  Meeting & Church St Cont'd
Watson, Alexander, Factor, 15 East Bay Cont'd
Watson, John, Cabinet Maker & Upholsterer, 26
  King St
Watson, Lydia, Widow, 5 Friend St
Watt, James, Grocer, 29 Church St Cont'd
Watts, Robert, Grocer, 52 Queen St
Weathers, Thomas, Shipwright, 5 Cock Ln
Weatherston, William, Tailor, 31 Broad St
Webb, Benjamin, Planter, 27 St Philip's St
Webb, John, Esq, 1 Moore St
Webb, William, Teller, State Bank, 1 Moore St
Weir, Francis & Co, Merchants, 1 Geyer's N Whf
Weissinger, John, Baker, 25 E King St Road
Welch, George, Cabinet Maker, 21 Pinckney St
Welch, George, Tobacco Picker, 1 W Lowndes St
Welch, John, Cabinet Maker, 150 Meeting St

Welch, Mary, Widow, 165 Meeting St
Welch, Thomas G, Carver & Guilder, 26 Pinckney
  St.
Wells, Francis, Mrs, Widow, 23 Elliott St
Wells, Rachel, 21 Beaufain St
Wells, Richard, Boat Builder, 24 Bay Cont'd
Wells, Samuel B, Sullivan's Auction Store, 26
  Hasell St
Wells, Samuel, Capt, Mariner, 26 Hasell St
Welsh, Edward, Wharfinger, Fitzsimmon's Whf
West, James, Dr, Physician
West, Thomas, Capt, Mariner, 6 East Bay Cont'd
Westerburg, John, Shipwright, 8 S Cock Ln
Westermeyer, Andrew, Merchant, Goldsmith &
  Jeweller, 19 Union St
Western, Thomas, Merchant, 10 Beaufain St
Weston & Mazyck, (Isaac M), Merchants, 10 Broad
  St
Weston, Plowden, Planter, 31 Queen St
Weyman, Edward, Surveyor, Custom House, Res,
  N Cannon St, Islington
Whaley, Mary, Mrs, Planterss, 293 King St
Whalley, George, Merchant, 122 Tradd St
Whalley, Thomas, Grocer & Boarding House, 38
  Bay Cont'd
Wharry, David, Grocer, 289 King St
Wheeler & Christie, Commission Merchants, 7
  Crafts' N Whf
Wheeton, Thomas, Grocer, 7 Berresford Al
White, Frances, Mrs, Mantua Maker, 103 King St
White, George R, Factor, Prioleau's S Whf E
  End, Res., 27 Bay Cont'd cor Centurion St
White J B, Student at Law, Hampstead
White, James, Grocer, 129 Queen St.
White, John, Factor, 4 Geyer's N. Whf, Res, 124
  Meeting St
White, Sarah, Seamstress, 13 South Bay
Whiting, John, Turner in General, 156 Meeting St
Whitley, Thomas, Grocer, 17 Amen St
Whitlock, Charles C, Comedian cor Mill & Huston
  St over Cannon's Bridge
Whitney, Thomas H, Carver & Frame Maker, 39
  Church St
Whittimore, Retire, Mrs, Widow, 151 Meeting St
Wigfall, Thomas, Planter, 46 George St
Wightman, John T, Painter & Glazier, Berresford
  Al
Wightman, William, Goldsmith & Jewellery Store,
  185 Meeting St.
Wightman, William, Teacher of Mathematics, 31
  Church St
Wilcox, James, Grocer, 14 N Bull St
Wilcox, Jeremiah, Painter & Glazier, 6 Montague
  St.
Wilhemi, J, Boarding House, 21 East Bay cor
  Tradd St
Wilkenson, Mary, Boarding House, 26 Union St
Wilkie, William, Col, 29th Regiment, 9th Brigade,
  15 Magazine St

Wilkins, William, Constable
Wilkinson, Abner, Commission Merchant, 30 Queen St
Wilkinson, Susan, Mrs , 3 S E Cannon St
Williams, Charles, Boatman, Moser's Lot, 109 Meeting St
Williams, David R , Planter, A M late Firm Freneau & W
Williams, Isham, Whf Owner, William's Whf
Williams, John, District Deputy Sheriff, Fort Mechanic
Williams, John, Grocer, 1 & 24 Berresford's Al
Williamson, Abraham, Soap Boiler, 9 S E Cannon St.
Williamson, Abraham, Tallow Chandler, 4 N Champneys St
Williamson, Hannah, Seamstress, 6 Lodge Al
Williamson, John, Merchant, 3 Faber's Range, Chisolm's Whf
Williman, ----, Mrs (Dr J), Widow, 211 King St
Williman, Christopher, Planter, 211 King St
Williman, George, Chair Maker, 64 ¾ Tradd St
Williman, George, Planter, 9 N W Boundary St
Williman, Jacob, Tanner & Currier, 1 S E Montague St
Willis, Henry, Baker, 23 East Bay Cont'd
Wilson, A , Planter, 8 Federal St
Wilson, James, Butcher, 82 Queen St
Wilson, Jehu, Student At Law, 9 Society St
Wilson, John, Cabinet Maker, 126 Meeting St
Wilson, John, Mariner, 5 Lodge Al
Wilson, John, Soap Boiler, 88 Meeting St
Wilson, Robert & Son, Physicians, 88 Church St
Wilson, Robert, Capt , Mariner, 2 Hasell St
Wilson, Robert, Dr , Physician, 87 Broad St
Wilson, Robert Jr , Dr Physician, 36 Meeting St
Wilson, Samuel, Dr , Physician, 43 Broad St
Wilson, Thomas, Planter, 5 S Minority St
Winchester, Jonathan, Carpenter, 2 S E Cannon St
Windsor, Thomas, Capt , Mariner, No Name Al.
Wing, Freeman, Capt , Mariner, 14 Guinard St.
Winkens, Ann M , Grocery Store, 11 Mazyck St
Winkins, John H , Grocer & Boarding House, 36 Union St
Winn, Joseph, Eating House & Tavern, Lodge Al
Winn, Joseph, Merchant, 9 Beaufain St
Winstanley, Thomas, Late Intendant, Attorney at Law, East Bay St
Winthrop, Joseph, His Swedish & Danish Majesties Consul
Winthrop, Joseph, Merchant 147 Bay, Res , 57 Tradd St
Wish & Bryan, Merchants, 148 Broad St
Wiss, Peter, Merchant Tailor, 2 King St.
Wissman & Lorent, Merchants, 135 Bay, Res , 52 Tradd St
Witte, M J , Merchant, 120 Tradd St

Wittich, C & F., Goldsmith & Jewellers, 25 Broad St
Witticker, Richard, Boarding House, 4 Chalmer's Al
Woddrop, John, Merchant, 9 East Bay
Wolf, Frederick, Mrs , Widow, 78 Mazyck St
Wolf, Rachael, Mrs , Widow, 259 King St
Wolfe, John, Grocer, 182 King St
Wood, James, Cotton Cleaner, 2 Pitt St , Harleston's Green
Wood, Patrick, Mrs , Widow, 80 Meeting St
Wood, William, Custom House Inspector, 15 Archdale St
Woodill, Susannah, Boarding House, 4 Price's Al
Woodman & Smith, Store Keepers, 76 King St
Woodmancy, John, Boarding House, 13 W King St Road
Woodworth, Darius, Capt , Mariner, 35 East Bay Cont'd
Worthington, Joseph, Upholsterer, 5 W King St Cont'd
Wrad, James, School Master, 104 Church St
Wragg, Charlotte, Miss, Plantress, 82 East Bay
Wragg, Quash, Wheelwright, 8 W Middle St
Wragg, Samuel, Planter, 5 Front St
Wrainch, John, School Master, 154 Meeting St
Wrainch, Richard, Scavenger & Carolina Coffee House Keeper, 115 Tradd St
Wright, Elizabeth, Miss, Plantress, 9 Orange St
Wurdemann, J G , Grocery Store, 9 Queen St
Wyatt, Delia, 25 Pinckney St
Wyatt, Lemuel, State Constable, 4 Chalmer's Al
Wyatt, Peter, Lumber Merchant, at his Mills, S W End of Lynch St , Ashley River
Wylie, William, Gunsmith, 73 Church St
Ximeno, Francis, Capt , Mariner, at Mrs John S Adams, 98 Bay
Yates, D , Mrs , Boarding School, 2 Port St
Yates, Jeremiah, Merchant, Port St
Yates, Joseph, Cooper Beale's Whf , Res , 11 Church St Cont'd
Yates, Seth, Shipwright, Lynch's Ln
Yaymin, Elizabeth, Pinckney St , over Cannon's Bridge
Yeadon, Richard, Teller, National Bank, 272 King St
Yeadon, William, Attorney at Law, 18 King St
Yeer, Jacob, Shoe Maker, 92 Queen St
Yong, Sarah, Mrs , 4 E New St
You, Elizabeth, Mrs , Widow, 31 Archdale St
Young, Joseph, Grocer, 152 Meeting St
Young, Mary, Mrs , Widow, 21 Friend St
Young, William, Merchant, 6 Champneys St
Zealey, Joseph, Butcher, 263 King St
Zeylstra, Peter, Merchant Ship Chandler, 64 Bay
Zilia, Laurence, Seamstress, 8 Ellery St.
Zill, William, Baker, 29 Union St Cont'd

Chapter 3

THE 1807 DIRECTORY

Like the 1806 directory, the one for 1807 was compiled by J J Negrin using the title of *Negrin's Directory for the Year 1807: Containing Every Article of General Utility* (Charleston: J J Negrin, 1807, 197 pages) This volume is better organized that the previous one with the lists of officers, etc in the front of the book The listing of individuals does not begin until page 101 A one page supplement can be found at the end The persons listed there have been included in the following alphabetized list Entries for 3,083 can be found here

———

Abbott, William, Merchant, Chisolm's Whf, Res , 1 Centurian St
Abelard, Anthony, Shop Keeper, 5 Middle St
Abendanone, Joseph, 224 King St
Abrahams, Isaac, Vendue Master, 4 Bedon's Al
Abrahams, Moise, 224 King, 24 Hasell St
Ackis, John E , Shoe Maker, 17 Union St
Adams & Lawrance, Factors, 5 Chisolm's N Whf
Adams, David, Merchant, 37 Hasell St
Adams, E M , House Carpenter, 21 Pinckney St
Adams, John S , Merchant, 98 East Bay
Adickes, E J , Chester County
Aertsen, Hester, Widow, 66 Church St
Aiken, William, Merchant, 3 East King St Road
Air, George, Carpenter, 10 Archdale St
Air, James A , Dr , 72 Tradd St
Aitchson, William, Merchant, 145 East Bay
Akeen, C , Widow, 31 Pinckney St
Akin, Ann, Mrs , Misses Boarding School, 117 King St
Akin, Thomas, Dr , 117 King St
Aldrich, Robert, at Thomas's Book Store, 121 Broad St
Alexander, Abraham, Store, 131 King St
Alexander, David, Merchant, 10 Broad St
Alexander, Joseph, Grocer 16 Church St , Res , 19 Tradd
Alfred, ——, Mrs , Widow, 47 East King St Road
Aiken, Martyn, Notary Public & Justice of Peace, 27 Archdale St
Allan, John, Capt , 109 King St
Allan, Mason & Ewing, Merchants, 113 Tradd St
Allan, Thomas, Planter, 7 Charles St
Allan, William, Factor, 10 Blake's Whf

Allan, William, Merchant, 12 Broad St , Res , 5 Federal St
Allen, John, Carpenter, 160 King St
Alline, Dominique, Hair Dresser, 40 Meeting St
Allison, William, Boat Builder, 3 Hard Al
Allport, John, Smith & Farrier, 113 King St
Alston, J W , Planter, 3 Front St
Alstyne, Mathew W , Grocer, 20 Elliott St
Ampau, E , Baker, 6 W King St Road
Ancklem, Clarender, Midwife, 53 Church St
Ancrum, James, Planter, 30 Hasell St
Ancrum, William, Planter, 22 Ellery St
Anderson, ——, Mrs , Shop Keeper, 38 Church St Cont'd
Anderson, Ann, Mrs , cor Middle & Minority St
Anderson, George, Capt , Spring St
Anderson, Hannah & Son, Merchants, 18 Tradd St
Anderson, John, House Carpenter, W King St Cont'd
Anderson, Rebecca, Mrs Widow, Spring St
Anderson, William, Stay Maker, 204 Meeting St
Annely, G W , Merchant, 1 S W Middle St
Anthony, John, Harness Maker, 192 Meeting St
Antonio, Manoel, Merchant, Columbia
Arle, Mary, Boarding House, 7 Union St
Armstrong, Hester, Seamstress, 44 Tradd St
Arthur, George, Carter, 43 George St
Artman, Peter, Coach Maker, 21 Archdale St
Ash, Elizabeth, Mrs , Widow, 5 Lamboll St
Ash, Hannah, Mrs , 19 King St
Ash, John, Planter, 17 South Bay
Ash, Samuel E & Co , Coach & Harness Maker, 149 Meeting St
Askew, Ann, Widow, 24 Archdale St
Assalit, Joseph, French Tutor, 163 Meeting St
Atkins, William, Victualler, Columbia St
Atmar, Ralph, Out Door Clerk, State Bank, 28 Church St Cont'd
Austin, Catharine, Shop Keeper, 47 East Bay
Austin, William, Broker, 91 Meeting St & 42 Church St
Axon, Jacob, Bill Book Keeper, S C Bank, Res , 61 Meeting St
Aydelot, Joshua, Mercantile, Chalmers Al
Ayrault, Peter, Merchant, 118 East Bay
Azevedo, R D , Dry Goods Store, 76 King St
Bacot, Henry, Attorney at Law, 16 Tradd St
Bacot, Thomas W , Postmaster & Cashier S C Bank, 99 Tradd St
Badger, James, Corn Store, 134 Meeting St
Bagshaw, Robert, Planter, W Pinckney St , Cannonborough
Bailey & Waller, Merchants, 121 Broad St
Bailey, George, Attorney at Law, State House Square
Bailey, George G , Commission Store, 187 Meeting St.
Bailey, H B , Boarding House, 187 Meeting St
Bailey, Henry, Attorney at Law, State House Square

Bailly, Anthony, Shoe Maker, 5 Unity Al
Baker, —, Mrs, 4 N. Wentworth St Cont'd
Baker, Francis, Mason, 38 King St
Baker, J J, Grocer, 20 East Bay
Baker, Samuel, Planter, 5 St Philip's St
Baker, Thomas, Mason, 38 King St
Balke, J, Capt, Whf. Owner, President, State Bank, Res., 5 South Bay
Ball, Archibald, Planter, 5 S E Cannon St
Ball, Bryant, Planter, 90 East Bay
Ball, Elizabeth, Widow, 5 Church St
Ball, James, Merchant, 34 Church St
Ball, John, Jr, Planter, 12 Hasell St
Ball, John, Planter, 31 Hasell St
Ball, Thomas, Mrs, 9 Church St Cont'd
Ballon, Andrew, Grocer, 54 Meeting St
Bampfield, George, Mrs, Widow, N Charlotte St
Bampfield, Peter, 19 Magazine St
Bampfield, Thomas J & Henry, Planters, 19 Magazine St
Banhoste W J, Book Keeper, Accountant, 16 Archdale St
Banks, Charles, Merchant, 110 Tradd St
Baptiste, Jean, Goldsmith, 11 Queen St
Barden, Kinsey & Thomas, Factors, 10 Crafts, Res, 51 Tradd St
Bargoyne, William, Dr, Apothecary & Druggist, 147 Broad
Barker Joseph S, Merchant, 94 East Bay, Res, 1 Anson St
Barkman, —, Mr, 28 Church St
Barksdale, Thomas, Jr, Planter, 90 Tradd St.
Barnett, Sam, Planter, 11 Wall St
Baron & Wilson, Physicians, 218 Meeting St
Baron, Alexander, Dr, 53 Broad St
Baron, John, Wine Merchant, 11 East Bay
Barquet, John, Umbrella Maker, 41 Meeting & 39 Queen St
Barrelli, Torre & Co, Print Seller & Mathematical Instrument Maker, 32 Broad St
Barreyre, Peter, Baker, 9 Berresford St
Barsh, David & Henry, Planters, Amelia Township, Lewisburgh County
Barville de Langlois, Refugee, St. Domingo, 25 Society St
Barville, Mitchell, Cabinet Maker, 25 Society St
Basden, Laurence, Ship Weight, 14 Pinckney St
Bass & Fordham, Mast, Block & Pump Makers, cor Gillion St & and East Bay
Bass, Thomas, Mast, Block & Pump Maker, 84 East Bay
Bateman, —, Mrs, Widow, 12 Friend St
Bateman, Edward, Hair Dresser, 28 Quince St
Bateman, Isaac, Pump Maker, Boundary St, W. King St
Bates, William, Comedian, Savage St
Bathell, Benjamin, Mill Wright, 1 Trott St.
Baunay, Peter J, Baker, 107 Queen St
Beach, Mary, Mrs, Widow, 22 King St

Beale, John E, Whf Owner, 32 Bay
Bean, James, Mariner, Lodge Al.
Beard F, Teller, S C Bank, Blackbird Al
Beard, W, Mrs, Widow, 104 Broad St
Beard, W, Porter, S C Bank, 34 Church St
Beath, David, Merchant, 19 East Bay
Beattie, Edward, Merchant, 46 East Bay
Beatty, Robert, Merchant, 28 Broad St
Beauchee, Francis, Black & Gun Smith, 5 Queen St
Bedrew, Joseph, Accountant, 32 Pinckney St
Bee, —, Mrs, Widow, 5 Cumberland St
Bee, John S, Factor, Crafts' Whf, Res, Tradd St
Bee, Peter Smith, Planter, 22 Church St
Bee, Thomas, Jr
Bee, Thomas, Judge, Admiralty Court of S C, 4 Short St
Bee, William, Planter, 14 Church St Cont'd
Beedil, Francis, Cigar Manufacturer, Limehouse Court
Beekman A, Painter & Glazier, 69 Meeting St
Beekman, Eliza, Widow, 17 East Bay Cont'd
Beekman, J F, Grocer, cor Magazine & Beaufain St.
Beekman, Sam, Pump Maker, 129 East Bay, Res, 28 Hasell St
Beggs & Coan, S W cor King St Road & Vanderhorst St
Beggs, John, Painter & Glazier, 87 King St
Bell, David, Book Keeper, 7 Society St
Bell, Rose, 52 Queen St
Bellard, Fillete, Grocer, 3 Middle St
Belleanton, Amelia, 9 Quince St
Bellinger, George, Dr, Planter, 24 Mazyck St
Bellinger, Mary, Widow of Edmund, Plantress, Res, W Pinckney St, Cannonborough
Bellisle, Peter, Baker & Grocer, 5 Maiden Ln
Belser, Christian, Victualler, E King St Road
Belser, Jacob, Butcher, E Read St
Belsher, R, Merchant, 7 East King St Road
Belthall, D, Capt, Mariner, 8 Wall St
Benden, David, Store, 242 King St.
Benden, Henry, 203 King St
Bennet, John, Grocer, 3 Union St
Bennett, H, Custom House Store Keeper, 22 King St
Bennett, John, Merchant, 11 Meeting St Store, East Bay
Bennett, Thomas, Jr, Lumber Merchant, at his Mills, Bull St
Benoist, C, Chair Maker, 3 Meeting St Cont'd
Benoist, J B, Baker, 138 Meeting St
Benoist, John, Capt, Mariner, 4 Maiden Ln
Benoit, Therese, see Hanotau
Benson, Laurence, Grocer, 233 King St
Bentham, J, Notary Public and Q U., 39 East Bay
Bering, Ann, Mrs, Dry Goods Store, 192 King St
Bering, John, Jeweller, 192 King St
Berkheim, Myer, Capt, Mariner, 4 Berresford

Bernard, Rene, Perfumer, 4 Tradd St
Berney, John, Insurance Broker, 28 King St
Bernstine, Henry, Grocer, N W cor Boundary & Coming St
Berranger, J D B, Grocer, 98 East Bay
Berry, ——, Mrs, Milliner, 49 Broad St
Berry, Hesley, Tailor, 19 Trott St
Berry, Sam, Grocer, 33 Queen St
Besden, Laurence, Shipwright, 14 Pinckney St
Besseleu, Charles, Carpenter, 29 Beaufain St
Besseleu, Elizabeth, Mrs, Nurse, 29 Beaufain St
Besseleu, Lewis, Cabinet Maker, 29 Beaufain St.
Besseleu, Mark Anthony, 29 Beaufain St
Beswicke, J, Wharfinger, Prioleau's, 3 Society St
Beswicke, S, Mrs, School Mistress, 3 Society St
Bethune, A, Merchant, 11 Broad St, Res, Pinckney St, Cannonborough
Beven, F, House Carpenter, 16 Union St Cont'd
Bianchi, Gaetano, Grocer, 10 Queen St
Bicaisse, Clodius, Cabinet Maker, 135 Meeting St
Bieller, Joseph, Butcher, 23 Archdale St
Bigelow, Elizabeth, Widow, 2 Meeting St
Billings, S, Livery Stables, 214 King St
Billings, Samuel, Livery Stables and Res, 67 & 68 Tradd St
Billings, Thomas, Boarding House, 11 Union St Cont'd
Bingley, N, Capt, Mariner, Hard Al
Bird, Barnaby, Custom House Boatman, Holmes Lot, Church St Cont'd
Bishop, Jane, Mrs, 77 Queen St
Bixby, Nathaniel, Merchant, 8 Crafts' Whf, Res, 35 King St
Bize, Daniel, Carpenter, Meeting St Road 2d above the Inspection
Bizeuil, Julian, Grocer, 80 Church St
Black & Birnie, Iron Mongers, 11 Broad St
Black & Yates, Coopers, Beale's & Crafts' N Whf
Black, James, Shipwright, 92 East Bay
Black, Johanna, Widow, 9 Guignard St
Blacklock, William, Merchant, 134 East Bay
Blackwood, Thomas, 19 East Bay, Res., 37 Tradd St
Bladen, Mary Ann, Mrs, Widow, 23 Guignard St
Blaikie, Elizabeth, Widow, 4 Church St
Blair, James, Vendue Master, Commission Merchant, 2 Stoll's Al
Blair, William, Shipwright, 2 Clifford St
Blake, Peter, Assistant Work House
Blake, W Ward, Grocer, 121 Queen St
Blakeley, Robert, Merchant, 4 E King St Cont'd
Blakely, Seth, Tailor, 2 Elliott St
Blamyer, W., Accomptant, 31 Society St
Blancken, George, Grocer, cor Lynch's Ln & Bay
Bland, Richard, Boarding House, 5 Union St
Blanken, George, Grocer, cor New Bay St & Lynch's Ln.
Blewer, Catharine, Widow, 48 E King St. Road

Blewer, Peter, Grocer & Wagon Yard, 60 E King St. Road
Blochay, Alexander, Capt, 49 Church St
Blome & Baumay, Bakers, 107 Queen St.
Blome, John, Surgeon, 107 Queen St
Bloomstock, M, Grocer, cor St Philip's & Liberty
Blue, Daniel, Jeffersontown, Georgia
Blume, Andrew, Butcher, 22 Hasell St
Boisgerard, C & F, Merchants, Crafts' N Whf, Res, 196 King St
Bollough, E, Shoe Maker, 88 Queen St
Bolton, Richard, Shop Keeper, 7 Laurens St
Bomkamper, Frederick, Grocer, 8 W Wall St
Bones & Adger, Store, 160 King St
Bonnald, ——, Capt, 10 Meeting St
Bonneau, E S, Mrs, Widow, 45 George St
Bonneau, John, 59 Broad St
Bonnell, ——, Capt, Lynch's Ln
Bonsall, Elizabeth, Mrs, 5 Wentworth St
Bonthron, John, Grocer, 90 Queen St
Booner, Christian, Grocer & Wagon Yard, 40 East King St Road
Boquet, Elizabeth, Mrs, Widow, 15 St Philip's St
Borch, Peter, Fruit Shop, 87 Queen St.
Bouchanneau, Isaac, Carpenter, Wolfe St
Bouchanneau, Sarah, Widow, Drake St, Hampstead
Bounetheau, Elizabeth, Mrs, 69 Church St
Bounetheau, G M. (J.P), Clerk of Council, Printer, 3 Broad St
Bourg, P, French Teacher, E Wall St
Bours, Luke, Merchant, 25 Elliott St
Boutan, Peter Bernard, Merchant, Citizen, U S, 104 E Bay
Bowen, Nathaniel, Rev, 7 Lamboll St
Bowhay, Joseph, Butcher Stall 23, Res, 18 E King St Road
Bowie, Joseph, Butcher, W St Philip's St Cont'd
Bowles, T, Maj, Planter, cor Drake & Nassau St, Hampstead
Bowman, Ann, Widow, 147 Meeting St
Bowman, John, Esq, N W End Montague St
Boyd, Benjamin, Merchant, 134 King St
Boyd, William, Merchant, 2 Chisolm's N Whf, Res, 103 Church St
Boyer, Jacob, Shop Keeper, 18 King St. Road
Boyle, James, Grocer, 10 Union St
Bozman, Hardy, Overseer, 12 Lamboll St
Bozman, Ralph, Mariner, 3 Smith's Ln
Braddock, Christian, Butcher, Cannon St
Bradford, Christiana, Mrs, Music Store, 136 Broad St
Bradley, Charles, Printer, 3 West St
Bradley, Moses, Butcher, 1 Bull St
Brady, Mathew, Merchant, 63 E King St Road
Bragdon, Daniel, Capt, 16 Scarborough St
Brailsford, John, Jr, Planter, 5 East Bay
Brailsford, Mary, Widow, 22 Tradd St
Brailsford, Robert, Planter, 4 West St

59

Brailsford, William, Planter, 18 Beaufain St
Brainerd, Elijah, Shoe Store, 102 King St
Brandon, David, Confectioner, cor. Meeting St
  Cont'd & Boundary
Branford, Mary, Mrs, Widow & Plantress, 17
  Legare
Brebner, Archibald, Gentleman, King St Road near
  the Forks
Bremar, Francis, Esq, 2 miles W King St Road
Brenan, Martin, Grocer, South Bay
Brenan, Mathew & Richard, Merchants, 146 Broad
  St.
Bride, E, Mrs, Umbrella Maker, 186 Meeting St
Bride, Eleanora, Boarding School, 25 Meeting St
Bright, Sam, Shoe Store, 32 Pinckney St
Brisbane, William, Planter, 19 Legare St
Brissat, F A, Baker, 2 Trott St
Broadfoot, James & Co, Merchants, 151 Bay, Res,
  7 Cumberland St
Broadfoot, William, Merchant, 26 Wentworth St
Broan, Mary, Mrs., 12 E Bay Cont'd
Brochard, C, Mrs, 2 Maiden Ln
Brockway, Samuel, House Carpenter, 84 King St
Brodie, Alexander, Col, Academy, 104 Broad St
Brodie, Rob, House Carpenter & Lumber Measurer,
  56 Tradd St
Broneaud, Daniel, Mason, 11 Maiden Ln
Brooks & Potter, Merchants, 6 Crafts' S Whf
Broskei, Sarah, Mrs, Boarding House, 21 E Bay
Bross, John, Grocer, 10 St Philip's St
Broughton, Ann, Miss, 1 Mazyck St
Brown, —, Mrs, 59 Tradd St
Brown & Hyams, Auctioneers & Commission
  Merchants, N E of the Exchange
Brown, Alexander, 14 Union St
Brown, Daniel, Capt, 2d, Two Friends, 23 East
  Bay Cont'd
Brown, Daniel, Capt, 31 Church St Cont'd
Brown, Daniel, Grocer, 100 Church St
Brown, James, Capt, 14 Union St
Brown, John, Mariner, 65 Queen St
Brown, Joseph, Custom House Inspector, Prioleau's
  Whf, S E End
Brown, Joseph, Grocer, 51 Queen St
Brown, Joshua, Vendue Master & Commission
  Merchant, Res, W Short St
Brown, Laurence, Grocer, N E Prioleau's Whf
Brown, Lemuel, Grocer, N E End Prioleau's Whf
Brown, Mary, Boarding House, 7 Union St
Brown, Moses, Drum Major, 50 King St, Barber
  Shop, 7 Union St
Brown, Rebecca, Widow, 22 St Philip's St
Brown, Sam, Mariner, 31 Church Cont'd
Brown, Sam S, 147 King St
Brown, Samuel, Broker, 162 King St
Brown, Sarah, Dry Goods Store, 77 King St
Brown, Sarah, Shop Keeper, 77 King St
Brown, Thomas, Capt, Anson St

Brown, William, Boarding House, Chalmers Al
Brown, William, Capt, 5 Guignard St
Brown, William, Capt, Savannah Packet, 5
  Guignard St
Browne, James, City Marshal, 123 King St
Brownlee, John, Merchant, 16 St Philip's St
Bruckner, D, Commission Merchant, 7 N
  Montague St
Bryan, Jonathan, Merchant, 39 Hasell St
Bryant, John, Clerk, Market, 14 W King St Road
Bryce, Nicholas, Auctioneer & Commission
  Merchant, 5 N Champneys St
Buchanan, Archibald, Brass Founder, 96 Bay, Res,
  11 Society St
Buckle, Elizabeth, Widow, 54 Broad St
Budd, Abigail, Mrs, Boarding House, 40 Church
  St
Buford, Elizabeth, 19 Broad St
Buist, G, Rev Dr, Rector, Scottish Presbyterian
  Church, Principal of the College, 3 Church St
  Cont'd
Bulit, Jacob, Shop Keeper, 164 King St
Bulkley & Rose, Ship Chandlers, 22 East Bay
Bulow, John & Charles, Merchants, 166 King St
Bunce, Jacob, Boat Builder, Hard Al
Bunel, Angelique, 6 Berresford St
Burch, Henry I, Merchant, 71 Queen St
Burchell, Thomas, Planter, Charles St
Burges, Mary, Dry Goods Store, 250 King St
Burgherding, Peter, Boarding House, back of 126
  Queen St
Burk, D, Shop Keeper, 26 Guignard St
Burkett, Mary, Boarding House, Chalmers Al
Burkmeyer, John, Butcher Stall 8, Res, 2 N
  Wentworth
Burn, John, Grocer, 131 Meeting St
Burnet, Andrew, Planter, 198 Meeting St.
Burnet, Forster, Ornamental Painter, 2 Tradd St
Burnham, Thomas, House Carpenter, 94 Queen St
Burr, Mary, Mrs, Mantua Maker, cor Pinckney &
  Charles
Burr, Nehemiah, Capt, cor Pinckney & Charles
Burrows, Frederick, Pilot, 5 Trott St.
Bussacker, Charles, Grocer, 24 Union St
Butle, —, Mrs, 212 Meeting St
Butler, Charles P, Jeweller, 238 King St
Butler, Daniel, Rigger, 9 Chalmers Al
Butler, Joseph, City Deputy Sheriff, 220 Meeting
  St
Butler, Joseph, Planter, 88 Tradd St
Butler, Robert, Capt, Mariner, 3 Minority St
Butler, William, Boarding House, 7 Chalmers Al
Buzsse, —, Madame, Widow & Grocer, 81
  Meeting St
Bynum, Turner, Misses Academy, 178 King St
Byrne, Patrick, Sail Maker, Champneys S Whf,
  Res, 13 Pinckney St
Byrnes & Bennett, Merchants, 114 East Bay

Byrnes, Joseph, Merchant, Res , 34 Pinckney St
Bythewood, Thomas, Capt , 3 Quince St
Cabeuil, Renard L , Factor, 12 Broad St
Calder, Alexander, Cabinet Maker & Upholsterer,
  29 Broad St
Calder, Alexander, Planters Hotel, Meeting St cor
  Queen
Caldwell, John, Carpenter, N W cor of College &
  Green St
Caldwell, S , Widow, Dry Goods Store, 92 King St
Caldwell, William A , Merchant, Blake's Whf
Caldwell, William, Merchant, 1 Blake's Whf
Callaghan, John, Merchant, 5 Elliott St
Calvert, Elizabeth, Mrs , Boarding House, 232
  Broad
Calvert, John, Mason, 275 King St
Cambridge, James H , Vendue Master, Beale's Whf
Cambridge, Tobias, Vendue Master, End Vendue
  Row & Beale's Whf , Res , 6 Orange St.
Camel, John, Guardsman, 19 Union St Cont'd
Cameron, Alexander, 13 Middle St
Cameron, Alexander, Dray Keeper, 88 Meeting St
Cameron, David, Butcher, 4 N Cannon St
Cameron, John, Mariner, Jones Court
Cameron, Lewis, Merchant, 23 Church St
Cammer, Peter, Grain Store, E King St Cont'd
Campbell, ——, Mrs , Milliner, 195 Meeting St
Campbell, Alexander, Capt , Mariner, 14 Amen St
Campbell, Archibald, Merchant, 95 Church St
Campbell, Elizabeth, Mrs , Widow, 132 Broad St
Campbell, M'Millan, Vendue Master &
  Commission Merchant, 5 S Champney St , Res ,
  12 St Philip's
Cannady, Henry, Grocer, 32 Pinckney St
Cannon, Martha, Miss, Plantress, W End Boundary
  Cannonborough
Cantor, J , Merchant, 13 Legare St
Cantor, Jacob, Accomptant & Interpreter, 116 Tradd
Cantor, Joshua, Limner, 13 Legare St
Cantor, Manning, Comedian, Savage St
Cape, Brian, Factor, Nichols' Whf
Cape, Thomas, Planter, 51 Mazyck St
Card, John, Baker, 1 Parsonage Ln
Cardozo, David, Lumber Merchant, 17 King St
Carew, Edward, Block, Pump Maker, Etc , 4 S
  Ellery St , Res , 33 Pinckney
Carew, Mary, Widow, 64 Church St
Carmand, Peter & Son, Tailors, 130 King St
Carmichael, Elizabeth, Mrs , Boarding House,
  Lynch's Ln.
Carmichael, George, Grocer, 164 do
Carn, Susannah, Mrs , Plantress, 17 Archdale St
Carns, Samuel, Rope Maker, St Philip's St Cont'd
Carns, T W , Book Keeper, 26 St Philip's St
Carpenter, Ann, Seamstress, 2 Longitude Ln.
Carpenter, Joseph, Butcher Stall 15, Res , 10 S
  Cannon
Carr, ——, Mr., Butcher, 39 East King St Road

Carr, Ann, Mrs , Widow, 14 Quince St
Carr, Charles, Tailor, 20 Wentworth St
Carrere, Charles, French Teacher, 7 Meeting St
Carrere, Francis, Tailor, 25 Union St
Carroll, Bartholomew, Planter, 8 N W. Boundary
  St
Carroll, James P , Planter, 27 St Philip's St
Carroll, John, Merchant, 102 East Bay
Carson, Elizabeth, 5 Charles St
Carson, James, Merchant, 7 Broad St., Res , 78
  Tradd St
Cart, John, Factor, Cochran's Whf , Res 9 N W
  Bull St
Cart, Sarah, Mrs , Widow, 7 Kinloch's Court
Carter, Elizabeth, Widow, 7 St Philip's St
Carter, George, Physician, S. W End 64 Tradd St
Cartin, John, Boarding House, 12 Union St Cont'd
Carver, William & Co , Farrier & Livery Stables, 1
  Kinloch's Court
Carvin, Elizabeth, Madame, 28 Church St
Case, Amasa, Grocer, 14 Union St Cont'd
Caseaux, Dominic, Dry Goods Store, 207 King St
Casey, Benjamin, Coach Maker, 116 Broad St
Cashman, John & Co , Grocers, 28 Union St
Cassin, P C , Merchant, 4 Crafts N Whf
Cassin, Patrick, Merchant, 104 Tradd St.
Cate, William, Boarding House, 34 Union St
Callet, M , Boarding House, Berresfords Al
Catonet, Peter, Merchant, 118 Broad St.
Cattle, William, Planter, 75 Tradd St
Caught, Thomas, Ship Builder, 31 East Bay Cont'd
Cavaroc, Francis, Umbrella Maker, 28 Queen St
Cave, Thomas, Distiller, Mazyckborough
Caw, Rachel, Mrs , Plantress, 1 Legare St
Cellery, Peter, Hair Dresser, 3 Elliott St
Chalmers, Daniel & Henry, Planter, 119 Broad St
Chambers, ——, Mr , Attorney at Law, 119 Broad
  St.
Chambers, A., Mrs , Boarding House, 42 Elliott St
Chambers, Ann, Seamstress, Chalmers Al
Chambers, William, Boarding House, 21 Union
Chambers, William Seth, Capt , Sullivan's Island
  Packet
Champlin, Joseph, Grocer, 14 Elliott St
Champney, John, Wharf Owner & Planter, 92 King
  St
Champy, A Edme, Madame, 130 Meeting St
Chancognie, Simon J., Merchant, 13 Laurens St
Chanet, Anthony, Dry Goods Store, 8 Queen St
Chanler, ——, Mrs , Widow of Dr Charles, 17
  Society St
Chanler, Catharine, Mrs , 50 Broad St
Chanler, John White, Rev , 52 Broad St
Chapman, Joseph, House Carpenter & Grocer,
  Boundary W of King St near Lowndes St
Charles, Andrew, Merchant, Firm Hopkins &
  Charles, 14 Liberty St
Chase, Archiles, Capt , 8 Laurens St

61

Chasteau, C , Dr , 36 Union St
Chatelain, Maria L , 4 Trott St
Chatters, Henry, House Carpenter, 8 Friend St
Chen, ——, Dr , 30 Meeting St & 8 Friend St
Cheves, Langdon, Attorney at Law, Firm Peace &
  Co , State House Square
Child, Elizabeth, Mrs , Milliner & Mantua Maker,
  101 King
Chinners, Frances, Widow, 19 East Bay Cont'd
Chion, Catherine, Seamstress, St Philip's St
Chion, Elizabeth, 14 Society St
Chion, J F, Merchant, at Mr Dulles
Chisolm, Alexander, Planter, 187 King St
Chisolm, George, Factor & Wharf Owner,
  Chisolm's Whf , Res., 30 Church St Cont'd
Chitty, W. J , Porter, State Bank, 30 Wentworth St
Choinard, Charles P , Grocer, 16 St Philip's St
  cor George
Chollit, Alexander, Distiller, 2 S E Coming St
Chouler, Mary, Mrs , Widow, 37 Beaufain St
Chrietsburg, Conrad, Butcher, South Bay, Res , 4 S
  Cannon
Christie, Alexander, Merchant, 93 Church St
Christie, James, Merchant, 9 Crafts N Whf.
Chupein, Lewis, Merchant Perfumer, 37 Broad St
Church, ——, Capt , Meeting St Cont'd
Church, Slocum, Carpenter, cor Boundary &
  Meeting St. Cont'd
Church, Thomas, Capt , 68 Queen St
Claims, Martin, House Carpenter, 2 Blackbird Al
Clancy, Michael, Grocer, 120 Tradd St
Clark, Curtis, Commission Merchant, 106 Queen
Clark, David, Watch Maker, 9 Anson & 21 Broad
  St
Clark, Isabella, Seamstress, 7 Union St Cont'd
Clark, James, Coach Maker, 75 Meeting St
Clark, James, Tailor, 12 Elliott St
Clarkson, William, 7 Champney St , Res , 9 Moore
  St
Clastrier, Maximin, Starch & Powder Manufacturer,
  S W Vanderhorst St
Claude, ——, Mr , Comedian, 24 Queen St
Clayton, Jane, Widow, 59 E King St Road
Cleapor, Charles, Sail Makers Loft 5, Nichols'
  Whf , Res , 17 Ellery St
Cleary, John R , School Master, 20 Hasell St
Cleary, Robert W , Harbor Master, 20 Hasell St
Clement, Sarah, Mrs , Widow, 44 Queen St
Clift, Mathew, Millwright, 89 Meeting St
Clissey, Raimond, Coach & Harness Maker, 79
  Church
Club, Alexander, Merchant, 7 & 117 Tradd St.
Coate, William A , Grocer, 4 Prioleau's N Range
Coates, ——, Mrs , Widow, 14 Bedon's Al
Coates, Thomas, Capt , Proprietor of Coates Row,
  Res., King St Road
Cobia, Daniel, Butcher, 12 Berresford St
Cobia, Francis, Carpenter, 15 Berresford St

Cochran, Charles B , State Treasurer, 67 Meeting
Cochran, John, Capt , 185 East Bay
Cochran, Margaret, Mrs , Store, 242 King St
Cochran, Robert E , Federal Marshal, 6 Wentworth
Cochran, Susanah, Mrs , Widow, 122 E Bay
Cochran, Thomas, 32 Queen St & at the Fire
  Insurance Office
Cocote, ——, Madame, 2 Maiden Ln
Codd, Francis, Planter, 80 Queen St
Coffskey, Ann C , Confectioner, 88 King St
Cogdell, J. S, Attorney at Law, 2 St Michaels Al
Cogdell, Mary Ann E , Mrs , Boarding School, 1 St
  Michaels Al
Cogdell, R W , Factor, 19 Mottes Whf
Cohen & Moses, Auctioneers & Commission
  Merchants, S of the Exchange
Cohen, B , Grocer, N Cannon St , Store, M's Bluff
Cohen, C , Widow, 6 Society St
Cohen, Jacob & Co , Auctioneers & Commission
  Merchants, Vendue Row
Cohen, Jacob, Dry Goods Store, 247 King St
Cohen, Jacob J , Merchant, 54 King St
Cohen, Joseph, Sexton, Synagogue, near
  Synagogue, Hasell St
Cohen, Margaret, Widow, 6 Beaufain St
Cohen, Mordicai, Merchant, 124 King St
Cohen, Moses, Merchant, 198 King St
Cohen, Philip, Vendue Master, 10 Orange St
Cohen, Samuel, N Cannon St
Cohen, Solomon, Shop Keeper, 164 King St
Coils, Margaret, Seamstress, 19 Pinckney St
Coit & Fraser, Factors, 3 Crafts' N Whf
Colbard, W , Mariner, back of 12 Union Cont'd
Colcock, M , Mrs , Misses Boarding School, 6
  Lamboll St , Summer Res , N W cor Boundary
  & Mill St , Cannonborough
Cole, Sarah, Nurse, 30 King St
Coleman, Benjamin, Grocer, 33 Union St
Coleman, Sylvester, Merchant, 182 King St
Colhoun, J., Lighthouse Master, Lighthouse Island
Colley, Thomas, Grocer, 16 Linguard St
Collier, W , Savannah Stage Office, 189 Meeting
  St
Collins, Ann, 42 Queen St
Collins, Catherine, Mantua Maker, 21 Berresford
Collins, Mary, Mrs., Widow, 18 Hasell St
Colzy, Christian, Merchant Tailor, 29 Church St
Condy & Raguet, Merchants, 31 East Bay
Condy, Jeremy, Notary Public Conveyancer, 31
  East Bay
Connolly, J , Capt , Mariner, 17 Meeting St
Connor, Bryan, Merchant, 116 Queen St
Conover, William, Printer, cor Meeting & Federal
  St
Constance, ——, Mr , Saddler, 23 Pinckney St
Conton, John, Dr , Vanderhorst St
Conyers, Elizabeth, Mrs , Misses Boarding House
  School, 264 King St

Conyers, William M , Capt , Mariner, Harbor
Master, 27 Pinckney St
Cook, Samuel, Tailor, 17 Tradd St.
Cook, Susannah, Seamstress, 1 Linguard St
Cooper, Sarah, Widow, School Mistress & Clear
Starcher, 8 West St
Cooper, William, Shoe Maker, 255 Linguard St
Coram, Francis, Factor, Prioleau's S Whf , Res , 22
George St
Coram, Thomas, Painter & Engraver, 70 Queen
Corbett, Samuel, Tavern Keeper, 191 Meeting St
Corbett, T , Jr , Planter, 1 Ropers Ln
Corbett, T , Sr , Planter, Mill St , Cannonborough
Cordes, Elizabeth, Mrs , Plantress, 39 Wentworth
Cordier, Peter, Grocer, 58 E King St Road cor
Read St
Corkel, Thomas, Mariner, 9 Cock Ln
Corker, Thomas, Shipwright, cor Maiden Ln
Pinckney St
Cormick, Thomas, Grocer & Contractor, 71 E Bay
Cormier, Francis, Shipwright, 21 N W Wall St
Cornells, John & B , Grocers, 72 Meeting St
Cornely, James, Carpenter, 20 E King St Road
Cornwall, Samuel, Carpenter, Henrietta St
Corre, Jacob, 6 Queen St
Corrie, Alexander & Co , Vendue Master &
Commission Merchants, Exchange Al , Res , 1
Short St
Corrie, Samuel, Wheelwright, 10 W King St Road
Cortney, E , Wine Merchant, Apply to S Smith
Cott, Thomas, Shipwright, 137 East Bay
Cottingham, Ann, Mrs , Widow, 8 Bedon's Al.
Cotton, Ann, Boarding House, 14 Berresford Al
Cotton, J W , Carver & Guilder, 63 Meeting
Cotton, William, Accomptant, 31 Elliott St.
Coudrognan, ——, Madame, 34 Union St Cont'd
Cournand, ——, Madame, Vanderhorst St
Courtney, Humphrey, Merchant, 34 Meeting St
Courtney, James, Merchant, Meeting St
Courty, John, Grocer, 30 Union St
Coventry, Alexander, Dyer, 85 Tradd St
Cowen & Co , Saddlers & Harness Makers, W
King St Cont'd
Cowen & Hurlbut, Saddler & Trunk Makers, 139
King St
Cowen, John, Rigger, 36 East Bay Cont'd
Cox & Shepherd, Printers, Editors of the Times,
124 Tradd St
Cox, James, Merchant, Firm Tunno & Cox, 10
Church St Cont'd
Cox, John, Mason, 2 Federal St
Cox, Joseph D , Carpenter, 127 Meeting St
Cox, Thomas C , Proprietor, Times, 20 Meeting St
Cox, Thomas, Coach Maker, 1 Clifford St
Coy, Jonathan W & Co , Grocers, 13 Elliott St
Coyles, Margaret, Miss, 19 Pinckney St.
Cozzens, Elizabeth, Mrs , Boarding House, S
Linguard St

Crafts, Abraham, Notary Public, 84 Meeting St
Crafts, William & Ebenezer, Merchants & Whf
Owners, Crafts Wharves, Res , 21 Church St
Craib, Thomas, House Carpenter, 26 Beaufain St
Crane, Joseph & Co , Shoe Store, 31 Church St
Cranston, James, Broker, 36 Church St
Crask, Philip, Painter & Glazier, 12 Pinckney St
Crass, Mathew W , Mason, 4 Kinloch's Court
Craven, H , Miss, Seamstress, 60 Church St
Crawford & Lloyd, Druggist and Chemists, 15
Broad St
Crawford, Alexander, Painter & Glazier, 213
Meeting St
Crawford, James, Grocer, 120 King St
Crawford, John, Wharfinger, Vanderhost Whf ,
Res , 7 Tradd St
Crawford, William, at Mr O'Conners, King St
Crawley, ——, Miss, School Mistress, 12 Stolls Al
Crawley, Hannah, Widow, 105 Broad St
Creighton, Edward, Hair Dresser, 5 & 12 Union St
Cont'd
Creighton, James, Hair Dresser, 4 Elliott St
Creighton, Joseph, Hair Dresser, 12 Union St
Creighton, Perth, Hair Dresser, Unity Al
Creighton, Samuel, Hair Dresser, 19 Union St
Cont'd
Crever, Valentine, Guardman, 26 Trott St
Cripps, John S , Merchant, 52 Meeting St
Crocker & Hitchbourn, Merchant Crafts N Whf ,
Res , 24 Tradd St
Croft, Edward, Attorney at Law, 44 Meeting St
Croft, Peter, Col , Factor, Cordes St , Res.,
Hampstead
Cromwell, O , Sheriff's Office, Res , 9 Stolls Al
Crosbey, Josiah, Capt , Grain Merchant, 23
Scarsborough St , Store, 4 Mottes Whf
Cross, George, Capt , Merchant, 1 Federal St
Cross, George W , Attorney, Office 52 Meeting St
Cross, James, Black & Fancy Dyer, 177 Meeting
St
Cross, John, Carpenter, 8 Society St
Cross, John, Dyer & Scourer, 21 Hasell St
Cross, Samuel, Chair Maker, Quince St
Crouch, Abraham, Notary Public, Counting House,
Res , 84 Meeting St
Crovat, Peter, Merchant, Descourdres & Co
Crow, John, Book Binder, 77 Church St
Crowell, Jeremiah, Grocer, 93 Queen St
Cruckshanks, D , Boot & Shoe Store, 120 Queen St
Cruckshanks, D , Tanner, Amhearst St , Hampstead
Cruger, Elizabeth, Mrs , Widow, 7 Guignard St.
Cruger, Elizabeth, Mrs , Widow, 30 Meeting St
Crunkshanks, William, Boot and Shoe Store, 40
Elliott & 29 Queen
Cuckow, William, Pilot, Hard Al
Cudworth, Benjamin, Stewart, Orphan House
Cudworth, Nathaniel, Porter National Bank, Res ,
17 Magazine

Cuigno, Lewis, Tobacconist, 27 Union St
Culliat, Elizabeth, Boarding House, 123 East Bay
Cummings, John, Carpenter, 39 Church St Cont'd
Cunningham, ——, Mrs, Widow of Col C,
  Hampstead
Cunningham, Charles, Merchant, 70 King St Road
Cunningham, John, Merchant & Commissioner,
  Cotton Warehouse Company, 148 King St.
Curtis, Francis, Master of the Poor House
Custer, James, Factor, 2 Wentworth St
Custer, James, Factor, Prioleau's Whf, Res., S.
  Wentworth
Cutler, F John & Co, Grocers, N Charlotte St
Cutter, Robert, Capt, Mariner, 7 Smiths Ln
D'Oyley, Daniel, Merchant & Whf Owner,
  D'Oyley's Whf, late Ropers
Dabney & Parmele, Merchants, 16 Tradd St
Dabney, William, Merchant & Grocer, 101 Church
  St
Dacosta, Joseph, Broker, 2 Wentworth St.
Dailey, William, Grocer, 132 King St
Daingee, Francis, Store Keeper, 6 Queen St
Daker, Charles, Grocer, 134 Meeting St
Daker, Frederick, Grocer, 147 Meeting St
Dalcho, Frederick, M D, Res, 108 Tradd St cor
  Church
Dalgleish, Adam, Grocer, 82 Meeting St
Dalgleish, Adam, Grocer, S W cor Queen &
  Mazyck St
Dalton, Grace, Widow, 7 Linguard St
Dalton, James, Dr, Apothecary & Chemist, Church
  St. N W cor Tradd St
Dampsey, Mary, Grocer, 23 Scarborough St
Dandy, Timothy, Shoe Store, 13 Broad St
Daniel, Margaret, Mrs, Pastry Cook, 22 Archdale
  St
Danton, James, Carter, cor St Philip's &
  Wentworth
Darby, Arteman B, Deputy Surveyor General
Darby, John, Grocer, 16 Archdale St
Darby, John, Grocer, 7 Ellery St
Darby, Robert A, Tailor, 75 East Bay
Darrell, Nicholas, Capt, Mariner, 7 Cumberland St
Dart & Simons, Factors, Crafts S Whf
Dart, Benjamin S, Factors, Res, 28 Tradd St
Dart, Isaac M, Attorney & Factor, Crafts Whf,
  Res, 3 S W Montague St
Dart, J. S, Res., 28 Tradd St.
Dart, John M., Attorney at Law, Res, 28 Tradd St
Dastas, ——, Messrs, Merchants, 4 King St
  Cont'd
Datty, Marc, French Academy, 24 Wentworth St
Daty, Julie, Madame, Misses Boarding Academy,
  24 Union St
Davega, Moses, Shop Keeper, 3 King St Cont'd
David, Jacob, Dry Goods Store, 157 King St
Davidson & Blocker, Merchants, 71 E King St
  Road

Davidson, Gilbert, Merchant, 17 Broad St
Davidson, John, Charleston Librarian, State House,
  Res, 5 Society St
Davidson, Sibella, Mantua Maker, 65 Meeting St
Davis & Carroll, Merchant, 101 East Bay
Davis, Israel, Store Keeper, 128 King St
Davis, John M, Marine Insurance Broker, 36 E
  Bay
Davis, John, Merchant, 29 Wentworth St
Davis, Matilda, Seamstress, 27 Wentworth St
Dawes, Hugh P, Factor & Commission Merchant,
  Office Gadsden's Whf
Dawnie, Robert, Tin Plate Worker & Plumber, 15
  Tradd
Dawson, Ann, Mrs, 39 Beaufain cor King St
Dawson, Isaac, Capt, 8 Minority St.
Dawson, John & William, Merchants, 115 East Bay
Dawson, John, Esq, 2 East Bay Cont'd
Dawson, John, Jr, Merchant, Res, 6 N Bull St
Dawson, John, Merchant, 67 E King St Road
Dawson, William, Firm J & W, 9 Church St
Dayton, Shipwright, E Pinckney St,
  Cannonborough
Deas, Charles & Thomas, Factors, 1 Motte's Whf
Deas, David, Attorney at Law, 66 Tradd St
Deas, Henry, Esq, Planter, 1 Friend St
Deas, James, Attorney at Law, 1 East Bay Cont'd
Deas, Robert, Dr, Planter, 57 Queen St
Deas, Thomas H, Factors, 294 King St
Debesse, J J, Merchant, 117 King St
Debougarin, D, Madame, Seamstress, 17 Hasell St
Debow, Garrett, Grocer, 68 East Bay
Debow, J, Grocer, cor Church & Moore St
Debow, William, Dr, Druggist, 43 East Bay
Deglanne, John, Mariner, 28 Pinckney St
Delaire & Canut, Merchants, 95 East Bay
Delaire, A, Merchant, 9 East Bay Cont'd
Delalande, J P, Broker, 22 Guignard St
Delany, Daniel, House Carpenter, 11 St Philip's St
Delap, John, Mariner, 73 Church St
Delavincendiere, ——, 10 W King St Cont'd
Deleon, Jacob, Vendue Master, 3 N E Vendue
  Row, Res, 5 New St
Deliesseline, F G., Merchant, 12 Mottes Whf
Delisle, J. G, Dr, 14 Queen St
Delorme, John Francis, Planter, 42 Broad St
Demelliere, ——, Monsieur, Painter, 193 Meeting
  St
Demontmain, Lewis Claude H, 85 King St
Dempsay, Judah, Shop Keeper, 28 Queen St
Dener, George, Tanner & Currier, 9 Mazyck St
Dennis, Elizabeth, Mrs, 240 King St
Dennison, James, Capt, 38 Elliott St
Denny, James, Boarding House, 35 Union St
Denny, Thomas, Physician, 48 Broad St
Denoon, David, Mrs, Widow, 38 Trott St
Denton, Ann, Widow, Mantua Maker, 69
  Wentworth

Depass, Ralph, Vendue Master, 8 S Champneys St
Depau, Francis, Merchant, 7, 8, 9 & 10 Mottes
Whf.
Desaussure, H. W , Esq , Attorney at Law, 206
Meeting
DeSaussure & Ford, Attornies at Law, Office 29
Tradd
Desclaux, Joseph, Shop Keeper, 21 Wall St
Desclaw, Joseph, Mariner, 2 N E Wall St
Descoudres, L P & Co , Dry Goods Store, 117
King St
Desel, Christian, Cabinet Maker, 50 Broad St & 52
King St
Desiree, L , Shop Keeper, 40 King St
Desiree, Maria, Cigar Maker, 25 Wentworth St
Desjardins, J A , Merchant, 22 King St Road
Desportes, P , Grocer, 88 East Bay
Desrivaux, ----, Monsieur, 29 Union St
Desrivaux, Melanie, Cake Shop, 107 Queen St
Detargny, Marin, Rev , Minister of the French
Protestant Church, 75 Church at Parsonage House
Deveaux, Barn , Attorney at Law, Office 101 Tradd
St
Deveaux, Jacob, Gentleman, 16 King St
Devillers, L , Professor of Music, 258 King St.
Dewar, Robert, Director, S C Bank, Res , 82 Tradd
St
Dewees, William, Factor, 2 Prioleau's S Range,
Res , cor Charlotte & Alexander St
Mazyckborough
Diamond, John, Surveyor, 119 Meeting St
Dickinson, Francis, Attorney at Law, 35 Meeting St
Dickinson, J F , Merchant, 122 Tradd St
Dickinson, S , Stables & Wagon Yard Keeper, 143
King
Dickinson, Samuel, Vendue Master & Commission
Merchant, 5 Champneys
Dieckert & Co , Grocers, 71 East Bay
Diedericks, Franz & Co , Merchants, 116 Tradd St
Dile, Peter, Baker & Confectioner, 21 Queen
Dill, Jane E , Mrs , Widow, 9 Prices Al
Dillon, Thomas P , Grocer, 11 Union St Cont'd
Dixon, J , Tallow Chandler, 18 W King St Road
Dobbins, Rosa, 1 Parsonage Ln
Doggett, Henry, Lumber Whf South Bay, Res , 45
Tradd
Domec, Marc, Merchant, 112 King St
Donaldson, James, House Carpenter, 103 Tradd St.
Donaldson, Mary, Mrs , Milliner & Dress Maker,
107 Broad St
Donneo, Daniel, Boarding House, 9 Union St
Dorrell, ----, Mrs., Widow, 3 Water St
Dorrell, Jane, Boarding House, Chalmers Al
Dorrell, Robert, Factor, 3 N W Boundary St
Dougherty, John, Stucco Plasterer, N E cor
Charlotte & Washington St , Mazyckborough
Doughty, Thomas, Factor, 2 Mottes Whf , Res , 4
Anson

Doughty, W , Esq , Planter, 2 E Smith St ,
Harlestons Green
Douglas, Alexander, Tailor, 14 Elliott St
Douglas, James, Accomptant & Collector, 106
Queen St
Douglas, James K , Merchant, 89 Church St
Douglas, James, Turner, back of 62 Meeting St
Dowling, Archibald, Dry Goods Store, 78 King St
Dowme, Robert, Tin Plate Worker & Plumber, 15
Tradd
Drayton, John, Esq., Late Governor, Planter, N.
Montague St
Drayton, Thomas, Planter, 31 Wentworth St
Drayton, William, Attorney at Law, 97 Tradd St
Drennis, George, Baker, 34 Beaufain St cor St
Philip's St
Dressler, Hance, Grocer, 60 Meeting St
Drews, Henry, Shop Keeper 7 Prioleau's N Whf
Drouillard, M. J , Middle St
Drummond, James, Boot & Shoe Store, 33 Elliott
St
Dubarry, Stephen, Grocer, 93 King St
Dubert, Frederick, Grocer, 49 E King St Road
Dubois, John, Tailor, Quince St
Dubois, Peter, Carpenter, 14 S Cannon St
Duff, Mary, Shop Keeper, 24 Queen St
Duffus, John, Merchant, 35 Elliott St
Duggan, J & T , Masons & Plasterers, E St
Philip's St. Cont'd.
Duhadway, C B , Saddler & Harness Maker, 31
Broad St
Dulles, Joseph, Merchant
Dumaine, John, Chemist, 19 Ellery St
Dumouchel, Elizabeth, 25 Church St
Dumoutet, John B , Goldsmith & Jeweller, 120
Broad
Duncan, John, Merchant, 68 E King St Road
Duncan, John, Merchant, N Bull St
Duncan, Patrick, Tallow Chandler, E Pinckney St ,
Cannonborough
Dunwoody, Samuel, W Pitt St.
Duplat, Rose, Goldsmith, 11 Queen St
Dupont, Delorme, cor Wall & Pitt St
Dupont, John, Planter, 34 Church St
Dupont, Joseph, Grocer, 181 Meeting St
Duprat, Raymond, Commission Broker, 3d story
116 Queen St
Dupre, Benajmin, Livery Stables, 37, 38 & 81
Church
Dupre, James, House Carpenter, 4 Wall St
Durbec, Joseph, Grocer, 133 Queen St
Durrett, George, Livery Stables, Bank Square
Dutch, Stephen, Factor, 9 Union St. Cont'd
Duvall, Catherine, Mrs , Widow, 107 Church St
Duvall, Joseph, Shoe Maker, Quince St
Duvall, Philip, Planter, Spring St , Cannonborough
Duvergie, Catharine, 55 Trott St
Dyer, Daniel, Vintner, Whim Court

Dyre, Kendall, at Mr Hislops, Queen St
Eager, Sarah, Seamstress, Williams' Whf
Eason, Robert, Vendue Master & Commission
  Merchant, 4 S Champney St, Res, 22 King St
Easterby, George, Capt, 31 Guignard & 11
  Pinckney St
Easton, Sarah, 25 Beaufain St
Eaton, Robert, Shipwright, 46 Tradd St
Eberly, Barbara, Widow, 18 Guignard St
Eckert, Robert D, Grocer, 6 Church St
Eckhard, Jacob, Professor of Music, Organist,
  German Church, 14 George St
Eden, William, Turner, 6 Amen St
Edgworth, ——, Miss, Misses Boarding School, 2
  West St
Edwards, Alexander, Esq, Judge, Recorder of
  Inferior City Court, 3 St Michaels Al
Edwards, Catherine, Mrs, Widow, 3 S W Lynch's
  St
Edwards, Edward, Planter, Pinckney St,
  Cannonborough
Edwards, George, Planter, 90 Tradd St
Edwards, Isaac, Factor, 1 S. End Prioleau's Whf,
  Res, 10 Friend St
Egleston, John, Merchant & Grocer 67 East Bay
  cor Queen St, Res, 99 East Bay
Ehney, George, Carpenter, 4 Smith St
Ehney, Peter E, Tailor, 281 King St
Ehney, William F, Porter, S C Bank, Res, 26
  Beaufain St
Ehney, William, Tailor, Whim Court & 1 Elliott St
Ehrick, John M, Merchant, 7 Crafts' N Whf & 74
  Queen St, Res, 1 St Philip's St
Eleizer, Elisha, City Deputy Sheriff, 25 Guignard
  St
Elf, Ben, Cartman, 5 Charlotte St, Mazyckborough
Elfe, Benjamin, Planter, Amhearst St
Elfe, Thomas, Carpenter, 7 Mazyck St
Elford, James, Capt, Navigation School, 34 Union
  St Cont'd
Elfrid, Johan, Grocer, 2 Union St
Elliott, ——, Miss, 17 Legare St
Elliott, Benjamin, Attorney at Law, 17 Legare St
Elliott, Charles, Planter, 290 King St
Elliott, Samuel J, Printer, 8 Ellery St
Elliott, T O, Mrs, Plantress, 15 Legare St
Elliott, Thomas, Planter, 5 Gibbes St
Ellis, Elizabeth, Dry Goods Store, 13 Queen St
Ellis, Thomas, Jr, Carpenter, 5 Amen St
Ellis, Thomas, Sr, Wood Measurer, 14 Scarborough
Ellis, William, Boarding House, 30 Union St
  Cont'd
Ellison, John, Store Keeper, 52 King St
Ellison, William, Merchant, Columbia
Elmore, Dorcas, Mrs, Widow, 4 Mazyck St
Elsworth, John, Gauger of City Council, 130 Queen
  St
Elsworth, Susanah, Seamstress, 6 Lodge Al

Elsworth, Theophilus, Gauger, Custom House, Res,
  E Pitt St & 130 Queen St
Elsworth, Thomas, Mariner, 6 Lodge Al
Emanuel, Flora, Mrs, Shop, 45 East Bay
Emanuel, Nathan, Dry Goods Store, 233 King St
Emard, Susannah, Confectioner, 42 Meeting St
England, Alexander, Baker, 100 Tradd St
Ernest, Jacob, Tailor, 22 Queen St
Eschausse, William, Mattress Maker, 42 Meeting
  St
Estill, Sarah, Seamstress, 25 Beaufain St
Etenaud, Stephen, Gentleman, 12 Beaufain St
Evans, James, Shoe Maker, 10 N Bull St
Evans, John, Boot & Shoe Maker, 126 Meeting St
Evans, L, House Carpenter, 35 Queen St
Evans, Thomas, Guardman, 5 Lodge Al
Evringham & Bingham, Factors, 5 Champneys Whf
Evringham, John, Merchant, 39 East Bay Cont'd
Ewing, Alexander, Merchant, 3 Chisholm's Whf,
  Res, 1 Bedon's Al
Ewing, John, Merchant, 214 Meeting St
Faber, Charles, Rev, Minister, German Church, 2
  S W Lynch St, Harleston Green
Faber, Christian H, 16 Berresford St
Faber, John C, Whf Owner & Warden, 92 East
  Bay
Faber, William, Merchant, Cochran's Whf, Res, 25
  George St
Fair, John, Boot & Shoe Maker, 141 King St
Fair, Richard, Boot & Shoe Maker, 94 King St
Fair, Robert, Boot & Shoe Maker, 190 King St
Fair, William, Tanner & Currier, cor Bull & Pitt
  St
Fairchild, Aaron, Black Smith, Ham's Whf, Res,
  13 George St
Fairley, Hance, Cabinet Maker, 66 Meeting St
Fanning, Maria M, Milliner, 117 King St
Farley, James, Boot & Shoe Maker, 27 Broad St
Faroux, Nicholas, Grocer, 106 King St
Faure, ——, Miss, Mantua Maker, Cumberland St
Faures, Sophie, Madame, Widow, 4 S Minority St
Faust, Jeremiah, Boarding House, 201 King St
Faust, Lewis, Butcher, 55 East King St Road
Fayolle, Peter, Dancing Master, 260 King St
Fayssoux, Ann, Widow, 67 Tradd St
Febve, Benjamin, 30 Society St
Fell, Elizabeth, Mrs, Millinery Store, 24 Broad St
Feraud, Alexander, Merchant, 152 King St
Ferguson, ——, Mr., Academy, 186 Meeting St.
Ferguson, Ann, Mrs, Widow, 3 Liberty St
Ferguson, Edmond, Carpenter, 1 Berresford St
Fernald, Dennis, Guardman, 4 Union St
Fiddy, William B, Merchant, 2 S Gillion St
Fields, William, Mrs, Widow, at Mr Cleapors
Fife, Mary, Mrs, Widow, 8 Coming St
Fillettte, Francis, Jeweller, 11 Queen St
Fillison, Thomas, Boarding House, 7 Lodge Al
Finch, Joseph, Nail Manufactory, 8 Gillion St.

Findley, Jacob, Mason, 36 King St
Firmont, Anthony, Capt, Henrietta St
Fisher & Hitchcock, Saddlers & Harness Makers,
  191 King St
Fisher, James, Esq, 16 South Bay
Fisher, Philip, 3 Cliffords Al
Fitzgerald, James, Hair Dresser, 12 Union St
Fitzgerald, L, House & Ship Painter, Governor's
  Bridge
Fitzpatrick, James, Trader, Chalmers Al
Fitzpatrick, Peter, Tailor, 106 Tradd St
Fitzsimons, Christopher, Merchant & Whf Owner,
  Res, 73 East Bay
Fitzsimons, Dolly, Magazine St
Flagg, George, Jr, Painter & Glazier, 11 E Bay
  Cont'd
Flagg, George, Sr, Esq, 212 King St
Flagg, Samuel H, Dr, Dentist, 26 Queen St
Fleming, James, Grocer, 41 Tradd St
Fleming, Robert, Merchant, 135 King St cor
  George
Fleming, Thomas, Store & Wagon Yard, 42 E
  King St Road
Fleming, William, Merchant, 23 E King St Road
Fletcher, Thomas, Merchant, 1 Crafts' S Whf
Flint, Joseph, Grocer, 31 Union St Cont'd
Floderer, John, Grocer, 2 Smiths Ln
Flogel, Samuel, Mariner & Grocer, 165 Meeting St.
Florance, Zachariah, Dentist, 126 King St
Florin, Ann, Seamstress, Cumberland St
Florin, Lucas, 32 Guignard St
Fogartie, Christian, 14 Ellery St
Fogartie, James, Factor, Cordes St, Res, 15
  Scarborough
Fogartie, Mary, Mrs, Widow, 14 Ellery St
Folker, John Casper, Planter, 38 Beaufain St
Follin, Augustus, Shop Keeper, 103 King St
Follin, Michael, Tobacconist, 89 King St
Footman, J W, Grocer & Wagon Yard, 24 King
  St Road
Forbes, Alexander, Commission Merchant, 17
  Elliott St
Forbes, John, Tin Plate Worker, 189 King St
Ford, Jacob, Attorney at Law, 29 Tradd St
Ford, John, Boarding House, 32 Union St
Ford, Timothy, Barrister, 208 Meeting St
Fordham, Rich, Block & Pump Maker, Governor's
  Bridge, 59 Church St, Firm Bass & Fordham
Forrest, ——, Madame, Widow, 1 Minority St
Forrest, Aberdeen, Cooper, N Boundary St
  between Meeting & King St Cont'd
Forrest, Charity, Mrs, Widow, 2 Hasell St &
  Meeting
Forrest, T H, Cooper D'Oyley's Whf, Res, 106
  Church St
Forrester, Robert, Constable, 1 Society St
Forrester, Susanah, Widow, Nassau St,
  Mazyckborough

Forsyth, Walter, 51 Tradd St
Foster, John, Grocer, Unity Al
Foster, Nathan, Grocer, 30 Elliott St
Foster, Robert, Merchant, 16 Elliott St
Foster, Thomas, Out Door Clerk, National Bank,
  Res, 285 King
Foucard, Peter J, Music Master, 255 King St
Fouchy, Josephine, Madame, 119 King St
Fouchy, Olimpie & Sisters, 12 Ellery St
Fowke, Mary, Mrs, Plantress, 2 Union St Cont'd
Fowle, Nathaniel, Watch Maker, 3 Broad St
Fowler, James H, Boot & Shoe Maker, 20 Union
  St
Fowler, John, Carpenter, Longitude Ln
Fowler, John, Lumber Merchant, Gibbes St
Frances, ——, Capt., Mariner, 2 Union St Cont'd
Frances, Amelia, Mrs, Boarding House, 30 Church
Fraser, ——, Mrs, Widow, Plantress, 27 King St
Fraser, James, Capt, Planter, Thomas St,
  Cannonborough
Fraser, John, 224 Meeting St
Fraser, John, Maj, Planter, 80 Tradd St
Fraser, Mary James, Mrs, Widow, 1 East Bay
Fraser, Thomas, Planter, 3 Laurens St
Frazer, John M, Carpenter, 26 Trott St
Frean, Margaret, Mrs, Dry Goods Store, 70 King
  St
Frederick, G. W., Mason, 3 Meeting St
Freeman, E William, Mrs, Widow, 91 Tradd St
Freer, Charles, Planter, 7 N Wentworth St Cont'd
Frenando, Joseph, Rigger, 73 Church St
Freneau, Peter, Esq, 34 George St
Friday, William, Butcher, 6 N Cannon St
Friend, Ulrick, Butcher, 6 N Cannon St.
Frink, Thomas, Wharfinger, Beale's Whf, Res, 38
  Pinckney St
Frish, Charles, Merchant, 181 King St
Frobus, Henrietta, Boarding House, Chalmers Al
Fronty, Michael, Dr, Physician, 11 Moore St
Frost, Elizabeth, Mrs, Widow, 9 W St
Fuller, Oliver, Capt, Mariner, 57 Meeting St
Fullilove, Thomas, Millwright, 26 Trott St
Fulmer, John, Coach Maker, 3 Blackbird Al
Furches, John, Tailor, 20 Queen St
Furman, Richard, Rev, Mr, Minister, Baptist
  Incorporated Church, 10 Church St
Furman, Wood, A. B Academy, 1 Stolls Al
Futerell, James, Teller, S C Bank
Futhey, Hartley, 10 Queen St
Gabeau, Anthony, Tailor, 190 Meeting St
Gabeau, James, Cooper, 6 Crafts' N Whf
Gabeau, James, Cooper, Crafts' S Whf, Res, 5
  Laurens St
Gabeau, John, Mast, Block & Pump Maker, 1
  Gillon's Whf
Gabenatte, Anthony, Guardman, 4 Georges Al
Gadsden, ——, Mrs, Widow of Gen, 16 Front St,
  Gadsden's Green

Gadsden, James W., 73 Queen St
Gadsden, M , Mrs., Widow, 19 Front St
Gadsden, Philip, Whf Owner, Merchant, 8 Front St , Counting House, Gadsden's Whf
Gadsden, Thomas, Planter, Ashley River Road
Gaigou, Theodore, Meeting St Cont'd
Gaillard & Mazyck, Factors, 6 Chisolm's N Whf
Gaillard, Eleanor, Mrs , Widow, 78 East Bay
Gaillard, T, Attorney at Law, 45 Meeting St
Gaillard, Theodore, Factor, N W Montague St
Galbraith, Robert, Carpenter, 17 George St
Gallagher, S S T D , Rev , Roman Catholic Church, 28 Wentworth St
Gallaway, Alford, Pilot, 4 Lynch's Court
Galleger, William, Grocer, 44 Tradd St
Galluchat, J , Merchant, cor Tobacco & King St
Gandouin, John, Merchant Hatter, Etc , 58 E Bay
Gantt, E , Mrs , Misses Boarding School, 45 Trott St
Garden, Adam, Boot & Shoe Maker, Cliffords Al
Garden, Alexander, Dr , Physician, 16 East Bay Cont'd
Garden, Alexander, Planter, N E cor Coming & Bull St
Garden, Martha, Widow, 22 Beaufain St
Gardener, John, Black Smith, Governor's Bridge, Res , 5 Maiden Ln
Gardener, Ruth, Widow, 19 Quince St
Gardener, Sophia, Seamstress, Archdale St.
Garrick, Frederick, Confectioner, 37 Queen St
Gasper, Francis, Shipwright, 21 Trott St
Gaujan, P B , Gentleman, Hampstead
Gaultier, Joseph, Vendue Master, 271 King St
Gayner, Thomas, Boarding House, 6 Lodge Al
Geddes, Henry, Merchant, 176 King St
Geddes, John, Attorney at Law, 119 Broad St
Geddes, Robert , Merchant, 156 King St
Gedney, Isaac, House Carpenter, 12 George St
Gefkin, Henry, Deputy Sheriff, 18 Mazyck
Gell, John, Livery Stables, N Bank Square
Gennerick, J F , Merchant, 150 King St
Gensel, John, 2 Coming St
George, James, Shipwright, 33 East Bay Cont'd
George, Mary, Mrs , Shop Keeper, 204 King St
George, Peter, Scrivener, 30 Tradd St
Gerald, Mary, Seamstress, Limehouse Court
Gere, Greenman, Shipmaster, 98 Church St.
Geres,——, 1 St Philip's St
Gervais, Mary, Mrs., Plantress, 85 Broad St
Gervais, R L , 85 Broad St
Geyer, John, Capt , Merchant, Chisolm's Whf.
Gibbes, John, Planter, 121 Meeting St
Gibbes, Lewis, Planter, 8 South Bay
Gibbes, Robert R., Planter, 8 South Bay
Gibbes, Sarah, Widow, Plantress, 13 Meeting St.
Gibbs, W. H , Master in Equity, 4 Orange St
Gibbs, George, Baker, 29 Elliott St
Gibbs, Mary, Widow, Plantress, 285 King St.

Gibson & Broadfoot, 843 East Bay
Gibson, Alexander C , Grocer, 234 King St
Gibson, James, Coach Maker, 55 Meeting St
Gibson, Robert, Black Smith, 4 Archdale St
Gibson, Robert, Store Keeper, 232 King St
Gidiere, ——, Madame, Liquor Store, 10 E King St Cont'd
Gidney, Isaac, Carpenter, 12 George St
Gilbert, Joseph, Brick Maker, Back of 25 Church St Cont'd.
Gilchrist, Adam, Merchant, 16 E Bay, Res , 12 Church St
Gill, Isaac, Watch Maker, 236 King St
Gilliland, W H., Tailor, W King St Road
Gillispie & Mackay, Merchants, 30 East Bay
Gillon, Ann P , Mrs , Widow, 2 W Wall St
Gilmon, Zadock, Merchant, 8 Crafts' Whf
Gissendenner, L , Widow, Nurse & Mantua Maker, S Bull St
Gissendenner, Susanah, Widow, 24 Beaufain St
Gist, N & F , Merchants, 146 King St
Given, Mary, Shop Keeper, 42 East Bay Cont'd
Gleise, Stephen, Dr , 252 King St
Glemet, Lewis, Shop Keeper, 5 King St Road
Glen, John, Merchant, 15 Ellery St
Glen, John, Planter, 54 Tradd St & 13 Legare St
Glover, Charles, Mesne Conveyance, 3d Story, State House, Res , S cor Bull & Smith St , Harleston
Glover, Joseph, Dr , Physician, Dispensary, 14 Archdale
Glover, Wilson, Planter, 2 Meeting St
Gobert, Charles, Merchant, 5 Motte's Whf
Godfrey, Catherine, Widow, 76 Tradd St
Godwin, E S , 21 Hasell St
Goldsmith, Morris, Store Keeper, 112 King St
Gomez, Jacob, Store Keeper, 245 King St
Good, Sarah, School Mistress, 42 King St
Goodtown, Peter, Mariner, 136 Meeting St
Gordan, William, Grocer, 87 King St
Gordon, A , Mason, 101 Queen St
Gordon, James, Merchant, 26 East Bay
Gordon, John, Scavenger, New East Bay St
Gordon, Margaret, Widow, Plantress, 4 Parsonage Ln
Gordon, Mul, Mason, 6 W King St
Gordon, T., Cashier, Counting House, 18 Church St Cont'd
Gosjan, ——, Monsieur, 10 W Meeting St Cont'd
Gough, John Parker, Physician, 220 Meeting St
Gould, Thomas, Painter & Glazier, 23 George St
Gowdey, Margaret, 45 Broad St
Gowen, Sarah, Laundress, 22 Trott St
Gradick, Christian, Butcher, Mary St , Wraggsborough
Grado, Mariano, Boarding House, 13 Union St Cont'd
Graeser, Jacob, Col , Merchant, 100 Queen St

Grant, A, Merchant, 92 Church St, Res., 15 Friend St.

Grant, James, Printer, 7 Union St
Grant, Joseph, Rigger, 31 Pinckney St
Graves, Charles, Factor, Res, 55 Tradd St
Gray, Benjamin, Lumber Merchant, 4 N Montague St
Gray, Caleb, Tailor, 140 King St
Gray, Henry, Justice of Peace, cor of Liberty & King St
Gray, William, Mason, Whim Court
Gray, William, Merchant, 7 East Bay
Green, Benjamin, Grocer, 17 Union St Cont'd, Res, 20
Green, Edmund, Factor, 6 Champneys St & 145 Broad
Green, Sarah, Seamstress, 21 Beaufain St
Green, William, Boarding House, Elliott St Cont'd
Green, William J, Grocer, 40 Union St
Greenland, George, Factor, 32 Meeting St
Greenwood, William, Jr, Agent, 1 Ellery St
Greenwood, William, Sr, Planter, 20 Beaufain St
Greffin, Peter, Merchant, 142 Broad St
Gregorie, James, Jr, Merchant, 133 Broad St, Res, 95 Church St
Gregorie, James, Sr, Merchant, 133 Broad St
Greiner, Charles, Watch Maker, E King St Cont'd
Greiner, Meinrad, Merchant, 9 East King St Cont'd
Grice, C E, Merchant, 16 Broad St
Grice, Caleb E, Merchant, 123 Tradd St
Grierson, James, Tavern Keeper, 65 East Bay
Griffin, Mary, Widow, Shop Keeper, 41 E Bay Cont'd
Grimball, Elizabeth, Mrs, Plantress, 21 South Bay
Grimball, P J, Carpenter, 4 Swintons Ln
Grimke, John J, Associate Judge, 6 Front St
Grippon, John, Grocer, 42 Elliott St
Groasman, Henry, Wharffiller, 6 W Coming st
Groning, Lewis & R, Merchants, 8 East Bay
Gros & Lee, Cabinet Makers, 76 Meeting St
Groscoll, Anthony, Instrument Maker & Turner, cor of Church & Chalmers Al
Groshon, Andrew, Painter & Glazier, 53 Meeting St
Groves, Ann, 6 Cliffords Al
Groves, Samuel, 20 Federal St
Gruau, Francis Paul, Mariner, 35 Hasell St
Grubee, Hermand, Grocer, 59 Church St
Gruber, Catherine, Widow, N Wentworth St Cont'd
Gruber, Christian, Clerk of the Market, 15 Berresford
Guerlain, Lewis H., Merchant, Fitzsimmon's Whf.
Guest, ——, Mrs, Widow, Plantress, 85 Meeting St.
Guilbert, Eugene, Professor of Music, cor Wall & Pitt St
Guilou, Samuel, Tailor, 109 Queen St

Gunn, William, Gun & Black Smith, 5 Queen St
Gurnier, Joseph, Mariner, 17 Trott St
Gurry, Catherine, Widow, Meeting St Cont'd
Gyles, Thomas, Accomptant, 26 Elliott St.
Hacket, Jane, Mrs, 1 Parsonage Ln
Hagood, Johnson, Attorney at Law, 2 Archadale St
Haig, David, Cooper, Crafts' Whf, Res, 132 Meeting
Hall, ——, Misses, 13 Guignard St
Hall, Daniel, Factor, 2 State House Square
Hall, George, Dr, Physician of the Marine Hospital, 2 East Bay Cont'd
Hall, James, Stone Cutter, 5 Ellery St
Hall, Jane, Nurse & Seamstress
Hall, Thomas, Clerk, Admiralty & Register Copy Right, 33 Broad St
Hall, Thomas, Mason, S W End Vanderhorst St
Hall, William & Co., Merchants, 22 Broad St
Hall, William, Capt, Mariner, 7 Front St
Halliday, Hugh, Cooper, 6 N Champncy St
Ham, Thomas, Teacher, N Amhearst St
Hamett, Margaret, Widow & Seamstress
Hamett, Thomas, 49 Trott St.
Hamilton, James, Maj, Merchant, 9 Pinckney St
Hamilton, James, Planter, Pinckney St, Cannonborough
Hamilton, Marlborough S, Academy, 102 Broad St
Hamilton, Mary Ann, Boarding House, 8 Union St
Hamilton, Paul, Esq (Late Governor), Planter, 1 E Bay
Hamilton, Rachel, Miss, 98 King cor Parsonage Ln
Hampton, William, Cabinet Maker, 64 Meeting St
Hands, Jane, Mrs, School Mistress, 58 Church St
Hanmer, John, Seaman at Mr Roche's, Church St
Hannah, Hannah, Widow, 43 East Bay Cont'd
Hanothau, Therese & Sister, Fruit Shop, 25 Church St
Hanson, Thomas, Carpenter, 5 Berresford St
Happold, John, Butcher, Coming St opposite Burial Ground
Happold, John Philip, Butcher, 10 N W Boundary St
Harby, Rebecca, Mrs, Widow, 5 Orange St
Harcourt, John, Hair Dresser, 16 Mazyck St
Harding, Gardner, Tailor, 5 Stolls Al
Hare, Frances, Mrs, Widow, 16 Amen St
Harleston, Edward, Planter, 19 St Philip's St
Harleston, Elizabeth, Mrs, Plantress, 94 Tradd St
Harleston, Nicholas, Planter, 3 W Bull St
Harleston, William, Planter, 90 Broad St
Harper, James, Baker, 43 Tradd St
Harris, Andrew, 10 W King St Cont'd
Harris, Hyam, Dry Goods Store, 3 Queen St
Harris, Jacob, Store Keeper, Queen St near the Bay
Harris, John, Drayman, 125 Meeting St
Harris, Moses, Dry Goods Store, 187 King St
Harris, Tucker, Dr, 71 King St

Harrison, George, Nail & Ironmongery, 19 Church St
Harrison, Thomas, Rigger, cor Vanderhorst & St Philip's St
Harrison, William P, Printer, Whim Court
Hart, Daniel, Vendue Master, 54 East Bay
Hart, Nathan, Store, 183 King St
Hart, Rachel, Dry Goods Store, 277 & 228 King St
Hart, Simon Moses, 227 King St
Harth, John, Planter, N W End South Bay
Hartt, Moses, Carpenter, 1 Society St
Harvey, Elizabeth, Widow, 120 Meeting St
Harvey, Elizabeth, Widow, 2 Short St
Harvey, James, Carpenter, Fort Mechanic
Harvey, John, Grocer, 29 Union St
Harvey, John S, Printer, 120 Meeting St
Harvey, Mary, Widow, 82 Queen St
Harvy, Benjamin, Capt, Planter, Thomas St, Cannonborough
Haskell, E, Planter, 1 Front St
Haskett, Samuel, Saddler & Harness Maker, 121 King St
Haslett, John, Merchant, 10 East Bay, Res, 61 Church
Haslett, John, Sr, Glass & Color Store, 62 East Bay
Hatch, R, Capt, Mariner, 14 Union St. Cont'd
Hatter, E B, Mrs, Widow, 32 Queen St
Hattier, Henry, Grocer, 117 East Bay
Hauck, John, Grocer, 10 Anson St cor Laurens
Hawes, Mary, Widow, 10 Amen St
Hay, George, Shoe Store, 22 Elliot St.
Hayda, David, Grocer, 154 Meeting St
Haydon, Mathew, Boarding Officer, W Meeting St Road
Haydon, William, Custom House Inspector, E St Philip St Cont'd
Hayes, David, Mariner, 6 N Chalmers Al
Haynsworth, Lee P, Merchant, 39 East Bay
Hazlehurst, Robert & Co, Merchants, 14 East Bay
Hazlehurst, Robert, Merchant, 8 Front St.
Heath & Byrne, Sail Makers Loft, Champneys Whf
Heath, J. D., Attorney at Law, State House Square
Heath, James, Sail Maker, 3 S W Wall St
Hedderly, William, Bell Hanger & Founder, 36 Queen St
Heffernan, John, Cabinet Maker, 95 Tradd St
Heffernan, Michael, 10 Beaufain St
Heir, Henry, Drayman, 5 N W Boundary St.
Henderson, D, Lock Smith & Bell Hanger, 24 Queen St & Grocery Store, 24 East Bay Cont'd
Henderson, Elizabeth, Boarding House, 15 Trott St.
Henderson, Robert, 2 Pinckney St
Hendrickson, B, Carpenter, W Meeting St Road
Hennequin, J B Olman, Confectioner, 126 Queen St.
Henon, Thomas, Gun Smith, 22 Queen St

Henry, Ann, Mrs & Son, Millinery & Dry Goods Store, 118 Tradd St
Henry, Jacob, Merchant, 7 W King St Road
Henson, Archibald, Carpenter, 1 N Minority St
Henson, Thomas, 5 Berresford St
Henwood, Samuel B, Accomptant, 33 Society St
Herbemout, Nicholas, French Tutor, 213 Meeting St
Herd, Banjamin F, Grocer, 138 Queen St
Heriot, R, Merchant, Crafts' S Whf., Res, 2 Middle
Herron, John, Merchant, 142 King St
Herts & Poot, Dry Goods Store, 132 King St
Hessley, John, Tailor, 34 Queen St
Heynes, James, Grocer, 41 Union St
Heyns, James, Grocer, 4 Union St.
Heyward, Hannah, Mrs., Plantress, 10 Legare St
Heyward, Nathaniel, Planter, 25 East Bay Cont'd
Heyward, Samuel, Capt, Mariner, 11 Mazyck St
Heyward, Thomas, Planter, 221 Meeting St
Hibborn, Susanah, 27 King St.
Hill, Asa, Butcher Stall 6, Res, 2 N Cannon St
Hill, Charlotte, Widow, 16 Magazine St
Hill, Francis C, Painter, 28 Archdale St
Hill, Hannah, Mrs, Misses Boarding House, 19 Meeting
Hill, Helena, Mrs., Widow, Blake St, Hampstead
Hill, Henry, Coach Maker, 25 Guignard St
Hill, Paul, Distiller, Cane Wire Worker, Clerk of the German Church, 28 Archdale St
Hill, Thomas, Clothes Warehouse, 26 Church St
Hillegas, Philip, Distiller, 29 W King St Road
Hillman, ——, Mrs, Boarding House, 18 East Bay
Himely, J J, Merchant, 76 Church St.
Hinchman, Daniel R, Merchant, 71 East Bay
Hinds, Thomas, Attorney at Law, 33 Broad St
Hinson, Sarah, Nurse, 266 King St
Hinson, Susan, Seamstress, Mosers Lot, 209 Meeting
Hippius, Plebe, Mrs, 8 Pinckney St
Hislop, Christiana, Nurse, 3 Union St Cont'd
Hislop, John, Carpenter, 61 Church St
Hislop, Robert, Lumber Merchant, 1 Laurens St
Hislop, Robert, Tailor, 113 Queen St
Hobrecker & Rho, Gun Smiths, 91 King St
Hodge, E. Mantua Maker, Meeting St Cont'd
Hodgson, Martha, Nurse, 41 King St.
Hoey, Ann, Grocer, 5 King St
Hoff, John, Printer & Book Seller, 6 Broad St
Hogarth, William Jr, Shoe Maker, 3 East Bay Cont'd
Hollan, Andrew, Mariner & Counting House Waterman, 37 Church St Cont'd
Holland, ——, Mrs, Widow, 9 Parsonage Ln
Hollard, John, Custom House Officer, 12 Church St. Cont'd
Hollinshead, William, Rev Dr, Pastor Independent Church, 7 Maiden Ln

Holloway, Richard, Carpenter, 7 Archdale St
Holmes, Andres & Co, Merchant, 116 East Bay, Res, 4 Pinckney St
Holmes, Benjamin, Merchant, 12 King St Road
Holmes, Charles, Islington, N W Cannon St
Holmes, J B, Advocate & Planter, 6 Meeting
Holmes, Mary, Mrs, Widow, 8 St Philip's St
Holmes, Thomas, Carpenter, N Bull St
Holmes, Thomas, Custom House Inspector, 2 Linguard St
Holmes, William & Co, Vendue Master & Commission Merchant, Res, 129 East Bay S W cor Coming & Boundary
Honeywood, Arthur, Engraver, 59 Meeting St.
Honeywood, Elizabeth, Mrs, Widow, 59 Meeting St
Honour, John, Saddler, 20 Coming St
Hook, E, Mrs, Widow, Blake St, Hampstead
Hope, Jonathan, City Hotel, 55 East Bay
Hopkins & Charles, Merchant, 125 East Bay
Hopkins, Ebenezer, Grain Merchant, 10 Union Cont'd
Hopper, Elizabeth, Widow, Butcher, Alexander St
Hopton, Robert, Carpenter, 3 S Bull St
Horden, John, Tobacconist, 35 Broad St, 167 Meeting St
Horlbeck, Henry, Mason, 3 Moore St
Horlbeck, John, Jr., Mason, 9 Moore St
Horlbeck, John, Sr, Mason, 9 Moore St
Hornby, ——, Miss, Boarding School, 225 King St
Horry, Elias, Planter, 225 Meeting St
Horry, Harriett, Mrs, Plantress, 59 Tradd St
Horry, Jonah, Planter, Mazyckborough, cor. Charlotte & Elizabeth St
Horry, Lynch, Planter, 81 Broad St
Horry, Thomas, Planter, 27 Meeting St
Hort, Robert S, Attorney at Law, 18 George St
Houlton, James, Broker, 4 Cumberland St
House, Samuel, Q U and Notary Public, Comptrollers Office
Houston, James, House Carpenter, 5 Wall St
Howard, John, Mason, 21 George St
Howard, Richard, Cooper, Gillion St, Res, 35 Society
Howard, Robert, Tax Collector, Exchange, Res, 1 George St
Howell, Thomas, Capt, Lynch's St
Huff, John, Carpenter & Boarding House, 6 Unity Al
Huger, Ann J, Mrs, Widow, Plantress, 88 Broad
Huger, Carlos, Tailor, 7 Queen St Cont'd
Huger, Daniel, Late Secretary of State, 81 Queen St
Hughes, Edward, Jr, Merchant, 55 King St
Hughes, Edward, Teacher, Misses Academy, 79 Tradd
Hughes, John, Merchant, Chisolm's Whf., Res., 30 Church St Cont'd

Humbach, ——, Mr., Butcher, 26 King St Road
Humbert, Godfrey, Carpenter, Lynch's Ln
Hume, ——, Mr, 214 Meeting St
Hume, James, Grocer, 289 King St
Hume, John, Planter, 11 Wentworth St
Hume, John, Planter, W Smith St
Hunt, John, Merchant, 85 Church St
Hunt, Joseph, Capt, Mariner, 64 Wentworth St.
Hunt, Thomas, Planter, 51 Tradd St
Hunter, ——, Mrs, Dry Goods Store, 108 Queen St
Hunter, ——, Mrs, Widow of William, Tailor, 7 Elliott St Cont'd
Hunter, John, Hair Dresser, 108 Queen St
Hunter, John, Shoe Maker, 21 Church St Cont'd
Hurr, Abagail, Mrs, Widow, 241 King St
Hussey, Brian, Pilot, 13 Water St
Huston, James, Merchant Tailor, 27 Church St
Hutchins, Thomas, Gentleman, 12 Society St
Hutchinson, Ann, Mrs, 8 N Bull St
Hutchinson, Ann, Widow, Lynch's Ln
Hutchinson, Charlotte, Miss, 8 N Bull St
Hutchinson, E A, Merchant, 106 East Bay
Hutchinson, H, Capt, Mariner, 11 Champneys St
Hutchinson, Jeremy, near 1 Mile Stone, Meeting Road
Hutchinson, L, Mrs, Widow, 4 Federal St
Hutchinson, Samuel, Boarding House, Chalmers Al
Hutton, Frederick, Tailor, 4 Cumberland St
Hutton, James, Factor, 12 South Bay
Huxham, ——, Miss, Millinery Store, 13 Tradd St
Hyams, David, Store, 170 King St
Hyams, Hanah, Dry Goods Store, 98 King St
Hyams, Samuel, Dry Goods Store, 122 Queen St
Ingels, Catherine, Seamstress, 30 Pinckney St
Ingles, Thomas, Hair Dresser, 40 Meeting St
Inglesby, Henry, Mans Mercer & Merchant Tailor, 96 Broad St
Inglesby, William, Sr, Planter, 23 Tradd St
Ingraham, Nathaniel, Capt, Merchant, 149 King St
Ireland, Benjamin, Carpenter, 94 Queen St
Ireland, Edward, Cart Keeper, 18 W. King St. Road
Irvin, Moses, Shoe Maker, 16 Trott St.
Irvine, James, 34 Church St Cont'd
Irving, John, Capt, 12 Legare St
Irving, Mathew, Dr, 7 Meeting St
Isaacs, A, Vendue Master, Champney St, Res, 4 Bedon's Al
Isaacs, J, Mrs, Grocer, King St Road
Ivers, Sophia, Seamstress, 11 Berresford St
Izard, Henry, Planter, 1 Meeting St
Izard, Ralph, Mrs, Sr, Widow, 1 Meeting St
Izard, Ralph, Planter, 99 Broad St
Jacks, James, Merchant Jeweller, 125 Broad St
Jackson, Jonathan, Rev, W. Pitt St, Gadsden's Green
Jackson, Martha, Milliner, W King St Cont'd
Jackson, Mont, Deputy Sheriff, 10 Berresford Al
Jackson, William, Shoe & Boot Store, 77 East Bay

Jacobs, Barnard, Clothing Store & Public Chair
  Keeper, 50 East Bay
Jacobs, Elizabeth, 10 Queen St
Jacobs, Fanny, Seamstress, 115 Meeting St
Jacobs, Hyam, Merchant, 29 Meeting St
Jacobs, Samuel, Dry Goods Store, 211 King St
Jahan, Joseph, Architect Builder, 5 W Meeting St
  Cont'd
James, Holloway, Factor, Chisolm's S Whf
James, John, Carpenter, 8 Orange St
James, Robert, Carpenter, 31 King St
Jamieson, Rebecca, Widow, 18 Beaufain St
Javain, Peter, Dry Goods Store, 83 King St
Jeannerett, C, Collection Clerk, State Bank, Res, 5
  East Boundary St
Jearden, Louis, Grocer, 13 Trott St
Jeffers, Mary, Mrs., Plantress, Pinckney St,
  Cannonborough
Jenkins, ——, Mrs, Plantress, 20 South St
Jenkins, Edward, Rev Dr, Pastor, Episcopal
  Church, Res, 10 Lamboll St
Jenkins, Elias, Mason, 12 Liberty St
Jenkins, Michael, Planter, 2 Legare St
Jennings, Elizabeth, Mrs, Widow, 4 New St
Jerry, James, Attorney at Law, 62 Tradd St
Jesse, Sarah, Miss, S E cor Broad & King St
Jessop, J, Private Boarding House & Livery
  Stables, 243 King St
Jewell, Ben, Merchant, 59 East Bay
Jocelin, Henry, Cabinet Maker, 13 Amen St
Joffar, Sarah, Plantress, Harleston St.
Johnson, ——, Miss, 3 Amen St
Johnson, ——, Miss, Seamstress, 15 Wall St
Johnson, Barbara, Doctress, Widow, 9 Wentworth
Johnson, Benjamin, Capt, 15 Pinckney St
Johnson, Blanchy, Seamstress, Quince St
Johnson, David, Grocer, 157 King St
Johnson, J & Co, Merchant, 11 Champney
Johnson, J, Black Smith, Gillion St, Res, 87 Bay
  St or at his Foundary, King St Road
Johnson, Jabez W, Watchmaker, 119 Meeting
Johnson, John, Carpenter, 1 Blackbird Al
Johnson, John, Esq, 158 King St
Johnson, John, Hair Dresser, 16 Ellery St
Johnson, Joseph, Dr, Apothecary and Druggist, 5
  Broad St
Johnson, Mary, Miss, Plantress, South Bay
Johnson, Mary, Widow, Seamstress, 24 Beaufain
Johnson, Rachel, Boarding House, 2 Swinton Ln
Johnson, W P, Merchant, 158 King St
Johnson, William, Black Smith, 6 East Bay Cont'd
Johnson, William, Judge Admiralty, 1 Charles St.
Johnson, William, Sr, Black Smith, 10 Charles St.
Johnston, Alexander, School Master, 44 Trott St
Johnston, Christian, Sail Maker, Wingfields Loft, on
  Beale's Whf
Johnston, David, Deputy Collector, Custom House,
  Res, 22 Mazyck St

Johnston, Edward, Grocer, 23 Union St Cont'd
Johnston, J W, Attorney at Law, 83 Queen St,
  Office 48 Broad St
Jones, ——, Mrs, Pastry Cook, 42 Tradd St
Jones, Abner, Tailor, Amen St
Jones, Elizabeth, Widow, Tailoress, 7 Maiden Ln
Jones, Henry J, Merchant, 27 George St
Jones, Henry, Merchant, 18 Church St
Jones, Henry, Shipwright, 20 Pinckney St.
Jones, Jacob, Planter, Pinckney St, Cannonborough
Jones, Jehu, Tailor, 110 Broad St, Res 42 Tradd
Jones, Joseph, Merchant, 14 Tradd St
Jones, Nancy, Seamstress, Jones Court
Jones, Nathaniel, Merchant, 8 Tradd St
Jones, Robert W, Cabinet Maker, 29 King St
Jones, Samuel, S C Bank, 1 Guignard St
Jones, Samuel, Store, 248 King St
Jones, Snelling, 3 Beaufain St
Jones, Thomas, President, S C Bank, 2 Guignard
  St cor Charles St
Jones, William, Planter, 3 S Charlotte St
Jordon, Christopher, Grocer, 2 King St
Joseph, ——, Sausage Maker, 7 King St
Joseph, Joseph, Shop Keeper, 133 King St
Jourdan, Hanah, Seamstress, 51 Wentworth St
Jousset, John, Capt, Mariner, 19 Amen St
Just, George, Guardman, Chalmers Al
Just, John, 165 Meeting St
Kaifer, John J, Butcher, King St Road
Kamp, Catherine, Widow, 11 Cliffords Al
Kanpson, Herman, Carpenter, Vanderhorst St
Karwon, Thomas, Planter, 2 Hasell St
Kay, George M, Dry Goods Store, W King St.
  Cont'd
Kay, James, Grocer, 21 Meeting St
Kay, Mary, Widow, Boarding House & Seamstress,
  11 Bedon's Al
Keating, Elizabeth, 91 Church St.
Keating, William, Broker & Commission Merchant,
  Beale's Whf, Res Columbia St
Keddle, Charles, Merchant, 127 Broad St
Keenan, George, Merchant, 23 Chruch St Cont'd
  & 66 E King St Road
Keenan, Thomas, Grocer, 1 Church St
Kehnle, J, Custom House Weigher, S Boundary St
Kehr, John D, Commission Merchant, 110 East
  Bay
Keils, Peter, Carpenter, 11 E King St Road
Keith, Isaac, Rev Dr, Pastor, Independent
  Presbyterian Church, 50 Tradd St
Keith, Silvanus, Merchant & Whf Owner, 109 East
  Bay
Kelly, Christopher, Grocer, 11 Union St
Kelly, John, Pilot, 5 Guignard St
Kelly, Mary, Mrs, Store, 114 King St
Kelly, Michael, Merchant, 87 Tradd St
Kelly, William, Butcher, Hampstead
Kemnitz, Francis F, Merchant, 2 Smiths Ln

Kennedy, Ann, Mrs , N Charlotte St ,
Mazyckborough
Kennedy, Edward, Merchant, 5 Crafts' S Whf ,
Res , 10 Moore
Kennedy, James B , Merchant, 69 Tradd St
Kennedy, James, Planter, 8 Mazyck St
Kennedy, John, Accomptant, Jones Court
Kennedy, P , Grocer, 82 Meeting St & 53 Tradd
St
Kennedy, William, Tailor, Cock Ln
Kenny, John, Mariner, 8 Guignard St
Keon, William, Boarding House, Chalmers Al
Ker, Henry & John, Merchants, 10 Tradd St
Ker, John, Grain Inspector, 16 Society St
Kern, John F , Merchant, 185 King St
Kerr & Wadsworth, Corn Store & Grocery, 13
Archdale
Kerr, Andrew, Merchant, 126 Broad St
Kershaw, Charles, Factor, 23 East Bay
Kikland, Joseph, Dr , Physician, Dispensary, 34
Broad St
Kimball & Rand, Merchants, 15 Queen St
Kimball, George, Shoe Store, 110 Queen St
King, James, Grocer, 23 King St
King, John, Grocer, 5 Tradd St
King, Mary, Miss, 11 Amen St
King, Mary, Miss, Boarding House, Chalmers Al
King, William, Boarding House, 9 Union St
King, William, Grocer, 201 King St
Kingman, E , Shoe Store, 180 Meeting St
Kinmont, David, Black Smith, New East Bay St
Kirk, J & Lukens, Merchants, 56 East Bay
Kirk, John, Boarding House, 23 East Bay Cont'd
Kirkpatrick, James, Merchant, 84 Church St
Kittleband, David, House Carpenter, 7 Stolls Al
Knarston, James, Mill Wright, 3 S Spring St ,
Hampstead
Knell, Yates & Co , Merchants, Meeting St Road
Knox, Sarah, Mrs , Boarding House, 4 Meeting St
Knust, Henry, Grocer, 66 Broad St
Kochler, Aldophus, Tailor, 2 Beaufain St
Koffskey, Ann C , Grocer, 88 King St
Kohne, Frederick, Merchant, 28 East Bay
Kreps, Ann, Mrs. & Son, Bakers, 12 W King St
Cont'd.
Kugley, John, Carpenter & Whf Builder, 15
Mazyck
L'homaca, D , Dr , Physician, 23 Elliott St , Res ,
168 King St
Laats & Zylstra, Druggist, Paint & Oil Store, 138
King
Labat, David, Shop Keeper, 119 Queen St
Labatut, Peter, Drawing Master, 81 King St
Labaussay, ——, Baker, 3 E King St Cont'd.
Laborde, Francis, Livery Stables & Public Chairs,
173 King
Laborde, Henriette, Fruit Shop, 253 King St

Lacassagne, Mary, Refugee, St. Domingo, 9 Middle
St
Lacombe, Geraud, Tobacconist, 108 King St
Lacombe, John Benoit, Capt , 4 Maiden Ln
Lacombe, Stephen, Dr , 3 Maiden Ln.
Lacoste, Stephen, Merchant, 9 Magazine St
Lacroix, H , School Mistress, 16 Archdale St
Ladeveze, Joseph, Merchant, 85 King St
Ladson, ——, Mrs., Widow, 88 Tradd St
Ladson, James, Maj , Planter, 13 Meeting St
Lafar, Peter & John, Goldsmith & Jewellers, 15
Meeting St
Lafarque, ——, Madame, 119 King St.
Laffont, John & Co , Coopers, Motte's Whf
Lafilley, Francis, Book Keeper, 4 Wentworth St
Lagrande, Francis, Dr , 25 Union St Cont'd
Laidler, William, Capt , Mariner, Blackbird Al
Lajus, Paul, Confectioner, 139 Broad St
Lamb, David, Merchant, 2 Bedon's Al
Lambert, Jane, Mrs , 13 Friend St
Lampton, Catherine, Widow, 15 Quince St
Lance, Lambert, Mrs , Widow, 81 Queen St
Landrie, ——, Madame, Widow, Shop Keeper, 6
Beaufain St
Lane, Ann, Mrs , Widow, 11 Friend St
Lane, Joseph, Carpenter, 40 Trott St
Lane, Robert, Merchant, 108 East Bay
Lange, J H & Co , Merchant, 18 East Bay
Lange, Jacob, 1 Church St Cont'd
Langley, John, Merchant, 11 Middle St
Langley, William, S Montague St
Langlois, DeBarville, Refugee, St Domingo, 19
Federal St
Langlois, Maria, Madame, Boarding School, 94
Tradd St
Langstaff & Frink, Wharfingers, Beale's Whf , 36
Trott St
Langton, John, Grocer, 123 Queen St
Lanneau, Bazile, 1 S W Pitt St cor Beaufain
Lants, Sarah, Widow, 62 Wentworth St
Lapenne, Joseph, Grocer, 59 E. King St Road cor
Read St
Lapier, Amy, Seamstress, Prices Al
Lapierre, Bernard, Cabinet Maker, 175 Meeting St
Laporte, R., 19 Wall St
Laroche, Elizabeth, Widow, Seamstress, 29
Beaufain
Larrey, Robert, Carpenter, 57 Church St
Lartigan, Dominick, Grocer, 145 Meeting St
Latham, Daniel, Distiller, 1 Hasell St
Latham, Joseph, Distiller, Cannonborough
Latthausen, J W , at Mr Mauran, 15 Tradd St
Laughlin, Mary, Shop Keeper, 70 King St
Laurence, Henry, Planter, 28 East Bay Cont'd
Laurens, Peter, Grocer, 167 King St
Laval, Jacint, Sheriff, Charleston District, Office,
State House, Res., 16 Pinckney St
Lavaulan, Paul, Trader, 193 Meeting St

Lawrence, Elizabeth, Mrs , Widow, 18 Pinckney St
Lawrence, Robert D , Attorney at Law, 83 East Bay
Lawrence, Sarah, Mrs , Widow, 44 George St
Lawrence, Vincent, Capt , Merchant, 38 Society St
Lawson, William, Fruit Shop, 87 Queen St
Lawton, Winburn, Planter, Lynch's Ln
Lazarus, Jacob, Dry Goods Store, 144 King St
Lazarus, Marks, Store Keeper, 102 King St
Leadbetter, Agnes, Mrs , School Mistress, 9 Liberty St
Leatch, Catherine, Seamstress, 39 Church St Cont'd
Leaumont, R , Professor of Music, N W cor Middle & Minority St
Leavitt, Joshua, Grocer, 112 East Bay
Lebby, Nathaniel, Mast & Pump Maker, Governor's Bridge, Res , 55 Church St
Leblong, Henry, Shoe Maker, 7 Liberty St
Lebreton, John B , Store Keeper, 2 Queen St
LeBruce, Martha, Plantress, 226 Meeting St
Lecat, ——, Madame, Confectioner, 89 King St
Lecat, P., Professor of Music, 89 King St.
Lechais, A , Assistant Post Master, 13 Church St
Leduc & Danjou, Grocers, 117 Queen St
Lee & Beekman, Auctioneers, 128 East Bay
Lee, Abigail, Seamstress, 222 Meeting St.
Lee, John & Co , Merchants, 206 King St
Lee, Stephen, Attorney at Law, Clerk, Inferior Court, 55 King St
Lee, Stephen, Planter, 40 Broad St
Lee, Thomas, Comptroller General, Office 3d Story Guard House, Res , 17 Society St
Lee, Timothy, Factor, 14 Crafts' N Whf
Lee, William, Merchant, 1 Archdale St
Leefe, ——, Mr , Merchant, 23 Elliott St
Lefeve, John, Glass Engraver, 181 Meeting St
Legare, Elizabeth, Mrs , Widow, 2 Mazyck St
Legare, James, Planter, 2 New St
Legare, John, Planter, Santee, 5 Anson St
Legare, Mary, Mrs , Plantress, 10 Wall St
Legare, Mary, Mrs , Widow, 283 King St
Legare, Solomon, Planter, 19 Friend St.
Legare, Thomas, Planter, 1 Gibbes St
Lege, J M , Dancing Master Academy, 104 Queen St
Legg, Catherine, Mrs., Widow, 7 St Philip's St.
Legg, Joseph, Store Keeper, 184 King St
Legge, Ann, Mrs , Widow, 57 Trott St
Lehre, ——, Mr , Accomptant, 8 Middle St
Lehre, Ann, Mrs., Widow, 25 St Philip's St
Lehre, Thomas, Planter, 272 King St
Lelly, Stephen & Sibley, Turpentine Distillers, Mazyckborough, Grocery Store, Governor's Bridge
Lemake, Christian, Grocer, 27 Wentworth St cor St Philip's St
Lengle, John, Merchant, 14 N W Middle St

Lenormant, Andrew, Goldsmith & Jeweller, 101 King
Lenox, Samuel, Merchant, 8 Beaufain St
Leroy, Joseph, Hair Dressser, 98 Church St
LeRoy, Joseph, Hair Dresser, 28 Church St
Leseigneur, Vincent, Dr , 4 E Savage St , Res , Hospital for Negroes, S W End cor Broad & Savage St
Lesene, Thomas, Merchant, 127 Broad St
Lesley, Henry, Capt., Mariner, 6 Trott St
Lester, J , Seamstress, 37 King St
Leuder, F , Mrs , Confectioner, 27 Queen St , Candle & Soap Manufactory, 6 W. Meeting St
Leven, L , Dry Goods Store, 194 Meeting St
Levrier, Peter, Rev , French Teacher, 42 Meeting St
Levy, Ann, Dry Goods Store, 187 King St
Levy, Bella, Shop Keeper, 267 King St
Levy, Lyon, Clerk in the Treasury, 189 King St
Levy, Manuel, Store, 230 King St
Levy, Moses C , Store, 217 King St
Levy, Nathan, Shop Keeper, 115 King St
Levy, Ruben, Broker, 18 Magazine St
Levy, Samuel S , Grocer & Dry Goods Store
Levy, Simon, Store, 229 King St
Levy, Solomon, Merchant, 100 N W cor Broad & King St
Levy, Solomon, Store, 53 King St
Lewis, ——, Mr , Grocer, Governor's Bridge
Lewis, Ann, Shop Keeper, 60 Church St
Lewis, Isaac, Merchant, 20 Broad St
Lewis, John, Factor, W Alexander St
Lewis, John, Grocer, 22 Union St.
Lewis, Joseph, 31 Archdale St & at the Times Office
Lexier, ——, Madame, Rutledge St
Leyles, Marian, Seamstress, 5 George St
Liddle, Delila, Seamstress, Cock Ln
Liddle, John, Custom House Inspector, Cock Ln
Lieben, Israel D , Broker & Commission Merchant, 43 East Bay
Lightwood, Edward, Attorney at Law, 220 Meeting St , Office, Thomas Parker Esq
Lightwood, Elizabeth, Mrs , Widow, 220 Meeting St
Limehouse, Robert, Lumber Measurer, 64 Tradd St
Lindsay, Robert, Carpenter, 27 Church St Cont'd
Ling, Philip, Coach Maker, 9 Guignard St
Linguard, Mary, Mrs , Widow, 65 Church St
Lining, Charles, Attorney at Law, Ordinary, Charleston District, 3 Legare St
Little, Ann, Widow, Boarding House, 6 Union St
Little, Robert, Carpenter, 3 Pinckney St
Little, Robert, Lumber Merchant, Fitzsimmons' Whf.
Livingston, J H , Printer, 79 Queen St.
Livingston, John, Tailor, 41 King St
Livingston, Robert Y , Merchant, E King St Road

Lloyd, Daniel, Mrs , Widow, 7 Bedon's Al
Lloyd, Henry, Boarding House, 5 Union St Cont'd
Lloyd, John, Jr (B T), W End Bull St
Lloyd, John, Jr , Factor, 166 Meeting St
Lloyd, John P , Bedstead & Venetian Blind Maker,
Etc , 80 Meeting St
Lloyd, John, Sr , Planter, 60 Tradd St
Lloyd, Joseph, Dry Goods Store, 229 King St
Lock, Emily, Miss, Savage St
Lockwood, Joshua, Planter, 1 Smiths Ln
Lockwood, Joshua, State Bank, Res , 40 Broad St.
Lockwood, Thomas P , Glass & China Store, 87
Church
Logan, C M , Factor, Chisolm's Whf
Logan, Christian M , Factor, Chisolm's Whf , Res ,
31 Tradd St
Logan, George, Dr , Physician, Dispensary, Res ,
111 Queen
Logan, J V , 31 Tradd St
Logan, Thomas, Grocer, 43 Church St
Long, John, Butcher, Cannonborough
Long, John, Merchant, 31 Clifford St
Long, Mary, Nurse, 4 George St
Lopez, Aron, Merchant, 214 King St
Lopez, David, Commission Merchant, 126 East Bay
Lord, Jacob N , Boot & Shoe Maker, 2 W King
Cont'd
Lorent & Steinmetz, Merchants, New Firm
Lorent, Knipping & Steinmetz, Merchants, 135 &
136 East Bay, Res , 52 Tradd St
Loret, ——, Madame, 1 Longitude Ln
Lorez, John, Dry Goods Store, 111 King St
Lothrop, Seth, Merchant, 109 East Bay & 2
Prioleau's N Whf
Love, Elizabeth, Seamstress, 23 St Philip's St
Loveday, Sarah, Mrs , Widow, 10 Moore St.
Lovell, J S , Merchant, 80 Tradd St
Lovell, John, Revenue Cutter, 35 Broad St
Lovett, William, Carpenter, 3 Lamboll St
Low, James, Mariner, 35 Church St. Cont'd
Lowe, John, Jeweller, 33 Church St
Lowndes, James, Planter, 215 Meeting St.
Lowndes, Jane, Mrs , Plantress, 7 Church St
Lowndes, John, Grocer, 62 Meeting St.
Lowndes, Thomas, 89 Broad St
Lowndes, William, Planter, 89 Broad St
Lowrey, Charles, Tailor, 45 Church St
Lubet, John, 10 Wentworth St.
Lucas, John, Lumber Merchant, Lucas' Mills,
Cannonborough
Lucas, Jonathan, Planter & Mill Owner, Pinckney
St , Cannonborough
Lucian, Alexander, Baker, E Pinckney St ,
Cannonborough
Lukens & Co , Merchants, Quince St
Lukens, John, Merchant, 56 E Bay, Res , 6 Hasell
St.
Lundquest, Magnus, Shipwright, 9 Pinckney

Lusher, George, Merchant, 74 East Bay
Luther, Giles, Shoe Store, 186 Meeting St
Lynah, James, Dr , Physician, 47 Meeting St
Lynch, Thomas, Mason, 4 West St
Lyon, Mordicai, Shop Keeper, 225 King St
M'Afee, John, Carpenter, 9 Liberty St
M'Allister, Benjamin, Capt , Grocer, 4 Prioleau's
Whf
M'Allister, John, Butcher, 56 East Bay
M'Beth, Henry & Co , Merchants, 138 East Bay
M'Beth, Henry & Son, Merchants, 138 East Bay
M'Beth, James, Merchant, 137 East Bay
M'Beth, John, Shoe Maker, 40 Elliott St
M'Bride, Mary, Mrs , 57 East Bay
M'Call, Ann, Mrs , Widow, 105 Church St
M'Call, Elizabeth, Mrs , 14 Meeting St
M'Call, Hicks, Attorney at Law, 12 Meeting St
M'Call, James, Planter, Opposite 1 Mile Stone
M'Call, John, Grocer, 188 Meeting St
M'Call, John H , Planter, 105 Church St
M'Call,——, 3 King St
M'Calla, Thomas H , Dr , Physician, 10 Elliott St
M'Cann, Edward, Clerk, Fish Market, 6 Prices Al
M'Cardle, John, Constable, 16 Hasell St
M'Cardle, Patrick, State Constable, 5 Chalmers Al
M'Clarichdie, ——. Mrs , Midwife, 77 Meeting St
M'Cleish, ——, Mrs , School Mistress, 26 Queen St
M'Cleish, Alexander, Brass Founder &
Mathematical Instrument Maker, 56 Meeting St ,
Res , 9 St Philip's
M'Clure, John, Merchant, 2 cor Champneys Whf
M'Cormick, Elizabeth, Boarding House, Champneys
Whf
M'Cormick, William, Grocer, 21 E Bay cor Tradd
St
M'Couarta, Margaret, 5 Beaufain St
M'Credie, David & Co , Merchants, 8 Broad St
M'Credie, Jane, Mrs , Widow, 42 East Bay Cont'd
M'Credie, William, Millinery, 209 King St
M'Dannell, Sarah, Grocer & Wagon Yard, 16 W
King St Road
M'Donnald, ——, Mr , Carpenter, 1 Cliffords Al
M'Donnald, ——, Mrs , Widow, 10 Beaufain St
M'Donnald, Christopher, Grocer, 269 King St
M'Dow, Preceptor, S Montague St
M'Dowall & Co , Grocers, 24 Pinckney St
M'Dowall, Alexander, Merchant, 32 Broad St
M'Dowall, Alexander, Saddler, 80 King St
M'Dowall, James, Merchant, 64 King St
M'Dowall, John, Merchant, 144 King St
M'Dowall, John, Merchant, 169 King St
M'Dowall, Patrick, Merchant, 143 Broad St
M'Elmoyle, William, Grocer, 276 King St
M'Farlane, Catherine, Widow, 36 Hasell St
M'Fie, Dugald, Merchant, 27 Church St Cont'd
M'Gann, Patrick, Watchmaker, 132 East Bay

M'Gillivray, Alexander H , Vendue Master & Commission Merchant, 43 East Bay, Res , 36 Tradd St

M'Ginness, Patrick, Grocer, 70 King St

M'Ginness, Peter, Grocer, 15 Ellery St

M'Grath, Edward, Architect, 5 & 26 Archdale St

M'Grath, Michael, Merchant, Nichols' Whf

M'Gregor, Neil, Planter, S W End Vanderhorst St.

M'Hugh, Francis, Builder, South Bay

M'Hugh, John, Merchant, 17 Scarborough St

M'Intosh & Foulds, Cabinet Makers, 133 Meeting St

M'Intosh, Elizabeth, Widow, 66 Church St

M'Kay, Barbara, Shop Keeper, 1 Quince St

M'Kay, Malcolm, Grocer, 53 ½ Tradd St

M'Kee, ——, Mrs , Shop Keeper, 277 King St

M'Kee, John, Mason, 277 King St

M'Kenzie & M'Neill, Merchants & Grocers, 123 Broad

M'Kenzie, Ann, Butcher, Spring St

M'Kenzie, Callen, Merchant, E King St Cont'd

M'Kenzie, Catherine, Seamstress, Prices Al

M'Kenzie, Elizabeth, Boarding House, 3 N Unity Al

M'Kenzie, Hannah, Mantua Maker, 53 Queen St

M'Kernan, James, Wharfinger, Keith's Whf , Res 8 Church St

M'Kerns, Michael, Grocer, 28 Union St

M'Key, John, Dr , Physician, Jailer, Magazine St

M'Kinley, Donald, Merchant, 19 Elliott St

M'Kinnie, Isaac, 165 Meeting St

M'Lachlan, Campbell & Co , Merchants, 16 Tradd St

M'Lachlin, Philip, Capt , Mariner, 264 Meeting St

M'Lean, ——, Mr , Gentleman, 259 King St.

M'Leod, John, Overseer, 17 W King St Road

M'Millan, Ann, Mrs , Widow, 77 Tradd St

M'Millan, John, Merchant, Chisolm's Whf

M'Millan, Richard, Merchant Stables & Wagon Yard, 7 East King St Cont'd

M'Millan, Thomas, Carpenter, 77 Tradd St

M'Neal & Walton, Merchant, 3 E King St Cont'd

M'Neal, Catherine, Shop Keeper, 36 Hasell St

M'Neal, Nathaniel, Gentleman, 49 King St

M'Neil, Neil, Capt , Mariner, 144 East Bay, Res 21 King

M'Owen & Hagood, Merchants, Vanderhorst's Whf

M'Pherson, Duncan, Store Keeper, 72 King St

M'Pherson, John, Mrs , Plantress, 99 Broad St

M'Pherson, Peter, Candle Manufactory, Cannon St

M'Quiston, Archibald, Store, 79 King St

M'Ray, Malcolm, Grocer, 54 Tradd St

M'Taggart, David, Merchant, 7 Cumberland St

M'Whan & Nephew, Merchants, 19 Broad St , Res Gadsdens Ln.

Macadam, James & Co , Merchants, 153 East Bay, Res. S W End Cannon St , Cannonborough

Macaulay, Daniel, Merchant, 111 Tradd St

Macaulay, Son & Co , Merchants, 18 Broad St

Mackay, Elizabeth, Mantua Maker, 14 Quince St

Mackay, Sarah, Widow, 54 Wentworth St

Madelmond, John, School Master, 151 Meeting St

Madlemond, ——, Madame, Shop Keeper, 112 Queen St.

Maguire, F & J , Boot & Shoe Makers, 44 Broad St

Magwood, Robert, Physician, 99 Queen St

Magwood, Simon, Factor, Blake's Whf , Res , 99 Queen St

Maheo, Louis, Merchant, 42 Broad St & 11 King St Road

Maine, John, Commission Merchant, Motte's Whf , 43 East Bay Cont'd

Mair, Ann, Mrs , Widow, 43 Church St Cont'd

Mair, Brice & Co , Merchants, 135 East Bay

Makky, John, Builder, 113 Meeting St

Malcomb, ——, Mrs , 6 Mazyck St

Malton, Thomas, Gentleman, 6 Mazyck St

Manigault, Gabriel, Planter, 5 Amen St

Manigault, Joseph, Planter, cor E Meeting St Road

Mann, Colin, Cigar Maker, 54 Church St

Mann, Margaret, Boarding School, 7 Trott St

Mann, Spencer John, Merchant, Motte's Whf , 20 Federal St

Manning, Flora E , Widow, Store, 54 East Bay

Mansui, ——, Monsieur, Cigar Maker, 25 Union St Cont'd

Manuel, E , 13 Bull St

Manuel, Philip, Tailor, 42 Queen St , Res , 5 Clifford Al

Marchal, Francis, Professor of Music, 40 Church St

Marchant, Peter T , Courier Office, 16 East Bay Cont'd

Marcie & Co , Grocers, 33 Pinckney St

Margart, John H , Black & White Smith, 66 Meeting St , Res , 2 Blackbird Al

Marian, Christopher, Unity Al

Markley, Abraham, Merchant, 122 King St

Marks, Humphrey, Merchant, 137 King St & 10 W. King St Cont'd

Marks, Joseph, Grocer, 125 Queen St

Marks, S M , Shop Keeper, 127 King St

Marlen, Edward, Sr Custom House Inspector, Cock Ln.

Marlen, W C , Cabinet Maker, Whim Court

Marsden, ——, Mr , Factor, S Amherst St

Marsh, James, Shipwright, 24 Guignard St

Marshall, ——, Mrs , Misses Boarding School, 74 Tradd St

Marshall, Ellen, Mrs , 19 Wall St

Marshall, Helena, Shop Keeper, 27 E Wall St

Marshall, J , Cutler & Surgeon's Instrument Maker, 194 Meeting St

Marston, David, Commission Merchant, 3 Crafts'
  N Whf.
Martin, ----, Monsieur, Cigar Maker, 17 Union St
Martin & Ricard, Grocers, 8 N Prioleau's Whf
Martin, Charles, Mason, 17 Scarborough St
Martin, Christian, Grocer, 5 N Prioleau's Whf
Martin, Henry, 10 Meeting St Cont'd
Martin, Jacob, Book Keeper S C Bank, Res, 174
  Meeting St
Martin, John P., Merchant, 10 Wentworth St
Martin, Nicholas, Mason, 114 Meeting St
Martin, Philip B, Butcher, Hampstead
Martin, Thomas & Co., Merchants, Chisolm's Whf
  & 79 East Bay
Martindale, James C, Merchant, W King St
  Cont'd
Mashbourn, Nicholas, Carpenter, 92 East Bay
Mason & Co, Merchants, 113 Tradd St
Mason, Sarah, Mrs, Boarding School, 109 Church
  St.
Massot, H, Watch Maker, cor Queen & Meeting
  St.
Mathew, James, 3 Anson St
Mathews, Benjamin, Mrs, Widow, 1 S Bull St
Mathews, George, Vendue Master & Commission
  Merchant, S E cor Bull & Rutledge St
Mathews, James, Attorney at Law, 83 East Bay
Mathews, James, Shoe Maker, 23 King St
Mathews, John, Mrs, Plantress, Harleston Green
Mathews, John, Planter, N Bull St
Mathews, Martha Ann, Plantress, 3 W New St
Mathews, Mary, Seamstress, E Pitt St
Mathews, Sarah, Mrs, S W cor Rutledge &
  Wentworth St Cont'd
Mathews, Thomas, Planter, 13 Lamboll St
Mathews, William, Planter, W Rutledge St
Mauger, John, Ship Broker, 24 East Bay
Mauran, John R, Carolina Coffee House, 115
  Tradd St
Maury, ----, Mrs, Millinery Store, 139 King St.
Maury, Everest, Teacher, Piano Forte, 139 King St
Maxwell, Harriot, Mrs, 48 Meeting St
May, James, Grocer, 3 Tradd St.
May, John, Tavern Keeper, 180 King St
Mayberry, Thomas, Steward, Marine Hospital, 58
  Queen St
Mayerick, Samuel, Merchant, 2 W King St Road,
  Res., E Boundary, St. opposite Orphan House
Mazyck, Daniel, Planter, N E cor Smith &
  Montague St
Mazyck, N, 10 Broad St., Res, 86 Meeting St
Mazyck, Stephen, Planter, 5 Short St
Mazyck, William, 3 Archdale St, Firm Gaillard &
  Mazyck
Mead, James, Grocer, N E cor. Quince & Hasell
Meagher, Martin B., Mariner, 22 Wall St
Meagher, Mary, Boarding House, 36 East Bay
  Cont'd

Mealy, John, 2d Lt City Guard, 26 Trott St
Mecomb, Joseph, Merchant, 155 King St
Medows, George, Boot & Shoe Maker, Vanderhorst
  St
Meeds, William, Coffee House, 1 S E cor Cannon
  & Coming St Cont'd
Meeks, Sarah, Widow, 4 St. Philip St
Meentz, D C A, Grocer, 180 King St
Megrath, Michael, Commission Merchant, Keith's
  Whf
Meine, John, Factor, 44 East Bay Cont'd
Mellard, James H, Rev, Methodist Church, N W
  cor Pitt & Boundary St (Parsonage House)
Mellicham, S L., Planter, 2 S Montague St
Melmies, Anthony, Turner, 137 Meeting St
Mensey, Robert, Boot Maker, 71 Meeting St
Menud, John B G, 19 Ellery St
Meriam & Perry, Merchants, 1 Crafts' N Whf
Mersey, John, Mariner, 53 Church St
Metivier, Stephen & Francis, Bakers, 139 Meeting
  St
Meurset, John, Silver Smith, 21 Broad St
Mey, Florian C, Merchant, Mey's Whf, Res, 43
  Pinckney St
Michael, Henry, Public Chair Keeper, 1 Parsonage
  Ln
Michel, Marie, Madame, Veuve, 6 W Coming St
Middleton, Ann, Mrs., Plantress, 95 Broad St
Middleton, Arthur, 95 Broad St
Middleton, Henry, Planter, N Montague St
Middleton, Mary, Widow, Seamstress, 1 Cliffords
  Al
Middleton, Solomon, Tailor, 129 King St
Miles, Michael, Vendue Row, 7 George St.
Miley, Peter, Deputy Sheriff, 4 St Philip's St
Millar, Nicholas, Baker, 16 George St
Millar, William, Baker, 23 Queen St
Miller, Anson, Shipwright, 18 N W Wall St
Miller, Benjamin, Butcher, Opposite the One Mile,
  King St Road
Miller, Catherine, Boarding House, 19 Society St
Miller, Christopher, Confectioner, 37 Queen St
Miller, Elizabeth, Boarding House, Chalmers Al
Miller, Elizabeth, Widow, 161 King St
Miller, Frederick, Butcher, 57 King St Road
Miller, Frederick, Guardsman, 3 Union St Cont'd
Miller, J D., 2 East Boundary St cor Wall
Miller, James, Merchant, 110 Tradd St
Miller, James, Sr, Merchant, Chisholm's Whf
Miller, James, Wine Merchant, 61 East Bay
Miller, John H., Notary Public and Q U, 134 East
  Bay, Res., 15 Guignard
Miller, John James, Carpenter, W End Wentworth
  St Cont'd
Miller, John T., House Carpenter, 9 Laurens St
Miller, Martha, Goldsmith & Jeweller, 35 Queen St
Miller, Mathew, Goldsmith & Jeweller, 40 Queen
  St

Miller, William, Chalmers Al
Miller, William, Tailor, 102 Queen St
Milligan, F , 3 Washington St , Mazyckborough
Milligan, Joseph, Shop Keeper, 69 King St
Milligan, Joseph, Store Keeper, 73 King St
Milligan, Thomas, Accomptant, 1 Stolls Al
Milligan, William, Merchant, 124 East Bay, Res ,
    48 Church St Cont'd
Milligan, William, Shipwright, 27 Hasell St
Mills, Andrew, Carpenter, 6 Magazine St
Mills, Rebecca, Mrs , Widow, 48 E Bay Cont'd.
Mills, Thomas, Merchant, 108 Tradd St.
Milner, George, Black Smith, 72 Church St , Chair
    Makers Shop, 52 Church St.
Minot, Dorcas, 5 Smiths Ln
Minot, John & Benjamin, Factors, 6 East Bay
Minot, William, Planter, 2 Gibbes, St
Miott, John, Lumber Measurer, N Amhearst St
Mishaw, John, Grocer, 4 East Bay Cont'd
Mitchell, Alexander, Harness Maker, 78 Meeting St
Mitchell, Andrew, Stucco Plasterer, 2 Short St
Mitchell, Ann E , Mrs , Widow, Plantress, 25 Wall
Mitchell, Ann, Mrs , Plantress, 118 Meeting St.
Mitchell, Dennison & Co , Coopers, Vanderhorst's
    Whf
Mitchell, Elizabeth, Widow, 9 Amen St
Mitchell, James, Cooper, Vanderhorst's Whf , 18
    Meeting St
Mitchell, James D , Attorney at Law & Secretary to
    the Late Governor, 213 Meeting St
Mitchell, James, House Carpenter, 6 West St
Mitchell, John, Boarding House, 23 Union St
Mitchell, John, Col , Notary Public and Q U , 29
    East Bay, Res , 7 Magazine St
Mitchell, L , Capt , Mariner, 20 Berresford St
Mitchell, Mills, W End Boundary St
Mitchell, Thomas, Pilot, 276 King St
Mitchell, Thomas, Pilot, New East Bay St
Modern, James, Mariner, 3 Ellery St
Moise, A & H , Vendue Master & Commission
    Merchants, Vendue Row
Moise, Cherry, Broker & Agent for J Cohen &
    Co , Res , 98 Tradd St
Moles, ——, Mrs , Store, 193 King St
Moles, James, Black Smith, 193 King St.
Moncrieffe, John, Carpenter, 9 East Bay Cont'd
Moncrieffe, John, Merchant, 1 Church St
Moncrieffe, Mary, Mrs., Widow, 82 Tradd St
Monefeldt, Esaias, Merchant, 119 East Bay, Res.,
    119 Tradd St
Monnar, Lewis, Hair Dresser, 2 & 21 Queen St
Monpoey, Honore, Grocer, 118 King St
Montamar, ——, Madame, Shop Keeper, 2 King St
    Road
Montel, Anthony, Shop Keeper, 288 King St
Mood, Peter, Goldsmith & Jeweller, 222 King
Moodie, Benjamin, His Britannic Majesty's Consul,
    65 Tradd St.

Mooney, Patrick, Merchant, Champneys Whf , Res ,
    8 S Cannon St & 21 Tradd St
Mooney, William, Merchant, 9 Broad St
Moore, H H , 186 Meeting St
Moore, John E , Planter, 33 Trott St
Moore, Joseph, Drayman & Public Chair Keeper, 8
    East Bay Cont'd
Moore, Mary, Widow, Grocer, 196 Meeting St
Moore, Philip, Cabinet Maker, 28 Meeting St
Moore, S W , Accomptant, Lynch's Ln
Moran, Christian, Boarding House, Chalmers Al
Mordicai, D & Co , Vendue Master & Commission
    Merchants, Exchange Row
Mordicai, David, Commission Merchant, 14
    Guignard
Mordicai, Jacob, Broker, 250 King St
More, P J , Dr , Surgeon, Dentist & Midwife, 47
    King St
Morford, E , Book Store, 132 Broad St
Morgan, Benjamin, Grocer, 12 Middle St
Morgan, E B , Sash Maker, Meeting St Road
Morgan, Henry, Boarding House, 18 Amen St
Morgan, Isaac, Carpenter, Parsonage Ln
Morphy, Don Diego, His Catholic Majesty's Consul
    for Spain, 79 Meeting St
Morris, Elizabeth, Shop Keeper, 33 East Bay
    Cont'd
Morris, Thomas, Col , Merchant, 17 Legare St
Morris, Thomas, Factor Gadsden's Whf , 58 Trott
    St
Morrison, James, Cooper, 1 Cochran's Whf
Morrison, John, Capt , Mariner, 89 Tradd St
Morrison, John, Clerk to M'Dowell & Co., Res ,
    Prices Al
Morrison, Rebecca, Widow, 98 Wentworth St
Morrison, Spencer, Grocer, Elliott St Cont'd
Mortimer & Heron, Merchants, 14 Broad St
Mortimer, Edward, Merchant, 6 Anson St
Morton, Alexander, Grocer, 231 King St
Morton, Joseph, Drayman, 5 W Pitt St , Harleston
    Green
Moser, Myer, Firm Cohen & Moses, 86 Broad
Moser, Philip, Dr , Apothecary & Druggist, 124
    Broad St , Res , 1 New St
Moses & Isaacks, Vendue Master & Commission
    Merchants, 7 S Champneys St
Moses, Chapman, Store, 116 King St
Moses, Henry, Shop Keeper, 51 East Bay
Moses, Isaac C , Merchant, 96 & 237 King St
Moses, Isaiah, Store, 197 King St
Moses, Lyon, Broker, 18 Archdale St
Moses, Philip & Sons, Coopers, 20 King St
Moses, Philip, Store, 36 King St
Moses, Solomon, Constable, 191 King St
Motherin, James, Boarding House, 11 Charles
Motta, E D L., Auctioneer & Commission
    Merchant, Exchange Row, Res , 48 Tradd St

Motte, A & F Sauvalle, Merchants, 11 Motte's Whf
Motte, Abraham, Whf Owner Stores, 14, 15, 16, 17 & 18 Motte's Whf, Res 41 Church
Motte, Francis, Factor, Vanderhorst's Whf, Res 209 Meeting St
Motte, J A., Store Keeper, 75 King St
Motte, Mary, Mrs, Widow, 217 Meeting St
Mouat, John, Mrs, Widow, 32 Beaufain St
Mouat, John, Out Door Clerk, S C Bank, 32 Beaufain St
Moubray, Martha, Mrs, 90 King St
Moubray, William, Baker, 29 W King St
Moulin, Peter, Shop Keeper, 251 King St
Moultire, William A, Planter, E Pinckney St, Cannonborough
Moultrie, A, Advocate at Law, 2 Cumberland
Moultrie, Ann, Mrs, Plantress, 62 Tradd St
Moultrie, H, Mrs, Plantress, Town
Moultrie, James, Dr, Port Physician, 87 Meeting
Moultrie, William, Gen, Butcher, Town
Mouzon, Christian, Boot & Shoe Maker, 4 Church
Muck, Philip, Music Master, 254 King St
Muckenfuss, Henry, 3 N Wentworth St Cont'd
Muckenfuss, Michael, Cabinet Maker, 53 King St
Muir, William, Merchant, 8 Magazine St
Mulin, Rose, Mantua Maker, 31 Trott St
Mulin, Sarah, Widow, 7 Church St
Muller, F, Shoemaker & Guardman, 3 Union
Mulligan, Bernard, Wharfinger, 12 Champneys Whf
Munch, Philip H, German Hotel, 127 East Bay
Muncreeffe, John, Jr, Carpenter, 9 East Bay Cont'd
Muncreeffe, John, Sr, Carpenter, 9 East Bay Cont'd
Muncreeffe, Susanah, Mrs, Widow, 34 Hasell St
Munds, Israel, Rev, Academy, 6 Union St Cont'd
Munro, Catherine, Mrs, Midwife, 43 Elliott St cor E Bay
Munro, John, Boarding House, 123 East Bay
Munro, John, Jewellery Store, 8 Elliott St
Munro, Thomas, Boarding House, 38 Union St
Munsell, John, Grocer, Chalmers Al
Murden, Jeremiah, Merchant, 2 Prioleau's S. Whf
Murley, Samuel, Merchant, 77 East Bay, Res Charlotte St
Murphy, ——, Mrs, Boarding House, 15 Elliott St
Murray, ——, Mrs, Seamstress, 43 King St.
Murray, Charlotte, Mantua Maker, Chalmers Al
Murset, Amelia, Widow, 21 Archdale St
Mushett, J, Black Smith, 10 Ellery St, Res 68 Meeting St
Myer, Michael, Auctioneer, 7 Clifford St
Myers, Andrew, Guardman, 5 Cliffords Al
Myers, John, Guardman, 5 Clifford Al
Myers, Samuel, Tailor, 208 King St
Mylne, James, Mrs, 31 Union St Cont'd

Myzyck, Hannah, Seamstress, 53 Queen St
Naar, Moise, Shop Keeper, 43 King St
Nathan, Nathan, Shop Keeper, 124 King St
Nathan, Solomon, Shop Keeper, 228 King St
Navarro, Esther, Boarding House, Magazine
Neal, Robert, Boarding House, Chalmers Al
Negrin, J J, Editor & Printer of L'Oracle, Interpreter & Tutor of the French & English Languages, 106 Queen St
Neilson, James, Merchant, 35 Elliott St
Neilson, James S, Attorney at Law, Prothonotary Office, 176 Meeting St
Nelson, Erasmus, Grocer, 32 Archdale St
Nelson, Isaac, Boarding House, 51 E King Road
Nelson, Jane, Mrs., Widow, 73 Church St
Neufville, ——, Miss, 75 Queen St.
Neufville, Edward, Planter, 89 Broad St
Neufville, Elizabeth, Mrs, 75 Queen St
Neufville, Isaac, Book Keeper, National Bank, 8 N Wentworth St Cont'd
Nevile, Joshua, Cabinet Maker, 40 Tradd St
Newford, Mary, Seamstress, 13 Mazyck St
Newton, Anthony, Butcher, 12 S Cannon St
Newton, James, Boot & Shoe Maker, 17 Tradd
Newton, Mary, Butcher, 28 Society St
Newton, Mary, Widow, Butcher, N Cannon St
Nichols, George, Factor, 18 Scarborough St
Nipper, David H., Book Binder, 100 King St
Nobbs, Samuel, Custom House Inspector, Shoe Store, 191 King St
Noble, John, Dr, Apothecary & Druggist, 173 King St
Noel, Ann, Mrs, Mantua Maker, 66 King St
Noel, William, Professor of Music, 66 King St
Noldens, Peter, Merchant Tailor, 116 Queen St
Nolen, James, Carpenter, 19 Mazyck St
Norris, Martha, Widow, 9 Water St
Norry, J C F, Tobacconist, 20 George St
North & Webb, Factors, Chisolm's S Whf
North, Susannah, Widow, 38 Tradd St.
North, William, Navigation Teacher, Astronomer, Etc, 98 Church St
Norton, W W, Merchant, 163 Meeting St, Res, 21 Guignard St
Nowel, J, Commission Merchant, 17 Berresford
Nowell, Thomas S, Discount Clerk, S C Bank, 32 George St
Nuffer, Mary, N W End Wentworth St Cont'd
Nugent, Margaret & Daughters, 13 Lamboll St
Nye, Philip, Merchant, 15 Elliott St
O'Brian, Mary, Widow, Shop Keeper, 17 Wall St
O'Conner, Thomas, Clerk, Hay Market, South Bay, Grocer, 1 King St
O'Hara, Charles & Henry, Merchants, 144 Broad St
O'Hara, Charles, Merchant, 6 Smiths Ln
O'Hear, James, Accomptant, N Bull St
O'Kelly, John, Tutor at the College, Res, City Hotel

O'Lane, Catherine, Widow, 270 King St
O'Neale, Charles, Merchant, Firm Pagan &
O'Nealey, 152 King St
O'Neale, E , Mrs., Widow, Nurse, 3 George St
Oakford, Mary, Widow, Lynch's Ln
Oats, John, Grocer, 280 King St
Oats, Mary, Widow, 6 Meeting St Cont'd
Oeland, John, Grocery Store, 8 Union St Cont'd
Ogden, G W , Clothier & Salesman, 49 E Bay
Ogest, Joseph, Shoe Maker, 6 Amen St
Ogier, L & Co , Factors, 9 Crafts' S Whf, Res 20
   Friend St.
Ogier, Thomas, Merchant, 146 East Bay, Res 74
   Tradd St
Ogilvie, J A , Mrs , Plantress, Islington,
   Cannonborough
Ohlweiller, M , Baker & Grocer, 14 Church St
Ohring, Magnus, 19 Amen St
Ohter, Lewis, Tailor, Cliffords Al
Oliphant, David, Painter, 9 Ellery St
Oliphant, Thomas, Upholsterer, 64 Meeting St
Oliver, James, Butcher, 43 King St Road
Oliver, James, Mason, St Phillips St Cont'd
Oliver, Joseph, Grain & Commission Merchant, 6
   Motte's Whf
Oliver, Sarah, Boarding House, 7 East Bay Cont'd
Oliver, Stephen, Butcher, 45 East King St Road
Osborn, Richard, Factor, 1 Blake's Whf
Osborn, Thomas, Planter, 6 South Bay
Otto, Frederick, Boarding House, 4 Lodge Al
Otto, Hannah, Widow, 7 Federal St
Ottolenqui, Abraham, Teacher, 2 Berresford St
Otwell, John D., Shoe Store, 20 Elliott St
Otzell, John, Grocer, 99 King St
Owen, John, Merchant, 27 Tradd St
Owen, John, Millwright, W End Bull St
Owen, Thomas, Mariner, 40 Pinckney St
Pabarte, John, Refugee, St Domingo, 17 George St
Pagan, & O'Neale Archibald, Merchants, 151 King
Page, J W , Shoe Store, 27 Elliott St
Pagels & Co , Grocers, 27 Coming St
Paine, Thomas & Son, Merchants, 13 Hasell St
Palmer, Job, Carpenter, Clerk, Independent
   Congregational Church, Meeting St , Res 32 Trott
   St
Palmer, John, Sergeant City Guard, 44 Church St
Paque, F Gabriel, Architect Builder, 106 King St
Parker, Ann, Mrs , Dry Goods Store, 221 King St
Parker, Ann, Mrs., Widow, 3 Legare St
Parker, Catherine, Mrs , Millinery Store, 180
   Meeting
Parker, Florida, Mrs , Widow, 29 Guignard St
Parker, George, Planter, 90 East Bay
Parker, Isaac, Planter, 9 Legare & 3 Gibbes St
Parker, John, Merchant, 3 New St
Parker, John, Planter, 159 East Bay, Res 9
   Archdale St
Parker, Mary, Mrs , Widow of John, 6 George St

Parker, Phineas, Dyer, 89 Meeting St
Parker, Samuel, Planter, 44 George St
Parker, Thomas, District Attorney Office, State
   House Square, Res , 33 Meeting St.
Parks, Samuel, Shoe Store, King St
Patch, Frances, Widow, Seamstress, 24 Beaufain St
Paterson, Hugh, Notary Public, Insurance Broker,
   82 Church
Patterson, Ann, Widow, Seamstress, 24 Beaufain St
Patterson, David, Capt , Mariner, Lynch's Ln
Paul, D , Merchant, 224 King St
Pavielle, ——, Madame, 14 Wall St
Paxton, Henry H , Merchant, 11 Blake's Whf , Res ,
   15 King St
Payne, ——, Capt , 13 Hasell St
Payne, W. R , Stone Cutter, 77 King St
Payne, William, Commission Broker, 131 Broad St
Peace & Cheves, Joseph, Attornies at Law, State
   House Square, Summer Res , Hampstead, cor
   Drake & Nassau St
Peak, John, Carter, 24 George St
Peake, S , & Co , Iron Mongery Store, 12 Tradd St
Pearce & Tillinghast, Reuben, Shoe Store, 8 Elliott
Pearce, John, Painter & Glazier, 5 Bedon's Al
Pearce, Temple & Co , Shoe Store, 187 Meetng St
Pearson, Benjamin, Capt , Mariner, 22 Scarborough
   St
Peck & Wallace, Grocers, 2 Queen St
Peigne, Lewis, 7 & 8 Berresford St
Pellissier, John B , Store Keeper, 53 East Bay
Pemble, David, Tailor, 11 Tradd St
Pennall, James, Merchant, 9 W King St Road
Pennington, Edward, Lt , Revenue Cutter, 5
   Blackbird Al
Pepoon, Benjamin, Grain Merchant, 15 Queen St ,
   Store 118 Blackbird Al
Pepoon, Joseph P , Corn Store, 235 King St
Perdrian, Peter, Carpenter, 7 Smith Ln
Perinchief, Frances, Mrs , Widow, 7 Archdale St
Perman, George, Capt , 4 Stolls Al
Peronne, Caesar, Capt , Mariner, 13 Liberty St
Peronneau, John, Hair Dresser, 212 King St
Peronneau, William, Planter, 9 George St
Perrie, Isabella, Mrs., Midwife, 96 Queen St
Perry, Ann D , Mrs., Widow, Plantress, N. Bull St
Perry, Helen, Widow, Plantress, 33 W King St
   Road
Peter, Vincent, Grocer, 39 Elliott St
Peters, Mary, Widow, 110 Queen St
Petrie, Alexander, Factor, 1 Orange St
Petrie, George, School Master, 9 Federal St
Petsch, Julius, Book Binder, Stationer & Book
   Store, 123 Tradd St., Res , 21 Society St
Peyssou, Lewis, Goldsmith & Jeweller, 58 East Bay
Peyton, John, Counting House, Res , Lynch's Ln
Pezant, J L , Grocer, Market Square, Boundary St
Philips & Gardner, Merchants, 3 Prioleau N Range
Philips, Dorothea, Mrs , Widow, 69 Queen St

Philips, John, Painter & Glazier, 14 King St
Phillips, ----, Mr , Dry Goods Store, 189 King St
Phillips, ----, Mrs , Widow, 60 King St
Phillips, E. & B., Boot & Shoe Store, 23 Elliott &
86 Church St
Phillips, James & Co , Shoe Store, 90 Church St
Phillips, Sophia, Mrs , 50 Church St
Phrow, John L , Tin Plate Worker, W King St
Cont'd.
Pichon, ----, Madame, 33 Union St Cont'd
Pieckenpack, John, Grocer, 22 Coming St
Piercy, ----, Rev , Mr , 15 Front St
Pillans, Ann, Mrs , Widow, 110 Tradd St
Pillot, John, Grocer, 53 E King St Rd
Pillot, Onesime, Grocer, 6 Elliott St
Pilsbury, Amos, School Master, 4 Guignard St
Pincel, William, Tin Plate Worker, 184 Meeting St
Pinckney, C C , Gen , Planter, 1 East Bay Cont'd
Pinckney, Charles, Esq , Planter, Governor of State
of S C , 222 Meeting St
Pinckney, Frances S., Mrs , 14 Legare St
Pinckney, Roger, Planter, 42 George St
Pinckney, Thomas, Jr , 34 Trott St
Pinckney, Thomas, Maj , Planter, 42 George St
Pinckney, Thomas, Planter, 100 Broad St
Piot, Ambrose, Hair Dresser, 107 King St
Placide, Alexander, Manager, Charleston Theatre, &
Dancing Master, 93 Broad St , Vauxhall Garden
Plater, Henry, Guardman, 11 George's Al
Plissonneau, John, Grocer, 44 King St
Plissonneaur & Bork, Sail Maker, 119 E Cochran's
Whf
Plum, E., Broker, National Bank Square
Plumer, Mary, Mrs , Boarding House, 5 Tradd St
Plumet, John, Dr , 45 King St
Poague, ----, Mrs , Plantress, 75 Tradd St
Pogson, Milward, Rev Dr , St James Goose Creek
& St Johns Berkley, 4 Laurens & Gadsdens
Green
Poincignon, P A , Tinplate Worker, 12 Queen St
Poissenot, Joseph, Mrs , Shop Keeper, 18
Berresford St
Pollock, Solomon, Mrs , 4 N Bull St
Polony, John L , Dr , Physician, 30 Society St
Porcher, Isaac, Planter, 8 Charlotte St ,
Mazyckborough
Porter, John, Saddler & Harness Maker, 161 King
St & 8 W King St Cont'd
Porter, William, Auctioneer & Commission
Merchant, Exchange Row, Res , 56 Queen St
Postell, Edward, Chair Maker, Jones Court
Postell, William, Capt , Planter, 39 George St
Potter & Robertson's, Rope Walk, E Meeting St
Road
Potter, John, Merchant, 19 Broad St
Potter, Washington, Merchant, 262 King St
Poujaud, A , Merchant, 179 King St

Poulnot, Edward, Capt , Mariner, 20 Church St
Cont'd
Poulnot, Nicholas, Boot & Shoe Maker, 39 Meeting
St
Poupel, Jeanne M , Madame, Widow, 112 Queen
St
Powell, ----, Mrs , Widow, 12 Wall St
Power & Welsh, Ship Chandlers, Grocers, Etc , 80
East Bay
Poyas, John E , Dr , Planter, 29 Meeting St
Pratt, John, Capt , Mariner, 21 Elliott St
Pratt, Samuel H , Merchant, Grocery Store, 107
East Bay & 21 W King St Road
Prentice, John, Coach & Chair Maker, 30 Archdale
St
Presley, M & C , Misses, Mantua Makers, 16
Meeting St
Presley, William, Merchant & Grocery Store, King
St Cont'd
Preveaux, Elizabeth, Mrs , Plantress, 16 Berresford
St
Prevost, ----, Mrs , Mantua Maker, 151 Meeting St
Prevost, Elizabeth, Seamstress, 59 Church St
Price, John, Merchant, 8 Church St Cont'd
Price, Thomas W , Planter, 7 Friend St
Price, William, Planter, 2 Orange St
Prieur, V , Madame, 179 King St
Primrose, Catherine, Mrs , Widow, 21 St. Philip's
St
Primrose, Robert, Accomptant, 21 St Philip's St
Prince, Charles, Tin Plate Worker, 246 King St
Prince, Harriot, Mrs., Widow, 3 New St
Prince, Joseph, Cooper, Fitzsimmon's Whf , Res , 9
Maiden Ln
Prince, William, Tailor, 10 Queen St
Pringle, John J , Attorney General, 93 Tradd St
Pringle, Robert, Dr , Physician, 18 Queen St
Pringle, Thomas, Grocer, W King St Cont'd
Prioleau, A E., Mrs , Widow, 83 Queen St
Prioleau, Isaac, Factor, 49 Meeting St
Prioleau, J C , Capt , Merchant, 76 East Bay
Prioleau, J , Wharfinger, Crafts' Whf , Res , Maiden
Ln
Prioleau, Jane B , Mrs , School Mistress, 10 Maiden
Ln
Prioleau, Philip G , Dr , Physician, 51 Broad St
Prioleau, Samuel, 83 Queen St
Prioleau, Samuel, Factor, Whf Owner, Prioleau's
Whf , Res , 49 Meeting St.
Prioleau, Thomas G , 83 Queen St
Pritchard, Joseph, Factor, Wharfinger & Lumber
Merchant, Gadsden's Whf , Res , 57 King St
Pritchard, Paul, Jr , Shipwright, Res , 37 Hasell St
Pritchard, Paul, Sr , Shipwright, Gadsden's Whf ,
Res , 5 Middle St
Pritchard, S , Mrs , Plantress, 170 Meeting St
Pritchard, William, Jr , Shipwright, William's Whf ,
Res , 2 Charles St.

Pritchard, William, Sr, Shipwright, 1 Pinckney St
Purcell, Arabella, Mrs, Widow, 10 East Bay Cont'd
Purcell, Joseph R, Land Surveyor, 11 George St.
Purse, Elizabeth, Mrs, Mantua Maker, 117 Broad St.
Purse, William, Watchmaker & Jeweller, 117 Broad St
Purvis, William, Merchant, cor Boundary & Middle St
Quain, Maria, Boarding House, 14 Union St Cont'd
Quash, Robert, Planter, 91 Broad St
Query, ——, Mrs, Widow, 27 Society St
Query, Thomas, Book Binder, 27 Society St
Quigging, ——, Mrs, Boarding House, 27 Union St Cont'd
Quin, Thomas F, Grocer, 22 Quince St, Res W Meeting St Cont'd
Quinby, Joseph, Carpenter & Grocer, 6 & 7 Pinckney St
Quinlon, Michael, Grocer, cor Mazyck & Magazine St
Radcliffe, Thomas, Mrs, Widow, Plantress, 39 & 40 George St
Rade, J C, Dr, Physician & Apothecary, 226 King St
Rain, Samuel, Pilot, 6 Stolls Al
Raine, Thomas, Grocer, Meeting St Road
Ramage, F, Mrs, Boarding House, 35 Tradd St
Ramley, ——, Mrs Barbara, Laundress, 5 Coming St
Ramsay, David, Dr., Physician, 106 Broad St
Ramsay, George, Shop Keeper, 25 Church St. Cont'd
Ramsey, John, Dr, Planter, 299 King St
Randell, Elizabeth, Mrs, Widow, 76 Queen St
Rantin, William & Co, Grocer, 101 Church St
Ravenel, Daniel J, Justice of Peace, State Secretary Office
Ravenel, Daniel, Planter, 115 Broad St
Rawliingston, T W, Merchant, Chisolm's S Whf
Raworth, George, Trimmer, 78 Meeting St
Rawston, Elizabeth, Milliner & Mantua Maker, 47 Broad St
Raynal, Lewis, Accountant, Counting House
Raynal, P E B, Goldsmith, 105 Tradd St
Read, James, Mrs, Widow, W Read St
Read, William, Dr., Physician, 19 Church St Cont'd
Reader, Philip, Shoe Store, 80 King St
Rebb, Adam, Baker, 32 Union St Cont'd
Rechon, David, Tailor, 110 King St
Redman, Samuel, Painter, 26 Hasell St.
Reed, John & Co, Shoe Store, 62 King St
Reeves, Enos, Jeweller, 112 Broad St
Reiar, Henry, Grocer, Williams' Whf, S Bay
Reid, Alexander, Watch Maker, 128 King St

Reid, George, Notary Public & Agent for the Batavian Kingdom, 12 East Bay
Reid, Jacob, Gen, 44 East Bay Cont'd.
Reid, John, Mrs, Widow, 36 Church St
Reid, Mary C, Widow, 36 Church St
Reigne, John, Baker, 9 Elliott St
Reilley, James, Saddler & Harness Maker, 24 Church St
Remondo, Peter, Fruit Shop, 141 Broad St
Remoussin, Daniel, Planter, 33 Beaufain St
Remoussin, M P D, Planter, St Domingo, 30 Beaufain St
Renauld, John, Fruit Shop, 34 Tradd St
Rennie, George, Marble Cutter, 62 Broad St
Renty, John, Tailor, 3 Chalmers Al
Rephell, Joseph, Cigar Maker, 8 Water St
Reside, William, Cabinet Maker, 77 Church St
Revel, George, Merchant, N Montague St
Reynolds, Elizabeth, Grocer, Quince St
Rhind, Elizabeth, Mrs, 11 N W Wentworth St Cont'd
Rhodes & Otis, Factor, 13 East Bay
Rhyn, Evan, Dry Goods Store, 134 Broad St
Ricard, Francis, Grocer, 35 East Bay
Ricardo, R J & Co, Store Keepers, 240 King St
Richards, Samuel, Editor of the City Gazette, 6 Bedon's Al
Richardson, J B, at his Seat, Jamesville
Richardson, James, 4 S Bull St
Richardson, Thomas, Merchant, 122 Tradd St.
Ridgway, ——, Mrs, Boarding House, 18 Union St.
Ridgway, John, Constable, 18 Union St
Rigaud, Peter, Soap & Candle Manufactory, 10 W Meeting St. Road
Righton, F, Mrs., 3 Stolls Al
Righton, Joseph, Cooper, 1 Water St
Righton, M'Cully, Esq, 2 Water St
Riley, Robert, Accomptant, 27 Beaufain St
Ring, D A, Painter & Glazier, 97 King St
Rivers & Penners, Grocers, South Bay
Rivers, Elizabeth L, Widow, 1 Society St
Rivers, Frances, Mrs, Widow, 172 King St
Rivers, Francis, Planter, 12 Amen St
Rivers, Francis, Umbrella Maker, Quince St
Rivers, Gracia, Mrs, Widow, cor Short & Mazyck St
Rivers, Samuel, Shipwright, 6 Water St
Rivers, Thomas, Jr, 47 Trott St
Rivers, Thomas, Planter, 2 Stolls Al
Riviere, Jean P, Grocer, 124 Queen St
Riviere, Marie Louis Ferret, Fruit Shop, 144 Meeting
Roach, William, City Treasurer, Exchange, Res, 2 Society
Roberts, Adam, Mariner, 23 Beaufain St
Roberts, William, Coach Maker, 66 Meeting St
Robertson, Alexander, Baker, 100 Tradd St
Robertson, Alexander, Baker, 40 Union St

Robertson, George, Merchant, King St Cont'd,
Res, Boundary St
Robertson, John, Merchant, 8 Crafts' S Whf, Res,
47 Church St Cont'd
Robertson, Samuel & George, Merchants, Opposite
the Tobacco Inspection
Robin, Andrew, Broker, 177 Meeting St
Robinet, Francis, Cooper, 124 East Bay
Robings, Thomas J, Boot & Shoe Maker at Mr
Rouse's
Robinson & Long, Merchants, 136 King St
Robinson, Mary, 36 Queen St
Robinson, Peter, Painter & Glazier, 8 Parsonage Ln
Robinson, William, Insurance Broker, 36 East Bay
Robinson, William, Merchants & Planters Hotel, 60
East Bay
Robiou, Charles, Merchant, E cor King St Cont'd.
& Boundary St
Roche, John, Grocer, 78 Church St
Rodes, ——, Dr, 11 Legare St
Rodgers, Samuel, Organist, St Michael's Church, 4
N Wentworth St Cont'd
Rodrigues, Moise, Merchant, 130 King St
Roe, Gilbert, Umbrella Maker, East King St
Cont'd
Roger, Abraham, Shoe Maker, 8 Water St
Rogers, Christopher, House Carpenter, 25 Tradd St
Rogers, Elizabeth, Mrs, Widow, 115 Meeting St
Rogers, James, Corn Store, 39 Trott St
Rogers, Ralph, Merchant, 26 Church St Cont'd
Rogers, Sarah, Mrs, Widow, 26 Church St Cont'd
Roh, Jacob, Black & White Smith, 91 King St
Rolman, John, Boarding House, 4 Union St
Roper, Thomas, Maj, Planter, 71 East Bay
Rose, ——, Misses, 14 Broad St
Rose, Ann, Widow, 23 Society St
Rose, Henry, Merchant, 21 Motte's Whf., Res,
Montague St
Rose, John S, Factor, 81 Tradd St
Rose, Salem, Carpenter, Blackbird Al
Ross, David, Tailor & Habit Maker, Liberty St
Ross, John, 224 Meeting St
Ross, John, Merchant, at Mr John Woddrop
Ross, Mary, Nurse, 12 Moore St
Ross, Thomas, Grocer, 202 King St
Rosse, Paul, Print Seller & Frame Maker, 31 Broad
St
Rossignol, ——, Madame, Refugee, St Domingo,
17 N W. Wall St
Rou, M, Cabinet Maker, 17 George St
Roupell, E, Mrs, Plantress, 73 Tradd St
Rouse, William, Maj., Tanner & Currier, 70
Meeting St
Roussel, Alexander, Shoe Maker, 210 King St
Rousseneaur, ——, Madame, 16 Wall St
Rout, ——, Mrs, Widow, 16 Friend St
Roux, Lewis, Merchant & Liquor Store, 37 East
Bay, Res, 153 Meeting St

Rowand, Charles E, Planter, 2 Friend St
Rowed, John, Merchant, 114 Tradd St
Rowley, Ann, Widow, 257 King St
Ruberry, John, Carpenter, 65 Tradd St
Ruberry, William, Carpenter, 66 Tradd St
Ruddock, Samuel A, (A M) Academy, 20 Church
St
Ruhlman, George, Tailor & Boarding House, 4
Union
Rulain, Catherine, Miss, 270 King St
Russell, ——, Mrs, Mantua Maker, 9 Cliffords St
Russell & Ames, Hatters, 4 Broad St
Russell & Co William, 34 Elliott St
Russell, Benjamin, Mason, 29 Guignard St
Russell, Daniel, Carpenter, 2 Ellery St
Russell, Elizabeth, Plantress, 73 Tradd St
Russell, John, Black Smith, Governor's Bridge &
Williams' Whf, Res 97 Wentworth St
Russell, Mary, Seamstress, 9 Trott St
Russell, Nathaniel, Merchant, 16 East Bay
Rutledge, Charles, Planter, S W cor Wentworth St
Cont'd & Rutledge St
Rutledge, Edward, Planter, Boundary St W of
King St
Rutledge, Frederick, Planter, 59 Tradd St
Rutledge, Henry, Maj, Planter, 25 Wentworth St
Rutledge, Hugh, Judge of the Court of Equity, 15
St Philip's St
Rutledge, John, Col, 25 Wentworth St
Rutledge, John, Mrs, Widow, 14 St Philip's St
Rutledge, John, Planter, E Alexander St
Rutledge, Sarah, Miss, 22 Church St
Rutledge, William, 7 Anson St
Rutledge, William, N E cor. Chapel & Elizabeth
St, Mazyckborough
Ryan, Elizabeth, Mrs, Store, 52 East Bay
Ryan, James, Register in Equity, S Bull St
Ryer, Henry, Grocer, Williams' Whf, South Bay
Saint Cellery, Peter, Hair Dresser, 3 Elliott St
Salmon, David D, Saddler & Harness Maker, W
King St. Cont'd
Saltus, ——, Mr, Ship Joiner, 21 Guignard St
Saltus and Yates, Ship Chandlers, 41 East Bay & 2
Crafts' S Whf
Samory, Claude Nicholas, Grocer, 19 Queen St
Samory, Sally, 53 Meeting St
Sanderson, Christian, Grocer, 90 Meeting St
Sandford, John, Corn Store & Carver & Guilder, 41
Queen St.
Sandoz, Frederick, Watchmaker & Jeweller, 138
Queen St
Sanford, Moses, School Master, German Friendly
Society School, 6 Archdale St
Santi, Angelo & Co, Merchants & Confectioners,
81 King St
Sarrazin, Jonathan, Esq, 12 Wentworth St
Sasportas, ——, 245 King St.
Sass, Jacob, Cabinet Maker, 34 & 35 Queen St

Sauvalle, Francis, Store, 20 Motte's Whf, Res , 18 Berresford

Savage, Martha, Mrs., Widow, cor Broad & Savage

Savage, Samuel, Carpenter, S Cannon St

Savala, Joseph, Fruit Shop, 99 King St

Saydam, Guardman, 5 Lodge Al

Sayre, Stephen, Ship Joiner, Pritchard's Whf, Res , 33 Guignard St

Schem & Falconet, Watch Makers, 138 Broad St

Schem, J Francis, Watch Maker, 138 Broad

Schirer, John, Gun Smith, 177 Meeting St

Schirmer, John E , Cooper, Keith's Whf, Res , 95 Queen St

Schirmer, John F , Grocer, 70 East Bay

Schmitzer, Frederick, Grocer, Quince St

Schmitzer, Henry, Butcher, Spring St

Schmitzer, John A , Grocer, 48 King St

Schnell & Smitzer, Grocers, Cochran's Whf

Schreiner, N , Mrs , Grocer, cor George & Coming

Schroebel, John, Grocer, 35 King St Road

Schultz, Christoper, Grocer, 40 East Bay Cont'd

Schutt, Margaret D , Mrs , 56 Tradd St

Schwartz, John, Grocer, 40 East Bay Cont'd

Scott, Alexander, Dry Goods Store, 38 Queen St

Scott, Ann, Shop Keeper, 37 Queen St

Scott, James, Auctioneer & Commission Merchant, cor Champney St & Vendue Row, Res , 101 Tradd

Scott, John, Watch Maker & Jeweller, 111 Broad St

Scott, Thomas, Merchant, 83 Church St.

Scott, William, Merchant, 154 King St

Screven, Thomas, Mrs , Widow, 110 Church St

Seabrook, Benjamin, Planter, 1 N W Bull St

Sears, Stephen, Ship Joiner, 33 Guignard St

Seaver, Abraham, House Carpenter, 36 Pinckney St

Seavey, John, Butcher, 31 W King St Road

Secress, ——, Mrs , Boarding House, cor Amen & Union St Cont'd

Secress, Martin, Capt , cor Amen & Union St. Cont'd

Segerstrom, J G , Grocer, 2 Elliott St Cont'd

Seixas, J M., Mercantile, 69 King St

Serand, Francis J , Baker, 13 Quince St

Serjeant, Mary, Dry Goods Store, 204 King St

Seyle, Samuel, Harness Maker, 199 King St

Seyler, Precilla, Seamstress, cor Bull & Coming St.

Shaady, Michael, Boarding House, 5 Lodge Al

Shabrick, Thomas, Merchant, 151 E Bay, Res , 18 S Bay

Shackelford, Mary, Mrs , Boarding House, 114 Queen St & on Sullivan's Island

Shand, Robert, Custom House Inspector, 6 S Linguard St

Sharp, John, Mast, Pump & Block Maker, Governor's Bridge, Res , 19 Guignard St

Shaw, Richard, Tailor, 12 Lamboll St

Shaw, Terrance, Stucco Plasterer, N Montague St

Shaw, Walter E , St Philip's St Cont'd

Shecut, John L , Dr , Apothecary & Druggist, 220 King

Shepherd, James, Harness Maker, 7 Coming St

Shepherd, Samuel, 26 Pinckney St

Shepherd, Thomas, Mariner, 19 Pinckney St

Shepherd, Thomas, Proprietor of Times, 14 Water St

Shepherd, Thomas R , Planter, 33 W King St Road

Shirer, John, House Carpenter, 5 S W Coming St

Shirlock, William, Ironmongery Store, 175 King St

Shrewsbury, Edward, Ship Carpenter, 12 Guignard St.

Shrewsbury, Jeremy, House Carpenter, 12 Guignard St

Shrewsbury, Mary Ann, Mrs , Widow, 12 Guignard St

Shrewsbury, Stephen, Book & Collector Clerk, S C Bank, Res., 8 Cumberland St.

Shroder, John & Cuttler, Grocers, 5 Hasell St

Sibley, Joseph, Grocer, 40 East Bay

Simmons, Francis, Planter, 18 Legare St

Simmons, John, Planter, Coming St

Simmons, Joseph, Grocer & Liquor Store, 42 East Bay cor. Broad St

Simmons, Thomas, Planter, Smith St

Simmons, William, Tailor, 6 S Bull St

Simms, William, Tavern & Store, 20 W King St Road

Simons, C D , Custom House Weigher, 82 Tradd St

Simons, Dart, 7 Crafts' S Whf, Res., W Washington

Simons, James, 56 King St

Simons, James D , Rev , 82 Tradd St

Simons, Keating & Son, Factors, Res , 3 Orange St

Simons, Keating L , Attorney at Law, 3 Orange St

Simons, Keating, Planter, 3 Orange St.

Simons, Sampson, Shop Keeper, 105 King St

Simons, Samuel, Shop Keeper, 192 King St

Simons, Sarah R , Mrs , Plantress, 58 Tradd St

Simons, Saul, Jr , Tin Plate Worker, 149 Meeting St

Simons, Simon, Mariner, 13 Wall St.

Simpson, John, Planter, 11 Magazine St

Simpson, Lidia, Seamstress, Cumberland St

Simpson, Margaret, Plantress, 111 Church St

Simpson, William, Planter, 2 Minority St.

Sims, E. & J H Winkins, Boarding House, 36 Union

Sims, William, House Carpenter, W King St Cont'd.

Sims, William, Millwright, W King St Road

Sinclair, Alexander & Co , Merchants, 3 Blake's Whf

Singleton, Mary, Mrs , Widow, 3 Trott St

Singleton, Sarah, N Boundary between King & Meeting St Cont'd

Singleton, Tabitha, Seamstress, 19 Trott St

Sisk, Susannah, Mrs, Boarding House, 13 Amen St
Skirving, Charlotte, Mrs, Widow, 16 Church St
Skirving, William, Col, Planter, Ladson &
   Skirvings Court, 13 Meeting St
Slade, Laben, Shipwright, 9 Pinckney St
Slade, Margaret, Boarding House, 8 Stolls Al
Slann, Ann C, Miss, Seamstress, W Pitt St.
   Harleston
Slawson, Henry, Baker
Slawson, Nathaniel, Baker, 14 Maiden Ln
Smallwood, Richard, Custom House Weigher, 22
   Pinckney St
Smart, John T, Boot & Shoe Maker, 113 Broad St,
   Res, 31 Broad St
Smerdon, Elias, Secretary & Orator, Marine
   Insurance Company & Notary Public, Ropers Ln
Smerdon, Henry, Marine Insurance Broker, Ropers
   Ln
Smilie, Susannah, Mrs, Widow, 7 South St
Smiser, Hannah, Mrs., 48 Church St
Smith, ——, Dr, Physician, N Amhearst St
Smith, ——, Misses, 74 Tradd St
Smith, ——, Mrs, Boarding House, 7 Broad St
Smith, Agnes, Mrs., Boarding House, 10 Mazyck
   St
Smith, Agnes, Mrs, Plantress, 10 Mazyck St
Smith, Ann, Mrs, Widow, E Read St
Smith, Benjamin, Planter, 15 Church St Cont'd
Smith, Daniel, Assessor, City Tax Collector,
   Exchange, 5 Society St
Smith, Edward, Attorney, 24 Coming St
Smith, Elizabeth, Store Keeper, 157 King St
Smith, Elizabeth, Widow, E Pitt St
Smith, George, Carpenter, 7 Middle St
Smith, George, Elias, Cabinet Maker, 115 Meeting
   St
Smith, George, Professor of Music, 63 Tradd St
Smith, George S D, Book Keeper, City Gazette,
   26 Meeting St
Smith, Gregorie O, Merchant, 133 Broad St
Smith, Henry, Shipwright, 6 Maiden Ln.
Smith, James, Carpenter, 5 Guignard St, Res, 9
   Beaufain St
Smith, James, Rigger, 22 Union St Cont'd
Smith, John (L.L.D), Academy, 83 Broad St
Smith, John, Clerk of St Philip's Church, 84 Queen
   St
Smith, John R, Planter, Cannon St
Smith, Josiah, Cashier, National Bank, Res, 8
   Anson St
Smith, M'Pherson, Planter, Drake St, Hampsted
Smith, Margaret, Shop Keeper, 187 King St
Smith, Marian, School Mistress, 69 Church St
Smith, Mary, Mrs, Widow, 71 Chruch St
Smith, Mary Roger, Mrs, Widow, 3 Coming St
Smith, Morton Wilks, Accomptant, 21 Friend St.
Smith, Naomi, Miss, 4 Coming St
Smith, O'Brien, Planter, 11 Church St

Smith, Peter, Capt, Lumber Merchant & Whf
   Owner South Bay, Res, 23 Mazyck St
Smith, Peter, Planter, 2 South Bay
Smith, Peter, St Andrews Parish, 288 King St
Smith, Rebecca, Mrs, Widow, 73 Queen St
Smith, Roger Moore, Mrs, Widow, 5 West St
Smith, Samuel, Factor, 39 Broad St
Smith, Samuel, Grocer, 10 Champney St
Smith, Samuel, Miniature Painter, 2 Champneys St
Smith, Samuel W, Attorney at Law, 105 Broad St
Smith, Sarah, Boarding House, Chalmers Al
Smith, Sarah, Mrs, Widow, 22 Church St
Smith, Thomas B, Hampstead
Smith, Thomas, Capt, Merchant, 69 Tradd St
Smith, Thomas, Grocer & Liquor Store, 182 King
   St
Smith, Thomas, Planter, Charlotte St,
   Mazyckborough
Smith, Thomas Rhett, Planter, 56 Tradd St or at
   Col Skirving's Court, 13 Meeting St
Smith, Thomas Y & M W, 21 Friend St
Smith, Thomas Y, Accomptant, 21 Friend St
Smith, Whiteford, Grocer, 56 Church St
Smith, William, Carpenter, 26 N Wall St
Smith, William, Ironmonger, 21 Elliott St
Smith, William L, Attorney at Law, 82 East Bay
Smith, William S, Attorney at Law, 38 Broad St
Smith, William, Shipwright, Ham's Whf., Res, 11
   Pinckney St
Smith, William, Sr, Merchant, Fitzsimons' Whf,
   Res, 42 Pinckney St
Smylie & Patterson, Merchants, 105 East Bay
Smyth, John & Co, Merchants, 5 E King St Road
Smyth, John, Planter, 33 Hasell St
Snitter, Bristol, Rope Maker, Rope Ln alias Broad
   Court
Snowden, Ann, Mrs, Widow, 3 Quince St
Sollee, John, Proprietor, City Theatre, 26 Church St
Solomon, Alexander, Store, 188 King St
Solomon, Chapman, Shop Keeper, 185 King St
Solomon, Joseph, Shop Keeper, 163 King St
Solomon, Levy, Store Keeper, 63 East Bay
Solomon, Mark, Dry Goods Store, 159 King St
Solomon, Solomon, Dry Goods Store, 186 King St
Somarsall, Thomas, Merchant, 5 Crafts' St. Whf
Somers, Rosa, Mantua Maker, 54 Queen St
Soult, John Francis, Commissary of the Commercial
   Relations for the French Empire, 85 Meeting St
Sparks, Thomas, Mrs, 39 Queen St
Sparrow, James, Butcher, 6 S E Cannon St,
   Cannonborough
Spears, James, Carpenter, 3 Society St
Speissegger, John, Musical Instrument Maker, 4
   Hasell
Spencer, Joseph, Capt, Mariner, 16 Queen St
Spencer, Sebastian, formerly Shoe Maker, 168
   Meeting St

Spencer, William & George, Masons, 168 Meeting
  St
Spidle, Elizabeth, Widow, 4 Clifford St
Spidle, John G , Builder, 24 Archdale St
Spring, John, Powder Inspector & Silver Smith, 4
  Blackbird Al
Stank, Christopher, Grocer, 279 King St
Stanyarne, James, Planter, 18 South Bay
Starkey, Susannah, Widow, Seamstress, 3 Meeting
  St
Starr, Walter, Shop Keeper, 209 King St
Steel, John, Book Keeper, State Bank, Res , Hasell
Steinmyer, G W , Baker, S Boundary opposite
  Lowndes
Stent, John H , Mason, 78 Queen St
Stent, John, Jr , Carpenter, 19 Mazyck St
Stephen, William, Factor, 10 Laurens St
Stephen, William, Merchant, 72 East King St
  Cont'd
Stevens, Daniel, Coach Maker, 96 Meeting St
Stevens, Daniel, Col , Supervisor, 30 George St
Stevens, Jervis H , City Sheriff, Exchange, Res , 68
  Tradd St & Bee St , Cannonborough
Stevens, William S , Dr , Physician, 46 East Bay,
  Res , 19 King St
Stewart, Ann & Margaret, Misses, Boarding School,
  12 Moore St
Stewart, Christian, Attorney at Law, 1 Wentworth
  St
Stewart, Daniel , Planter & Glazier, 104 King St
Stewart, R , Planter, 14 Society St
Stewart, William, Academy, 44 Church St
Stiff, Richard, Accomptant, 4 Beaufain St
Stock, Thomas, Dr , M D , Lynch's Ln
Stocker, Henry & Co , Boat Builders, Governor's
  Bridge, Res , 9 Charles St.
Stockwell, Samuel, Comedian, Savage St
Stodder, John, Boarding House, 27 Union St
Stoll, Catherine, 17 Magazine St
Stoll, John H , Turner, 22 Hasell St
Stone, Isabella, Mrs , Widow, 2 W Coming St
Stone, Thomas, Mason, 6 Coming St
Stoney, John, Merchant, 8 Motte's Whf , Res , 2
  Front St
Stoops, Benjamin T , Boot & Shoe Maker, 2 Broad
  St
Stowe, Richard R., Capt , Mariner, 122 Meeting St
Street, ——, Capt , Mariner, 23 Wall St
Strobel & Co , Merchants, 109 Tradd St
Strobel, J , Tanner, Meeting St , Res , S Boundary
Strobel, Jacob, Butcher, Meeting St Market, Res.,
  104 King St
Strobel, John, Tanner, Blackbird Al
Strobel, Lewis, Capt , City Guard, 49 East Bay
Strobel, Mary E , Widow, Tanner, 118 Meeting
Stroecker, J , Black Smith, 154 Meeting St
Stromer, Henry M , Grocer, 86 King St
Strother, Mary, Widow, 3 Blackbird Al

Stroub, George, Carpenter, 2 Blackbird Al
Stroub, Jacob, Carpenter, 2 Blackbird Al.
Stuart, William, Tailor, 3 Amen St
Sturgis & Lovell, Josiah, Merchants, 4 Crafts' S
  Whf , Res , 40 Church St Contd
Suares, David, Mercantile, 68 King St , Res , 21
  Berresford
Suares, Jacob, Grocer, 249 King St
Suares, Jacob, Rev , Synagogue, Hasell St
Sullivan, Timothy, Auctioneer & Commission
  Merchant, N Vanderhorst's Whf , Res , 27
  Guignard St
Sully, Mathew, Comedian, 6 Savage St.
Summers, Rossetta, Mantua Maker, 54 Queen
Sutherland & Reader, Boot & Shoe Store, 130
  Queen St
Sutherland, James, Accomptant, 25 Elliott St
Sutton, Ephraim, Capt , Mariner, Lynch's Ln
Swain, Mark, Pilot, 3 Stolls Al
Swain, Rebecca, Mrs , Widow, 3 Stolls Al
Swan, Robert, Carpenter, 133 Meeting St
Swaney, William, Cabinet Maker, 52 Queen St
Sweeney, Brian, Grocer, 5 East Bay Cont'd.
Sweeney, James & Thomas, Grocers, 14 Queen St
Sweet, ——, Mrs , Widow, 115 Queen St
Sweetzer, John R , Saddler, 218 King St
Swinton & Miles, Factors, Chisolm's Whf , Res , 2
  Laurens St
Swinton, Hugh, Planter, 74 Meeting St
Syfan, John, Butcher, 44 East King Road
Symonds, Hannah, Mrs , 3 Guignard St
Taffs, Margaret, Widow, N Cannon St
Taggart, Mary, Mrs , Widow, 17 Meeting St
Talvande, Rose, Madame, 102 Tradd St
Tardy, Alexander, Tin Plate Worker, 131 Queen St
Tarone & Co., Anthony, Print Sellers, Etc , 30
  Broad St
Tarraf, Philip, Rigger, Cock Ln.
Tarrer, Elizabeth, Swintons Ln
Tate, James, Capt , Mariner, 115 Queen St
Tavel, Frederick, Merchant, 13 Motte's Whf , Res ,
  8 East King St Road
Taylor, Joseph, Capt , Mariner, 3 Charles St
Taylor, Joseph, Shipwright, Hard Al
Taylor, Margaret, Widow, 17 Guignard St
Taylor, Maria, Mantua Maker, 3½ Smith St
Taylor, Paul, Carpenter, 75 S Cannon St
Taylor, Samuel , Attorney at Law, 83 Queen St
Taylor, Sarah, Widow, 10 Quince
Taylor, Susannah, Widow, 274 King St
Taylor, Teressa, Seamstress, St Philip St
Taylor, William, Planter, S E End Lynch's St
Teasdale, Isaac, Merchant, 21 Ellery St
Teasdale & Son, Merchants, 4 East Bay
Teasdale, John, Merchant, 2 East Bay
Techer, John, Grocer, Johnson & M'Kenzie's Whf ,
  South Bay
Teddeman, ——, Mrs , Widow, 3 Front St

Teddeman, Philip, Dr , 22 Wentworth St
Temple, Pearce & Co , Shoe Store, 110 Queen &
187 Meeting St.
Thayer, E , Broker, 43 Elliott St , Res , 49 Tradd
Thayin, Lewis S , Cradle Manufactory, Columbia
St
Theus, Dinah, Nurse, 32 Wentworth St
Theus, Simeon, Collector, 239 King St
Thevenin, P , Refugee, St Domingo, Boundary W
King
Thomas, E S, Bookseller & Stationer, 121 Broad
St.
Thomas, Francis, National Bank, C D , 29
Archdale
Thomas, John D , Grocer, Tradd St
Thomas, John, Grocer, 31 Union St
Thomas, John, Hair Dresser, 178 Meeting St
Thomas, John J , Merchant, E Middle St
Thomas, John, Store Keeper, 37 Broad St
Thomas, Mary Lamboll, Mrs , Widow, 12 King St
Thomas, S , Cannon St., Cannonborough
Thomas, Sarah, Quince St
Thomas, Sarah, Seamstress, 37 Union St.
Thomas, Stephen, Merchant, 7 E. King St Cont'd
Thompson, Aaron, Factor, 13 Crafts' N Whf , Res ,
3 Quince St
Thompson, Alexander, Mason, 21 Trott St
Thompson, Hannah, Seamstress, 32 Pinckney St
Thompson, J , House Carpenter, 22 Beaufain St
Thompson, James, Boarding Officer, Custom
House, 11 Hasell St
Thompson, James, Capt , Quince St
Thompson, James D., Deputy Sheriff, 18 Amen St
Thompson, Lesley, Tailor, 95 Church St
Thompson, Margaret, Shop Keeper, 21 Beaufain St
Thompson, Rufus, Shoe Store, 65 King St
Thorne, John G , Sail Maker, Beale's Whf , Res ,
10 Bedon's Al
Thornton, Asa, Academy, 17 Ellery St
Thorpe, Thomas, 112 Tradd St
Threadcraft, Bethel & Co , Watch & Clock Makers,
235 King St.
Thwing, David, Ship Joiner, Governor's Bridge,
Res , 2 Parsonage Ln
Thwing Edward, House Carpenter, 73 Meeting St
Time, Joseph, 22 Trott St
Time, Joseph, Monsieur, Confectioner, 80 Meeting
St
Timmons, William, Merchant, 12 Laurens St
Timothy, Benjamin F, School Master for the S C
Society, 199 Meeting St
Tobias, Judith, Widow, 202 King St
Tofel, John, Confectioner, 142 Broad St
Tomkins, Joseph, Mariner & Boarding House, 13
Ellery St.
Tongue, Abraham, School Master, 2 Berresford St
Toomer, Ann, Mrs , 7 Legare St
Torrans, ——, Miss, 32 Queen St

Torres, Abraham, Shop Keeper, 84 King St
Torrey, William, Capt , Mariner, 7 S End New St
Tourette, Thomas, French Bording House, 171
Meeting St
Toussiger, Margaret, Widow, 4 Water St
Tovey, Henry, Mast, Pump & Block Maker, 100
East Bay, Res , 38 Hasell St
Trajetta, Philip, Music Master, 4 Cumberland St
Trapier, ——, Mr , Planter, S Alexander St ,
Mazyckborough
Trenholm, William, Grocer & Grain Merchant, 3 N
Prioleau's Whf
Trescott, Edward, Planter, 108 Broad St
Trescott, William, Attorney at Law, 108 Broad St
Trezevant, Lewis, Associate Judge, Court of
Sessions and Common Pleas, 273 King St
Trezevant, Peter, Discount Clerk, State Bank, 98
Queen
Trouche, Adel, Madame, Refugee, St Domingo, 9
Middle St
Troup, Elizabeth, Mrs., Widow, 72 Queen St
Truchelet, Joseph, Merchant & Baker, 128 Queen
St
Truelle, James, Tobacconist, 38 Union St Cont'd
Tucker, Charles S , Factor, 49 East Bay
Tucker, Mary, Mrs , 24 East Bay
Tucker, Mary, Mrs , Seamstress, Mosers Court
Tucker, Sarah, Mrs , 108 Church St
Tunno & Price, Merchants, 7 Chisolm's N Whf., 5
Church St Cont'd
Tunno, Adam, Merchants, 27 East Bay
Tunno, Cox, Merchants, 27 East Bay
Tunno, William, Planter, 81 East Bay
Turnbull, Gavin, Comedian, 59 Queen St
Turnbull, James, Lumber Merchant, South Bay
Turnbull, Robert J , Attorney at Law, 8 Meeting St
Turnbull, Sarah, Widow, Boarding House, 1 Bank
Square
Turner, ——, Mrs , Widow, 4 W King Cont'd
Turner, Ann, Widow, 4 Legare St
Turner, Elizabeth, Seamstress, 14 Berresford St
Turner, Thomas, Capt , Dancing Master, Whim
Court
Turner, William, Shop Keeper, 12 Mazyck St.
Turpin, William, Esq , Planter, 149 King St
Tyler, Benjamin, School Master, St Philip's St
Cont'd
Ulmo, A , Dr , Apothecary & Druggist, 176
Meeting St
Ulrick, Samuel, Tanner & Currier, W Pitt St ,
Harleston Green
Ummensetter, James, Tanner & Currier, 17
Beaufain St
Ummensetter, John, Tanner & Currier, Pitt &
Beaufain St
Underwood, Thomas, Boot & Shoe Maker, 103
Queen

Underwood, William, Boarding House, Chalmers Al
Uttice, Thomas, Boarding House, 8 Union St
Valance, Moses & Son, Traders, 42 Tradd St
Vale, Elizabeth, Widow, Alexander, N W cor Cannon & Thomas St
Valk, Jacob R , Merchant, Crafts' N Whf., Res , Church
Vanderberg, J F , Rigger, 5 Charles St
Vanderbuffe, James, Mariner, 10 Berresford St
Vanderherchen, A Taylor, 1st Lt City Guard, 210 King St
Vanderhoff, Cornelius, Shoe & Boot Maker, 130 King
Vanderhorst & Tailor, Factors, Vanderhorst's Whf
Vanderhorst, Arnoldus, Gen , Planter, 16 East Bay
Vanderhorst, John S , Merchant, 15 East Bay
Vanhagan, George, Grocer, 12 Anson St
Vanhost, W J , Mercantile, 26 Meeting St.
VanRhyn, A E , Miss, Merchant, 134 Broad St
Vardel, Robert, Carter, Drake St , Hampstead
Vardel, Thomas Addison, Mason, 21 St Philip's St
Vaughn & Alley, Merchants, Prioleau's Whf
Vaughn, James, Merchant, Elliott St Cont'd
Vaughn, Jesse, 12 East King St Cont'd
Venneaud, Abraham, Tailor, St Philip's St
Vernon & Co , Goldsmith & Jeweller, 140 Broad St
Verree & Blair, Auctioneers & Commission Merchants, N Vendue Row
Verree, Joseph, Vendue Master, 3 Church St
Verree, Mary, Mrs., Widow, 3 Church St
Verree, Rebecca, Mrs , Widow, Distillery, Mazyckborough
Verree, Samuel & Robert, Merchants, 3 Church St
Vesey, Charles M , Book Keeper, Fitzsimmons' Whf , 5 Parsonage Ln
Vesey, John, Mercantile, W King St Road
Vesey, Joseph, Capt , Academy, 13 N W Middle St
Vesey, Joseph, School Master, 3 Parsonage Ln
Vidal, ——, Monsieur, Shop Keeper, 80 Church St
Vigie, Anthony, Tobacconist, late Planter, St Domingo, 20 Archdale St
Vignier, Arnoldus, Merchant Tailor, 13 Broad St.
Villers, ——, Mrs , 52 Queen St
Vincent, Elizabeth, Mrs , Boarding House, 5 Tradd St
Vincent, Peter, Shipwright, 23 Guignard St
Vincent, Thomas, Capt , Mariner, 5 Tradd St
Vinro, Sarah, Widow, 26 Union St Cont'd
Virgent, Elizabeth, Mrs., Widow, S Amhearst St , Hampstead
Visseulk, Thomas, Gentleman, 3 Berresford St
Wagner, George, Planter, 101 Broad St
Wagner, Paul, Grocer, 183 Meeting St
Wainwright, Ann, Mrs , Widow, 265 King St

Walden, Joseph & Co , Crafts' Whf , Opposite Scale House
Waldo, Joseph W , Druggist & Physician, 152 King St
Walker & Evans, Marble Cutters, 24 Trott St
Walker, Caleb, Carpenter, 14 Magazine St
Walker, Edward, Capt , 121 Broad St
Walker, Robert, Cabinet Maker, 39 Church St
Walker, William, Cabinet Maker, 12 Archdale St
Wall, Richard, Boarding House, Chalmers Al
Wallace & Lawrence, Brass Founders, 11 Ellery St
Wallace, James, Custom House Officer, cor Boundary & Lowndes St
Wallace, Thomas, Cabinet Maker, 25 Queen St
Waller, Charlotte, Mrs , Widow, 13 Magazine St
Wallsley, Joseph, Boarding House, 29 Union St
Walsh, Edmond, Grocer, 2 Amen St & 5 Union St Cont'd , Res , 18 Friend St
Walton, William & Co , S W cor King St Cont'd , 2 Boundary St , Store 9 Broad St
Ward, Daniel, Master, Work House, 65 Queen St
Ward, James, Attorney at Law, 47 Church St
Ward, James M , Attorney at Law, Bee St., Cannonborough
Ward, John, Attorney at Law, 3 East Bay
Ward, Sarah, Mrs , Widow, 210 Meeting St
Waring & Haynes, Factors, 11 Blake's Whf
Waring, Daniel, Attorney at Law, 13 Scarborough St
Waring, Mary, Mrs , Widow, 32 Wentworth St
Waring, Morton & Son, Factors, 152 East Bay & 55 Broad St
Waring, Morton A , Factor, 11 Liberty St
Waring, Thomas, Planter, Charlotte St , Mazyckborough
Waring, Thomas, Sr., Naval Officer, 38 Meeting St
Warley, ——, Misses, 26 Beaufain St
Warley, Feliz, 8 Trott St
Warner, Penelope, Widow, 202 Meeting St
Warnock, Joseph, Boarding House Stables, 15 Queen
Warnock, Joseph, Jr., Carpenter, N Montague St
Warren, John, Capt , 9 Linguard St
Warren, Samuel, Col , Planter, St. James Santee, Isaac M Dart's Factor
Wartenberg & Kippenberg, Grocers, 30 Queen St
Washington, William, Gen , Planter, Res , 22 South Bay
Watson & Ferguson, Grocers, 60 & 61 King St
Watson, Alexander, Factor, 15 East Bay Cont'd
Watson, John, & Co , Merchants, 7 East Bay
Watson, John, Cabinet Maker & Upholsterer, 26 King
Watson, Kirk & Co , Boarding House, 15 Union St
Watson, Lydia, Widow, 5 Friend St
Watson, Nathaniel, Chair Maker, 21 Queen St
Watson, W , Grocer & Dry Goods Store, 75 Meeting St

Watt, James, Grocer, 29 Church St Cont'd
Watts, Robert, Fruit Store, 14 Friend St
Weathers, Thomas, Shipwright, 5 Cock Ln
Weatherston, William, Tailor, 31 Broad St
Weaver, Joseph, Portrait Painter, 105 Church St
Webb, Catharine, Widow, Plantress, 4 Friend St.
Webb, John, Esq , 1 Moore St
Webb, William, Teller, State Bank, 1 Moore St
Weir, Francis & Co , Merchants, 4 Chisolm's N Whf
Welch, George, Tobacco Picker, 1 W Lowndes St
Welch, John, Cabinet Maker, 150 Meeting St
Welch, Susannah, Widow, 13 St Philip's St
Welch, T G , Carver & Guilder, 24 Society St
Well, Rachael, 21 Beaufain St
Wells, Charlotte, Widow, 24 Beaufain St
Wells, Francis, Mrs , Widow, 250 King St
Wells, Moses, Shoe Maker, 21 Beaufain St
Wells, Richard, Boat Builder, 24 Bay Cont'd & Williams' Whf
Wells, Thomas B , Vendue Master, 20 Wentworth St
Wesner, Henry P , Baker, 19 Coming St
Westermeyer, Andrew, Merchant Goldsmith & Jeweller, 19 Union St
Weston & Mazyck (Isaac M), Merchants, 10 Broad
Weston, Paul, Dr , Chapel St
Weston, Plowden, Planter, 31 Queen St
Weyman, Edward, Major, Surveyor, Counting House, Res , 7 West St
Whalley, T , Grocer & Boarding House, 38 E. Bay Cont'd
Wheeler & Scott, Commission Merchants, 12 Crafts' N Whf
Wheeton, Thomas, Grocer, 7 Berresford St.
Whightman, John P , Painter & Glazier, Berresford Al.
Whitaker, Richard, Boarding House, 4 Chalmers Al
White, Charles, Cabinet Maker, 36 Broad St
White, Francis, Mrs , Mantua Maker, 78 King St
White, G K , Factor, Cordes St
White, George R , Factor, Prioleau's S Whf, Res , 48 Trott St
White, J B , Student at Law, 10 Middle St
White, James, Grocer, 129 Queen St
White, John, Factor, Chisolm's N Whf , Res , 124 Meeting St
White, John P & Co , Merchants, 21 Vendue Row
White, Lucy, Widow, 30 Pinckney St
Whiting, John, Turner in General, 156 Meeting St
Whitley, Thomas, Grocer, 17 Amen St
Whittemore, Retire, Mrs , Widow, 151 Meeting St
Wigfall, ——, Mrs , Widow, 46 George St
Wigfall, Robert, Dray Owner, 21 Beaufain St
Wightman, William, Goldsmith & Jeweller, 185 Meeting
Wilcox, James, Grocer, 14 N Bull St
Wilcox, Jeremiah, 14 N. Bull St

Wildman, Seymore, Shoe Store, 105 King St
Wilkinson, Mary, Boarding House, 26 Union St
Wilkinson, Susan, Mrs , 3 S E Cannon St
Will, Susannah, Widow, 25 Beaufain St
Willard, Joseph, 55 Queen St
William, Hannah, Seamstress, 9 Lodge Al
Williams, Ann, Mantua Maker, 174 King St
Williams, Benjamin Paul, Factor, Cordes St cor Commerce
Williams, David R , Planter, A M , late Firm Freneau & Williams
Williams, Henry, 88 Meeting St
Williams, Isham, Whf Owner, Williams' Whf
Williams, James, Counting House, 35 Union St Cont'd
Williams, John (D D S), 46 Wentworth St
Williams, Mary, Shoe Maker, 24 Trott St
Williams, Rachael, Grocer, 66 East Bay
Williamson, Abraham, Soap Boiler, 9 S E Cannon St
Williamson, Abraham, Tallow Chandler, 12 N Champneys St
Williamson, Charles, Custom House Boatman
Williamson, John, Merchant, 2 Lodge Al
Williamson, Maria, Seamstress, 15 Guignard St
Williman, Christopher, Planter, 211 King St
Williman, George, Planter, N W Boundary St.
Williman, J , Mrs , Dr , Widow, 211 King St
Williman, Jacob, Tanner & Currier, 1 S E Montague
Willis, ——, Mrs , 23 East Bay Contd
Wilson & Paul, Merchant & Grocers, 23 Broad St
Wilson, Charlotte, Widow, Plantress, N Bull St
Wilson, Hugh, Capt , Planter, 293 King St
Wilson, James, Butcher, 82 Queen St
Wilson, James, Jr , Merchant, 120 East Bay
Wilson, John, Cabinet Maker, 126 Meeting St
Wilson, John, Grocer, East Meeting St Cont'd
Wilson, Robert & Son, Physicians, 97 Church St
Wilson, Robert, Capt , Mariner, 2 Hasell St.
Wilson, Robert, Dr , Physician, 87 Broad St
Wilson, Robert, Jr , Dr , Physician, 36 Meeting St
Wilson, Robert, Plasterer, 10 Linguard
Wilson, Samuel, Dr., Physician, 36 Meeting St
Wilson, Sarah, Widow, Quince St
Wilson, Thomas, Planter, 16 Society St
Winchester, Jonathan, Carpenter, 2 S E Cannon St
Wing & Thomas, Coach Makers, 23 Hasell St
Wing, Freeman, Capt , Mariner, 2 Charles St
Winkins, John H , Grocer & Boarding House, 36 Union
Winn, Joseph, Deputy Sheriff, 11 Beaufain St
Winstanley, Thomas, Attorney at Law, 86 East Bay
Winthrop, Elizabeth, Mantua Maker, 13 Friend St
Winthrop, Joseph, His Swedish & Danish Majesty's Consul, 52 Tradd St
Winthrop, Joseph, Merchant, 147 & 148 East Bay
Wish & Bryan, Merchants, 130 Broad St

Wiss, Peter, Saddler & Harness Maker, 200 King
St
Witt, John, Grocer, 34 King St
Wittich, C. & F., Goldsmiths & Jewellers, 25 Broad
Woddrop, John, Merchant, 9 East Bay
Wolf, Rachel, Mrs , Widow, 7 Orange St
Wood, & Lowery, Grocer, 7 Elliott St
Wood, A , Mrs , Grocer, 1 King St Road
Wood, A , Tavern Keeper, 97 Queen St
Wood, James, Engraver, Etc , Boundary St , W of
King St
Wood, William, Custom House Inspector, 15
Archdale St
Woodman & Smith, Store Keepers, 84 King St
Woodmancy, John, Boarding House, 19 W King
Road
Woodward, John H , Teacher, 114 Queen St
Worthington, Elizabeth, Store Keeper & Wagon
Yard, 8 King St Road
Wragg, Samuel, Maj , Planter, 5 Front St
Wrainch, John, School Master, 154 Meeting St
Wraine, Adam, Shipwright, 24 Pinckney St
Wright, Elizabeth, Miss, Plantress, 9 Orange St
Wurdemann, J G , Grocer, 9 Queen St
Wyatt, Lemuel, State Constable, 4 Chalmers Al
Wyatt, Peter, Lumber Merchant, at his Mills, S W
End Lynch's St , Ashley River
Yates & Black, Inspectors & Cooper, 5 Crafts' N
Whf
Yates, D , Mrs , Boarding School, South Bay
Yates, Elizabeth, Grocer, 3 Union St
Yates, Jeremiah, Merchant, South Bay
Yates, Joseph, Cooper, Beale's Whf , Res , 11
Church Cont'd
Yates, Samuel, Capt , Mariner, Lynch's Court
Yates, Seth, Shipwright, Lynch's Court
Yeadon, Richard, Teller, National Bank, 18 King
St
Yeadon, William, Attorney at Law, 51 Meeting St
Yoer, Jacob, Shoe Maker, 92 Queen St
You, John, Assistant Book Keeper, National Bank,
Res , 25 Archdale St
Young, W. P , Printer & Book Seller, 41 Broad St
Young, William, Merchant, 6 Champneys St.
Zealey, Joseph, Butcher, 263 King St
Zelotus, Prince, Mariner, Anson St
Zilia, Laurence, Seamstress, 8 Ellery St
Zylk, John, Wheelwright, 7 Liberty St
Zylstra, Peter, Merchant & Ship Chandler, 64 E
Bay

Chapter 4

THE 1809 DIRECTORY

The 1809 directory was compiled by Richard Hrabowski and published using the title of *Directory for the District of Charleston Comprising the Places of Residence and Occupation of the White Inhabitants of the Following Parishes, To Wit – St. Michael, St. Philip, St. Philip on the Neck, St John (Colleton), Christ Church, St James (Santee), St. Thomas and St Dennis, St Andrew, St John (Berkeley), St Stephen and St James (Goose Creek)* (Charleston: John Hoff, 1809, 160 pages) The directory of individuals can be found on pages 3-112 The supplemental information was listed at the back of the volume As indicated by the title this directory covers the Charleston District Hrabowski was able to do this because he was also appointed to take the 1810 census in the area

This directory is very poorly organized The editor made no effort to alphabetize names except to put them under the correct initial letter In addition, he usually lists all the individuals on a given street whose names begin with a particular letter. This results in a considerable amount of confusion and duplication Some people have the exact entry more than once Also, individuals who owned businesses at two or more locations have more than one entry. The exact duplications have been eliminated in the 4,411 entries that follow, but the multiple listings at different addresses have been retained In some instances, it is clear that the same person has businesses at more than one location; for others, it is possible that two people have the same name Also, the entries from the outlying parishes are grouped together at the end of the regular listings in the original directory but have been given in alphabetical order here

----

Abbott, Barbara, 39 Society St
Abendanon, Jacob, Shop Keeper, 240 King St
Abendanon, Joseph, Shop Keeper, 240 King St
Abernethie, John J , Clerk, 36 Queen St
Abernethie, Mary, 36 Queen St
Abrahams, Abraham, Store Keeper, Edisto Island
Abrahams, Jacob, Shop Keeper, 4 Queen St
Abrahams, Samuel, Store Keeper, Edisto Island
Abrams, Levy I , Shop Keeper, 257 King St
Adams, Benjamin, Planter, Wadmalaw Island
Adams, David, Factor, 21 Ellery St
Adams, David, Factor, Stoll's Al

Adams, DeLeisslin, Factors, Chisolm's N Whf (Counting House)
Adams, E , Sullivan's Island
Adams, John, Merchant, 14 Laurens St
Adams, Samuel, Planter, St Stephen's, 40 miles
Adams, William, Planter, Wadmalaw Island
Addison, James, Planter, St Stephen's, 40 miles
Addison, Josiah, Planter, St Thomas', 8 miles
Adel, Thomas, 31 Pinckney St
Adger, James, Shop Keeper, 159 King St
Adkins, Catharine, Butcher, Coming St
Aertsen, Esther, School Mistress, 67 Church St
Aiken, Ann, School Mistress, 2 Cumberland St
Aiken, Ann, Seamstress, 31 Pinckney St
Aiken, Thomas, Physician, 2 Cumberland St
Aiken, William, Store Keeper, King St Rd
Aints,——, Shop Keeper, 20 Church St
Airs, George, Carpenter, 12 Archdale St
Airs, William, Overseer to Harleston Estate, Berkeley, 28 miles
Alexander, Abraham, Shop Keeper, 131 King St
Alexander, David, Merchant, 10 Broad St
Alexander, Joseph, Merchant, 90 Queen St
Alexander, S , Capt , Mariner, 139 East Bay St
Alexander, William, Overseer to Thomas Palmer, St James', Santee, 33 miles
Allan, William, Merchant, 5 Federal St
Alldrige, Robert, Wharfinger, 3 Stoll's Al
Allen, John, Mariner, 111 King St
Allen, John, Planter, St Thomas', 19 miles
Allen, John W., 30 Pinckney St
Allen, Josiah, Cabinet Maker, 2 Bank Square
Allen, T , Planter, 8 miles from Charleston, Christ Church Parish
Allen, William, Merchant, 20 East Bay St
Allen, William, Merchant, Store, 112 East Bay St
Allene, Dominique, Hair Dresser, 39 Meeting St Al.
Allix, Lucien, Baker, Sullivan's Island
Allport, John, Smith Farrier, 113 King St
Allspice, Catharine, Confectioner, 189 King St
Allston, William, Planter, 13 King St
Allwood, James, Planter, St Stephen's, 40 miles
Amberson, Jonas, Grocer, 2 Market St
Amie, Chre, Madame, Seamstress, 9 Ellery St
Amos, John, Carpenter, John's Island
Ampo, ——, Baker, King St Rd
Anbinnal, Mary, 14 Church St
Ancrum, James H , Planter, 36 Church St Cont'd
Anderson, ——, Boatman, Sullivan's Island
Anderson, Hannah, Store Keeper, cor of Broad & Church Sts
Anderson, John, Carpenter, Cannon's Bridge
Anderson, John, Grocer, Charlotte St
Anderson, Philip, Planter, St James', Santee, 30 miles
Anderson, Samuel, Gardner, Hampstead
Anderson, W C., Capt , Mariner, 204 Meeting St.

Anderson, William, Stay Maker, 204 Meeting St.
Andre, ——, Madame, 19 Trott St
Andrews, Moses, Block Maker, 28 Elliott St
Angel, Justus, Store Keeper, 22 Elliott St
Annely, George Wilding, Clerk, 1 Middle St
Annotta, T, Fruiterer, 25 Church St
Anthony, J C, Soap & Candle Manufacturer, St Mary's St
Anthony, John, Harness Maker, 192 Meeting St
Antonio, Peter, Cigar Maker, 35 Broad St
Antz, Levy, Planter, St Thomas', 12 miles
Arms, Sarah, Seamstress, 178 Meeting St
Armstrong, Ann Matilda, 37 Broad St
Armstrong, Esther, 3 Smith's Ln
Armstrong, J, Overseer to William Matthews, 32 miles, St James' Santee
Armstrong, W, Overseer to F Cordes, St John's, Berkeley, 38 miles
Arnaut, ——, Black Smith, 33 Motte St
Arthur, George, Factor, John St
Arthur, Peter S, Planter, St James' Santee, 37 miles
Artope, George, Superintendent, Santee Canal, St Stephen's, 53 miles
Ash, Elizabeth, 7 Lamboll St
Ash, John, Planter, South Bay
Ashby, Thomas, Planter, St Thomas', 18 miles
Assalit, Joseph, Teacher at College, 158 Meeting St
Atchinson, William, Merchant, 23 Church St
Atchison, Adam, Clerk, King St Rd
Atchison, Robert, Clerk, 19 East Bay St
Atchison, William, Merchant (Counting House), 145 East Bay St
Atkinson, Mary, Planter, 70 Broad St
Atkinson, Michael, Carpenter, 9 Wentworth St
Atwell, John D, Boot & Shoe Store, 77 East Bay St
Atwell, John D, Shoe Store, 17 Tradd St
August, Charles, Cabinet Maker, 99 Queen St
Auld, Issac, Physician, Edisto Island
Aunard, Moise, Peddlar, 255 King St
Aurauza, B, Blacksmith, 9 Motte St
Austin, Catharine, Shop Keeper, 47 East Bay St
Austin, John, Jewelller, 112 Broad St
Austin, William, Broker, 91 Meeting St
Austin, William, Jr, cor. of Pitt & Wentworth St
Axon, Edward, Carpenter, 64 Broad St
Axon, Jacob, Clerk, S C Bank, 63 Broad St
Axon, John, Planter, Berkeley, 52 miles
Axon, John, Planter, St James' 42 miles
Ayrault, Peter, Merchant, 117 East Bay St
Backstrom, John S, Grocer, 2 Elliott St
Bacot, Henry H, Attorney, 26 Tradd St
Bacot, Peter, Attorney, 99 Tradd St
Bacot, T W, Cashier, Bank of S C, Postmaster, 99 Tradd St
Badger, James, Painter, 135 Meeting St

Baggot, Randal, Overseer to Roger Pinckney, St Thomas Parish, 24 miles
Bagnell, Aben, Overseer to Smith, St James' Goose Creek, 19 miles
Bagshaw, Robert, Planter, Cannonborough Road
Bailey, Benjamin, Planter, Edisto Island
Bailey, David, Merchant, Book Seller, 25 Broad St
Bailey, Edward, Planter, Edisto Island
Bailey, Gabriel, Attorney, 2 Blackbird Al
Bailey, Henrietta, Boarding House, 6 Liberty St
Bailey, Henry, Attorney, 2 Blackbird Al
Bailey, Henry, Planter, Edisto Island
Bainki, George, Band Box Maker, 10 Queen St
Bairfeild, James, Overseer to John B Holmes, St. John's, Berkeley, 33 miles
Bakeman, John, Grocer, cor of Mazyck & Beaufain Sts
Baker, Alpheus, School Master, St Stephen's, 53 miles
Baker, Amey, School Mistress, Wentworth St
Baker, Fanny, 20 Trott St
Baker, John J., Grocer, 20 East Bay St.
Baker, John, Mariner, Kinloch Court
Baker, Joseph, Carpenter, Boundary St
Baker, Noah D, Dyer, 150 Meeting St.
Baker, Samuel, Planter, 6 St Philip's St
Baker, Samuel, Planter, St Andrew's Parish, 17 miles
Balck, John, Ironmonger, 11 Broad St
Baldrick, Thomas, Planter, St James' Goose Creek, 10 miles
Bale, Elizabeth, Umbrella Maker, 185 Meeting St
Baleys, Samuel, Tanner, Pitt St
Ball, Archibald, Planter, John's Island
Ball, Elias, Planter, St John's, Berkeley, 35 miles
Ball, Eliza, Planter, John's Island
Ball, Elizabeth, Widow, 5 Church St
Ball, Isaac, Planter, St John's, Berkeley, 33 miles
Ball, James, Merchant, 87 Church St
Ball, John, Jr, Planter, St John's, Berkeley, 32 miles
Ball, John, Planter, St John's, Berkeley, 35 miles
Ball, Sarah, 9 Church St Cont'd
Ballantine, Alexander, Coach Maker, 54 Meeting St
Ballard Thomas, Overseer to Thynes, St John's, Berkeley, 36 miles
Bampfield, James, Factor, 15 Friend St
Bampfield, Thomas, Clerk, Counting House, 15 Friend St
Banare, Peter, Baker, 94 King St
Banks, Charles, Merchant (Counting House), Craft's S Whf
Banks, Charles, Merchant, 1 Logan St
Banks, Thomas, Tavern Keeper, Four Mile House
Bannister, John, Overseer to Theus, St John's, Berkeley, 60 miles
Bannister, Sampson, Overseer to Theus, St John's, Berkeley, 60 miles

Barber, Henry, Planter, St John's, Berkeley, 45 miles
Bardold, ——, City Guard, 21 Berresford St
Bardsden, Laurens, Ship Carpenter, East Bay St
Baring, John, Shop Keeper, 194 King St
Barker, Jacob, Overseer to Daniel Ravenall, St John's, Berkeley, 40 miles
Barker, Joseph Sandford, Merchant (Custom House), 101 East Bay St
Barker, Joseph Sandford, Merchant, corner of 12 Anson St & Society St
Barkley, James, Shop Keeper, King St Road
Barkley, Robert, Overseer to Thomas Corbett, Jr, St John's, Berkeley, 30 miles
Barksdale, George, Planter, Christ Church Parish, 4 miles
Barksdale, Mary, Planter, 90 Tradd St
Barksdale, Mary, Planter, Christ Church Parish, 18 miles
Barksdale, Thomas, Planter, Christ Church Parish, 14 miles
Barnett, Elisha, Planter, St James' Santee, 48 miles
Barnett, Francis, Planter, Christ Church Parish, 24 miles
Barnett, Samuel, Planter, St James' Santee, 26 miles
Barney, ——, Custom House Boatman, Holme's Lot
Baron & Wilson, Physicians, (Shop) cor of Water & Meeting Sts
Baron, Alexander, Jr, Physician, 45 Meeting St
Baron, Alexander, Physician, 53 Broad St
Baron, Benjamin, Planter, Four Holes
Barrelli & Torry, Opticians, 32 Broad St.
Barrenger, John, Grocer, cor of South Bay & King St
Barrett, Benjamin, Planter, St John's, Berkeley, 45 miles
Barrier, Jean, Shop Keeper, 14 Motte St
Barron, John, Wine Merchant, 11 East Bay St
Barry, Peter, Boot & Shoe Maker, 31 Broad St
Barry, Sarah, Shop Keeper, Market St
Barry, William, Silver Plater, 10 Trott St
Bartless, Henry, Blacksmith, 24 cor of Middle & Laurens St
Barton, George, Planter, Christ Church Parish, 11 miles
Barton, John B., Painter, 60 Church St
Bartrand, James, Baker, 8 Berresford's Al
Bascomb, Benjamin, Clerk, 89 Church St
Bates, John, Overseer, Wadmalaw Island
Battker, J A, Grocer, 30 Union St
Battker, J, Grocer, 24 Union St
Bauny, Peter, Shop Keeper, 89 King St
Bay, Anderson, Attorney, 197 Meeting St.
Bay, E. H, Judge, Common Pleas & Sessions, 197 Meeting St
Bay, John, Merchant, 197 Meeting St
Bay, William, Merchant, 197 Meeting St.

Baylock, David, Hunter, St Stephen's, 46 miles
Baylock, Richard, Hunter, St Stephen's, 46 miles
Beals, Joseph, Scrivener, 122 King St
Beard, Elizabeth, Widow, 29 Trott St
Beard, Frederick, Teller, S C Bank, 118 Meeting St Road
Beard, William, Porter, Bank of S C, 35 Church St
Beath, David, Grocer, 20 Tradd St
Beath, Perman, Grocers, 19 East Bay St
Beattie, Edmond, Merchant, 3 West St
Beatty, Robert, Store Keeper, 28 Broad St
Beaudrot, Joseph, School Master, 31 Pinckney St
Becaise, Claude, Cabinet Maker, 136 Meeting St
Beckett, James, Planter, Edisto Island
Bedal, Francis, Painter, 60 Church St
Bee, Barnard E, Attorney, 5 Short St
Bee, Eliza, Widow, 11 Amen St
Bee, James S, Clerk, 11 Amen St
Bee, John, Carpenter, 11 Amen St
Bee, John S, Factor, 103 Church St
Bee, Peter Smith, Planter, 22 Church St
Bee, Thomas, Judge, Federal Court, 5 Short St
Bee, William, Planter, 14 Church St Cont'd
Beekman, Adolph, Painter & Glazier, 69 Meeting St
Beekman, Elizabeth, 17 East Bay & Minority St
Beekman, Samuel, Pump Maker, 28 Hasell St
Beggs, James, Store Keeper, 163 King St
Beile, John C, Shop Keeper, 219 King St
Bell, Ann, Nurse, 6 Moore St
Bell, David, Clerk, 6 Society St
Bell, John James, Planter, St Stephen's, 50 miles
Bell, Mary, Tavern Keeper, St James' Goose Creek, 22 miles
Bellard, Antoine, Shop Keeper, 15 Amen St
Bellinger, William, Planter, St Andrew's Parish, 10 miles
Bellisle, Peter, Baker & Grocer, 87 East Bay St
Belshaw, Robert, Store Keeper, King St Road
Beltzer, Christian, Butcher, King St Road
Beltzer, Jacob, Butcher, Hampstead
Benay, Frank, Overseer to P Ray, St John's, Berkeley, 45 miles
Bennett, Henry, Deputy Collector, Custom House, 2 Anson St
Bennett, John, Grocer, 2 Union St
Bennett, John H, Planter, Christ Church Parish, 15 miles
Bennett, John Swinton, Planter, James Island
Bennett, Margaret, Planter, Christ Church Parish, 4 miles
Bennett, Sarah, Planter, Wadmalaw Island
Bennett, Thomas, Jr., Lumber Merchant, Lynch St
Bennett, Thomas, Sr, Planter, James Island
Bennoist, John, Planter, Christ Church Parish, 15 miles
Bennoist, Peter, Planter, Wadmalaw Island

Bennoist, William, Planter, Christ Church Parish, 15 miles
Benoist, Charles, Chair Maker, 7 Blackbird Al
Benoist, Daniel, City Scavenger, 4 Mazyck St
Benoist, John B , Baker, 138 Meeting St
Benoist, Philip, Planter, St John's, Berkcley, 36 miles
Benson, Laurence, Shop Keeper, 214 King St
Bentham, James, Clerk, 39 East Bay St
Bentham, James, Notary Public & Q U., 39 East Bay St
Bentham, William, Capt , Mariner, 39 East Bay St
Bequaise, Mary, 224 King St
Berbant, Samuel, Tailor, 76 East Bay St
Bermond, ——, Physician, 90 Church St
Bernard, M , Store Keeper, 54 King St
Bernard, Rene, Hair Dresser & Perfumer, 4 Tradd St
Berney, John, Insurance Broker (Counting House), 29 East Bay St
Berney, John, Insurance Broker, 11 Archdale St
Bernstine, Henry, Grocer, Boundary St
Berry, Andrew, Lt of Revenue Cutter, Bull St
Bessilicu, Elizabeth, Nurse, 27 Beaufain St
Beswick, John B , Clerk, 121 Meeting St Road
Bethel, Benjamin, Millwright, 89 Meeting St
Bethune, Angus, Merchant, Cannonborough Road
Betsel, Mary, Planter, Christ Church Parish, 18 miles
Bevin, Thomas, Boot & Shoe Store, 3 Elliott St.
Bianki, George, Band Box Maker, 10 Queen St
Bigilow, Elizabeth, Meeting St Road, next to Piquet Guard House
Billings, Samuel, Livery Stable, 68 Queen St
Bingley, N , Capt , Mariner, 9 Middle St
Bins, ——, Mrs , Planter, St John's, Berkeley, 46 miles
Bins, Michael, Planter, St. Stephen's 46 miles
Bins, Stephen, Planter, St Stephen's 46 miles
Bird, Richard, Overseer to Alexander Broughton, St John's, Berkeley, 41 miles
Bird, Sarah, Nurse, 6 Mazyck St
Birnie, William, Merchant, 22 Elliott St
Bissierre, Theodore, Tailor, 43 Queen St
Bixby, Nathan, Merchant, 35 King St
Bizuel, Julien, Shop Keeper, 80 Church St
Black, Christian, Chair Maker, 9 Guignard St
Black, William, Cooper, 11 Broad St
Black, William, Cooper's Shop, Craft's S Whf
Black, William, Planter, St Andrew's Parish, 10 miles
Blackley, John, Clerk, 52 King St
Blacklock, William, Merchant, (Counting House), 135 East Bay St
Blacklock, William, Merchant, Bull St
Blackman, Thomas, Planter, Wassmasaw, 29 miles
Blackwood, John, Store Keeper, 171 King St

Blackwood, Thomas, Merchant (Store), 17 East Bay St
Blackwood, Thomas, Merchant, 39 Tradd St
Bladen, Mary Ann, Widow, 11 Wentworth St
Blair, James, Vendue Master, 2 Stoll's Al
Blair, John K., Clerk, 19 East Bay St
Blair Napier, Vendue Master, (Store), Champney St
Blair, William, Ship Carpenter, 6 Mazyck St
Blake, John, Capt President of State Bank, South Bay
Blakely, Robert, Store Keeper, 186 King St
Blamyer, William, Jr , Factor (Counting House), 152 East Bay St
Blamyer, William, Jr , Factor, 27 Society St
Blanch, Matlame, 47 Trott St
Blanck, Martin, Capt , Mariner, 4 Wall St
Blancke, Christian, Clerk, 8 East Bay St
Bland, Richard, Boarding House, 120 Queen St
Blier, Andrew, Wheel Wright, King St Road
Block, Nathaniel, Cabinet Maker, Wentworth St
Blocker, James, Merchant, King St Road
Blom, John, Confectioner, 107 Queen St
Bloomstock, Michael, Grocer, 3 Liberty St
Bluer, Peter, Grocer, King St Road
Bluit, James, Shoe Maker, St Stephen's, 52 miles
Blythwood, Thomas, Mariner, 3 Kinloch Court
Boinneau, S , Overseer to E Rutledge, St John's, Berkeley, 30 miles
Boisgerard, C & F , Merchants (Counting House), Craft's S Whf.
Boisgerard, C & F., Merchants, 197 King St
Bolchez, Alexander, Capt , Mariner, 108 Meeting St.
Bold, William, Planter, 4 Tradd St
Bollough, Elias, Custom House Inspector, 18 Berresford St
Bollough, George & Brother, Planters, Christ Church Parish, 17 miles
Bollough, James, Planter, Christ Church Parish, 15 miles
Bolton, Martha, Planter, Christ Church Parish, 4 miles
Bompkemper, Frederick, Grocer, Cannon St
Bonaus, John, Goldsmith, 142 Broad St
Bonetheau, Gabriel, M C C , Justice of the Peace, & Printer, 35 Trott St
Bonneau, ——, Widow, St James' Goose Creek, 16 miles
Bonneau, Arnoldus, Planter, Christ Church Parish, 25 miles
Bonneau, Eleanor, 45 George St
Bonneau, Elisha, Planter, St James' Santee, 40 miles
Bonneau, Elizabeth, Planter, Christ Church Parish, 22 miles
Bonneau, Henry, Planter, Christ Church Parish, 32 miles
Bonneau, John, 56 Broad St.

Bonnel, John, Capt., Mariner, 5 Lynch's Ln
Bonsall, Elizabeth, 5 Wentworth & St Philip's St
Bonthron, Henry, Clerk, 92 Queen St
Bonthron, John, Grocer, 92 Queen St
Boone, Sarah, Planter, 85 Meeting St
Boone, Thomas, Planter, Christ Church Parish, 10 miles
Booner, Christian, Tavern Keeper, 114 Queen St
Booth, William, Mariner, 7 Motte St
Boothroyd, Jabez, Merchant, 77 Meeting St
Borch, Peter, Grocer, 65 East Bay St
Borvil, Joseph, Butcher, St Philip's St Cont'd
Boss, John, Capt., Merchant, 40 East Bay St
Boucheneau, Sarah, Hampstead
Bouchet, Anthony, Cutler, 133 Queen St
Bouchet, Marie, 12 Motte St
Bouchett, James, Planter, St Stephen's, 46 miles
Bouchett, John P., Planter, St James' Santee, 35 miles
Bouchett, Michael, Blacksmith, St Stephen's, 46 miles
Bouchus, Frederick, Black Smith, 124 Queen St
Bounetheau, E W., Carpenter, Trott St
Bounetheau, Elizabeth, Widow, 68 Church & Amen St
Bounetheau, G M., Printer, Clerk of City Council, Justice of Peace, Printing Office, 1 Broad St
Bounetheau, Gabriel, M C C., Justice of the Peace & Printer, 35 Trott St
Bourdon, J S., 7 Middle St
Bournos, L F., Clerk, 28 East Bay St
Bours, Luke, Vendue Master, 106 East Bay St
Bousquet, Peter, Shop Keeper, 215 King St
Boutland, —, Madame, 27 Guignard St
Bowen, John, Planter, St James' Goose Creek, 24 miles
Bowen, Nathaniel, Rev., 68 Tradd St
Bowler, Rutherford, Overseer to Moore, St Thomas' Parish, 8 miles
Bowles, Ann, School Mistress, Orphan House
Bowles, John, Printer, 41 Broad St
Bowman Daniel, Planter, Four Holes
Bowman, James, Shipwright, Christ Church Parish, 15 miles
Bowman, Sabina, Planter, Montague St.
Bowman, Sarah, Planter, Wassmasaw, 40 miles
Bowman, Thomas, Planter, Wassmasaw, 31 miles
Boyd, Benjamin, Store Keeper, 134 King St
Boyd, William, Merchant (Counting House), Chisholm's Whf
Boyd, William, Merchant, 34 East Bay & Minority St.
Boyeman, John, Overseer to Dr E Jones, St. Andrew's Parish, 13 miles
Boyer, J F., Grocer, King St Road
Boyer, Mary, 5 Clifford St
Brabant, James, Overseer to Mrs Bennett, Christ Church Parish, 10 miles

Brabant, James, Planter, Christ Church, 6 miles
Bradford, Christina, Music Store, 55 East Bay St
Bradham, James, Planter, Four Holes
Bradley, Charles, Printer, 1 Maiden lane
Bradley, Henry, Planter, St John's, Berkeley, 35 miles
Bradley, Matthew, Lumber Merchant, 4 Short St
Bradwell, Isaac, Planter, Four Holes
Brailsford, Edward, Dr., Planter, Cannonborough Road
Brailsford, Edward, Physician, St James' Goose Creek, 20 miles
Brailsford, Elizabeth, 125 Meeting St
Brailsford, John, Planter, 5 East Bay St
Brailsford, John, Planter, St James' Goose Creek, 9 miles
Brailsford, Joseph, Clerk, 34 Hasell St
Brailsford, Mary, 22 Tradd St
Brandford, Mary, Planter, 17 Legare St
Brandon, David, Distiller, 1 Meeting St Road
Brandt, H F., Dr., Physician, 15 Pinckney St
Brandt, James W., Capt., Planter, Christ Church Parish, 4 miles
Brandt, Thomas, School Master, St Stephen's, 50 miles
Brattel, William, Painter, Bull St
Breach, Peter, Tailor, St John's, Berkeley, 52 miles
Brecker, Jacob, Blacksmith, St. James' Goose Creek, 19 miles
Brecker, John, Overseer to Charles Smith, St James' Goose Creek, 18 miles
Brecker, Lewis, Tavern Keeper, St James' Goose Creek, 18 miles
Breid, Matthew, Carpenter, 29 Church St Cont'd
Bremar, Henry, Dentist, Trott St
Brenan, M & R., Merchants, 146 Broad St
Brian, John, Planter, St Thomas' Parish, 21 miles
Brian, Lydia, Planter, St Thomas' Parish, 21 miles
Brickell, James, St John's, Berkeley, 45 miles
Bride, Elizabeth, Umbrella Maker, 185 Meeting St
Bridie, Eleanora, School Mistress, 25 Meeting St
Bridie, Robert, Vendue Master, 74 Church St
Bridy, Jane, Store Keeper, 162 King St
Bright, Susannah, Boarding House, 4 Lodge Al
Brindley, John George, Planter, St James' Goose Creek, 23 miles
Brindley, John, Planter, St James Goose Creek, 24 miles
Bringley, William, Planter, Boundary St
Brisack, —, Motte St
Brisbane, Willaim, Planter, Meeting St
Brisbane, William, Planter, St Andrew's Parish, 9 miles
Briscoe, Sarah, 40 East Bay St
Bristoe, Philip, Overseer to F Marion, St John's, Berkeley, 45 miles
Brit, Stephen, Wheel Wright, 6 Liberty St

Broadfoot, James, Merchant, cor. of Meeting & Tradd St
Broadfoot, William, Merchant, (Counting House), 143 East Bay St
Broadfoot, William, Merchant, cor of Meeting & Tradd St
Broadham, Mary, Planter, Four Holes
Brockway, Martha, 174 King St
Brockway, Samuel, House Carpenter, 86 King St
Brodie, John, Lumber Merchant, 58 Tradd St
Brooks & Potter, Merchants (Counting House), Vanderhorst's Whf
Brooks, Frederick, Mariner, 76 Queen St
Brooks, Thomas, Tailor, 11 Tradd St
Bross, John, Tavern Keeper, Sullivan's Island
Broughton, Ann, Planter, 1 Mazyck St
Broughton, John P , Planter, St John's, Berkeley, 28 miles
Broughton, Mary, Planter, St John's, Berkeley, 28 miles
Broughton, Peter, Capt , Planter, St John's, Berkeley, 33 miles
Broughton, Thomas, Jr , St John's, Berkeley, 28 miles
Brown, ——, Mrs , Planter, Coming St
Brown, Alexander, Clerk, 166 King St
Brown, Ann, Seamstress, 13 Ellery St
Brown, Daniel, Capt , Boarding House, 35 Church St Cont'd
Brown, Daniel, Grocer, 100 Church St
Brown, Elizabeth, Planter, Christ Church Parish, 25 miles
Brown, James, Overseer to Wigfall, St James' Goose Creek, 21 miles
Brown, Jane, Spinner, Orphan House
Brown, John, Grocer, 35 Broad St
Brown, John, Grocer, Market St
Brown, John, Planter, Wassmasaw, 29 miles
Brown, Jonathan, Mariner, 1 Parsonage Ln.
Brown, Joseph, Custom House Officer, 36 East Bay St
Brown, Joseph, Grocer, 51 Queen St.
Brown, Joshua, Vendue Master, 205 King St
Brown, Joshua, Vendue Master, Store, Exchange St.
Brown, Mary, King St Road
Brown, Mary, Tavern Keeper, St James' Goose Creek, 20 miles
Brown, Michael, Cabinet Maker, 99 Queen St
Brown, Rebecca, Seamstress, 17 Trott St
Brown, Robert, Planter, John's Island
Brown, Samuel, Custom House Boatman, 23 King St
Brown, William, Boarding House, 24 Union St
Brown, William, Boarding House, 9 Union St
Browne, Alexander, Shop Keeper, 13 Motte St
Browne, Alexander, Shop Keeper, 15 Motte St
Browne, G W , Ropewalk, Hampstead
Browne, Harriett Lowndes, Planter, 61 Tradd St

Browne, James, City Marshall, 123 King St
Browne, Samuel, Commission Broker, 163 King St
Browne, William, 26 Queen St
Browne, William, Carpenter, 123 King St
Browning, Gideon, Planter, Wassmasaw, 31 miles
Browning, Peregrin, Overseer to James Legare, John's Island
Browning, William, Overseer to Beltzer, St James' Goose Creek, 14 miles
Brownlee, John, Merchant, 14 St Philip's St
Brune, ——, Overseer to Col Shubrick, Bull's Island
Bruner,——, Overseer to Mrs Legare, Christ Church Parish, 10 miles
Brunston, John, Carpenter, 6 Meeting St Road
Brunswick, Stephen, Grocer, 92 East Bay St
Bryan, Daniel, Clerk, 194 Meeting St
Bryant, Jane, Widow, King St Road
Bryce, Henry, Merchant, 143 East Bay St
Bryce, Nicol, Vendue Master, (Store), Champneys St
Bryce, Nicol, Vendue Master, 118 Church St
Brynes, Patrick, Sail Maker, 12 Pinckney St
Buchanan, Archibald, Brass Founder, Shop 91 East Bay St
Buckhannan, Angus, Wheel Wright, 1 Back St
Buckiman, Tailor, 29 Church St
Buckingham, John, Boot & Shoe Maker, 8 Broad St
Budd, Abigal, Boarding House, 40 Church St
Buford, Catharine, Seamstress, 9 Archdale St
Buist, Mary, Planter, 2 Church St Cont'd
Bulet, Peter, Clerk, King St Road
Bulkley, Rose, Ship Chandlers (Store), 22 East Bay St
Bulkley, Stephen, Ship Chandler, 118 King street
Bull, Elizabeth, Planter, St Andrew's Parish, 12 miles
Bull, William S , Capt , Planter, St Andrew's Parish, 12 miles
Bulow, John & Charles, Merchants, 166 King St
Bunch, James, Planter, St James' Goose Creek, 22 miles
Bunch, Lydia, Planter, St John's, Berkeley, 35 miles
Bunell, Angelica, 45 King St
Burboyne, ——, Tinman, 246 King St
Burbridge, Jonathan, Planter, St James' Goose Creek, 25 miles
Burbridge, Richard, Planter, St James' Goose Creek, 25 miles
Burch, Henry T , Merchant, 13 Parsonage Ln.
Burckmyer, John, Butcher, Wentworth St
Burdell, John, Planter, St. John's, Berkeley, 65 miles
Burden, Kinsey, Planter, 6 Logan St
Burden, Kinsey, Planter, John's Island
Burden, Thomas, Factor, 6 Logan, St

Burdick, Benjamin, Mariner, 19 Amen St
Burger, Charles, Clerk, 48 Church St
Burger, George, Clerk, 143 East Bay St
Burger, William, Clerk, 30 East Bay St
Burgoyne, William, Druggist, 147 Broad &
  East Bay St
Burien, Daniel, Blacksmith, 16 Society St
Burke, John, Mariner, 20 Guignard St
Burn, Alexander, Carpenter, St James' Goose
  Creek, 10 miles
Burn, James, Planter, 54 Meeting St
Burn, John Alexander, Overseer to Shakelford, St
  James' Santee, 42 miles
Burn, John, Grocer, 131 Meeting St Road &
  Society St
Burness, James, Planter, St Thomas' Parish, 18
  miles
Burnet, Foster, Painter, 46 East Bay St
Burnett, Benjamin, Carpenter, John's Island
Burnham, Thomas, House Carpenter, 23 St. Philip's
  St
Burns, Francis, Boarding House, 6 Union St
Burns, Michael, School Master, James Island
Burrbridge, John, Overseer to Henry Deas, St
  James' Goose Creek, 21 miles
Burrbridge, Thomas, Planter, St. James' Goose
  Creek, 26 miles
Burridge, L, Mariner, Coming St
Burrows, Mary, Seamstress, 6 Trott St
Busket, ——, 255 King St
Bussacker, Charles, Grocer, 24 Union St.
Butcher, Mary, Seamstress, Boundary St.
Butler, Charles P, Goldsmith & Jeweller, 236 King
  St
Butler, Daniel, Shop Keeper, 17 Motte St
Butler, Joseph, Deputy Sheriff, 112 Meeting St
Butler, Joseph, Planter, 5 Friend St
Butler, Robert, Capt, Inspector of the S C
  Insurance Company, 3 Minority St
Butler, Thomas, Planter, St James' Santee, 42
  miles
Butman, Ebenezer, Clerk, King St Road
Byer, Henry, Grocer, South Bay
Bynum, John, School Master, James Island
Bynum, Turner, Factor, 7 Blackbird Al
Byrnes, Patrick, Sail Maker, 12 Pinckney St
Cabaneau, F, Umbrella Maker, 28 Queen St
Caine, ——, Mrs, 6 Berresford's Al
Cairborne, George, Planter, St Andrew's, 15 miles
Calder, Alexander, Boarding House & Planter's
  Hotel, 47 Church & Queen St
Calder, Henry, Planter, Edisto Island
Calder, James, Cabinet Maker, 38 Meeting St
Caldwell, John, Carpenter, 1 College St
Caldwell, Samuel, Carpenter, Washington St
Caldwell, William A, Merchant, 106 East Bay,
  Dwelling, New St
Caldwell, William, Carpenter, 1 College St

Caloff, Henry, Planter, Race Ground
Calvert, Elizabeth, Boarding House, 21 Church St
Calwell, Sarah, Seamstress, 6 Society St
Cambridge, Elizabeth, 6 Orange St
Cambridge, James H, Vendue Master, Trott St
Camer, James, Planter, Race Ground
Cameron, David, Butcher, Cannon St
Cameron, Lewis, Boarding House, 23 Church St
Cameron, Richard, Clerk, 71 Meeting St
Cammer, Peter, Shop Keeper, 21 Wall St
Campbell, Alexander, Mariner, 14 Amen St
Campbell, Ann, Planter, Wadmalaw Island
Campbell, Archibald, Merchant, 96 Church St
Campbell, Colin, Merchants, 39 Church St
Campbell, Elizabeth, Shop Keeper, 165 King St
Campbell, Jane, Seamstress, Mazyckborough
Campbell, M'Millan & Co, Vendue Masters, Store,
  Champneys St, Dwelling, 12 St Philip's St
Campbell, Mary, Planter, 11 Church St
Campbell, Mary, Planter, John's Island
Canter, Abraham, Clerk, 23 Tradd St
Canter, Emanuel, Merchant, 6 Savage St
Canter, Jacob, Merchant, 116 Tradd St.
Canter, John, Limner, 23 Tradd St
Canter, Joshua, Limner, 13 Legare St
Canton, John, Physician, 27 Archdale St
Cape, Brian, Factor, 13 Anson St
Capers, Gabriel, Planter, Wadmalaw Island
Carendeffer, A, Physician, 42 George St
Carew, Edward, Pump & Block Maker, 35
  Pinckney St.
Carew, Edward, Pump & Block Maker, Shop, East
  Bay St
Carey, John, Tallow Chandler, King St Road
Carey, Thomas, School Master, Edisto Island
Carmand, Francis, Tailor, 232 King St
Carmichael, George, Tobacconist, 104 King St
Carnacan, Richard, Clerk, 113 Tradd St
Carne, Thomas W, Messenger of Council, Clerk to
  Commissoners of Streets, 26 St Philip's St
Carnes, Benjamin, Planter, 12 Legare St
Caroylle, Peter, Rigger, Boundary St
Carpenter, Joseph, Butcher, Cannon St
Carr, James, Butcher, Washington St
Carr, James, Grocer & Livery Stable, King St Road
Carrere, Charles, Teacher of French, 83 Meeting St
Carrere, Francis, Tailor, 7 Queen St
Carroll, Bartholomew, Planter, Boundary St
Carroll, James Parsons, Planter, Boundary St
Carslen, John, Grocer, 27 Anson St
Carson, James, Store, 10 Broad St, Dwelling, 78
  Tradd cor Orange St
Cart, John, Jr, Factor, Bull St.
Cart, John, Lumber Merchant, Bull St
Cart, Sarah, 1 Kinloch Court
Carter, George, Physician, 65 W end Tradd St
Carter, I C, Mariner, 33 Elliott St.
Carthers, Robert, Black Smith, 116 Broad St

Cartherwood, John, Watch Maker, 117 Queen St
Caruth, John, Capt , Mariner, 1 Lynch's Ln
Casey, Benjamin, Coach Maker, 116 Broad St
Cashman, John, Grocer, 7 King St
Casken, John, Carpenter, 54 Queen St
Cassin, Patrick, Merchant, 104 Tradd St
Catonnet, Peter, Shop Keeper, 243 King St.
Cattle, William, Planter, St Andrew's, 16 miles
Caught, Thomas, Shop Keeper, 130 East Bay St
Chambers, William, Grocer, 8 Motte St.
Chambers, William, Planter, St Andrew's, 16 miles
Champey, Edmond, Attorney, 22 Society & cor
  Meeting St
Champion, Richard Lloyd, Planter, St Andrew's, 12
  miles
Champlin, Jane, 5 Church St Cont'd
Champneys, John, Planter, 95 King St
Chancognie, Simon Jude, French Consul, 15
  Laurens St
Chandler, Elizabeth, 52 Broad St cor Orange St
Chanet, Anthony, Shop Keeper, 8 Queen St
Chanler, Catharine, Widow, 9 Federal St
Channer, C J , Tailor, 160 King St
Chapman, Joseph, Grocer, King St Road
Charles, Andrew, Merchant, 10 Elliott St
Charley, ——, Boatman, Sullivan's Island
Charlotte, ——, Madame, 170 Meeting St
Chase, A., Capt , Mariner, 9 Laurens St
Chase, P W , Carpenter, 16 Middle St
Chatteau, Charles, Shop Keeper, 21 Trott St
Chazel, Francois, Store Keeper, 19 Church St
Cheves, Langdon, Attorney General, 37 Meeting St
Chew, Sarah, Seamstress, Hampstead
Childs, Elizabeth, Shop Keeper, 101 King St
Chion, J F , Merchant, 86 King St
Chionard, Charles, Grocer, Sullivan's Island
Chisolm, Alexander, Planter, 287 King St
Chisolm, George, Factor, 34 Church St Cont'd
Chisolm, Robert, Physician, Edisto Island
Chisolm, Taylor, Factor (Counting House),
  Chisolm's Whf
Chitty, Ann, Seamstress, 10 Berresford St
Chitty, William John, Assistant Clerk to State Bank,
  St Philip's St
Choat, Thomas, Mariner, 7 Anson St
Chouler, Mary, Seamstress, 108 Meeting St.
Chrietzburg, Conrad, Butcher, Cannon St
Christian, ——, Butcher, Mazyckborough
Christian, Charles, Merchant (Counting House), 116
  East Bay, Dwelling, Queen St
Christian, Charles, Merchant, 6 New St
Christie, Alexander, 94 Church St
Chritzberg, George, Shop Keeper, 52 Anson St
Chupein, Lewis, Hair Dresser, 137 Broad St
Church, Margaret, Seamstress, Wentworth St
Cills, ——, Mrs , Seamstress, 19 Pinckney St
Clabby, Richard, Store Keeper, 147 King St
Clairfont, John, Candle Manufacturer, Hampstead

Clancy, Michael, Store Keeper, King St Road
Clapp, Henry, Coach Maker, 94 Queen St
Clark, Bartholomew, Grocer, 233 King St
Clark, David, Watch Maker, 41 Anson St
Clark, J W , Capt , Mariner, 113 Meeting St
Clark, James, Coach Maker, 1 Back St
Clark, Richard, Boatman, Sullivan's Island
Clarke, James, Boarding House, 32 Union St
Clarke, James, Planter, Edisto Island
Clarke, James, Tailor, 10 Elliott St cor Bedon's
  Al
Clarke, John, Cabinet Maker, 29 King St
Clarkson, William, Factor, 8 Champneys St ,
  Dwelling, cor Meeting & Hasell St
Clarkson, William, Jr , Merchant, 27 St Philip's St
Clarkson, William, Rev , Wadmalaw Island
Clastrier, Maxemin, Starch Powder Manufacturer,
  Vanderhorst St
Clastriere, Mary, 256 King St.
Cleapor, Charles, Sail Maker, 17 Ellery St
Cleary, John R , School Master, 19 Hasell St
Cleary, Nathaniel Green, Clerk, Sheriff's Office, 19
  Hasell St
Cleary, Robert Washington, Surveyor U I O , 122
  East Bay St
Clement, Sarah, Widow, 45 Queen St
Clifford, Henry, Clerk, 2 Hard Al
Clime, Martin, Carpenter, 1 Blackbird Al
Clissey, Raymond, Coach Trimmer, 79 Church St
Clouet, Joseph, Baker, Boundary St
Clough, Thomas, Merchant (Counting House),
  Craft's N Whf
Clough, Thomas, Merchant, 129 Broad St
Coates, Catharine, Planter, Race Ground
Coates, William A , Grocer, Prioleau's N Whf
Cobia, Christiana E , Planter, Montague St
Cobia, Daniel, Butcher, Montague St.
Cobia, Francis, Carpenter, 30 Archdale St
Cobia, Nicholas, Planter, 4 Miles House, King St
  Road
Cochran, Benjamin, Overseer to Carson's Estate,
  Wadmalaw Island
Cochran, Charles B., State Treasurer, 70 Meeting
  St
Cochran, Margaret, Shop Keeper, 242 King St
Cochran, Robert, Capt , Planter, Ship Yard, King St
  Road
Cochran, Robert E , Federal Marshall, 9 George St
Cochran, Susannah, Planter, 12 Church St
Cochran, Thomas, Factor (Counting House), 120
  East Bay St
Cochran, Thomas, Factor & Commission Merchant,
  32 Queen St
Cock, J S H , Capt., Mariner, 33 Church St
Coclcock, Job, 108 Church St
Cogan, James B , Grocer, 1 Market St
Cogdell, John S , Attorney, 2 St Michael's Al

Cogdell, M A E, Boarding School, 1 St Michael's Al,

Cogdell, Richard, Clerk, 1 St Michael's Al

Cohen, Jacob & Co, Vendue Masters, Store, Champneys St

Cohen, Jacob, Keeper of Synagogue, 21 Hasell St

Cohen, Mordecai, Store Keeper, 124 King St

Cohen, Moses, Store Keeper, 198 King St

Cohen, Philip, Vendue Master, 10 Orange St, Store, Champneys St

Cohen, Solomon J, Store Keeper, 165 King St

Cohen, Solomon, Shop Keeper, King St

Cohkler, Frederick, Tanner, Coming St

Coit, Fraser, Factors (Counting House), Chisolm's Whf

Coit, Jonathan, Factor, 19 Meeting St

Colbert, William, Boatman, Sullivan's Island

Colcock, Mellisscent, Boarding School, 8 Lamboll St

Cole, Jacob, Clerk, 116 Queen St

Cole, John, Mariner, Church St

Cole, Joseph, Boot & Shoe Maker, 3 Broad St

Cole, Richard, Ship Carpenter, Cannon St

Coleman, Benjamin, Grocer, 33 Union St

Coleman, Benjamin, Shop Keeper, 166 King St

Coleman, Margaret, Sewing Mistress, Orphan House, Boundary St

Coleman, Samuel, Mariner, 5 Lodge Al

Coleman, Sylvester, Store Keeper, 142 King St

Colley, John, Clerk, 43 Church St

Colley, Thomas, Grocer, 2 Linguard St

Collier, William, Boarding House, 189 Meeting St

Collins, Catharine, Seamstress, 46 Queen St

Collins, John, Clerk, 18 Hasell St

Collins, Manassah, 42 Queen St

Collins, William, Mariner, 8 Laurens St

Collogier, Antonio, Grocer, Sullivan's Island

Collynon, Mitchell, Confectioner, East Bay St

Colzy, Charlemagne, Tailor, 29 Church St

Condy & Raguet, Merchants, Store, 123 East Bay St.

Condy, Jeremiah, Merchant, 178 Meeting St

Condy, Jeremiah, Merchant, 31 Church St.

Connelly, John, Grocer, Market St

Connelly, M H, Planter, 17 Meeting St

Conyers, Elizabeth, School Mistress, 264 King St

Conyers, William, Harbor Master, 27 Pinckney St

Cooke, Samuel, Tailor, 63 Church St

Cooper, Henry, Shop Keeper, 61 Church St

Cooper, James, Capt, Merchant, Church St

Cooper, Jane, Nurse, 25 King St

Cooper, Jonathan, Capt, Mariner, 3 Lynch's Ln

Cooper, Matthew, Merchant (Counting House), Craft's East Bay Range

Cooper, Matthew, Merchant, 7 Broad St.

Coram, Francis, Wood Measurer, 29 George St

Coram, Thomas, Painter & Engraver, 70 Queen St

Corbett, Thomas, Jr, Planter, Mill Tract St

Corbett, Thomas, Sr, President, S C Insurance Co, cor. of Cumberland & Church St

Cordier, Peter, Store Keeper, King St Road

Cordoza, David, Lumber Measurer, 17 King St

Corkell, Thomas, Mariner, Cock Ln

Corker, Thomas, Ship Carpenter, 32 Pinckney St

Cormia, Francois, Ship Carpenter, 19 Wall St

Cormick, Thomas, Merchant, 5 Maiden Ln

Cornell, Benjamin, Clerk, Market St

Cornell, John, Baker, 164 King St

Corre, Margaret, Widow, 54 King St

Corrie, Samuel, Wheelwright, King St Road

Corvan, Joseph, Clerk, 178 King St

Cost, Louis, Merchant, 4 Berresford St

Coste, Velve, 6 St Philip's St.

Cotton, Ann, Boarding House, 3 Parsonage lane

Coullion, Lewis, Grocer, Sullivan's Island

Courtney, Humphrey, Merchant, 34 Meeting St

Courtney, John, Grocer, 135 Meeting St

Cousins, Elizabeth, Shop Keeper, 13 Amen St

Couzons, Thomas, Clerk, 52 King St

Coventry, Alexander, Dyer, 84 Tradd St

Cowan & Hurlburt, Saddlers, 194 King St

Cowan, John, Rigger, 36 Church St

Cowen, Henry, Saddler, 40 Church St

Cox, James, Merchant, 10 Church St Cont'd

Cox, Joseph, Planter, John's Island

Cox, Thomas C, Printer & Editor of the Times, 20 Meeting St

Cox, Thomas, Coach Maker, 1 Clifford St

Crafts, William, Jr, Attorney, 88 Broad St

Crafts, William, Merchant, 88 Broad St

Cramais, ——, 6 Trott St

Crask, Philip, Painter, 11 Pinckney St

Craston, James, Broker, 15 Friend St

Crawford & Vanderhorst, Wharfingers, Vanderhorst's Whf

Crawford, Gabriel, Planter, Edisto Island

Crawford, Grizzy, 4 Church St

Crawford, James, Grocer, 71 Meeting St

Crawford, John, Druggist, 15 Broad St

Crawford, John, Wharfinger, 77 Queen St

Crawford, Thomas, Student of Medicine, Orange St

Crayou, Valentine, Guard Man, 19 Trott St

Creiger, Clinton, Mariner, 23 Berresford's Al

Creswell, James, Brass Founder, 81 Meeting St

Cripps, John Splatt, Planter, 51 Meeting St

Crocker, Hichburn, Merchants (Counting House), Craft's N Whf

Croft, Arnold, Clerk, Hampstead

Croft, Edward, Attorney, 35 Meeting St

Croft, Peter, Factor, Hampsted

Cromwell, ——, Brick Layer, 6 Back St

Cromwell, Charles, Capt, Mariner, 9 Stoll's Al

Cromwell, Jeremiah, Grocer, 32 Church St

Cromwell, Oliver, Attorney, 9 Stoll's Al

Crosby, Joseph, Capt, Grain Merchant, 39 Anson St

Cross, George, Capt., Merchant, 206 Meeting & cor Tradd St
Cross, George Warren, Attorney, 206 Meeting & cor Tradd St
Cross, Matthew William, Brick Layer, 3 Kinloch Court
Crouch, Abraham, Notary Public, Counting House, 122 Meeting St
Crovat, Peter, Store Keeper, 117 King St
Crow, Harman, City Guard, 37 Broad St
Crow, John, Book Binder, 12 Broad St
Crowley, Hannah, Boarding House, 105 Broad St
Crowther, Thomas, Saddler & Harness Maker, 78 Meeting St
Cruckshanks, Daniel, Boot & Shoe Maker, 119 Queen St
Cruckshanks, William, Boot & Shoe Maker, 26 Broad St
Cruger, Elizabeth, 30 Meeting St
Cruger, Elizabeth, 7 Guignard St
Cruger, Nicholas, Planter, 20 Federal St
Cuckoo, William, Pilot, 1 Hard Al
Cudworth, Benjamin, Steward to Orphan House, Boundary St
Cudworth, Nathaniel, Porter to the National Bank, 20 Mazyck St
Cugley, John, Carpenter, Mazyck St
Cummings, Esther, Shop Keeper, 52 East Bay St.
Cummins, John, House Carpenter, 41 Church St Cont'd
Cunningham, ——, Boarding House, 5 Union St.
Cunningham, Charles, Merchant, Hudson St
Cunningham, Elizabeth, Planter, King St Road
Cunningham, John, Planter, 148 King St
Cunningham, Richard, Capt., Planter, 148 King St
Curtis, Ephraim, Carpenter, 42 Anson St
Curtis, Francis, Keeper of the Poor House, Mazyck St
Cutler, J F., Grocer, Mazyckborough
Cutter, Ann, Seamstress, 7 Kinloch Court
Cutter, Isaac, Merchant, 276 King St.
Cyrus, Richard, Cabinet Maker, 29 King St
D[pages 25 & 26 of directory missing, part of 27 is torn]
D'Azeordo, Rachael, Shop Keeper, 74 King St.
Dabney, William, Grocer, 8 Hasell St
Dabrois, Charles, 5 Minority St
Dacosta, Isaac, Physician, 8 Orange St
Dalcho, Frederick, Physician, 135 Broad
Daley, Richard, Mariner, 29 King St
Dalgliesh, Adam, Grocer, 82 Meeting St.
Dalton, Grace, Seamstress, 2 Linguard St
Damgee, Francis, Shop Keeper, 6 Queen St
Dangerfield, William, Capt., Planter, Wassmasaw, 32 miles
Daniel, William, Mariner, 27 Berresford's Al
Daniell, Lewis, Lumber Merchant, 18 Middle St
Danjou, Ferdinand, Grocer, 86 King St

Danner, John, Overseer to B Roper, St. Andrew's, 16 miles
Dantzman, George, Merchant (Counting House), Craft's Whf
Darby, John, Grocer, 13 Archdale & cor Beaufain St
Darby, Robert A., Tailor, 76 East Bay St
Darrell, John S., Capt., Deputy Harbor Master, 35 Anson St
Darrell, Josiah, Clerk, 35 Anson St
Dart, Isaac Motte, Factor, Montague St
Dart, Simmons, Factors (Counting House), Craft's Whf
Dastas, Matthew, Billiard Table Keeper, Coming St
Datart, John, Planter, St Stephen's, 50 miles
Datty, Mark, Boarding School, Wentworth St
Davega, Moses, Vendue Cryer, 26 Meeting St
Davergore, ——, Madame, 19 Wentworth St
David, Jacob, Shop Keeper, 111 King St.
Davidson, James, Merchant, 6 Orange St
Davidson, John, Librarian, 34 Meeting St
Davidson, William, Overseer to Yeadon, St Andrew's, 16 miles
Davis, ——, Overseer, Charleston Neck
Davis, ——, Overseer to Read, St John's, Berkeley, 30 miles
Davis, Abel, Planter, St John's, Berkeley, 47 miles
Davis, Charles, Upholsterer, 100 Queen St
Davis, Francis, Overseer to Thomas Tunno, St John's, Berkeley, 60 miles
Davis, Izrael, Shop Keeper, 112 King St
Davis, Jesse, Planter, St John's, Berkeley, 50 miles
Davis, John M., Insurance Broker
Davis, John, Merchant, Wentworth St
Davis, John, Miller to Henry Laurence, St John's, Berkeley, 31 miles
Davis, John, Planter, St John's, Berkeley, 60 miles
Davis, John, Store Keeper, King St Road
Davis, Thomas, Tavern Keeper, St John's, Berkeley, 45 miles
Davis, William, Grocer, Rutledge St
Davize, Dominique, Merchant, 50 East Bay St
Dawsey, William, Planter, St John's, Berkeley, 40 miles
Dawson, Ann, Montague St.
Dawson, Ann, Widow, Boundary St
Dawson, John, Jr., Merchant, cor of Bull & Rutledge St
Dawson, John, Sr., Planter, 2 East Bay & cor Guignard St
Dawson, John, Store Keeper, King St Road
Deaglish, George, Slater, 4 cor of Mazyck & Queen St
Deas, Charles, Factor, Wentworth St
Deas, David, Planter, St James' Goose Creek, 22 miles
Deas, Robert, Planter, 57 Queen St
Deas, Thomas H., Factor, 81 East Bay St

Debesse, John, Merchant, 122 King St
Debord, John, Brass Founder, 49 East Bay St
Deboumoint, Charles, Shop Keeper, 22 Beaufain St
DeBow, Garret, Vendue Master, 7 East Bay St
Deckard, Rebecca, Planter, Christ Church Parish, 11 miles
Decker, Charles, Grocer, 46 Wentworth St
Degland, Blaise, Mariner, Meeting St Road
Degland, V, Madame, Shop Keeper, 25 Wall St
Dehay, Andrew, Overseer to D Deas, St James' Goose Creek, 22 miles
Dehay, Benjamin, Overseer to Keating Simons, St John's, Berkeley, 29 miles
Dehay, James, Planter, Wassmasaw, 32 miles
Dehay, Mary, Planter, Wassmasaw, 31 miles
Delaire, James, Merchant (Counting House), 39 East Bay St
Delaire, James, Merchant (Counting House), 95 East Bay St
DeLaire, Stephen, Baker, 17 Wall St
DeLalande, A J P, Broker, 21 Guignard St
DeLamotta, Emanuel, Vendue Master, Store, Exchange St
Delany, James, Planter, St Stephen's, 44 miles
Delany, James, Ploughman, St Stephen's, 50 miles
Delany, Vincent, Planter, St Stephen's, 50 miles
Delap, Elizabeth, Nurse, East Bay St
DeLeiben, Hannah, Shop Keeper, 96 King St
Deleissline, F G, Factor, 112 Queen St
Deliessline, John, Planter, Dewee's Island
Delisle, John G, Physician, 5 Cumberland St
DeLoire, Breard & P Taslet, 78 East Bay St
Dempsey, Michael, Soap Manufacturer, Meeting St
Dempsey, Thomas, Grocer, 30 Wall St
Dener, George, Tanner, 9 Mazyck St
Dennis, James, Boarding House & Constable, 39 Union St
Denoon, Margaret, Widow, 38 cor of Wentworth & Meeting St
Dent, John, Capt, U S Navy, Mazyckborough
Depau, Francis, Merchant, 16 East Bay St
Depestre, Hector, Planter, Daniel's Island, 7 miles
Deportes, Peter, Grocer, 88 East Bay St.
Derreer, Anthony, Boot & Shoe Maker, 9 Trott St.
Deschamps, F, Planter, St James Santee, 41 miles
Descleaux, Peter, Grocer, King St. Road
Descoudres, L P & Co, Shop Keepers, 117 King St.
Desgraves, M., Planter, 1 Maiden Ln
Dessaussure, D, Mrs, Montague St
DeTollenaire, Charles, Planter, St John's, Berkeley, 42 miles
Detroit, ——, Madame, 1 Minority St
Deveaux, Barnwell, Attorney, 40 Church St
Deveaux, John, Planter, Edisto Island
Devenau, Abraham, 105 Queen St
Devilliers, Louis, Professor of Music, 258 King St
Dewees, William, Factor, Mazyckborough

Dewees, William, Jr, Factor, Mazyckborough
Diamond, John, Surveyor, 9 cor of Blackbird Al & Meeting St
Dickenson, Samuel, Vendue Master, 133 Broad St
Dickinson, Francis, Attorney, 14 Moore St
Dickinson, Joseph, Carpenter, Cannonborough Road
Dickinson, Samuel, Vendue Master, Store, Champneys St
Dickson, John, Clerk, King St Road
Dickson, Samuel, School Master, 13 King St.
Dieckert, J A, Grocer, 4 Market St
Dignum, James, Brick Layer, Edisto Island
Dill, Peter, Baker, 23 Queen St
Dill, Susannah, Planter, 274 cor of King & Price's Al
Disher, Lewis, Cabinet Maker, 29 King St
Disher, Mary, Seamstress, Lowndes St
Ditmore, John, Carpenter, Hampstead
Dixon, John, Soap Manufacturer, King St Road
Dixon, Robert, Butcher, King St Road
Doll, Elizabeth, Nurse, 19 Motte St
Domac, Mark, 170 King St
Don, Alexander, Carpenter, 21 Society St
Donaldson, William, Carpenter, 14 King St
Donnelly, Amherst, Planter, St John's, Berkeley, 32 miles
Donnevan, ——, Mrs, Widow, Charleston Neck
Donnevan, Daniel, Boarding House, 35 Union St.
Door, Daniel, Mariner, St James' Santee, 38 miles
Door, Thomas, Shoe Maker, St James' Santee, 36 miles
Dorcham, Daniel, Overseer to A Edwards, St James' Goose Creek, 20 miles
Dorrett, Jane, Boarding House, 10 Berresford's Al
Dorrill, James, Planter, Christ Church Parish, 12 miles
Dorrill, Joseph, Planter, Christ Church Parish, 10 miles
Dorrill, Mary, Planter, Christ Church Parish, 10 miles
Dorrill, Rebecca, Planter, Christ Church Parish, 11 miles
Dorrill, Robert, Factor, Boundary St.
Dorrill, Robert, Planter, Christ Church Parish, 12 miles
Dougherty, John, Plasterer, 16 Wall St
Dougherty, William, Plasterer, 16 Wall St
Doughty, William, Planter, Smith St
Douglas, Alexander, Tailor, 20 Queen St
Douglas, C, Clerk, 123 Broad
Douglas, Thomas, Factor, 14 Anson St
Douglas, William, Grocer, 8 Union St
Douglass, James, Turner, 39 East Bay St
Doumoutett, I B, Jeweller, 120 Broad
Dowling, Archibald, Brick Layer, 105 King St
Dowling, Edward, Brick Layer, 11 Berresford St
Downing, Cage, Planter, St John's, Berkeley, 48 miles

Downing, George, Planter, St. Stephen's, 45 miles
Downing, Micajah, Planter, St Stephen's, 45 miles
Downing, Samuel, Planter, St John's, Berkeley, 44 miles
Doyle, Thomas, Shop Keeper, 59 East Bay St
Doyle, Thomas, Tavern Keeper, Moncks Corner
Drayton, Charles, Dr., Planter, St Andrew's, 13 miles
Drayton, John, Governor, Commander in Chief, cor Rutledge & Bull St
Drayton, Rebecca, Planter, Hampsteaed
Drayton, Thomas, Planter, St Andrew's, 14 miles
Drayton, William, Attorney, 3 State House Square
Drege, ——, Madame, Shop Keeper, 34 Motte, St
Drennes, Martha, Baker, 32 cor of Beaufain & St Philip's St
Dresler, Hanse, Grocer, 60 Meeting St
Driggers, Daniel, Planter, St James' Goose Creek, 21 miles
Drouilliet, Jean, Baker, 40 Union St
Drury, Robert, Overseer, Wadmalaw Island
Druss, Louisa, 104 Queen St
Dubac, Francis, Shop Keeper, 138 Meeting St
Dubard, P L, Hair Dresser, 68 Meeting St
Dubarry, Stephen, Shop Keeper, 93 King St
Dubert, Frederick, Grocer, King St Road
Dubois, ——, Madame, Seamstress, Boundary St
Dubois, John, Tailor, 51 Anson St
Dubois, Louis, Paper Hanger, 93 Queen St
Dubois, Nicholas, Tailor, 127 Queen St
Dubois, Peter, Carpenter, Cannon St.
Dubois, Robert, Gardener, King St Road
Dubois, Samuel, Overseer to Pinckney, St James' Santee, 42 miles
Dubose, Joseph, Planter, Christ Church Parish, 24 miles
Dubose, Samuel, Jr, Planter, St Stephen's, 53 miles
Dubose, Samuel, Sr., Planter, St Stephen's, 52 miles
Dudler, Ezekiel, Shop Keeper, 43 Wentworth St
Dudler, Rebecca, Seamstress, 43 Wentworth St
Dueston, Stephen, Carpenter, Trott St
Duff, Mary, Shop Keeper, 16 Berresford's Al
Duffus, John, Clerk, 4 Short St.
Dugan, Thomas & John, Brick Layers & Plasterers, St Philip's St Cont'd
Duggan, Thomas, Grocer, Forks of the Road
Duke, Francis, Tailor, King St Road
Dukes, William, Planter, St Stephen's, 45 miles
Dulles, Joseph, Store Keeper, 103 Broad
Dumain, Toubert, Ship Carpenter, 12 Middle St.
Dumaine, John, Physician, 83 East Bay St
Dumoit, Adelaide, Seamstress, 15 Wall St
Dunbar, William, Tavern Keeper, Four Miles House
Duncan, Alexander, Blacksmith, 11 Ellery St
Duncan, John, Merchant, Bull St
Duncan, Margaret, Seamstress, Mazyck St

Duncan, Patrick, Soap & Candle Manufacturer, Cannonborough Road
Dunham, Thomas, Carpenter, 8 Amen St
Dunmyer, Joshua, 102 Queen St
Dunn, John, Grocer, Market St
Dunnasan, John, Planter, King St Road
Dupeau, Francis, Merchant, 31 Society St
Dupeiry, John, Pitt St
Duplatt, J B, Goldsmith, 58 East Bay St
Dupont, Joseph, Grocer, 181 Meeting St
Dupre, Benjamin, Livery Stables, 37 Church St
Dupre, Cornelius, Factor, 11 Hasell St
Dupre, Francis, Shop Carpenter, 21 Ellery St
Dupre, James, Carpenter, John St
Duprey, ——, Madame, 26 Society St
Durban, John J, Hatter, 176 Meeting St
Durby, Joseph, Grocer, King St Road
Durnad, ——, Overseer to Johnson, St James' Goose Creek, 23 miles
Durrett, George, Livery Stable, 1 Bank Square
Duval, Pierre, King St Road
Dwight, Samuel, Planter & Physician, St John's, Berkeley, 56 miles
Dyer, Thomas, Carpenter, Sullivan's Island
Dyson, Thomas, Lock Keeper, Santee Canal, St John's, Berkeley, 42 miles
Eaden, John, Planter, Christ Church Parish, 11 miles
Eady, ——, Overseer to W M Taylor, Folly Island
Eady, Elizabeth, Planter, St John's, Berkeley, 45 miles
Eason, James, Ship Carpenter, 16 Wentworth St
Eason, Robert, Ship Carpenter, 9 Wentworth St
Eason, Robert, Vendue Master, 22 King St
Eason, William, Planter, 15 Wentworth St
Easterby, George, Capt, Mariner, 10 Pinckney St
Easterly, Silas, Planter, St James' Goose Creek, 22 miles
Easton, Sarah, Seamstress, 8 Ellery St
Eaton, Edward, Boatman, Sullivan's Island
Eckard, Jacob, Musician & Organist of St Michael's Church, 47 Tradd St
Eckells, John, Planter, Wassmasaw, 28 miles
Eckert, Robert D, Grocer, 6 Church St
Eden, James, Planter, Christ Church Parish, 16 miles
Edes, ——, Capt, Mariner, Longitude Ln
Edings, William, Planter, Edisto Island
Edmonston, Charles, Merchant (Counting House), Craft's S Whf
Edmonston, Charles, Merchant, 48 Church St Cont'd
Edwards, Alexander, City Recorder, 3 St Michael's Al
Edwards, Edward, Planter, St. John's, Berkeley, 45 miles
Edwards, George, Planter, 261 King St
Edwards, Isaac, Factor, 11 Friend St

Edwards, John, Merchant, 106 East Bay St
Edwards, John, Overseer to Gibbes, John's Island
Edwards, John, Planter, St John's, Berkeley, 38 miles
Edwards, Sugar, Overseer to T Broughton, St John's, Berkeley, 30 miles
Eggleston, John, Grocer, 1 Ellery St
Eggleston, John, Grocer Store, Fish Market
Ehney, Peter, Planter, Christ Church Parish, 18 miles
Ehney, William Frederick, Out Door Clerk, State Bank, 24 Beaufain St
Ehney, William, Tailor, 88 Tradd St
Ehrick, John Mathais, Merchant, 1 St Philip's St
Elanat, Maria, Shop Keeper, 125 Queen St
Elf, Benjamin, Carpenter, Hampstead
Elf, George, Planter, St Thomas', 10 miles
Elf, Thomas, Carpenter, Boundary St
Elf, Thomas, Jr, Carpenter, Boundary St
Elford, James M, Teacher of Navigation, 1 Motte St
Elfrid, John, Constable, 1 Union St
Elliott, Charles, Planter, St Andrew's, 19 miles
Elliott, Elizabeth, Shop Keeper, 27 Motte St
Elliott, John, Boatman, Sullivan's Island
Elliott, Joseph, Custom House Officer, 80 King St
Elliott, Juliet, Planter, 30 George St
Elliott, Mary, 15 Legare St
Elliott, S I, Printer, 10 Maiden Ln
Elliott, Thomas O, Planter, St Andrew's, 16 miles
Elliott, Thomas, Planter, St Andrew's, 19 miles
Elliott, William, Custom House Officer, 5 Gibbes St
Ellis, Ann, Planter, St James' Santee, 43 miles
Ellis, David, Carver, 31 Anson St
Ellis, Mary, Planter, Edisto Island
Ellis, Samuel, Planter, St James' Santee, 43 miles
Ellis, Thomas, Carver, 31 Anson St
Ellis, Thomas, Tailor, 46 Broad St
Ellis, Thomas, Wood Measurer, 31 Anson St
Ellison, James, Clerk, 52 King St
Ellison, John, Store Keeper, 52 King St
Ellsworth, Frederick, Capt, Mariner, Pitt St
Elmore, Dorcas, Seamstress, 20 Hasell St
Elsworth, John Theophilus, Gauger, 10 Queen St
Elsworth, Theophilus, Gauger, Custom House, Pitt St
Eltenaud, Stephen, Baker, 17 Beaufain St
Emanuel, E F., Shop Keeper, 45 East Bay St
Emanuel, Isaac, Store Keeper, 196 King St
Emanuel, Nathan, Store Keeper, 233 King St
Emarrett, P, Cabinet Maker, 157 Meeting St
Emmerson, Jonas, Grocer, 291 King St
England, Alexander, Baker, 98 Tradd St
English, Mary, Planter, Christ Church Parish, 20 miles
English, William, Overseer to Pinckney, St James' Santee, 42 miles

Emphord, John, Cabinet Maker, 28 Meeting St
Eschausse, William, Mattress Maker, 43 Meeting St
Eustis, Thomas, 12 Union St
Evans, —, Mrs (James), Planter, Christ Church Parish, 10 miles
Evans, —, Overseer to Theodore Gaillard, St John's, Berkeley, 37 miles
Evans, Daniel, Shoe Maker, St James' Santee, 32 miles
Evans, David, Mariner, Christ Church Parish, 4 miles
Evans, George, Physician, St. John's, Berkeley, 28 miles
Evans, James, Shoe Maker, 66 Tradd St
Evans, James, Stone Cutter, 31 Trott St
Evans, John, Shoe Maker, 148 Meeting St
Evans, John, Tailor, St James' Santee, 28 miles
Evans, Leacraft, House Carpenter, 238 King St
Evans, Thomas, Planter, Christ Church Parish, 11 miles
Evans, William, Overseer, St Andrew's, 15 miles
Evans, William, Planter, Christ Church Parish, 9 miles
Evans, William, Shoe Maker, 12 Union St
Everhart, Susan, Mantua Maker, 14 Society St
Everingham, John, (Counting House), Bailey's Whf
Everingham, John, Merchant, 139 East Bay St
Eves, Joseph, Ship Carpenter, East Bay St
Ewing, Alexander, Merchant, 1 Bedon's Al
Ewing, Alexander, Merchant, Chisolm's N Whf
Ewing, James, Planter, 114 Meeting St
Faber, Charles, Rev, Pastor of German Church, 7 West St
Faber, Christian H, Factor, 145 cor of Meeting & Hasell St
Faber, I C., Jr, Clerk, S C. Bank, 93 East Bay St
Faber, John C, Rev, 93 East Bay St
Faber, William G, Lumber Merchant, 29 George St
Fabre, Christian Henry, Factor (Counting House), 93 East Bay St
Fair, John, Boot & Shoe Maker, 128 King St
Fair, Richard, Shoe Maker, 190 King St.
Fairbrother, John, Painter, 28 Church St Cont'd
Fairbrother, John, Painter, Shop, 2 Tradd St
Fairchild, Aaron, Blacksmith, 15 George St
Fairchild, Robert, Planter, Edisto Island
Fairly, Hance, Cabinet Maker, 67 Meeting St
Fairweather, Richard, Grocer, 136 Meeting St
Famonruse, O, Shop Keeper, King St Road
Farn, Elizabeth, Planter, 32 Hasell St.
Farr, John, Planter, John's Island
Farr, Sarah, Planter, Cannonborough Road
Farrell, Benjamin, Overseer to Shoolbread, St James' Santee, 42 miles
Fastbender, S., Gardner, King St. Road

Fastbender, William, Gardner, King St. Road
Faulckner, Robert, Merchant, 23 Church St
Faur, —, Madame, Seamstress, 13 Moore St
Fauretta, Thomas, Shop Keeper, 171 Meeting St
Faussoux, Ann, Planter, 67 Tradd St
Faust, Jeremiah, Grocer, Market St
Fawksworth, Robert, Overseer to J Prioleau, St
John's, Berkeley, 43 miles
Fawksworth, S , Overseer to Baldric, St James'
Goose Creek, 8 miles
Fay, Obadiah, Overseer to John Huger, St
Thomas', 44 miles
Fayolle, Peter, Professor of Dancing, 260 King St
Fayssoux, James H , Physician & Planter, St
John's, Berkeley, 40 miles
Fearman, Anthony, Mariner, Boundary St
Fell, Elizabeth, Planter, 29 Wall St
Fell, Thomas, Tinman, 6 Price's Al
Fell, William, Ship Carpenter, 29 Wall St
Felt, William, Planter, Goddard's Island, 7 miles
Ferguson, Ann, Planter, 2 Liberty St
Ferguson, Daniel, Boot & Shoe Maker, 111 Broad
St
Ferguson, Edmond, Carpenter, 1 Clifford Al
Ferguson, John, Overseer to Leavitt, Daniel's
Island, 6 miles
Ferguson, Samuel, Planter, 2 Liberty St
Fernando, Joseph, Mariner, 8 Amen St
Feurshaw, Margaret, Planter, James Island
Fewaux, Elizabeth, Planter, Wassmasaw, 28 miles
Fickling, Henry, Planter, John's Island
Fickling, Isaac, 102 Queen St
Fiddy, William, Store Keeper, King St Road
Field, Elizabeth, Widow, 94 Broad St
Field, Rebecca, Nurse at Orphan Hospital,
Boundary St
Fields, Caleb, Clerk at Courier Office, 30 Church
St
Fife, Mary, Coming St
Finches, John, Tailor, 160 King St
Findlay, Henry, Planter, St James' Santee, 42 miles
Findlay, Jacob, Overseer to Isaac Parker, St
Thomas, 9 miles
Fink, Thomas, Factor, 38 Pinckney St
Fintch, Joseph, Nail Manufacturer, 167 Meeting St
Fisher, George A , Saddler, 191 King St
Fisher, James, Capt , Mariner, 108 Church St
Fisher, James, Merchant, cor of South Bay & King
St
Fisher, Philip, 5 Clifford Al
Fitch, Joseph, Clerk, 106 East Bay St
Fitz, John, Guard Man, 18 Trott St
Fitzgerald, Matthew, Butcher, King St Road
Fitzpatrick, Peter, Tailor, 106 Tradd St
Fitzsimons, Christopher, Distillery, Anson St
Fitzsimons, Christopher, Merchant Distiller, 29
Hasell St
Flagg, George, Jr , Painter, 11 East Bay St

Flagg, George, Painter, 215 King St
Flagg, William, Mariner, 27 East Bay St
Fleming, James, Grocer, 41 Tradd St
Flemming, Henry, Store Keeper, 135 King St
Flemming, Michael, Clerk, King St Road
Flemming, Robert, Shop Keeper, King St Road
Flemming, Thomas, Store Keepers, 156 King St
Flint, Joseph, Grocer, 31 Motte St
Floderer, John, Grocer, 14 Church St
Florence, Zakariah, Dentist, 221 King St
Florentine, Mary Ann, Seamstress, Boundary St
Florin, Lucas, Merchant, 32 Guignard St
Flotard, John & Charles, Merchants, 167 King St
Floyd, John, Planter, St James' Santee, 28 miles
Fludd, Daniel, Planter, South Bay
Fogartie, Christian, 12 Wall St
Fogartie, James, Capt , Factor, 32 Anson St
Fogartie, Stephen, Capt , Planter, St Thomas', 14
miles
Folker, John Caspar, Planter, 38 Beaufain St
Folker, John H , Clerk, 38 Beaufain St
Folker, Joseph, School Master, 3 Wentworth St
Folker, Thomas P , Physician, 38 Beaufain St
Folley, John, Rigger, 64 East Bay St.
Follin, A & N F , Tobacconists, 151 Meeting St
Follin, A F & Co , Tobacconists, 92 King St
Follin, Thomas, Planter, Four Holes
Follin, William, Planter, Four Holes
Folmer, John, Chair Maker, 6 Blackbird Al
Footman, John W , Broker, 289 King St
Forbes, Alexander, Merchant, 18 Elliott St
Forbes, John, Tinman, 193 King St
Forbes, William, Tinman, 246 King St
Ford, Ebenezer, Planter, King St Road
Ford, Jacob, Attorney, Office, 29 Tradd St
Ford, Timothy, Attorney, 209 Meeting St
Fordham, Benjamin, Block & Pump Maker, Shop,
Fish Market
Fordham, Benjamin, Pump & Block Maker, 23
Ellery St
Fordham, Joseph, Pump & Block Maker, Boundary
St
Fordham, Richard, Blacksmith, Boundary St
Fordham, Richard, Ship Carpenter, Boundary St
Forest, Charity, Widow, 2 Hasell St
Forrest, Thomas Hunter, Cooper, 262 King St
Forrester, Susannah, Seamstress, Hampstead
Forster, Archibald, Guardman, 14 Hasell St
Forsyth, Walter, Merchant, 3 West St
Fort, John, Planter, St James' Santee, 42 miles
Foster, Henry, Out Door Clerk, Branch Bank, 164
Meeting St
Foster, Mary, Widow, 158 Meeting St
Foster, Nathan, Grocer, 30 Elliott St
Foster, William, Clerk, 164 Meeting St
Foucard, P I., Musician, 255 King St
Fouches, —, Madame, 180 Meeting St.

Foultz, William, Overseer to Daniel Ravenell, St John's, Berkeley, 41 miles
Fourneau, John, Pilot, 7 St Michael's Al
Foutaine, Jane, 73 Church St
Fowke, Mary, Planter, 7 Church St
Fowler, James, Lumber Merchant, 2 Gibbes St
Fowler, John, Carpenter, 5 St Michael's Al
Fowler, Michael, Planter, St Thomas', 22 miles
Fowler, Richard, Planter, Christ Church Parish, 3 miles
Fox, Patrick, Clerk, King St Road
Frampton, William, Clerk, King St Road
Francis, Joseph, Stone Cutter, 17 Pinckney St
Franklin, James, Mariner, 2 Linguard St
Fraser, Charles, Attorney, 27 King St
Fraser, Charles, Attorney, Office, 24 Tradd St
Fraser, James, Capt., Gardener, King St Road
Fraser, Sarah, Planter, Ashley Ferry, 10 miles
Fraser, T L S, Planter, 38 Hasell St
Fraser, Thomas, Planter, 38 Hasell St
Frazer, I M, Carpenter, 34 Trott St
Frazer, John, Factor, 3 Wentworth St
Frazer, Joseph, Ferry Keeper, Haddril's Point, Christ Church Parish, 3 miles
Frean, Benjamin, Shop Keeper, Store, 281 King St
Frean, Margaret, Store Keeper, 69 King St
Frean, William, Grocer, Store, 205 cor. of King St & Market St
Frederick, Washington, Planter, John's Island
Free, Rineard, Tailor, 38 Union St
Freeman, Benjamin, Planter, Wadmalaw Island
Freeman, Elizabeth, Planter, 91 Tradd St
Freeman, Josiah, Overseer to Matthews, John's Island
Freeman, Mary, Planter, Wadmalaw Island
Freeman, Richard, Jr, Planter, John's Island
Freeman, Richard, Sr, Planter, John's Island
Freer, Daniel, Carpenter, Wadmalaw Island
Freer, Margaret, Planter, James Island
Freer, Mary, Planter, 3 Wentworth St
Freer, Mary, Planter, John's Island
Freneau, Peter, Printer & Editor of City Gazette, 34 George St
Friend, Ulric, Baker, 22 East Bay St
Frierson, John, Planter, St John's, Berkeley, 45 miles
Fripp, Charles, Planter, John's Island
Frish, Charles, Shop Keeper, 181 King St
Frisk, R N & Co, Grocers, 32 Archdale St
Fromento, Augustine, Perfumer & Hair Dresser, 13 Broad St
Fronty, Michael, Physician, 11 Moore St
Frost, Elizabeth, Planter, 8 West St
Frow, John L, Magazine St
Fry, George Washington, School Master, St John's, Berkeley, 55 miles
Fulks, William, Overseer to Ravenell, St John's, Berkeley, 40 miles

Fuller, Benjamin, Planter, St Andrew's, 15 miles
Fuller, Catharine, Planter, St. Andrew's, 15 miles
Fuller, Christopher, Physician, Ashley Ferry, 10 miles
Fuller, Thomas, Merchant, 23 Church St
Fullilove, Thomas, Cotton Gin Maker, King St Road
Furman, Richard, Rev, Pastor, Baptist Church, 10 Church St
Furr, Jacob, Planter, King St Road
Futterell, James, Teller, S C Bank, 35 King St
Gabean, James, Cooper's Shop, Craft's Whf
Gabeau, Anthony, Tailor, 190 Meeting St
Gabeau, John, Pump & Block Maker
Gadsden, C E, Rev, St John's, Berkeley, 33 miles
Gadsden, Hugh Dawes, Factor, Gadsden's N Whf
Gadsden, James, Factor & Lumber Merchant (Counting House), Gadsden's Whf
Gadsden, James, Factor, 112 East Bay St
Gadsden, James W, Planter, 72 Queen St
Gadsden, John, Attorney, 112 East Bay St
Gadsden, Martha, Planter, East Bay St
Gadsden, Philip, Factor, 112 East Bay St
Gadsden, Thomas, Planter, King St Road
Gaillard, Bartholomew, Planter, St John's, Berkeley 39 miles
Gaillard, Charles, Clerk, Boundary St
Gaillard, Charles, Sr, Surveyor, St James' Santee, 44 miles
Gaillard, David, Planter, St James' Santee, 44 miles
Gaillard, Harriott, Planter, Pineville, St Stephen's, 52 miles
Gaillard, I B, Coach Trimmer, Boundary St
Gaillard, James, Planter, St Stephen's, 50 miles
Gaillard, John, Overseer, St James' Santee, 40 miles
Gaillard, Mazyck, Factors (Counting House), Chisolm's Whf
Gaillard, Peter, Capt, Planter, St John's, Berkeley, 56 miles
Gaillard, Peter, Planter, 164 Meeting St.
Gaillard, Theodore, Jr, Planter, St John's, Berkeley, 37 miles
Gaillard, Theodore, Judge, Court of Equity, 6 Short St
Gaillard, Thoedore, Factor, Montague St
Gaillard, William, Planter, St. James' Santee, 46 miles
Gainer, Thomas, Mariner, 35 Motte St
Galbraith, Robert, Carpenter, 17 George St
Galean, James, Cooper, 47 Motte St
Gallagher, Simon Felix, Rev, Minister of the Roman Catholic Church, Magazine St
Gallahan, Frederick, Shop Keeper, 38 East Bay St
Galloway, Alfred, Pilot, 3 Lynch's Court
Galloway, James, Clerk, 98 Queen St
Galloway, Thomas, Planter, St John's, Berkeley, 58 miles

Gandouin & Chamois, Hatters, 180 Meeting St
Gandouin, Isidore, Store Keeper, 10 Queen St
Gandouin, John, Hatter, 58 cor of East Bay &
    Unity Al
Gano, Samuel, Carpenter, Boundary St
Gappin, William, Wheelwright, 153 Meeting St
Gardeire, Joseph, Shop Keeper, 10 Queen St
Garden, Alexander, Planter, Coming St
Garden, Harriett, Planter, 16 East Bay St
Gardner, John, Blacksmith, 37 Society St
Gardner, John, Blacksmith, Shop, 92 East Bay St
Garey, James, Planter, St James' Santee, 42 miles
Garey, Peter, School Master, St James' Santee, 32
    miles
Garner, Ann, Planter, 31 Beaufain St
Gaskins, Amos, Planter, St John's, Berkeley, 60
    miles
Gates, Jacob, Boarding House, Wagon Yard, King
    St Road
Gaultier, Joseph, Vendue Master, 271 King St
Gay, John T , Tinman, Market St
Geddes & Croft, Office, 35 Meeting St
Geddes, Henry, Merchant, King St Road
Geddes, John, Attorney, 119 Broad St
Geddes, Robert, Store Keeper, 160 King St
Gedney, Isaac, Mariner, 32 St Philip's St
Geffkin, Henry Charles, Carpenter, 5 Society St
Geffkin, Henry, Lumber Measurer, 5 Society St
Gense, Thomas, Physician, 14 Elliott St
Gensel, John, Steward to Marine Hospital, 3 Back
    St
George, James, Ship Carpenter, 32 East Bay St
George, Mary, Shop Keeper, 7 Market St
Gercke, Frederick, Confectioner, 37 Queen St
Gerdier, Margaret, Store Keeper, 175 King St
Gerry, ——, Madame, 2 Meeting St
Gervais, Paul, Rev., Planter, 4 Legare St
Geyer, Elizabeth, Seamstress, 24 King St
Geyer, John, Planter, Christ Church Parish, 4 miles
Gibbes, George, Baker, 29 Elliott St
Gibbes, John, Planter, 120 Meeting St
Gibbes, Robert, Overseer, Christ Church Parish, 6
    miles
Gibbes, William Hasell, Master in Equity, 43 Broad
    St
Gibbes, William, Planter, James Island
Gibbs, Robert R , Planter, John's Island
Gibson, Broadfoot & Co (Custom House), 150 East
    Bay St
Gibson, James, Coach Maker, 54 Meeting St
Gibson, Robert, Shop Keeper, 232 King St
Gibson, William, Clerk to Chisolm & Taylor, 35
    Church St. Cont'd
Gibson, William, Merchant, Co-partner of Gibson &
    Broadfoot, 7 Broad St
Gideon, Benjamin, Coach Maker, 54 Meeting St.
Gierardeau, John, Planter, John's Island
Gilbert, I E , Trunk Maker, 16 Beaufain St

Gilbert, John C , Merchant, 6 Berresford St
Gilbert, John, Carpenter, Edisto Island
Gilbert, Joseph, Brick Layer, 22 Church St Cont'd
Gilbert, Seth, Wharfinger, 1 Lynch's Court
Gilchrist, Adam, Merchant, President National
    Branch Bank (Counting House), cor of Craft's N
    Whf & East Bay
Gilchrist, Adam, President of National Branch
    Bank, 12 Church St
Gilchrist, John, Clerk, 4 Mazyck St.
Giles, Matilda, Seamstress, 40 Tradd St
Giles, Othniel J , Deputy Sheriff & Justice of Peace,
    16 King St
Gill, Isaac, Watch Maker, 194 Meeting St
Gill, John, Livery Stable Keeper, 3 Bank Square
Gilles, Alexander, Store Keeper, 185 King St
Gillespie, John & Co , Merchants, 30 East Bay St
Gillespie, John, Overseer to J Ball, St John's,
    Berkeley, 35 miles
Gilliland, W H , Tailor, 158 King St
Gillman, Zadock, Merchant, Store, Crafts' N Whf ,
    31 Church St
Gillon, Ann, School Mistress, 2 Wall St
Giraud, Francis, Clerk, Lynch St
Gisendanner, Susannah, Widow, 24 Beaufain St
Gisendaner, Lucretia, Seamstress, Bull St
Gist, ——, Mrs , Planter, St Andrew's, 16 miles
Gist, N. & F , Store Keepers, 146 King St
Gladden, Joseph, Carpenter, 65 Tradd St
Glashard, ——, Madame, Seamstress, 42 Wentworth
    St
Glass, Ebenezer, Weaver, Wentworth St
Gleamet, Louis, Shop Keeper, King St Road
Gleize, Henry, Physician & Druggist, 259 King St
Glen & Daniell, Factor & Lumber Merchant,
    Gadsden's Whf
Glen, John, Factor & Lumber Merchant, Middle St
Glen, Margaret, Planter, 55 Tradd St
Glen, Marshall, Planter, Daniel's Island, 6 miles
Glen, Martha, Planter, Daniel's Island, 6 miles
Glover, Charles, Planter, Bull St
Glover, Joseph, Physician, 22 Beaufain St
Glover, Sanders, Overseer, St Thomas', 9 miles
Glover, Wilson, Planter, 2 Meeting St
Glymp, C Henry, Lock Keeper, Santee Canal, St
    Stephen's
Godard, Rene, Merchant, 56 King St
Godet, John, Shoe Maker, 27 Trott St
Godfrey, Sarah, Seamstress, Magazine St
Godhur, William, Planter, James Island
Goedekean, Ida, Seamstress, 39 King St
Goldsmith, John, Peddlar, 255 King St
Gomez, Philip, Store Keeper, 245 King St
Good, Francis, Grocer, Hampstead
Good, Sarah, 42 King St
Goodwin, Samuel, Overseer to Miles, St Andrew's,
    12 miles
Gordon, A. W , Merchant, 129 Broad St

Gordon, Irvin, Clerk, City Gazette, Office, 2 Whim Court
Gordon, James & Co , Merchants, 26 East Bay St
Gordon, James & John, Brick Layers, 101 Queen St
Gordon, John, Lumber Measurer, 2 Whim Court
Gordon, John, Scrivener, 15 Wentworth St
Gordon, Martha, Seamstress, 7 Parsonage lane
Gordon, Thomas, Capt , Cashier, Custom House, 18 Church St Cont'd
Gordon, Thomas, Clerk, 56 Church St
Gordon, William Edward, Butcher, Neck Road
Gordon, William, Grocer, 87 King St
Gouelleton, Boarding House, 177 Meeting St
Gough, ——, Brick Layer, 82 Meeting St
Gough, John, Physician, 119 cor of Meeting St & Lightwood's Al
Gould, Patrick, Soap & Candle Manufacturer, Washington St
Gould, Thomas, Painter, 24 George St
Gourdine, Samuel, Planter, St John's, Berkeley, 34 miles
Gourell, Peter, Shop Keeper, 70 Church St
Gourlay, Ann, 21 Church St Cont'd
Gourlay, James, Boot & Shoe Maker, 31 Broad St
Gourlay, John, Tanner, 3 Magazine St
Gourlay, John, Tanner, Hampstead
Goutin, Madaline, 26 Trott St
Gowdy, Margaret, Widow, 45 Broad St
Gradick, Christian, Butcher, Cannon St
Grado, Marian, Grocer, 5 Motte St.
Graham, Angus, Planter, Christ Church Parish, 9 miles
Graham, Archibald, Store Keeper, King St. Road
Graham, Margaret, 25 Berresford's Al
Graham, Michael, Grocer, 28 Union St.
Graham, Susannah, Seamstress, Church St
Graham, Thomas, Cabinet Maker, 67 Meeting St
Grand, Nicholas, Planter, 6 Cumberland St
Grant, Alexander, Merchant, 93 Church St
Grant, Hary, Merchant, 2 Savage St
Grant, James, Printer, 14 Guignard St
Graser, Jacob Conrad, Merchant, 14 Archdale St
Graves & Toomer, Factors (Counting House), Chisolm's Whf
Graves, Charles, Planter & Factor, 56 Tradd St
Graves, James, Planter, Boundary St
Graves, Massey, 8 Smith Ln
Gravolez, ——, Harness Maker, 192 Meeting St
Gray, Benjamin, Lumber Merchant, Montague St
Gray, Henry, Justice of Peace, 125 King St
Gray, Ruth Ann, Seamstress, 1 Whim Court
Gray, William, Merchant, 113 Tradd St.
Grayer, John, Planter, St John's, Berkeley, 46 miles
Grayer, John, Planter, St Stephen's, 44 miles
Gready, Andrew, Printer, 16 Elliott St
Gredless, Owen, Planter, St James' Santee, 48 miles

Green, Daniel, Clerk, Inspection St
Green, Daniel, Mariner, Moore St
Green, Edmond, Factor, 145 Broad St
Green, Elizabeth, Planter, St John's, Berkeley, 52 miles
Green, John Gray, Tavern, Ashley Ferry, 10 miles
Greenhill, Hume, Carpenter, 64 W end of Tradd St
Greenland, George, Factor, 31 Meeting St
Greenland, George, Jr , Planter, St Thomas', 13 miles
Greenland, William, Factor, 31 Meeting St
Greenwood, William, Merchant, 21 Beaufain St
Greffin, Peter, Store Keeper, 186 King St
Gregor, Alexander, Physician, John's Island
Gregorie, James, Merchant, 95 Broad St
Gregorie, M C , 18 Anson St
Gregson, Thomas, Assistant Clerk, Branch Bank, 24 Beaufain St
Griffen, Ephraim, Cabinet Maker, 14 Archdale St
Griffen, Mary, Seamstress, 29 Pinckney St
Griffin, Charles, 3 Meeting St
Griffin, Christopher, Clerk, 186 Meeting St
Griggs, Isaac, Attorney, 37 East Bay St
Grimball, Elizabeth, Planter, South Bay
Grimball, M P , 10 Beaufain St
Grimke, John F , Judge, Court of Common Pleas & Sessions, 36 East Bay St
Grimke, Thomas, Attorney, 36 East Bay St
Griner, Charles, Watchmaker, 173 Meeting St
Gripper, John, Cooper, 42 Elliott St
Griswold, Ebenezer, Mariner, 2 Elliott St
Griswold, M , Tailor, 29 Church St
Groles, Antonio, Confectioner, 113 King St.
Groning, Lewis R , Merchants, 8 East Bay St
Grooms, George, Overseer to P Pritchard, Daniel's Island, 7 miles
Grooms, John H , Overseer to Wragg, St John's, Berkeley, 30 miles
Grooms, John H , Planter, St James' Goose Creek, 26 miles
Grooms, Sarah, Tavern, St Andrew's, 8 miles
Gros, John, Cabinet Maker, 79 Meeting St
Grove, Samuel, Merchant, 56 East Bay St
Gruber, ——, Butcher, Hampstead
Gruber, Catharine, Widow, Wentworth St
Gruber, Charles, Capt of Magazine Guard, Neck, 4 miles
Gruber, Christian, Butcher, 15 Berresford St
Guerard, Philip, Baker, 140 Meeting St
Guerin, Francis, Planter, St Andrew's, 16 miles
Guerin, Robert, Planter, Neck Road
Guerineau, Joseph, Shop Keeper, 37 King St
Guering, Robert, Tailor, 102 Queen St
Guibert, Eugene, Musician, 1 Wall St.
Guieu, A J , Clerk, King St. Road
Guieu, L P , Clerk to Joseph Dullas, 33 East Bay St
Guigan, Theodore, Planter, East Bay St

Guild, Samuel, Carpenter, St Stephen's, 52 miles
Guilliott, ——, Miller to John B Holmes, St John's, Berkeley, 33 miles
Guillou, Samuel, Tailor, 103 Queen St.
Gulder, John, Miller, St John's, Berkeley, 32 miles
Gunn, William, Blacksmith, 5 Queen St
Gunter, Edward, Ironmonger, 113 East Bay St
Gunther, P F , Tailor, 11 Queen St
Gurry, Caleb, Mrs , Planter, St Stephen's, 50 miles
Gurry, Theodore, Planter, St Stephen's, 50 miles
Guy, James, Tailor, Boundary St
Gyles, John, Clerk, 187 Meeting St
Gyles, William, Clerk, 187 Meeting St
Hackell, Philip, Grocer, 1 Bull St
Hacker, Benjamin, Ship Chandler, 17 East Bay Cont'd
Hacket, William, Overseer, St James' Santee, 28 miles
Hackett, Jane, Boarding House, 61 King St
Hadden, Gardner, Tailor, 6 Stoll's Al
Haffer, Elizabeth, Widow, 32 Queen St
Haffernal, John, Cabinet Maker, 95 Tradd St
Hagen, Richard, Grocer, King St. Road
Hagerman, J F , Clerk, 4 Tradd St.
Hagood, John, Factor, 116 Tradd St (Custom House), Vanderhorst's Whf
Hahnbaum, George, Carpenter, Bull St
Haig, David, Cooper, 132 Meeting St
Haig, David, Cooper Shop, Craft's Whf
Haig, Robert, Carpenter, 44 Wentworth St
Hailes, Daniel, Overseer to Samuel Dubose, St Stephen's, 50 miles
Hailes, James, Planter, St Stephen's, 48 miles
Hall, ——, Mrs , Boarding House, 2 Elliott St
Hall, B. A , Seamstress, East Bay Cont'd
Hall, Daniel, Factor, 2 State House Square
Hall, Elisha, Overseer to James Simons, St Andrew's, 12 miles
Hall, James, Stone Cutter, Market St
Hall, Sarah, 10 Meeting St
Hall, Thomas, Capt , Planter, Register of the District Court of the U S , 33 Broad St
Hall, William & George, Merchants, Store, 22 Broad St
Hall, William, Capt , 37 East Bay Cont'd
Hall, William, Merchant, 125 Broad St
Halliday, Hugh, Cooper, 1 Champneys St
Halsall, William, Butcher, 17 cor of Guignard St & Maiden Ln
Halsey, James, School Master, St James' Santee, 36 miles
Halt, George, Physician, 1 East Bay Cont'd.
Ham, Thomas, Clerk, Washington St
Hambert, Godfrey, Carpenter, 8 Lynch's Ln
Hamilton, David, Clerk, 132 East Bay Cont'd.
Hamilton, James, Merchant & Planter, 113 Tradd St

Hamilton, James, Overseer to Thomas Porcher, St John's, Berkeley, 45 miles
Hamilton, John, Ship Carpenter, 3 Guignard St
Hamilton, Marlborough, School Master, 102 Broad St
Hamilton, Thomas, Blacksmith, Wentworth St
Hamlin, Cornelius, Planter, St Thomas', 20 miles
Hamlin, Elisha, School Master for C F Society, 2 West St
Hamlin, Frances, Planter, Christ Church Parish, 9 miles
Hamlin, Samuel, Planter, St Thomas', 19 miles
Hamlin, Thomas, Planter, Christ Church Parish, 10 miles
Hammett, Thomas, Collector of Accounts, 7 Bedon's Al
Hammond, William, Clerk, 14 Trott St
Hanck, John, Grocer, 42 Anson St
Hancock, Richard, Boarding House, 34 Union St.
Hanmer & Gibson, Grocers, Sullivan's Island
Hannah, Andrew, Merchant, 8 Broad St
Hannahan, John, Factor, 7 Whim Court
Hannahan, Samuel, Overseer to Dr Townsend, Wadmalaw Island
Hannahan, William, Planter, Edisto Island
Hanscomb, James, Physician & Planter, John's Island
Hanscomb, Thomas, Planter, John's Island
Happoldt, John, Butcher, Cannon St
Happoldt, John Philip, Butcher, Cannon St
Harby, Isaac, School Master, Edisto Island
Hare, Francis, Shop Keeper, 16 Union St
Haris & Pool, Shop Keepers, 132 King St
Harleston, Edward, Planter, St John's, Berkeley, 33 miles
Harleston, Nicholas, Planter, St John's Berkely, 32 miles
Harleston, William, Planter, St John's, Berkeley, 34 miles
Harper, James, Baker, 43 Tradd St
Harper, Thomas, Grocer, 42 cor of Tradd & King St
Harrel, Jacob, Planter, St John's, Berkeley, 55 miles
Harriott, Barnabas, Blacksmith, 26 Church St Cont'd
Harris, Charles, Overseer to N Harleston, St John's, Berkeley, 32 miles
Harris, Elizabeth, Shop Keeper, 182 King St
Harris, Jacob, Shop Keeper, 201 King St
Harris, Martha, School Mistress, 6 Trott St
Harris, Tucker, Physician, 71 King St.
Harrison, Francis, Grocer, Mazyck St
Harrison, Francis, Grocer, Rutledge St
Harrison, George, Jr , Hardware Store, 64 Meeting St
Harrison, George, Overseer to Sarah Legare, St James' Santee, 30 miles

Harrison, John, Overseer to Rev M'Leod, Wadmalaw Island
Harrison, Thomas, Rigger, St Philip's St
Harrison, William Primrose, Boarding House, 106 East Bay Cont'd
Harry, Thomas, Planter, Four Holes
Hart, Daniel, Store Keeper, 54 East Bay St
Hart, Dorcus, School Master, 16 Society St
Hart, John, Clerk, 150 King St
Hart, Joseph, Store Keeper, 53 East Bay St
Hart, Moses, Carpenter, Boundary St
Hart, Nathan, Shop Keeper, 120 King St
Hart, Simon Moses, Shop Keeper, 227 King St
Harth, John, Lumber Merchant, W End of South Bay
Harth, William, Merchant, W End of South Bay
Harts, H M , Shop Keeper, 166 King St
Harvey, Archibald, Clerk, 24 Society St
Harvey, Arnold, Planter, Wassmasaw, 31 miles
Harvey, Benjamin, Capt , Planter, James Island
Harvey, Benjamin, Planter, Cannonborough Road
Harvey, Catharine, Seamstress, 16 Ellery St
Harvey, Henry, Coach Maker, 7 Clifford St
Harvey, John, Planter, St John's, Berkeley, 38 miles
Harvey, John, Printer, Cock Ln
Harvey, Mary, Seamstress, 82 Meeting St
Harvey, Samuel, Mariner, 3 Guignard St.
Haskett, Samuel, Saddler & Harness Maker, 121 King St
Haskins, Sarah, Planter, James Island
Haslett, John, Merchant, 10 East Bay St
Hatch, Robert, Capt , Mariner, 14 Motte St
Hatchet, Thomas, Store Keeper, St John's, Berkeley, Moncks Corner
Havda, David, Grocer, 154 Meeting St
Hawes, Benjamin, Ship Carpenter, 10 Amen St
Hawes, Nathaniel, Mariner, 58 Church St
Hawie, Thomas, Planter, 10 East Bay St
Hayden, Matthew, Custom House Clerk, Hampstead
Hayes, David, Grocer, Sullivan's Island
Hayne, Stephen, Planter, St Stephen's, 45 miles
Haynsworth, John, Store Keeper, King St Road
Hazell, George, Planter & Physician, St Thomas', 27 miles
Hazlehurst, Robert, Merchant, 14 East Bay St.
Headwright, James, Planter, St James' Goose Creek, 22 miles
Heath & Byrne, Sail Makers, Loft, Bailey's Whf
Heath, James M , Sail Maker, 3 Wall St
Heath, John D , Attorney, 50 Broad
Hedderly, William, Bell Hanger, 86 Queen St
Hedley, John, School Master, 109 Church St
Hedrick, John, Sail Maker, 24 East Bay Cont'd
Hemmitt, Charlotte, 14 Elliott St
Henderson, Daniel, Gunsmith, 23 Queen St
Hendlen, John, Planter, James Island
Hendrickson, B , Carpenter, Hampstead

Hennon, Thomas, Gun Smith, 113 Broad St
Henry, Ann & Son, Store, 22 Elliott St
Henry, Ann, Shop Keeper, 98 King St
Henry, Ann, Store Keeper, 6 Wentworth St
Henry, Eliza, Boarding House, 19 Berresford's Al
Henry, Jacob, Store Keeper, King St Road
Henry, Julian, Cabinet Maker, 184 Meeting St
Henwood, Thomas, Clerk, 29 Society St
Herchart, Daniel, Butcher, King St Road
Herring, Esther, Planter, St John's, Berkeley, 50 miles
Herriott, Roger, Commission Merchant, 2 Middle St
Herriott, Roger, Merchant (Counting House), 120 East Bay Cont'd
Herron, Charles, Tailor, 20 Motte St
Herron, David, Carpenter, 2 Federal St
Herron, John, Tailor, 27 Church St
Herron, Samuel, Merchant, 14 Broad St
Hervient, Fourgeaud, Baker, 6 Maiden Ln
Heslie, John, Tailor, East Bay St
Heuston, Thomas, School Master, 44 Church St
Heyns, James, Grocer, 19 Coming St
Heyward, Elizabeth, Planter, 120 Meeting St
Heyward, Hannah, Planter, 10 Legare St.
Heyward, Nathaniel, Jr , Planter, 26 East Bay Cont'd
Heyward, Nathaniel, Sr , Planter, 26 East Bay Cont'd
Heyward, Samuel, Capt , Factor, 20 Mazyck St
Heyward, William, Planter, 10 Legare St
Heyward, William, Planter, 26 East Bay Cont'd
Hibben, James, Capt , Planter, Christ Church Parish, 3 miles
Hicks, Joseph, Carpenter, Pitt St
Hicks, Thomas, Overseer to Reynolds, Wadmalaw Island
Higden, Bailey, Planter, John's Island
Higham, Thomas, Merchant, 23 East Bay St
Highland, John, Overseer to John Ward, John's Island
Hill, Andrew, Ship Carpenter, 8 Berresford's Al
Hill, Asa, Butcher, Cannon St
Hill, Duncan Henry, Mariner, 106 East Bay St
Hill, Hannah, School Mistress, 112 Meeting St
Hill, Henry, Wheel Wright, 7 Maiden Ln
Hill, Paul, Wire & Cane Worker, 28 Archdale St
Hill, R C , Painter, 28 Archdale St
Hillegas, Philip, Distiller, Coming St Cont'd
Hilliard, Nathaniel, Mariner, 2 Pinckney St
Hillman, Ann, Boarding House, 19 East Bay St
Himeley, John James, Merchant, 20 Broad St
Hindley & Gregorie, Merchants (Counting House), Chisolm's Whf
Hindley, Thomas H , Merchant, 95 Broad St
Hinds, David, Overseer to C Cordes, St Stephen's, 50 miles
Hinds, David, Physician, St Stephen's

109

Hinds, John, Tavern Keeper, St James' Goose Creek, 17 miles
Hinds, Starling, Planter, St John's, Berkeley, 34 miles
Hinds, Thomas, Planter, Christ Church Parish, 19 miles
Hingen, Thomas, Carpenter, 5 Berresford St
Hippias, Phebe, Seamstress, 47 Pinckney St
Hixham, Elizabeth, Milliner, 13 Tradd St
Hobrecker, J C, Blacksmith, 5 Market St
Hodge, David, Cabinet Maker, 62 Meeting St
Hodge, Eleanor, 1 Laurens St.
Hoey, John, Grocer, 2 King St.
Hoff, John M, Deputy Clerk of Market, 7 Wall St
Hoff, John, Printer Book Seller, 6 Broad St
Hoff, Philip, Printer, Broad St
Hoffman, George, Grocer, 32 Church St
Hoffman, Zachariah, Physician, 286 King St
Hogarth, Mary, Shop Keeper, 26 Wall St
Hogarth, William, Boot & Shoe Maker, 2 East Bay Cont'd
Hogarth, William, Shoe Maker, 37 Union St
Holinsby, Elizabeth, Planter, James Island
Holland, John, Boatman, Sullivan's Island
Holland, John, Carpenter, 13 St Philip's St
Holland, John, Deputy Naval Officer to Custom House, 187 Meeting St
Hollinshead, William, Rev, Minister of Independent Church, 8 Maiden Ln
Holloway, Daniel, Merchant, 97 Queen St
Holmes, Charles, Custom House Officer, 26 Guignard St
Holmes, Daniel, Planter, James Island
Holmes, Isaac, Planter, John's Island
Holmes, J Bee, Planter (Dwelling, Meeting St), St John's, Berkeley, 33 miles
Holmes, James, Clerk, 12 East Bay St
Holmes, John, Brick Layer, 26 George St
Holmes, John, Planter, John's Island
Holmes, John W, Planter, James Island
Holmes, Joseph, Clerk, 177 King St
Holmes, Margaret, 44 Pinckney St
Holmes, Margaret, Matron at Orphan House, Boundary St
Holmes, Mary, 8 St Philip's St
Holmes, Sanford N, Clerk, 273 King St
Holmes, Thomas, Carpenter, St John's, Berkeley, 50 miles
Holmes, Thomas, Tavern, Quarter House, 6 miles
Holmes, William & Co, Vendue Store, 127 East Bay St
Holmes, William, Vendue Master, Boundary St
Holwell, Thomas, Boatman, 1 Lynch's Court
Honeywood, Arthur, Engraver, 59 Meeting St
Honeywood, Elizabeth, Blacksmith, 59 Meeting St
Honore, John, Saddler, 21 Coming St
Hood, Abraham, Planter, St. Stephen's 45 miles
Hood, Nathaniel P, Grocer, 16 Elliott St.

Hopkins & Charles, Merchants (Counting House), Vanderhorst's Whf
Hopkins, Charles, Planter, St James' Santee, 41 miles
Hopkins, Ebenezer, Grain Merchant & Grocer, 10 Motte St
Hopkins, John N, Merchant, 19 Meeting St
Hopson, George, Broker, 45 Anson St
Hopwood, William, Hatter, 41 Queen St
Hordon, John, Tobacconist, 131 Coate's Row, East Bay St
Horlbeck, Henry, Brick Layer, 3 Moore, St
Horlbeck, John, Jr, Brick Layer, 8 Moore, St
Horlbeck, John, Sr, Brick Layer, 8 Moore St
Hornby, Elizabeth, School Mistress, 58 Meeting St
Horry, Elias Lynch, Planter, St Andrew's, 18 miles, Dwelling, W End of Broad St
Horry, Elias, Planter, 124 Meeting St
Horry, Harriott, Planter, 61 Tradd St.
Horry, Jonah, Planter, Washingon St
Horry, Thomas, Planter, 27 Meeting St
Hort, Robert, Attorney (Office, Coate's Row), Hampstead
Hort, William, Planter, Christ Church Parish, 4 miles
Horwood, Mary, Nurse, 3 Meeting St
Horwood, William, Tailor, 3 Meeting St
Houlton, James, Collector of Accounts, 5 Cumberland St
Houlton, Thomas, Harness Maker, 16 Guignard St
Houzeal, David, Clerk, 122 Queen St
Howard, Alexander, Factor & Commission Merchant, 1 George St
Howard, John, Brick Layer, 22 George St.
Howard, Richard, Cooper, 18 George St
Howard, Robert, Tax Collector, 1 George St
Howard, William, Clerk, 1 George St
Howarth, Benjamin, Physician & Planter, St John's, Berkeley, 51 miles
Howe, Michael, Stone Cutter, 32 Pinckney St
Howell, Jeremiah, Gardener for Agricultural Society, Neck, 5 miles
Hrabowski, Richard, Factor & Commission Merchant, Coate's Row, East Bay St
Hubbert, John, Boarding House, 1 Berresford's Al
Hubble, Seares, Mariner, 40 East Bay Cont'd
Hubert, Charles, Cannon St
Hudgins, William, Overseer to Cunningham, St John's, Berkeley, 27 miles
Hudson, James, Overseer to Dr Chisolm, Edisto Island
Hudson, John, Overseer to Paterson, St John's, Berkeley, 36 miles
Hueston, James, Carpenter, 17 Middle St
Hueston, James, Tailor, 27 Church St
Huet, Louis, Grocer, 9 Anson St
Huff, Abigal, 244 King St

Huff, Jacob, Planter, St James' Goose Creek, 22 miles
Huff, John, Carpenter, 2 Unity Al
Huff, John, Overseer to S Mazyck, St James' Goose Creek, 18 miles
Huff, Samuel, Maj , Tavern Keeper, St James' Goose Creek, 25 miles
Huffman, ——, Overseer, St Andrew's, 12 miles
Huger, Ann, Planter, 90 Broad St
Huger, Daniel, Planter, St Andrew's, 8 miles
Huger, Daniel, Secretary to the Governor, 80 Queen St
Huger, Elizabeth, Planter, 13 East Bay Cont'd
Huger, John, Capt , Planter, St Thomas', 17 miles
Huggins, Jacob B , Planter, Christ Church Parish, 20 miles
Huggins, Nathaniel, Overseer, Cat Island, Christ Church Parish
Huggins, William, Planter, Christ Church Parish, 16 miles
Hughes, Edward, School Master, 79 Tradd St
Hughes, Eliza, Planter, St. Stephen's, 46 miles
Hughes, John, Wharfinger, 5 Lamboll St
Hughes, Malachi, Planter, St Stephen's, 46 miles
Hughes, Thomas, Planter, Cannon St
Hume, John, Planter, cor of Wentworth & Smith St
Humphries, John, Coach Trimmer, 1 Back St
Hunt, Joseph, Mariner, Wentworth St
Hunt, Mary, Boarding House, 5 Champneys St
Hunt, Thomas, Planter, 53 Tradd St
Hunter & Ross, Grain Merchant, Store, 120 Tradd St
Hunter, James, Clerk, Cannonborough Road
Hunter, James, Grain Merchant, 8 Church St
Hunter, John, Shop Keeper, 119 King St
Hunter, Letitia, Seamstress, 8 Ellery St
Hurd, Benjamin, Shop Keeper, 13 Society St
Hurd, Sarah, Shop Keeper, 11 Motte St
Hurst, James, Overseer to M'Beth, St John's, Berkeley, 33 miles
Hussey, Brian, Pilot, 13 Water St
Hutchet, Charles, Store Keeper, 102 East Bay St
Hutchins, Samuel, Brick Layer, 20 Hasell St
Hutchinson, Ann, Planter, East Bay St.
Hutchinson, E A , Merchant, 10 East Bay Cont'd
Hutchinson, Jeremiah, Jr , Carpenter, St Andrew's, 12 miles
Hutchinson, Maria, Seamstress, 5 Beaufain St
Hutman, Frederick, Tailor, South Bay
Hutton, James, Factor, W End of South Bay
Huxford, Harleck, Planter, St John's, Berkeley, 38 miles
Hyams, David, Vendue Master, 169 King St
Hyams, Samuel, Shop Keeper, 121 Queen St
Hyer, Henry, Drayman, Boundary St
Hylliard, ——, Boarding House, Sullivan's Island
Hyslop, Christiana, ·Nurse, 33 Motte St

Hyslop, Hannah, Seamstress, 4 Lynch's Court
I'On, Jacob Bond, Planter, Christ Church Parish, 22 miles
Icardin, Lewis, Grocer, 15 Trott St
Icobia, Henry, Guardman, 107 King St
Inglesby, Henry, Tailor, 90 Broad St
Inglesby, William, Planter, 24 Tradd St
Ingraham, Henry, Navy Agent, 293 King St
Ingraham, Nathaniel & Son, Navy Agents (Custom House), 154 East Bay St
Ingraham, Nathaniel, Navy Agent, 293 King St
Innes, John, Coach Trimmer, 116 Broad St
Ireland, Benjamin, Carpenter, 94 Queen St
Irvine, Matthew, Physician, 7 cor of Meeting & Smith's Ln
Isaac, Abrahams, Vendue Master, Store, Champneys St
Isaacs, Abraham, Vendue Master, 4 Bedon's Al
Izard, Ellis, Planter, 1 Meeting St.
Izard, Henry, Planter, 1 Meeting St
Izard, Ralph, Lt , Planter, St. Andrew's, 15 miles
Izard, Ralph, Planter, St Andrew's, 12 miles
Izard, Richard, Planter, 90 Broad St
Jacks, James, Goldsmith & Jeweller, Store, 125 Broad St
Jacks, James, Goldsmith, 7 George St
Jackson, E., Miss, Planter, St John's, Berkeley, 45 miles
Jackson, Hugh, Clerk, 233 King St
Jackson, John, Planter, St Thomas & St Dennis, 8 miles
Jackson, John, Planter, Wassmasaw, 28 miles
Jackson, M , Tavern Keeper & Deputy Sheriff, St James' Goose Creek, 23 miles
Jackson, R , Miss, Planter, St John's, Berkeley, 45 miles
Jackson, Robert, Carpenter, Fort at Sullivan's Island
Jackson, William, Boot & Shoe Maker, 77 East Bay St
Jackson, William, Weaver, St James' Santee, 42 miles
Jacob, Edmond, Tailor, Mazyck St
Jacobs, Barnard, Shop Keeper, East Bay St
Jacobs, Hyman, Shop Keeper, 30 Meeting St
Jacobs, Samuel, Shop Keeper, 211 King St
Jahan, Joseph, Carpenter, 2 Meeting St. Cont'd
James, John, Deputy Sheriff, 47 Broad St
James, Samuel, Carpenter, Sullivan's Island
Janti, ——, Monsieur, Shop Keeper, 23 Anson St
Jardin, John A , Shop Keeper, King St
Jaresset, John, Mariner, 16 Trott St
Jarman, John, Planter, Race Ground
Jarman, Thomas, Planter, St. James' Santee, 42 miles
Jarrowt, Mary, Planter, Christ Church Parish, 15 miles
Jaudon, Daniel, Planter, St. James' Santee, 48 miles
Javan, Peter, Shop Keeper, 83 King St

Jeannerett, Christopher, Teller, State Bank, 128 Broad

Jeffords, Elizabeth, Planter, Christ Church Parish, 15 miles

Jeffords, John H , Planter, James Island

Jeffords, John, Planter, Christ Church Parish, 19 miles

Jeffords, John, Tailor, 48 Pinckney St

Jenkins, Benjamin, Sr , Planter, Wadmalaw Island

Jenkins, Christopher, Planter, Edisto Island

Jenkins, Elias, Brick Layer, 12 Liberty St

Jenkins, Joseph, Planter, Edisto Island

Jenkins, Martha, Planter, Legare St

Jenkins, Micah, Planter, 4 Legare St

Jenkins, Micah, Planter, John's Island

Jenkins, Phoebe, Planter, John's Island

Jenkins, Richard, Planter, John's Island

Jenkins, Robert, Planter, Edisto Island

Jenkins, Samuel, Planter, Wadmalaw Island

Jennings, Elizabeth, Widow, 1 New St

Jerril, Race, House Carpenter, 24 Guignard St

Jervey, David, Planter & Physician, Christ Church Parish, 17 miles

Jervey, James, Attorney, 140 Meeting St

Jervey, Thomas, Capt , Mariner, 18 Church St Cont'd

Jessop, Jeremiah, Tavern Keeper, 117 Queen St

Jewell, Benjamin, Store Keeper, 59 East Bay St.

Joel, Thomas, Planter, St Thomas', 16 miles

Johns, John, Shop Keeper, 3 cor of Coming & Wentworth

Johnson, Andrew, Planter, St Thomas & St Dennis, 23 miles

Johnson, Ann, Seamstress, 5 St Philip's St

Johnson, Archibald, Overseer to Mishau, St James' Santee, 34 miles

Johnson, Benjamin, Ship Carpenter, 58 Anson St

Johnson, Charles, Clerk, 52 Broad St

Johnson, David, 45 Queen St

Johnson, Elizabeth, School Mistress, 8 Wentworth St

Johnson, Hans, Grocer, 24 Pinckney St

Johnson, Jabez W , Watchmaker, 179 Meeting St Cont'd

Johnson, John, Attorney, 82 Queen St

Johnson, John, Carpenter, Louisville, St Thomas', 12 miles

Johnson, John, Jr , Blacksmith, Charlotte St

Johnson, John, Justice of Peace, 164 King St

Johnson, Joseph, Physician & Druggist, 5 Broad St

Johnson, Joshua, Planter, Christ Church Parish, 5 miles

Johnson, Peter, Printer, 6 Meeting St

Johnson, Robert, Mrs , Planter, St Thomas & St Dennis, 7 miles

Johnson, Thomas, Boot & Shoe Maker, 32 Broad St

Johnson, William, Blacksmith, 59 Anson St.

Johnson, William, Judge of Supreme Court of U S , 1 Anson St

Johnston, Barbara, Midwife, 24 King St

Johnston, Edward, Grocer, 23 Motte St

Johnston, Gardner, Ship Carpenter, 8 Water St

Johnston, John, Carpenter, 40 King St

Johnston, Mary, Widow, South Bay

Johnston, Thomas, Grocer & Wagon Yard, King St

Johnstone, John, Merchant, 23 Church St Cont'd

Joiner, Jesse, Planter, Four Holes

Jones & Harper, Cabinet Makers, 14 Archdale St

Jones, Abner, Tailor, 15 cor of Meeting & Guignard St

Jones, Abraham, Shop Keeper, 86 King St

Jones, Charles, Market St

Jones, Edward, Dr , Planter, St Andrew's, 13 miles

Jones, Elias, Overseer to Schackelford, St James' Santee, 28 miles

Jones, Henry John, Merchant, 28 Society St

Jones, Henry, Ship Carpenter, 20 Pinckney St

Jones, Henry, Store Keeper, 18 Church St Cont'd

Jones, James L , Tavern Keeper, St Andrew's, 7 miles

Jones, John, Planter, Christ Church Parish, 11 miles

Jones, John, Tailor, 102 Queen St

Jones, Joseph, Grocer, 14 Tradd St

Jones, Mary, Widow, 29 King St

Jones, Noah, Attorney, 8 Hasell St

Jones, Noah, Attorney, Office, Tradd St

Jones, Paul T , Clerk at S C Bank, 12 King St

Jones, Rollin, Patroon, St John's, Berkeley, 36 miles

Jones, S C , Book Keeper, S C Carolina Bank, 1 Guignard St

Jones, Sarah, Seamstress, 131 East Bay St

Jones, Thomas, Custom House Boatman, Church St

Jones, Thomas, Factor, 3 cor of Coming & Wentworth

Jones, Thomas, President, S C Bank, 2 Guignard St

Jones, Thomas, Tailor & Planter, St James' Santee, 35 miles

Jones, William, Blacksmith, St Stephen's, 43 miles

Jones, William, Boarding House, 27 Berresford's Al

Jordan, Christopher, Coach Trimmer, 6 Anson St

Josef, ——, Madame, 15 Trott St

Joseph, Lewis, Sausage Maker, 27 Union St

Josephs, Joseph, Store Keeper, 133 King St

Jost, John, Grocer, 50 Anson St

Jourdon, Daniel, Planter, St John's, Berkeley, 44 miles

Jourdon, Elizabeth, Planter, St Thomas & St Dennis, 19 miles

Joy, Benjamin, Planter, Christ Church Parish, 12 miles

Joy, Daniel, Overseer to C. Air, Christ Church Parish, 6 miles

Joy, William, Overseer to Ellsworth, Christ Church
Parish, 3 miles
June, Stephen, Blacksmith, St Stephen's, 50 miles
Jurgens, Christian, Baker, Vanderhorst St
Just, George, Sergeant in City Guard, 37 Broad St
Kahnley, John, Custom House Officer, Boundary
St
Kakely, George, Capt , Planter, Wentworth St
Kalchoffen, J J , Overseer, King St Road
Kanapauge, Joseph, Shoe Maker, 23 Trott St
Kanapauge, William, Silversmith, 23 Trott St
Kartman, Frederick, Sergeant in City Guard, 107
King St
Kay, Ann, Shop Keeper, 19 Motte St
Kay, Mary, Boarding House, 11 Bedon's Al
Kean, Jacob, Jr , Planter, St Stephen's, 40 miles
Kean, Jacob, Planter, St Stephen's, 40 miles
Kean, Zion, Planter, St Stephen's, 40 miles
Keatly, James, Planter, St Stephen's, 40 miles
Keckley, George, Capt , Planter, St James' Goose
Creek, 25 miles
Keckley, John, Cabinet Maker, 49 King St
Keckley, Mitchael, Planter, St James' Goose Creek,
20 miles
Keenan, George, Shop Keeper, King St Road
Keenan, Thomas, Grocer, cor of Church & Water
St
Keilly, John, Clerk to William Pritchard, Sr , 1
Trott St
Keisch, John, Grocer, Cochran's Whf
Keith, George, Carpenter, 29 Society St
Keith, Isaac S , Rev , Pastor, Independent Church,
50 Tradd St
Keith, S., Mrs , Planter, 7 Meeting St
Keith, William, Tailor, 27 cor of Church & Water
St
Keller, Philip, Planter, Four Holes
Kelly, Christopher, Cannonborough Road
Kelly, Christopher, Shop Keeper, 207 King St
Kelly, Jacob W , Grocer, King St Road
Kelly, John, Pilot, 6 Guignard St
Kelly, Mary, Store Keeper, 114 King St
Kelly, Michael, Merchant, 19 Tradd St
Kelly, Susannah, Seamstress, 6 Meeting St
Kemnitz, Frederick, Grocer, 2 Smith's Ln
Kempson, Harman, Carpenter, Vanderhorst St
Kennedy, Ann, Charlotte St
Kennedy, E , Merchant (Counting House), Craft's
Whf
Kennedy, E , Mrs , Tavern Keeper, St John's,
Berkeley, 36 miles
Kennedy, Edward, Merchant, 2 Moore St
Kennedy, James, Planter, 8 Mazyck St
Kennedy, James, Planter, Shipyard
Kennedy, John, Planter, St John's, Berkeley, 36
miles
Kennedy, John, Sullivan's Island
Kennedy, Lionel H , Attorney, 8 Mazyck St

Kennedy, Peter, Grocer, 53 Tradd St
Kenny, John, Grocer, 146 Meeting St
Kent, William, Blacksmith, St John's, Berkeley, 53
miles
Keorvin, Elizabeth, 27 St Philip's St
Ker, John, Hatter, 15 Elliott St
Ker, William, Clerk, 15 Elliott St
Kern, John Frederick, Merchant, 187 King St
Kerr & Wadsworth, Grocers, 13 Archdale St
Kerr, Andrew, Merchant, 126 Broad St
Kershaw, Charles, Factor, 23 East Bay St
Kerwan, Thomas, Planter, St Thomas', 18 miles
Keyser, Mary C , Butcher, King St Road
Khone & Maxwell, Merchants (Counting House),
East Bay St
Khone, John Frederick, Merchant, 73 Queen St
Kidd, George, Clerk, Beale's Whf
Kiddle, Charles, Merchant, 127 Broad St
Kiels, Peter, Shop Keeper, 172 King St
Kilconie, Anthony, 1 Broad St
Kilkenny, Teddy, Clerk, 53 Tradd St
Kimball, George, Grocer, 204 King St
King, Alexander, Sullivan's Island
King, Benjamin, Carpenter, St Philip's St.
King, George, School Master, St Stephen's, 52
miles
King, James, Grocer, 23 King St
King, John, Merchant, 109 Tradd St
King, John, Merchant, Store, 8 Tradd St
King, Mitchell, Teacher, College St
King, Robert, Overseer to Thomas Palmer, St
Stephen's, 43 miles
King, William, Boarding House, 23 Union St
King, William, Planter, Four Holes
Kingdon, ——, Tailor, 108 Tradd St
Kingman, Eliab, Inspector, Custom House,
Cannonborough Road
Kinkaid, Alexander, Cabinet Maker, 84 Tradd St
Kinmont, David, Blacksmith, 2 East Bay St
Kirk, Henry, Pilot, 27 Elliott St
Kirk, John D , Boarding House, 30 Berresford's Al
Kirk, John, Merchant, 56 East Bay St
Kirk, John, Shop Keeper, Mazyckborough
Kirk, Robert, Tavern Keeper, St John's, Berkeley,
53 miles
Kirkpatrick & Douglas (Counting House), Bailey's
Whf
Kirkpatrick, Jane, Mantua Maker, 5 Smith's Ln
Kirkpatrick, John, Merchant, 89 Church St
Kirkpatrick, Joseph, Physician & Druggist, 82
Church St
Kittleband, David, Carpenter, 28 Elliott St
Knox, John, Ship Carpenter, 3 Guignard St
Knox, Mathew, Cryer of the Court of Common
Pleas & Sessions, Mazyckborough
Knox, Sarah, Shop Keeper, 22 Church St Cont'd
Knox, Walter, Carpenter, 2 Green St.
Knust, Henry, Grocer, 59 Broad St

Koffskey, Ann, Shop Keeper, 88 King St.
Kogler, Jacob, Butcher, Hampstead
Kough, Owen, Clerk, 4 Broad St
Kreps, Ann, Baker, 164 King St
Kunhart, William, Clerk to David Bailey, 25 Broad
St
Laat, Joseph, Lumber Measurer, 2 Kinloch's Court
Laats, Mary M , Clerk, 141 King St
LaBarbandauh, Alexander, Shop Keeper, 6 Middle
St.
Labatut, ——, Monsieur, Limner & Teacher of
the French, 3 St Philip's St
Labatut, ——, Monsieur, Musician, 84 King St
Laborde, Francis, Livery Stables, 173 King St
LaCaisson, ——, Madame, 5 Middle St
Lacey, John, Pilot, 27 Elliott St
Lacey, Thomas, Carpenter, 35 Trott St
Lacomb, ——, Cigar Maker, 109 King St
Lacombe, Benoit, 4 Maiden Ln
Lacombe, Stephen, Physician, 3 Maiden Ln
Lacoste, Charles, Shop Keeper, 180 King St
Lacoste, Stephen, President, Union Insurance Co ,
54 Broad St
LaCoudre, K , Physician, 147 Meeting St
Ladevize, James, Shop Keeper, 87 King St.
Ladson, Eliza, School Mistress, 8 Whim Court
Ladson, James, Planter, St Andrew's, 15 miles
Lafar, Joseph, Cooper, 155 Meeting St
Lafar, Peter & John, Goldsmiths, 155 Meeting St
Laffilly, Francis, Clerk, Wentworth St
Lafin, Mary, Shop Keeper, 77 King St
Lafond, Henrietta, 13 Guignard St
Lafond, John, Cooper, East Bay Cont'd
Laginsandieu, ——, Monsieur, Store Keeper, King
St Road
Laidler, William, Capt , Mariner, 5 Blackbird Al
Lajust, Paul, Confectioner, 139 Broad St
Lamb, David, Merchant, 96 Tradd St
Lamb, Thomas, School Master, 105 Queen St
Lambert, Francis, Beer Merchant, 187 Meeting St
Lame, ——, Tinman, 158 Meeting St
Lance, Lambert, Mrs , 12 Friend St
Lance, Sarah, Planter, 80 Queen St
Lane, John, Merchant, 2 Lynch's Ln
Lane, Robert, Wine Merchant, 2 Laurens St
Lane, Robert, Wine Merchant, Store, 109 East Bay
Cont'd
Lang, I H & Co , Merchants (Store), 18 East Bay
St.
Lange, I H., Merchant, 1 Church St Cont'd
Langley, William, Montague St
Langlois, Maria, School Mistress, 46 Tradd St.
Langlois, Mitchel, 18 Federal St
Langstaff & Frink, Store, Beale's Whf
Langstaff, Benjamin, Factor, 34 Trott St
Langton, John, Grocer, 122 Queen St cor Motte
St
Lanneau, Basil, Tanner, Pitt St

Lanneau, Peter, Mariner, 25 Federal St
Lapin, Joseph, Shop Keeper, King St Road
Laport, Rene, Merchant, 99 Meeting St
Larbe, Joseph, Shoe Maker, 132 Queen St.
Lardon, Louis, Shop Keeper, 224 King St
Large, John, Boat Builder, Sullivan's Island
LaRoache, James, Planter, Wadmalaw Island
LaRoche, Eliza, Seamstress, 27 Beaufain St
LaRoussitur, P L , Silversmith, Magazine St
Larry, Robert, Carpenter, 57 Church St
Lartego, Montague, Shop Keeper, 2 Linguard St
Lartigue, John, Confectioner, 41 Meeting St
Latham, Daniel, Distiller, 1 Hasell St
Latham, Daniel, Jr , Merchant, 1 Hasell St
Latvison, L , Planter, 22 Guignard St
Lauderhausen, William, Billiard Table, 103 East
Bay Cont'd
Laughridge, David, Clerk, 113 King St.
Laundry, Elizabeth, Seamstress, 24 Pinckney St
Laurence, Henry, Planter, St John's, Berkely, 31
miles
Laurence, Peter, Merchant, 19 Beaufain St
Laurens, Henry, Planter, East Bay Cont'd
Laval, Jacint, Capt , U S Army, 16 Pinckney St
Laval, Jacinth, Jr , Planter, James Island
Lavauden, Paul, Shop Keeper, 193 Meeting St
Lavert, ——, Fruiterer, 28 Queen St
Lavieux, Elizabeth, Shop Keeper, 230 King St
Lawrence, Nathaniel, Brass Founder, 66 Meeting St
Laws, Robert, Planter, Wassmasaw, 40 miles
Lawson, William, Grocer, 90 Queen St
Lawton, William, Planter, James Island
Lawton, Winborn, Planter, James Island
Layton, Louisa, Planter, St John's, Berkeley, 55
miles
Lazarus, Marks, Merchant, 103 King St
Lazarus, Michael, Merchant, 124 King St
Leaes, John J , Merchant, 12 Middle St
Leaumont, Robert, Musician, 63 Meeting St
Leavitt, Horatio, Clerk to David Bailey, 25 Broad
St
Leavitt, Joshua, Planter, Daniel's Island, 6 miles
Lebat, Catharine, Shop Keeper, 118 Queen St
LeBreton, John, Store Keeper, 2 Queen St
Lecat, Francis, Teacher of Violin, 89 King St
Lechaise, Andrew, Assistant Postmaster, 13 Church
St
Ledbetter, Agens, Seamstress, 9 Liberty St
Leduc & Danjou, Grocers, 19 cor Church & Tradd
St
Lee & Haynsworth, Store Keepers, King St Road
Lee, Dorothea, Planter, 40 Broad St
Lee, George, Mariner, 29 Berresford's Al
Lee, Paul S H , Clerk, Comptroller's Office, 175
Meeting St
Lee, Stephen, Secretary of State, 87 Tradd St
Lee, Thomas, Cabinet Maker, 80 Meeting St
Lee, Thomas, State Comptroller, 35 Society St

Lee, Timothy, Factor (Counting House) 7 East Bay St

Lee, Timothy, Factor, 3 Trott St

Lee, W C, Tobacconist, 150 Meeting St

Lee, William, Clerk, Inferior City Court, 122 King St

Lee, William, Merchant, 8 Federal St

Leech, Catharine, Nurse, 40 Church St Cont'd

Leefe, Benjamin, Vendue Master, 35 Elliott St

Leefe, Benjamin, Vendue Master Store, Champneys St

Lefeve, John, Shop Keeper, King St

Legare, —, Mrs., Planter, 284 King St

Legare, Daniel, Physician & Planter, Christ Church Parish, 9 miles

Legare, Elizabeth L, Planter, 4 Society St

Legare, James, Planter, 10 New St

Legare, James, Planter, John's Island

Legare, Mary, Planter, John's Island

Legare, Nathan, Mrs, Planter, Christ Church Parish, 10 miles

Legare, Sarah, Planter, 15 Anson St

Legare, Solomon, Jr, Planter, 19 Friend St

Legare, Solomon, Planter, St John's, Berkeley, 35 miles

Legare, Thomas, Planter, 1 Gibbes St

Legare, Thomas, Planter, John's Island

Legay, —, Mrs, Planter, Christ Church Parish, 6 miles

Legere, —, Keeper of Magazine, Christ Church Parish, 6 miles

Legge, Ann, 52 Trott St

Legge, J H., Clerk, 52 Trott St

Legge, Joseph, Planter, Race Ground

Legge, Thomas W, Clerk, 52 Trott St

Leggett Sarah, Planter, Christ Church Parish, 14 mi

Legoux, —, Dentist, 25 Trott St.

Legrande, —, Physician, 65 Church St

LeGray, John, Tailor, 110 Queen St

Lehre, Ann, Planter, St Stephen's, 40 miles

Lehre, Thomas, Planter, 272 King St

Leitch, Neil, Clerk, 34 East Bay St

Lelane, Aaron W, Rev, Christ Church Parish, 3 miles

Lemaitre, John, Hatter, 179 King St

Lemke, Christian, Grocer, 36 Beaufain St

Lenorment, Andrew, Silversmith, 220 King St

Lequeux, Benjamin, Planter, St Stephen's, 50 miles

Lequeux, John, Wharfinger, 35 Anson St

Lequeux, Samuel, Overseer to Ann Thomas, St Stephen's, 50 miles

Lequeux, Sims, Planter, St John's, Berkeley, 28 miles

Leroy, Joseph, Gardner, Lowndes St

LeRoy, F, Physician, 141 Meeting St

Lesesne, Ann, Planter, St Thomas', 12 miles

Lesesne, Daniel, Planter, St. Thomas', 21 miles

Lesesne, Hannah, Planter, 42 East Bay Cont'd

Lesesne, Isaac, Capt, Mariner, 43 East Bay Cont'd

Lesesne, Mary, Planter, St Thomas', 12 miles

Lesesne, Peter, Planter, St Thomas', 18 miles

Lesesne, Thomas, Merchant, Coming St

Lesherin, John B, Grocer, King St Road

LeSignett, Vincent, Physician, 3 Savage St

Leslie, Henry, Mariner, 55 Anson St

Leslie, Sarah, Boarding House, 26 Union St

Leveen, Lewis, Clerk, 139 King St

Leverett, William, Writing Master, College

Levingston, Robert Y, Clerk, 31 George St

Levrier, —, French Teacher, 43 Meeting St

Levy, Emanuel, Shop Keeper, 48 East Bay St

Levy, Jacob C, Clerk, 217 King St

Levy, Lyon, Clerk, State Treasury Office, 189 King St

Levy, Moses C, Shop Keeper, 217 King St

Levy, Nathan, Store Keeper, 115 King St

Levy, Reuben, Broker, Cock Ln.

Levy, Samuel, Constable, 1 Swinton's Ln

Levy, Simon, Shop Keeper, 231 King St

Levy, Solomon, Store Keeper, 100 Broad St

Lewis, F, 44 Queen St

Lewis, John, Carpenter, 13 Archdale St

Lewis, John, Clerk, Mazyckborough

Lewis, John, Grocer, 22 Union St

Lewis, John, Merchant, 126 Broad St

Lewis, Joseph, Clerk, 31 Archdale St

Lewis, William, Cabinet Maker, 99 Queen St

Lewis, William, Overseer to S Prioleau, St James' Goose Creek, 21 miles

Ley, Francis, Custom House Officer, Cannon St

Libby, Catharine, 18 George St

Libby, Nathaniel, Planter, Christ Church Parish, 5 miles

Libby, William, Ship Carpenter, 2 Society St

Liblong, Henry, Shoe Maker, 5 Liberty St

Liddle, John, Shop Keeper, 4 Minority St

Liddle, William, Overseer to T Gourdine, St Stephen's, 50 miles

Lightburn, Francis, Capt, Planter, Wadmalaw Island

Lights, William, Overseer to E Mortimer, Christ Church Parish, 9 miles

Lightwood, Elizabeth, Planter, 119 Meeting St

Lilly & Sibley, Grocers, Shop, 90 East Bay Cont'd

Limbackker, John, Planter, James Island

Limehouse, Robert, Lumber Merchant, 55 W end Tradd St

Lincoln, Henry, School Master, Hampstead

Lindershein, Christian, Carpenter, Lowndes St

Lindsay, John L, Butcher, King St. Road

Lindsay, Robert, Carpenter, 25 Church St Cont'd

Lindsay, William, Merchant, 103 East Bay Cont'd

Lindsay, William, Merchant Store, 70 East Bay St

Ling, Philip, Chair Maker, 9 Guignard St

Ling, Robert, Coach Maker, 1 Back St

Linguard, Mary, 66 Church St

Lining, Charles, Ordinary, Charleston District, 8 Legare St
Lining, Mary, Planter, St Andrew's, 19 miles
Linson, Thomas, Planter, St Stephen's, 43 miles
Little, John, Turner, 192 King St
Little, Robert, Lumber Merchant, 3 Pinckney St
Livings, James, Pilot, 5 Lynch's Court
Livingston, Henry, Clerk, 135 King St
Livingston, J H , Printer, 78 Queen St
Lloyd, John, Factor, 166 Meeting St
Lloyd, John, Factor, Bull St
Lloyd, John P , Venetian Blind Maker, 97 Meeting St
Lloyd, Joseph, Store Keeper, 65 King St
Lockey, George, Planter, Boundary St
Lockhart, Thomas, Planter, St John's, Berkeley, 60 miles
Lockwood, Joshua, Jr , Assistant Clerk, State Bank, 40 Broad St
Lockwood, Joshua, Sr , Planter, Smith's Ln
Logan, Ann, Seamstress, 257 King St
Logan, George, Physician & Druggist, 1 Moore St
Logan, George R , Attorney, 47 Church St
Logan, Honoria, Planter, 33 Tradd St
Logan, Thomas, Grocer, 43 Church St
Logan, William, Register of Mesne Conveyance, Cannonborough Road
Long, John, Butcher, Cannon St
Long, John, Store Keeper, 136 King St
Long, Josiah, Overseer, Iehawsa Island
Long, Rachel, Boarding House, 16 Elliott St
Long, Robert, Capt , Mariner, 4 Clifford St
Longbothom, B T , Dentist, 54 Meeting St
Longford, Ann R , Seamstress, 13 Liberty St
Longguest, Magnus, Ship Carpenter, 8 Pinckney St
Lopez, Aaron, Shop Keeper, 30 Beaufain St
Lopez, David, Vendue Master (Counting House), 126 East Bay Cont'd
Lopez, David, Vendue Master, 237 King St
Lopez, John, Grocer, 25 East Bay Cont'd
Loppincoot, Jacob, Merchant, 70 King St
Lord, Jacob N , Boot & Shoe Maker, 155 King St
Lord, John, House Carpenter, 24 Guignard St
Lorent & Steinmentz, Merchants, 52 Tradd St
Lorent & Steinmitz, Merchants (Counting House), 28 East Bay St
Lothrop, S H , Merchant, 108 East Bay Cont'd
Love, Elizabeth, Seamstress 30 Trott St
Loveday, Sarah, 10 Moore St
Lovell, Josiah Sturges, Merchant, 295 King St
Lowe, John, Goldsmith, 114 Broad St
Lowndes, Thomas, Planter, 91 Broad St
Lowndes, William, Planter, Ashley River, back of Race Ground
Lowry, Charles, Tailor, 45 Church St
Lowry, Charles, Wheelwright, 6 Liberty St.
Lowry, Daniel, Planter, Edisto Island
Lowry, Henry, Planter, Edisto Island

Lowry, Isham, Overseer to M Jenkins, John's Island
Lucas, Jonathan, Jr , Planter, Mills, Boundary St
Lucas, Jonathan, Planter & Millwright, Christ Church Parish, 4 miles
Ludeman, John, Deputy Federal Marshal, 67 Meeting St
Luder, Francis, Confectioner, 27 Queen St
Lukens, John, Merchant, 6 Hasell St
Lusher, George, Merchant, 73 East Bay St
Luther, Giles, Boot & Shoe Store, 176 Meeting St
Luther, Simeon, Boot & Shoe Maker, 176 Meeting St
Lynah, Edward, Planter, 95 Meeting St
Lynah, James, Physician, 47 Meeting St
Lynch, Clarke, Milliners, 111 Tradd St
Lynch, Thomas, Brick Layer, 4 West St
Lynes, John, Overseer to Mrs Thomas, James Island
Lynes, Samuel, Overseer to Motte, St John's, Berkeley, 28 miles
Lynn, John, Factor, 6 East Bay Cont'd
Lyon, Mordecal, Shop Keeper, 225 King St
Lyons, Isaac, Planter, Wassmasaw, 31 miles
Lyons, Zachariah, Planter, St Andrew's, 14 miles
M'Adam, James, Merchant, Cannon St
M'Adams, James & Co , Merchants (Custom House), 32 East Bay St
M'Auley & Son Co , Merchants, 18 Broad St
M'Auley, Daniel, Merchant, 14 Broad St
M'Beth, Henry, Co , Merchants, Store, 138 Coate's Row
M'Beth, Sarah, Nurse, 268 King St
M'Bride, James, Druggist, 57 East Bay St.
M'Bride, James, Physician, St Stephen's, 50 miles
M'Bride, John, Overseer to Smith's Estate, St Thomas & St Dennis, 22 miles
M'Bride, Mary, Planter, St James' Goose Creek, 22 miles
M'Bride, Mary, Shop Keeper, 57 East Bay St
M'Call, Ann, Widow, 105 Church St
M'Call, Duncan, Clerk & Boarding House, Meeting St
M'Call, Hext, Attorney, 14 Meeting St
M'Call, James, Planter, King St Road
M'Call, John, Grocer & Boarding House, 188 Meeting St
M'Call, John H , Planter, St John's, Berkeley, 28 miles
M'Call, L B , Grocer, South Bay
M'Calla, Thomas H , Physician, 29 Anson St
M'Callister, John, Planter, St Stephen's, 46 miles
M'Calpin, Henry, Overseer to E Harleston, St John's, Berkeley, 33 miles
M'Cann, ——, Mrs , 3 Price's Al
M'Cants, Ann, Planter, James Island
M'Cants, David, Planter, St John's, Berkeley, 58 miles

M'Cants, James, Overseer to Porcher, St John's, Berkeley, 37 miles
M'Cants, John, Millwright to Keating Simons, St John's, Berkeley, 30 miles
M'Cants, John, Planter, St. John's, Berkeley, 58 miles
M'Cants, Nathaniel, Planter, St John's, Berkeley, 42 miles
M'Cartey, John, Constable, 4 Motte St
M'Cay, Joseph, School Master, 6 Archdale St
M'Cay, Malcolm, Grocer, 54 cor of Legare & Tradd St.
M'Cleish, Agnes, 8 Anson St
M'Cleish, James, Brass Founder, 93 East Bay St
M'Cleish, Mary, School Mistress, 121 Broad St
M'Clure, Patrick, Grocer, cor of Meeting & Trott St
M'Clymont, Gilbert & Co, Grocers, 90 Meeting St
M'Conny, James, Overseer to Kerwan, St Thomas & St Dennis, 18 miles
M'Cormick, Elija, Coming St
M'Cormick, Richard, Attorney, 112 Meeting St
M'Cormick, William, Grocer, 123 Tradd St
M'Coy, Charles, Planter, St Stephen's, 45 miles
M'Coy, John, Clerk, King St Road
M'Coy, William, Planter, St. Stephen's, 44 miles
M'Crady, ——, Shop Keeper, 105 King St
M'Crady, David, Merchant, 8 Broad St
M'Crady, Hannah, Merchant, 8 Broad St
M'Crady, Jane, East Bay Cont'd.
M'Cready, Mary Ann, Milliner, 209 King St
M'Cullow, Matthew W, Planter, St John's, Berkeley, 28 miles
M'Cume, Archibald, Planter, St James' Goose Creek, 20 miles
M'Dannell, Sarah, Tavern Keeper, King St Road
M'Donnald, Adam, Planter, St Stephen's, 46 miles
M'Donnald, Christopher, Grocer, 269 King St
M'Donnald, Susannah E, Planter, 15 Beaufain St
M'Dougall, John, Tailor, Edisto Island
M'Dow, Robert, Planter, King St Road
M'Dow, William, School Master, Montague St
M'Dowall, Alexander, Saddler, 80 King St
M'Dowall, Andrew, Clerk, 64 King St
M'Dowall, James, Store Keeper, 64 King St
M'Dowall, John, Planter & Tax Collector, St Thomas & St Dennis, 21 miles
M'Dowall, John, Shop Keeper, 168 King St
M'Dowall, John, Store Keeper, 144 King St.
M'Dowall, Sarah, Boarding House, 36 Union St
M'Dowell, James, Boot & Shoe Maker, 31 Broad St
M'Elmolye, William, Grocer, 276 King St
M'Evoy, ——, Physician, 20 Wentworth St
M'Faight, John, Mariner, 22 East Bay St.
M'Farlane, Clerk, 119 Queen St
M'Farlane, James, Carpenter, 29 Church St Cont'd.

M'Farlane, M, Clerk, 123 cor. of Church & Broad St
M'Fie, Dougald, Merchant, 24 Church St Cont'd
M'Gall, Elizabeth, Planter, 14 Meeting St
M'Gann, Patrick, Watch Maker, 132 Coate's Row
M'Gillivray, Alexander, Vendue Master, 6 Lynch's Ln
M'Gillivray, Alexander, Vendue Master Store, East Bay St
M'Ginness, K, Tailor, 129 King St
M'Grath, John, Clerk, 106 East Bay St
M'Grath, Jones, Merchant, 40 Church St, Store, Keith's Whf
M'Greal, Thomas, Clerk, 181 King St
M'Gregor, Laurence, Planter, St James' Santee, 44 miles
M'Gregor, Neil, Gardner, Vanderhorst St
M'Guffy, Anthony, Clerk, 31 cor Church St & St Michael's Al
M'Guinness, Joseph, Millwright, Christ Church Parish, 4 miles
M'Guire, Hugh, Tailor, 26 Church St
M'Kee, Abel, Ship Joiner, 34 East Bay Cont'd
M'Kehn, Uphy, Seamstress, 28 George St
M'Kehn, William, Brick Layer, 28 George St
M'Keirnan, John, Cooper, 179 Meeting St
M'Kelvey, Robert, Col, Planter, St John's, Berkeley, 50 miles
M'Kendry, John, Overseer to Fred Simons, John's Island
M'Kenzie, Ann, Seamstress, Hampstead
M'Kenzie, Elizabeth, Boarding House, 3 Unity Al
M'Kenzie, Henry, Butcher, Cannon St
M'Kenzie, Henry, Butcher, Hampstead
M'Kenzie, John, Grocer, 83 cor of Broad & Broughton's Lot
M'Kenzie, Thomas, Overseer to John Brian, St Thomas & St Dennis, 21 miles
M'Kernon, Brass Founder, 3 Federal St
M'Kie, John, Brick Layer, 277 King St
M'Kimmey, Charles, Clerk, East Bay St
M'Kindlay, Dugald, Merchant, 34 East Bay St
M'Kinlay, John, Grocer, Inspection St
M'Lachlan & Smith, Merchants, 6 Tradd St
M'Lane, Susannah, Seamstress, 8 Wall St
M'Lauchlan, Philip, Capt, Mariner, 14 Water St
M'Lean, Margaret, Shop Keeper, Boundary St
M'Leland, Mary, Nurse, Orphan House
M'Lenclhen, Archibald, Planter, St James' Santee, 37 miles
M'Leod, Donald, Rev, Pastor, Presbyterian Church, Edisto Island
M'Leod, Normand, Planter, Edisto Island
M'Leod, Robert, Planter, Edisto Island
M'Means, James, Overseer to Hanscomb, John's Island
M'Means, William, Overseer to Clark, Wadmalaw Island

M'Millan, Duncan, Overseer to T Pinckney, St.
James' Santee, 42 miles
M'Millan, John, Merchant (Counting House),
Chisolm's Whf
M'Millan, Richard, Boarding House, 179 King St
M'Millan, Thomas, Carpenter, 77 Tradd St
M'Neil & Co., Grocers, 123 Broad St
M'Neil & Walton, Store Keeper, 181 King St
M'Neil, Catharine, Shop Keeper, 36 Hasell St
M'Neil, Neil, Capt, 21 King St
M'Neil, Neil, Capt, Merchant, Store, 121 Broad St
M'Neill, Samuel, Clerk, 31 cor Church & St
Michael's Al
M'Nillage, Alexander, Planter, Christ Church
Parish, 5 miles
M'Nillage, Sail Maker, 17 Ellery St
M'Norton, Alexander, Overseer to William Eddings,
Edisto Island
M'Owen, Patrick, Merchant, 21 cor of East Bay &
Tradd St
M'Owen, Patrick, Merchants, Store (Custom
House), 44 Coate's Row
M'Pherson, Duncan, Shop Keeper, 72 King St
M'Pherson, Peter, Soap & Candle Maker, Cannon
St
M'Pherson, Susannah, Planter, 98 Broad St
M'Quiston, Archibald, Shop Keeper, 79 King St
M'Riddle, Benjamin, Clerk, 156 King St.
Macbeth, James, Merchant, 4 Lamboll St
Macguire, ——, Shoe Maker, 148 Meeting St.
Mackay, Barbara, Planter, King St Road
Mackay, James, Clerk, 5 Champneys St
Mackey, John, Jailer, Magazine St
Mackey, Mungo, Planter, Edisto Island
Mackie, James, Merchant, King St Road
Mackintosh & Foulds, Cabinet Makers, 62 Meeting
St
Macnamara, John, Merchant, 5 Elliott St
Madan, John, Brass Founder, Wentworth St
Madden, James, Attorney, 46 King St
Madelmont, ——, School Master, 5 Cumberland St
Magrath, Edward, Carpenter, 26 Archdale St
Magwood, Robert, Physician, 99 Queen St
Magwood, Simon, Factor, 99 Queen St
Maigy, Charles, Shop Keeper, 160 King St
Mair & Fraser, Gardeners, King St Road
Mair, Brice, Co , Merchants, Store, 134 Coate's
Row
Mair, James, Planter, John's Island
Mairs, Simon, Shop Keeper, 184 King St
Makkay, Jane, Widow, 112 Meeting St
Malcom, Thomas, Clerk, 2 Short St
Mall, James, Merchant (Counting House), Craft's
Whf
Mall, James, Merchant, 21 cor of East Bay &
Tradd St
Mallard, Elisha, Planter
Mallard, James, Planter, Four Holes

Manherl, Charles, Store Keeper, 135 Queen St
Manigault, Joseph, Planter, Meeting St Road
Mann, John, Brick Layer, 36 King St
Mann, Spencer John, Planter, Christ Church Parish,
12 miles
Manning, Edward, Tailor, 113 King St
Manning, James, Planter, Wassmasaw, 34 miles
Manry, Eaverish, Shop Keeper, 183 King St
Mansuy, ——, Tobacconist, 2 Trott St
Maquire, James, Boot & Shoe Maker, 100 Tradd St
Marchant, Peter, Physician, King St. Road
Marey, Abraham, Tavern Keeper, St John's,
Berkeley, 35 miles
Margart, John H , Blacksmith, Blackbird Al
Marine, Margaret, Widow, 80 East Bay St
Marion, Elizabeth, Planter, St John's, Berkeley, 60
miles
Marion, Francis, Jr , Planter, St John's, Berkeley,
45 miles
Marion, Francis, Planter, St John's, Berkeley, 53
miles
Marion, Mary Esther, Planter, St John's, Berkeley,
60 miles
Marion, Robert, Planter & Representative to
Congress, St Stephen's, 53 miles
Marion, Samuel, Planter, St James' Goose Creek,
21 miles
Markely, Abraham, Merchant, 122 King St
Markely, B A , Attorney, 122 King St
Marker, Mary, Boarding House, 14 Friend St
Marks, Alexander, Store Keeper, 136 King St
Marks, Humphrey, Store Keeper, 136 King St
Marks, Joseph, Grocer, 165 Meeting St
Marks, Mark, Vendue Cryer, 28 Wentworth St.
Marks, Sarah, Shop Keeper, 126 King St
Marlan, Nathaniel, Planter, St John's, Berkeley, 45
miles
Marlen, Edward, Jr , Tailor, 25 King St
Marlen, William, Cabinet Maker, 2 Price's Al
Marley, Peter, Deputy Sheriff, 4 St Philip's St
Marlin, Edward, Jr (Counting House), 10 Guignard
St
Marr, Ann, 44 Church St Cont'd
Marsan, Mary, 7 Friend St
Marsden, Benajmin, Vendue Master, Hampstead
Marsh, James, Ship Carpenter, 28 Guignard St cor
Anson St
Marsh, James, Shipyard, Gadsden's Whf
Marshall, C., Planter, 72 Tradd St
Marshall, Eleanor, Shop Keeper, 33 Wall St
Marshall, Elizabeth, School Mistress, 86 Tradd St
Marshall, John, Cabinet Maker, Cont'd of Meeting
St
Marshall, John, Cutler, 53 Meeting St
Marshall, John, Jr , Clerk, State Tax Office, 106
King St
Marshall, L F , Seamstress, 58 Broughton's Lot
Marshall, Mary S , 52 cor of Orange & Broad St

Marshall, William, Vendue Master, Champneys St
Marshall, William, Vendue Master, cor of Whim
Court & King St
Marszorati & Co., Print Sellers & Mathematicians,
30 miles
Martin, ----, Madame, 9 Wall St
Martin, Charles, Brick Layer, 34 Anson St
Martin, Christopher, Shop Keeper, Boundary St
Martin, Henry, Carpenter, 16 St Philip's St
Martin, Jacob, Book Keeper, S C Bank, 174
Meeting St
Martin, James, Clerk, 97 East Bay St
Martin, John C , Brick Layer, Trott St
Martin, John, Merchant, 17 Amen St
Martin, John Nicholas, Brick Layer, 115 Meeting
St
Martin, John Peter, Merchant, 39 Wentworth St
Martin, John, Ship Carpenter, 12 Middle St
Martin, John, Teller, Branch Bank, 8 Coming St.
Martin, Lewis, Cigar Maker, 17 Union St
Martin, Thomas & Co , Merchants (Counting
House), Chisolm's Whf
Martin, Thomas H , Brick Layer, 4 Mazyck St
Martin, Thomas, Merchant, 57 cor of Friend &
Broad
Martindale, James Cannon, Store Keeper, 167 King
St.
Marveraus, M S , Grocer, 63 Church St
Mashburne, Nicholas, House Carpenter, Cock Ln
Mason, George, Merchant, 58 Queen St
Mason, Robert, Planter, Edisto Island
Masset, Horatio, Watch Maker, 96 Queen St
Masset, Simon, Grocer, 64 Broad St
Mastwarn, William, Grocer, Market St
Mathews, Edmond, Rev , Planter, St Andrew's, 16
miles
Mathews, George, Vendue Master, Bull St
Mathews, James, Attorney, 14 Anson St
Mathews, John R , Planter, Edisto Island
Mathews, Mary, Planter, 74 Queen St
Mathews, Mary, Planter, John's Island
Mathews, Philip, Rev , Planter, St James' Santee,
43 miles
Mathews, Thomas, Mrs , Planter, St. Andrew's, 17
miles
Mathews, Thomas, Planter, John's Island
Mathews, William, Planter, John's Island
Mathews, William, Planter, Rutledge St
Mathews, William, Planter, St James' Santee, 32
miles
Mathine, ----, Planter, Wassmasaw, 29 miles
Matthews & Thomas, Planter, 95 Church St
Matthiesen, C F , Store Keeper, 129 Queen St
Mattuce, John, Butcher, Alexander St.
Mauger, John, Ship Chandler, 24 East Bay St.
Mauran, John R., Merchant, 75 Queen St
Maurel, M , Planter, 4 Parsonage Ln
Maverick, Samuel, Merchant, Boundary St

Maverick, Samuel, Merchant, Store 154 King St
Maxey, Frances, Planter, Edisto Island
Maxey, Joseph, Overseer to John Ward, John's
Island
Maxwell, Nathaniel G , Factor, Lynch St
Maxwell, Robert, Merchant, 50 Meeting St
May, Gracey, Planter, Wassmasaw, 33 miles
May, John, Boarding House, 180 cor of Federal &
King St
Mayberry, Thomas, Col , 22 Mazyck St
Mayer, John George, Attorney, 6 Motte St
Mays, James, Grocer, 3 Tradd St
Mazyck, Alexander C , Planter, 87 Meeting St
Mazyck, Alexander, Planter, St James' Santee, 35
miles
Mazyck, Daniel, Planter, Charlotte St
Mazyck, Mary, Planter, 2 Church St
Mazyck, Nat B , Merchant Store, 129 Broad St
Mazyck, Nataniel B , Merchant, 86 Meeting St
Mazyck, Paul, Planter, 3 cor Archdale St &
Magazine St
Mazyck, Paul, Planter, St James' Santee, 35 miles
Mazyck, Stephen, Planter, St John's, Berkeley, 38
miles
Mazyck, William, Factor, 3 cor of Archdale &
Magazine St
Mead, James, Grocer, 31 Hasell St. cor Anson St
Meads, William, Printer, Vanderhorst St.
Mealy, John, Lt of City Guard, Picquet Guard
House, Meeting St
Meed, William, Merchant's Hotel, 60 East Bay St.
Meentz, D C. A , Shop Keeper, 180 King St
Megee, William, Rev , Minister, Pitt St
Meggett, William, Capt , Planter, Edisto Island
Meise, Charles B & Co , Store Keepers, 66 King
St
Meissig, John, Fisherman, Broughton's Lot
Mellesemont, Andrew, Hair Dresser, 29 Motte St
Mellmase, Antoine, Turner, 136 Meeting St
Melpin, Archibald, Overseer to W A Deas, St
James' Goose Creek, 15 miles
Melrose, Thomas, Overseer to Hugh Rose, Christ
Church Parish, 18 miles
Mench, Henry, Shop Keeper, 25 Motte St.
Mendez, Aaron, Tinman, 246 King St
Mensey, Robert, Shoe Maker, 12 Ellery St
Mentzing, ----, 24 Queen St.
Menude, John, Planter, 83 East Bay St
Mercea, John, Grocer, 33 Pinckney St
Mersaill, Dominique, Coach Maker, 54 Meeting St
Mersailles, James, Shop Keeper, King St Road
Meshaw, John, Grocer, 4 cor. Pinckney & East Bay
Cont'd.
Messervy, Philip, Capt., Mariner, 7 Meeting St
Messroon, James, Capt , Mariner, 55 Coate's Row
Metevier, John, Baker, 139 Meeting St
Mey, Florian Charles, Merchant, 43 Pinckney St
Meyer, ----, City Guard, 69 Meeting St

119

Meyer, David, Confectioner, 18 Berresford St
Michaw, Abraham, Planter, St James' Santee, 34 miles
Middleton, Arthur, Planter, St Andrew's, 16 miles
Middleton, Henry, Planter, Montague St cor of Pitt St
Middleton, Mary, Seamstress, 85 Queen St
Middleton, Solomon, Tailor, 129 King St
Middleton, Thomas, Mrs., Planter, St Andrew's, 13 miles
Mikell, Elizabeth, Planter, Edisto Island
Mikell, Ephraim, Jr., Planter, Edisto Island
Mikell, Ephraim, Sr, Planter, Edisto Island
Mikell, John Calder, Planter, Edisto Island
Mikell, John, Sr, Planter & Tax Collector, Edisto Island
Mikell, Mary, Planter, Edisto Island
Milan, ——, Gardner, Hampstead
Miles, John, Factor (Counting House), Chisolm's Whf
Miles, John, Factor, 5 Coming St
Miles, Rebecca, Widow, 45 East Bay St
Miles, W, Mrs, Planter, St Andrew's, 15 miles
Millar, James, Sr, Merchant (Counting House), Chisolm's Whf
Millar, James, Sr, Merchant, 44 Anson St
Miller, Amelia, Mantua Maker, 39 Church St Cont'd
Miller, Andrew, Merchant, 6 Friend St
Miller, Archibald Edward, Printer, 102 Broad St
Miller, Benjamin, Butcher, King St Road
Miller, Benjamin, Tailor, 91 East Bay St
Miller, Catharine, Boarding House, 10 Federal St
Miller, Charles, Confectioner, 60 King St
Miller, Frederick, Butcher, King St Road
Miller, Frederick, Grocer, South Bay
Miller, Frederick, Shoe Maker, Vanderhorst St
Miller, George, Store Keeper, King St Road
Miller, Jacob, Rope Maker, Coming St
Miller, James, Wine Merchant, 61 East Bay St
Miller, Jane, 124 Meeting St
Miller, John David, Silver Smith, Boundary St.
Miller, John T, Carpenter, 10 Laurens St
Miller, Joseph, Boarding House, 21 Union St
Miller, M, Goldsmith, 40 Queen St
Miller, Nicholas, Baker, 16 George St
Miller, Robert, Drayman, 8 East Bay Cont'd
Miller, Samuel, Overseer to Bond I'on, Christ Church Parish, 20 miles
Miller, Samuel Stent, Printer, Boundary St
Miller, William, Baker, 74 Meeting St
Miller, William, Tailor, 102 Queen St
Miller, William, Tailor, 12 Berresford St
Milligan, Joseph, Shop Keeper, 73 King St.
Milligan, William, Merchant, 48 Church St Cont'd.
Millikan, Thomas, Vendue Master, 75 Broad St
Mills, Edmond, Miller to P. Broughton, St John's, Berkeley, 30 miles

Mills, Samuel, Rev, Protestant Methodist Church, Pitt St
Mills, Thomas, Rev, Planter, King St Road
Milner, George, Blacksmith, 72 Broad St
Minora, Baptist, 245 King St
Minott, Benjamin, Factor, 4 Gibbes St
Minott, Dorcas, Seamstress, 24 King St
Minott, William, Planter, 4 Gibbes St
Miott, Alexander, Clerk, 22 King St
Miott, Harriott, Widow, Hampstead
Miskelly, Daniel, Overseer to the Estate of Jenkins, John's Island
Missou, ——, Madame, Laurens St
Missout, ——, Madame, 4 Middle St
Mitchell, Alexander, Saddler & Harness Maker, 82 Meeting St
Mitchell, Andrew, Plasterer, 1 Clifford Al
Mitchell, Ann D, Widow, 117 Meeting St
Mitchell, Ann, Planter, 84 Meeting St
Mitchell, J. H, Justice of the Peace & Q U, 15 Guignard St
Mitchell, James, Block & Pump Maker, 63 Church St
Mitchell, James, Cooper, 18 Meeting St
Mitchell, James D, Attorney, 117 Meeting St
Mitchell, James D, Attorney, Wentworth St
Mitchell, John Hinckely, Notary Public & Q U (Office), 133 Coate's Row
Mitchell, John, Mariner, 19 Union St
Mitchell, John, Notary Public and Q U, 29 East Bay St.
Mitchell, Mary, Coming St
Mitchell, Thomas, Pilot, 19 Guignard St
Mitchell, Thomas, Planter, 23 Hasell St
Mitchell, William N, Planter, St John's, Berkeley, 28 miles
Mitchell, Joseph, Ship Carpenter, St James' Santee, 23 miles
Mathews, Robert, Overseer to Elias Ball, St John's, Berkeley, 29 miles
Moderne, James, Mariner, 1 Motte St
Moise, Aaron, Store Keeper, Store, 55 King St
Moise, Aaron, Vendue Master, 81 Tradd St
Moise, Cherry, Vendue Master, 98 Tradd St
Moise, Hyam, Vendue Master, 7 Orange St
Moles, James C, 142 Meeting St
Moles, Margaret, Store Keeper, 173 King St
Moll, John, Grocer, Boundary St
Mompoey, ——, Mrs, 3 Bull St
Monar, Lewis, Hair Dresser, 21 Queen St
Moncrieff, John, Merchant, 9 Meeting St
Monies, John, Merchant, 9 Broad St
Monies, William, Merchant, 9 Broad St
Montane, Anthony, Cigar Maker, King St. Road
Montesquieu, Rene, Tinman, 158 Meeting St
Montgomery, Peter, Shoe Maker, 12 Ellery St
Mood, Peter, Silversmith, 223 King St
Moodie, Benjamin, British Consul, 57 Tradd St

Mooney, Charles, Merchant, 21 cor of East Bay & Tradd St
Mooney, James, Store Keeper, 174 King St
Mooney, Patrick, Merchant, 1 Orange St
Mooney, Patrick, Merchant, Store, 6 Champneys St
Moore, Burgess, Tavern Keeper, St. John's, Berkeley, 62 miles
Moore, Henry H , Teacher, College
Moore, James, Carpenter, Pitt St
Moore, James, Ship Carpenter, 19 Middle St
Moore, John E , Planter, St. Thomas & St Dennis, 8 miles
Moore, John, Lock Keeper, Santee Canal, St John's, Berkeley, 42 miles
Moore, Joseph, Drayman, 8 East Bay Cont'd
Moore, Philip, Cabinet Maker, 28 Meeting St
Moore, Richard, Painter, 29 Wentworth St
Moore, Stephen West, Merchant, 2 Archdale St
Moorhead, Thomas, Factor, 99 Queen St
Mordecai, David, Vendue Master, 16 Berresford St
Mordecai, Debow, Vendue Master, Exchange St.
Mordecai, Isaac, 52 Wentworth St
Mordecai, Jacob, 22 Trott St
Mordecai, Joseph, Gunsmith, 4 Liberty St
Mordecai, Sarah, 22 Trott St
More, P I , Physician, 47 King St
Moreton, Alexander, Grocer, 231 King St
Moreton, Elizabeth, 202 Meeting St
Moreton, John, Planter, St James' Goose Creek, 26 miles
Morford, Willington & Co, Printers, Stationers, Editors of the Courier, 133 Broad St
Morgan, Benjamin, Boatman, 18 Middle St
Morgan, Benjamin, Boatman, Sullivan's Island
Morgan, C B., Carpenter, Hampstead
Morgan, Isaac C , Carpenter, Montague St
Morgan, James, Ship Carpenter, East Bay Cont'd
Morphey, Diego, Spanish Consul, 84 Meeting St
Morris, Christopher G , Clerk, 58 Wentworth St
Morris, Elizabeth, Mantua Maker, 6 Lamboll St
Morris, John, Overseer to Johnson, St James' Goose Creek, 23 miles
Morris, Lewis, Col., Planter, 115 Meeting St
Morris, Lewis, Jr., Planter, 115 Meeting St
Morris, Thomas, Jr , Clerk, 58 Wentworth St
Morris, Thomas, Merchant, 58 Wentworth St
Morrison, Ann B , Milliner, 9 Tradd St
Morrison, John, Capt , Merchant, 89 Tradd St
Morrison, John, Cooper, Shop, 119 East Bay St.
Morrison, Rebecca, Midwife, 63 Church St
Morrison, Richard F , Planter, Capers Island
Morrison, Spencer, Grocer & Boatman, Gadsden's N Whf.
Morrison, Spencer, Grocer & Boatman, 2 Elliott St Cont'd
Mortimer & Herron, Merchants (Counting House), Chisholm's Whf
Mortimer, Ann, Seamstress, John St

Mortimer, Edward, Merchant, 16 Anson St
Moser, Philip, Physician & Druggist Shop, 124 Broad St
Moser, Philip, Physician & Druggist, 8 Logan St
Moses, David, Auctioneer, 49 cor of King & Broad St
Moses, Fisher, Printer, 49 cor of King & Broad St
Moses, Henry, Shop Keeper, 51 East Bay St
Moses, Hetty, Mantua Maker, 8 Guignard St
Moses, Isaac C , Merchant, 273 King St.
Moses, Isaiah, Shop Keeper, 197 King St
Moses, Izrael, Cooper, 49 cor of King & Broad St
Moses, Levy, Store Keeper, 68 King St
Moses, Lyon, Merchant, 18 Swinton's Ln
Moses, Myer & Co , Vendue Master, Champneys St.
Moses, Myer, Vendue Master, 55 King St
Moses, Philip, Merchant, 49 cor of King & Broad St
Moses, Solomon, Shop Keeper, 194 King St
Motta, Emanuel de la, Vendue Master, 48 Tradd St
Motta, Sarah, 23 Tradd St
Motte, Abraham, Factor, 79 East Bay St.
Motte, Alexander B , Planter, St John's, Berkeley, 28 miles
Motte, Frances, Mrs , Planter, St James' Santee, 42 miles
Motte, Francis, Factor, 210 Meeting St
Motte, Mary, Planter, St John's, Berkeley, 28 miles
Mouatt, Mary, Planter, Boundary St
Moubray, William, Baker, 206 King St
Moulan, Peter, Shop Keeper, 252 King St
Moulin, Rose, Embroiderer, 55 Wentworth St
Moultrie, ——, Mrs , Planter, 6 Cumberland St
Moultrie, James, Physician, 11 St Philip's St
Moultrie, William, Planter, St John's, Berkeley, 43 miles
Mouren, Christopher, Boarding House, Mazyck St
Mouzon, Charles, Boot & Shoe Maker, 46 Church St
Muck, Philip, Professor of Music, 254 King St
Muckenfuss, Elizabeth, Widow, 53 King St
Muckenfuss, Henry, Brick Layer, Wentworth St
Muerset, John, Silversmith, 21 Broad St
Muir, Charles, Capt , 17 Meeting St
Muir, William, Merchant, Magazine St
Muir, William, Overseer to Robert Browne, John's Island
Mulligan, Barnard, Merchant, 3 Champneys St.
Mulligan, Francis, Justice of the Peace, Washington St
Mulligan, William, Ship Carpenter, 18 Wall St
Munch, Philip H , Grocer, Market St
Muncrieff, John, Carpenter, 9 East Bay Cont'd
Muncrieff, Susannah, 34 Hasell St
Munds, Israel, Rev , 6 Motte St
Munroe, Catharine, Midwife, 23 Society St.
Munroe, John, Mariner, 2 Champneys St

Munroe, John, Watchmaker, 36 cor of Elliott & East Bay St
Munroe, Robert, Cooper, 36 cor of Elliott St & Coate's Row
Murchison, M , Overseer to Dr Drayton, St Andrew's, 13 miles
Murden, Jeremiah, Merchant, 8 Stoll's Al
Murley & Naylor, Merchants, Store, 71 East Bay St
Murphy, ——, Boatman, Sullivan's Island
Murphy, Patrick, Grocer, Sullivan's Island
Murphy, Patrick, Shop Keeper, Cannon St
Murphy, Sarah, Boarding House, 41 East Bay St
Murray, Joseph James, Planter, Edisto Island
Murray, William, Overseer to J Manigault, St James' Santee, 29 miles
Murray, William, Ship Carpenter, 56 Anson St
Murrell, Martha, Planter, Christ Church Parish, 23 miles
Murrell, Robert, Clerk, 8 Kinloch Court
Mushett, John, Blacksmith, 71 Meeting St
Mushett, John, Blacksmith, Shop, 10 Ellery St
Myers, Michael, Shop Keeper, 24 Queen St.
Myers, Samuel, Tailor, 208 King St
Myrick, ——, Overseer to David Deas, St. John's, Berkeley, 26 miles
M[?]dray, Starling, Wheelwright, St Stephen's, 43 miles
M[?]us, Stephen, Overseer to Tennant, St James' Goose Creek, 21 miles
Nagel, Christian, Clerk, 14 Church St
Nagle, Elizabeth, Shop Keeper, 278 King St
Nankeville, George, Rev., St Thomas', 26 miles
Napier, Thomas, Vendue Master, 19 East Bay St
Naser, Casper, Tinman, 162 King St
Naser, Frederick, Cabinet Maker, 38 Meeting St
Nasted, Frederick, Cutler, 52 Meeting St
Nathan, ——, Mrs , Planter, St Stephen's, 50 miles
Nathan, Nathan, Shop Keeper, 124 King St
Nathan, Solomon, Shop Keeper, 62 East Bay St
Nathans, Nathan, Shop Keeper, 222 King St
Naylor, Thomas, Merchant, 71 East Bay St
Neal, Robert, Shop Keeper, King St Road
Nebbins, John, Mariner, 7 Society St
Neil, Charles, Merchant, 106 East Bay St
Nell, Jesse, Rope Walk, Hampstead
Nelson, Christopher, Mariner, 5 Lodge Al
Nelson, George, Grocer, Market St
Nelson, Isaac, Tailor, King St Road
Nelson, James S , Attorney, 18 Queen St
Nelson, Jane, Seamstress, 73 Church St.
Nelson, Mary, Seamstress, 288 King St
Nelson, William R , Mariner, 73 Church St
Nervis, Ann, Boarding House, 20 Union St
Nesbit, Maria, Planter, 13 King St
Nesbitt, Alexander, Planter, St John's, Berkeley, 24 miles
Nesbitt, James, Overseer, King St Road

Nettles, George, Planter, Wassmasaw, 40 miles
Nettles, James, Planter, Wassmasaw, 31 miles
Nettles, Joseph, Planter, Wassmasaw, 31 miles
Nettles, Malachi, Planter, Wassmasaw, 40 miles
Nettles, William, Planter, Wassmasaw, 31 miles
Netzell, John, Confectioner, 107 King St
Neufville, Ann, School Mistress, 168 King St.
Neufville, Isaac, Discount Clerk, National Bank, 4 Laurens St
Neville, Joshua, Cabinet Maker, 30 Tradd St
Nevin, Thomas, Mariner, 17 Wentworth St
Newell, Jesse, Planter, Meeting St Road
Newman, Charles, Grocer, 196 Meeting St
Newman, F C & Speirs, Grocers, 10 Archdale St
Newman, Thomas, Planter, St John's, Berkeley, 62 miles
Newton, Ann, Planter, 4 Gibbes St
Newton, Anthony, Butcher, Cannon St
Newton, Mary, Butcher, Cannon St.
Neyle, Susannah, Planter, 21 Tradd St
Nicholson, James, Attorney, Cannonborough Road
Nicholson, James, Gunsmith, 177 Meeting St
Nipper, David, Bookbinder, 100 King St
Nizer, Dominique, Physician, 111 King St
Nobbs, Samuel, Weigher to Custom House, St Philip's St Cont'd
Noble, John, Physician, 176 King St
Noiset, Philip, Gardner, Hampstead
Nol, James, Carpenter, 19 Mazyck St
Nolden, Eliabeth, Shop Keeper, 89 King St
Nopey, Peter, Carpenter, St James' Santee, 32 miles
Norris, John, Brick Layer, 27 George St
Norris, Joseph, Mariner, 18 Union St
Norris, Martha, Seamstress, 21 East Bay St
Norroy, John C F , Tobacconist, 20 George St
North & Webb, Factors (Counting House), John's Island
North, Susannah, Shop Keeper, 38 Tradd St
North, William, Teacher, 180 King St
Northrop, Amos P , Attorney, Office, 105 Broad St
Northrop, Amos P , Attorney, Pitt St
Norton, John, Shop Keeper, South Bay
Nowell, John, Merchant, 117 East Bay St
Nowell, John, Merchant, 3 Berresford St
Nowell, Thomas, Discount Clerk, S C Bank, 7 Mazyck St
Nugent, Margaret, Mantua Maker, 12 Lamboll St
Nye, Philip, Merchant, 30 Church St
Nye, Philip, Merchant, Store, 16 Broad St
Nyler, Ephraim, Millwright, John's Island
O'Conner, Thomas, Grocer, 1 King St
O'Donevan, M., School Master, 120 Broad St
O'Driscoll, Cornelius, Capt., Mariner, 21 Elliott St
O'Hara, Charles & Henry, Merchant, 144 Broad St
O'Hara, Charles, Merchant, 6 Smith's Ln
O'Hara, Daniel, Merchant, 144 Broad St
O'Harra, Henry, Merchant, 7 Cumberland St

O'Harra, S, Painter, 78 Meeting St
O'Hear, James, Planter, St Andrew's, 16 miles
O'Neal, Charles, Store Keeper, 195 King St
O'Neal, Elizabeth, Nurse, 2 Clifford St.
Oats, Mary, Seamstress, 7 Meeting St Cont'd
Oaxford, Mary, 4 Lynch's Ln
Oeland, John, Store Keeper, 30 East Bay Cont'd
Ogden, G W, Merchant Tailor, 121 East Bay
  Cont'd
Ogelvie, J A, Planter, Cannon St
Ogier, Lewis & Co, Factors (Counting House),
  Craft's Whf
Ogier, Lewis, Factor, 20 Friend St
Ogier, Thomas, Merchant, Tradd St
Ohlweiller, Michael, Grocer, Market St
Oliphant, David, Painter, 17 Berresford St
Oliver, James, Brick Layer, Vanderhorst St
Oliver, James, Carpenter, Neck Road
Oliver, Joseph, Merchant, Store, 94 East Bay
  Cont'd
Oliver, Stephen, Butcher, King St Road
Olman, Henry, Confectioner, 126 Queen St
Oring, Magnus, Mariner, 1 Trott St
Orrock, A M, Store Keeper, 195 King St
Osborne, C, Mrs, Planter, South Bay cor Legare
  St
Osborne, Charles, Factor, South Bay cor. Legare St
Otto, Hannah, Seamstress, 7 Society St
Ottolingin, Abraham, Store Keeper, 195 King St
Otzell, John, Grocer, 99 King St
Owen John, Factor, 27 Tradd St
Owens, David, Jr, Overseer to Isaac Edwards, St
  John's, Berkeley, 60 miles
Owens, David, Overseer to Isaac Edwards, St
  Thomas, 12 miles
Owens, William, Jr, Planter, St John's, Berkeley,
  58 miles
Owens, William, Planter, Wassmasaw, 28 miles
Packer, James, Planter, St. John's, Berkeley, 42
  miles
Packer, James, Planter, Wassmasaw, 43 miles
Packer, Robert, Planter, St John's, Berkeley, 45
  miles
Packer, Samuel, Planter, St John's, Berkeley, 42
  miles
Pagan & O'Neal, Merchants, 169 King St. Road
Pagat, Christian, Grocer, 2 St Philip's St
Page, William, Gardener, Race Ground
Pagels, Christopher, Shop Keeper, Wentworth St.
Paice, ——, Guilder, 7 Maiden Ln
Paine, Joseph, Clerk, 13 Hasell St
Paine, Stephen, Capt, Mariner, 13 Hasell St.
Paine, Thomas, Jr, Surveyor, 13 Hasell St
Paine, Thomas, Merchant, 13 Hasell St.
Palmer, Job, Carpenter, Wentworth St
Palmer, John, Capt, Planter, St. Stephen's, 53 miles
Palmer, John, Planter, St John's, Berkeley, 56
  miles

Palmer, John, Sergeant, City Guard, 44 Church
  St
Palmer, Joseph, Planter, St John's, Berkeley, 54
  miles
Palmer, Thomas, Planter, St Stephen's, 43 miles
Panty, George, Planter, St James' Santee, 42 miles
Paque, F G, Grocer, 106 King St Road
Parker, Ann, 28 King St
Parker, Benjamin, Planter, Daniel's Island, 8 miles
Parker, Catharine, Store Keeper, 119 King St Road
Parker, Florida, Seamstress, 26 Guignard St
Parker, George, Merchant, cor of Fitzsimons Whf
  & East Bay St
Parker, Isaac, Planter, 9 Legare St
Parker, John, Jr, Attorney, Pitt St
Parker, John, Merchant, 10 New St
Parker, John P, Overseer to Prioleau, St Stephen's,
  50 miles
Parker, John, Planter, Pitt St
Parker, Moses, Planter, St John's, Berkeley, 60
  miles
Parker, Phemas, Dyer, 89 Meeting St
Parker, Samuel, Merchant, 14 George St
Parker, Sarah, Planter, 9 Legare St
Parker, Thomas, Attorney, Federal Court, 33
  Meeting St
Parkinson, John, Coach Trimmer, 72 Church St
Parks, John, Blacksmith, 15 Trott St
Parks, Samuel, Boot & Shoe Store, 82 King St
  Road
Parmelo, David, Merchant, Stoll's Al
Parrot, Nancy, Planter, John's Island
Parsons, Joseph, Gardner, Hampstead
Pascal, Jeremiah, Printer, cor of Queen & Motte St
Paslet, Lewis, Cigar Maker, 3 Motte St
Patch, Nathaniel, Mariner, 6 Clifford's Al
Paterson, Hugh & Co, Insurance Brokers (Custom
  House), 36 East Bay St
Paterson, Hugh, Insurance Broker, 11 Meeting St
Paton, John, Clerk at Custom House, Magazine St
Patrick, Philip, Clerk, 205 King St. Road
Patterson, Ann, Widow, 1 Lynch's Ln
Patterson, James, Boatman, Sullivan's Island
Patterson, John, Planter, Edisto Island
Patterson, Samuel, Grocer, 126 Meeting St
Patterson, William, Overseer to H Horry, St
  James' Santee, 50 miles
Paul, John, Fruiterer, 28 Queen St
Paxton, Henry William, Merchant, 15 King St.
Payne, Letitia, Hampstead
Payne, W H, Stone Cutter, 76 King St Road
Payne, William, Commission Merchant & Vendue
  Master, 131 Broad St
Payne, William, Vendue Store, cor of Gillion St &
  East Bay St
Peagler, Henry, Planter, St Stephen's, 52 miles
Peak, John, Carter, 25 George St

Pearce, George B., Boot & Shore Store, 106 King St Road
Pearce, John, Overseer to Samuel Dubose, St Stephen's, 53 miles
Pearce, John, Planter, 6 St Michael's Al
Pearce, John, Planter, St Stephen's, 40 miles
Pearce, Moses, Planter, St Stephen's, 40 miles
Pearce, Reuben, Boot & Shoe Store, 106 King St Road
Pearce, Timothy, Planter, St Stephen's, 40 miles
Pease, Samuel, Shipwright, Christ Church Parish, 4 miles
Pebart, John, 19 George St
Pedrio, Peter, Carpenter, 8 Smith's Ln
Pedro, James, Overseer to Dupre's Estate, St James' Santee, 47 miles
Peigne, Lewis, Merchant, 7 Berresford St
Peignie, James L, Cabinet Maker, 7 Berresford St
Peircy, John F., Maj., Planter, St James' Santee, 28 miles
Pellissier, I B, Shop Keeper, 228 King St Road
Peltzer, Anthony, School Master, 3 Short St
Pemble, David, Merchant Tailor, 11 Tradd St
Pennall, James, Store Keeper, King St Road
Penner, John, Grocer, South Bay
Pennington, Edward, Lt, Revenue Cutter, 3 Blackbird Al
Penny, John, Miller, Mills, Boundary St
Pepoon, Benjamin, Grain Merchant, 15 Queen St
Pepoon, Joseph, Grocer, 234 King St Road
Pepoon, Joseph P, Grain Merchant & Grocer, 17 Friend St
Pepoon, Loring, Clerk, 16 Broad St
Pepper, John, Planter, Christ Church Parish, 4 miles
Percy, William, Rev, Pastor of St Philip's Church, East Bay St.
Perdue, John, Book & Shoe Maker, 2 Lamboll St
Perenchiel, Frances, Boarding House, 7 Archdale St
Perow, Joseph, Carpenter, 9 Clifford's Al
Perritt, James, Overseer to P Porcher, St John's, Berkeley, 52 miles
Perritt, Thomas, Overseer to Elias Horry, St James' Santee, 46 miles
Perrone, Caesar, Longitude Ln
Perroneau, William, Planter, South Bay
Perry, Ann, Planter, Bull St
Perry, Eleanor, Planter, King St. Road
Perry, Isabella, Midwife, 97 Queen St
Perry, Joseph, Clerk, Society St
Perry, Philip, Overseer, St. James' Goose Creek, 9 miles
Petch, Julius, Book Binder & Stationer, Store, 1 Broad St
Petch, Julius, Stationer & Book Binder, 8 Mazyck St.
Peter, Vincent, Grocer, 39 Elliott St
Peters, George, School Master, Orphan House

Peters, John, Mariner, 22 Pinckney St
Peters, William, Ship Carpenter, 26 Pinckney St
Peterson, Jonn, Clerk, King St Road
Petray, Lewis, Clerk, 180 King St Road
Petrie, George, Collector of Accounts, 9 Society St
Pett, Francois, Planter, 136 Meeting St
Peupel, ——, Madame, Boarding House, 111 Queen St
Peyre, Francis, Planter, St Stephen's Parish, 40 miles
Peyssou, Lewis, Goldsmith, 142 cor of Union & Broad St
Peyssoux, M R, Shop Keeper, 129 King St
Peyton, Richard Henry, Attorney, 58 King St Road
Pezant, J L, Grocer, Boundary St
Phelon, Edward M, Grocer, cor of Queen & Meeting St
Philbing, John, Planter, St James' Goose Creek, 10 miles
Philips, John, Grocer, 10 Union St
Phillips, Aaron, Shop Keeper, 78 King St Road
Phillips, Benjamin, Planter, St James' Santee, 26 miles
Phillips, E B, Shoe Store, 23 Elliott St
Phillips, Elizabeth, Planter, Christ Church Parish, 3 miles
Phillips, Gardner, Merchants, 97 East Bay St
Phillips, James, Shoe Store, 31 cor of St Michael's Al & Church St
Phillips, John, Cabinet Maker, 69 Queen St
Phillips, John, Painter, 8 Elliott St
Phillips, John, Rev, School Master, 15 Pinckney St
Phillips, Samuel, Clerk, 97 East Bay St
Phillips, William, Planter, St James' Santee, 26 miles
Phipps, William, Pilot, 2 Champneys St
Phyney, Josiah, Pilot, 2 Champneys St
Picault, Francois, Tailor, 22 Queen St
Pickenpack, John, Shop Keeper, 9 Coming St
Pickens, Ezekiel, Planter, St Thomas', 25 miles
Pickering, Martha, Planter, John's Island
Picket, Albert, Shop Keeper, 15 Motte St
Pierra, ——, Madame, Seamstress, 12 Ellery St
Pierre, Jerome, Planter, 29 Beaufain St
Pierson, Benjamin, Mariner, Boundary St.
Pierson, Ephraim, Shop Keeper, 5 Middle St
Pierson, James, Merchant, 12 Broad St
Pillans, R & J, Bakers, 110 Tradd St.
Pillot, Omne, Grocer, 6 Elliott St
Pillsbury, Amos, School Master, 4 Guignard St
Pillsbury, Samuel, Export Inspector, Custom House, 4 Anson St
Pilot, John, Grocer, King St Road
Pinckeny, Charles, Planter, 121 Meeting St
Pinckeny, Frances S, Planter, 14 Legare St
Pinckeny, Roger, Planter, 14 Legare St.
Pinckney, Charles Cotesworth, Gen, Planter, East Bay St

Pinckney, Roger, Planter, St. Thomas', 24 miles
Pinckney, Thomas, Jr, Capt, Planter, St James'
Santee, 42 miles
Pinckney, Thomas, Lt in U S Navy, 285 King St
Pinckney, Thomas, Maj, Planter, 40 George St.
Pinckney, Thomas, Planter, 1 Federal St
Piot, Ambrose, Hair Dresser, 108 King St Road
Pittman, William, Overseer to William Cordes, St
Stephen's, 50 miles
Placide, Alexander, Comedian, 194 Broad St
Plant, Henry, Ship Carpenter, 23 Beaufain St
Platt, Tilman, Planter, St James' Goose Creek, 21
miles
Plissounneau, John, Shop Keeper, 41 King St
Plumer, Mary, Boarding House, 5 Tradd St
Plummer, F John, Clerk, 1 Raper St.
Plummett, Antoine, Shop Keeper, 45 King St
Poague, Harriet, Planter, 73 Tradd St
Pogson, Millwood, Rev, Planter, St John's,
Berkeley, 27 miles
Pogson, Milwood, Rev, Planter, 8 New St
Pohl, Elias, Shop Keeper, 224 King St. Road
Poincignon, P A, Tinman, 12 Queen St
Poller, George, Planter, Four Holes
Pollock, Gavin, Shop Keeper, Wentworth St
Poppingham, ——, Planter, St James' Goose Creek,
20 miles
Porcher, George, Planter, St John's, Berkeley, 42
miles
Porcher, Isaac, Planter, St Stephen's, 50 miles
Porcher, P, Mrs., Planter, St John's, Berkeley, 37
miles
Porcher, Philip, Planter, St Stephen's, 50 miles
Porcher, Samuel, Capt, Planter, St. Stephen's
Parish, 53 miles
Porcher, Thomas, Planter, St John's, Berkeley, 45
miles
Porter, Abijah, Overseer to Legare, St John's,
Berkeley, 36 miles
Porter, Benjamin R, Cabinet Maker, 149 Meeting
St
Porter, John, Store Keeper, 157 King St Road
Porter, Lewis, Mariner, 22 Beaufain St.
Porter, William L, Merchant, (Counting House)
Chisolm's Whf
Porter, William L, Merchant, 17 Elliott St
Porter, William, Mariner, 28 Berresford's Al
Porter, William, Vendue Master, 56 Queen St
Porter, William, Vendue Master, Store, Champneys
St
Postell, Catharine, Seamstress, 24 St. Philip's St
Postell, Phillip, Planter, Mazyckborough
Postell, William, Planter, 39 George St
Postell, William V, Wheel Wright, 24 St. Philip's
St
Potter, John, Merchant, 19 Broad St
Potter, Washington, Merchant, 76 Church St.
Poujaud, Augustus, Grain Merchant, 112 Tradd St

Poulnot, Nicholas, Shoe Maker, 39 Meeting St
Poulton, Edward, Capt, Grocer, cor of Church St
Cont'd & Water St
Powell, John, Butcher, King St Road
Powell, William, Overseer to Beltser, St James'
Goose Creek, 22 miles
Power, Edward, Ship Chandler, 80 East Bay St
Power, James, Teacher, John's Island
Poyas, Elizabeth, Seamstress, 7 Lynch's Ln
Poyas, H. S, Planter & Physician, 29 Meeting St
Poyas, John E, Planter & Physician, 29 Meeting St
Poyas, John Lewis, Carpenter, Race Ground
Pratt, John, Capt, Mariner, 3 Laurens St
Pratt, S H, Store Keeper, King St Road
Preacher, Gimrod, Planter, Wassmasaw, 29 miles
Prebble, George, Capt., Mariner, 25 Queen St
Preguit, ——, Shoe Maker, 41 Meeting St
Prentice, ——, Fencing Master, 8 Ellery St
Prenville, Shop Keeper, 28 Pinckney St
Pressly, Margaret, Seamstress, 116 Meeting St
Pressly, William, Store Keeper, 177 King St Road
Prevost, Peter, Mariner, 14 Church St
Preyle, J F, Watch Maker, 12 Tradd St
Price, John, Grocer, 141 cor. of Union & Broad St
Price, Moses, Carpenter, Boundary St
Price, Thomas, Planter, Lynch St
Price, Thomas, Rev, Planter, John's Island
Price, William, Planter, 2 Orange St
Prieur, M E M, 61 Meeting St
Primrose, Robert, Merchant, 21 St Philip's St
Prince, Charles, Tinman, 246 King St Road
Prince, Clement L, Ferry, Lamprier's Point, Christ
Church Parish, 4 miles
Prince, John, Clerk, 68 cor Amen & Church St
Prince, Joseph, Planter, King St Road
Prince, William, Tailor, 10 Queen St
Pringle, James, Planter, 197 Broad St
Pringle, John Julius, Planter & Attorney, 93 Tradd
St
Pringle, Robert, Planter, 17 Archdale St
Pringle, Thomas & Co, Shop Keepers, 170 King
St Road
Prioleau, Elias, Clerk, 15 Ellery St.
Prioleau, Elizabeth H, Seamstress, 82 Queen St
Prioleau, James, Merchant, 49 Meeting St
Prioleau, Jane B, School Mistress, 15 Ellery St
Prioleau, John C, Planter, 38 Broad St
Prioleau, John, Clerk, 15 Ellery St
Prioleau, P G, Physician, 51 Broad St
Prioleau, Samuel, Attorney, 82 Queen St
Prioleau, Thomas, Physician, 82 Queen St
Prioleau, Thomas, Physician, St. John's, Berkeley,
39 miles
Prior, William, Lock Keeper of Santee Canal, St
John's, Berkeley, 36 miles
Pritchard, Benjamin, Printer, 30 Wall St
Pritchard, Joseph, Merchant, 50 King St Road
Pritchard, Paul Jr, Ship Carpenter, 37 Hasell St

Pritchard, Paul, Planter & Ship Carpenter, Daniel's Island, 7 miles
Pritchard, Susan, Planter, Christ Church Parish, 5 miles
Pritchard, William, Jr, Ship Carpenter, 2 Anson St
Pritchard, William, Sr, Ship Carpenter, 1 Pinckney St
Prizgar, Catharine, Seamstress, 70 Queen St
Procurer, John, Brick Layer, 100 Queen St
Proys, Peter, Clerk, 5 Champneys St
Purkey, Henry, Planter, St John's, Berkeley, 50 miles
Purse, William, Goldsmith, 117 Broad St
Purvis, William, Merchant, Hampstead
Pye, Joseph, Planter, St John's, Berkeley, 55 miles
Pye, Peter, Jr, Planter, St. John's, Berkeley, 53 miles
Pye, Peter, Planter, St John's, Berkeley, 55 miles
Pye, William, Planter, St John's, Berkeley, 56 miles
P[?]do, Ann, Planter, Capers Island
P[?]ing, Overseer to Colonel Shubrick, Bull's Island
P[?]o, William, Planter, Capers Island
Quash, Robert, Planter, 93 Broad St
Quash, Robert, Planter, St Thomas', 29 miles
Querard, Henry, Shop Keeper, 102 King St
Query, Thomas, Bookbinder, 13 Motte St
Quiggin, Mary, Boarding House, 7 Lodge Al
Quin, Thomas F, Grocer, Clifford St
Quinby, Joseph, Grocer, 46 Pinckney St
Quinlon, Michael, Grocer, cor of Mazyck & Magazine St
Quinnon, Dennis, Grocer, 62 King St
Raborn, David, Overseer to Lightwood, James Island
Rabson, Andrew, Tailor, 3 Union St
Racte, Jacob, Guardman, Cock Ln
Radcliffe, I W, Tailor, 96 Broad St
Radcliffe, L. C., Planter, cor of George & Meeting St
Rade, I C, Physician & Druggist, 226 King St
Railston, Robert, Overseer to Richard Jenkins, John's Island
Raine, Samuel, Pilot, 7 Stoll's Al
Raine, Thomas, Grocer, Hampstead
Ramadge, John, Sullivan's Island
Rambert, Elisha, Shoe Maker, St James' Santee, 36 miles
Ramilie, John, Overseer, St Andrew's, 14 miles
Ramily, Christopher, Carpenter, St James' Santee, 30 miles
Ramsay, David, Physician, 106 Broad St
Ramsay, John, Physician, Coming St
Ramsay, Mary, Widow, Hampstead
Randall, Elizabeth, Planter, 44 Meeting St.
Randell, George, Commission Merchant, 45 Tradd St

Ransier, Peter, Custom House Officer, Holmes' Lot, Church St Cont'd
Rantin, William, Grocer, 101 Church St
Rantling, Godfrey, Carpenter, Edisto Island
Rasdale, John William, Shop Keeper, 16 Hasell St
Ravenel, Paul, Planter, St John's, Berkeley, 44 miles
Ravenel, Rene, Planter, St John's, Berkeley, 42 miles
Ravenell, Catharine, Planter, 115 Broad St
Ravenell, Daniel, Deputy Secretary of State, 15 Queen St
Ravenell, Henry, Planter, St John's, Berkeley, 42 miles
Ravenell, Stephen, Planter, St. John's, Berkeley, 42 miles
Rawlinson, ----, Mrs, Planter, St Stephen's, 50 miles
Raworth, G F, Saddler, 76 Meeting St
Ray, Peter, Capt, Tavern Keeper, St John's, Berkeley, 45 miles
Ray, William, Rigger, Cock Ln.
Raynald, T, Secretary & Auditor, Union Insurance Co, 41 Church St
Read, Jacob, Gen, Planter, Charlotte St
Read, William, Physician & Planter, St John's, Berkeley, 30 miles
Reader, Philip, Shoe Store, 183 King St
Reainey, John, Shop Keeper, 5 Meeting St
Reardon, James, Tavern Keeper, St James' Goose Creek, 23 miles
Rechon, David, Tailor, 111 King St
Redhammer, J, Planter & Ferry Keeper, Strawberry, 30 miles
Redhammer, Peter, Overseer to Ball, St John's, Berkeley, 31 miles
Rees, L N, Physician, 10 Wall St
Reid, Alexander, Watch Maker, 128 King St
Reid, Elenor, Widow, Hampstead
Reid, George, Notary Public & Q U, 12 East Bay St
Reid, John & Co, Shoe Store, cor of Queen & King St
Reid, John, Wheel Wright, 173 Meeting St
Reid, Margaret, Boarding House, 1 Archdale St
Reid, Mary C, 36 Church St
Reid, William Warrant, Clerk, 1 Elliott St
Reigne, John, Baker, 9 Elliott St   ·
Reilly, George, Tavern Keeper, Sullivan's Island
Reilly, James, Saddler & Harness Maker, 28 Church St. Cont'd
Reily, Robert, Clerk, 27 Beaufain St
Reisher, Joseph, Cutler, 64 Church St
Remley, Barbara, Widow, Coming St
Remondo, Peter, Store Keeper, 67 King St
Remouit, L, Limner, 53 Meeting St
Remousin, Arnold, Planter, 29 Beaufain St
Remousin, Augustus, Planter, 29 Beaufain St

Remousin, Henry, Planter, 29 Beaufain St
Remousin, Paul D , Planter, 29 Beaufain St
Remousin, Pluton, Planter, 29 Beaufain St
Renaud, ——, Monsieur, Grocer, Sullivan's Island
Renauld, John, Grocer, 34 Tradd St
Rennie, George, Stone Cutter, 58 Broad St
Repault, Joshua, Planter, St John's, Berkeley, 33 miles
Reside, William, Cabinet Maker, Church St
Revell, George, Wharfinger, cor of Rutledge & Bull St
Revierre, John P , Shop Keeper, 123 Queen St
Reynolds & Ash, Coach Makers, 169 Meeting St
Reynolds, Benjamin, Planter, Wadmalaw Island
Reynolds, Christopher, Store Keeper, 48 Anson St
Reynolds, Jonathan, Planter, Wadmalaw Island
Reynolds, William, Planter, Wadmalaw Island
Rhederick, George, Carpenter, 94 Queen St
Rhind & Bruce, Merchants, Store, 108 East Bay St
Rhind, Eliza, Widow, Wentworth St
Rhodes & Otis, Factors, 13 East Bay St
Rhodes, Josiah, Grocer, Market St
Rhodes, Thomas, Mariner, 5 Anson St
Ria, Richard, Overseer to N Venning, Christ Church Parish, 7 miles
Ria, Samuel, Overseer to James Hibben, Christ Church Parish, 3 miles
Ricard, Francis, Grocer, 35 East Bay St
Ricardo, B I, Shop Keeper, 77 Church St
Rice, William, Clerk, 87 East Bay St
Rich, David, Overseer to Henry Findlay, St James' Santee, 42 miles
Richards, Elijah, Clerk, 30 Elliott St
Richards, Samuel, Printer, 19 East Bay Cont'd
Richardson, James, Mariner, Bull St
Richardson, Thomas, Merchant, 2 Wentworth St
Richbourg, James, Planter, St John's, Berkeley, 62 miles
Richmond, Elias, Carpenter, 94 Queen St
Richmond, John, Hair Dresser, 23 King St
Rico, Porto, Guardman, Wentworth St
Rigaud, Peter, Planter, Cannon St.
Riggs, Thomas, Mariner, 18 Guignard St
Righton, Florence, 25 Eliott St
Righton, Joseph, Cooper, 1 Water St
Righton, M'Cully, Cooper, 2 Water St
Rignet, ——, Madame, 27 Wall St
Riley, William, Planter, Wassmasaw, 28 miles
Ring, D A , Painter, 29 Broad St
Rish, George, Overseer to Hopkins, St James' Santee, 41 miles
Rivers, Charles, Planter, James Island
Rivers, Francis, 171 King St
Rivers, Francis, Jr , Planter, James Island
Rivers, Francis, Planter, 12 Union St
Rivers, Francis, Sr , Planter, James Island
Rivers, Gracia M , Clerk, Elliott St

Rivers, Gracia, Planter, St John's, Berkeley, 34 miles
Rivers, Henry S , Planter, James Island
Rivers, John, Grocer, South Bay
Rivers, Samuel, Ship Carpenter, 5 Water St
Rivers, Stiles, Planter, Edisto Island
Rivers, Susannah, Planter, James Island
Rivers, Thomas, Jr , Butcher, 11 Wentworth St
Rivers, William C., Planter, James Island
Rivers, William, Planter, James Island
Rivierre, Joseph, Blacksmith, 62 Church St
Roach, Nash, City Inspector, 2 Society St
Roach, William, City Treasurer, 2 Society St
Roberts, Catharine, Seamstress, 1 Clifford St
Roberts, Enos, Planter, St John's, Berkeley, 45 miles
Roberts, Francis, Saddler & Harness Maker, 116 King St
Roberts, Lynch, 107 Broad St
Roberts, Owen P , Carpenter, 37 Trott St
Roberts, Peter, Planter, St Stephen's, 40 miles
Roberts, Rebecca, Widow, 49 King St
Roberts, Robert, Planter, St Thomas', 10 miles
Roberts, William, Custom House Officer, 5 Anson St.
Roberts, William, Overseer, St John's, Berkeley, miles
Robertson, George, Store Keeper, Boundary St
Robertson, John, Carpenter, 9 East Bay Cont'd
Robertson, John, Factor, 47 Church St Cont'd
Robertson, John, Factor, Craft's Whf
Robertson, John, Miller, Christ Church Parish, 4 miles
Robertson, M A , Nurse at Orphan House, Boundary St
Robertson, Samuel & George, Store Keepers, cor Vanderhorst & King St
Robertson, Thomas, Ship Carpenter, 1 Pinckney S
Robinson & Banks, Tavern Keepers, 191 Meeting St
Robinson & Long, 176 King St
Robinson, James, Assistant at Work House, Magazine St
Robiou, Charles, Store Keeper, Boundary St
Roche, John, Grocer, 78 cor of Berresford's Al & Church St
Rochefort, Amelia, Store Keeper, 78 King St
Roddy, James, Merchant, 116 Tradd St
Roddy, James & Co , Merchants (Counting House Bailey's Whf
Roderigue, Abraham, Shop Keeper, 210 King St
Rodgers, Samuel, Musician, Wentworth St
Rogers, Christopher, 25 Tradd st
Rogers, Ralph, Clerk, 23 Church St Cont'd.
Rogers, Robert W., Planter, St. John's, Berkeley, miles
Rogers, Sarah, Planter, 23 Church St Cont'd
Rogers, Sarah, Planter, James Island

Rogers, Shadrack, Hunter, St Stephen's, 40 miles
Roh, Jacob, Blacksmith, 91 King St
Rolong, Robert, Brick Layer, 203 King St
Ropell, Elizabeth, Planter, 71 cor of Friend &
  Tradd St
Roper, Benjamin Dart, Planter, 1 Legare St
Roper, Benjamin, Planter, St Andrew's, 16 miles
Roper, Thomas, Col , Planter, 72 East Bay St
Roper, William, Planter, 5 East Bay St
Rose, ——, Mrs , Boarding House, Sullivan's Island
Rose, Ann, Seamstress, 37 Beaufain St.
Rose, George, Ship Chandler, 126 Broad St
Rose, Henry, Merchant, 42 Broad St
Rose, Hugh, Planter, 38 East Bay Cont'd
Rose, Hugh, Planter, Christ Church Parish, 20 miles
Rose, Hugh, Planter, State House Square
Rose, John S., Store Keeper & Clerk at Custom
  House, 9 Maiden Ln
Rose, Joseph, Tailor, 5 Whim Court
Rose, Rebecca, Planter, 6 Smith's Ln
Rose, William, Planter, John's Island
Ross, Ann, Widow, 1 Liberty St.
Ross, Benjamin, Carpenter, 67 W end of Tradd
  St
Ross, Daniel, Lumber Merchant, 65 W end of
  Tradd St
Ross, David, Tailor, 46 Broad St.
Ross, Eliza, Nurse, 6 Moore St
Ross, James, Clerk, 135 King St
Ross, William, Store Keeper, Boundary St
Rouchell, Louis, 28 Wall St
Roulain, Catharine, Seamstress, 33 King St
Rouse, Christopher, Brick Layer, cor of Market &
  Meeting St
Rouse, James, Coach Maker, cor of Market &
  Meeting St
Rouse, John, Clerk at Custom House, cor of
  Market & Meeting St
Rouse, Joshua, Tanner & Currier, cor of Market &
  Meeting St
Rouse, William, Intendant & Tanner, cor of Market
  & Meeting St
Rouse, William, Jr , Tanner, cor of Market &
  Meeting St
Rout, Catharine, School Mistress, 16 Friend St
Roux, Lewis, Merchant, 152 Meeting St
Roux, Lewis, Merchant, (Counting House) 37 East
  Bay St
Rowan, Charles, Planter, 2 Friend St
Rowand, Robert, Planter, 48 Meeting St
Rowed, John, Merchant, 24 East Bay St
Royall, William, Planter, James Island
Ruberry, John, Carpenter, Magazine St
Ruberry, William, Carpenter, 68 West End of Tradd
  St
Ruchet, Charles, Hatter, 69 East Bay St.
Rudd, Butlingham, Planter, Four Holes,
Rudd, Elias, Planter, Four Holes

Rudd, Ely, Planter, Four Holes
Rudd, Jane, Planter, Four Holes
Ruddock, George, Carpenter, St John's, Berkeley,
  32 miles
Ruddock, S A , Surveyor & Clerk of St Michael's
  Church, 20 King St
Ruhlman, George, Tailor, 3 Union St
Rumbly, John, Overseer to Thomas Horry, St
  Andrew's, 17 miles
Runnett, Sarah, Boarding House, 9 Berresford's Al
Rush, Joseph, Physician, John's Island
Russel, Benjamin, Brick Layer, 29 Guignard St
Russel, Daniel, House Carpenter, 24 Guignard St.
Russel, John, Blacksmith, 15 Wentworth St
Russell, John, Blacksmith Shop, Governor's Bridge
Russell, John, Hatter, 4 Broad St
Russell, Margaret, Shop Keeper, 106 King St
Russell, Nathaniel, Merchant, 23 Meeting St
Russell, William, Merchant (Counting House), 186
  East Bay St
Russell, William, Merchant, 23 Church St Cont'd
Russell, William, Overseer to H Horry, St James'
  Santee, 44 miles
Rutledge, Benjamin, Silversmith, 105 Tradd St
Rutledge, Charles, Planter, cor of Wentworth &
  Rutledge St
Rutledge, Edward, Planter, St John's, Berkeley, 28
  miles
Rutledge, Frederick, Planter, 61 Tradd St
Rutledge, Hugh, Judge, Court of Equity, 15 St
  Philip's St.
Rutledge, John, Clerk, 130 Broad St
Rutledge, John, Col , Planter, Wentworth St
Rutledge, Sarah, Planter, cor of St Philip's &
  Boundary St
Rutledge, William, cor George & Anson St
Rutureau, Charles, 110 King St
Ryan, Elizabeth, Widow, 72 East Bay St
Ryan, James, Register in Equity, Bull St
Ryan, Thomas, Merchant, 72 East Bay St
Sacal, ——, Overseer at Davidson's, Neck
Safford, John, Mariner, 13 Laurens St
Sallaneres, A H , Hudson St.
Salters, Thomas, Ship Joiner, 32 Guignard St
Salts, Susan, Boarding House, 2 Longitude Ln
Samora, Pierre, Shop Keeper, 80 Church St
Samory, Claude, Grocer, 19 Queen St
Sampson, Elias & Co, Grocers, 23 Mazyck St
Samuel, H , Watchmaker, 17 Society St
Sandall, John, Planter, St John's, Berkeley, 40
  miles
Sandall, John, Planter, St. Stephen's, 40 miles
Sanders, John, Planter, St Thomas & St Dennis, 11
  miles
Sanders, Martin, Planter, Christ Church Parish, 9
  miles
Sanders, Peter, Overseer to Marion, St John's,
  Berkeley, 43 miles

Sanders, William, Jr, Planter, St Thomas & St Dennis, 11 miles
Sanders, William, Planter, Christ Church Parish, 3 miles
Sanders, William, Sr, Planter, St Thomas & St Dennis, 10 miles
Sanderson, John, Grocer, Market St
Sandford, John, Grocer, 103 East Bay St
Sandford, John, Grocer, 68 East Bay St
Sandford, Moses, School Master, 1 Cumberland St
Sandhill, John, Planter, St James' Santee, 28 miles
Sandon, F A, Goldsmith, 134 Queen St
Sandoz, I F, Grocer, Market St
Santi, Angelo, Confectioner, cor King & Clifford St
Sargent, David, Shop Keeper, 244 King St
Sargent, John, Clerk, 231 King St
Sargent, John H, Printer & Proprietor of the Strength of the People, 113 Queen St
Sargent, John, Jr, Clerk, 241 King St
Sarrazin, Jonathan, Merchant, 10 Wentworth St
Sarsedas, David, Vendue Master, 36 George St
Sass, Jacob, Cabinet Maker, 35 Queen St
Saunders, I B, Clerk, King St Road
Savage, Ann, Store Keeper, 118 Broad St
Savage, Martha, Widow, cor of Broad & Savage Sts
Savaller, Joseph, Shop Keeper, 100 King St
Saverance, Robert, Shoe Maker, Christ Church Parish, 15 miles
Savowski, Peter, Shop Keeper, 9 Trott St
Sayer, Stephen, Ship Joiner, 33 Guignard St
Sayer, Stephen, Ship Joiner, Shop, 93 East Bay
Schackelford, Mary, Planter, St James' Santee, 41 miles
Schamfie, I H, City Guard, 6 Kinloch Court
Schem, J F, Watchmaker, 138 Broad St
Schirer, Elizabeth, Coming St
Schirer, John, Carpenter, Coming St
Schirmer, J E, Cooper, 95 Queen St
Schmidt, Elizabeth, Widow, Pitt St
Schmidt, John William, Physician, 3 Bedon's Al
Schnanenburger, Jacob, Grocer, 183 Meeting St
Schnell, John J, Grocer, 48 King St
Schodde, Margaret, Milliner, 117 King St
Schooler, Thomas, Gunsmith, St Stephen's, 52 miles
Schoulters, Abraham, Blacksmith, 26 Church St. Cont'd. cor Lynch's Ln
Schrierle, John M, Carpenter, 7 Friend St.
Schroder, John & Co, Grocers, Market St
Schroder, John A, Grocer, 49 Anson St.
Schroebel, John, Grocer, King St. Road
Schuffle, Thomas, Planter, St. Andrew's, 15 miles
Schultz, Christopher, Grocer, East Bay St
Schultz, John, Overseer to Mrs Thompson, St James' Santee, 32 miles
Schutt, Margaret D, Merchant, 6 Coming St.

Schwartz, John, Grocer, Clerk, Church St Cont'd cor Lynch's Ln
Scott, Ann, Shop Keeper, 38 Queen St
Scott, Benjamin, Overseer to Daniel Mazyck, St John's, Berkeley, 40 miles
Scott, Elizabeth, Planter, James Island
Scott, George, Carpenter, 9 Trott St
Scott, James, Vendue Master, 101 Tradd St
Scott, James, Vendue Master, Store, Champneys St
Scott, John, Overseer to Joseph Jenkins, Edisto Island
Scott, Thomas, Merchant, 4 Church St
Scott, W M, Merchant, 76 Meeting St
Scott, William, Millwright, 1 Beaufain St
Scott, William, Planter, Christ Church Parish, 3 miles
Scott, William, Store Keeper, King St Road
Scovil, Oliver, Grocer, 11 Union St
Screven, Thomas, Planter, Hampstead
Screven, Thomas, Planter, St James' Goose Creek, 8 miles
Seaborn, Thomas George, Ship Carpenter, 31 Berresford's Al
Seabrook, Ann, Planter, Wadmalaw Island
Seabrook, Benjamin, Planter, Edisto Island
Seabrook, Gabriel, Planter, Edisto Island
Seabrook, Joseph B, Planter, Edisto Island
Seabrook, Joseph, Planter, Edisto Island
Seabrook, Mary, Planter, Edisto Island
Seabrook, Thomas Bannister, Planter, Edisto Island
Seabrook, William, Planter, Edisto Island
Sealy, David, Overseer to Robert Quash, Christ Church Parish, 25 miles
Seare, Joseph, Wheel Wright, 72 Church St
Seares, Isaac, Mariner, Neck Road
Seavay, John, Butcher, King St Road
Secrets, Martin, Capt, Mariner, 24 Motte St
Segerstrom, Jane, Grocer, 4 Elliott St Cont'd
Seigbert, Joseph, Grocer, 19 Middle St
Seixas, Isaac M, Shop Keeper, 195 King St
Semonet,——, Planter, 29 Church St
Semyen, Amarinthia, Planter, cor Stoll's Al & Church St
Sereches, ——, Mrs, Planter, St. Andrew's, 19 miles
Sergeant, P T, Grocer, 7 East Bay St
Severs, Abraham, House Carpenter, 37 Pinckney St
Seyle, Samuel, Saddler & Harness Maker, 199 King St
Seyler, Priscilla, Widow, Coming St
Seymore, Isaac, Capt, Mariner, 29 King St
Shackelford, William F, Planter, St John's, Berkeley, 42 miles
Shand, Robert, Inspector at Custom House, 7 Linguard St
Sharp, John, Block & Pump Maker, 75 East Bay St
Shaw, Eliza, Seamstress, 13 Trott St
Shaw, Mary, 78 Meeting St

Shaw, William, Cooper, 95 Queen St
Shaw, William D , Merchant, East Bay cor Blakes Whf
Shaw, William D , Merchant Store, 32 East Bay St
Shecut, J L E W , Physician, President of Homespun Co , 216 King St
Sheergold, Sarah, Planter, Edisto Island
Sheerman, James, Capt , Mariner, 14 East Bay St
Sheerwood, John, Planter, Wassmasaw, 7 miles
Sheley, Michael, Cock Ln.
Shepheard, Thomas Radcliffe, Planter, King St Road
Shepherd, James, Harness Maker, 10 Coming St
Shepherd, Thomas, Rigger, Mazyckborough
Sheppard, Christiana, Widow, 34 Pinckney St
Sheppard, Rachel, Seamstress, 112 King St
Shervin, James, Clerk, Lucas' Mills, Boundary St
Sherwood, Barnet, Brick Layer, 117 Meeting St
Shields, Henry, Clerk, 231 King St
Shinar, John, Grocer, 151 Meeting St
Shirer, John, Gunsmith, 177 Meeting St
Shirras, Alexander, Merchant, 21 Church St.
Shirtliff, William, Merchant, 12 Laurens St
Shiveley, George, Grocer, 117 Meeting St
Shoolbred, James, Planter, cor Legare & Lamboll Sts
Shorthouse, Thomas, Merchant, 6 Hasell St
Shrewsbury, Edward, Ship Carpenter, 18 Wentworth St
Shrewsbury, Jeremiah, House Carpenter, 12 Guignard St
Shrewsbury, S , Clerk, S C Bank, cor of East Bay & Laurens St
Shubrick, Richard, Physician, Neck Road
Shubrick, Thomas, Col , Planter, Neck Road
Shubrick, Thomas, Jr , Neck Road
Sibley, Joseph, Grocer, 40 East Bay St
Sickles, Duncan, Deputy Sheriff, 7 St Michael's Al
Signus, John, Hair Dresser, 93 East Bay St
Sigwald, Thomas, Cabinet Maker, 9 Berresford St
Sillman, James, Boot & Shoe Maker, 31 Broad St
Simmons, Andrew, Boot & Shoe Maker, 15 Tradd St
Simmons, Charles, Weigher at Custom House, 8 Cumberland St
Simmons, Francis, Planter, John's Island
Simmons, James, Rev., Pastor, St Philip's Church, 96 Church St
Simmons, John, Clerk, 95 Tradd St
Simmons, John, Overseer to John Geyer, St Thomas & St. Dennis, 17 miles
Simmons, Joseph, Grocer, cor of East Bay & Broad St.
Simmons, Sarah Ruth, Planter, 60 Tradd St
Simmons, Thomas, Assistant Steward, Marine Hotel, Queen St
Simmons, Thomas, Planter, John's Island

Simmons, William, Tailor, 2 Bull St
Simms, James, King St Road
Simms, William, Carpenter, Hudson St
Simms, William, Store Keepers, King St Road
Simons, Anthony, Factor, Washington St
Simons, Benjamin B , Physician, 15 East Bay St
Simons, Edward, Planter, St John's, Berkeley, 36 miles
Simons, Hannah, Seamstress, 14 Pinckney St
Simons, Harry, Keeper of U S Arsenal, cor of Smith & Wentworth St
Simons, I Bee, Factor, (Counting House), Craft's Whf
Simons, James, Planter, St Andrew's, 11 miles
Simons, John, Mariner, 14 Pinckney St.
Simons, Joseph, Physician, 176 King St.
Simons, K & Sons, Factors, (Counting House) Chisolm's Whf
Simons, Keating, Factor, 4 Orange St
Simons, Keating Lewis, Attorney, 3 Orange St
Simons, Maurice & Lewis, Factors, 4 Orange St
Simons, Sampson, Shop Keeper, 195 King St
Simons, Samuel, Shop Keeper, 193 King St
Simons, Simon, Mariner, 3 Hard Al
Simons, Susannah, Planter, 10 Liberty St
Simpson, John, Planter & Justice of Peace, Magazine St
Simpson, Michael, Shop Keeper, 178 King St
Simpson, Preeson, Dentist, Cannonborough Road
Simpson, William, Planter, 2 Minority St
Simpson, William, Planter, St John's, Berkeley, 36 miles
Sims, Elizabeth, Boarding House, 32 Berresford's Al
Sims, James, Overseer to Samuel Porcher, St John's, Berkeley, 55 miles
Sinclair, Alexander, Merchant, 18 East Bay St
Sinclair, Alexander, Merchant, 19 East Bay St
Singletary, James G , Clerk, 35 Church St Cont'd
Singletary, John Jink, Planter, Four Holes
Singletary, Joseph, Overseer to Wigfall, St Thomas & St Dennis, 18 miles
Singletary, Michael, Planter, Four Holes
Singleton, Benjamin, Crockery Store, 9 Broad St
Singleton, Mary, Boarding House, 3 Trott St
Sinkclair, Charles, Planter, St Stephen's, 50 miles
Sinkclair, Margaret, Planter, St John's, Berkeley, 60 miles
Sinkclair, William, Planter, St. John's, Berkeley, 60 miles
Sisk, Susannah, Nurse, 70 Church St
Skillings, John, Planter, St John's, Berkeley, 50 miles
Skirving, Bethia, Planter, 11 George St
Skirving, C , Mrs , 16 Church St Cont'd
Skirving, William, Col , Planter, 17 Church St. Cont'd
Skrine, Tacitus G , Clerk, 274 King St

Slade, Labin, Mariner, 49 Pinckney St
Slade, Margaret, Boarding House, 8 Stoll's Al
Slawson, Nathaniel, Baker, 90 King St.
Slowick, John, Grocer, 282 King St
Slowman, Mary, Seamstress, 131 East Bay St
Smallwood, Richard, Custom House Officer, 21
Pinckney St
Smart, John T, Boot & Shoe Maker, 7 St
Michael's Al
Smart, Samuel, Planter, St Andrew's, 8 miles
Smart, William, Overseer to Bowman's Estate, St
James' Santee, 50 miles
Smeiser, Frederick, Grocer, 46 cor of Trott &
Anson St
Smerdon, Elias, Secretary & Auditor of S C
Insurance Co., 1 Raper St
Smerdon, Henry, Broker, 1 Raper St
Smerdon, Henry, Broker, Office, 23 East Bay St
Smiezer, Henry, Butcher, Mazyckborough
Smilie & Patterson, Grocer, East Bay, Store, 104
East Bay St
Smilie, Susannah, Planter, 11 Legare St
Smith, ——, Shop Keeper, 191 King St
Smith, Agnes, 10 Mazyck St
Smith, Agnes, Boarding House, 7 Broad St
Smith, Allen, Planter, Four Holes,
Smith, Ann, Planter, 7 St Philip's St
Smith, Benjamin, Planter, 15 Church Cont'd
Smith, Caroline, Mantua Maker, 1 Price's Al
Smith, Caroline, Mantua Maker, 6 Wentworth St
Smith, Charles, Planter, St James' Goose Creek, 18
miles
Smith, Charles, Planter, Wassmasaw, 29 miles
Smith, Christopher, Keeper of Baan, 132 King St
Smith, Daniel, City Assessor & Enquirer, 4 Society
St
Smith, Eliza, Shop Keeper, 161 King St
Smith, Ezekiel, Planter, Four Holes
Smith, Francis, Planter, St Stephen's, 40 miles
Smith, George, Carpenter, Cannon St
Smith, George, Merchant, 40 Anson St
Smith, George, Overseer to P Thompson, St
John's, Berkeley, 60 miles
Smith, Henry Middleton, Planter, St James' Goose
Creek, 18 miles
Smith, Henry, Shop Keeper, 161 King St.
Smith, Hugh, Merchant, 7 Broad St
Smith, James, Boot & Shoe Maker, 3 Broad St
Smith, James, Capt , Planter, Christ Church Parish,
6 miles
Smith, James, House Carpenter, 11 Beaufain St
Smith, James, Overseer to W Bull, St Andrew's,
12 miles
Smith, James, Rigger, 21 Motte St
Smith, Jane, Planter, 21 Friend St
Smith, John, Boarding House, 25 Union St
Smith, John, Boarding House, 7 Union St.
Smith, John, Butcher, King St Road

Smith, John, Clerk, 18 East Bay St
Smith, John, Clerk, St Philip's Church, 84 Queen
St
Smith, John M , Merchant, 5 Orange St.
Smith, John, Planter, King St ,
Smith, John, Planter, Wassmasaw, 29 miles
Smith, John, School Master, 187 Broad St
Smith, John, Ship Carpenter, Washington St
Smith, Joseph, Boatman, Sullivan's Island
Smith, Josiah, President of National Branch Bank,
40 Anson St
Smith, Mary, Mantua Maker, 19 Middle St
Smith, Mary, Planter, 7 Coming St.
Smith, Mary, Widow, 71 Church St
Smith, Mathew, Planter, Four Holes
Smith, Neomi, Planter, 8 Coming St
Smith, O'Brien, Maj , Planter, 11 Church St
Smith, P M S , Planter, St Thomas & St Dennis,
16 miles
Smith, Paul, Clerk, 60 Meeting St
Smith, Peter, Factor, 28 Mazyck St
Smith, Peter, Planter, 290 King St
Smith, Peter, Planter, St Andrew's, 16 miles
Smith, Peter, Planter, St Stephen's, 40 miles
Smith, Peter, Planter, W end South Bay
Smith, Rebecca, Boarding House Keeper, 16 Broad
St
Smith, Rebecca, Planter, 71 Queen St
Smith, Richard, Cabinet Maker, 28 Meeting St
Smith, Robert, Ship Carpenter, Sullivan's Island
Smith, Samuel, Attorney, 105 Broad St.
Smith, Samuel, Factor, 39 Broad St
Smith, Samuel, School Master, S.C Society,
Meeting St
Smith, Samuel, Sr , Grocer, 4 Champneys St
Smith, Sarah, Planter, 7 Coming St
Smith, Sarah, Widow, 22 Church St
Smith, Thomas Rhett, Planter, 12 Meeting St
Smith, Thomas, Rigger, 9 Trott St
Smith, Thomas Young, Clerk, 21 Friend St
Smith, Walter, Overseer to Faussoux, St John's,
Berkeley, 40 miles
Smith, Whitford, Jr , Brick Layer, 56 Church St
Smith, Whitford, Sr , Grocer, 56 Church St
Smith, William, Boot & Shoe Maker, 3 Broad St
Smith, William, Carpenter, 32 Wall St
Smith, William Loughton, Planter, 82 East Bay cor
Amen St
Smith, William, Mariner, 2 Lodge Al
Smith, William, Merchant, 42 Pinckney St
Smith, William, Planter, Four Holes
Smith, William, Prothonotary, Bull St
Smith, William, Ship Carpenter, Washington St
Smizer, Hannah, Widow, 48 Church St
Smylie, Andrew, Grocer, 39 Hasell St
Smylie, John, Planter, Wadmalaw Island
Smyth, John & Co., Store Keepers, King St. Road
Smyth, John, Planter, 8 George St

Snell, Frederick, Planter, Wassmasaw, 28 miles
Snell, John, Planter, Four Holes
Snowden, Ann, Boarding House, 129 Broad St
Snowden, C B , Attorney, 129 Broad St.
Snowden, W E , Clerk, 129 Broad St
Solan, Timothy, Store Keeper, Monck's Corner
Sollee, John, City Theatre, 24 Church St
Solomon, Mark, Shop Keeper, 127 King St
Solomons, Aaron, Shop Keeper, 161 King St
Solomons, Alexander, Shop Keeper, 177 King St
Solomons, Chapman, Shop Keeper, 188 King St
Solomons, Solomon, Shop Keeper, 128 King St
Somarsall, Thomas, Insurance Broker (Custom
    House), 26 East Bay St
Somarsall, Thomas, Insurance Broker, 45 George
    St
Somarsall, William, Merchant, John's Island
Sommers, James, Planter, 2 Friend St
Sothrop, Seth, Merchant, 109 East Bay Cont'd
Soults, Ludrick, Overseer to Ball, St John's,
    Berkeley, 35 miles
Sparkman, William, Overseer to Henry Izard, St
    John's, Berkeley, 55 miles
Sparks, Rachael, Seamstress, 39 Queen St
Sparrow, James, Butcher, Cannon St
Spears, Mary, School Mistress, 3 Society St
Spears, Thomas, Lock Keeper, Santee Canal, St
    John's Berkeley, 45 miles
Speisseger, J , Musical Instrument Maker, cor
    Hasell & Anson St
Spelzer, Archibald, Carpenter, 123 Meeting St
Spencer, George, Brick Layer, Hampstead
Spencer, J H., 16 Queen St
Spencer, Sebastian, Shoe Maker, Hampstead
Spidle, Elizabeth, Widow, 3 Clifford St
Spidle, John George, Carpenter, 24 Archdale St
Spiers, Christian, Grocer, 10 Archdale St.
Spindlar, Mary, Nurse, Orphan House
Spring, John, Messenger to the Governor, Powder
    Inspector & Arsenal Keeper, 4 Blackbird Al
Sprott, ——, Overseer to Thomas Mathews, John's
    Island
St Memin, ——, Limner, 90 Church St
Stack, Thomas, Overseer to T Barksdale, Christ
    Church Parish, 22 miles
Stafford, James, Mariner, East Bay St
Stagg, J D , Merchant, 129 Broad St
Staggers, George, Planter, Wassmasaw, 33 miles
Stan, Joseph G , Grocer, Market St
Stanyard, Ann, Planter, John's Island
Star, Anthony, Grocer, 92 East Bay St
Starling, Maxfield, Carpenter, St James' Santee, 32
    miles
Steadman, Charles I., Sheriff, Charleston District,
    Mazyckborough
Steadman, Thomas, Book Keeper, State Bank,
    Mazyckborough
Steel, John, Weaver, Orphan House

Steele, John, Shop Keeper, 159 King St
Steelman, George, Planter, St Stephen's, 40 miles
Steiker, John, Grocer, Market St
Steinman, C W , Baker, Boundary St
Stent, Ann, Planter, James Island
Stent, John, Jr , Carpenter, Mazyck St
Stent, John, Sr , Planter, James Island
Stent, Robert, Carpenter, Wentworth St
Stephens, William, Clerk of Market, 11 Laurens St
Stevens, ——, School Master, 5 Cumberland St
Stevens, Charles, Planter, St Stephen's, 50 miles
Stevens, Daniel, Planter, 30 George St
Stevens, Daniel, Supervisor's Office, 24 Tradd St
Stevens, Elizabeth, Widow, 36 Anson St
Stevens, Jervis H , City Sheriff, 64 Tradd St
Stevens, John, Mariner, 17 Wentworth St
Stevens, Thomas, Coroner, Charleston District, 33
    East Bay St
Stevens, William S , Physician, 19 King St
Stevens, William W , Physician, Shop, 43 East Bay
Steward, Charles, Scrivener, 1 Wentworth St
Steward, E M , Seamstress, 59 Queen St.
Stewart, Alexander, Bookbinder, 1 Broad St
Stewart, Ann, School Mistress, 12 Moore St
Stewart, Catharine, Seamstress, 13 Berresford St
Stewart, Robert, Planter, 8 Friend St
Stewart, Samuel, Clerk, 231 King St
Stewart, William, Overseer to Heyward, St Thomas
    & St Dennis, 28 miles
Stewart William, School Master, 44 Church St
Stiff, Richard, Clerk, Magazine St
Stiles, Jane, Planter, James Island
Stine, Samuel, Tailor, 15 Meeting St
Stocker, Henry, Boat Builder, 57 Anson St
Stocker, Henry, Boat Builder, East Bay St
Stoll, Catharine, Seamstress, Magazine St
Stone, Charles, Planter, James Island
Stone, Isabella, Widow, Coming St
Stone, John, Overseer to Motte, St James' Santee,
    42 miles
Stone, Margaret, Seamstress, 13 Berresford's Al
Stone, William, Musician, 55 East Bay St
Stoney, John, Merchant, 32 East Bay Cont'd
Stoops, B T , Shoe Maker, Mazyck St.
Stopes, Hendrick, Gardner, James Island
Street, Alexander, Charleston Neck
Strobel, Jacob, Butcher, Hampstead
Strobel, Martin, Attorney, 8 Meeting cor Smith's
    Ln
Strobell & Aspinall, Merchants (Counting House),
    147 Broad St
Strobell, Benjamin, Merchant, 42 Broad St
Stroble, John, Tanner, 118 Meeting St
Stroble, Lewis, Capt , City Guard, 47 East Bay St
Strohecker, John, Blacksmith, 156 Meeting St
Stromer, Henry M , Grocer, 64 Meeting St
Strother, Thomas, Planter, Wassmasaw, 32 miles
Stroup, Jacob, Carpenter, 2 Berresford St

132

Stuart, Normand, Grocer, Bull St
Sturges & Lovell, Merchants, (Counting House),
Craft's Whf
Sturgis, Josiah, Merchant, 42 Church St Cont'd
Suares, Jacob, Rev , Pastor of Hebrew
Congregation, 21 Hasell St
Suau, Peter, Merchant, Bull St
Sucker, Christopher, Butcher, King St Road
Sullivan, Daniel, Clerk, 36 Queen St
Sullivan, Timothy, Vendue Master, 38 Anson St
Sullivan, Timothy, Vendue Master, Exchange St
Sully, Mathew, Comedian, 7 W end Savage St
Sully, Mathew, Sr., Custom House Officer, 7 King
St
Surran, Francis, Grocer, 11 Anson St
Sutcliff, Elias, Four Mile House
Sutcliffe, J E , Carpenter, 7 Berresford St
Suwarrez, Isaac, Shop Keeper, 244 King St
Swain, Luke, Pilot, 7 Stoll's Al
Swain, Rebecca, 5 Stoll's Al
Swan, Robert, Carpenter, 133 Meeting St
Swan, William John, Clerk, East Bay St
Sweeney, Bryan, Tavern Keeper, Watson's Garden,
King St Road
Sweeney, Esther, Seamstress, 3 Whim Court
Sweeney, James, Merchant, 6 Mazyck St
Sweeney, Patrick, Overseer to W Pritchard, Christ
Church Parish, 5 miles
Sweeney, Thomas, Clerk, 36 Queen St
Swift, William, Shop Keeper, 140 King St
Swinton, Hugh, Factor, Cannon St
Swinton, Hugh, Planter, Long Island
Swinton, James, Factor, (Counting House)
Vanderhorst's Whf
Swinton, James, Factor, Hampstead
Swinton, Susannah, 75 Meeting St
Switzer, John R , Saddler & Harness Maker, 218
King St
Syfan, Charles, Gardner, Race Ground
Syfan, John, Butcher, King St Road
Taggart, Mary, Widow, 17 Meeting St
Talbot, Mathew, School Master, St Thomas', 21
miles
Taraff, Philip, Rigger, Cock Ln
Tardy, Alexander, Tinman, 131 Queen St
Tate, James, Capt , Mariner, 114 Queen St
Tate, William, Carpenter, St James' Goose Creek,
10 miles
Tatem, William, Clerk, 73 East Bay St
Taussiger, Margaret, Widow, 4 Water St
Taylor, Alexander, Capt , Mariner, 8 Blackbird Al
Taylor, Barnard, Blacksmith, St. Stephen's, 46
miles
Taylor, Charlotte, Boarding House, 19 Berresford
St
Taylor, Elizabeth, School Mistress, 71 Queen St.
Taylor, Francis, Accountant, Friend St
Taylor, John, Mariner, 22 Berresford St

Taylor, John, Planter, St John's, Berkeley, 40 miles
Taylor, Joseph, Brick Layer, 19 Coming St
Taylor, Joseph, Capt , Mariner, 3 Anson St
Taylor, Josiah, Factor, 10 Lamboll St
Taylor, Margaret, Seamstress, 8 Blackbird Al
Taylor, Maria, Mantua Maker, 4 Smith's Ln
Taylor, Paul, Brick Layer, St Stephen's, 46 miles
Taylor, Paul, Carpenter, Cannon St
Taylor, Sarah, Planter, St John's, Berkeley, 40
miles
Taylor, William M , Planter, Beaufain St
Taylor, William M , Planter, Folly Island
Taylor, William Malcolm, Planter, Beaufain St W
end
Teasdale, John & Son, Merchants, 2 East Bay St
Teasdale, John & Son, Store, 4 East Bay St
Teasdale, Richard, Clerk, 2 East Bay St
Telfer, Robert, Clerk, 96 Church St
Temple & Peters, Shoe Store, 187 Meeting St
Templer, John, Neck Road
Tennant, Charles, Physician, St James' Goose
Creek, 21 miles
Tennant, James, Tailor, 9 Wentworth St
Tennant, Robert, Clerk, 92 Church St
Tew, Charles, Q U & Notary Public, Wentworth
St
Thackam, Judith, Seamstress, 94 Meeting St
Tharin, Lewis, Sr , Candle Manufacturer, Columbus
St
Thayer, Ebenezer, Broker, 49 Tradd St , Office,
Elliott St
Theus, Martha, Planter, John's Island
Theus, Mary, Planter, St John's, Berkeley, 60 miles
Theus, Simeon, Collector, Custom House, 239 King
St
Thick, William, Boat Builder, 32 Pinckney St
Thomas, ——, Machinist at Theatre, New St
Thomas, Ann, Planter, St Stephen's, 50 miles
Thomas, Bridget, Seamstress, 8 Archdale St
Thomas, Francis, Discount Clerk, Branch Bank, 29
Archdale St
Thomas, James, Clerk, Lynch St
Thomas, John, Grocer, 37 Broad St
Thomas, John, Hair Dresser, 178 Meeting St.
Thomas, John, Merchant, 106 East Bay St
Thomas, John, Shop Keeper, 263 King St
Thomas, Joseph, Coach Maker, 21 Hasell St
Thomas, Mary L , Planter, 12 King St
Thomas, Samuel, Clerk, 177 King St.
Thomas, Samuel, Physician, 14 George St
Thomas, Sarah, Shop Keeper, 23 East Bay St
Thompson, ——, Mrs , 24 King St
Thompson, Aaron, Brick Layer, 36 Trott St
Thompson, Abiel, School Master, Christ Church
Parish, 3 miles
Thompson, George, Mariner, 10 Anson St
Thompson, Hugh, Overseer to Admiral Graves, St
John's, Berkeley, 32 miles

Thompson, James B., Shop Keeper, 44 Tradd St
Thompson, James, Boarding Officer, Port of
Charleston & Keeper, Carolina Coffee House, 114
Tradd St. cor Bedon's Al
Thompson, Jane, Planter, James Island
Thompson, John, Coach Maker, 54 Meeting St
Thompson, John, Mariner, 6 Anson St
Thompson, Leslie, Tailor, 95 Church St
Thompson, Lewis, Planter, St. James' Goose Creek,
20 miles
Thompson, M , Overseer to Estate of Lee, St
John's, Berkeley, 27 miles
Thompson, Margaret, Shop Keeper, Beaufain St.
Thompson, Rebecca, Planter, Cannonborough Road
Thompson, William, Boot & Shoe Maker, 29 St
Philip's St
Thompson, William, Ship Carpenter, 108 East Bay
St
Thorn, J G , Sail Loft, Beale's Whf
Thorne, John G , Sail Maker, 10 Beadon's Al
Thornhill, John, Merchant, 119 King St
Thornley, James, Planter, Wassmasaw, 33 miles
Thornley, John, Planter, Wassmasaw, 28 miles
Thornton, Catharine, Seamstress, George St
Threadcraft, Bethel, Watchmaker, 235 King St
Thrower, Evan, Overseer to Peter Gaillard, 60 miles
Thwing, Edward, Grocer, 73 Meeting St
Thynnes, William, Santee Canal Store Keeper, St
John's, Berkeley, 33 miles
Times, Joseph, Guardman, 1 Society St
Timmons, William, Merchant, Hampstead
Timothy, Ann, School Mistress, 69 Tradd St
Timrod, Henry, Tobacconist, St Philip's St Cont'd.
Tobias, Judith, Widow, 202 King St
Todd, John, Jr , Planter, James Island
Todd, John, Sr , Planter, James Island
Todd, Richard, Clerk, 118 East Bay St
Tofel, John, Confectioner, 80 Meeting St
Tongue, Susannah, Planter, 45 Church St Cont'd
Toomer, Ann, Widow, 7 Legare St
Toomer, Anthony, Physician, Christ Church Parish,
10 miles
Toomer, Henry B , Factor, Cannonborough Road
Torry, E & Co , Block & Pump Makers, 80 East
Bay St
Torry, Ezekiel, Pump & Block Maker, 277 King St
Torry, William, Capt , Mariner, 7 New St
Tourrell, Richard, Boarding House, Sullivan's
Island
Tovey, Henry, Block & Pump Makers, 100 East
Bay St
Tovey, Henry, Pump & Block Maker, 38 Society
St
Townsend, Daniel, Planter, Edisto Island
Townsend, John, Planter, Wadmalaw Island
Tracey, John, Overseer to J Geddes, St Andrew's,
16 miles
Trenholm, George, Capt , Mariner, Prioleau's Whf

Trenholm, William, Jr , Merchant, Meeting St Road
Trenholm, William, Merchant, Prioleau's Whf
Trescott, Edward, Planter, 103 Broad St
Trescott, John, Physician, 108 Broad St
Trescott, William, Attorney, 108 Broad St
Trezyant, Peter, Discount Clerk, State Bank, 4
Stoll's Al
Truchelut, Joseph, Store Keeper, 128 Queen St
Truchelut, Joseph, Store Keeper, 85 King St
Tucker, Charles Smith, Clerk, 188 Church St
Tucker, Sarah, Widow, 108 Church St
Tucker, William B , Porter, State Bank, 108 Church
St
Tunis, Charles, Clerk to Rhodes & Otis, 5 Tradd St
Tunno, Cox, Merchants, 27 East Bay St
Tunno, Jarah, Planter, 64 Tradd St , W end
Tuno, Thomas, Merchant, 8 Church St Cont'd
Tuny, John, Carpenter, 26 Archdale St
Turnbull, Gavin, School Master, 21 Mazyck St
Turnbull, James, Carpenter, South Bay
Turner, Jane, Widow, 155 King St
Turner, William, Clerk, 36 King St.
Turner, William, Guardian, Boundary St
Turpin, William, Merchant, 149 King St
Twing, David, Ship Chandler, 5 Parsonage Ln.
Twing, David, Ship Joiner, East Bay St
Tydiman, Esther, Planter, 33 East Bay St
Tydiman, Philip, Planter, Wentworth St
Tyler, Benjamin, School Master, St James' Goose
Creek, 17 miles
Ulmo, Anthony, Physician & Druggist, 18 Queen
St
Ulmore, Samuel, Planter, Wassmasaw, 33 miles
Ulrick, Samuel, Tanner, Pitt St
Umback, Jacob, Butcher, King St Road
Ummansetter, John, Tanner, 19 Beaufain St
Underwood, William, Market St
Urquart, James, Clerk to Charles Kershaw, 23 East
Bay St
Vale, Elizabeth, Widow, Cannon St
Valence, Moses, 249 King St.
Valk, Jacob R , Store Keeper, King St
Van Rhine, A E , Store Keeper, 134 Broad St
Vanden, John, Tailor, 4 Union St
Vanderberg, John, Rigger, 30 Pinckney St
Vanderherchen, Andrew, Lt of City Guard, 212
King St
Vanderhoff, Cornelius, Boot & Shoe Maker, 142
King St
Vanderhoff, Cornelius, Shoe Maker, 112 Meeting
St
Vanderhorst, Arnoldus, Gen , Planter, 15 East Bay
St
Vanderhorst, Arnoldus J , Planter, Christ Church
Parish, 10 miles
Vanderhorst, John, Factor, 15 East Bay St
Vanderhorst, Richard, Planter, St James' Santee, 28
miles

Vanvelson, Rachael, Planter, St Stephen's, 46 miles
Vardell, Robert, Tailor, Hampstead
Vardell, T A, Brick Layer, 21 St Philip's St
Varence, Adam, Ship Carpenter, 22 East Bay St
Varner, Peter, Jr, Planter, Wassmasaw, 32 miles
Varner, Peter, Sr, Planter, Wassmasaw, 32 miles
Vassault, Thomas, Shop Keeper, 109 cor of Church & Union St
Vaughn & Alley, Merchants, Priolcau's Whf
Vaughn, Jesse, City Scavenger, 31 Wall St
Vaugn, John B, Planter, 106 Queen St
Veira, Joseph, Lumber Measurer, 246 King St
Vellas, Peter, Confectioner, 189 Meeting St
Venning, Nicholas, Brick Layer, 3 Kinlock Court
Venning, Nicholas, Planter, Christ Church Parish, 6 miles
Venning, Samuel, Planter, Christ Church Parish, 5 miles
Vernon, Nathaniel, Jewellier, 136 Broad St
Verree, Joseph, Capt, Vendue Master, 3 Church St
Verree, Joseph, Vendue Master, Store, Exchange St
Verree, Mary, 3 Church St
Verree, Robert, Merchant, 3 Church St
Verree, Samuel, Silversmith, 3 Church St
Vesey, Charles, Clerk, 8 Parsonage Ln
Vesey, Joshua, Capt, School Master of Fellowship Society, 38 King St
Vidal, John, Shop Keeper, 185 Broad St
Vigier, Julia, Cigar Maker, 20 Archdale St
Villard, Louis, Cutler, 108 Queen St
Villeponteaux, Benjamin, Planter, St John's, Berkeley, 45 miles
Villeponteaux, Drake, Planter, St John's, Berkeley, 45 miles
Villeponteaux, William, Planter, St John's, Berkeley, 45 miles
Vincent, James, Black Smith, Charlotte St
Vincent, Thomas, Merchant, 21 East Bay St
Vonhagen, George, Grocer, Vanderhorst St
Wade, Joseph, Carpenter, 94 Queen St
Wadling, Benjamin, Overseer to Elfe, Daniel's Island, 8 miles
Wagner, Ann, Planter, 101 cor. King St & Broad St
Wagner, Mary, Seamstress, 7 Trott St
Wainwright, Ann, Planter, 265 cor of Tradd & King St
Waite, Rosanna, Planter, St Stephen's, 53 miles
Wakefield, Benjamin, Merchant, Mill Tract St
Walden, Elisha, Planter, St James' Goose Creek, 24 miles
Walden, Joseph & Co., Merchants (Counting House), Crafts' N Whf
Waldo, J W, Physician, 154 King St
Waldon, Joseph & D, Merchants, 40 Church St
Walker, ——, Mrs., Planter, Christ Church Parish, 19 miles

Walker, Caleb, Carpenter, cor Mazyck St & Magazine St
Walker, Francis, Clerk, 146 Broad St
Walker, John, Chair Maker, 78 Meeting St
Walker, John, Clerk, 47 Church St
Walker, John, Planter, Christ Church Parish, 7 miles
Walker, Robert, Cabinet Maker, 39 Church St
Walker, Samuel, Tailor, Boundary St
Walker, Tandy, Clerk, 185 King St
Walker, Thomas, Stone Cutter, 32 Trott St
Walker, William, Cabinet Maker, 3 Beaufain St
Wall, Richard, Boarding House, 24 Berresford's Al
Wallace, James, Custom House Officer, Boundary St
Wallace, James, Overseer to Ball St Johns, Berkeley, 32 miles
Wallace, Robert, Brass Founder, 66 Meeting St
Wallace, Thomas, Cabinet Maker, 99 Queen St
Waller, Charlotte, Widow, Magazine St
Walters, Catharine, Nurse, 6 Moore St.
Walters, Rebecca, Shop Keeper, 2 Berresford's Al
Walton, William & Co, Store Keepers, 151 King St
Walton, William, Merchant, 150 cor Boundary St & King St
Walton, William, Overseer to J Lucas, Jr, St Thomas & St Dennis, 23 miles
Wansley, Joseph, Boarding House, 29 Union St
Ward, Daniel, Master of Work House, cor of Mazyck & Queen St
Ward, James, Attorney, 6 Logan St
Ward, John, Planter & Attorney, 3 East Bay St
Ward, Sarah, Planter, 210 Meeting St
Ward, Thomas, Painter & Glazier, 8 Kinloch Court
Warham, ——, Mrs, Planter, St Andrew's, 19 miles
Warham, Mary, Planter, 123 Meeting St
Waring & Hayne, Factor, Chisolm's Whf
Waring, Henry, Planter, 30 Anson St
Waring, Horatio S, Student of Medicine, 32 Meeting St
Waring, Morton & Son, Factors, 152 Custom House
Waring, Morton, Factor, 55 Church St
Waring, Susan, Planter, 32 Wentworth St
Waring, Thomas, Naval Officer, 32 Meeting St
Waring, Thomas, Planter, Charlotte St
Wark, John, Tallow Chandler, Cannonborough Road
Warley, Felix, Cashier, State Bank, 8 Trott St
Warley, Felix, Jr, Attorney, 8 Trott St
Warley, M A E, 26 Beaufain St
Warley, Martha, Planter, St John's, Berkeley, 52 miles
Warley, Paul, Planter, St Thomas & St Denis, 24 miles
Warley, William, Physician, 8 Trott St
Warner, John, Magazine St
Warner, Penelope, Shop Keeper, 203 Meeting St
Warnock, John, Attorney, 45 Broad St

Warren, John, Mariner, 1 East Bay St
Warren, Joseph, Rev , Episcopal Minister, Edisto Island
Warren, Samuel, Col , Planter, St James' Santee, 48 miles
Wartenberg & Knippenberg, Grocers, 33 Queen St
Washington, William, Gen , Planter, 3 cor of Church St Cont'd & Fort St
Washington, William, Jr , Planter, 4 Church St Cont'd
Watkins, John, Ship Chandler, St Thomas & St Dennis, 25 miles
Watson, Alexander, Factor, 15 East Bay St
Watson, James, Mariner, 15 Union St
Watson, James, School Master, Stoll's Al
Watson, John, Cabinet Maker, 26 King St
Watson, William, Shop Keeper, 72 Meeting St
Watts, James, Grocer, 29 Church St Cont'd
Watts, Robert, Mariner, 55 Queen St.
Waugh, W & A , Merchants, 122 Tradd St
Way, ——, Mrs , Planter, James Island
Weatherly, William, Brick Layer, 12 Liberty St
Weathers, Thomas, Boat Builder, Cock Ln.
Weaver, Peter, Shoe Maker, Lowndes St
Webb, Burgess, Pilot, 22 East Bay St
Webb, Daniel C , Factor, Mill Tract
Webb, John, Merchant, 227 East Bay St
Webb, William, Planter, St James' Santee, 37 miles
Webb, William, Teller, State Bank, Cannonborough Road
Webber, Samuel, Rigger, 27 Anson St
Webster, William R , Coach Maker, 54 Meeting St
Weir, M'Fee & Co, Merchants, Chisolm's Whf.
Weir, Sarah, Seamstress, 178 Meeting St
Weissinger, John, Baker, 175 King St
Welling, William, Harness Maker, Clifford St
Wells, Eliza, Seamstress, 114 Meeting St.
Wells, Frances, Widow, 251 King St
Wells, John, Planter, St James' Santee, 40 miles
Wells, Richard, Boat Builder, 135 East Bay St.
Wells, Richard, Boat Builder, Shop, East Bay St
Wells, Samuel, Mariner, 20 Trott St
Wells, William H , Planter, St James' Santee, 46 miles
Wellshy, William, Overseer to Stile's Estate, Wadmalaw Island
Wellsman, James, Pilot, 1 Lynch's Court
Welsh, Edward, Capt., Mariner, 2 Logan St
Welsh, George, Picker of Tobacco, Lowndes St
Welsh, Jesse, Miller, Neck Road
Welsh, Mary, 163 King St
Welsh, T. G , Carver & Guilder, 80 Meeting St
Wernhoff, B I , Gardner, King St Road
Werts, Rebecca, Planter, Christ Church Parish, 9 miles
Wescott, Mary, Planter, Edisto Island
Wescott, Randolph, Planter, Edisto Island
Wescott, Thomas, Planter, Edisto Island

Wescott, William, Planter, Edisto Island
Wesner, Frederick, Carpenter, 199 King St
Wesner, Henry P , Baker, 20 Coming St
West, Thomas, Mariner, 80 East Bay St
Weston, Paul, Physician, Stoll's Al
Weston, Plowden, Planter, 31 Queen St
Weston, William, Planter, Wadmalaw Island
Weyman, Edward, Maj , Surveyor of the Port of Charleston
Whaley, George, Planter, Four Holes
Whaley, Joseph, Planter, Edisto Island
Whalley, Mary, Widow, 1 Lamboll St
Wheelden, Elias, Planter, Christ Church Parish, 3 miles
Wheelden, Elisha, Planter, Christ Church Parish, 16 miles
Wheelden, John, Ship Carpenter, 32 Pinckney St
Wheeler, George, Clerk, 38 Wentworth St
Wheeler, William, Planter, St. Thomas & St. Dennis, 22 miles
Whilder, Catharine, Planter, St John's, Berkeley, 55 miles
White & Power, Painters, 106 Tradd St
White, Ann, Mantua Maker, St Mary's St
White, Ann, Planter, Christ Church Parish, 21 miles
White, Gudlip, Cabinet Maker, 36 Broad St
White, Henry, Mariner, 14 Wall St.
White, James, Clerk, 4 Champneys St
White, James, Grocer, 66 East Bay St
White, James, Shop Keeper, 31 Meeting St
White, John B , Attorney, 104 Broad St
White, John, Factor, 122 Meeting St
White, John, Factor, Merchant (Counting House), Chisolm's Whf
White, John K , Factor, 40 Society St cor East Bay St
White, John P , Vendue Master, 55 East Bay St
White, John P , Vendue Master, Store, Champneys St
White, John, Planter, Christ Church Parish, 13 miles
White, Josiah, Boarding House, 2 Berresford's Al
White, William Richard, Planter, Wadmalaw Island
Whitehouse, Catharine, Planter, St John's, Berkeley, 55 miles
Whitesides, John, Planter, Christ Church Parish, 8 miles
Whitesides, Moses, Planter, Christ Church Parish, 8 miles
Whitesides, Thomas, Planter, Christ Church Parish, 15 miles
Whitley, John, Brick Layer, 16 Ellery St
Whitley, Thomas, Grocer, 3 Market St
Whitney, Archibald, Baker, 34 Beaufain St
Whitney, John, Mariner, 136 East Bay St
Whitney, John, Turner, 88 Meeting St
Whittemore, Hannah, Seamstress, 9 Society St
Wienges, John, Grocer, 36 Union St
Wigfall, Levy D , Planter, 92 Tradd St

Wigfall, Levy D. , Planter, St James' Goose Creek, 21 miles
Wigfall, Thomas, Planter, St Thomas & St Dennis, 13 miles
Wiggins, W C , Grocer, 144 Meeting St
Wightman & Hembert, Boot & Shoe Makers, 15 Hasell St
Wightman, John Thomas, Turner, 26 Hasell St
Wightman, William, Painter & Glazier, 26 Hasell St
Wightman, William, Painter, 133 Meeting St
Wilcox, Jeremiah, Painter, Bull St
Wildman, ——, Merchant, 1 Cumberland St.
Wildman, Seymore, Hatter, 189 King St
Wilhelmi, J P , Clerk to Groning, 33 George St
Wilkinson, Abner, Clerk, Market St
Wilkinson, Susanna, Widow, Cannon St
Will, C , Seamstress, Montague St
Will, Warren Robert, Brick Layer, Montague St
Willard, Diana, Boarding House, Magazine St
Williams, Abner, Coach Maker, 54 Meeting St
Williams, Benjamin Paul, Planter, St James' Goose Creek, 22 miles
Williams, Isham, Planter, William's Whf
Williams, James G , Custom House Officer, 2 Motte St
Williams, Margaret, Planter, Wadmalaw Island
Williams, Simpson, Pilot, 107 Church St
Williams, Stephen, Planter, Four Holes
Williams, William, Hair Dresser, 174 King St
Williams, William, Overseer to S M M'Donnald, St John's, Berkeley, 34 miles
Williams, William, Tailor, 102 Queen St
Williamson, Abraham, Tallow Chandler, Cannonborough Road
Williamson, Hannah, Seamstress, 50 Anson St
Williamson, John, Capt , Merchant, East Bay (Counting House), Motte's Whf
Williamson, John, Mariner, 18 Amen St
Williman, Christopher, Planter, 213 King St.
Williman, George, Coach Maker, 116 Broad St
Williman, George, Tanner, Boundary St
Williman, Jacob, Tanner, 1 Montague St
Willington, A S , Printer, 7 New St
Willis, I. H , Clerk, 116 Meeting St
Willson, Elias, Planter, St. John's, Berkeley, 55 miles
Willson, George, Planter, St John's, Berkeley, 55 miles
Willson, James, Planter, St. John's, Berkeley, 55 miles
Willson, Russel, Overseer to H Horry, St James' Goose Creek, 18 miles
Wilson & Paul, Grocers, 23 cor of Church & Broad St
Wilson, Algernon, Planter, 11 Society St
Wilson, Hugh, Jr , Planter, Wadmalaw Island
Wilson, Hugh, Planter, James Island

Wilson, Isaac M , 4 Archdale
Wilson, James, Plasterer, 10 Clifford St
Wilson, John, Grocer, Meeting St
Wilson, John, Physician, Wassmasaw, 30 miles
Wilson, Judy, Planter, Wassmasaw, 40 miles
Wilson, Mary, Seamstress, 123 Meeting St
Wilson, R , Dr., & Son, Druggist, Store, 97 Church St
Wilson, Rebecca, Boarding House, 63 Meeting St
Wilson, Robert, Mariner, 2 Hasell St
Wilson, Robert, Physician, 36 Meeting St
Wilson, Robert, Sr , Physician, 189 cor Mazyck & Broad St
Wilson, Samuel, Physician, 4 Archdale, cor Magazine St
Wilson, Stephen, Merchant, 4 Archdale
Winchester, Jonathan, Carpenter, Vanderhorst St
Wing, F , Mariner, 20 Middle St
Wingwood, Chavel, Overseer to James Scott, Christ Church Parish, 7 miles
Wingwood, John, Overseer to Jeffords, Christ Church Parish, 15 miles
Wingwood, Susan, Planter, Christ Church Parish, 11 miles
Winn, Joseph, Merchant, 16 Beaufain St
Winstanley, Thomas, Attorney, 86 East Bay St
Winter, James, Planter, St James' Goose Creek, 35 miles
Winters, James, Planter, Wassmasaw, 32 miles
Winters, Jane, Planter, Wassmasaw, 33 miles
Winthrop, Joseph, Merchant (Counting House), Vanderhorst's Whf
Winthrop, Joseph, Merchant, Danish & Swedish Consul, 59 Tradd St
Wish & Bryan, Merchants, 130 Broad St
Wish, John, Weaver, Wentworth St
Wish, Thomas, Clerk, 59 Queen St
Wish, William, Merchant, 130 Broad St
Wiss, Peter, Tailor, 200 King St
Witherspoon, I R , Physician, Christ Church Parish, 18 miles
Witte, John, Grocer, 34 King St
Witter, Benjamin, Planter, James Island
Witter, Joseph, Overseer to Thomas Hall, Christ Church Parish, 11 miles
Witter, Mary, Planter, James Island
Witter, Susan, Planter, John's Island
Witter, William, Tailor, James Island
Wittington, ——, Overseer to M E Marion, St John's, Berkeley, 60 miles
Wodrop, John, Merchant, 9 East Bay St
Wolfe, ——, Shop Keeper, 164 King St
Wolfe, Jacob, Clerk, 28 East Bay St
Wood, Absalom, Tavern Keeper, 98 Queen St
Wood, James, Baker, St Philip's St
Wood, John, Clerk, 7 Elliott St
Wood, John Thomas, Surveyor, St. James' Santee, 35 miles

Wood, Margaret, Seamstress, 15 Archdale St
Wood, Robert, Tavern, St Andrew's, 6 miles
Wood, William, Grocer, Boundary St
Wood, William, Planter, Edisto Island
Wooden, Charles, Pilot, 20 Pinckney St
Woodman & Smith, Store Keeper, 105 King St
Woodman, Eliza, Mantua Maker, 23 Beaufain St
Woodman, John H , School Master, 1 Cumberland
  St
Woodmancy, John, Grocer, King St Road
Woodrouffe, Eliza, Boarding House, 31 Church St
Woods, Alley, Shop Keeper, 40 Church St Cont'd
Woods, John, Beale's Whf
Woody, John, Carpenter, St James' Santee, 50
  miles
Wooley, Thomas, Clerk, 227 East Bay St.
Wragg, Sarah, Planter, 35 East Bay St.
Wrainch, John, School Master, 150 Meeting St
Wright, Elizabeth, 9 Orange St
Wright, James, Planter, St Stephen's, 45 miles
Wright, Jeremiah, Planter, St Stephen's, 45 miles
Wright, Lachlan, Planter, 1 Green St
Wright, Robert, Millwright, James Island
Wrightman, William, Goldsmith, 185 Meeting St
Wurdemann, I G , Grocer, 9 cor of Union &
  Queen St
Wyatt, Elizabeth, Widow, 55 Church St
Wyatt, John, Ship Carpenter, 55 Church St
Wyatt, Peter, Lumber Merchant, Mills, Lynch St
Wyetker, Richard, Grocer, 31 Union St
Wylie, John, Merchant, 23 Church St
Yates, Deborah, School Mistress, Fort St , South
  Bay
Yates, Jeremiah, Planter & Ship Chandler, Fort St.
Yates, Joseph, Cooper, 11 Church St Cont'd
Yates, Joseph, Cooper's Shop, Beale's Whf
Yates, Samuel, Capt , Mariner, 5 Lynch's Court
Yates, Samuel, Ship Chandler, Store, 41 East Bay
  St
Yates, Seth, Ship Carpenter, 6 Lynch's Court
Yates, William, Attorney, 18 King St
Yeaden, Richard, Teller, National Branch Bank,
  Bull St
Yoer, Jacob, Boot & Shoe Maker, 93 Queen St.
You, John, Clerk, National Bank, 25 Archdale St.
Young, Ball, Tobacconist, 1 Elliott St Cont'd
Young, Martin, Grocer, Market St
Young, Thomas, Planter, 21 Friend St
Young, W P., Printer & Bookseller, 41 Broad St
Young, William, Merchant, 205 King St
Young, William, Merchant, Store, 3 Champneys St
Zealy, Joseph, Shop Keeper & Butcher, 275 King
  St
Zilk, John, Wheel Wright, 6 Liberty St.
Zimmerman, George, Overseer to G Axon, St
  James, Santee, 42 miles
Zylstra, John, Oil Color Man, 38 East Bay St.
Zylstra, Peter, Oil Color Man, 64 East Bay St

Chapter 5

THE 1813 DIRECTORY

The 1813 directory was compiled by Joseph Folker under the title of *A Directory of the City and District of Charleston; and Stranger's Guide: Containing Considerable Subjoined Matter, on Different Subjects, For the Year 1813* (Charleston: G M Bounetheau, 1813, 128 pages)

Folker, who operated an academy on Minority Street, has his listing of individuals on pages 1-87 with the rest of the volume containing supplemental information Like the 1809 directory, this one is also poorly alphabetized; for example Alston and Austen appear before Adger In addition, Folker has subheadings for some names but will list other family names under those headings Finding an individual can thus be difficult The 2,325 entries (a shorter number than in 1806, 1807, and 1809) below have been arranged in correct order

----

Abell & Terry, Grocers, 52 Tradd St
Abrahams, Judith, Store Keeper 193 King St
Abrahams, Samuel, 376 King St.
Adams, Benjamin, Planter Wacrontaw Island
Adams, David & Son, Factors, Custom House, Chiholm's Whf
Adams, Ezekiel M'Lean, Carpenter, 29 Pinckney St
Adams, Samuel, Planter, Wacrontaw Island
Addison, James, Planter, St Stephen's (40 miles)
Addison, Joseph, Planter, St Thomas' (8 miles)
Adger, James, Store Keeper, Brownlee's Row
Adger, Robert, Store Keeper, King St Road
Aikin, William, Merchant, King St Road
Airs, George, Custom House Inspector, 12 Archdale St
Airs, Thomas, Shipwright, Langstaff's Whf, Res, 3 Wall St
Akin, Ann, Mrs, Boarding School, 6 Cumberland St
Akin, Thomas, M D., 6 Cumberland St.
Albanac, Peter, Tailor, 136 Queen St
Aldrich, Robert, Wharfinger, Chisolm's Whf, Res, 35 Elliott St
Alexander, Abraham, Clerk & Auditor of the Custom House, Res, 122 King St.
Alexander, Abraham, Jr, Store Keeper, 122 King St
Alexander, David, President, Union Insurance Co, 10 Broad St
Allan, William, Merchant, 1 Vendue Range, Res, Berresford St

Allen, John D, Planter, St Thomas' Parish (19 miles)
Allen, Josiah, Cabinet Maker, Meeting St
Allen, William, Factor, Custom House, Blake's Whf, Res, Liberty St
Allston & Simons, Factors, Custom House, Blake's Whf
Alston, Joseph, His Excellency, 13 King St
Alston, William, Planter, 13 King St
Ancrum, J H, Planter, Stono (18 miles)
Anderson, Hannah, Store Keeper, 16 Tradd St
Anderson, Isabella, Widow, Grocer, 32 Market St
Anderson, Philip, Planter St Stephen's Parish (50 miles)
Anderson, William, Stay Maker, 229 Meeting St
Andrews, Moses, Mast, Block and Pump Maker, East Bay, Res, 14 Logan St
Annelly, George W, Merchant, 1 Middle St
Anthony, John, Harness Maker, 158 King St
Arthur, John, Factor, John St, Wraggsborough
Arthur, P S, Planter, St James', Santee (52 miles)
Artman, Peter, Coach & Chair Maker, 9 Archdale St
Ash, Elizabeth, Mrs, Planter, 9 Lamboll St
Ash, John, Planter, 16 South Bay
Ashby, Thomas, Christ Church Parish (18 miles)
Aspinall, Nicholas, Merchant (Strobel & Aspinall), Res, Washington St
Assalit, Joseph, Professor of the Languages, 14 Elliott St
Atwell & Kingman, Shoe Store, 101 Broad St
Austen, Catharine, Widow, 68 East Bay
Austen, James, Carpenter, 68 East Bay
Austen, Samuel, Carpenter, 68 East Bay
Austin, John, Jeweller, 90 Broad St
Austin, William, Jr, School Master, 194 Meeting St
Austin, William, Sr, Broker, 107 Meeting St
Averell & Cooper, Shoe Store, 284 King St
Axson, ——, Clerk, S C Bank, 62 Tradd St
Axson, Ann, St John's, Berkeley (54 miles)
Axson, John, Planter, St Stephen's (52 miles)
Axson, Samuel E, Carpenter, Adams St
Ayrault, Peter, Merchant, 235 East Bay
Bacot, Henry H, Attorney at Law, 24 Tradd St
Bacot, Peter, Attorney at Law
Bacot, Thomas W, Cashier, S.C. Bank and Post Master, 84 Broad St
Badger, James, Painter & Glazier, 106 Wentworth St
Bailey, David, Merchant, 15 Meeting St
Bailey, Henry, Attorney at Law, 3 Blackbird Al.
Baird, Frederick, Teller, S C Bank, Res, Boundary St
Baird, William, Porter, S.C. Bank, 35 Church St
Baker, Alpheus, Classical Teacher, Cannonborough
Baker, Joseph, Carpenter, Boundary St
Baker, Noah D, Dyer and Scourer, 170 Meeting St

Baker, Richard B , Weigher, Custom House
Baker, Samuel, Grocer, 5 St Philip's St
Ball, Isaac, Planter, East Bay St (St John's, Berkley, 24 miles)
Ball, John, Jr , Planter, Hasell St (St John's, Berkeley, 24 miles)
Ball, John, Planter, East Bay St (St. John's, Berkeley, 24 miles)
Bampfield, James, 37 George St
Bampfield, Thomas, 37 George St.
Banister, John, St John's Berkley (60 miles)
Baquet, Peter, Store Keeper, 309 King St
Barker, J Sanford, Merchant, 220 East Bay, Res , cor Anson & Society Sts
Barker, James, Truss Maker & Military Embroiderer, 9 Pinckney St
Barrelli, Torre & Co , Opticians & Print Sellers, 35 Broad St
Barrett, Benjamin, St John's, Berkely (40 miles)
Barreyre, Peter, Store Keeper, 104 King St
Barron, Alexander, Jr., M D , 45 Meeting St
Barron, Alexander, M D., cor Broad and Orange Sts
Barron, John, Wine Merchant, Exchange, Res , 19 Tradd St.
Barry, Peter, Last Maker, 130 Queen St
Barthelemi, Rene, 7 Wentworth St
Bartless, Henry, Blacksmith, 24 Middle St
Barton, Mary, Mrs Mantua Maker, 16 George St
Barville, M , Cabinet Maker, 31 Society St
Bates & Perkins, Merchants, 5 Champneys St.
Battker, John Andrew, Grocer, 101 East Bay
Bauney, Peter, Store Keeper, 33 King St
Bay, Andrew, Attorney at Law, 8 Meeting St
Bay, Elihu H , Judge, Court of Common Pleas and Sessions, 8 Meeting St
Bay, John, Merchant, 8 Meeting St
Baynot, Reny, Grocer, 39 King St
Bazuels, Juliana, Grocer, 84 King St
Beard, John, Baker, 160 Meeting St
Bee, Barnard E , Attorney at Law, 5 Short St
Bee, J Simmons, Commission Merchant and Vendue Master, 107 Broad St
Bee, J Smith, Planter, 5 Coming St
Bee, James, Factor, 129 Church St
Bee, Joseph, 5 Hasell St
Bee, Thomas, Attorney at Law, 129 Church St
Beecher, Maria, Widow, 12 King St
Beekman, ——, Mrs , Widow, 1 Hasell St
Beekman, Adolph, Painter and Glazier, Meeting St
Beekman, Samuel, Mrs , Widow, Hasell St
Bees, William, Carpenter, St. Philip's St., Neck
Beggs, James, Store Keeper, 167 Kng St
Beile, John C , Merchant, 80 King St
Belcher, Elias, Capt , 87 Wentworth St.
Belisle, Peter, Grocer & Baker, 105 East Bay
Bell, Alexander, Carpenter, 13 Tradd St
Bell, David, Book Keeper, 9 Society St

Bell, Mary, Tavern Keeper, St James, Goose Creek (22 miles)
Belser, Christiana, Mrs , Widow, King St Road
Belz, Christian, Grocer, 207 Meeting St
Benjamin, Ezra, Capt , 117 Tradd St
Bennett, Henry, Deputy Collector Customs, Res , Anson St
Bennett, Isaac S K , Attorney at Law, Office, 228 Meeting St , Res , 9 Montague St
Bennett, J H , Planter, Christ Church Parish
Bennett, John S , Planter, James Island
Bennett, Joseph, Attorney at Law, 9 Montague St
Bennett, Sarah, Planter, Wadmalaw Island
Bennett, Swinton, Brick Layer, Bull St
Bennett, Thomas, Jr , Hon , Intendent, Bull St W End
Bennett, Thomas, Sr , Planter, 9 Montague St
Benoist, Eliza, Planter, St John's, Berkeley (40 miles)
Benoist, J B , Baker, 159 Meeting St
Benoist, John, Planter, Christ Church Parish (15 miles)
Benoist, Philip, Planter, St John's, Berkley (55 miles)
Benoist, William, Planter, Christ Church Parish (15 miles)
Benson, L , Merchant, 306 King St
Bentham, James, Merchant, 372 King St
Bentham, Mary, Mrs , 372 King St
Bentham, Robert, Attorney at Law, 372 King St
Bentham, William, Capt., Mariner, 372 King St.
Bernard, Reine, Hair Dresser, 2 Tradd St
Berney, John, Marine Insurance Co , 50 East Bay, Res , 11 Archdale St
Berney, Robert, Marine Insurance Co , 50 East Bay, Res , 11 Archdale St
Bery, Piere, Grocer, 57 Church St
Beswick, ——, Mrs , School Mistress, 32 George St
Beswick, John, Lumber Measurer, 32 George St
Bethune, Angus, 75 Broad St
Bigelow, Elizabeth, Mrs , Widow, 130 Meeting St
Billing's Livery Stables, 52 Church St
Bingley, Edward, Grocer, 9 Market St
Bingley, Nathaniel, Capt , Society St
Bins, Michael, Planter, St Stephen's Parish
Bins, Stephen, Planter, St Stephen's Parish
Black & Birnie, Merchants, 11 Broad St
Black & Law, Boot & Shoe Makers, 24 Broad St
Black & M'Dowall, Merchants, 78 King St
Blacklock, William, Merchant, 260 East Bay Res , 1 Bull St
Blackwood, John, Store Keeper, King St Road
Blackwood, Thomas, Merchant, Chisolm's Whf., Res , Pitt St
Blair, James, Vendue Merchant, 126 Tradd St
Blair, Napier & Co. Vendue Masters, 2 Vendue Range
Blake, John, 3 South Bay

Blake, Margaret, 3 South Bay
Blamyer, William, Jr, Factor, D'Oyley's Whf
Blane, Andrew, Wheelwright, Meeting St Road
Blewer, Peter, Mrs, Store Keeper, King St Road
Blome, John, M D 113 Queen St
Bloodgood, S, Store Keeper, 213 King St
Bloom, Andrew, Butcher, King St Road
Bloomstock, M, Grocer, 3 Liberty St
Boles, Abiel, School Master, Orphan House
Bonneau, John, Factor, Blake's Whf, Res., 59
    Broad St
Bonnell, John, Capt, 14 Lynch's Ln
Bonseil, Mary, Mrs, Widow, 48 Wentworth St
Booker, Ann, Grocer, 374 King St
Booth, William, Capt., 70 Anson St
Borch, Peter, Grocer, 83 East Bay
Boudo, Lewis, Jeweller, 117 Queen St
Boulineau, ——, Madam, Store Keeper, King St
    Road
Bounetheau, E, Mrs, 13 Cumberland St
Bounetheau, Edward W, Carpenter, Montague St
Bounetheau, G M, Q U., Clerk of Court &
    Printer, Office, E Bay, Res, 108 Wentworth St
Bounetheau, J W, Printer, 13 Cumberland St
Bours & Bascome, Vendue Masters, Prioleau's S
    Range
Bousquet, Peter, Store Keeper, 309 King St
Bowles, Ann, School Mistress, Orphan House
Bowman, John, Mrs, Widow, Planter, 20 Beaufain
    St
Boya, Jacob, Store Keeper, King St Road
Boyd, John, Mariner, 38 Elliott St
Boyd, William, Merchant, Chisolm's Whf, Res, 1
    Minority St
Bradford, Christiana, Mrs, Music Store, 18 King
    St
Bradley, Charles, Printer, 14 Maiden Ln
Bradley, Elizabeth, Mrs, Widow, 5 New St
Brailsford, Alexander M, 111 Tradd St
Brailsford, Edward, M D 4 New St
Brailsford, Elizabeth, Miss, 250 Meeting St
Brailsford, James, 111 Tradd St
Brailsford, John, Planter, 41 Hasell St
Brailsford, Mary, Mrs, 111 Tradd St
Braly, Mary, Mrs, 5 Wentworth St
Brander, James, Silversmith, 109 Queen St
Bremar, Henry, Dentist, 6 Maiden Ln
Brindlay, J G, Grocer, 5 West St.
Brisbane, William, Planter, 15 Meeting St
Broadfoot, James, Merchant, 26 Cumberland St
Broadfoot, William, Merchant, 8 Coates' Row
Brodie, Robert, Jr, Lumber Measurer, 56 Tradd St
Brodie, Robert, Lumber Measurer, 56 Tradd St
Brooks & Potter, Merchants, 1 Vanderhorst's Whf
Bross, John, Tavern Keeper, Sullivan's Island
Broughton, Ann, Miss, 1 Mazyck St.
Broughton, Daniel, 26 Society St

Broughton, Mary, Mrs, Planter, St John's Berkeley
    (28 miles)
Broughton, Peter, Planter, St John's, Berkley (28
    miles)
Broughton, Philip P, Planter, St John's Berkeley
    (28 miles)
Broughton, Thomas, Planter, St John's, Berkeley
    (28 miles)
Brown & Tunis, Factors, 31 East Bay
Brown, Alexander, Merchant, 138 King St
Brown, Daniel, 125 Tradd St
Brown, George W, Rope Walk, Meeting St Road,
    Hampstead
Brown, Harriet, Mrs, 59 Tradd St
Brown, John, Grocer, 38 Broad St.
Brown, John, Planter, Cannonborough
Brown, John, Wassamasaw (29 miles)
Brown, Jonathan, Mariner, 1 Parsonage Ln
Brown, Joshua, Vendue Master, Vendue Range,
    Res, 12 New St
Brown, Robert, John's Island
Brown, Samuel, Planter, Mazyckboro
Brown, Sarah, School Mistress, 191 Meeting St
Brown, William, Boarding House, 1 Archdale St
Brown, William, Boatman, 56 Elliott St
Brown, William, Mariner, 136 Elliott St
Browne, James, Coroner & Justice of the Peace, 49
    Wentworth St
Browne, Samuel, Broker, 232 King St
Brownlee, John, Merchant, 14 St Philip's St
Bryant, John, Planter, 38 Hasell St
Bryant, Lydia, Mrs, Planter, 38 Hasell St
Bryant, Sarah, Mrs, Planter, King St Road
Bryce, Henry, Merchant, 268 East Bay
Bryce, Nicol, Vendue Master, 8 Vendue Range
Buchan, ——, Rev Dr, 3 Lynch St
Buchanan & M'Cliesh, Brass Founders, 111 East
    Bay
Buchanan Daniel, Tailor, 110 Church St
Budd, Abigail, Mrs, Boarding House, 40 Church
    St
Bulet, Peter, Porter House, Prioleau's Whf.
Bulkley & Rose, Ship Chandlers, 39 East Bay
Bulkley, James, Ship Chandlers, 208 East Bay
Bulkley, Stephen, Ship Chandlers, 134 King St
Bull, W S, Mrs, Lamboll St
Bull, William A, Planter, St. Andrew's Parish (13
    miles)
Bulow, J & C, Merchants, 391 King St
Bunch, James, Shop Keeper, Forks Road
Burage, Laurence, Capt, Hampstead
Burden, Thomas, Factor, cor King & South Bay
    Sts
Burger
Burger, Charles, Accomptant, 63 Church St
Burger, George, Accomptant, 63 Church St
Burger, Samuel, Deputy Secretary of State, 63
    Church St
Burger, William, Accomptant, 63 Church St

Burgoyne, William, M D., Druggist, cor. East Bay & Broad St
Burke, Walter, Capt , 6 Anson St
Burnet, Foster, Oil & Color Shop, 101 East Bay
Burns, John, 3 Washington St
Burns, William, Gardner, Islington Butcher's Row
Burrows, Mary, Mrs , Widow, Wentworth St
Busacker, Charles, Grocer, 33 State St
Busche, Marcia, Grocer, 298 King St
Butler, Charles P., Jeweller, 335 King St.
Butler, Joseph, Deputy Sheriff, 112 Meeting St
Butler, Thomas, Planter, St James', Santee (42 miles)
Butman, Ebenezer, Store Keeper, King St Road
Byrd, John J , School Master, 124 Wentworth St
Byrne, Henry, Sail Maker, 13 Pinckney St
Byrne, Patrick, Sail Maker, 13 Pinckney St
Cahusac, John, Planter, St John's, Berkeley (52 miles)
Calder, Alexander, Planter's Hotel, 25 Church St
Caldwell, & Kyd, Store Keepers, King St Road
Caldwell, William A , Vendue Master, Vendue Range
Calhoun, John, Keeper, Light House, Folly Island
Calvert, ——, Mrs , Boarding House, 83 Church St
Cambridge, Tobias, Mrs , 7 Orange St
Camer, James, Planter, Race Ground (2 miles)
Cameron, Lewis, 109 Tradd St
Campbell & Milikin, Vendue Masters, 3 Vendue Range
Campbell, A , Capt , 135 East Bay
Campbell, John, Rev , Beaufort, St Helena
Campbell, M'Millan, 218 East Bay
Cannon, ——, Miss, Planter, Cannonborough
Canter, Benjamin, Cabinet Maker, 64 Broad St
Canter, Emanuel, Merchant, Savage St
Canter, John, Limner, 64 Broad St
Canter, Joshua, Limner, 64 Broad St
Canter, Sarah, Mrs , Widow, Savage St
Cape, Bryan, Factor, 21 Anson St
Cape, John, Planter, John's Island (8 miles)
Capers, Gabriel, Planter, Wadmalaw
Caquett & Co , Chocolate Manufactory, 112 Queen St
Cardozo, David, Master, Free School No 1, 47 Tradd St
Cardozo, Isaac, Accomptant, 47 Tradd St
Cardozo, Jacob, Lumber Measurer, 47 Tradd St
Carew, Edward, Mast, Block & Pump Maker, 206 East Bay
Carmand, T , Merchant Tailor, 328 King St
Carne, T W , & Co , Merchants, 136 King St
Carolan's Boot & Shoe Store, 35 Church St
Carpenter, Joseph, Butcher, Cannonborough
Carr, James, Butcher, Cannonborough
Carr, James, Purser to the Navy, 23 Anson St
Carrere, Charles, Classical Teacher, 60 Broad St
Carroll, Bartholomew, Boundary St

Carroll, John Parsons, Planter, Boundary St
Carson, James, Merchant, 10 Broad St , Res , 86 Tradd St
Carsten, John, Grocer, 21 Anson St.
Cart, John, Factor, Bull St
Cart, John, Jr , Bull St
Cart, Sarah, Kinloch's Court
Carter, George, M D , 64 Tradd St
Caruth, John, Capt , King St Road
Carvalho, ——, Rev Mr , 29 Hasell St
Carvalho, David, 29 Hasell St
Casey, Benjamin, Coach & Chair Maker, 95 Broad St
Cassin, Patrick, Vendue Master, Vendue Range, Res , 5 Pinckney St
Castagnow, Bernard, Blacksmith, Queen St
Cathewood, John J , Watch Maker, 32 Broad St
Catonet & Feraud, Grocers, 21 Queen St
Caught, Mary, Shop Keeper, 140 East Bay
Caught, Thomas, Shipwright, 140 East Bay
Chalmers, Margaret, Mrs , Grocery Store, 233 East Bay
Champlain, J , Lt , U S Artillery, 95 Tradd St
Champlin, Jane, Mrs , Boarding House, 212 Meeting St.
Champneys, John, Planter, 105 King St
Chancoigne, ——, Mons , 16 Laurens St
Chanet & Duquercron, Grocers, 216 King St
Chaplin, William, Planter, John's Island
Chapman, Joseph, Grocer, 394 King St
Childs, Eliza, Mrs., Store Keeper, 112 King St
Chitty, Charles, Clerk, Sheriff's Office, 191 Meeting St
Chitty, John W , Collection Clerk, State Bank, St Philip's St
Chrietsburgh, Thomas, 42 Pinckney St
Christian, Charles, Merchant, 236 East Bay St
Christie, Alexander, Baker, 118 Church St
Chubb, William, Planter, Four Holes (40 miles)
Chupein, Lewis, Hair Dresser, 114 Broad St
Churr, John, Grocer 309 King St
Clark, David, Watch Maker
Clark, Elizabeth, Shop Keeper, 188 King St
Clark, James, Tailor, 12 Elliott St
Clark, Joseph W , Capt , 9 Orange St
Clark, Mary, Mrs , Millinery Store, 186 King St
Clarkson, William, Factor, 8 Champneys St
Clarkson, William, Jr , Factor, 3 Motte's Whf
Clayson, E , Grocer, Cannonborough
Clayton & Young, Tailow Chandlers, Butcher's Row
Cleapor, Charles, Sail Maker, Lothrop's Whf , Res , 24 Ellery St
Cleary, Nathaniel Greene, Sheriff, Charleston District, Res , 36 Wentworth St
Cleland, G , Hat Store, 200 King St
Clement, Pinckney, Planter, St Thomas' Parish (8 miles)

Clement, William, State Treasurer's Office, Guard
House
Clemmmons, E , Mrs , Boarding House, 265 East
Bay
Clery, John R , 36 Wentworth St
Clifford, Henry, Factor, Mey's Whf , Res , Hard Al
Clissy, Raymond, Coach & Chair Maker, Shop, 103
Church St , Dry Goods Store, Etc , Res , 141 King
St
Cobia, Christiana E , Montague St
Cobia, Daniel, Butcher, Montague St
Cobia, Francis, Butcher, Hampstead
Cobia, Francis, Carpenter, Hampstead
Cobia, Nicholas, Planter, Four Mile House (4 miles)
Cochran, ——, Mrs , Widow, 132 East Bay
Cochran, Charles B., President, Union Bank, 32
Society St
Cochran, Margaret, Mrs , Store Keeper, 342 King
St
Cochran, Robert E , Federal Marshall, 15 Society
St
Cochran, Robert, Sr., 71 Meeting St
Cochran, Thomas, Factor, 32 Queen St
Cockfield, Mary, Mrs , Planter, St John's
Cockoo, William, Pilot, Hard Al
Cogdell, A E , Mrs , Widow, Boarding House, 1 St
Michael's Al
Cogdell, John S , Attorney at Law, 2 St Michael's
Al
Cogdell, Roger, Clerk, Planters & Mechanics Bank,
1 St. Michael's Al.
Cohen, & Lazarus, Merchants, 146 King St
Cohen, John, Grocer, cor Laurens & Middle St
Cohen, Joseph, Sexton, Synagogue, 27 Hasell St
Cohen, Moses, Store Keeper, 228 King St
Cohen, Philip, Auctioneer, 8 Vendue Range
Cohen, Solomon, Store Keeper, 165 King St
Colcock, John, Mrs , Boarding School, 10 Lamboll
St
Cole, John, Capt , 44 Tradd St
Cole, Joseph, Boot & Shoe Maker, 2 Broad St
Cole, Margaret, Boarding House, 58 Elliott St
Cole, Richard, Shipwright, Langstaff's Whf , Res.,
St Philip's St
Coleman, Benjamin, Grocer, King St Road (2
miles)
Coleman, Sylvester, Merchant, 11 Beaufain St.
Collier, William, Accomptant, 125 Wentworth St
Collins, ——, Mrs , Mantua Maker, 20 Hasell St
Collins, John, Accomptant, 20 Hasell St
Compton, Jesse, Hatter, 152 King St
Condy & Raguet, Merchant, 242 East Bay, Res., 99
Meeting St
Connelly, Jeremiah, Capt , 17 Meeting St
Connover, Eliza, Mrs , School Mistress, 17 Society
St
Conyers, William, Harbor Master, Office,
Exchange, Res , 29 Pinckney St

Cook, Samuel, Boarding House, 14 Queen St
Cooper, James, Capt , 161 East Bay
Coram, Francis, Factor, Prioleau's Whf
Coram, Thomas, Mrs , Widow, 80 Queen St
Corbett, Thomas Jr , Planter, Cannonborough
Corbett, Thomas, President, Insurance Company,
Res., 1 Cumberland St
Cordes, William, Planter, St John's (52 miles)
Corker, Thomas, Shipwright, 22 Pinckney St
Cornell, Banjamin, Clerk, 47 Elliott St
Corr, Charles, Tailor, 15 Queen St
Corrie, Samuel, Wheelwright, King St Road
Courtney, Edward, Mrs Boarding House, 10
Champneys St
Courtney, Edward S , Store Keeper, 10 Champneys
St
Courtney, Humphrey, Wine Merchant, 32 Meeting
St
Courty, John, Boarding House, 24 State St
Couterier, Elias, Planter, St John's, Berkeley (55
miles)
Couterier, Isaac Jr., Planter, St John's, Berkeley
(53 miles)
Couterier, Isaac, Planter, St John's, Berkeley (53
miles)
Couterier, Jospeh, Planter, St John's, Berkeley (60
miles)
Coventry, Alex, Dyer & Scourer 92 Tradd St
Cowen, John, Rigger, 140 East Bay
Cowing, Henry, & Co , Merchant, 137 King St
Cox, ——, Capt , 189 East Bay
Cox, Thomas C , Editor, Times, 20 Meeting St
Cox, Thomas, Coach & Chair Maker, 26 Broad St
Crafts, Thomas, Attorney at Law, 10 New St
Crafts, William, Jr , Attorney at Law, 10 New St
Crafts, William, Sr , Whf Owner, 10 New St
Craig, Thomas, Accomptant, Vendue Range
Cranston, James, Broker, 13 Mazyck St
Crask, Philip, Painter & Glazier, 12 Pinckney St
Crawford, John, Factor, Compting House,
Vanderhorst's Whf
Cregier, Peter, Grocer, 132 Queen St
Cripps, John, Planter, 51 Meeting St
Crocker, D , Merchant, Craft's N Whf
Croft, Arnold, Factor, Johnson's Whf , Res ,
Hampstead
Croft, Peter, Factor, Johnson's Whf., Res ,
Hampstead
Cron, Hartman, Grocer, 70 Church St
Crosby, Josiah, Capt , 47 Anson St
Cross, George, Capt , 231 Meeting St
Cross, George Warren, Attorney at Law, Office,
227 Meeting St , Res , 231 Meeting St
Crouch, Abraham, 247 Meeting St.
Cruckshanks, Daniel, Boot & Shoe Maker, 127
Queen St
Cruckshanks, William, Boot & Shoe Maker, cor.
Beresford's Al & Chruch St

Cudworth, Benjamin, Bull St
Cudworth, Nathaniel, 7 Boundary St
Cunningham, John, Merchant, Wraggsborough
Cunningham, Richard, Planter, Charlotte St,
  Wraggsborough
Curtis, Frances, Matron, Poor House, Mazyck St
Curtis, Francis, Master, Poor House, Mazyck St
D'azevado, R, Mrs, Store Keeper, 81 King St
D'Oyley, Daniel, Whf Owner, 28 East Bay
Dalcho, F, Rev Dr, Cannonborough
Dalton, James, Druggist & Chemist, cor Church &
  Tradd Sts
Danford, ——, Mrs., School Mistress, Lynch's Ln
Dangerfield, William, Planter, St John's
Daniel, Lewis, Lumber Master, Langstaff's Whf
Danjou, Lewis, Grocer, cor Church & Tradd Sts
Darby, Robert A, Tailor, 94 East Bay
Darrell, James, Christ Church Parish (12 miles)
Darrell, John S, Capt, 23 Middle St
Darrell, Joseph, Christ Church Parish (10 miles)
Darrell, Josiah, Accomptant, 23 Middle St
Darrell, Nicholas, Captain, 122 Church St
Darrell, Robert, Factor, Magwood's Whf, Res, 99
  Wentworth St
Dart, Benjamin, Factor, 26 Tradd St
Dart, J M, Factor, Chisolm's S Whf, No 7,
  Res, Montague St
Dart, John S, Attorney at Law, 26 Tradd St
Datant, John, Planter, St John's, Berkley (50 miles)
Datty, Mark, Boarding School, 70 Wentworth St
Davenport, Samuel, Merchant, Crafts' N Whf
David, Charles, Upholsterer, Church St
David, Jacob, Shop Keeper, 6 Market St
Davidson, Gilbert, Planter, 61 Broad St
Davis, David, Tavern, Forks of the Road
Davis, Jesse, Planter, St John's, Berkeley (50
  miles)
Davis, John, M, Notary Public, 40 East Bay, Res,
  Cannonborough
Davis, John, Store Keeper, King St Road (1 Mile)
Davis, Thomas, Capt, Zigzag Court
Davis, W. G., Blacksmith, 187 King St
Davis, William, Grocer, Cannonborough
Dawes, Hugh P, Factor, Gadsden's Whf
Dawsey, William, Planter, St. John's, Berkley (48
  miles)
Dawson, John, Cashier, State Bank, Res, Bull St
Dawson, John, Mrs, Widow, Montague St
Dawson, John, Shipwright, Montague St
Day, George, Tailor, 85 King St
Dearson, William, Grocer, Gadsden's Whf.
Deas, Charles, Factor, Custom House, 99 East Bay
Deas, David, Planter, 73 Tradd St
Deas, Henry, Planter, 1 Friend St
Deas, Thomas, Merchant, 99 East Bay
Deas, William A, Planter, St Philip's St (N. End)
Debesse, J. J, Merchant, 16 Archdale St
Debow, Garrett, 28 Archdale St

Debow, John, Coach & Chair Maker, 29 Hasell St
Debow, William, Druggist, 104 East Bay
Debrier, Francis, Store Keeper, King St Rd
Decamp, F, Planter, St James', Santee (36 miles)
Decamp, James, 45 Wentworth St
Decotes, A, Clothes Warehouse, 64 East Bay St
Dehon, ——, Right Rev Dr, South Bay
Delaire & Canut, Factors, Motte's Whf
Delaney, James, Planter, St. Stephen's (44 miles)
Deleon, Abraham, Medical Store, 246 King St,
  Res, 38 Tradd St
Deleon, Jacob, Vendue Master, 38 Tradd St
Delettre, Albert, Factor, Mey's Whf.
Deliesseline, F G, Factor, 265 East Bay
Delon, Mordecai, 38 Tradd St.
Dempsey, Thomas, Grocer, 7 Minority St
Dener, George, Tanner, 11 Mazyck St
Dennison, James, Cooper, 48 East Bay
Denny, Thomas, M D, 13 Broad St
Denoon, ——, Mrs, Widow, 104 Wentworth St
Dent, John, Commodore, 160 East Bay
Depass, Joseph, Vendue Master, Vendue Range
Depass, Mary Ann, Store Keeper, 119 East Bay
Depau, Francis & Co, Factors, Motte's Whf
Depester, Hector, Planter, Daniel's Island
Desaussure, H A, Attorney at Law, 37 King St
Descoudres & Crovat, Merchants, 143 King St
Desel, Charles, Cabinet Maker, 53 Broad St
Desgar, Henry, Confectioner, King St. Rd
Desportes, Peter, Grocer, 107 East Bay
Deveaux, Jacob, Factor, 6 Cumberland St
Deveaux, John, Planter, Edisto Island
Deveaux, Thomas, Vendue Master, 149 East Bay,
  Res, Bull St
DeVillers, A, Book & Stationery Store, 51 Broad
  St
DeVillers, L, Music Store, 52 Broad St
Dewar, Robert, Director, S C Bank, 90 Tradd St
Dewees, John, Clerk, Prioleau's Whf., Res,
  Mazyckborough
Dewees, William, & Sons, Factors, Prioleau's Whf,
  Res, Mazyckborough
Diamond, John, Surveyor, 155 Meeting St
Dick, J & Co, Merchants, 341 King St
Dickinson, Francis, Attorney at Law, 18
  Cumberland St
Dickinson, J F, Grocer, 128 Tradd St
Dickinson, Joseph, Carpenter, Cannonborough
Dickinson, Samuel, Vendue Master, 6 Vendue
  Range
Dickson, Samuel, 172 King St.
Dieckert, John, Grocer, 4 Market St
Diederichs, F F & Co., Merchants, 120 Tradd St
Diele, Peter, Baker, 341 Queen St
Diesher, William, Accomptant, King St Rd
Ditmore, John, Carpenter, Hampstead
Dixon, John, Tallow Chandler & Soap Boiler, King
  St Road

144

Dixon, Robert, Butcher, King St Rd
Doglaine, ——, Madam, King St Rd
Dominique, R, Capt, 19 Cumberland St
Donaldson, William, Carpenter, 37 Beaufain St
Donn, Alexander, Carpenter, 33 Soeity St
Donnally, ——, Capt, 1 Gillon St
Doughty, Thomas, Factor, Martin's Whf, Res, 22 Anson St
Doughty, William, Planter, Harleston's Green, Smith's St
Dove, William P, Ship Joiner, Mey's Whf
Dowling, Archibald, Grocer, 3 King St
Dowling, Edward, Brick Layer, 6 Society St
Downie, Robert, Tin Plate Worker, 5 Tradd St
Downing, Samuel, St John's, Berkley (44 miles)
Doyles, Thomas, Tavern, Monk's cor (32 Mile)
Drabe, Christian, Grocer, 33 Archdale St
Drayton, Charles, M D, 145 Meeting St
Drayton, John, Judge, Federal District Court of S C, 9 Logan St
Drayton, Rebecca, Widow, Planter, Hampstead
Drayton, Thomas, Planter, 93 Wentworth St
Drayton, Thomas, Planter, St Andrew's Parish (14 miles)
Drayton, William, Col, U S Infantry, 12 Meeting St
Drayton, William, H, M D, 93 Wentworth St
Drensler, Hans, Grocer, 60 Meeting St
Drews, Henry, Grocer, 10 Lynch's Ln
Driggers, Daniel, Plasterer, 21 Goose Creek
Drummond, James, Boot & Shoe Maker, 130 Queen St
Dubec, Francis, Store Keeper, 41 King St
Dubert, Frederick, Grocer, King St Road
Duboise, Lewis, Paper Hanger, 97 Queen St
Dubose, Samuel, Planter, St Stephen's (52 miles)
Duffus, John, Accomptant, 3 Short St
Duffy, Francis, Grocer, South Bay
Duggan, Thomas, Plasterer, St Philip's St
Duhadaway, C B, Cap & Harness Maker, 32 Broad St
Duke, John, Printer, 8 Amen St
Dumaine, George, M D. & Druggist, 90 King St
Dumas, Peter, Store Keeper, 113 King St
Dumontet, J B, Jeweller & Military Store, 90 Broad St
Duncan, Alexander, Blacksmith, 26 Pinckney St
Duncan, John, Merchant, Bull & Pitt Sts
Duncan, Patrick, Tallow Chandler, Cannonborough
Dunmyer, Christian, Butcher, Meeting St Rd
Dunn, John, Grocer, 186 Meeting St
Duplat, John, Jeweller, 75 East Bay
Dupont, J B, Boot & Shoe Maker, 221 Meeting St.
Dupont, John, Planter & Master, Work-House, 34 Church St
Dupont, Joseph, Crockery & Glass Store, 210 Meeting St

Dupre, Cornelius, Factor, D'Oyley's Whf., Res, 7 Minority St
Dupre, James, Carpenter, Meeting St Road
Durang, J B, Umbrella Maker, 50 Broad St
Durban, A, Hatter, 294 King St
Duval, Peter, Grocer, Butcher's Row
Duval, Peter, Shoe Maker, Anson St
Dyott, John, Dentist, 85 Meeting St
Eagar, Sarah, Boarding House, Williams' Whf
Eason, Robert, Vendue Master, 4 Society St
Easton, James, Shipwright, 62 Anson St
Eckhard, Jacob, Music Master, 12 George St
Eckhard, Jacob, Music Master, 12 George St
Eckhart, Ann, Shop Keeper, 192 King St
Edmondston, Charles, Merchant, 224 Meeting St
Edwards & Legge, Factors, Prioleau's Whf
Edwards, Edward, Planter, Cannonborough
Edwards, Isaac, Friend St
Edwards, John, Planter, St John's (38 miles)
Egleston, John, Grocer, 207 East Bay, Res, 210
Ehney, William, Tailor, 310 King St.
Ehrenpford, J P, Cabinet Maker, 27 Broad St
Ehrick, J M, Merchant, Res, 259 East Bay
Elbridge, Elizabeth, Mrs, Widow, 18 Society St
Elfe, Benjamin, Brick Layer, Pitt St
Elfe, Benjamin, Jr Clerk, Hampstead
Elfe, Benjamin, Sr, Hampstead
Elfe, George, Planter, St Thomas' Parish
Elfe, Thomas, Carpenter, Pitt St
Elfe, Thomas, Jr Lt, U S Army, Pitt St
Elford, J M., Navigation School, 23 State St
Elizer, Eleazer, Justice of the Peace, 376 King St
Elliott & Bacot, Office, 88 Broad St
Elliott, Amarintha, Mrs, Planter, 13 Legare St
Elliott, Barnard, Mrs, Planter, 30 George St
Elliott, Benjamin, Attorney at Law, 25 Meeting St
Elliott, Charles, Attorney at Law, 5 Gibbes St
Elliott, Eliza, Mrs, Store Keeper, 115 King St
Elliott, Mary, Mrs Planter, 11 Legare St
Elliott, Thomas C, Planter, 5 Gibbes St
Ellis, Thomas, Wood Measurer, 40 Anson St
Elsinore, Alexander, Clerk, 9 Market St
Elsinore, James, Accomptant, 89 East Bay
Elsworth, F, Captain, Wentworth St
Elsworth, John T, Gauger, Custom House, 10 Maiden Ln
Elsworth, Theophilus, Gauger, Custom House, 109 East Bay
Emerson, Jonas, Grocer, 10 Middle St
Emmanuel, Isaac, Clerk, 196 King St
England, Alexander, Baker, 105 Tradd St
Enn, English, Grocer, 17 King St
Enslow, Joseph, Cooper, 6 Wentworth St, 1 St Philip's St
Erving, John, Lt First Regiment, U S Artillery, 95 Tradd St
Evans, George, M D, St John's (28 miles)
Evans, James, Marble Cutter, 38 Wentworth St

Evans, John, Shoe Maker, 179 Meeting St
Evans, Leacraft, Carpenter, 337 King St
Evans, Thomas, Planter, Christ Church Parish
Everard, William, Dyer & Scourer, 30 Society St
Ewing, Alexander, Merchant, Chisholm's Whf,
    Res, 2 Lynch's Ln
Faber, Christian H, Factor, 213 East Bay, Res, 253
    King St
Faber, John C, 213 East Bay
Faber, John C, Jr Assistant Clerk, S C Bank, 213
    East Bay
Faber, P A, Dr, Medical Store & Res, 255 King
    St.
Faber, William G, Lumber Merchant, Faber's (late
    Gadsden's) Whf, Res, 21 George St
Fair, John, Boot & Shoe Maker, 136 King St
Fair, Richard, Boot & Shoe Maker, 170 King St
Fairley, Hance, Cabinet Maker, 67 Meeting St
Fairweather, R, Grocer, 154 Meeting St
Farr, Elizabeth, Mrs, 100 Meeting St
Farr, John, Wharfinger, M'Cormick's Whf, Res,
    100 Meeting St.
Faust, Jeremiah, Grocer, Market St
Fayolle, Peter, Dancing Master, 359 King St
Fell, Thomas, Tinner, 130 Tradd St
Feraud, Alexander, 209 King St
Ferguson, Ann, Mrs, Planter, 2 Liberty St
Ferguson, James, Aide to Maj Gen Pinckney, 2
    Liberty St
Ferguson, John, 21 Friend St
Ferguson, Samuel, M D, 2 Liberty St
Fewaux, Eliza, Planter, Wassmasaw (28 miles)
Finch, Joseph, 191 Meeting St
Fisher, George A, Saddler, 287 King St
Fisher, James, Merchant, 52 Meeting St
Fitzpatrick, P, Tailor, 114 Tradd St
Fitzsimons, C, Factor, Fitzsimons' Whf, Res, 37
    Hasell St
Flemming, James, Grocer, 39 Tradd St
Flemming, John, Store Keeper, King St Rd
Flemming, Matthew, Grocer, cor Tradd St & East
    Bay, Res., 130 Tradd St
Flemming, Thomas, Merchant, 187 King St
Flemming, Thomas, Merchant, 361 King St
Flinn, ——, Rev Dr, South Bay
Flint, Joseph, Grocer, 92 East Bay
Flodore, John, Grocer, 29 Tradd St
Florance, Z, Merchant, 316 King St
Florin, Henry, 37 Guignard St
Flotard & Co, Store Keepers, 230 King St
Flyn & Neville, Grocers, Magazine St
Fogartie, James, City Marshal, 41 Anson St
Fohn, A & F, Tobacconists, 174 Meeting St
Foissin, Esther, Mrs, Widow, 103 Tradd St
Folker, James, Accomptant, 38 Beaufain St
Folker, John C., Justice of the Peace, 38 Beaufain
    St
Folker, John Hinds, Merchant, 51 King St

Folker, Joseph, Academy, 10 Minority St
Folker, Patrick Hinds, 38 Beaufain St
Folker, Thomas P, M D, Medical Store, Etc,
    Res, cor Church & Elliott Sts
Forbes, John, Tin Plate Worker, 276 King St
Ford & Desaussure, Attorney at Law, Office, 27
    Tradd St
Ford, Jacob, Attorney at Law, Office, 27 Tradd St
Ford, Timothy, Attorney at Law, 232 Meeting St
Fordham, Benjamin, Pump & Block Maker, 204
    East Bay
Fordham, Joseph, Pump & Block Maker, 31
    Guignard St
Forrester, Susannah, Hampstead
Foster, Nathan, Grocer, 47 Elliott St
Fowke, Mary, Mrs, Planter, 7 Church St
Fowler, Michael, Planter, St Thomas'
Fowles, William, Cabinet Maker, 60 Meeting St
Fraser, ——, Major, Planter, Meeting St Rd
Fraser & Coit, Factors, Custom House, D'Oyley's
    Whf
Fraser, Alexander, 42 Pinckney St
Fraser, Charles, Attorney at Law, 22 Tradd St
Fraser, James, Planter, King St Rd
Fraser, James Staunton, Printer, Gazette Office
Fraser, Sarah, Ashley Ferry (10 miles)
Frazer, John M, Carpenter, 41 Wentworth St
Frean, Martha, Mrs, Widow, 106 Meeting St
Frean, William, Grocer, 295 King St
Frederick, Naested, Store Keeper, 22 Broad St
Freeman, Benjamin, Planter, Wadmalaw
Freeman, Josiah, Planter, John's Island
Freeman, Mary, Mrs, Planter, Wadmalaw
Freeman, Richard, Jr, Planter, John's Island
Freeman, Richard, Planter, John's Island
Freneau, Peter, 35 George St
Frink, Thomas, 44 Pinckney St.
Frish, Charles, Store Keeper, 263 King St
Fronty, Michael, M D, 225 King St
Frost, Thomas, Mrs, Widow, 10 West St
Fry, Jacob, Tanner, King St Rd
Fuller, Benjamin, Planter, St Andrew's (12 miles)
Fuller, Catharine, Mrs, Widow, 45 Tradd St
Fuller, Christian, M D., Ashley Ferry (12 miles)
Fuller, Oliver, Capt, Merchant, 56 Meeting St
Fuller, William, Hatter, 87 King St
Fulmer, John, Chair Maker, Blackbird Al
Furman, R, Rev Dr, 10 Church St
Furman, Richard, M. D, 10 Church St
Furman, Wood, Classical Teacher, 136 Church St
Futterell, James, Teller, S C Bank, 35 King St
Gabeau, Anthony, Tailor, 215 Meeting St
Gabeau, Daniel, Accomptant, 215 Meeting St
Gabeau, James, Cooper & Packer, Crafts' N Whf
Gabeau, John, Pump, Block & Mast Maker, 215
    Meeting St
Gabeau, Simon, Capt, 215 Meeting St
Gadsden, C., Rev, 7 George St.

Gadsden, James, 7 George St.
Gadsden, James W., Planter, Cannonborough
Gadsden, John, City Attorney, 7 George St
Gadsden, Philip, 7 George St.
Gadsden, Thomas, Mrs., 12 Meeting St
Gaillard & Mazyck, Factors, Chisolm's Whf
Gaillard, Bartholomew, St John's (39 miles)
Gaillard, Charles, Surveyor, St James', Santee
Gaillard, David, Planter, St James', Santee
Gaillard, James, Pineville
Gaillard, John, Hon., Planter, St James', Santee (40 miles)
Gaillard, Peter, Planter, St John's (52 miles)
Gaillard, Theodore, Factor, Montague St
Gaillard, Theodore, Judge, Court of Equity
Gaillard, Theodore, Jr., St John's (37 miles)
Gaillard, William, Planter, St James', Santee (48 miles)
Gallagher, F., Rev Dr., 90 Wentworth St.
Galloway, James, Grocer, cor East Bay & Pinckney Sts
Garden, Alexander, Maj., Planter, 55 Tradd St
Gardner, Ann, Mrs., Widow, 40 Hasell St
Gardner, John, Blacksmith, Fish Market, Res., 40 Society St
Gardner, John, Merchant, 215 East Bay
Gardouin, Isidore, Hat Store, 76 East Bay
Garnier, Joseph, Grocer, 77 Church St.
Gates, ——, Mrs., Widow, King St Rd
Gaugdeau, Theodore, Planter, Meeting St Rd
Gaultier, Joseph, 89 Tradd St
Geddes, John, Hon., Attorney at Law, 98 Broad St
Geddes, Robert, Merchant, King St Rd
Gefkin, Christiana, Mrs., Widow, 8 Society St
Gefkin, Henry, Carpenter, 19 Mazyck St
Gell, John, Livery Stables, Bank Square, Res., Cannonborough
Gentil, A., Shop Keeper, 31 Anson St
George, James, Shipwright, 88 East Bay
George, John, Grocer, 246 East Bay
Gervais, Paul T., Rev., 10 Legare St
Geyer, John, Capt., 18 Lynch's Ln
Gibbes, George, Baker, 40 Elliott St.
Gibbes, John, Planter, 141 Meeting St
Gibbes, Robert, Planter, 7 South Bay
Gibbes, William H., Master in Equity, 46 Broad St
Gibbes, William, Planter, James Island
Gibson, James, Tannery, 138 Meeting St
Gibson, Robert, Store Keeper, 330 King St.
Gibson, William H., 138 Meeting St
Gidere, ——, Madam, Store Keeper, 209 King St
Gidere, John J., Store Keeper, 209 King St
Gilbert, Seth H., Wharfinger, D'Oyley's Whf
Gilchrist, Adam & Son, Merchants, 261 East Bay
Giles, Othniel J., State Coroner, 28 King St
Gill, Isaac, Watch Maker, 219 Meeting St
Gilliland & Co., Merchants, 175 King St
Gilliland, William H., Tailor, 199 King St.

Gilman, Zaddock, Merchant, 8 Crafts' N. Whf.
Glen, John, Teller, Planters and Mechanics Bank
Glen, Martha, Mrs., Widow, 19 Montague St
Glenn, Margaret, Mrs., Widow, 59 Tradd St
Glieze, Henry, M D., cor Anson & Market Sts
Glover, Charles H., M D., 21 Beaufain St
Glover, Charles, Notary Public & Q U., 68 East Bay
Glover, Joseph, M D., 10 Rutledge St
Glover, Sanders, Planter, St Thomas'
Glover, Wilson, Planter, 2 Meeting St
Godard, Rene, Broker, 61 King St
Godet, John, Grocer, 153 Meeting St
Good, Francis, Shop Keeper, Meeting St Rd
Goodman, Duke, Store Keeper, 177 King St Rd
Gordon, C P., Wharfinger, Crafts' Whf
Gordon, James, Brick Layer, 106 Queen St
Gordon, James, Merchant, 43 East Bay
Gordon, John, Brick Layer, 106 Queen St
Gordon, William E., Butcher, Hampstead
Gordon, William, Grocer, 96 King St
Goss, William, 8 West St
Gough, John P., M D., 244 Meeting St
Gough, R S., Planter, 13 Liberty St
Gourdine, Samuel, Planter, St. John's, Berkeley (34 miles)
Gourly, John, Tanner, Hampstead
Gradick, Christian, Butcher, Butcher Row
Grado, Marian, Boarding House, State St.
Grady, John, Grocer & Boarding House, cor Church St & Berresford Al
Graham, Thomas, Cabinet Maker, 58 King St
Grahame, Archibald, Merchant, King St. Rd
Grainer, Charles, Watch Maker, 88 Meeting St
Grant & Duboise, Tailors, 107 Church St
Grant, Alexander, Merchant, 116 Church St
Grantt, James, Printer, Washington St
Graves, Charles, Factor, 54 Tradd St
Graves, Charles, Jr., 54 Tradd St
Gray & Corby, Blacksmiths, 16 Queen St
Gray, Henry, Justice of the Peace, 273 King St
Gray, William, Merchant, 278 East Bay
Gready, Andrew P., Printer, 106 Wentworth St
Gredless, Owen, Planter, St James', Santee
Greeland, George, 31 Meeting St
Green, Edmund, Factor, 119 Broad St
Green, Edmund, Jr., Factor, 119 Broad St
Green, Elizabeth, Planter, St John's (52 miles)
Green, John, Grocer, 18 Queen St.
Greenhill, Hume, Carpenter, Adams St
Greenland, William P., Factor, Prioleau's Whf
Greenwood, William, Merchant, 21 Beaufain St
Gregory, Maria, Mrs., Widow, 26 Anson St
Griggs, Isaac, Attorney at Law, State St.
Grille, Claude, Hat Store, 152 King St
Grimke, ——, Doctor, 153 East Bay
Grimke, Frederick, Attorney at Law, 153 East Bay

Grimke, Thomas F, Judge, Court of Common Pleas & Sessions, 153 East Bay
Grimke, Thomas S, Attorney at Law, 37 Church St
Grisson, John, Fruit Store, 52 Elliott St
Groning, L & R, Merchant, 25 East Bay, Res, 15 Montague St
Gros, John, Cabinet Maker, 25 Hasell St
Groschong, T, Cigar Maker, 97 East Bay
Gruber, Charles, Captain, Magazine Guard (Neck)
Gruber, Christian, Accomptant, Meeting St Rd
Gue, J F, Tin Plate Worker, 13 Market St
Guerineau, Joseph, Grocer, 362 King St
Guerineau, Joseph, Store Keeper, 39 King St
Gunter, P F., Tailor, 123 East Bay
Hagen, Richard, Store Keeper, King St Rd
Hagood, John, Merchant, 10 St Philip's St
Hahahan, Broker, St Philip's St (Neck)
Hahnbaum, ——, Mrs, Boarding School, 18 Guignard St
Hahnbaum, George, Carpenter, 18 Guignard St
Haig, David, Cooper, 150 Meeting St
Haig, Robert, Carpenter, 111 Wentworth St
Hall, James, Stone Cutter, 56 Church St
Hall, Thomas, 36 Broad St
Hall, William & George, Merchants, 104 Broad St
Hall, William, Jr, M D, 152 East Bay St
Hall, William, Warden, 152 East Bay St
Halsall, William, Butcher, cor Guignard St & Maiden Ln
Ham, Thomas, Commission Merchant, Motte's Whf
Hamilton, David, Wharfinger, Fitzsimons' Whf
Hamilton, John, Shipwright, 5 Anson St
Hamilton, Malborough, School Master, cor Meeting & Queen Sts
Hammet, Thomas, Vendue Master, 46 Wentworth St
Hanckell, Christian, Rev, 19 Society St
Hancock, George, Cabinet Maker, 3 Hard Al
Hannah, Alexander, Merchant, 8 Broad St
Hannah, Andrew, Merchant, 8 Broad St
Happoldt, J P., Butcher, Hampstead
Harby, Isaac, Classical Teacher, 17 Berresford St.
Harleston, Edward, Planter, 23 St Philip's St.
Harleston, Nicholas, Planter, Bull St.
Harleston, William, Planter, St John's (33 miles)
Harper, J, Musical Instrument Maker, 320 King St
Harper, James, Baker, 42 Tradd St
Harper, Thomas, Hat Store, 70 East Bay
Harris, E, Hat Store, 212 Meeting St
Harris, Jacob, Store Keeper, 226 King St
Harris, Tucker, M D., 78 King St
Hart, Elizabeth, Mrs, Store Keeper, 79 East Bay
Hart, John, Accomptant, 18 King St
Hart, Nathan, Store Keeper, 13 King St
Hart, Simon Moses, Store Keeper, 19 Elliot St
Hart, William, Accomtpant, 20 King St
Harth, John, Lumber Merchant, South Bay

Harth, William, Lumber Merchant, Gibbes St
Harvey, Arnold, Planter, Wassamsaw (31 miles)
Harvey, Benjamin, Capt, Planter, Cannonborough
Harvey, Elizabeth, Mrs., Widow, 14 Maiden Ln
Harvey, Mary, Mrs, Widow, School Mistress, 36 Society St
Hasell, Andrew, Planter, 17 South Bay
Haskell, ——, Maj, Planter, 155 East Bay
Haskett, Samuel, Saddle & Harness Maker, 165 King St
Haskins, Sarah, Widow, 10 Blackbird Al
Haslett, John, Merchant, 27 East Bay
Hattier & Son, Store Keepers, 173 King St
Hauck, John, Grocer, 8 Laurens St
Hawes, Benjamin, 21 Hasell St
Hawes, Mary, Mrs, Widow, 21 Hasell St.
Hawes, Nathaniel, 21 Hasell St
Hayda, David, Store Keeper, 177 Meeting St
Hayne, Stephen, Planter, St Stephen's
Hazlehurst, Robert, Merchant, 8 Church St
Hazzard, John, Ship Joiner, 2 Hard Al
Heath, John D, Attorney at Law, 34 Meeting St
Hedderly, William, Bell Hanger, 86 Queen St
Hedley, John, Rev, D D, Classical Teacher, 46 Tradd St
Helfred, John, Constable, Boarding House, Champneys St
Helsey, John, Tailor, 81 Meeting St
Hendrichson, B, Carpenter, Hampstead
Henry, Alexander, Merchant, King St Rd
Henry, Jacob, Store Keeper, King St Rd
Henry, Julien, Cabinet Maker, 168 Meeting St
Henry, Mary, Mrs., Midwife, 108 King St. Rd
Hentz, M C, Boarding School, 5 Meeting St.
Henwood, Thomas, Accomptant, 2 St Philip's St
Herbert, John, Grocer, 5 East Bay
Herd, Benjamin F, Factor, Prioleau's Whf
Heriot, Roger, Factor, Blake's Whf
Heriot, Roger, Mrs, Young Ladies Academy, cor King & Boundary Sts
Hertz, H. M, Store Keeper, 160 King St.
Hertz, Jacob, Merchant, 12 Beaufain St
Heulan, Jonty, M D & Druggist, 25 Meeting St
Hewitt, Thomas, Grocer, 19 King St
Heyward, Nathaniel, Jr, Planter, 144 East Bay
Heyward, Nathaniel, Planter, 144 East Bay
Heyward, William, Planter, 144 East Bay
Hill, Christian G, Carpenter, 29 Archdale St
Hill, Francis C, Ornamental Painter, 29 Archdale St
Hill, Paul, Wire & Cane Worker, 29 Archdale St
Hobrocker, I. C, Blacksmith, Market St
Hoff, John M, Clerk of the Markets, 7 Middle St
Hoff, John, Stationer & Printer, 117 Broad St
Hoff, Philip, Stationer & Printer, 117 Broad St
Holland, ——, Mrs, Boarding House, 49 Meeting St.
Holland, Edward, 49 Meeting St

Holland, John, Boarding House, 49 Meeting St
Hollinshead, William, Rev, D D, Maiden Ln
Holmes, ——, Notary Public, 46 East Bay
Holmes, Harriet, Mrs, Widow, 10 Lynch's Ln
Holmes, John B, Recorder, 6 Meeting St
Holmes, Joseph B, Accomptant, 44 East Bay
Holmes, Margaret, Matron, Orphan House
Holmes, William, Butcher, Coming St (Neck)
Holmes, William H., Factor, Gadsden's Whf
Holmes, William, Vendue Master, Boundary St
Holton, James, Cumberland St
Hopkins, J M. Merchant, East Bay, cor
  Magwood's Whf.
Horden, Eliza, Mrs, Grocer, Wentworth St
Horlbeck, Henry, Brick Layer, 14 Cumberland St
Horlbeck, John, Brick Layer, 18 Cumberland St
Horry, Elias L, Planter, 65 Broad St
Horry, Harriet, Mrs, Planter, 61 Tradd St
Horry, Thomas, Planter, 25 Meeting St
Hort, William, Planter, Christ Church (237 Mile)
Houchet, Charles, Store Keeper, Queen St
Hough, Wade, Merchant, East Bay
Houston, James, Carpenter, 17 Middle St
Howaith, Benjamin, M D, St John's (51 Mile)
Howard, Alexander, Deputy Comptroller
Howard, John, Brick Layer, 140 Meeting St
Howard, Richard, Cooper, Gillon St
Howard, Robert, Maj, Painter, 31 Hasell St
Howard, William, Deputy Surveyor General,
  Hampstead
Howe & Fitch, Merchants, 232 East Bay
Howe, Michael, South Bay
Howe, S, Shoe Store, 74 Meeting St
Hubbard, Elisha, Grocer, Tradd St
Hudson, Joseph, Capt, Liberty St
Huff, Jacob, Planter, Goose Creek
Huger, Daniel, 80 Queen St.
Huger, Daniel F., Attorney at Law, 36 Meeting St.
Huggins, William, Planter, Christ Church Parish
Hughes, Edward, Planter, Dorchester
Hughes, Edward, Young Ladies Academy, 87 Tradd
  St
Hughes, John, Accomptant, 6 Lamboll St
Hughes, Mahehi, Planter, St Stephen's
Hull, Latham, Vendue Master, Vendue Range
Hume, John, Planter, 61 Wentworth St
Hume, Robert, Planter, 61 Wentworth St
Hunt, John F, Attorney at Law, 50 Church St
Hunt, Thomas, Attorney at Law, 41 Broad St.
Hunter, John, Millinery Store, 138 King St
Hunter, Randad, Shoe Maker, 15 Elliot St
Hussy, Bryan, Capt, 12 Water St
Huston, James, Merchant Tailor, 61 Church St.
Hutchins, Samuel, Brick Layer, 3 Hasell St
Huxford, Harleck, Planter, St John's (55 miles)
Hyams, David, Archdale St
Hyams, Isaac, Store Keeper, 108 King St
Hyams, Samuel, Vendue Master, 5 Vendue Range

I'on, Jacob Bond, Planter, Christ Church Parish
Inglesby, Henry, Merchant Tailor, 107 Tradd St
Inglesby, William, Planter, 57 Broad St
Ingraham, Henry, Merchant, 293 King St.
Ingraham, Nathaniel, Merchant, 293 King St
Ireland, Benjamin, Carpenter, 107 Queen St
Irvine, Matthew, M. D, 7 Meeting St
Isaacks, A. M, Grocer, 76 Meeting St
Isaccks, Abraham, Vendue Master, 10 Vendue
  Range
Izard, Henry, Planter, St Andrew's
Izard, Ralph, Planter, 79 Broad St
Izard, Ralph, Planter, St Andrew's
Jackson, Hugh, Wharfinger, Bailey's Whf
Jackson, John, Planter, Wasamsaw
Jackson, Montague, Deputy Sheriff, City & District
  of Charleston, 17 Archdale St
Jackson, William, Boarding House, 213 Meeting St
Jacobs, Cecilia, Store Keeper, 69 East Bay
Jacobs, Hyam, 27 Meeting St
James, Jacks, Jewellers, 105 Broad St
James, John, Carpenter, 196 Meeting St
Jaques, D, Silversmith & Plater, 17 Wentworth St
Jarman, John, Race Ground (2 miles)
Javain & Co, Grocers, 95 King St
Jeanerett, Christopher, Teller, State Bank, Wall St
Jeanerett, John, Accompant, 15 King St
Jeffords, John, Planter, Christ Church Parish
Jeffords, John, Tailor, 8 Pinckney St
Jenkins, Benjamin, Planter, Wadmalaw
Jenkins, Christopher, Planter, Edisto Island
Jenkins, Elias, Brick Layer, 11 Liberty St
Jenkins, Joseph, Planter, Edisto Island
Jenkins, Micah, Planter, 10 Legare St
Jenkins, R, Planter, John's Island
Jenkins, Robert, Planter, Edisto Island
Jenkins, Samuel, Planter, Wadmalaw
Jervey, James, Clerk, Federal Court, 223 Meeting
  St
Jessop, Jeremiah, Grocer, 124 Queen St
Joel, Thomas, Planter, St Thomas' (16 miles)
Johnson & Fordham, Blacksmiths, 9 Gillon St
Johnson, Andrew, Grocer, 45 Tradd St
Johnson, Andrew, Planter, St Thomas' Parish
Johnson, Benjamin, Shipwright, Johnson's Whf
Johnson, Charles, 46 Anson St
Johnson, Hans, Grocer, 26 Pinckney St
Johnson, Joseph & I A, M D & Druggists, 105
  Broad St.
Johnson, Jabez W, Watch Maker, 201 King St
Johnson, John, 226 King St
Johnson, John, Carpenter, 42 King St
Johnson, John, Furnace, Etc, Res, Washington St,
  Mazyckborough
Johnson, Thomas, Boot & Shoe Maker, 130 Queen
  St
Johnson, William, Blacksmith, 59 Anson St

Johnson, William, Hon., Federal Judge,
   Cannonborough
Johnston, Edward, Grocer, 23 State St
Johnston, Peter, Printer, 3 Amen St
Johnston, Thomas, Store Keeper, King St Rd
Jones, Abraham, Cabinet Maker, 5 Beaufain St
Jones, Edward, M. D, St Philip's St (Neck)
Jones, Henry, Shipwright, 20 Pinckney St
Jones, Joseph, 12 Tradd St.
Jones, Margaret, Mrs, Widow, 30 King St
Jones, Paul, Assistant Clerk, S C Bank
Jones, Samuel B, Book Keeper, S C Bank, 1
   Guignard St
Jones, Thomas, Factor, Mey's Whf, Res, 77 Queen
   St
Jones, Thomas, President, S C Bank, 2 Guignard
   St
Jones, Thomas, Store Keeper, Prioleau's Whf
Jost, John, 1 Market St
Jourdon, Daniel, Planter, St John's (44 miles)
Julian, Joseph, Carpenter, 120 Meeting St
Just, George, 38 Pinckney St
Kanust, K, Grocer, 68 Broad St
Keating & Cassin, Store Keepers, King St Rd
Keckeley, George, Planter, Goose Creek (25 miles)
Keckeley, Michael, Planter, cor Coming &
   Boundary Sts
Keckley, John, Cabinet Maker
Keels, ——, Mrs, Widow, Store Keeper, 206 King
   St Rd
Keely, Sebastian, Inspector, Custom House,
   Cannonborough
Keenan, George, Merchant, 66 King St. Rd.
Keith, George, 9 Society St
Keith, I, Rev Dr., 49 Tradd St
Keith, Sylvanus, Merchant, 137 King St
Kelly, Christopher, Union Tavern, Cannonborough
Kelly, James, Grocer, Cannonborough
Kelly, John A, Store Keeper, 129 King St
Kelly, John, Pilot, 16 Guignard St
Kelly, Joseph, Grocer, 39 Anson St.
Kelly, Mary, Mrs, Widow, Store Keeper, 129 King
   St.
Kelly, Mary, Mrs, Widow, 38 Lamboll St
Kelly, Michael, Merchant, 51 East Bay
Kemnitz, F., Grocer, 395 King St
Kempson, Harman, Carpenter, 2 Vanderhorst St
Kennedy, E, Mrs, Tavern Keeper, St John's (36
   miles)
Kennedy, Edward, (of the Custom House), 21
   Mazyck St
Kennedy, James, Capt, Planter, 10 Mazyck St
Kennedy, John, Planter, St John's (36 miles)
Kennedy, Lionel H., Attorney at Law, 43 Broad St
Kennedy, Peter, Grocer, 51 Tradd St
Ker, Andrew, Merchant, 87 Church St
Kern & Perry, Grocers, 268 King St
Kerr, Adam, 388 King St

Kerr, John, 388 King St
Kerr, Joseph, 388 King St
Kerr, William, Accomptant, 388 King St
Kershaw, Charles, Factor, 121 Church St
Kerwan, Thomas, Planter, St Thomas' (18 miles)
Kiddle, Charles, Merchant, 17 Broad St
King & Jones, Merchants, 6 Tradd St.
King, Benjamin, Carpenter, St Philip's St.
King, Mary, Mrs, Grocer, 23 King St
King, Mitchell, Attorney at Law, Office, 2 St
   Michael's Al.
King, William, Planter, Four Holes
Kippenberg, Andrew, Grocer, 37 Queen St
Kirk, Alexander, Merchant, 47 East Bay
Kirk, John, Grocer, 2 King St
Kirk, John, Merchant, 74 East Bay
Kirk, Robert, Planter, St John's (53 miles)
Kirkland & Akin, M D & Druggist, 107 Church
   St
Kirkpatrick & Douglas, Factors, Bailey's Whf
Kittleband, David, Carpenter, 14 Logan St
Kittleband, J, Carpenter, 14 Logan St
Kneiff, Francis, Grocer, 24 Archdale St
Knough, John, Saddler, King St Rd
Knox, John F, Shipwright, (Pritchard & Knox), 34
   Guignard St
Knox, John, Keeper, Hay Market, Gadsden's Whf
Kohler, Frederick, Tanner, King St Rd
Kohne & Maxwell, Merchants, 263 East Bay
Kohne, Frederick, Merchant, 67 Broad St
Kugley, John, Carpenter, 17 Mazyck St
Kunhardt, William, Wharfinger, Bailey's Whf
Kurtze, Ludolph, Grocer, Washington St.
Labarben, Alexander, Teacher of the French, 67
   King St
Labassy, Peter, Baker, King St. Rd
Labat, Catharine, Mrs, Store Keeper, 126 Queen St
Labatut, A, Limner, 84 Meeting St
Laborde, Francis, Livery Stables, 246 King St
Labreton, J B, Store Keeper, 321 King St
Lacomb, ——, Monsieur, Tobacconist, 120 King St
Lacombe, Stephen, M. D, 15 Maiden Ln
Lacoste, Charles, Store Keeper, 217 King St
Lacoste, Stephen, Mrs, Widow, King St Rd
Lacoudre, G, M. D & Druggist, 166 Meeting St
Ladaveze, R & A, Store Keepers, 94 King St
Lafan, E G, Master, Free School No 4, 199 King
   St
Lafar, David B, Cooper, Magwood's Whf, Res,
   163 Meeting St
Lafar, Joseph D, Cooper, Blake's Whf, Res, 163
   Meeting St
Lafar, P X. & J J, Gold & Silversmiths, 163
   Meeting St
Laffilly, Francis, Accomptant, 17 Wentworth St
Lafon, John, Cooper, 212 East Bay
Lagrange, Lewis, M D, 88 Church St
Laidler, William, Capt, 6 Blackbird Al

150

Lamb, David, Merchant, Blake's Whf, Res, 104 Tradd St

Lamb, James, Merchant, Blake's Whf, Res, 104 Tradd St

Lamb, Thomas, Classical Academy, 112 Queen St.

Lambert, Francis, Porter House, 81 East Bay

Lancaster, —, Shipwright, Williams' Whf

Lance, Lambert, Mrs, Widow, 86 Queen St

Lance, William, Attorney at Law, 1 St. Michael's Al

Lane, Robert, Mrs, Widow, St Philip's St

Laneau, Basil, Tanner, 1 Pitt St.

Lang, John H, Merchant, East Bay

Langton, John, Book Keeper, Planters & Mechanics Bank, 101 Broad St

Lanswerall, Benjamin C, Tailor, 61 Church St

Lapiere, Bernard, Cabinet Maker, 95 Meeting St.

Laporte, Rene, Meeting St Rd

Larry, John, Book Keeper, 75 Church St

Larry, Peter, Carpenter, 75 Church St

Larry, Peter, Jr, Brick Layer, 75 Church St

Lartigue, J, Confectioner, 83 King St

Latham, Daniel, Sr, Distiller, 2 Hasell St

Lathan, Daniel, Jr, Merchant, 2 Hasell St

Lathan, Richard L, M D, 3 Hasell St

Laurens, Henry, Planter, 169 East Bay

Laval, Jacint, Planter, Goose Creek (23 miles)

Lawrence, E, Mrs Widow, 18 Pinckney St

Lazarus, Jacob, Vendue Master, 217 East Bay

Lazarus, Mark, 114 King St

Lazarus, Michael, Store Keeper, 146 King St

Lecat, F, Musician, 26 Ellery St

Lechais, Andrew, Deputy Post Master, 49 King St

Lee, —, Mrs, Midwife, 5 Ellery St

Lee, Dorothy, Mrs, Planter, 96 Broad St.

Lee, Paul S H, Planter, 96 Broad St

Lee, Stephen, Brick Layer, 36 Hasell St

Lee, Thomas, Cabinet Maker, 69 Market St

Lee, Thomas, Comptroller, Office, Guard House, Res, 48 Society St

Lee, William, Attorney at Law, Office, Exchange, Res, 4 George St.

Lee, William C., Tobacconist, 172 Meeting St

Lee, William, Clerk, Union Bank, King St Rd

Leefe, Benjamin, Vendue Master, Vendue Range, Res, 10 Meeting St.

Legare, Francis, Planter, 3 New St

Legare, James, Planter, 3 New St

Legare, Solomon, Planter, 32 Friend St

Legare, Thomas, Planter, 1 Gibbes St

Legge, John H, Factor, Prioleau's Whf, Res, 130 Wentworth St

Legge, Joseph, Planter, Race Ground

Legrand, Lewis, Hair Dresser, 123 King St

Lehre, —, Dr, Mrs., 33 Beaufain St

Lehre, Thomas, Col, 371 King St

Leitch & Kidd, Grocers, 283 King St

Leland, A W, Rev, 15 Legare St

Leland, B & I, Merchants, 239 East Bay

Lequeux, Benjamin, Planter, St Stephen's (50 miles)

Lequeux, John, Merchant, 35 Anson St

Lequeux, Sims, Planter, St John's (28 miles)

Leslie, Henry, Capt, 69 Anson St

Lessene, —, Captain, 16 Society St

Lessene, Daniel, Planter, St Thomas' (21 miles)

Lethbridge & Co, Merchants, 89 East Bay

Levy, Abraham, Jeweller, 155 King St

Levy, B, Printer, Meeting St Rd

Levy, Elias, Accomptant, 278 King St

Levy, Emanuel, Store Keeper, 63 East Bay

Levy, Jacob, Saddler, 37 Meeting St

Levy, Lyon, Deputy State Treasurer, 278 King St

Levy, Reuben, Broker, 71 Anson St

Levy, S, Store Keeper, 277 King St

Levy, Simon, Store Keeper, 150 King St

Levy, Solomon, Store Keeper, 52 King St

Lewis, David, Store Keeper, 254 King St

Lewis, John, Grocer, 13 East Bay St

Lewis, John, Merchant, 1 Middle St

Lewis, John, Store Keeper, 53 King St

Lindsay, John L, Butcher, Cannonborough

Lindsay, William, Merchant, 87 East Bay St, Res, 130 Church St

Ling, John, Merchant, cor Church & Tradd Sts

Ling, P, Coach Maker, 11 Ellery St

Ling, R & P, Coach Makers, 41 Market St

Lining, Charles, Attorney at Law, 6 Legare St

Lining, Edward, Attorney at Law, 6 Legare St

Lipman, Abraham, Watch Maker, 101 King St.

Little, Robert, Lumber Merchant, Motte's Whf, Res, Charlotte St, Mazyckborough

Livingston, Alexander, Tailor, 10 Archdale St

Livingston, Gordon, Grocer, 168 King St

Livingston, R Y, Book Keeper, Union Bank, 42 Society St

Lloyd, John, Deputy City Sheriff, 190 Meeting St

Lloyd, John, Factor, Bull St

Lloyd, John P, Venetian Blind Maker, 111 Meeting St

Lloyd, Joseph & Son, Merchants, 55 King St

Lockwood, Joshua, Teller, State Bank, 1 Smith's Ln

Logan, C M, Commission Merchant, 50 Church St.

Logan, George, Dr, 15 Cumberland St

Logan, George R, Attorney at Law, 51 Broad St

Logan, William, Planter, Goose Creek (25 miles)

Lopez, —, Mrs, Store Keeper, 336 King St

Lopez, Aaron, 26 Ellery St

Lopez, John, Grocer, 75 Meeting St

Lord, Archibald, U. S Navy, 9 Mazyck St

Lord, Jacob N, Shoe Maker, Brownlee's Row

Lorent & Steinmetz, Merchants, 45 East Bay

Lothrop, Samuel, Whf Owner, Lothrop's Row

Lothrop, Seth, Whf Owner, Lothrop's Row

Lovell, Josiah, Merchant, 399 King St
Lowndes, Thomas, Planter, 71 Broad St
Lowndes, William, Hon , Member of Congress,
Ashley River (2 miles)
Lowrey, Charles, Tailor, 78 Church St
Lowrey, Daniel, Planter, Edisto Island
Lowrey, Henry, Planter, Edisto Island
Lucas, Jonathan, Mills, Cannonborough
Lucas, Jonathan, Planter, Christ Church Parish
Lukens, John, Cashier, Union Bank, 6 Hasell St
Lusher, George, Merchant, 199 East Bay
Luther & Stall, Boot & Shoe Store, 211 Meeting St
Lyles, Z , Baker, 15 Cumberland St
Lynah, E , Dr , Planter, Widow, 47 Meeting St
Lynah, Edward, Mrs., Widow, 47 Meeting St
Lynah, James, 47 Meeting St
Lynn, John, Factor, Gadsden's Whf
Lyons, Isaac, Mineral Water Warehouse, 62 East
Bay
Lyons, Isaac, Planter, Wassamsaw (31 miles)
M'Bain, James, Sail Maker's Loft, Motte's Whf
M'Beth, James, Commission Merchant, 5 Lamboll
St
M'Call & Hays, Attorneys at Law, 115 Church St
M'Call, Ann, Mrs , Widow, 130 Church St
M'Call, Beckman, Accomptant, 130 Church St
M'Call, James, Planter, King St Rd
M'Call, John H , Planter, St John's (28 miles)
M'Calla, ——, Mrs , Dr , 38 Anson St
M'Candlish, William, 16 Tradd St
M'Cants, Ann, Mrs , Planter, James Island
M'Cants, David, Planter, St John's (58 miles)
M'Cants, James, Planter, St John's (27 miles)
M'Cants, John, Planter, St John's (58 miles)
M'Cants, Nathaniel, Planter, St John's (42 miles)
M'Cauley & Co , Merchants, 18 Broad St
M'Cauley, Daniel, Jr , Merchant, 9 Broad St.
M'Cauley, George, Merchant, 119 Church St
M'Cay, Barbara, King St Rd
M'Cay, L. R , Classical Teacher, 76 Broad St
M'Chesh, James, Brass Founder, 15 Pinckney St
M'Cormick & Egan, Attorneys at Law, 83 Broad
St
M'Cready, William, Carpenter, 184 King St
M'Donnald, Adam, Planter, St Stephen's (46 miles)
M'Donnald, Christopher, Grocer, 361 King St
M'Donnald, Sarah, Boarding House, 260 King St
M'Donnald, Susannah E , Planter, 11 Beaufain St.
M'Dowall & Black, Merchants, 79 King St.
M'Dowall, Alexander, Saddler & Harness Maker,
88 King St
M'Dowall, Andrew, Merchant, 79 King St
M'Dowall, James, Merchant, 79 King St
M'Dowall, John, Merchant, 174 King St
M'Dowall, John, Planter, St Thomas' (21 miles)
M'Dowall, Robert, Boot & Shoe Maker, 60 Church
St
M'Elmoyle, William, Grocer, 24 King St

M'Farland, James, Carpenter, 247 Meeting St
M'Fie & Calder, Merchants, Bailey's Whf
M'Gann, Patrick, Watch Maker, Coates' Row, East
Bay
M'Gillivray, Alexander, Vendue Master, 247 East
Bay, Res , 17 Lynch's Ln
M'Hough, Francis, Carpenter, 3 West St.
M'Intosh, John, Cabinet Maker, 62 Meeting St
M'Kay, James, Merchant, 9 Broad St
M'Kay, Malcolm, 52 Tradd St.
M'Kee, Abel, Ship Joiner, Shop, Fish Market Whf
M'Kee, John, Brick Layer, 378 King St
M'Kenzie, Ann, Mrs., Widow, Hampstead
M'Kenzie, Henry, Butcher, Hampstead
M'Kenzie, John, Grocer, 103 Church St
M'Kinlay, Dugald, Merchant, 52 East Bay
M'Kinney, ——; Factor, Blake's Whf
M'Lachlan & Smith, Merchants, Tradd St
M'Lachlin, Philip, Captain, George St
M'Lean, Lachlan, Capt , 3 Logan St
M'Leod, Donald, Rev , Edisto Island
M'Leod, Normand, Planter, Edisto Island
M'Leod, Robert, Planter, Edisto Island
M'Millan, John R , Attorney at Law, 212 King St
M'Millan, Richard, Wagon Yard, 212 King St.
M'Millan, Samuel, Attorney at Law, 212 King St
M'Nance, James, Boot & Shoe Maker, 124 Tradd
St
M'Neil, ——, Capt , (Late of the U S), 19
Montague St
M'Neil, John P , Merchant, 203 King St.
M'Neil, Neil, Capt , King St.
M'Neill, John, Grocer, South Bay
M'Neill, Neill & Co., Grocers, Broad St
M'Nellage & Byrne, Sail Maker's Loft, Bailey's
Whf.
M'Pherson, Duncan, Store Keeper, 79 King St
M'Pherson, Susannah, Mrs , Planter, 77 Broad St
Mackay, John & Co , (Investigator), 57 East Bay
Macnamara, John, Merchant, 6 Elliot St
Magnet & Hanson, Grocers, 53 East Bay
Magrath & Jones, Merchants, Lothrop's Whf
Magrath, John, Merchant, Fitzsimons' Whf , Res ,
201 East Bay
Maguire, Hugh, Merchant Tailor, 93 East Bay
Magwood & Patterson, Factors, Magwood's Whf
Magwood, Robert, M D , 79 Queen St
Magwood, Simon, 79 Queen St
Maillard, John, Wharfinger, Vanderhorst's Whf
Main, James, Cabinet Maker, 11 Society St
Mairs, Simon, Store Keeper, 252 King St
Malcom, John, Accomptant, 13 Short St
Manar, Nicholas, 13 Champneys St
Mann, John, Brick Layer, 38 King St
Mann, Spencer John, Planter, 64 Wentworth St
Marchant, Peter T , Planter, King St Rd
Margart, J H , Blacksmith, 136 Meeting St
Margat, Lewis, Baker, 43 Queen St

Marit, Pauline, Mattress Maker, 116 Queen St
Markley, Abraham, Merchant, 12 St Philip's St
Markley, Benjamin A, Attorney at Law, 110 Meeting St
Marks, Elias, King St Rd
Marks, H & Son, Store Keepers, King St Rd
Marks, Joseph, Grocer, 135 Queen St
Marley, Peter, Deputy District Sheriff, 141 East Bay
Marsh, James, Shipwright, Marsh's Whf
Marshall, John, Accomptant, 118 King St
Marshall, John, Merchant, 278 East Bay
Marshall, Mary, Mrs., Widow, 55 Broad St
Marshall, William, Shipwright, Washington St
Marshall, William, Vendue Master, Prioleau's S Range, Res, 2 Middle St
Martin, Charles, Brick Layer, 43 Anson St
Martin, Jacob N., Book Keeper, S C Bank, 197 Meeting St
Martin, John N, Brick Layer, 135 Meeting St
Martin, John P, Merchant, 63 Wentworth St.
Martin, Thomas & Co, Merchants, Martin's Whf
Martin, Thomas H, Brick Layer, 22 Mazyck St
Martin, Thomas, Merchant, 54 Broad St
Martindale, James C, Merchant, King St Rd
Mashburn, Nicholas, Shipwright, 17 Pinckney St
Mason, George, 10 Lynch's Ln
Massoretti & Co, Opticians, 20 Broad St
Mathews, Edmund, Rev, Planter, St Simons
Mathews, George, 70 Wentworth St
Mathews, James, Attorney at Law, 22 Anson St
Mathews, John R, Planter, Edisto Island
Mathews, Mary, Mrs, Planter, John's Island
Mathews, Philip, Rev, Planter, St Luke's (80 miles)
Mathews, Thomas, Mrs, Planter, St Andrews (17 miles)
Mathews, Thomas, Planter, Wadmalaw
Mathews, William, Planter, 3 Rutledge St
Mathews, William, Planter, John's Island
Mathews, William, Planter, Santee (29 miles)
Mattheussen, F, Store Keeper, 17 Queen St
Mauger, John, Ship Chandler, 41 East Bay
Maxey, Francis, Planter, Edisto Island
Maxwell, Robert, Merchant, 50 Meeting St
Mayberry, Thomas, Col, Boarding House, 47 Broad St
Mayer, John G, Attorney at Law, 75 Queen St
Mays, James, Grocer, 1 Tradd St
Mazyck, Alexander, Planter, St James', Santee (42 miles)
Mazyck, Daniel, Planter, Washington St, Mazyckborough
Mazyck, N B, Factor, 101 Meeting St
Mazyck, Paul, Planter, St James', Santee (35 miles)
Mazyck, Stephen, Planter, St John's (38 miles)
Mazyck, William, Factor, 1 Magazine St
Mead, James, Grocer, 5 Hasell St
Mease, Charles B, Merchant, 72 King St

Meeds, William, Merchant, Merchants Hotel, 73 East Bay
Menial, Charles, Mattress Maker, 16 Queen St
Mercier, James, Captain, 10 Washington St.
Mercier, Mathew, Grocer, State St
Messervey, ——, Captain, 220 Meeting St
Messkwarp, William E, Grocer, 116 East Bay
Messroon, James, Captain, 279 East Bay
Mey, Charles S & I, Merchants, Mey's Whf
Mey, F C, Merchant, 46 Pinckney St
Michael, Henry, Livery Stable, 18 Mazyck St
Michael, Peter, Hatter, 208 King St
Middleton, Arthur, Planter, 20 Meeting St
Middleton, H, Hon, Planter, 1 South Bay
Middleton, Mary, Mrs, Widow, 90 Queen St
Middleton, Solomon, Tailor, 154 King St
Middleton, Thomas, Mrs, Planter, St Andrews (15 miles)
Mikell, E, Jr, Planter, Edisto Island
Mikell, Ephraim, Planter, Edisto Island
Mikell, John C, Planter, Edisto Island
Mikell, John, Planter, Edisto Island
Miles, Ann, Mrs, Widow, 45 Tradd St
Miles, Jeremiah, Planter, St Paul's Parish
Miles, John, Planter, St Paul's Parish
Miles, William, Planter, St Paul's Parish
Milikin, Thomas, Vendue Master, 96 Church St
Miller, Abraham, Brick Layer, 23 Society St
Miller, Benjamin, Butcher, King St Rd
Miller, Catharine, Mrs, Widow, 23 Society St
Miller, Frederick, Butcher, King St Rd.
Miller, George, Store Keeper, King St Rd
Miller, Jacob, Rope Maker, Butcher's Row
Miller, James A, Deputy District Sheriff, 4 Minority St
Miller, Job, Brick Layer, 8 Blackbird Al
Miller, John, Accomptant, 23 Society St
Miller, John, Accomptant, Boundary St
Miller, John D, Goldsmith, Boundary St
Miller, Martha, Jewellery Store, 326 King St
Miller, Patrick, Merchant, 52 Anson St
Miller, Samuel S, Printer, Boundary St
Miller, W, Tailor, 108 Queen St
Miller, William, Baker, 78 Meeting St.
Miller, William, Grocer, Ashley River Bridge
Miller, William, Merchant, 52 Anson St
Millessime, Antoine, Hair Dresser, 7 Market St
Mills, Rebecca, Mrs, 22 East Bay
Mills, Thomas, Rev, King St Rd.
Minott, William, Carpenter, 4 Gibbes St
Miot, Charles, Carpenter, 56 Anson St.
Miot, John, Mrs, Widow, Hampstead
Mishaw, John, Grocer, 123 East Bay
Mitchell, Ann, Mrs, Widow, 8 George St
Mitchell, Ann, Mrs Widow, 242 Meeting St
Mitchell, James, Cooper, Vanderhorst's Whf
Mitchell, James D, Ordinary, Office, Guardhouse, Res, 75 Wentworth St

Mitchell, John H , Notary Public & Q U , 58 East Bay
Mitchell, John, Notary Public & Q U , 60 East Bay
Mitchell, Thomas, Planter, Daniel's Island
Moise, Aaron, Store Keeper, 86 King St
Moise, Cherry, Vendue Master, 9 New St
Moison, John, Gunsmith, 79 East Bay
Moles, ——, Mrs , Widow, Store Keeper, 218 King St
Moles, James C , Store Keeper, 197 King St
Monies, Hugh, Merchant, 46 East Bay
Monnar, Lewis, Hair Dresser, 2 Queen St
Monpoey, Honore, Grocer & Factor, Bull St
Montesqueux, Robert, Tinner, 184 Meeting St
Mood, John, Silversmith & Gilder, 304 King St
Mood, Peter, Silversmith & Gilder, 318 King St
Mooney, Ann, Store Keeper, 193 King St
Mooney, Patrick, Merchant, 1 Orange St
Moore, James, Ship Carpenter, 19 Middle St
Moore, P J , M D , 50 King St
Moore, Richard, Painter, Etc , 53 Wentworth St
Moore, Stephen W., Notary Public, Union Bank, 24 St Philip's St
Mordecai, David, Vendue Master, Prioleau's South Range
Morford, F , Bookstore, 112 Broad St
Morgan, Samuel, Boarding House, 8 Champneys St
Morris, Christopher G , Merchant, 262 East Bay, Res , 158
Morris, Lewis, Col , Planter, 239 Meeting St
Morris, Lewis, Jr , Col , Aide to Gen Pinckney, 239 Meeting St
Morris, Thomas, Jr , 158 East Bay
Morris, Thomas, Merchant, 158 East Bay
Morris, William, Planter, 239 Meeting St
Morrison, James, Cooper, 3 Champeys St
Morrison, John, Boarding House, 34 Chalmers' Al
Morrison, John, Captain, 97 Tradd St
Mortimer, Edward, Merchant, 24 Anson St
Morton, Alexander & Co , Grocers, 329 King St
Moser, Philip, M D , Broad St , Res , 12 Logan St
Moses, David, Vendue Master, Vendue Range, Res , Beaufain St
Moses, Fisher, Printer, Church St
Moses, Henry, Store Keeper, 77 East Bay
Moses, Isaiah, Jr., Store Keeper, 157 East Bay
Moses, Isaiah, Store Keeper, 287 East Bay
Moses, Israel, Cooperage, East of the Exchange, Res , Beaufain St
Moses, Joseph, Store keeper, 71 East Bay
Moses, Lyon, 18 Swinton's Land
Moses, Myer, Vendue Master, Vendue Range, Res , 35 Broad St
Moses, Simon, Store Keeper, 213 East Bay
Moses, Solomon, Constable, 277 King St.
Motta, De La, E , Vendue Master 2 Vendue Range
Motte, Abraham, Factor, 97 East Bay
Motte, Francis, Factor, 232 Meeting St

Motte, Mary, Mrs , Widow, Planter, 241 Meeting St
Moulin, Peter, Store Keeper, 350 King St
Moultrie, James, M D 13 Pitt St
Mouzon, Charles, Shoe Maker, 60 Church St
Muck, Philip, Music Store, 52 Broad St
Muckinfuss, Henry, Brick Layer, 75 Wentworth St
Muir, William, Merchant, 7 Magazine St
Muirhead, James, Accomptant, Blake's Whf
Mulligan, Bernard, Merchant, 178 King St
Mulligan, Francis, Justice of the Peace, King St Rd
Munch, Philip H , Grocer, 131 Tradd St
Muncrieff, ——, Miss, School, 129 East Bay
Muncrieff, ——, Mrs , Widow, 129 East Bay
Muncrieff, John, Planter, 9 Meeting St
Munds, ——, Mrs , School Mistress, State St
Munds, Israel, Rev , School Master, State St
Mungo, M'Key, Planter, Edisto Island
Munro, ——, Mrs , Boarding House, 55 East Bay
Munro, Catharine, Mrs , Midwife, 35 Society St
Munro, Robert, Cooper, Craft's N Whf.
Murden, Jeremiah, Merchant, Blake's Whf
Murley, Samuel, Merchant, Martin's Whf , Res , Mazyckborough
Murphy, Peter, Grocer, 279 King St
Murral, Robert, Accomptant, 4 Zigzag Court
Mushett, John, Blacksmith's Shop, Ellery St.
Myer, John, Grocer, 256 King St
Myers, Levy, M. D , 149 East Bay
Myers, Mordecai, Student at Law, 149 East Bay
Myers, Samuel, Tailor, Wentworth St
Nailor, Thomas, Factor, 90 East Bay
Naser, Casper, Tinman, St Philip's St. (Neck)
Naser, Frederick, Saw Pit, W End Beaufain St
Neal, Robert, Shop Keeper, 48 Anson St
Nelson, Christopher, Grocer, 44 East Bay
Nelson, George, Grocer, 70 Market St
Nelson, James, Attorney at Law, 30 Queen St
Nettles, George, Planter, Wassamasaw (40 miles)
Nettles, James, Planter, Wassamasaw (31 miles)
Nettles, Joseph, Planter, Wassamasaw (31 miles)
Nettles, Malachi, Planter, Wassamasaw (40 miles)
Nettles, W , Planter, Wassamasaw (31 miles)
Neufville, Isaac, Factor, Boundary St
Neville, Joshua, Cabinet Maker, 322 King St.
Newman, Charles, Boarding House, 222 Meeting St
Newman, Thomas, Planter, St John's (62 miles)
Newton, Anthony, Butcher, Butchertown
Newton, Mary, Mrs , Butcheress, Butchertown
Nipper, David H., Book Binder, 111 King St
Nisbett, Alexander, Mrs., Planter, 32 Hasell St
Nobbs Samuel, Weigher, Custom House, Res , St Philip's St
Noble, John & Co , M D. & Druggist, 179 King St
North & Webb, Factors, Chisolm's Whf
North, Richard B , Factor, Adams St
Norton, E , Mrs Widow, 13 South Bay

Nowell, John, 20 Berresford St
Nowell, Thomas, Discount Clerk, S C Bank, 21 Magazine St
O'Donnovan, M, Head Teacher, Charleston College
O'Driscol, Cornelius, Capt, 24 Friend St
O'Flinn, Morris, Master, Free School No 2, 89 Church St
O'Hara, Charles & Henry, Merchants, 9 Champneys St
O'Hara, Charles, Merchant, 9 Smith's Ln
O'Hara, Daniel, Merchant, 398 King St
O'Hara, Oliver, Factor, 9 Champneys St
O'Hear, James, Planter, 1 Smith St
O'Neal, Charles, Merchant, King St Rd
O'Sullivan, Charles, Planter, 31 Broad St
Oats, Mary, Seamstress, Meeting St Rd
Oeland, John, Store Keeper, 231 King St
Ogden, G W, Merchant Tailor & Salesman, 67 East Bay
Ogden, Robert, Attorney at Law, 13 Montague St.
Ogier, L, Factor, Crafts' Whf, Res, 83 Tradd St
Ogier, Thomas, Vendue Master & Commission Merchant, 12 Broad St
Ohlweiler, M, Grocer & Baker, 35 Meeting St
Oliphant, David, Painter, Etc, 149 Meeting St
Oliver, James, Brick Layer, King St Rd
Oliver, James, Butcher, King St Rd
Oliver, Joseph, Merchant, 214 East Bay
Oliver, Stephen, Butcher, King St Rd
Osborn, Catharine, Mrs, Widow, South Bay
Osborn, Richard, Factor, Counting House, 28 East Bay, Res, South Bay
Osburn, Charles, Factor, South Bay
Otis, John, Grocer, 102 East Bay
Otis, Joseph, Factor, 13 George St
Owen, John, Factor, 25 Tradd St
Owens, David, Planter, St John's (60 miles)
Owens, William, Jr, Planter, St John's (58 miles)
Owens, William, Planter, Wassamasaw (28 miles)
Page, J. W., Merchant, Champneys Whf
Paine, Joseph, Accomptant, 12 Hasell St
Paine, Stephen, Capt, 12 Hasell St
Paine, Thomas, Capt, 12 Hasell St
Painter, John, Secretary of City Guard
Palmer, Edward, Master, Free School No 5, Cannonborough
Palmer, Job, Carpenter, 98 Wentworth St
Pardiere, Bernard, Cigar Maker, 191 East Bay
Parker, Ann, Mrs, Widow, 71 Orange St
Parker, Benjamin, Planter, Daniel's Island (8 miles)
Parker, George, Merchant, Mazyckborough
Parker, Henry, Planter, Pitt St
Parker, Isaac, Planter, 7 Legare St
Parker, John, Attorney at Law, 58 Broad St
Parker, John, Merchant, 10 Short St
Parker, John, Planter, Pitt St
Parker, Samuel, Planter, 43 George St
Parker, Thomas, District Attorney, 32 Meeting St

Parker, Thomas, Jr, Attorney at Law, 32 Meeting St
Parkinson, J, Grocer, 179 Meeting St
Parks, ——, Rev, Mr, Planter, Dorchester (25 miles)
Parsons, Joseph, Planter, Hampstead
Paterson, Hugh, Secretary, Union Insurance Co., Res, 43 Society St
Patrick, Philip, Planter, King St Road
Patterson, Samuel, Merchant, 46 Hasell St
Patterson, William, Planter, St John's, Berkeley (35 miles)
Patton, William, Merchant, Back of Exchange
Paxton, Henry, Accomptant, 1 Short St
Payne, Letitia, Mrs, Widow, Hampstead
Payne, William & Son, Vendue Master & Commission Merchant, 110 Broad St
Peake, John, Factor, 24 George St
Peake, Oliver, Factor, 24 George St
Pearce, George P, Comission Merchant, 259 King St
Pearce, John, Planter, St Stephen's (40 miles)
Pearce, Moses, Planter, St Stephen's (40 miles)
Pearce, Reuben, Shoe Store, 117 King St
Pearce, Richard, Shoe Store, 286 King St
Pearce, Timothy, Planter, St Stephen's (40 miles)
Pedrieux, ——, Mrs, School Mistress, 4 Maiden Ln
Pedrieux, Peter, Carpenter, 4 Maiden Ln
Peel, John, Book Binder, 111 Broad St, Res, 7 Liberty St.
Pelzer, A, Teacher, 7 Archdale St
Pemble, David, Grocer, 2 Market St.
Pennington, Ann, Mrs, Store Keeper, 215 King St
Pepoon, Benjamin, Grocer & Grain Store, 15 Queen St
Pepoon, Joseph, Grocer, 100 Church St
Pepper, John, Planter, Christ Church Parish (4 miles)
Percy, Arnold, Tradd St
Percy, John, Maj, Planter, St James Santee
Percy, William, Rev, D D Tradd St
Perkins, E, Boot & Shoe Store, 76 Queen St.
Perman, George, Grocer, 36 East Bay
Peronneau, Henry W, Attorney at Law, Office, Meeting St, Res, 6 South Bay
Peronneau, William, Planter, 6 South Bay
Perot, George, Store Keeper, 20 Elliott St
Perriere, Gustavus, U S Coffee House, 77 East Bay
Peter, Vincent, Grocer, 40 Elliott St
Peters, George, School Master, 21 George St
Peters, John, Capt, 21 Pinckney St
Petrie, George, Collector of Accounts, 20 Society St
Petrowick, James, Grocer, Amen St.
Petsch, Julius, Book Binder, 109 Church St
Peyre, Francis, Planter, St Stephen's (40 miles)
Peysson, L, Jewellery Store, 65 East Bay

Pezant, I L , Grocer, Boundary St
Pezant, L , Grocer, 7 Maiden Ln
Phelon, E M , Maj , Grocer, 206 Meeting St
Philips, Aaron, Merchant, 71 King St
Philips, Alexander, Shipwright, 20 Society St
Philips, Benjamin, Planter, St James', Santee
Philips, Benjamin, Shoe Store, 119 Tradd St
Philips, Dorothy, Mrs , 69 Queen St
Philips, Ebenezer, Shoe Store, 92 King St
Philips, John & Co., Grocers, 33 Chalmer's Al.
Philips, John, Cabinet Maker, 69 Queen St
Philips, John, Painter & Glazier, 9 Elliott St
Philips, John, Rev Classical Teacher, 64 Meeting
St
Philips, William, Planter, St James', Santee (26
miles)
Picault, F , Theatre Coffee House, 18 Friend St
Pike, James, Shoe Maker, 15 Tradd St
Pillans, R & I , Bakers, 118 Tradd St
Pillot, O , Dry Goods & Grocery Store, 267 King
St
Pilsbury, Samuel, Export Officer, Custom House, 9
Anson St
Pinckney, Charles Cotesworth, Gen , 120 East Bay
Pinckney, Charles, Hon , Planter, 246 Meeting St
Pinckney, Henry, 30 Hasell St
Pinckney, Rodger, Planter, 97 Church St
Pinckney, Thomas, Jr , 30 Hasell St
Pinckney, Thomas, Jr , Maj , Planter, 78 Broad St
Pinckney, Thomas, Major General, 40 George St
Pinckney, Thomas, Planter, 30 Hasell St
Pineau, F , Grocer, 12 Market St
Pitt, Robert, Carpenter, 3 Magazine St
Pitt, William, Carpenter, 3 Magazine St
Placide, C , Widow, 74 Broad St
Pogson, Milwood, Rev., Planter, Goose Creek
Pohl, Elias, Store Keeper, 327 King St
Poincignon, P A , Tin Plate Worker, 118 Queen St
Porcher, George, Planter, St John's (42 miles)
Porcher, Isaac, Planter, St Stephen's (50 miles)
Porcher, Philip, Planter, St Stephen's (50 miles)
Porcher, Samuel, Planter, St Stephen's (53 miles)
Porcher, Thomas, Planter, St. John's (45 miles)
Porter, Benjamin, Cabinet Maker, 365 King St
Porter, John, Saddler, 189 King St
Porter, Peter, Blacksmith, 8 Lamboll St
Porter, William, Justice of the Peace, 88 East Bay
Potter, John, Merchant, 19 Broad St
Potter, Washington, Merchant, 33 East Bay
Poujaud, A , Grain Store & Commission Merchant,
8 Tradd St
Poulinot, N , Boot & Shoe Maker, 38 Meeting St.
Powell, John, Butcher, St Philip's St (Neck)
Power, Edward, Ship Chandler, 98 East Bay
Poyas, J E , M. D & Planter, 26 Meeting St
Pratt, John, Capt , 3 Laurens St
Prauninger, Leonard, Butcher, Butchertown
Prele, J F , Watch Maker, 41 Queen St

Prentice & Eager, Merchant, Back of Exchange
Prible, M , Mrs , Boarding House, 214 Meeting St
Price, James, Shoe Store, 31 Church St
Price, Thomas, Planter, 39 George St.
Price, Thomas, Rev , Planter, James Island
Price, William, Planter, 2 Orange St
Primerose, Robert, Merchant, 266 East Bay
Prince, Charles, Tinner, 344 King St
Prince, Clement L , Lamprier's Point (4 miles)
Prince, John, Accomptant, 13 Cumberland St
Pringle, Ann, Miss, Planter, 1 Legare St
Pringle, James R , Planter, 77 Broad St
Pringle, John J , Attorney At Law, 101 Tradd St
Pringle, Robert A , Planter, 48 Meeting St
Prioleau, ——, Miss, 27 Beaufain St
Prioleau, Elias, Accomptant, 22 Ellery St
Prioleau, Elias, Attorney at Law
Prioleau, Jane, Mrs , School Mistress, 22 Ellery St
Prioleau, John C , Capt , Factor, 65 Queen St
Prioleau, Philip G , M D , 55 Meeting St
Prioleau, Samuel, Attorney at Law, Office, cor
Meeting & Queen St , Res , 6 Short St
Prioleau, Thomas, M D , St John's (39 miles)
Pritchard & Shrewsbury, Shipwrights, Pritchard &
Shrewbury's Whf
Pritchard, Joseph, 62 King St
Pritchard, Paul, Shipwright, St Philip's (Neck)
Pritchard, William, Jr., 2 Anson St
Pritchard, William, Sr , Shipwright, Mey's Whf.
Pryton, R H., Attorney at Law, 63 King St
Purse, Thomas, Watch Maker, 54 Meeting St
Purse, William, Watch Maker, 96 Broad St
Purvis, William, Merchant, Hampstead
Quash, Robert, Planter, 99 Broad St
Query, Thomas, Book Binder, 25 Broad St
Quesrard, Henry, Accomptant, Vendue Range
Quilan, Michael, Store Keeper, 299 King St Road
Quin, Thomas F , Grocer, Meeting St. Road
Quinby, Joseph, Grocer, 6 Pinckney St
Rabb, Frances, Mrs , Grocer, 10 South Bay
Radcliffe, Thomas, Mrs., Planter, 38 George St
Rade, J C , M. D & Druggist, King St Road
Ramsay, David, M D., 87 Broad St
Rasdale, J W , Lt , City Guard, Picquet Guard
House
Ravenel, Catharine, Mrs , Widow, Broad St.
Ravenel, Daniel J , Secretary of State, Office, Guard
House, Res , 94 Broad St
Ravenel, Henry, Planter, St John's (42 miles)
Ravenel, John, 94 Broad St
Ravenel, Paul, Planter, St John's (44 miles)
Ravenel, Rene, Planter, St John's (42 miles)
Ravenel, Stephen, Planter, St John's (42 miles)
Rawlinson, T W , Merchant, Chisolm's Whf
Raworth, George F., Saddler & Harness Maker, 90
Meeting St
Ray, James, Factor, 90 East Bay
Read, Alexander, Watch Maker, 93 Broad St.

Read, George, Mrs., Widow, 106 Tradd St.
Read, Harleston, Planter, 64 Wentworth St
Read, Jacob, Gen , Cannonborough
Read, John, Shoe Store, 69 King St
Read, John, Wheelwright, 196 Meeting St
Read, William, M D , 62 Wentworth St
Reader, Philip, Shoe Store, 292 King St
Rechon, David, Tailor, 124 King St
Rechon, Lewis, Sail Maker, 124 King St
Reigne, John, Merchant, 95 East Bay
Reily, George, Tavern Keeper, 216 Meeting St
Reily, James, Saddler & Harness Maker, 28 Church St.
Reily, Robert, Accomptant, 244 East Bay
Remousin, Arnold, 31 Beaufain St
Remousin, Augustus D , 31 Beaufain St
Remousin, Daniel, 81 Queen St.
Remousin, Paul D , 31 Beaufain St
Remousin, Pluton, 31 Beaufain St
Renauld, John, Fruit Store, 32 Tradd St
Rendell, George, Accomptant, 152 King St
Revel, Hannah, Mrs , 47 Anson St
Reviere, J P , Fruit Store, 204 Meeting St
Reynolds, George, Coach & Chair Maker, 193 Meeting St
Rhodes & Saltus, Factors, Crafts' S Whf
Ricard, Francis, Grocer, 59 East Bay
Richards, Charles, Brick Layer, 8 Liberty St
Richards, Elijah, Grocer, 41 Elliott St
Richards, Frederick, Brick Layer, 8 Liberty St
Richardson, James, 8 Bull St.
Richardson, John S , State Attorney, Court House Square
Righton, ——, Mrs , 46 East Bay
Righton, Joseph, Cooper, 2 Water St
Righton, M'Cully, 3 Water St
Ring, D A , Painter, Smith's Ln
Rivers, Charles, Planter, James Island
Rivers, Francis, Jr., Planter, James Island
Rivers, Francis, Planter, 18 Pinckney St
Rivers, Francis, Planter, James Island
Rivers, Gracia, Mrs , Widow, 5 Short St
Rivers, Henry S , Planter, James Island
Rivers, John, Shipwright 6 Water St
Rivers, Joseph, Planter, 18 Pinckney St
Rivers, Samuel, Shipwright, 6 Water St
Rivers, Thomas, 8 Anson St
Rivers, William C., Planter, James Island
Rivers, William, Planter, James Island
Rivers, William, Shipwright, 6 Water St
Roach, Nash, Planter, 2 Society St
Roach, William, City Treasurer, Office, Exchange, Res , 2 Society St
Roberts, Enos, Planter, St John's (62 miles)
Roberts, F , Saddler & Harness Maker, 131 King St
Roberts, Peter, Planter, St John's (45 miles)
Roberts, William, Custom House, 128 Wentworth St

Robertson, Francis, Factor, Bailey's Whf
Robertson, George, Merchant, 202 King St
Robertson, James, Accomptant, Blake's Whf
Robertson, John, Merchant, King St Road
Robertson, John, Navy Agent, Crafts' S Whf, Res , 16 Meeting St.
Robertson, Philip, Merchant, Crafts' N Whf
Robertson, Samuel, Merchant, 202 King St
Roche, John, Grocer, 101 Church St
Roddey, James & Co , Merchant, Coates' Back Row
Rodgers, Christopher, 230 Tradd St
Rodgers, Elizabeth, Mrs , Widow, 314 Meeting St
Rodgers, John B , Accomptant, 240 East Bay
Rodgers, John R , Accomptant, 31 East Bay
Rodgers, Susannah, Mrs , School Mistress, 47 Wentworth St
Roh, Jacob, Blacksmith, 101 King St
Roper, Benjamin, Planter, 238 Meeting St
Roper, Thomas, Col , 89 East Bay
Roper, William, Planter, 22 East Bay
Rose, Christopher, Grocer, 10 South Bay
Rose, George, (of Bulkley & Rose), Merchant, 87 Church St
Rose, Henry, Merchant, Bailey's Whf
Rose, Hugh, Planter, 245 Meeting St
Rose, John, Merchant, 87 Church St
Rose, John, Planter, Dorchester
Rose, John S , Accomptant, 16 George St
Rose, William, Planter, John's Island
Ross, Ann, Mrs , Widow, 2 Liberty St.
Ross, Daniel, Saw Mill, West End Tradd St
Ross, David, Toll Receiver, Ashley River Bridge
Ross, James, Merchant, King St Road
Rotereau, Charles, Guardman, 123 King St
Roulain, Robert, Brick Layer, 42 George St
Rouse, Christopher, Brick Layer, 37 Market St
Rouse, David, 37 Market St
Rouse, James, Lt., U S Artillery, 37 Market St.
Rouse, John, 37 Market St
Rouse, William, Col , (Tannery), 37 Market St
Rouse, William, Jr , Capt , 37 Market St
Rout, Catharine, Boarding School, 19 Friend St
Roux, Frederick, Merchant, 164 Meeting St
Roux, Lewis, Merchant, 56 East Bay, Res , 175 Meeting St
Rowan, Robert, Planter, 48 Meeting St
Ruberry, John, Carpenter, 28 Mazyck St
Ruberry, William, Carpenter, 69 Tradd St
Ruddock, P A , Surveyor, 20 King St
Russell, Eliza, Mrs , Widow, 35 Guignard St
Russell, John, Blacksmith, 117 East Bay, Res , 124 Wentworth St
Russell, John, Hatter, 162 King St
Russell, Nathaniel, Merchant, 21 Meeting St
Rutledge, Charles, Planter, Wentworth St
Rutledge, Edward, Mrs , Widow, 102 Tradd St
Rutledge, Frederick, Planter, 62 Tradd St

157

Rutledge, Hugh, Attorney at Law
Rutledge, John, Col , Planter, 58 Broad St
Rutledge, States, 25 Anson St
Rutledge, William, 25 Anson St
Ryan Elizabeth, Mrs , Planter, 67 Wentworth St
Ryan, Elizabeth, Mrs , Widow, 91 East Bay
Ryan, James, Register in Equity, Office, Court
  House, Res , 8 Bull St
Ryan, John, Merchant, Motte's Whf
Ryan, Peter T , Distiller, 10 Anson St
Safford, James, Capt , 8 Pinckney St
Salter, Thomas R , Shipwright, Pritchard's Whf
Samory, E , Mattress & Bed Maker, 113 Queen St
Sampson, Elias, Grocer, cor St Philip & George
  St
Sanford, John, Grocer, 110 East Bay
Santy, Angelo, Confectioner, 41 Meeting St
Sarzedas, David, Jr , Vendue Master, Vendue
  Range, Res , 18 Queen St
Sass, Edward, Cabinet Maker, 38 Queen St
Sass, Jacob, Col , Cabinet Maker, 38 Queen St
Sass, William, Accomptant, 38 Queen St
Savage, Ann, Mrs , Millinery & Seeds Store, 315 &
  89 King St
Savage, Martha, Mrs , Planter, 2 Savage St
Sax, Henry, Grocer, 86 Church St
Schem & Sandoz, Watch Makers, 41 Meeting St
Schirer, John, Carpenter, 4 Coming St
Schirer, John, Gun Smith, 188 Meeting St
Schmidt, John, M D , Bedon's Al
Schnell, John J , Grocer, 51 King St
Schnierle, John M , Carpenter, 6 Friend St
Schrewsbury, Edward, Shipwright, 45 Society St.
Schrewsbury, Jeremiah, Carpenter, 13 Guignard St
Schriber, John, Overseer of the Roads, Neck
Schrimer, John E , Cooper Shop, Lothrop's Whf
Schroeder, John, Grocer, 3 Hasell St
Schroeder, John, Grocer, Queen St
Schultz, Abraham, Blacksmith, 19 Lynch's Ln
Schultz, John, Factor, Fitzsimmon's Whf
Schutt, Casper C , Mrs , Widow, 25 East Bay
Scott, James, Church St
Scott, William, M , Merchant, 15 Pinckney St
Scott, William, Millwright, 3 Beaufain St
Scriven, Rebecca, Miss, 12 Lynch's Ln
Scriven, Thomas, Planter, Goose Creek (8 miles)
Seabrook, Benjamin, Planter, Edisto Island
Seabrook, Gabriel, Planter, Edisto Island
Seabrook, Joseph B , Planter, Edisto Island
Seabrook, Joseph, Planter, Edisto Island
Seabrook, Thomas B , Planter, Edisto Island
Seabrook, William, Planter, Edisto Island
Seaver, Abraham, Carpenter, 43 Pinckney St
Seavy, John, Butcher, King St Road
Senet, Mariane, Store Keeper, 84 King St
Seyle, Samuel, Saddler, 289 King St
Seyler, Prescilla, Store keeper, 206 King St.
Shand, Robert, 14 Pinckney St

Sharp & Sheldon, Block & Pump Makers, 73
  Market St
Shaw, William D , Merchant, 240 East Bay
Shea, Richard, Boarding House, 7 Elliott St
Shecut, J L E W , M D , 49 Broad St
Shehe, Michael, Constable, 24 Tradd St
Sheively, George, Seeds Store, 173 Meeting St
Shephard, Thomas R , Planter, King St Road
Shepherd, James, Saddler, 313 King St
Shoolbred, James, Planter, 12 Lamboll St
Shorthouse, Thomas, Merchant, 210 East Bay, Res ,
  6 Hasell St
Shrewsbury, Stephen, Col , Clerk S C Bank, Res ,
  East Bay
Sibley, George B , Varnish Manufacturer,
  Washington St , Mazyckborough
Sibley, Joseph, Grocer, 1 Bailey's Whf
Siffy & Mintzing, Lumber Yard, 1 Back St
Simons, Benjamin B , M D , 32 East Bay
Simons, G , 4 Orange St
Simons, Hannah, Mrs , Seamstress, 104 Meeting St
Simons, Henry, Arsenal, 3 Bull St
Simons, James D , Rev , 13 St Philip's St
Simons, James, Maj , Planter, 3 Bull St
Simons, Joseph, Grocery & Liquor Store, 61 East
  Bay
Simons, Keating & Son, Factors, Martin's Whf ,
  Res , 4 Orange St
Simons, Keating L , Attorney at Law, 45 Broad St
Simons, Maurice, Factor, Blake's Whf , Res , 43
  Society St
Simons, Samuel, Merchant, 281 King St
Simons, Sedgwick L., 4 Orange St
Simpson, John, Planter, 60 Tradd St
Sinclair, Charles, Planter, St Stephen's (50 miles)
Sinclair, Margaret, Mrs , Planter, St John's (60
  miles)
Sinclair, William, Planter, St John's (60 miles)
Singellon, James M , Printer, 41 Wentworth St
Singellton, B , Glass & Crockery Store, 16 Broad
  St
Singellton, Moses, Tax Collector, St
  Bartholomew's (40 miles)
Singellton, Thomas, Accomptant, 16 Broad St
Singleton, Mary, Mrs , 3 Wentworth St
Sissell, William, Capt , 41 Queen St
Skrine, Tacitus G , Accomptant, Tradd St
Slawson, Nathaniel, Baker, 100 King St
Slorick, John, Grocer, 10 King St
Sluter, Jacob, Store Keeper, 280 King St
Smart, John T , Boot & Shoe Maker, 200 Meeting
  St
Smeisser, Frederick, Grocer, 57 Anson St
Smith, Agnes, Mrs., Boarding House, 7 Broad St
Smith, Allen, Planter, Four Holes
Smith, Ann, Mrs , Planter, 10 West End
Smith, Benjamin B., Attorney at Law, 230 Meeting
  St

Smith, Charles, Planter, 2 South Bay
Smith, Charles, Planter, Wassamasaw (29 miles)
Smith, Christopher, Keeper, Kolf-Baan, 73 Wentworth St
Smith, Daniel, City Assessor & Justice of the Peace, Office, Exchange, Res, Society St
Smith, Eliza, Mrs, Store Keeper, 164 King St
Smith, Ezekiel, Planter, Four Holes
Smith, Frances, Planter, St Stephen's (40 miles)
Smith, George, Carpenter, Middle St
Smith, George, Planter, 49 Anson St
Smith, Henry Middleton, Planter, Goose Creek
Smith, Hugh, Merchant, 7 Broad St
Smith, James & George, Grocers, Meeting St Road
Smith, James, Carpenter, 16 Beaufain St
Smith, James, Cutler, 92 Broad St
Smith, Jane, Mrs, Widow, School Mistress, 15 Pinckney St
Smith, Jean, Mrs, Confectioner, Queen St
Smith, John, Planter, Wassamasaw (29 miles)
Smith, John, Upholsterer, 17 Mazyck St
Smith, Josiah, 49 Anson St
Smith, Loughton, Mrs., Widow, Planter, 100 East Bay
Smith, Mary, Mrs, 8 Mazyck St
Smith, Mary, Mrs, Boarding House, 42 Elliott St
Smith, Matthew, Planter, Four Holes
Smith, Neomi, Miss, Planter, 8 Coming St
Smith, Peter, Lumber Merchant & Factor, South Bay, Res, 27 Mazyck St
Smith, Peter, Planter, St Stephen's (40 miles)
Smith, Peter, Warden, Planter, 2 South Bay
Smith, Richard, Cabinet Maker, 30 Broad St
Smith, Robert, Planter, 8 Legare St
Smith, Roger, Mrs, Planter, 12 Coming St
Smith, Samuel, Planter, 42 Broad St
Smith, Thomas, Factor, 88 Wentworth St
Smith, Thomas R, Planter, Ladson's Court
Smith, Whitefoord, Jr, Grocer & Beer House, 68 Church St
Smith, Whitefoord, Sr, Grocer, 74 Church St
Smith, William, Jr, Shipwright, Smith's Whf
Smith, William M, Planter, 101 Tradd St.
Smith, William, Planter, Four Holes
Smith, William S, Prothonotary, Court of Common Pleas and Sessions, Res, Bull St.
Smith, William, Sr, Factor, Johnson's Whf, Mazyckborough
Smyle, Andrew, Fitzsimon's Whf
Smyth, John & Co, Merchants, King St Road
Smyth, John, Queen St
Snowden, Ann, Mrs., Boarding House, 108 Broad St
Snowden, Charles, Rev, Planter, Pineville (50 miles)
Snowden, James, Accomptant, 108 Broad St.
Snowden, William E, Accomptant, 108 Broad St
Solee, John, City Theatre, 24 Church St.

Solomon, Alexander, Store keeper 258 King St
Solomon, Marks, 113 Meeting St
Solomon, Sarah, Store Keeper, 80 East Bay
Sommers, James, Accomptant, 260 East Bay
Spears, Mary, Mrs, Widow, 3 Society St
Speisseger, John, Musical Instrument Maker, cor Anson & Hasell Sts
Spidle, John, Carpenter, 25 Archdale St
Spring, John, Powder Receiver, Etc, Blackbird Al
Stanilaus, Huard, M D & Druggist, 74 East Bay
Stanley, Caleb, Grocer, 95 East Bay
Starr, Joseph, Grocer, 114 East Bay
Steedman, Charles J, Col, President, Planters & Mechanics Bank, Mazyckborough
Steedman, Thomas, Cashier, Bank of S C, Mazyckborough
Steel, John, Clerk, Planters & Mechanics Bank, Boundary St
Steel, John, Grocer, King St
Steinmetz, I A E, Merchant, 50 Tradd St
Stent, John, Jr, Carpenter, Mazyck St
Stent, John, Planter, James Island
Stent, Robert, Carpenter, Parsonage Ln
Stevens, Daniel, Col, Supervisor, 31 George St
Stevens, David, Commission Merchant, East Bay
Stevens, Jervis Henry, City Sheriff, Office, Exchange, Res, 64 Tradd St
Stevens, Thomas, Teller, United Bank, Meeting St
Stevens, William, Laurens St
Stevens, William, S, M D, 206 King St
Stewart, ——, Miss, Boarding School, Tradd St
Stewart, Charles, Attorney at Law, 44 Wentworth St
Stine, Samuel, Tailor, 130 King St
Stock, John, Planter, Ladson's Court
Stocker, Henry, Boat Builder, 205 East Bay
Stone, Isabella, Mrs., 35 Guignard St
Stone, John, 35 Guignard St
Stone, Thomas, Brick Layer, 35 Guignard St
Stoney, John, Merchant, Motte's Whf
Street, Timothy, Grocer, 165 Meeting St
Stroble, & Aspinall, Merchants, East Bay
Stroble, Jacob, Capt, City Guard, cor of King & Society Sts
Stroble, John, Capt, Bank, Boundary St.
Stroble, Lewis, Lt, City Guard, 13 Society St.
Stroble, Martin, Attorney at Law, 139 Meeting St
Strohecker, John, Blacksmith, 91 Meeting St
Suares, Isaac, 13 Friend St
Sullivan, Timothy, Vendue Master, Vendue S Range
Surau, J B, Shoe Store, 20 King St
Sutliff, E, Widow, Broad St
Swain, Luke, Pilot, 7 Stoll's Al
Sweeney, Esther, Mrs, 4 Smith's Ln
Sweeney, Frances, Mrs., 110 Tradd St
Sweeney, James, Merchant, 3 Minority St
Swift, William, Store Keeper, 117 King St

Swinton, Hugh, Planter, 19 Archdale St
Tallayand, Andrew, Boarding School, 82 Broad St.
Tastet, —, Monsieur, Dancing Master, 185 Meeting St
Tate, James, Capt, Merchant, 140 Queen St
Tavel, F, 1 Savage St
Taylor, James, Capt, 12 Anson St
Taylor, John, Planter, St John's (40 miles)
Taylor, Josiah, Factor, 13 Lamboll St.
Teasdale, John & Son, Merchants, 19 East Bay
Teasdale, John, Jr, Merchant, 19 East Bay
Teasdale, Richard, Accomptant, 19 East Bay
Telfer, Robert, Fancy Store, 33 Church St
Tennant, Moses, Grocer, 187 Meeting St.
Tennant, Thomas, Carpenter, 44 Queen St
Tew, Charles, Master, Free School No 3 & Q. U, 92 Wentworth St
Tharin, Lewis, Sr, Planter, Neck Road
Thayer, Ebenezer, Broker, 48 Tradd St
Thayer, Seth, Shoe Store, 99 King St
Theus, Simeon, Collector of the Port, 338 King St
Theus, Simeon, Jr., Factor, 338 King St
Thomas, E S, Editor, City Gazette, Office, 231 East Bay
Thomas, Francis, (late of the Branch Bank) 31 Archdale St
Thomas, John, Hair Dresser, 202 Meeting St
Thomas, Mary, Mrs, Widow, 12 King St
Thomas, Peter, Merchant, 61 King St
Thomas, Stephen, Merchant, 213 King St
Thompson, Alexander, Brick Layer, 42 Wentworth St
Thompson, George, Brick Layer, Magazine St
Thompson, James, Capt, Boarding Officer, Custom House, Res, Hasell St
Thompson, William, Ship Chandler, 227 East Bay
Thorne, John Gardner & Son, Sail Maker's Loft, East Bay, Res, 1 Cumberland St
Threadcraft, Bethel, Watch Maker, 334 King St
Thwing, David, Ship Joiner, 5 Parsonage Ln
Thwing, Edward, Grain store, cor Market & Meeting St
Thynnes, William, Store Keeper, Santee Canal, St John's (33 miles)
Tiddyman, Philip, M D, Planter, 84 Wentworth St
Timmons, George, Accomptant, 17 Tradd St
Timmons, William, Tax Collector, Office, Guard House, Res, Mazyckborough
Timrod, William H, Book Binder & Stationer 25 Broad St
Tobias, Judith, Store Keper, 292 King St
Todd, Jane, Widow, 4 Savage St
Tofel, John, Confectioner, 159 Meeting St
Toohey, Michael, Grocer, 106 Meeting St
Toomer, Ann, Mrs, Widow, 5 Legare St
Toomer, Henry B, Factor, Vanderhorst's Whf
Toomer, Joshua W, Attorney at Law, Office 93 Broad St, Res, Legare St.

Torree, Charles D, Optician, 100 Broad St
Torrey, E., Mast, Block & Pump Maker, 109 East Bay
Torrey, William, Capt, 11 New St
Tournier, D, Boot & Shoe Store, 178 Meeting St
Tovey, Henry, Mast, Block & Pump Maker, 249 East Bay
Towers, James, Carolina Coffee House, cor Tradd St & Bedon's Al
Townsend, Thomas, Carpenter, 2 Minority St
Trenholm, William, Grain Store, 127 Tradd St
Trescot, Edward, Planter, 80 Meeting St
Trescot, John S, M D., 60 Broad St
Trescot, William, Attorney at Law, 80 Meeting St
Trezevant, Peter, Discount Clerk, S C Bank, 4 Stoll's Al
Truchulet, John B, Grocer, 140 Queen St
Tucker, Charles S, Clerk, Office, Court House
Tucker, William, B, Register of Mesne Conveyance, Office, Court House
Tunis, Charles, Factor, 31 East Bay
Tunno, Adam, Merchant, 44 East Bay
Tunno, Thomas, Merchant, Chisolm's Whf, Res, 79 Tradd St
Tupper, Tristram, Merchant, 239 East Bay
Turnbull, Gavin, School Master, 96 Tradd St
Turnbull, James, Carpenter, 12 South Bay
Turnbull, R J, Attorney at Law, 1 Logan St
Turpin, William, Planter, 180 King St
Tyler, Joseph, Merchant, 237 East Bay
Ulmo, Anthony, M D & Druggist, 20 Queen St
Ummonsetter, John, Tanner, 19 Beaufain St
Valk, Jacob R, Vendue Master & Commission Merchant, Vendue Range, Res, 72 King St
Vanderbusche, C, Store Keeper, 98 King St
Vanderhorst, A, Gen, Planter, 32 East Bay
Vanderhorst, Arnoldus, Jr, Planter, St James', Santee (28 miles)
Vanderhorst, Richard, Factor, Vanderhorst's Whf
Vanning, —, Boot & Shoe Maker, 51 Elliott St
VanRhyan, A E, Miss, Store Keeper, 113 Broad St
Vardell, Thomas A, Brick Layer, 39 Anson St
Veny, Nathaniel, Grocer, 2 Washington St
Vernon, N., Jeweller, 115 Broad ST
Verree, Joseph, Capt., 3 Church St
Verree, Robert, Merchant, 3 Church St
Verree, Samuel, Silversmith, 3 Church St
Vesey, Joseph, School Master, 40 King St
Vidal, John, Confectioner, 117 Church St.
Villeard, L, Cutler, 115 Queen St
Villeponteaux, Benjamin, Planter, St John's (45 miles)
Villeponteaux, Duke, Planter, St John's (45 miles)
Villeponteaux, William, Planter, St John's (45 miles)
Villes, Peter, Confectioner, 59 East Bay
Vincent, Eliza, Mrs., Boarding House, 40 East Bay

Vincent, Lewis, Shoe Maker, 16 Amen St
Vincent, Thomas, 16 Cumberland St
Vincondrierre, P , Cigar Maker, 7 Wentworth St
Vion, ——, Madam, Store keeper, 93 King St
Wadsworth, William, Grocer, 15 Archdale St
Wagner, Ann, Mrs , St Philip's St
Walden, Joseph & Co., 6 Craft's N Whf
Walker & Evans, Marble Cutters, 37 Wentworth St
Walker, Caleb, Carpenter, 16 Magazine St.
Walker, John, Planter, Christ Church Parish (7
  miles)
Walker, Robert, Cabinet Maker, 53 Church St
Walker, William, Accomptant, 44 East Bay
Wall, Richard & Co , Grocers, cor King & Queen
  St
Wallace, James, Custom House Officer, Boundary
  St
Wallace, Robert, Brass Founder, 63 Meeting St
Wallace, Thomas, Cabinet Maker, 105 Queen St
Waller, William, Saddler, 47 Broad St
Walter, Jeremiah, Merchant, 128 Queen St
Walton, John, Merchant, 213 King St
Walton, William, Planter, Cannonborough
Wansley, Jospeh, Grocer, 8 Elliot St
Ward, James, Maj , Attorney at Law,
  Cannonborough
Ward, John, Col , Attorney at Law, 20 East Bay
Ward, Susannah, Mrs , 9 Legare St
Warham, Mary, Mrs , Widow, Planter, 17 Tradd St
Warham, William, Planter, 17 Tradd St
Waring & Hayne, Factors, Chisolm's Whf
Waring, Ann, Mrs , Planter, 82 Tradd St.
Waring, Horatio S , M D , 29 Meeting St
Waring, John, Mrs., Planter, 94 Wentworth St
Waring, Morton & Son, Factors, 269 East Bay
Waring, Morton, Federal Marshal, St Philip's St
Waring, Richard, M D & Planter, Dorchester
Waring, Thomas, Naval Officer, 29 Meeting St
Waring, Thomas, Planter, Wraggborough
Warley, Felix, Cashier, State Bank, Wentworth St
Warley, Felix, Jr , Capt , U S Infantry, Wentworth
  St
Warley, Jacob, Lt., U S Infantry, Wentworth St
Warley, M & A E , Misses, Beaufain St
Warley, William, M D , Boundary St
Warnock, John, Attorney at Law, Office, Court
  House, Res , 27 George St
Warnock, Thomas, Carpenter, King St Road
Warren, Joseph, Rev , Episcopal Minister, St.
  Thomas'
Warren, Samuel, Col , Planter, St James', Santee
  (48 miles)
Wartenburg, Peter, Grocer, 11 Market St
Washington, William, Mrs., Planter, 20 South Bay
Washington, William, Planter, 20 South Bay
Watson, Alexander, Accomptant, 235 East Bay
Watson, Alexander, Grocer, Amen St
Watson, William, Store Keeper, 127 King St

Waugh, W & A , Merchants, 258 East Bay
Wear, Sarah, Widow, 4 Wentworth St
Webb, Daniel, Factor, Cannonborough
Webb, John, Merchant, 245 East Bay
Weissinger, John, Mrs , Widow, King St Road
Wellesman, James, Branch Pilot, 15 Lynch's Ln
Welling & Ballantine, Harness Makers, 65 Meeting
  St
Wells, Richard, Boat Builder, East Bay
Wells, Thomas B , Accomptant, 18 Archdale St.
Welsh, Edward, 3 Archdale St
Welsh, Mary, Shop Keeper, King St
Welsh, N G , Keeper, Stranger's Burial Ground,
  Res , Archdale St
Welsh, Thomas, Carver, 45 Pinckney St
Wescott, Randolph, Planter, Edisto Island
Wescott, Thomas, Planter, Edisto Island
Wescott, William, Planter, Edisto Island
Wesner & Johnson, Carpenters, 8 New St
Wesner, Frederick, Carpenter, 61 Meeting St
Wesner, Henry P , Wharfinger, Chisolm's Whf
West, Thomas & Co , News Room, 213 Meeting St
West, Thomas, Capt , 20 Cumberland St
Weston, Paul, M D., Hampstead
Weston, Plowden, Planter, 31 Queen St
Weyman, Edward, Surveyor, Custom House
Whalley, George, Planter, Four Holes
Wheldon, Joseph, Accomptant, 14 Magazine St
White, Daniel, Butcher, Butchertown
White, Frederick, Accomptant, Vendue Range
White, George, Boarding House, 8 Chalmer's Al
White, George, Cabinet Maker, 120 Church St
White, George K , Factor, Prioleau's Whf , Res ,
  Boundary St
White, John B , Attorney at Law, 35 Broad St
White, John, Factor, Custom House, Chisolm's
  Whf , Res , 144 Meeting St
White, John P., Attorney at Law, 44 Pinckney St
White, John, Planter, Christ Church Parish
White, Richard, Planter, Wadmalaw
White, William, Grocer, 79 Church St
Whitesides, John, Planter, Christ Church Parish
Whitesides, Moses, Planter, Christ Church Parish (8
  miles)
Whitesides, Thomas, Planter, Christ Church Parish
Whiting, John, Turner & Grocer, 103 Meeting St
Whitney, Archibald, Baker, 297 King St
Whitney, James R , Steward, General Hospital, Fort
  Johnson
Whitney, Jedediah, Cabinet Maker, St Philip's St
Whitney, John, Capt , 3 Guignard St
Whitney, T H , Carver & Gilder, Beaufain St
Wiggins, William, Grocer, 164 Meeting St
Wightman, John J , Turner, 152 Meeting St
Wightman, William, Maj , Jeweller, 216 Meeting St
Wightman, William, Painter & Glazier, 152
  Meeting St

Wilhelmi, J P , Merchant, 25 East Bay, Res ,
  Butchertown
Williams, Ann, Mantua Maker, 198 King St
Williams, Isham, Planter, William's Whf
Williams, John, Boarding House, 14 Elliot St
Williams, William, Tailor
Williard, Joseph, 9 Magazine St
Williman, Christopher, Planter, 61 Broad St
Williman, George, Tanner, Boundary St
Williman, Jacob, Tanner, Montague St.
Willington, A S , Editor of Courier, 111 Broad St
Wilson, ——, Mrs , Widow, Boundary St
Wilson & Paul, Grocers, 23 Broad St
Wilson, Elias, Planter, St John's (55 miles)
Wilson, George, Planter, St John's (55 miles)
Wilson, Isaac, M D , 4 Archdale St
Wilson, James, Merchant, Chisolm's Whf
Wilson, James, Planter, St John's (55 miles)
Wilson, John, Carpenter, 127 Meeting St. Road
Wilson, John L , Attorney at Law, 29 East Bay
Wilson, John, M D , Planter, Wassamasaw (30
  miles)
Wilson, John, Surveyor, 10 Legare St
Wilson, John, Tallow Chandler, Meeting St Road
Wilson, Rebecca, Mrs , Nurse, 17 Meeting St
Wilson, Robert, M D , 69 Meeting St
Wilson, Samuel, Jr., M D , 4 Archdale St
Wilson, Samuel, M D , 4 Archdale St
Wilson, William H , Attorney, 4 Archdale St
Wincey, James, Blacksmith, Marsh's Whf
Winchester, Jonathan, Carpenter, Islington
Windsor, Thomas, Capt , 5 Maiden Ln.
Winstanley, Thomas, Attorney at Law,
  Mazyckborough
Winthrop, Joseph A., Merchant, Vice Consul of
  Sweden, 58 Tradd St
Winthrop, Joseph, Merchant, Vice Consul of
  Denmark, 58 Tradd St
Wiss, P. J , Licensed Billard Tables, 290 King St
Wittich, Charles, Porter, Planters & Mechanics
  Bank
Woddrop, John, Merchant, 26 East Bay
Wood, Absalom, Tavern Keeper, Mount Pleasant
Wood, Alley, Store Keeper, King St Road
Wood, James, Engraver, St Philip's St.
Wood, John, Surveyor, St James', Santee
Wood, William, Planter, Edisto Island
Woodman & Smith, Fancy Store, 116 King St
Woodmancy, J , Grocer, King St Road
Woodward, Esther, Widow, 5 Cumberland St
Wrainch, John, School Master, 173 Meeting St
Wright, Eliza, Miss, 10 Orange St
Wurdeman, John G , Grocer, 134 Queen St
Yates, Deborah, Mrs , Widow, School Mistress, 22
  South Bay
Yates, Jeremiah, Planter, 21 South Bay
Yates, Joseph, Packer & Compressor of Cotton, 225
  East Bay

Yates, Samuel, Capt , 5 Zigzag Court
Yates, Samuel, Jr , Ship Chandler, 48 East Bay
Yates, Seth, Mrs , Widow, 6 Zigzag Court
Yeadon, Richard, Planter, Bull St.
Yeadon, William, Attorney at Law, 83 Tradd St
Yoer, C A., Mrs , Milliner, 138 King St
You, John C , Master, Fellowship Society School,
  32 Archdale St
Young, William, Merchant, 3 Champneys St
Young, William, P , Printer, Book Seller &
  Stationer, 44 Broad St.
Zealy, George, Grocer, 31 King St
Zilk, John, Wheelwright, cor Boundary & Meeting
  Sts
Zylstra, John P , Oil & Color Shop, 66 East Bay
Zylstra, Peter, Mrs , Oil & Color Shop, 82 East Bay

www.ingramcontent.com/pod-product-compliance
Lightning Source LLC
Chambersburg PA
CBHW072249270326
41930CB00010B/2322